Lee and Grant

Lee and Grant

William M. S. Rasmussen and Robert S. Tilton

Virginia Historical Society, Richmond in association with D Giles Limited, London

© 2007 Virginia Historical Society

First published in 2007 by GILES
An imprint of D Giles Limited
D Giles Limited
2nd Floor
162-164 Upper Richmond Road
London SW15 2SL, UK
www.gilesltd.com

ISBN: 978-0-945015-26-0 (Softcover edition)
ISBN: 978-1-904832-36-2 (Hardcover edition)

All rights reserved

No part of the contents of this book may be reproduced, stored in a retrieval system, or transmitted in any form or by any means, electronic, mechanical, photocopying, recording, or otherwise, without the written permission of the Board of Trustees, Virginia Historical Society and D Giles Limited.

For the Virginia Historical Society: Photography coordinated by Muriel B. Rogers and Jeffrey Ruggles.

For D Giles Limited:
Copy-edited and proof-read by David Rose
Designed by Alfonso Iacurci, Anikst Design Limited, London
Produced by GILES, an imprint of
D Giles Limited, London
Printed and bound in Singapore

All measurements are in inches and centimetres

Front cover:
Robert Walter Weir, *Robert E. Lee* (detail), c.1852–55, oil on canvas, private collection, and Samuel Bell Waugh, *Ulysses S. Grant* (detail), 1869, oil on canvas mounted on plywood, The Abraham Lincoln Foundation of the Union League of Philadelphia

Frontispiece:
Jean Leon Gerome Ferris, *Let Us Have Peace, 1865* (detail), c. 1920, oil on canvas, Virginia Historical Society, Lora Robins Collection of Virginia Art

Contents

Presidents' Forewords 6

Acknowledgments 10

Introduction 12
- The Reinventing of Robert E. Lee – 1861-2007
- The Reinventing of Ulysses S. Grant – 1861-2007
- Beyond the Mythology:
  Intentions and Scope of This Project

I. The Decisions of 1861 48

II. Youth and Early Military Careers 76
- The Heritage of the Lee Family
- The Boyhood of Robert E. Lee
- Cousins at Arlington House
- Lee at West Point
- Engineering in the South, St. Louis, and Brooklyn
- The Grants of New England and Ohio
- The Reluctant Cadet
- Infantry Service in Missouri, Louisiana, and Texas

III. The Mexican War 122

IV. Crises of the 1850s 142
- Ambivalence Towards the Military
- Return to Civilian Life
- Prelude to War: Lee at Harpers Ferry
- Rejection of the Planter Lifestyle

V. The Civil War 176
- Lee in the East; Grant in the West
- Grant versus Lee: The Wilderness to Petersburg
- Appomattox

VI. Restoration of the Union 232
- Postbellum America: Lee, Grant, and National Reconciliation
- Washington College
- President of the United States

VII. Remembrance 302

Conclusion 324

Special Lenders 330

Notes 331

Index 347

Presidents' Forewords

Charles F. Bryan, Jr.
President and CEO, Virginia Historical Society

When I was growing up in a small town in Tennessee in the early 1960s, the Civil War fascinated me. Like many white southern boys, I had a photograph of my hero Robert E. Lee hanging prominently in my room. To me Ulysses S. Grant was the enemy. As I became a professional historian, however, and learned more about Grant, I came to look at him differently. I found that the more I knew about him, the more I admired him as a general and as a man. I hope that *Lee and Grant* will enable the reader to look again at these generals and when appropriate to reassess both their frailties and virtues, as I have done.

This book and the exhibition that it supports will provide as well a picture of their America, which will include discussions of the racial tensions that existed in the nineteenth century and that in some ways underlie our society today. Peculiar as it may seem, a century-and-a-half after Appomattox vestiges of the regional and racial biases that remained strong in rural Tennessee fifty years ago still linger. In *Lee and Grant* we attempt to put aside much of the mythology about the two generals that emerged in and remains a troublesome legacy from America's most tragic era. Underneath those myths one discovers stories about duty, honor, and idealism that are well worth remembering. Drs. William M. S. Rasmussen, Lora M. Robins Curator at the Virginia Historical Society, and Robert S. Tilton, Head of the Department of English at the University of Connecticut, have once again teamed to produce a compelling narrative. This is their fourth collaboration. On this 200th anniversary of Lee's birth, I invite you to explore in the pages that follow the lives of two of America's greatest heroes and a cross-section of the America in which they lived.

There is perhaps no better way to initiate the beginning of the end of regionalist interpretations of the Civil War than by the partnering of two historical societies that from the early nineteenth century have been the respective interpreters of southern and northern culture. I am indebted to my colleague Louise Mirrer, President and CEO of the New-York Historical Society, for co-producing this project. For the loan of key objects and the sharing of staff expertise, we also thank a group of institutions that joined our partnership: Washington and Lee University, The Museum of the Confederacy, The National Park Service (including Arlington House and White Haven), Stratford Hall—The Birthplace of Robert E. Lee, and the Civil War & Underground Railroad Museum of Philadelphia. We are indebted to the National Endowment for the Humanities for its support of this exhibition, and to the E. Rhodes and Leona B. Carpenter Foundation, and Washington and Lee University, with the assistance of the Joella and Stewart Morris Foundation, for support of this book.

Louise Mirrer

President and CEO, New-York Historical Society

My colleague Charles F. Bryan, Jr., President and CEO of the Virginia Historical Society, writes in his foreword of growing up in Tennessee, with Robert E. Lee as his hero. I grew up in New York, sharing a birthday with Ulysses S. Grant and in awe of his opulent tomb high above the Hudson River on Manhattan's Upper West Side. I read as much as I could about Grant and, though my heroes tended to be female and decidedly non-military, I tremendously admired Grant both as general and as president. Unlike my southern colleague, whose devotion to Lee meant abhorrence of Grant, I was raised, as I think many northerners of my generation were, to respect both men. I can still see the cover of a children's biography given to my brother as a gift in the late 1950s, which showed a stern, but handsome Lee on a horse, in full military dress. Though my family actively participated in the sixties civil rights movement, Lee was not, for us, a figure that provoked debates about the history of race in this country.

William M. S. Rasmussen and Robert S. Tilton's *Lee and Grant* explains, among other things, why this was the case. For many years the mythology surrounding the two generals overwhelmed the incidents in the lives of each that relate to the underpinnings and aftermath of the Civil War. The book's major achievement is thus, in my view, its presentation of the two men as they evince the dilemmas of American history—not only the legacy of slavery, secession and war, but also the rise of a powerful centralized government and the balance of military and civilian power.

I am very grateful to Charles Bryan for taking the initiative in the collaboration between the Virginia Historical Society and the New-York Historical Society that motivated this book as well as the complementary exhibitions on view at our institutions over the course of 2007–2008. I am also grateful to my New-York Historical Society colleagues, chief among them Linda S. Ferber, Vice President and Museum Director; Richard Rabinowitz, Senior Project Historian; Kathleen Hulser, Public Historian; Roy Eddey, Director of Museum Administration; and Jill Pazereckas, Research Associate. Josiah Bunting III has been an extraordinary guest project historian, and I am glad for the opportunity this venture gave us to become friends. We were fortunate to have the help also of John Y. Simon, editor of the Ulysses S. Grant papers. Above all, I would like to thank New-York Historical Society trustee and former board chair, Richard Gilder, for encouraging us in this endeavor, and for his great generosity to our splendid institution.

Acknowledgments

Two of our previous exhibitions, *Pocahontas: Her Life and Legend* (1994) and *George Washington: The Man Behind the Myths* (1999), examined the historical record of the lives of famous Americans and compared them to the works of writers and artists who recreated those lives, often adapting them to their own purposes. With the approach of 2007, the 200th anniversary of the birth of Robert E. Lee, we found another iconic figure whose real life has been pushed into obscurity by the myths surrounding it. The anniversary year seemed like an appropriate occasion to unravel the layers of regionalist glorification or damnation that have survived for nearly a century-and-a-half after the Civil War.

During the planning stage, Charles Bryan, president of the Virginia Historical Society, suggested to Louise Mirrer, president of the New-York Historical Society, that her institution produce a complementary Ulysses Grant exhibition, and that the two museums present both shows, either alternately or concurrently, to their respective audiences. After some discussion it was decided that the two shows should be combined as one. Grant's life has been as much obscured as Lee's; the regionalist adulation of one hero has often brought about a denigration of the other. Further, their somewhat parallel lives, which intersected on more than one occasion, had never before been compared. This perhaps surprising failure is yet another oddity that suggests the unhealthy persistence of regionalist interpretations of the Civil War. The vantage point gained by bringing together their biographies would shed new light on the stories of both generals.

Robert E. Lee and Ulysses S. Grant, each in his own way, helped to shape the American nation that emerged after the Civil War. Their long and event-filled lives spanned much of the nineteenth century. To help us maneuver a course through so rich and challenging a field of study, we asked four prominent historians to serve as consultants to the project: John Y. Simon, editor of *The Papers of Ulysses S. Grant* since 1967, Emory Thomas, author of *Robert E. Lee: A Biography* (1995), Josiah Bunting, author of *Ulysses S. Grant* (2004), and Ervin Jordan, author of *Black Confederates and Afro-Virginians in Civil War Virginia* (1995). We could not have assembled a better team. All were extraordinarily generous and warmly supportive, and each provided a good deal of guidance and a number of excellent suggestions. We owe to them a higher degree of thanks than can be registered here.

At the Virginia Historical Society, Jim Kelly, Nelson Lankford, Bob Strohm, Lee Shepard, Graham Dozier, and Jeffrey Ruggles provided support and advice. Jeffrey and Missy Rogers accomplished the Herculean task of gathering the 275 illustrations for this volume; Drew Gladwell assisted. Librarians Frances Pollard, John McClure, Margaret Kidd, and Greg Hansard helped us identify materials in the collection, and Bob Bergner conducted research. AnnMarie Price arranged the loans for the exhibition while Bill Obrochta planned the educational components. Stacy Gibford-Rusch conserved objects and Ron Jennings took photographs. We also thank Pam Seay and Risha Stebbins in the society's public affairs office. Dale Kostelny and Drew Gladwell assisted Charles Froom, who with his team at Archimuse provided the wonderful design of the exhibition. At the New-York Historical Society, we thank Linda Ferber, Roy Eddey, Kathleen Hulser, and especially Jill Pazereckas, who did yeoman work in that society's extensive collections. David Burnhauser, Emily Foss, and Heidi Nakashima arranged loans and conservation. Jill Reichenbach, Eleanor Gillers, Glenn Castellano, and Nicole Wells took photographs. We further thank Richard Rabinowitz, Lynda Kaplan, Eric Foner, David Blight, and John Hennessy for their suggestions. At Washington and Lee University, Peter Grover, Director of the Reeves Center, Pat Hobbs at Lee Chapel, history professors Holt Merchant and Taylor Sanders, and Lisa McCown in the special collections department at the Leyburn Library were as generous with their time and expertise as collaborators can be. Tom Litzenburg, former Director of the Reeves Center at Washington and Lee, encouraged us from the start. At the Museum of the Confederacy in Richmond we thank Waite Rawls, John Coski, Rebecca Rose, and Heather Milne. Andrew Coldren at the Civil War and Underground Railroad Museum in Philadelphia helped facilitate the generous loan of a Grant uniform. At Stratford Hall, we thank Paul Reber, Judy Hynson, and Ken McFarland, who have helped us throughout this project. At Arlington House, Kendall Thompson, Mary Troy, and Frank Cucurullo have answered all of our requests and questions with the graciousness that one comes to expect from the National Park Service, as have Mike Ward and Pam Sanfilippo at White Haven. Donald Tharpe, a private collector, has generously loaned several important Grant items to the exhibition. In Connecticut, we are indebted to Stacy Courtigiano for her wonderful work as a copy editor.

We have also been aided by the staffs at many museums, historical sites, libraries, and institutions, as well as by private individuals. We are particularly indebted to Alexander Acevedo, Terry Adams, William M. Anderson, David Cassedy, Suzanne Christoff, Bonnie Coles, Hillary Crehan, Daniela Stoffel Delprete, Amy Densford, Karie Diethorn, Sarah Duke, Lizanne Garrett, Keith Gibson, Lisa Kathleen Grady, Margaret Grandine, Peter Harrington, Debra Hashim, Patrick Hinely, Gary Hood, Diane Jacob, Tambra Johnson, Jennifer Jones, Wendy Kail, Tamera Kennelly, Russell Lewis, Richard Love, Olivia Mahoney, Ellen Martin, Alicia Mauldin, Rob Medina, Keya Morgan, James Mundy, Judith Pavelock, Dwight Pitcaithley, Geoffrey Platt, Sam Plourd, Elizabeth Pryor, David Reel, Susan A. Riggs, Cheryl Schnirring, Karen Schoenewaldt, Thomas F. Schwartz, Leslie Simon, Kristen Smith, Duane Sneddeker, James M. Sousa, Heather South, Alice M. Toebaas, Olga Tsapina, Rachel Waldron, William Whisler, James Zeender, and David Zeidberg.

The production of this catalog was underwritten by generous contributions from the E. Rhodes and Leona B. Carpenter Foundation and from Washington and Lee University, with the assistance of the Joella and Stewart Morris Foundation. The exhibition received major funding from the National Endowment for the Humanities.

At Giles Limited, we wish to thank Dan Giles and Sarah McLaughlin for taking on this predictably demanding project, for holding to their high standards as they brought the book to completion, and for maintaining the best of cheer throughout.

William M. S. Rasmussen
Richmond, Virginia

Robert S. Tilton
Storrs, Connecticut

Introduction

The Reinventing of Lee and Grant, 1861–2007

Thomas Eakins was nineteen years old in 1863 when Robert E. Lee's Army of Northern Virginia invaded Pennsylvania and threatened the town of Gettysburg. The young artist was among many residents of Philadelphia who anxiously followed the campaigns of the Civil War through newspaper accounts and word of mouth reports. Eakins would never fight, but he gave considerable thought to the national crisis that was unfolding before him. In 1871, after the death of Robert E. Lee and well into Ulysses S. Grant's first term as president, evidence of his continued concern about the lingering and possibly long-term effects of the war appeared in the form of a small painting (fig. 1). By then the tide of regional passions stirred by the conflict had in many areas subsided, thanks in part to the postwar efforts toward reconciliation made by both Lee and Grant.

Eakins, however, was still drawn to Appomattox. He sketched a dual portrait of the two generals pondering the results of the conflict that had shaken the nation to its core. At age twenty-seven, the artist who would become arguably the greatest American painter, was already a master at penetrating to the depths of the human condition. The protagonists are pensive; a plow and a bridled horse are visible in the background shadows, symbols of the agricultural existence that had been abandoned by many young men at the start of the war, an occupation that would be revived in the South thanks to the magnanimity of the Union commander. Eakins presents a tired, aged Confederate general, seated in full dress uniform. In defeat, Lee had to admit the tragic role fated to him in the national drama. Standing behind him in a dark uniform is the diminutive but sturdy figure of Grant, the profile of his head recognizable from a number of contemporary photographs. Victory had exacted a heavy toll in human life on both sides. Both figures seem to contemplate what has happened and what lies ahead.[1]

Both Lee and Grant did in fact give long and serious thought to the consequences of the war. In Mexico in the 1840s, these soldiers had experienced firsthand the cataclysm of battle and had been appalled by it. In the years leading up to their momentous decisions of 1861, both had been among the voices for the preservation of the Union. At Appomattox, they recognized all too clearly what had transpired. The surrender had brought an end to the killing locally, and had set the stage for the ending of the war, but enormous problems lay ahead. Both Lee and Grant are portrayed by Eakins as exhausted from their efforts, but with the presence of mind to be concerned about the nation's destiny.

By 1871, most Americans considered either Ulysses S. Grant (fig. 2) or Robert E. Lee (fig. 3) to be a hero. The reputations of the two generals, molded in part by a regional bias that would aggrandize the achievements of one often to the detriment of the other, would wax and wane over the next 140 years. Writers defending the "Lost Cause" of the Confederacy mythologized Lee as an invincible military genius and a man of character, the embodiment of what was best about the Old South. Literally scores of adulatory biographies were written, and images of Lee were to be found in many southern homes. What was worst about the Old South, however, the institution of slavery, would in the long run undo Lee's standing in American memory. By contrast, at the close of the war Grant was beloved in the North as the savior of the Union. However, the scandals brought about by Grant appointees during his presidential terms would tarnish the reputation of the victorious general who had been elected twice by popular votes of appreciation. Grant's virtues faded from public memory after he was laid to rest, but his military and political flaws would be remembered in the early twentieth century. During the final battles of World War I, the high mortality rate among Grant's troops in the last years of the Civil War was recalled; his presidential lapses in judgment would later be compared to the scandals of the Harding administration. More recently, thanks in large part to the editing and publication of the Grant Papers, his ability as a leader, his determination, and his stoicism have brought about a far more positive assessment of the general and president. Indeed, his major failing seems to have been his tremendous loyalty to his friends and to those to whom he had delegated authority.

Following Appomattox through the end of the nineteenth century, both Lee and Grant received considerable praise from their respective constituencies. However, while Lee was revered as the symbol of unvanquished southern pride, much more than was Jefferson Davis, Grant was not similarly admired in the North. Abraham Lincoln had been the personification of northern resolve. When Grant was victorious, he had shared the glory with Lincoln. Although Grant grew in symbolic stature when he was about to conquer Virginia, he would never become the emblem of Union hope akin to what Lee was in the South.

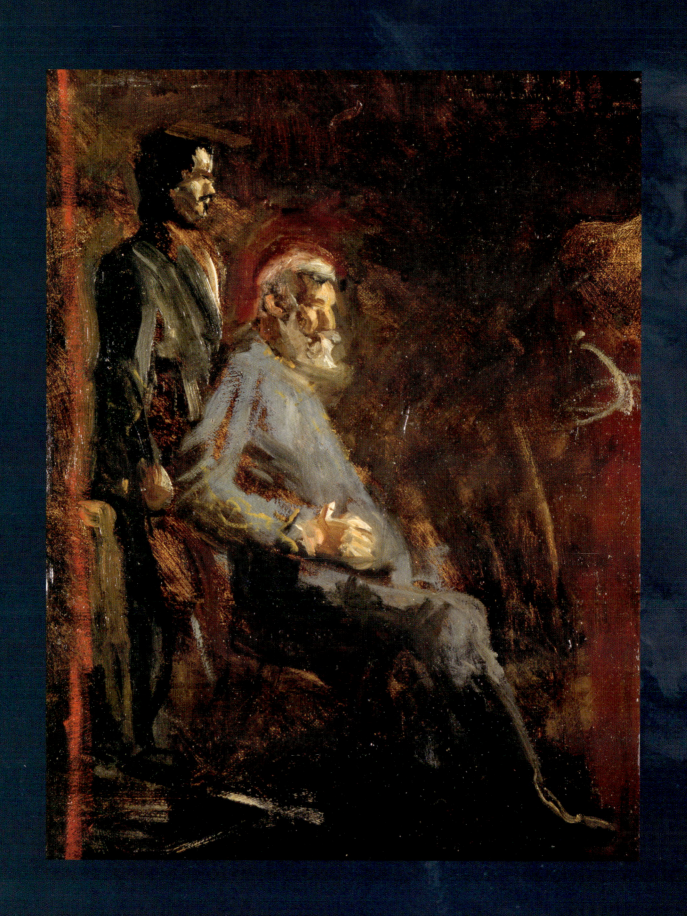

fig. 1.
Thomas Eakins, *Sketch of Lee and Grant at Appomattox*, c. 1871, oil on canvas mounted on fiberboard, 13⅛ × 10 in. (33.3 × 25.4 cm.), Hirshhorn Museum and Sculpture Garden, Smithsonian Institution, Gift of Joseph H. Hirshhorn, 1966 (photograph by Lee Stalsworth)

fig. 2.
Brady and Co., *Grant at Headquarters, Cold Harbor, Virginia*, June 11 or 12, 1864 (photograph courtesy of National Portrait Gallery, Smithsonian Institution)

fig. 3.
Julian Vannerson, *Robert E. Lee*, 1864 (photograph courtesy of Virginia Historical Society)

Although he rarely voiced his displeasure, Grant had long been annoyed about the high estimation in which Lee was held. After arriving in the East to assume command of the Union forces in 1864, he was reputed to have said to his more timorous lieutenants, "I'm tired of hearing about Bobby Lee. You'd think he was going to do a double somersault and land in our rear. Quit thinking about what he's going to do to you and think about what you're going to do to him." While traveling in Germany towards the end of his life, Grant broke what had been a long silence on the subject of Lee's reputation. He argued to a newspaper reporter that the accomplishments of his antagonist had been inflated from the start. During the war, northern generals had never received as strong support from the press as had Lee in the South. Grant's military predecessors had failed to use their great advantages in men and materials; when he did, Grant found himself in a position in which victory was expected, indeed inevitable, and his praise at the time was undermined by commentators who saw him as a "butcher" because of the high number of casualties on both sides. Grant recognized that his reputation had too often been diminished because his accomplishments were disparagingly compared to those of Lee, but he hoped, as it turned out in vain, that time would settle the comparison to his advantage.

> Lee was a good man, a fair commander, who had everything in his favor. He was a man who needed sunshine. He was supported by the unanimous voice of the South; he was supported by a large party in the North; he had the support and sympathy of the outside world.… Our generals had a hostile press, lukewarm friends and a public opinion outside.… Lee was of a slow, conservative, cautious nature, without imagination or humor, always the same, with grave dignity. I never could see in his achievements what justifies his reputation. The illusion that nothing but heavy odds beat him will not stand the ultimate light of history. I know it is not true.

After the war, while Grant's popularity was undeniable, the deification of Lee began in earnest. The vanquished general was believed by many observers to have been a better soldier, a better leader, and a better man.

At the turn of the century, as the construction of the last of the major monuments to Grant began, what had been a steady stream of Grant biographies slowed to a trickle. Books and articles about Lee, however, continued to increase in quantity. Southern sympathizers had adjusted their primary focus. Lee's character and his private life were now exalted. In the North, few biographers extolled Grant's domestic life. Indeed, for much of the twentieth century, Grant's vices unaccountably outshone his virtues.[2]

One of the reasons that the Lee cult continued while adulation for Grant faltered was based on the most obvious of motivations. The South had lost the war. There was no northern equivalent for such humiliation. Northern writers after Appomattox inherited no obligation to try to revamp the historical record, nor was there a need to defend the virtues of a lost way of life. There were no commensurate years of the personal and economic hardships that had followed defeat in the South. While in the industrialized North the view was forward, in the South it was often toward a nostalgic past. The voices coming from the postwar South were trying to exorcise demons; toward this end they invoked the saintly figure of their greatest leader. While Grant's achievements were undeniable, his adherents became fewer and fewer. As the memory of his extraordinary accomplishments began to fade, so too did Grant from the consciousness of the American public.

Historical hindsight is not 20/20 in either case. We undertook this project with a sense that one of the challenges was going to be seeing past the mythologies in an attempt to find the actual men. The notion of looking at them together, which we saw as somewhat novel, seemed to provide a platform from which one could view the emergence of each of these quite private individuals into the public sphere, and thereby allow for a reappraisal of their lives and careers that might bring a useful balance to the wildly varying, and often inaccurate, popular conceptions of both Lee and Grant. At the outset it will be useful to look briefly at the trajectories of their mythification and demystification, processes that have colored many of the scholarly and familiar perceptions of the great antagonists.

The Reinventing of Robert E. Lee, 1861–2007

Out of what seemed failure [Lee] helped to build the wonderful and mighty triumph of our national life, in which all his countrymen, north and south, share.

Theodore Roosevelt[3]

Either [Lee] knew what slavery meant when he helped maim and murder thousands in its defense, or he did not.

W. E. B. Du Bois[4]

Almost immediately after Lee's death, many white southern writers began to present him as an exemplary Christian leader. They focused on his character, which they said enabled him to endure the war and to exhibit a patriotic, conciliatory attitude in defeat. He was a man whose personal qualities were to be emulated, whose memory was to be valued for far more than his military accomplishments.

However, there was no doubt that Robert E. Lee had inherited slaves, that his father-in-law had owned many slaves whom Lee had managed, that a number of his relatives owned slaves, and that Lee's army had defended a government that wished to perpetuate slavery. While there was much to be admired about Lee, in their efforts to make him a symbol of the best that the slaveholding society of the Old South had to offer, such writers unknowingly began a process that would ultimately make Robert E. Lee the lightning rod for attacks against the slave society that had produced him. That said, although his United States citizenship would not be restored until 1975, for much of the first one hundred years after Lee's death, his persona as a soldier of knight-like virtue would be little challenged. Such adulation, which had started even before the war ended, was questioned early on by Lee himself.

Providence raises up the man for the time, and a man for this occasion, we believe, has been raised up in Robert E. Lee, the Washington of the second American Revolution.

Richmond *Dispatch*, February 7, 1865

In the fall of 1864, Edward Caledon Bruce composed a life-size oil portrait of Lee on the battlefield. The original does not survive, but a print made from the painting preserves the grandiose image (fig. 4). The painter mimicked the famous John Trumbull depiction of George Washington at Trenton, which had long been well known to Americans through engravings. It mattered little either to Bruce or to his viewers that Lee had enjoyed no victories in recent months. More important was that Confederate journalists had already compared Lee to Washington as a means to reinvent their military

fig. 4.
After Edward Caledon Bruce, *Robert E. Lee*, lithograph after the life-size portrait, oil on canvas, painted in 1864 and now lost (photograph courtesy of Gary Gallagher)

leader as a patriot and a man with the highest moral attributes. Bruce simply made use of a model that was already in vogue. The reality in 1864 was that Lee was losing in the field. He had made little progress since the Pennsylvania campaign of the preceding year. Yet the general's reputation was ever rising, in seemingly inverse proportion to his lack of success in battle.[5]

Lee's elevation during the war followed a curious path. In 1861 he had been severely criticized for his failed campaign in western Virginia. Then came a string of dramatic victories in 1862, starting when he repulsed McClellan's march on Richmond. As a consequence, by 1863 Lee had been reinvented as the hope of the Confederacy. He and the Army of Northern Virginia became the rallying symbols of the Confederate nation. His electrifying victory at Chancellorsville in April 1863 solidified the new image of Lee that Bruce would carry to canvas a year later. This seemingly invincible persona penetrated the northern psyche as well. After the war, Ulysses S. Grant would complain about the adulation given to Lee by the wartime northern press.

Many southerners even denied that the battle of Gettysburg, fought in July 1863, was a defeat for Lee. They rationalized that the general had not been routed from the field; he had stayed the night and had retired in order. The Pennsylvania campaign was only a setback. To many civilians in the South, more important than the outcome at Gettysburg was Lee's daring to take the initiative of moving the war into the North, which did keep Union armies from menacing Virginia for many months. He inspired both the soldiers of the Confederacy and their families back home, and his reputation, if not his successes, frightened many northerners. Bruce put on canvas a statement about strength and initiative in his image of a hero too great to allow for Confederate failure. The painting proved to be a balm to the Confederacy when it was displayed in Richmond during the darkest days of the war.

At the same moment when Bruce was immortalizing Lee on canvas, an equestrian sculpture of the general was conceived with the same adulatory theme. It was to have been a monumental piece of public art for Richmond, the Confederate capital. The sculptor was Frederick Volck, a Bavarian emigrant to Baltimore who had enlisted in the Confederate Bureau of Naval Ordnance and Hydrography. By 1864, his idea was well enough developed for it to be brought to the attention of Volck's commanding officer, Captain John Mercer Brooke. However, the sculpture could not be cast while the Confederacy struggled for its very survival. Following the war, Brooke assumed the professorship of physics and astronomy at the Virginia Military Institute in Lexington. There he introduced Volck to General Lee, his neighbor and the new president of Washington College. The sculptor made a life mask, which he used to produce both a bust and a fully detailed bronze model of the equestrian portrait (fig. 5). Volck had moved a step closer to the realization of his monumental vision, but the project was never carried any further.[6]

Had Volck's sculpture been cast full scale, it would inevitably have been associated with Thomas Crawford's statue *George Washington*, which had been erected on the grounds of the Capitol in Richmond

fig. 5.
Frederick Volck, *Robert E. Lee*, 1866, bronze,
36 × 28 in. (91.4 × 71.1 cm.), Virginia
Military Institute, gift of the artist

in 1858. Crawford's impressive monument, the first equestrian sculpture of Washington, had been admired by many visitors to the seat of the Confederate government. Lee would become his generation's symbol of southern strength, pride, and hope.

If he had succeeded in gaining by his sword all the South expected and hoped for, he could not have been more honored and lamented.
Mary Custis Lee to General R. H. Chilton, December 12, 1870[7]

The funeral of Robert E. Lee was not a spectacular event. Travel to Lexington was arduous in 1870, and the resident population there was small. The funeral no doubt would have been grander had it been held in Richmond, but still nothing comparable to the extravaganza that would be staged in New York City in tribute to Grant fifteen years later. The general's widow wished to believe that defeat in the Civil War did nothing to alter Lee's status with southerners. In this Mary Custis Lee was wrong. His defeat actually contributed to the process that elevated the general's reputation. Southern adulation for Lee became mixed with feelings of despair. That despondency, which remarkably survives to this day in some southern sympathizers, ignited a near deification of the general. After Appomattox, southerners identified him as the embodiment of the best values of their lost prewar civilization. The more they praised him, the more they praised their own way of life, which had been so rudely challenged and so greatly changed. They reassured themselves with the idea that if the Old South had produced so noble a leader as Lee, it must have been a great civilization.

The end of the Confederate threat, along with the passage of a few years, allowed even some embittered Unionists to recognize virtue in their former opponent. Lee, after all, had accepted defeat gracefully, had publicly supported reunification efforts, and had retired to the quiet life of a college president. Most northerners, however, would never fully forgive Lee for the choice that he had made to fight for secession, nor would they pardon him for the deaths and suffering that secession had caused in the North. Lee's generous postwar role would eventually fade from memory, and only the image of the Confederate general would be retained.

Among the first of the southern writers who recycled feelings of admiration for Lee as a means to counteract the despair that engulfed the region was John Esten Cooke, a former Confederate general and a well-known Virginia author. In 1871, Cooke praised Lee's character over his military prowess:

> The name of Lee is beloved and respected throughout the world. Men of all parties and opinions unite in this sentiment, not only those who thought and fought with him, but those most violently opposed to his political views and career.... His very enemies love the man. His private character is the origin of this sentiment.... The soldier was great, but the man himself was greater....
>
> The crowning grace of this man, who was thus not only great but good, was the humility and trust in God, which lay at the foundation of his character.

Cooke even criticized Lee for military mistakes, and, unlike later writers, he found no fault with the behavior at Gettysburg of Lee's lieutenant, James Longstreet. Instead, Cooke argued that Lee just got "carried away" by the confidence of his men, and he dared to add the opinion of a Federal officer who described the Confederate army at Gettysburg as if "drunk on champagne." To Cooke, Pickett's charge there "failed" and "the battle and the campaign failed with it."[8]

Almost immediately after the publication of Cooke's biography,

fig. 6.
George S. Cooke, *Jubal Anderson Early*, c. 1880s (photograph courtesy of Virginia Historical Society)

a highly vocal group of southern veterans suddenly had much to say about the campaigns in which they had participated. They had not dared to speak out while Lee was alive, but now they flaunted their association with him to their own advantage. Lee was again seen as a flawless commander by men who both admired his military accomplishments and valued his character. They gave adulation to a noble leader so that they might verify, to themselves and to the world, the validity of the cause for which they had sacrificed so much, and as a way of rebuilding their own lives and careers. Jubal Early (fig. 6), a former general in Lee's Army of Northern Virginia, became the principal spokesman. Embarrassed by what some people saw as his own wartime mistakes, Early had much to prove. John Warwick Daniel, Early's former chief of staff, saw the worship of Lee as a means for political advancement in postwar Virginia. Defiant and aggressive, Early, Daniel, and their cohorts seized control of Confederate history by deifying Lee and attempted to influence national opinion by heaping scorn on Grant, whom they described as a butcher and a drunkard, characterizations that have survived to this day. Among their other targets would be Jeb Stuart and James Longstreet; the latter had recently offended Confederate veterans by daring to criticize Lee's military decisions publicly. Just as bad, Longstreet had joined the Republican Party, the party of Lincoln, and had accepted a political office in Louisiana from his prewar friend, Ulysses S. Grant.[9]

At Lee's death in 1870, veterans in Lexington rallied to form the Lee Memorial Association. The director of the group was William N. Pendleton, Lee's former chief of artillery, who after the war served as rector of Grace Episcopal Church in Lexington and was a frequent visitor to the Lee home. In January 1872, Pendleton invited Early to deliver the annual Lee birthday address. In a three-hour oration that ran to fifty pages in print, the general chronicled Lee's campaigns. Early paid particular attention to his own activities, and laid out the battle strategies in ways that disavowed all criticism of both Lee and himself. The remarks were so well received that they were printed and widely read in the South, reaffirming for Early his leadership in the Lee cult.

Previously, the Lee Memorial Association had commissioned a "Lee Memorial Volume." The author was to have been Colonel Charles Marshall, Lee's former aide, who had ghostwritten some of the general's most important wartime correspondence, including Lee's last order to his troops. But when Marshall was denied access to confiscated Confederate military records, he abandoned the project. In the meantime, a local Baptist minister and a former chaplain in the Army of Northern Virginia, J. William Jones, had been preparing his own testimonial to Lee. He assumed authorship of the association's projected volume and was allowed access to Lee's private papers. By 1874, he had finished his *Personal Reminiscences, Anecdotes and Letters of General Robert E. Lee*. For help with the military portion of the book, which from the start was projected as its cornerstone, the author had turned to Early. In this way, thousands of new readers were introduced to Early's 1872 synopsis of Lee's campaigns. The first chapter, titled "The Soldier," is simply a reprinting of Early's oration.

As interesting as Early's military account is Jones's high assessment of Lee's character:

> It was my proud privilege to have known General Lee intimately....
>
> This first attempt at authorship I sent forth with a sincere desire that it may prove acceptable to the countless admirers of the great Confederate chieftain, that it may serve to give

fig. 7.
Edward Virginius Valentine, *Robert E. Lee*, 1875 (installed 1883), marble, L. 100½ in. (255.3 cm.), Lee Chapel, Washington and Lee University, gift of the Lee Memorial Association (photograph by Kevin Remington)

to all a higher appreciation of his noble character, and that it may prove a blessing to the young men of the country (more especially to those who "wore the gray"), by inducing them to study, in order that they may imitate, his shining virtues.[10]

In addition to the volume written by Jones, the memorial association in Lexington also commissioned what would become one of the most effective images used by the Lee cult, a statue that depicts the recumbent figure of the general (fig. 7). Lee's body had been interred beneath the chapel that the general had built for his students at Washington College. The place of worship became a shrine to the general. The association decided to dramatize the new status of the chapel by displaying a marble recumbent figure of Lee at center stage, on the main floor in an apse that would be added to hold it. Within days of her husband's death, Mary Custis Lee approved the association's plan. She recommended for the job Edward Valentine, a young Richmond artist already known to the family. In 1864, while studying in Berlin, Valentine had sculpted from photographs a statuette of Lee that was sold in England to raise funds to benefit disabled Confederate veterans. In May and June of 1870, he had sculpted a bust of Lee from life. Valentine had taken the measurements of Lee's face and body, apparently the only such statistics ever recorded.

Rarely in America had a recumbent statue been commissioned to honor the memory of a heroic figure. However, the setting dictated a sculptural type from a different tradition. Valentine showed Mrs. Lee photographs and drawings of recumbent figures in Europe that he knew, including the tombs recently sculpted in Berlin by Christian Daniel Rauch for Friedrich Wilhelm III, king of Prussia, and his wife Queen Louisa. The tradition of depicting a prostrate knight in battle attire atop his sarcophagus had its roots in the Middle Ages; it was therefore a fitting tradition to adapt to Lee, who was viewed in his day as a knight of the chivalrous culture that was Old Virginia.[11]

Valentine depicted Lee in his Confederate uniform, his sword at his side. The widow preferred to interpret this image as that of her husband asleep rather than dead, but for devotees of the Lee cult, the association of this flawless Christian soldier with the heroic knights of the Crusades was what gave the piece its power. In 1883, when the new apse and mausoleum were built and the recumbent figure was installed, Lee Chapel became a pilgrimage site akin to those of medieval Europe. For people who could not travel, photographs of the shrine by Lee's last photographer, the young Confederate veteran Michael Miley, served as souvenir relics.

The unveiling of Valentine's sculpture in 1883 was an occasion for what proved to be the second memorable oration delivered in Lexington. As with Jubal Early's famous three-hour discourse, John Warwick Daniel's remarks were also printed and widely disseminated. Daniel saw the Lexington speech as an opportunity to gain visibility. His association with Robert E. Lee might reverse his own failed political career, and he made good use of the opportunity. Southerners soon linked the untarnished memory of Lee with Daniel's own qualifications for political office. Twice previously he had been denied the Democratic nomination for Congress, and he had also lost a gubernatorial election. Following the Lexington event, Daniel enjoyed repeated political victories that eventually carried him to the United States Senate. His comments on Lee followed what was by then a familiar track; the only addition was a mention of Lee's final career at Washington College.

> When the true hero has come, and we know that here he is, in verity, ah! How the hearts of men leap forth to greet him.… In Robert Lee was such a hero vouchsafed to us and

to mankind, and whether we behold him declining command of the Federal army to fight the battles and share the miseries of his own people; proclaiming on the heights in front of Gettysburg that the fault of the disaster was his own; leading charges in the crises of combat; walking under the yoke of conquest without a murmur of complaint; or refusing fortunes to come here and train the youth of his country in the path of duty—here is ever the same meek, grand, self-sacrificing spirit.

Daniel focused on Lee's character, which had guided the decision-making process of 1861, had brought him victories against long odds, and had sustained Lee through the years following defeat. Daniel could not neglect the theme of the day—Lee's military prowess—and he elaborated on the general's "schemes of war and feats of arms [that were] as brilliant as ever thrilled the soul of heroism and genius with admiration." But, he pointed out, Lee's reputation as a moral man had much to do with his success because his troops were forever loyal to him and to what he stood for.[12]

Lee's character had stirred appreciation in the South since 1861, when his Christian morality had been lauded in newspaper accounts. His character had been addressed by John Esten Cooke in 1871, and it was a quality that even Jubal Early praised in 1872, partly because he could claim that a similar moral center was lacking in Grant: "Shall I compare General Lee to his successful antagonist? As well compare the great pyramid … to a pigmy perched on Mount Atlas. No, my friends, it is a vain work for us to seek anywhere for a parallel to the great character which has won our admiration and love." Lee's character was the crucial virtue that would be cited by every biographer for the next one hundred years.[13]

The Lexington faithful had generated a memorial book, a sculpture, and two well-received orations that had much to do with Lee's elevation during the decade-and-a-half following his death. During those same years, activities to memorialize Lee were also underway in the former Confederate capital. Twenty years would pass, however, before the Richmond efforts produced a monument.

From the start, Early had been at the center of the Richmond movement. He had organized the veterans of the Army of Northern Virginia into the Lee Monument Association. At almost the same moment, the Ladies' Lee Monument Association was formed. The ladies believed that mourning was their duty, and they were particularly adept at raising funds. Unlike just about everyone else, they were not intimidated by Early. The two groups shared a remarkably similar vision: they would re-inter the general in the former Confederate capital within an exceptionally grand monument. The ladies even knew precisely where he would be placed, in Hollywood Cemetery, where so many of them had tended to Confederate graves since 1861. Mary Custis Lee, however, would have nothing to do with this burial idea and would not agree to change the Lexington site.

Initially, the Lexington and Richmond organizations competed for the same revenues, which were scarce in the postwar South. Then Mrs. Lee asked that the recumbent statue for Lexington be finished first; Valentine delivered his sculpture in 1877 even though the chapel was not yet ready to receive it. Now free to move forward, the Richmond groups staged a sculptural competition that year, but it failed. They tried and failed again the following year.

In 1884, after some coaxing from the governor, who by good fortune was the general's nephew Fitzhugh Lee, the two Richmond groups united as a new Lee Monument Association. The governor assumed leadership of the effort. The partnership may have cost the ladies their separate identity, but they still had much to do with the success of the project. It was the ladies who initiated the sculptural competition of 1886 that yielded a successful design. The result was a large equestrian bronze that is the most impressive of the monuments to the general. Lee is projected not as a sleeping knight nor as the aggressive tactician that he actually was, but as a self-controlled and flawless soldier. He is as well, emphatically, a man of character. Intentionally, the sculpture rivals the Thomas Crawford equestrian monument to George Washington that embellishes the grounds of the Richmond Capitol. Viewers were meant to compare the two statues and the two men.

The commission process proved to be difficult, in part because the ladies and veterans had such different ideas about how to proceed. Jubal Early wrote the governor that if a Yankee sculpted the work, he would "get together all the surviving members of the Second Corps [of Lee's army] and blow it up with dynamite." Among those recruited by the ladies to judge the competition were Augustus Saint-Gaudens and John Quincy Adams Ward, both highly accomplished sculptors from the North. The competition was blind; no names were attached to the entries and northerners were allowed to participate. First prize was originally awarded to Charles Niehaus, a Cincinnati

fig. 8.
Jean-Antonin Mercié, *Lee Monument*, Richmond, 1886–90, bronze, scene of the unveiling (photograph courtesy of Virginia Historical Society)

sculptor who had yet to make a name for himself. However, on learning the names of the competitors, Saint-Gaudens argued that the most talented of the group actually was Jean-Antonin Mercié, a Frenchman whom he had known in the late 1860s in Paris. Mercié's original entry, which had depicted the horse rearing and Lee in the role of a conquering hero, had been rejected. The French sculptor was persuaded to submit a second design (fig. 8). In the revised model, the horse is as tranquil and self-contained as its rider. This was the general reinvented as a man of character, and so the design was accepted. The uniform and Lee's accouterments were faithfully copied from originals brought to Mercié's Paris studio by Sarah Nicolas

Randolph, the leader of the ladies' group, who was accompanied on her visits by the general's daughter, Mary Lee. Mercié was directed to cast the sculpture larger and build the base taller than had originally been proposed, so that the monument, at sixty-one feet, would stand barely taller than Crawford's *Washington*. Only the word "Lee" would be needed on the base to identify the subject.[14]

If the united Lee Monument Association struggled with the design process, it showed remarkable vision in placing the statue. Mercié's equestrian monument was made the focal point of an entirely new neighborhood west of the city. The principal axis was

appropriately named Monument Avenue. Newspapers estimated that the crowd at the unveiling in 1890 exceeded one hundred and fifty thousand people. Twenty-five thousand participated in the parade alone, which *The New York Times* reported took more than four hours to pass. The event was a high-water mark for the Lee cult. For decades white visitors to Richmond would make a pilgrimage to the statue. Photographs of it would proliferate. During the first half of the twentieth century, Lee's principal biographer, Douglas Southall Freeman, would reportedly salute it each day on his way to work. It was the Lee whom the people of Virginia and the South wanted to see, placed on a site that reminded them of his efforts to preserve their city and their nation.[15]

Richmond's African American newspaper, the *Richmond Planet*, recorded a different perspective on the festivities, one that would go little noticed for much of the next century: "Rebel flags were everywhere displayed and the long lines of Confederate veterans … told in no uncertain terms that they still clung to theories which were presumed to be buried for all eternity." The imposing Mercié sculpture, perhaps not surprisingly, would have much to do with the rejection of Lee by the black community of Richmond during the next century.[16]

The association of Lee with slavery was not new; it had been well established by the time of the 1890 unveiling. W. E. B. Du Bois would alert a wider audience to this issue. He castigated Lee as a fool and a traitor because "either he knew what slavery meant when he helped maim and murder thousands in its defense, or he did not." To this day, the problematic association of the general with the glaring evil of the society that produced him has yet to go away.[17]

Despite the protests of many African Americans, stories of Lee's exemplary character were often repeated at the end of the century. Lee was from the finest of families. He was linked to George Washington through his father's service and friendship, and later through his wife. He was devoted to a loving mother who had taught him duty and self-control. He detested slavery and opposed secession. As a commander he never blamed subordinates. After the war he advanced national reconciliation, and he sacrificed opportunities to attain personal wealth in order to educate the youth of the South. By 1890 little mention was made of his unblemished record at West Point, his outstanding record as a general, and his brave but ultimately hopeless stand against the numerical and material superiority of the North; in many ways, he was his character. By the time that Mercié's creation was finally hauled atop its massive pedestal, Lee's character had become intertwined with the story of the "Lost Cause" of the Confederacy. Contemporary accounts of Lee's life served to remind Americans of the North and South of the merits of the southern culture that had produced him.

Antebellum Virginia in particular had been romanticized; it was different, and somehow superior, to the rest of the Old South. Old Virginia was wistfully remembered by scores of authors who imagined a seemingly idyllic and enlightened plantation society, which they contrasted to the crass, urbanized, and industrialized present. Most of these writers were, of course, Virginians. The list includes the prolific but aging John Esten Cooke, along with newcomers George Cary Eggleston and Thomas Nelson Page. Page was arguably the best of the lot. His emotional tales from Old Virginia were read with tear-filled eyes in both the North and the South.[18]

Northerners were receptive to these stories. As the United States emerged as an international power with imperialist motives, northerners came to appreciate the military service and sacrifices that had been made by many southerners. They remembered the Civil War less in terms of victories and defeats and more for its stories of heroism and valor. Also, the nostalgia for the passing of a simpler, rural lifestyle was attractive because many in the North were worried about the dark side of the "Gilded Age," an era of excessive spending by a wealthy few while many suffered in poverty. They pondered a future dominated by increased immigration and industrialization.

[Lee was] a leader of men in war and peace, a champion of principles, a humanitarian, a man who devoted his entire life to the benefit of others without regard to himself.

Woodrow Wilson[19]

By the first years of the twentieth century, thanks to the effectiveness of southern writers, the rebel leader had been transformed into a national hero. In fact, a mania for Lee swept the country. As early as 1900, the *Chautauquan* placed Lee in "the first triumvirate of greatness" with Lincoln and Washington. In 1907 Theodore Roosevelt saw Lee's life as a "matter of pride to all our countrymen" and proposed the establishment of a national memorial.

In 1916 *Harper's* praised Lee as "the pride of the whole country." In 1924, Woodrow Wilson saw Lee's status as so high that it could not "be lifted to any new place of distinction by any man's words of praise." The general was, the former president said, "a leader of men in war and peace, a champion of principles, a humanitarian, a man who devoted his entire life to the benefit of others without regard to himself."[20]

This reinvention of Lee as a national hero allowed the now Senator John Warwick Daniel to mastermind the commissioning of a sculpture of the general for Statuary Hall in the U.S. Capitol. The year was 1903. For the preceding decade-and-a-half, Ulysses S. Grant had been honored with a series of equestrian monuments in northern cities. In 1900, a standing marble sculpture of the Union general had been unveiled in Washington in the rotunda of the Capitol. Three years later, a competition was staged to commission what would be the definitive sculptural monument to Grant, which was to be placed in Washington, D. C. on the mall directly below the Capitol. Lee's supporters knew that the centennial of his birth, 1907, was approaching. The time was right for the southern general to be honored in the nation's capital along with Grant.

In 1864, Congress had awarded to each state the privilege of presenting a pair of statues to Statuary Hall. Left to each state was the selection of which figures to honor, and few sculptures had been received prior to 1900. Because of this lengthy process, an image of Lee could be brought to the Capitol free of the tarnish of secession. The former "rebel," whom some congressmen of the Reconstruction era would have hanged for treason, would now be honored as one of the two figures from Virginia's past most worthy of national recognition. (The first, of course, was George Washington.) Past animosities, however, would delay the unveiling of both Virginia statues until 1934. Even at that date, the inclusion of Lee was not without controversy, especially among those northerners who had lost fathers and grandfathers in the conflict.

The sixty-five-year-old Edward Valentine welcomed the challenge offered by Senator Daniel. Valentine, however, clothed Lee in his Confederate uniform (fig. 9). He hadn't recognized that in the years since 1870 the general had been reinvented as a man of virtue and peace. In 1907, when the artist had virtually completed his work, his patron complained that the sculptor had depicted the wrong persona of Lee. The politically astute senator recognized

fig. 9.
Edward Virginius Valentine, *Robert E. Lee*, 1903–09, bronze, h. 78 in. (198.1 cm.), Statuary Hall, U.S. Capitol (photograph courtesy of Architect of the Capitol)

fig. 10.
Theodore E. Pine, *Robert E. Lee*, 1904, oil on canvas, 47 ½ × 36 ¾ in. (120.7 × 85.7 cm.), Washington and Lee University

that Americans in 1907 wanted to know Lee the private citizen:

> Though intense Confederate as I was and as loyal to memory as I am, my conviction is that Lee as presented to the nation should be in a plain citizen's coat, without mark or designation of rank or military distinction. When I first saw Lee in 1861 in Richmond, where he had gone to become Major General of the Virginia Forces, he wore plain citizen's dress. The moment my eye caught his face and figure, I was completely fascinated, and I said to myself "there is the greatest creature I ever looked upon." …
>
> The Confederacy was an episode of human history, and while Lee was the greatest General of history, except Napoleon, he is the greatest man of history excepting none. He should stand in the National Capitol in his greatest character.

Daniel added, "It matters not that your statue of him is about done. Let Virginia keep it and let her order, at any reasonable cost to be made by you, a statue of Lee in citizen's dress of heroic size to be presented to the United States."21

In 1904, Robert E. Lee, Jr. had published a loving account of his father's life entitled *Recollections and Letters of General Robert E. Lee*. The emphasis, predictably, was less on the general's military achievements than on his humanity. The reader is warmly welcomed into a caring family environment. The book received enthusiastic reviews nationwide and went through multiple printings. The younger Lee had given Americans the picture of the general that they wanted. Northerners could never love him as a soldier, but the son's account of the man was almost irresistible.

Also in 1904, Theodore Pine painted the portrait of Lee that has probably been reproduced more than any other canvas (fig. 10). The artist simply copied the upper portion of the photograph taken in Richmond in 1864 by Julian Vannerson. Pine was painting portraits in New York City as early as the 1850s. By 1904 he was an experienced artist, who for his health had moved to Asheville, North Carolina. There he found patrons more interested in looking at Lee's portrait than their own. In what was the year before he died, Pine

fig. 11.
Charles Francis Adams, Jr., relief sculpture at Washington and Lee University (photograph courtesy of Virginia Historical Society)

painted multiple versions of the Lee image. By the mid-1930s, one of the canvases had been given to Washington and Lee University. Over the years there were also gifts of a few small sculptures, but there was a strange absence in Lexington of any sort of monumental depiction of the general other than his sculpted figure in death.[22]

Vannerson's image of a remarkably handsome and spectacularly uniformed leader appealed in the South in 1904 because it both evoked thoughts of Old Virginia and reminded viewers of the character of Lee. The general seems like King Arthur, the creation of a culture based on honor and chivalry. He is remarkably calm, self-contained, and noble. Here, it could be reasoned by those who admired Lee, was the man who truly loved the Union and who by his temperate nature had worked to restore it after Appomattox.

Robert E. Lee is "one of our sacred men" whom we "consecrate" and "wish to resemble," and whom "you set on a high column, that all men looking at it, may be continually apprised of the duty you expect of them."

Charles Francis Adams, Jr., former Union general[23]

In Lexington, on the centennial of Lee's birth, a third memorable oration was delivered in the series that Jubal Early had made famous thirty-five years earlier. It was noteworthy because the speaker was a northerner (fig. 11). Charles Francis Adams, Jr. was a historian and president of the New England Historical Association. A direct descendant of Presidents John and John Quincy Adams and a former Union officer, he was not easily challenged as to his credentials to speak for all of America. Adams gave credibility to the new ideas about Lee, projecting him more as a nationalist than as a rebel general. He dared to state that all Americans owed Lee a debt of gratitude for his role in the difficult reconciliation process following the war. Even more surprising was his argument that Lee in fact had little choice on the secession issue. If I had been a Virginian in 1861, Adams said, my decision would have been the same.

The course set by Adams was followed by another New Englander of ancient lineage, Gamaliel Bradford. In 1912 he published a full-length biography entitled *Lee the American*. The book was well received in both the North and the South. To justify the nationalist theme signaled in the title, Bradford gave emphasis to Lee's role in reconciliation. To win the approval of more militant northern readers, however, he also stressed Lee's failures in life:

> I have referred ... to the immense importance of his general influence in bringing about reconciliation and peace. It is almost impossible to overestimate this ....
>
> Lee's life will always be regarded as a record of failure. And it is precisely because he failed that I have been interested to make this study of him .... America in the twentieth century worships success .... Here was a man who ... left an example that future Americans may study with profit as long as there is an America.

The works of Adams, Bradford, and even Pine are evidence of how some northerners had been complicitous in the projection of a highly favorable image of Lee to the nation.[24]

Southerners continued to portray Lee positively between 1920 and World War II. This was the era of the "Southern Renaissance" in literature. Towering amidst the best writers that the nation produced at this time was a southern historian who set out to vindicate the high standing given to Lee. His means would be to

fig. 12.
Jean Leon Gerome Ferris, *Let Us Have Peace, 1865*, c. 1920, oil on canvas, 23 × 30 in. (58.4 × 76.2 cm.), Virginia Historical Society, Lora Robins Collection of Virginia Art

present overwhelming factual evidence. Thanks to the Herculean efforts of biographer Douglas Southall Freeman, Lee's status would continue to rise.

Many Americans in the 1920s were interested in learning more about the colonial and antebellum past. Preservationists pointed to the two residences that were associated with Lee before 1861 as worthy of rescue. In 1925, Congress designated Arlington House, which sits within Arlington National Cemetery, as a national shrine that henceforth would be known as "The Robert E. Lee Memorial." Relics inherited by Mary Custis Lee from George Washington, which had been confiscated from the house in 1861, were returned by the government. In 1928, the Robert E. Lee Memorial Foundation was established to acquire and restore Stratford Hall, where Lee had spent his first eight years. *The New York Times*, which had endorsed the movement to reclaim Arlington House, devoted some thirty-one articles to Lee's birthplace. Organizations in two dozen states raised funds for Stratford, and Lady Astor (born Nancy Langhorne in Virginia) chaired a campaign in Great Britain. It had become fashionable among the educated and wealthy to revere the legacy of Robert E. Lee.[25]

It was also during the 1920s that the Philadelphia painter Jean Leon Gerome Ferris pictured Lee and Grant at Appomattox (fig. 12). This scene, which had been depicted by printmakers as early as 1865, can be viewed as evidence of both generals' status in America some sixty years after the event. Ferris's title, "Let us have peace," quotes the supposed words of the northern general at this solemn occasion. (Grant actually said "Let us have peace" three years later, as a campaign statement at the start of the presidential race of 1868.) The Union commander, who allowed magnanimous terms that helped to restore a measure of tranquility to the nation, is awarded his share of dignity, but the focal point of the painting is Lee. Both men, it seems, had come to the conclusion that the soon-to-be reunited states must be supported, but the burden would fall to Lee to convince his defeated countrymen.

By 1931, Lee's star had risen sufficiently for the United States Military Academy at West Point to reclaim the legacy of his tenure as superintendent. The general had been summoned to West Point in 1852 in recognition of the heroism that he had displayed during the Mexican War. His service as superintendent at the academy had been distinguished but had long been forgotten. Ernest Ludwig Ipsen was commissioned to create a flattering image of Lee as he appeared prior to the Civil War (fig. 13). Like Theodore Pine, Ipsen was a society portraitist in New York City. He worked from a Mathew Brady photograph taken about 1852. Although Brady had recorded Lee's handsome appearance as a civilian, Ibsen provided a full dress uniform for the brevet colonel of engineers. The impressive coat is actually much more ornate than the real one that Lee wore and that Robert W. Weir had painted from life in 1853 (see fig. 101).

Although many people had come to see Lee as a national hero, the true nature of the man who had led secessionist troops that slaughtered thousands of Union soldiers seemed elusive. The poet Stephen Vincent Benét was among those who questioned what had been said about Lee. He rejected the possibility that this "marble man" followed an uncomplicated creed of honor and spirituality, and searched instead for a more complex personality.

> A figure lost to flesh and blood and bones,
> Frozen into a legend out of life,
> A blank-verse statue—
> How to humanize
> That solitary gentleness and strength
> Hidden behind the deadly oratory
> Of twenty thousand Lee Memorial days,
> How show, in spite of all the rhetoric,
> All the sick honey of the speechifiers,
> Proportion, not as something calm congealed
> From lack of fire, but ruling such a fire
> As only such proportion could contain?
> The man was loved, the man was idolized,
> The man had every just and noble gift.
> He took great burdens and he bore them well,
> Believed in God but did not preach too much,
> Believed and followed duty first and last
> With marvelous consistency and force,
> Was a great victor, in defeat as great,
> No more, no less, always himself in both,
> Could make men die for him but saved his men
> Whenever he could save them—was most kind
> But was not disobeyed—was a good father,
> A loving husband, a considerate friend:
> Had little humor, but enough to play

fig. 13.
Ernest L. Ipsen, *Brevet Colonel Robert E. Lee, Superintendent USMA*, 1931, oil on canvas, 64 × 39 in. (162.6 × 99.1 cm.), West Point Art Collection, United States Military Academy, West Point, New York

Mild jokes that never wounded, but had charm,
Did not seek intimates, yet drew men to him,
Did not seek fame, did not protest against it,
Knew his own value without pomp or jealousy
And died as he preferred to live—sans phrase,
With commonsense, tenacity and courage,
A Greek proportion—and a riddle unread.
And everything that we have said is true
And nothing helps us yet to read the man,
Nor will he help us while he has the strength
To keep his heart his own.

Benét recalled comments from Lee's contemporaries about how difficult it was to get to know the actual man beneath the handsome façade, who "kept his heart a secret to the end/From all the picklocks of biographers." It would take a master locksmith to bring Lee the man to life. Fortunately, there was a volunteer ready to take up the task.[26]

Douglas Southall Freeman's four-volume biography, published in 1934, is some 2,100 pages in length. It was exhaustively researched and lucidly written. *R.E. Lee* won a Pulitzer Prize, and *The New York Times* decreed that the story of Lee was "complete for all time." Freeman, it must be said, repeated many of the adulatory arguments of his predecessors. The emphasis on character, the explanation of duty owed to one's family and to one's state, the accusation that subordinates failed in combat, and the celebration of postwar sacrifice for the good of the South and the nation were all familiar themes. What was different was the minute detail that Freeman offered as convincing, even irrefutable evidence that the old ideas were sound. Also extraordinary was the meticulous craftsmanship underlying his presentation. The result of Freeman's biography was that Lee's already high reputation rose to its apogee. Even northerners who detested the memory of the rebellion had to admit that Lee had at least a shred of greatness in him, and that Freeman was a brilliant historian.[27]

Freeman presented the general as a man of "simplicity and spirituality." Lee was projected as an uncomplicated figure whose conduct was determined by faith and by a strict code of behavior. The religious values could be understood, but his devotion to honor, duty, and self-control seemed almost unbelievable. In an effort to convince his readers that the general had no choice concerning decisions that many in the twentieth century disparaged, Freeman explained Lee's characteristic self-discipline:

> Because he was calm when others were frenzied, loving when they hated, and silent when they spoke with bitter tongue, they shook their heads and said he was a superman or a mysterious man.... They were mistaken.... What he seemed, he was—a wholly human gentleman, the essential elements of whose positive character were two and only two, simplicity and spirituality....
>
> Of humility and submission was born a spirit of self-denial that prepared him for the hardships of the war and, still more, for the dark destitution that followed it.... Through it all, his spirit of self-denial met every demand upon it.... And if one, only one, of all the myriad incidents of his stirring life had to be selected to typify his message, as a man, to the young Americans ... It occurred in Northern Virginia, probably on his last visit there. A young mother brought her baby to him to be blessed. He took the infant in his arms and looked at it and then at her and slowly said, "Teach him he must deny himself."

Freeman's scholarly approach brought credibility to the earlier accounts by Lee's comrades. Because of its length and scrupulous detail, *R. E. Lee* was hard to challenge.[28]

While Freeman was quick to defend Lee from detractors in

28 INTRODUCTION

seemingly every other sphere, he had relatively little to say on the subject of race. He did not envision that Lee would eventually be castigated on the score. Born, raised, and resident in an overtly racist society, Freeman could not have imagined that this would become a dominant issue. To those who argued that the general was harsh in the handling of the slaves owned by his father-in-law, Freeman answered that Lee was just as harsh in his treatment of his soldiers—he simply made both perform what he saw as their duties. To those who argued that Lee did not develop personal friendships with blacks, Freeman answered that Lee did not mistreat blacks nor did he dislike them. If Lee thought that blacks were less capable than whites and that they warranted a low position in society, he was not responsible for putting them in that position. To Freeman, Lee, for his time, place, and upbringing, was actually advanced in his sensitivity to the plight of African Americans.

For years Freeman had been a respected newspaper editor and radio commentator in the former Confederate capital. Following the enthusiastic reception of *R. E. Lee*, Americans who had become disillusioned by the tragedies of World War I and the Great Depression listened when Freeman pointed to Lee's strength of character and the South's ability to endure the heavy losses of war and economic misery. It is perhaps as much evidence of Freeman's influence in Virginia as of Lee's reputation there that a World War II recruiting poster was issued that asked for "Lee Navy Volunteers" (fig. 14). The new recruits would form a unit of 2,306 enlistees to be sworn in during the summer of 1942.[29]

[Lee was] one of the noblest Americans who ever lived, and one of the greatest captains known in the annals of war.
Winston Churchill[30]

Taken altogether, [Lee] was noble as a leader and as a man, and unsullied as I read the pages of our history.
Dwight David Eisenhower[31]

Comments such as those by Churchill and Eisenhower seem strange today. Did they dismiss racial discrimination in the Old South as condonable for its time and place, and so absolve Lee from recrimination on that score? As the Civil Rights Movement unfolded, many Americans began to recognize that the stance on race taken by many past and contemporary white commentators was unacceptable. As a consequence, Lee's reputation came under new scrutiny, in part because his family held slaves, but mainly because he had become the principal symbol of a nation that seemingly had been founded in order to perpetuate the peculiar institution.[32]

The Civil War Centennial, a celebration that focused on the military personae of both Lee and Grant, caused Americans to look anew at both generals. Grant's reputation began to rise, but where Lee was concerned this new attention undermined his status. Leaders of the Civil Rights Movement demanded a reassessment of the man whose army had defended slavery. Lee's reputation, like that of George Washington, who was suddenly seen as a slaveholder first and the "Father of His Country" second, began to plummet.

In 1977, the most adventurous of the historians who would challenge Freeman published a shocking rebuttal of *R. E. Lee*. Thomas Connelly gives 80 percent of *The Marble Man* to the mythologizing of Lee. Those pages provide a useful, detailed, and largely accurate summation of the literature published since the Civil War. But the last sixty pages present an original, and at times outrageous, interpretation of Lee's character:

> In truth, Lee was an extremely complex individual. Lee the man has become so intermingled with Lee the hero symbol that the real person has been obscured….
>
> Lee was neither serene nor simple. His life was replete with frustration, self-doubt, and a feeling of failure. All these were hidden behind his legendary reserve and his credo of duty and self-control. He was actually a troubled man, convinced that he had failed as prewar career officer, parent, and moral individual. He suffered the hardships of an unsatisfactory marriage, long absences from his family, and chronic homesickness for his beloved Virginia. He distrusted his own conduct. The specter of family scandals in the past, his unhappy marital situation, his strong Calvinistic obsession with sin—all united to make Lee fear for his self-control….
>
> … a man who is a great historical figure in his own right was shaped into what others wanted him to be, and has become something that he never was.

Connelly's suggestion that Lee was in fact a "complex individual" is fair; portrayals of the general had tended to be rather simplistic. His sketch of Lee as a troubled man who saw himself as a failure in

fig. 14.
I fought for Virginia. Now it's your turn! Join the Lee Navy Volunteers, 1942, 27 × 21 in. (68.6 × 53.3 cm.), World War II recruiting poster, Virginia Historical Society

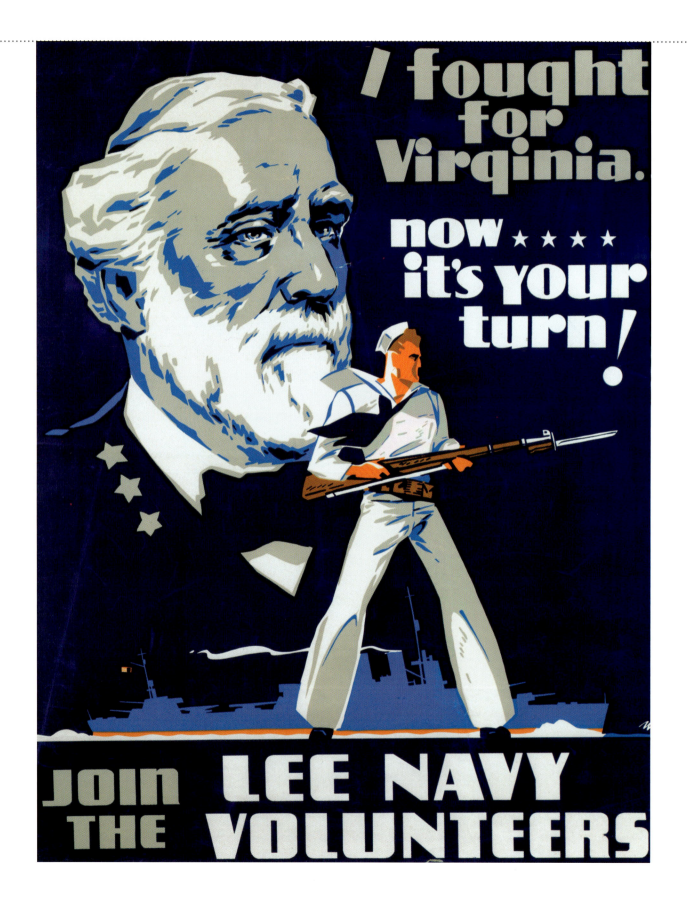

all of the important aspects of his life, however, stretches the available evidence beyond the bounds of credibility.[33]

General Lee's character has been an example to succeeding generations, making the restoration of his citizenship an event in which every American can take pride.

Gerald R. Ford[34]

In the mid-1970s, while Lee's character was under attack from a number of different directions, the federal government chose to honor him. After intense lobbying by southern regionalists, the general's citizenship was restored and his name was even given to a new Polaris submarine. Many northerners, however, remained indifferent to the idea of revering Lee, and a number of African Americans were vehement in their negative response. Through the 1980s and 1990s, the Confederacy and its figurehead were constantly impugned. In *Lee Considered: General Robert E. Lee and Civil War History* (1991), Alan T. Nolan brought forward evidence that Lee's views on race were not as benign as his followers would like to believe. The denigration of Lee as a slaveholder who led the fight to perpetuate slavery worked as well to undermine the mythologies that had been created about Lee, Old Virginia, and the Old South in general. The reputation of Lee had reached its nadir.

In June 1999, Lee's status as a symbol of racial hatred was made clear in Richmond. A portion of the city's newly restored Kanawha and Haxall canals was set aside as an outdoor history museum. Thirty giant banners depicting figures from Virginia's past were hung there. Included was an all too familiar image, the head and shoulders portion of the 1864 photograph of Lee by Julian Vannerson. The banner was soon defaced and ultimately had to be removed from the riverfront pantheon. City Council member Sa'ad El-Amin protested Lee's inclusion by equating the Confederacy with slavery and arguing that those who seek to glorify its soldiers and symbols are nostalgic for the rigid racial boundaries that had been maintained in Richmond for a century following emancipation. El-Amin compared Lee to Adolf Hitler and contended that Richmond's abundance of Confederate memorials on Monument Avenue offended African Americans in the majority-black city.[35]

Members of the Virginia Division of the Sons of Confederate Veterans responded to such attacks by rallying at the state Capitol. There they cheered the general as "the greatest American who has ever walked the face of this Earth." They paraded portraits of Lee with the caption "Carry Me Back [to Old Virginia]." A black scholar, Edward C. Smith, the director of the American Studies Program at American University, supported the protestors. "Robert E. Lee's name has been defiled," he said. The comparison of Lee to Hitler and the removal of a portrait of Lee from a history site he called "absolutely absurd" actions.[36]

The Richmond incident reaffirmed the association of Lee with both the Confederacy and its terrible institution. Barbara Ingram explained her perspective when the city council opened public hearings on the matter: "No amount of pretty words can change the cause for which Robert E. Lee stood." Former governor L. Douglas Wilder identified the problem when he asked, "What purpose is served by continuing to flaunt those images?"[37]

Four years later in Richmond, the executive board of the Robert E. Lee Council of the Boy Scouts of America, which represents the membership of twenty-four central Virginia counties, removed the general's name from its confederation. The group had honored Lee's name since 1942, the year that "Lee Navy Volunteers" had been recruited. The change "was the right thing to do," said scout executive Robert A. Tuggle. This decision sparked another public furor in central Virginia. Waves of letters, pro and con, were written to the local newspaper. Ross Mackenzie, editor of the *Richmond Times-Dispatch*, argued that the "good" general simply "went the wrong way." "Homages to Lee [are] symbols of the indefensible," he wrote, because "The Confederacy simply cannot be separated from slavery."[38]

In his *The Making of Robert E. Lee*, Michael Fellman challenges Freeman's interpretation of Lee's character. He sees a dark side to Lee's mind, and to southern society in general: "Lee was deeply antidemocratic, fearing that unprincipled demagogues in alliance with the undisciplined lower orders were destroying his genteel world." Fellman also suggests that "Only war could bring him fame and fulfillment." A bit later, he added fuel to the anti-Lee fires:

> Lee's star is fading, along with the passing of segregation, and fewer Americans, even in the Deep South, still venerate Lee uncritically….
>
> He was a leader in the Southern rebellion, in which so many fought so nobly for such a bad cause…. To accept Saint Robert would be to accept the code of the white South

fig. 15.
Joseph Edward Baker, *Ulysses S. Grant*, 1863, hand-colored lithograph, 22 ⅝ × 17 ⅜ in. (57.6 × 44.3 cm.), National Portrait Gallery, Smithsonian Institution

at face value, to deny the reality of terrible historical questions by embracing the willful self-blinding of hero worship. Like Connelly, Fellman oversteps what can be reasonably gleaned from the record. To suggest that Lee was a warmonger who was counting on a conflict to bring him "fame and fulfillment" seems simply wrong, and it is difficult for anyone to state, as Fellman does, that another person is "enigmatic, even to himself." It was perhaps inevitable that the passions of anti-Confederates who denigrated Lee would inspire neo-Confederates who poured praise on Lee. Equally exaggerated denunciations from both sides continue to this day.[39]

In 1931, before he abandoned plans to write his own biography of Lee, Allen Tate fumed,

> The longer I've contemplated the venerable features of Lee, the more I've hated him. It is as if I had married a beautiful girl, perfect in figure, pure in all those physical attributes that seem to clothe purity of character, and then had found when she had undressed that the hidden places were corrupt and diseased.

Lee has been clothed and undressed by apologists and detractors since 1861. While his image will inevitably continue to be linked to the society that reared him and the institution that was the law in the homeland that he chose to defend, during the past decade several scholars have published thoughtful and informative biographies that present a more balanced picture of the general. Prominent among these are the studies by Emory Thomas and Charles Roland, both in 1995, and Brian Holden Reid in 2005. Thomas's book is the only full-length biography that updates Freeman's scholarship with a realistic acceptance of Lee's fallibility and a fair treatment of his stance on race. In a follow-up essay written in 2005, Thomas acutely suggested that Lee is less a "marble man," as Stephen Vincent Benét described him, than he is a "malleable man," so many times has he been reinvented since 1861. In this study our challenge is to build on this work, and to consider whether Lee the man will ever be seen with true clarity.[40]

The Reinventing of Ulysses S. Grant, 1861–2007

Yet as the generations slip away, as the dust of conflict settles, and as through the clearing air we look back with keener wisdom into the nation's past, mightiest among the mighty dead loom the three great figures of Washington, Lincoln, and Grant.

Theodore Roosevelt[41]

Wasn't Grant supposed to be drunk a good part of the time during the Civil War? Certainly he was.

Ernest Hemingway (*For Whom the Bell Tolls*)[42]

Ulysses S. Grant's place in American memory would seem to be safe. He won the Civil War and saved the Union. The victorious general had become first in the hearts of his countrymen, many of whom were quick to see the parallel between Grant's achievements and those of George Washington. He was a self-made man, which had tremendous cachet in the postbellum United States, he had firm friendships with some of the most important men in the country, he had a stable, supportive family life, and he was twice elected president in consecutive referenda on his place in the nation's history. He had fought bravely against his last terrifying foe, throat cancer, and when he died more than a million people watched his cortege pass through the streets of Manhattan. While we now think of Lincoln as the greatest American of his moment, it is fair to say that many of their contemporaries would have cho-

fig. 16.
John Antrobus, *General Grant on the Battlefield*, 1863–64, oil on canvas, 84 × 64 in. (213.4 × 162.6 cm.), R. H. Love Galleries, Chicago.

sen the little general from Illinois.

Grant had won important victories for the Union in early 1862 at Forts Henry and Donelson and then at Shiloh, but few people at that date, North or South, knew much about him. Fewer knew what he looked like. Newspaper accounts of the campaigns gave hints about his personality, but there were relatively few photographs. Unlike McClellan, Halleck, and some other Union generals who from the start had captured the attention of the press and therefore had been paraded before the public, Grant had entered the war as an unknown and stayed that way for longer than anyone might have expected. By the summer of 1863, however, when he captured the seemingly impregnable fortress of Vicksburg, this fighting commander in the West could no longer be overlooked. Prints of the general began to appear. One of the first, by Joseph Baker, pictures Grant in the thick of combat (fig. 15). Baker capitalized on Grant's already established reputation for courage in the face of the enemy.

Congress and the president soon recognized the victorious commander. He was awarded a medal for Vicksburg. Lincoln lavished praise on the general and sent him off to rescue the nearly besieged city of Chattanooga. When Grant was successful there in November 1863, several paintings of the victor were commissioned. One is a life-size portrait that imagines the general's appearance on that battlefield (fig. 16). John Antrobus would at this early moment of Grant's public life attempt to provide the Union general with a stature akin to that of George Washington.[43]

Antrobus was an English emigrant to the South who had served briefly with a Confederate unit before he capriciously switched allegiance and moved to the North. In his endeavor to capture the essence of Grant, he attempted an overly ambitious canvas that is seven feet tall. A pastiche of the well-known John Trumbull print of George Washington at Trenton, the painting was intended to evoke grandeur appropriate to the moment. Grant is shown surveying the Battle of Chattanooga as it unfolds at Missionary Ridge. As in the Trumbull image, the general stands beneath the dark clouds of war, beside a broken cannon of the enemy, his horse held by an aide. Lincoln made a point of seeing this image when it was displayed in Washington.[44]

In the spring of 1864, the president promoted Grant to the position of general-in-chief with the rank of lieutenant general and reassigned him to the eastern theater. He was now in charge of all military operations, able to orchestrate the various Union armies in a coordinated effort. No longer would the Confederates be able to rush regiments from one battlefield to another to offset numerical weaknesses; Grant would do his best to keep them all fighting all the time. His victories continued, inspiring the Norwegian artist Ole Balling to celebrate the Union successes that would lead to ultimate victory by painting a portrait of Lincoln, followed by a grouping of *Grant and His Generals* (fig. 18).[45]

The twenty-six officers Balling depicted were actually scattered throughout the South. He did, however, sketch each of the portraits from life. He had found Grant at City Point, awaiting the collapse of Lee's army, and in the Valley of Virginia Balling tracked down Sheridan (pictured in the left foreground on the black horse that leads the others), but he had to wait until the end of the war to sketch many of the other officers, including Sherman (riding the white horse to Grant's immediate right). We don't know where he found George Armstrong Custer (second from the left), whose defeat in 1876 at Little Big Horn would undermine President Grant's attempts toward peaceful relations with the Plains Indian peoples.[46]

By the end of war, small black-and-white prints brought the story of the acclaimed general into the homes of grateful northerners. Even some southerners began to acknowledge a measure of appreciation for Grant, as they recognized that the terms imposed at Appomattox were in fact magnanimous. Grant had followed the spirit of reconciliation proposed by Lincoln, but on his own he had taken initiative. It was the general who decided to parole the soldiers of the Confederacy and who allowed officers to retain their sidearms. If the opinion of all Americans had been tallied in the months following Appomattox, Grant's popularity would have exceeded that of Lee.[47]

The best of the early biographies of Grant was penned in 1868, before his presidency, by Albert D. Richardson, who gathered information from some of the general's closest friends. He believed that "a destiny almost incredible awaited [Grant]." Richardson did not choose to "give all the minute details of Grant's achievements … but rather to show what made him the man he became— … what he thought, and hoped, and feared":

> Our war might have developed a leader profligate, corrupt, or uneasily ambitious, as so many great captains have been in the past. It gave us instead this pure, modest, simple-hearted man, who, loyal and admirable in private life, loved

fig. 17.
Ole Peter Hansen Balling, *Grant and His Generals*, 1865, oil on canvas, 23 × 36½ in. (58.4 × 92.7 cm.), National Portrait Gallery, Smithsonian Institution

himself last, and who always believed most enthusiastically in the United States of America. Invincibility in war, magnanimity in victory, wisdom in civil government, and unselfishness in all things—what are these, if they be not greatness?

Another of the first biographers, Henry C. Deming, emphasized the general's character and virtues:

> Nature endowed him with strength of will, an equable temper, a sound, practical, well-balanced understanding …. There is in him naught of that vacillation or oscillation which is fatal to all earnest decision …. Justice is with him a predominating attribute. He is devoted to the right ….
> He is faithful in his friendships; sincere in his professions; superior to all envy; generous in his appreciation and commendation of others; truthful, honorable, upright, in all his dealings and converse with his fellow-men; and ardent and tender in his domestic affections.

The devotion to his friends would prove to be more a detriment than a benefit during Grant's terms as chief executive.[48]

Scandals during the Grant presidencies inevitably weakened the general's reputation. Headlines in the press about his appointees accepting bribes were too shocking and too frequent to be ignored. In the end, however, the American public of the 1870s concluded that Grant had been betrayed by people he trusted, and that none of the scandals involved his connivance. Through all of his political misfortunes, Grant retained his place in the hearts of

fig. 18.
H. N. Tiemann & Co., *The Funeral of Ulysses Grant*, August 8, 1885, New York City (photograph courtesy of the New-York Historical Society Library)

fig. 19.
Thure de Thulstrup, *Grant from West Point to Appomattox*, 1885, watercolor, 24 × 18 in. (60.9 × 45.7 cm.), Anne S. K. Brown Military Collection, John Hay Library, Brown University

a large majority of the American people, many of whom wanted him to run for a third term.

Much was accomplished during Grant's two terms as president. He had faced challenges greater than those that had confronted nearly all of his predecessors in the office. There were international crises and a host of trials inherent in the reconstruction process and in western expansion. War with Great Britain was avoided; longstanding grievances were instead peacefully settled through arbitration. Grant refused to sacrifice American lives in the Cuban uprising that began as he took office, in the process quieting those who urged war with Spain. The president also established policies to advance the standing of both African Americans and Native Americans at a time when most white citizens were sadly insensible to the need.

Once out of office, Grant's popularity only increased. During a world tour of two-and-a-half years' duration, dignitaries from a number of countries honored Grant and the nation that he had saved. The general endured personal financial failure that was not his own doing with dignity, and he fought a painful cancer while he heroically drafted memoirs that would provide a handsome income for his family. When he died in 1885, Americans recognized that a giant figure in their history, a man equal to Washington and Lincoln, was gone.

The outpouring of appreciation for Grant would sustain his high reputation through the end of the century. He would be remembered as General Grant, a title that the public had never relinquished. This would have seemed appropriate to Grant, who devoted the twelve hundred pages of his memoirs to his biography up to 1865. The extraordinary success of the *Personal Memoirs of U. S. Grant* stands as the ultimate proof of the remarkably high reputation of the general at his death. Additional evidence of Grant's popularity at the close of the nineteenth century is abundant. Ninety-one biographies of him were published before 1900, and scores of prints were executed. A spectacular funeral, which preceded the planning of the grandest tomb that the nation would ever know, made clear his standing.[49]

James P. Boyd was one of several authors who produced biographies in the year of Grant's death. The obvious model for comparison was George Washington. Boyd wrote,

> As to men, none occupy the place of General Grant in the affections of the people …. His genius brought victory, and with victory, peace. The noblest tribute that can be paid mortal man is his by universal acclamation. "He made his foes his friends." …
>
> And now that he is dead there is universal mourning … he saved us as a people, a government, a solidified nation …. Though a larger and more perilous work than that of Washington, it was not unlike his. And as of him, an admiring, loving and grateful people will say: "First in war, first in peace, and first in the hearts of his countrymen."

There could be no higher praise than the famous words first spoken by Robert E. Lee's father.[50]

More than a million people would witness Grant's funeral in August 1885 (fig. 18). America had never seen its like. It seemed that nearly everyone in New York City was in attendance and that half of the buildings were draped in black. The route of the procession was made to stretch as far as was possible, from City Hall in lower Manhattan to Riverside Park in the upper northeast. A map of the route was published in advance to enable spectators to position themselves for the best view. Among those who marched in the seven-mile parade were President Grover Cleveland and former presidents Rutherford B. Hayes and Chester A. Arthur. Pallbearers William Tecumseh Sherman, Philip H. Sheridan, Simon Bolivar Buckner, and Joseph E. Johnston represented the Union and Confederate armies that they had once commanded.

fig. 20.
John Duncan, architect, *Grant's Tomb*, 1888–97, New York City (photograph by Robert Bradlow courtesy of New-York Historical Society Library)

Special trains from the South offered low fares "for those wishing to attend the Grant funeral in New-York." The anticipated "large crowds from the South" were a further measure of Grant's nationwide reputation at his death.[51]

The leading American lithography firm in the postwar era, L. Prang & Co. of Boston, proudly advertised the availability of artwork "which hitherto adorned only the parlors of the rich." The medium offered was the colorful chromolithograph. Prang reasoned that among the images that "every home" in 1885 had to have was a depiction of Grant. He commissioned what was probably a mourning picture (fig. 19). The artist was Thure de Thulstrup, a Swede who had served in the French Foreign Legion and in the Franco-Prussian War before studying art in Paris and New York, and who was well qualified to illustrate military scenes, the part of Grant's legacy that Prang thought would sell. Working in the *trompe l'oeil* tradition of illusion that was in vogue at the end of the nineteenth century as painters tried to compete with the skills of the photographer, Thulstrup depicted a portrait of the general that seems to rest on top of a larger sheet. Surrounding it are scenes that celebrate an illustrious military career.[52]

Thulstrup's narrative starts at the lower left with Grant's graduation from West Point and an episode from the Mexican War. Then it proceeds through Civil War victories to Grant's promotion by Lincoln to the rank of lieutenant general and the surrender at Appomattox. The chromolithograph made from Thulstrup's watercolor sold sufficiently well for Prang to issue a series of eighteen Civil War scenes during the next three years. Included are several of Grant's major victories.

What a man he is! what a history! what an illustration—his life—of the capacities of that American individuality common to us all ... this is what people like—and I am sure I like it.
Walt Whitman[53]

The demise of the general brought the question, "Grant's Memorial: What Shall It Be?" Those words are the title of an article that was published in 1885 in the *North American Review* by Karl Gerhardt, a young sculptor who had gained permission to take the death mask of Grant. Gerhardt's career had been furthered by Grant's friend Mark Twain; whether Twain's thoughts about the memorial underlie the ideas laid out by his protégé is not known. However, Gerhardt expressed the mood of the moment.

"As America is the greatest of modern nations," Gerhardt stated, Grant's memorial "should excel in grandeur any existing monument." "Shall it be an equestrian figure?" No, the sculptor answered. "Grant's life was complex," he was more than a soldier. "We should erect to his memory the grandest mausoleum or temple of modern times.... Let it be the combined work of our greatest architects, sculptors, and painters." In that way the memorial will have "architectural grandeur, statuary, bas-reliefs, and frescoes, illustrative of his life." And so it would be. A tomb would be built. Its grandeur would stand more as evidence of Grant's immense popularity than as an expression of his own personality.[54]

Grant was first laid to rest in a temporary tomb in Riverside Park. In 1888, the Grant Monument Association announced plans to replace that structure with a spectacular funerary memorial for "the grandest character of the century." It would be the largest tomb in North America. A competition was staged, and the greatest public fundraising campaign in history was launched. Some ninety thousand admirers from across the nation and the world contributed more than $600,000. The winning design (fig. 20), contributed by New York architect John Duncan, was modeled in part on one of the

fig. 21.
Daniel Chester French and Edward Clark Potter, *General Ulysses S. Grant*, modeled 1893–95, bronze, h. 174 in. (442 cm.), Fairmont Park Art Association, Philadelphia (photograph by Gregory Benson)

seven wonders of the ancient world, the tomb erected by the mourning wife of King Mausolus at Halikarnassos.[55]

Ground was broken for Grant's Tomb in 1891. Six years would pass as the immense edifice rose in granite and marble above the Hudson River. Within would be statues, along with murals depicting Grant's victories at Chattanooga and Vicksburg, and the surrender of Lee at Appomattox. A million people, including President William McKinley, attended the dedication of the tomb in 1897.

Karl Gerhardt had ended his editorial in the *North American Review* with the thought that the artwork in the tomb would "tell the story of his grand career to future generations." Few in 1885, or in 1897, anticipated that future generations of Americans would not be listening. The 1897 dedication of Grant's Tomb marked the high point of his popularity. The general's reputation would never again approach this pinnacle.

As New Yorkers basked in the honor of having provided the setting for the general's tomb, other northern cities looked for ways to memorialize Grant. Significant sculptural commissions were soon awarded in Philadelphia, Chicago, Washington, and the still separate city of Brooklyn. These monuments further document the cresting of Grant's popularity in the 1890s. Contrary to the sentiment expressed by Karl Gerhardt that an equestrian figure would tell viewers too little about Grant's life, it was in fact the general's military accomplishments alone that most Americans wanted to honor. The commissions for sculpture almost always called for Grant to be depicted in uniform, and often on horseback.

The general was sufficiently popular in Philadelphia for the Fairmont Park Art Association to form a Grant Memorial Committee only four days after his death. A competition was won by one of the great sculptors of the age, Daniel Chester French. Grant, clothed in winter gear, is presented as a formidable figure, the master horseman who controls his mount (fig. 21). Slow funding and the intervention of the Spanish-American War delayed the dedication of the monument until 1899. Chicago saw quicker results. An equestrian statue was sculpted in 1890 by the little-known Cincinnati artist Louis Rebisso and dedicated in Lincoln Park in 1891. In 1895 the Union Club of Brooklyn commissioned William Ordway Partridge to sculpt an equestrian monument that was dedicated in 1896, two years before Brooklyn became a borough of New York City.

The most important sculptures of Grant were produced for display in the nation's capital. In 1890, the Grand Army of the Republic voted to honor its general with a full-length sculpture to be placed in the rotunda of the U.S. Capitol (fig. 22). There it would bring honor to both Grant and his army. The commission was awarded to Franklin Simmons, an artist from Vermont whom Grant had admired decades earlier. After moving to Washington near the end of the Civil War, Simmons had sculpted a bust of the general. Grant was pleased with the effort, and he endorsed the young artist. It was therefore fitting that at the peak of his career Simmons was called back to the Capitol to take on this important task.[56]

In 1894, in what would be the first of two attempts, Simmons depicted a thoughtful Grant, still in uniform but laying aside his sword to pursue the peace that he had won. An olive branch is at his feet. The army rejected the effort. The G.A.R. would have Grant remembered as a soldier, not a soldier/statesman. Simmons's

fig. 22.
Franklin Simmons, *General U. S. Grant*, 1899, marble, h. 89 in. (226 cm.), Rotunda, United States Capitol, Washington, D. C (photograph courtesy of the Architect of the Capitol)

second model of a solid, thoughtful Grant was accepted. It was completed in 1899 and unveiled the next year, beside a sculpture of the other man who had preserved the Union, Abraham Lincoln.[57]

The idea for a second major piece for the city of Washington originated in 1895 with the Society of the Army of the Tennessee, veterans who had served under Grant in the West. Not to be outdone by the G.A.R., this army accomplished an even greater tribute to the general. In 1901, the Senate Park Commission engaged architect D. H. Burnham to redesign the landscape surrounding several of the principal federal buildings. Before the Civil War, the terrain had been made "picturesque" by A. J. Downing. The new plan called for a strictly geometric National Mall, the design that exists today. Dramatic vistas were formed. The east–west axis was to be terminated by focal points that would memorialize the wartime president and his general, the two figures who had saved the Union. The wish of the western veterans to honor Grant with a sculpture would be incorporated into the Park Commission's plan. They could not have asked for a more prominent site in all of Washington.

A competition was held in 1903 for the sculpture of Grant that would grace the National Mall. The little-known New York artist Henry Shrady won the commission, defeating twenty-six other contestants. Shrady had offered the grandest scheme of the lot. His sculptural group would be the largest that the nation had ever seen. Its components would stretch more than 250 feet across the lawn below the Capitol, forming a plaza almost the length of a football field. The sum of $250,000 was set aside for the project, making it the most expensive sculpture, or piece of art of any type, ever federally funded. The monument took time to complete, however, and was not dedicated until 1922.

The focus of the Shrady monument is a colossal statue of Grant seated atop his horse Cincinnati (fig. 23). Both rest on a marble base embellished with bronze bas-relief panels that depict marching soldiers carrying swords, flags, and rifles. Bronze, bellicose lions crouch at the four corners. Some thirty yards to the north and south are sculptural groups of soldiers in combat. In the *Cavalry Group*, seven horsemen mount a charge. In the *Artillery Group*, soldiers move forward with horses pulling a caisson and cannon. Visitors were expected to equate the achievements of Grant and Lincoln with those of Washington and Jefferson. As it turned out, the public paid great attention to the legacy of Lincoln. But as the years went by, less and less attention was given to the monument and the memory of Grant.[58]

The memorials on the mall in Washington have contributed to the reinventing of both Lincoln and Grant. The solid Henry Bacon building and within it the Daniel Chester French statue of a thoughtful Lincoln are inspiring. The Grant Memorial has failed to elicit comparable appreciation. The figure of a general surveying the landscape before him might seem timeless, an assuring symbol of the permanence of the Union, were the setting not so vast that it engulfs the sculpture. Grant disappears beneath the massive Capitol, which looms high behind him. That building is in fact the true focal point of Burnham's mall. Almost as problematic are the figures of the American soldiers who strain in combat—an activity that, sadly, is also timeless. The combat groups were set into place in 1912 and 1916, in time to be highly visible during the years of World War I. Combat losses in that conflict reminded many Americans of the high casualty figures during Grant's campaigns. Thus, Shrady's memorial actually contributed to the resurgence of Grant's persona as a "butcher." The lack of popularity of the Shrady memorial mirrored the decline in Grant's reputation.

The best biographers of Grant followed the lead of their Lee counterparts who preached the virtues of character. In 1898, Hamlin Garland, writing at the time that the general's two armies wanted only to remember his military achievements, set out to

fig. 23.
Henry Mervin Shrady, *General Ulysses S. Grant Memorial*, 1912–20, bronze, (central group) h. 17 ft. 2 in. (523 cm.), east end of National Mall, Washington, DC (photograph courtesy of National Park Service)

reveal in his biography what he called "the man Grant." He valued the war years as a period of personal growth for the general and defended the scandal-ridden president as personally incapable of corruption. He pointed in particular to Grant's considerable accomplishment of winning the appreciation of southerners.

> It has not been my intention to set down all the significant words and deeds of General Grant, nor to analyze all the official acts of President Grant, but to present the man Grant as he stands to-day before unbiased critics ….
>
> The section that deals with his command is not a history of the war with the South, … but the story of … his marvelous development during those four epic years ….
>
> The chapters on the Grant administrations attempt to show … that through all the complications of this period, through the weltering chaos of political knaveries and double-dealings, President Grant pursued a simple, straightforward course. He had in him small capacities for deceit or dishonesty ….
>
> He had the great happiness, also, of seeing the love and admiration of the whole people, North and South, come back to him ….

That men in the South had come to admire his strength of character had brought Grant comfort at the end of his life.[59]

To the detriment of Grant's reputation, few historians in the early twentieth century followed Garland's lead, in part because Grant had said little to explain his feelings or the motivations behind his actions, even to his friends. His former companions in arms had respected him, but tales about a leader who was revered in the way that Lee was were not forthcoming from Grant's lieutenants. The general's family also failed to make public much information about his private life. Julia Grant adored her husband and wrote of her love in her memoirs, but those remained unpublished until 1975. Not one of Grant's four children managed to recount warm stories of their father's domestic life as had Robert E. Lee, Jr. The youngest, Jesse Grant, eventually published *In the Days of My Father, General Grant* in 1925, but the book made little impact.

The general's good friend William Tecumseh Sherman declared

that Grant's "whole character was a mystery even to himself—a combination of strength and weakness." Here was part of the problem: even during his lifetime no one understood Grant. He made his decisions and offered few explanations. This method worked well for a general but poorly for a president. Josiah Bunting has used the term "silent serenity" to characterize Grant's disposition through life. The silence allowed a less than positive mythology to develop. It was said that Grant was a drunkard. Lincoln was reported to have joked about supplying whiskey to all his generals to get such good results. Others called him a dullard. Henry Adams quipped that the evolution from Alexander the Great and Julius Caesar, to Washington, to Grant disproved Darwin's theory. Such offhand comments did much to tarnish Grant's reputation over the years.[60]

Much in fact could have been celebrated about Grant's character. His sense of duty and honor, which he possessed as much as did Lee, was not widely remembered, nor was his self-restraint, which had sustained Grant through innumerable personal crises. His humanitarian philosophy, which was manifested in his attempts to better conditions for African Americans and Native Americans, was underemphasized, as was his loyalty to friends and colleagues. However, the truth about Grant's warm private relationships, his character, and his intellect would in the end come out. It is recorded in thousands of pages of his letters, military orders, speeches, and legislative drafts. Publication of *The Papers of Ulysses S. Grant* began in 1967.

Yet as the generations slip away, as the dust of conflict settles, and as through the clearing air we look back with keener wisdom into the nation's past, mightiest among the mighty dead loom the three great figures of Washington, Lincoln, and Grant. There are great men also in the second rank; for in any gallery of merely national heroes Franklin and Hamilton, Jefferson and Jackson, would surely have their place. But these three greatest men have taken their place among the great men of all nations, the great men of all time. They stood supreme in the two great crises of our history ....

Theodore Roosevelt,
speech delivered at Galena, IL, April 27, 1900

In an age of internationalism and American imperialism, Theodore Roosevelt, the outdoorsman and former Rough Rider, expressed the sentiments of many of his countrymen when he celebrated Grant's martial accomplishments. To his thinking, it was Grant's capability and decisiveness during times of crisis that earned him the highest acclaim. His Civil War accomplishments would not be famously recalled during World War I, however, in part because that conflict called for a negation of regionalism. The European war would "obliterate" what President Woodrow Wilson called the "last divisions between the North and South." Politicians dared not endanger national unity with references that might disrupt it. Thus, when in 1915 the Civil War commanders were pictured together, Grant in civilian clothes, on a newspaper poster created to celebrate the golden anniversary of the end of America's fraternal conflict (fig. 24), they were thought of as equals in their commitment to the peace and reunification that had been enjoyed by Americans for the following half century. Grant's persona as a tough commander was only rarely recalled, as in a speech delivered at his tomb in 1915 calling for military preparedness and denouncing the "peace-at-all-costs" men as the antithesis of Lincoln and Grant. A 1917 article in the *The New York Times* about America's most famous generals makes clear the disfavor into which Grant had fallen. Lee is ranked much higher, with the greats of all time, Hannibal, Alexander, Caesar, and Napoleon.[61]

The Great War did, however, bring to the fore the subject of casualties. In 1917, as Congress debated American entry into the fray, Senator Gilbert M. Hitchcock of Nebraska stated, "The awful sacrifices of life that must follow sicken my heart." President Wilson, recalling the carnage of a half-century before, worried that "the cost might be sufferings and sacrifices of such magnitude that those of the civil war would seem infinitesimal." German propaganda, which was crafted to deter American ingression, exaggerated potential casualties to the highest numbers that might seem credible. By the late 1920s, the association of Grant with such gruesome realities was sufficiently strong to be stated bluntly: "It is much the fashion to depict Grant as a dull butcher."[62]

Grant had appeared on both the new $50 Gold Certificate issued in 1913 and the new $50 Federal Reserve Note issued in 1914. The image there of an aging but thoughtful President Grant in civilian clothes, which survives on today's fifty dollar bill, gives no indication of the military background that had won the affection of his countrymen and had put him in the White House. Unfortunately,

fig. 24.
"Let Us Have Peace," The Golden Anniversary, April Ninth, 1865–1915, supplement of *The New York Times*, April 4, 1915, New-York Historical Society Library.

the Grant administrations would be seen as precedents for the term of Warren Harding that soon followed the armistice in France. The scandal that sent Secretary of the Interior Albert Fall and Secretary of the Navy Edwin Denby to prison for accepting bribes tied to naval oil reserves at Teapot Dome, Wyoming, was one of many humiliations that plagued the Harding administration. These episodes were matched in American history in number and severity only by those of the Grant years. In an article in *The New York Times* in 1924 entitled "Some Political Scandals in the History of the Nation," Grant's two administrations were reported as "the high-water mark of corruption in national affairs." More than half of the article neatly summarizes the Crédit Mobilier, Whiskey Ring, Indian Trading, and Black Friday scandals of Grant's era. When Harding complained that his friends kept him "walking the floors at nights" and worried about whether or not to expose the graft, the memory of Grant's excessive loyalty to bad friends was inevitably resurrected.[63]

By the late 1920s, the man who had been championed as the savior of the Union and the second George Washington had become so misunderstood that negative biographies that would have been unthinkable only a generation earlier began to appear. In 1928, William Woodward authored the most outrageous account of the general that had ever been published. Woodward ignored Grant's virtues, opting instead for a wholly different view of the general:

> Young Grant had a girl's primness of manner and modesty of conduct. There was a broad streak of the feminine in his personality. He was almost half-woman …. Grant was never immersed in love in the manner of the great lovers ….
>
> He did not want to kill animals, though he had no objection whatever to the killing of men; that is, to having them killed wholesale, in war ….
>
> Consider him as a sensitive child, pathetic in his hunger for love and approbation, and finding himself nicknamed "Useless" and the butt of village jokes ….
>
> There was no latent joy in Grant's life …. His emotions were buried, but not dead; they were buried alive ….
>
> But if there had been no Civil War what could we say of Grant?[64]

fig. 25.
Wilford S. Conrow, *Ulysses S. Grant*, 1941, oil on canvas, 27 × 23 in. (68.6 × 58.4 cm.), New-York Historical Society Museum, gift of George A. Zabriskie

In the same year, Stephen Vincent Benét offered a more tempered assessment. In *John Brown's Body*, the poet is not as kind to Grant as he is to Lee, but there is at least an attempt to speak of Grant's strengths. The southern general "followed duty first and last," and was "a good father, a loving husband, a considerate friend," but Benét saw the northern leader only as the public knew him. He was "a rider with a hard bit" who "wastes [his men] grimly." Grant is:

> … the chunky man from the West,
> Stranger to you, not one of the men you loved
> As you loved McClellan, a rider with a hard bit,
> Takes you and uses you as you could be used,
> Wasting you grimly but breaking the hurdle down.
> You are never to worship him as you did McClellan,
> But at the last you can trust him. He slaughters you
> But he sees that you are fed. After sullen Cold Harbor
> They call him a butcher and want him out of the saddle,
> But you have had other butchers who did not win
> And this man wins in the end.

Benét might also have said of Grant what he additionally said of Lee: the general kept his feelings to himself. Part of the reason that Grant has been so unappreciated is simply that many Americans to this day do not understand him.[65]

One writer of this era who appreciated Grant's enigmatic personality was John Frederick Charles Fuller, a career soldier. He had served as a major general in the British army, then as a military historian, strategist, and early theorist of modern armored warfare. Fuller became intrigued with the careers of Grant and Lee. Far removed in England, he was free to evaluate the two generals without the influence of regional prejudice. In 1929 he published *The Generalship of Ulysses S. Grant*. One New York reviewer wrote, "In flat defiance of the prevailing snobbish tendency to decry General Grant, Colonel Fuller … starts his book by declaring that 'he was the greatest strategist of his age, of the war, and, consequently, its greatest General.'" Four years later, Fuller ranked the northern general above his antagonist in *Grant & Lee, A Study in Personality and Generalship*.[66]

Fuller had been taught that Grant was a "butcher" and Lee one of the greatest generals in history. But on closer examination, he found "nothing like the Grant I had been led to picture." Grant's army was not ill-fed and ill-clothed, as was Lee's. Indeed, for his failure as a quartermaster, Lee must have been "one of the most incapable Generals-in-Chief in history." Of Grant, Fuller wrote:

> In the Pantheon of War he [Grant] has remained uncanonized …. Yet what did he do? He won the Civil War for the North, and so re-established the Union …. He fought some of the greatest campaigns in history; was never defeated, and after the war was twice chosen by his countrymen as their President. If there is not food for myth here, where shall we seek it? His story is as amazing as Napoleon's, and as startling as Lenin's; yet enigma he lived and enigma he died, and though occasion was propitious and circumstances were favourable, enigma he remains ….
>
> … He was one of those inscrutably simple men who from time to time appear in history, who manifest at some critical moment, and who being oblivious of their own greatness

and desiring no renown, set fire to an epoch; not by spectacular volcano belchings, but like a grey ember which is red hot at the centre.[67]

Grant the general was redeemed by Fuller. However, in the America of the 1930s, opinion about Grant's other public persona had yet to shift. In 1935, William B. Hesseltine found little to recommend the president in *Ulysses S. Grant: Politician*. He wrote an exhaustive volume (484 pages in twenty-six carefully structured chapters) that is a detailed review of an event-filled eight years. However, such chapter titles as "Forty Years of Failure," "Tarnished Halo," and "Political Fagots" alert the reader to the author's prejudices. Hesseltine saw a rude commoner who had risen to high power. In this fiftieth anniversary year of his death, Hesseltine did not have much that was positive to say about Grant's career as chief executive. The author does present Grant as a compassionate human being, but he also brings up the issue of drinking. If the question was raised with some seriousness about Grant's being a drunk, as it was in Hemingway's *For Whom the Bell Tolls* (1940), or humorously, as in the movie *Going My Way* (1944), where Father Fitzgibbon hides his whisky in the bookcase behind Grant's biography, most Americans by the 1940s would probably have answered in the affirmative.[68]

Perceptions of Grant began to change as the world moved closer to war. Even the usage of the term "unconditional surrender" again became suggestive. It had been mentioned with some frequency during World War I by Presidents Roosevelt and Taft, and by the supreme U.S. commander, General John J. Pershing. There was even an "Unconditional Surrender Club," headquartered in Michigan. Pershing had argued that unconditional surrender was essential if the enemy was to be kept from taking up arms again, but the originator of the idea was rarely credited. Two decades later, when Germany re-armed and initiated a second war, Americans would have reason to reconsider Grant's no-nonsense attitude toward one's enemies.[69]

In a speech delivered at Grant's Tomb in 1940, Admiral Clark Woodward warned that a "lack of preparedness made the Civil War so long." A year later, when veterans at Grant's Tomb called for aid for Britain and urged that "Hitler and his crowd … be whipped," Americans seemed to be reacquainting themselves with Grant's military legacy. In 1941, a trustee of the New-York Historical Society, George A. Zabriskie, commissioned a painting from society portraitist Wilford Conrow that he gave to the institution (fig. 25). The artist produced the image of President Grant that is well known today from the fifty dollar bill, a study that evokes thoughtfulness and firmness.[70]

In January 1943, President Franklin Roosevelt remembered the general when he resurrected the term "unconditional surrender" at a meeting with Winston Churchill at Casablanca, French Morocco. The demand that Grant had made famous at Fort Donelson was back, now describing what the Allies would expect of the Axis. The ploy seems to have boosted the morale of American troops. Reports in May 1943 of the surrender of German units in North Africa recount stories of American officers "snapping" to their "sweating" opponents "General Grant's famous terms, 'unconditional surrender.'" British military analysts actually came to fear that the term may have alarmed enemy forces too much; they complained that it caused the Italians to hesitate to topple Benito Mussolini and set up a revolutionary government. After President Roosevelt used it again in Hawaii in 1944 when discussing the fate of the Japanese, the premier of Japan, Kantaro Suzuki, warned that unconditional surrender "means nothing but outright death for all [our] people."[71]

Gertrude Stein saw a change in Americans that she linked to Grant's terms of surrender. On the day that victory in Europe was declared, she wrote that "there has been an unconditional surrender, and remember, it was General Grant … who invented for America that idea." The years between the two Roosevelts, she said, had brought easy success, easy money, easy everything. In contrast, the new generation had experienced the Depression and World War II. She had talked to those soldiers, and she mused, "In a queer way we have come back, we Americans, to more or less the pre-Civil War state of mind." She concluded that "we are going to be interesting again, be a sad and quiet people who can listen and who can promise and who can perform." The hope for a united America that Grant had expressed before the Civil War, and which his doggedness and talent had helped to achieve, now seemed within reach again.[72]

In 1950, Lloyd Lewis provided an account of the life of Grant before the Civil War in his posthumously published *Captain Sam Grant*. Initially a newspaper editor, Lewis turned to history, devoting five years of research to a projected multi-volume biography that was only partly completed at his death in 1949. Lewis believed that history did not have to be academic: good stories that happen to be true, he said, should be told with a joy that brings out the humanity in the protagonists. He presents an honest, personable, unpretentious, and remarkably talented Ulysses S. Grant who struggles against misfortune and human frailty to discover his abilities as a leader. The book ends with the colonel's accomplishment in June 1861 of persuading the members of his regiment to re-enlist:

> In the roar of laughter and cheers that went up Grant knew that his worries were over. The whoops of the men carried the promise of what they would do later in the day when 603 volunteered—"almost," as Grant said, "to a man."
>
> As the applause died, Grant heard [Congressman John A.] Logan present "your new commander, Colonel U. S. Grant," and cries of "Speech! Speech!" come up from the men. Grant stepped forward and said, in that low yet curiously penetrating and arresting tone which his voice at times possessed:
>
> "Men, go to your quarters!"
>
> The men looked at him, then at each other.
>
> They were in the Army now.[73]

With the approach of the Civil War centennial celebration of 1961–65, interest was revived in the conflict that had launched Grant's reputation. In those states that had been battlefields during the war, few residents failed to notice the anniversary. Many Americans took an interest in reconsidering what they knew about the history of the era. The leaders of the Union and Confederate armies were put under a new spotlight.

Regionalist viewpoints still prevailed in 1961. Many northerners had yet to accept Lee as a figure of national importance. The centennial would not change their inherent distrust of the rebel who had posed the greatest threat ever to the Union. Furthermore, leaders of the burgeoning Civil Rights Movement directed attention to the viewpoint of the enslaved Americans whom the secessionists had tried to hold in bondage. In this climate, the reputations of the two generals would move in opposite directions.

Americans were reminded that the man who had been so often neglected in their memory was in fact the victor who had preserved the Union. Lee was undeniably a military genius who had foiled the repeated assaults of Union generals, but Grant had defeated him. No matter how the story was told, it would have that same ending. Some southerners would never accept the man who conquered the Confederacy, but all had to concede that Grant possessed talent and determination in great measure. The time had come for a serious reconsideration of the northern commander.

The centennial inspired one of the better storytellers of American history to take on the recitation of Grant's campaigns. Bruce Catton offered the sort of detail that Freeman had given to Lee's Army of Northern Virginia. In *Grant Moves South* and *Grant Takes Command*, published respectively in 1960 and 1970, Catton recounted Grant's careers in the Western theater and then in the East. He credits the general where credit is due, but he offers none of the adulation that fills the pages of *R. E. Lee*. Instead, he is often painfully honest.

> There was nothing about Ulysses S. Grant that struck the eye; and this puzzled people, after it was all over, because it seemed reasonable that greatness, somewhere along the line, should look like greatness. Grant could never look like anything, and he could never make the things he did look very special; and afterward men could remember nothing more than the fact that when he came around things seemed to happen. The most they could say, usually, was that U. S. Grant had a good deal of common sense.[74]

In 1969, an enthusiastic appreciation of Grant finally appeared, the first since the end of the nineteenth century. The biographer, perhaps not surprisingly, was a direct descendant. Ulysses S. Grant III was the son of Grant's oldest child, Frederick. The younger Grant was a 1903 graduate of West Point who had ranked sixth in his class. He served as an aide to President Theodore Roosevelt in the White House, and enjoyed a military career that spanned four decades. At the close of World War II he retired with the rank of major general, and he served as chairman of the Civil War Centennial Commission from 1957 to 1961. Ulysses S. Grant III had been frustrated for half a century by the pervasiveness of the mythology that ridiculed his grandfather. In his opinion, neither historians, nor political writers, nor the public have understood the man. The younger Grant addressed the preface of *Ulysses S. Grant, Warrior and Statesman* to his own children:

> You should know more of the truth about him than has been told by the conventional historians, who have apparently never been able to understand him, and the political writers, who for some reason have hated him as the politi-

cians did …. [Even those] writing without malice or envy … have not fully seized and pictured the gracious, kindly, good man that the family knew him to be, the devoted husband and most affectionate father ….

Probably no great man has ever suffered as much as President Grant from the readiness of the public to accept false tales at their face value, and the tendency of writers of books and articles to repeat untruths, provided they were sensational enough to ensure sales ….

It may well be futile, therefore, to attempt to refute fables that have gained some sort of recognition by mere repetition. Ulysses S. Grant III could have further bolstered his grandfather's reputation by pointing to a record on racial issues that was progressive for his time. But like Lee biographer Clifford Dowdey, the grandson did not recognize in 1969 the new perspective from which many Americans would chose to evaluate the generals.[75]

Toward the end of his life, Ulysses Grant III could take hope in the inauguration of a project in which he would participate. This was the monumental publication of *The Papers of Ulysses S. Grant*, which have been edited by John Y. Simon since 1967. Grant, like Lee, was a prolific letter writer, and the celebrity of both men accounts for the survival of their papers in great numbers. During the past four decades, twenty-eight volumes of Grant's papers have been published, filling more than ten thousand pages. Simon has also edited and published *The Personal Memoirs of Julia Dent Grant* (1975), which presents fascinating information previously unavailable to the public about the family life of the general.

The *Papers* provide a biography of Grant that is extraordinarily rich in its detail, even more so than the meticulous account of Lee woven so eloquently by Freeman. One of Grant's strongest attributes was his ability to write lucidly. His modesty, humility, and honesty shine throughout the collection. The general, it turns out, is his own best defender. The publication of the *Papers* has been a key element in the major reassessment of Grant that is now underway. In the battle to bolster the reputations of Lee and Grant, the initiative has been seized by the North.

The *Papers* have also made possible the publication in recent years of a series of biographies of Grant that are as thoughtful and informative as the best of the newer books about Lee. Prominent among these are the studies by William S. McFeely (1982), which won the Pulitzer Prize for biography, Brooks D. Simpson (2000), Jean Edward Smith (2001), and Josiah Bunting III (2004).

Beyond the Mythology: Intentions and Scope of This Project

This attempt to conduct our own reappraisal of Lee and Grant will focus on bringing each man to life largely based on his own words and those of his contemporaries. When possible, letters and other written records, visual images, and decorative objects will allow us to have, if only for a moment, a clear view of each man as he understood himself and his place in the world. When dealing with these essentially private individuals who found themselves on the greatest stage in our nation's history, it can be difficult to sense the inner workings of either commander. On the other hand, what seems to be true about both Lee and Grant is that "what you see is what you get." Each had an unassailable self-image, each knew his own strengths and weaknesses, each had a personal code of correct behavior, and each believed that he had the power within to keep from bending under circumstances that would have broken the great majority of men. There are a surprising number of similarities in these two leaders who from their births, to their upbringings, to their beliefs, could not have been more different.

Rather than begin this study with their youth, we will commence with what became the defining period in the life of each future general, the weeks and days when both Lee and Grant had to choose to which side he owed allegiance in the impending conflict. For Lee, while he spoke often of his wish to preserve the Union, he was first and foremost a Virginian. For Grant, who had called a number of states home, it was the United States to which he had sworn an oath and for which he would, if necessary, lay down his life. For both, an adherence to a personal code of duty and honor was the only thing certain in a world that seemed to be collapsing around them.

I.

The Decisions of 1861

fig. 26.
Mathew Brady, *Robert E. Lee*, c. 1852 (photograph courtesy of Virginia Historical Society)

fig. 27.
Unidentified photographer, *Ulysses Grant*, 1863 (photograph courtesy of Library of Congress)

I can anticipate no greater calamity for the country than a dissolution of the Union. It would be an accumulation of all the evils we complain of, & I am willing to sacrifice every thing but honour for its preservation.

Robert E. Lee to his son Rooney Lee, January 29, 1861

We are now in the midst of trying times when every one must be for or against his country …. Having been educated for such an emergency, at the expense of the Government, I feel that it has upon me superior claims, such claims as no ordinary motives of self-interest can surmount.

Ulysses S. Grant to his father Jesse Grant, April 21, 1861

As the still youthful nation careened ever closer to what would become the Civil War, both Robert E. Lee and Ulysses S. Grant were faced with life-altering decisions. To each, self-interest, while never completely off the table, had to be suppressed when matters of great urgency were to be decided. Both men were governed by personal codes of honor and a steadfast allegiance to what each viewed as his homeland. In the end, Lee and Grant would follow paths that would also be taken by the majority of their respective southern and northern neighbors. For Lee, his successful career in the United States Army and his allegiance to the United States government could be trumped by only one set of relationships, those to his family and his home state of Virginia. In Grant's case, it was an allegiance to the nation more than to any particular locale in the North that led him to decide to take up arms once again, even though it would mean leaving the family life that he had finally regained. The character of each man, his beliefs about the duty that one owed to one's homeland, whether defined as a state or a nation, and the previous experiences that each had survived, made the decisions of 1861 predictable and inevitable. Our beginning with the moment that spring that changed each man's life and ultimately set the stage for his rise to national prominence will allow us to tell the story of their early lives with this chronological crossroads in mind.

* * * * * * * * * *

To each future general it must have seemed that events beyond his control were leading him toward the service to which he would ultimately pledge his life. For Lee (fig. 26), his sense of personal honor and his self-construction based on the life and career of the greatest American, George Washington, had been a touchstone. Bertram Wyatt-Brown, the author of a series of books on the subject of southern honor, has concluded that Robert E. Lee's decisions of 1861 are "inexplicable" without a thorough consideration of this code. Lee, after all, had told his son Custis that honor and fame are all that men should aspire to. He also stated on numerous occasions that he would sacrifice everything but honor to save the Union. But when he saw that his home state would be in the immediate line of fire, he felt he had no choice but to defend her.[1]

A strong sense of personal honor governed the life choices of Ulysses S. Grant (fig. 27) as well. Although his Civil War service began in the relatively safe northern Midwest, and so it might seem as though the lack of instantaneous repercussions from his decision might have made it easier to rationalize, Grant too was influenced by a code that was almost parallel to the formulation in the mind of the man who would become his great antagonist.

Among the cardinal principles of honor in the Old South were the defense of one's family and a loyalty to one's homeland. Such ideals had long been extant in the West; models were available from the poetry of Homer to the accounts of Tacitus, who pointed to similar phenomena governing honorable behavior among the Germanic tribes that he had observed. Such codes of honor demanded displays of personal bravery when challenged and did not tolerate disgrace. Death was always preferred to dishonor.[2]

The first and foremost reason for an exhibition of bravery and, if necessary, for the sacrifice of one's life, was to protect family. Robert E. Lee acknowledged this primal law. When a war, with its inevitable invasion of his home state, seemed imminent, Lee stated on a number of occasions that should a conflict begin, it would be his duty to defend his kin, and by extension, all of the citizens of Virginia. Further, as he told many of his correspondents, he would not raise his sword against his family or the people of his region. Evidence that such sentiments were widespread in prewar Virginia comes ironically from a letter from Grant's aunt, Rachel Grant Tompkins of Charleston (now West Virginia), who wrote to Grant's sister Clara in June of 1861, "if you can justify your Bro. Ulysses in drawing his sword against those connected by the ties of blood, … you are at liberty to do so, but [I] can not."[3]

Grant's aunt Rachel viewed "ties of blood" and allegiance to one's extended family, as did many southerners, as one aspect of a code that would ensure the survival of their way of life. Indeed, it can be argued that an understanding of such ties is crucial to gaining an appreciation of what drove Virginia and the rest of the Upper South out of the Union. The states of the Deep South had largely been settled by the sons and daughters of the border states; Virginia, especially, saw itself as the progenitor of much of the lower South. By the spring of 1861, a number of Virginia politicians had concluded that their commonwealth must come to the defense of its actual and figurative kin. Anything less would have been considered dishonorable, and therefore reprehensible.

For Grant, the defense of one's wife and children was just as certainly a guiding principle. Although his immediate family was safe in Illinois and would never be threatened by an invading Confederate army, Grant felt the disruption and loss that a war would bring to all Americans. He was also happy to use his military training; he believed that the war would end quickly and that he would be part of the process that would turn the nation back to its proper course. Ultimately, however, Grant would come to believe that the successful completion of his military assignments was critical because his own personal honor and that of his wife and children depended on it.

Interestingly, while concepts of loyalty to family and country were dominant in his mind, Grant, unlike Lee, had to find ways to deal with relations who were not always supportive of his position. With his characteristic attention to the larger matter at hand, Grant found the pro-southern sympathies of his slave-holding father-in-law in Missouri and his aunt Rachel in Virginia troublesome, but finally of no great concern. Like many in the divided state of Missouri, Colonel Frederick Dent said at the beginning of the conflict that he was pro-Union, but he was opposed to putting an army in the field to sustain the nation in its current form. A few months later Grant would command troops in that state, seemingly unconcerned that his men could conceivably have become an army of occupation should Missouri have gone over to the Confederacy.

It is difficult to overstate the importance of regional loyalty in the antebellum South. Mary Custis Lee acknowledged this when she explained that "as a man of honor" her husband "must follow the destiny of his State." The Lee and Carter ancestors of his father and mother, and the Custis, Fitzhugh, and Washington forebears of his wife's parents, had left a legacy of pride and patriotism that was linked inextricably to the history of Virginia. For Lee to have exiled himself from this heritage would have been unthinkable. He readily accepted the prevailing belief in his society that he had inherited a duty from the great Virginians who had gone before him to defend his state. In his case, that responsibility proved to be the trump card, his most important duty from which he would not shrink, more powerful even than his oath of allegiance to the United States as an army officer. Lee's father, "Light-Horse Harry" Lee, had provided what would become an exemplary sentiment for his youngest son at the time of the American Revolution: "Virginia is my country, her will I obey, however lamentable the fate to which it may subject me."[4]

In the North, while there certainly were state-based loyalties, in many cases ancestral roots had been taken up and transplanted westward. Families like the Grants, who had arrived in Massachusetts in the 1630s, were often dispersed across counties, and even states, and so there was less chance than in the South that a family legacy would be inextricably tied to a particular homeland. Ulysses S. Grant had been born in Ohio; by 1861 his military service had taken him south to Mexico, north to the Canadian border, and west to the Pacific coast; he had most recently been a resident of Missouri, and finally of Illinois. He felt no obligation to a particular state, but instead an allegiance to the whole of the American Union to which the midwestern regions belonged. This bond was as strong for Grant as was Lee's allegiance to Virginia; it pulled heavily on his conscience and would eventually call him to duty. He said as much after the fall of Fort Sumter, when he challenged all those around him to take a stand on secession.

Additional components of the southern code of honor also influenced Lee's behavior. Integral to this code was the opinion of one's peers. An individual's identity and status in society could be confirmed or denied by members of one's social class. Wyatt-Brown has observed that the most important categories by which southerners measured their peers were sociability, learning, and piety. Few Americans better exemplified these elements of gentility than did Robert E. Lee.

Lee loved to be sociable; he was strikingly handsome, and during his upbringing and military education he had learned to create an attractive appearance. The result was that Lee was remarkably self-assured in his role as a gentleman and officer. There is much evidence to support Wyatt-Brown's claim that Lee inspired others by his speech, bearing, and leadership, and that he moved with the grace of a proper Christian gentleman in the great majority of his dealings with everyone, including women, children, and even his slaves. He had a clear sense of how a person should treat those under his protection or command, and he often clothed his orders as polite requests, an untraditional style that evolved directly from his sense of the code of honor. A gentleman was allowed two ways to resolve differences. The first was violence, which, although it might seem ironic given his profession, was unacceptable to Lee. The other we might call quiet gentility. This practice allowed the general to avoid personal confrontation, which he intensely disliked, and it played a role in both his remarkable successes and his greatest failures.

Lee devoted many hours of reading to the Bible, the Episcopal Book of Common Prayer, and the code of self-discipline that Marcus Aurelius wrote as his *Meditations*. His piety was deeply ingrained in him by his mother and then reinforced by his wife and mother-in-law. He had developed an unquestioning faith that fatalistically accepted events as part of God's greater plan. Many in the South shared such a belief with Lee and admired him on this account. It is at times difficult to distinguish the wartime comments of Lee from those of Lincoln on the subject of Divine Providence.[5]

Gentility in society and peer review were seen differently in the antebellum North, where a self-made individual was appreciated more for his ingenuity than for his sociability. Such a climate worked to the advantage of Grant, who since his youth had been content with the solitude of his own company and never cared a great deal for the opinions of others. Here was a man who in the mid-1850s had little need for social interactions with his white neighbors while he labored in the fields side by side with slaves. By his own testimony, only once did Grant care about his appearance. Newly graduated from West Point, he had proudly modeled his officer's uniform, only to be ridiculed by both a child and a stable hand. After those experiences there would be no more catering to the superficiality of appearance. As an officer, Grant won the respect of his men not by his bearing or his breeding, but by his determination and his ability to achieve results. He seemed to believe that God would in the end decide matters in favor of the righteous, but he made no outward show of religious faith. Indeed, although his parents were religious, Grant never pursued an organized faith with any fervor. On his deathbed he would reject last rites.

Americans in the twenty-first century have been led to believe that the choices of allegiance made by Lee and Grant in 1861 were based largely on the dilemma of slavery. In fact, that issue had surprisingly little bearing on the decision-making of either. White southerners were not willing to sacrifice their lives in order to be slaveholders. Some seventy-five percent of the white male population in the South did not even own slaves. Also, the institution of slavery within the existing states was not in jeopardy in 1861. The newly elected President Lincoln had no power to end it, and most in the North wanted to avoid any confrontation on the issue. Many southerners, however, were willing to sacrifice their lives for the sake of honor. Slaveholders and nonslaveholders alike in the South resented the antislavery attacks by abolitionists such as William Lloyd Garrison and the efforts of northern congressmen to limit slavery because such instigations insulted their culture and implied a moral inferiority. The election of a president who saw slavery as a moral issue set the stage for the secession of the states of the Deep South. In response, Lincoln threatened a military invasion to quell the secessionists. At that point, obligations to family and region became commingled with the protection of slavery. Driven by a sense of honor to defend their plantation society, the border states joined their neighbors to the South in going to war.[6]

For Robert E. Lee the citizen, slavery was simply not an issue in 1861. The half-dozen slaves whom he had inherited from his mother had long ago been liberated, and his father-in-law's will, for which he was executor, ordered the manumission of the two hundred Custis slaves. Lee had no direct monetary stake in the slavery debate. Further, once the die was cast and the armies of the North and South were to take the field, he reiterated a theme that he had often stated previously. Lee made clear in 1861, on more than one occasion, that if he owned slaves, even if he owned every slave in the South, he would free them all to avoid secession and the break-up of the Union.

Slavery also played little part in Ulysses S. Grant's decision-making process. Like most Americans at the time, he never dreamed that an institution that was so widespread could ever be overturned, nor did he think that the problem was his concern. Besides, the slaves his wife owned who helped with her household duties made life much easier for his family. He was not an abolitionist, he later stated, nor did he think that slavery should necessarily come to an end. It was only midway into the war that Grant reached such a conclusion. By then, invading Union armies had liberated so many slaves that a tide had been broken loose that could not be turned. The Emancipation Proclamation can actually be seen as a document that was inspired by events in the field, as much as a call to slaves still in captivity to seek their freedom.

Lee and Grant were educated in a system that was predicated on the notion that the autonomy and safety of any individual soldier was secondary to the good of the whole; the men of the lower classes who made up the great majority of the fighting force were expendable if a military objective could be achieved. Both lived in a nation in which the rights and dignities that they would have expected for themselves were denied to a significant segment of the population on the basis of race. Neither man would have argued in 1861 that such rights and dignities should be universal. Lee, who often spoke against slavery, fought for the status quo; Grant, who rarely spoke against slavery, chose the side that would ultimately undermine the institution in its attempt to retain the political unity of the eighty-five-year-old nation. For each future commander, the life, liberty, and pursuit of happiness of any individual American, white or black, meant little in the context of the grand carnage that was about to erupt, a conflagration that we now understand to have been in large part about the bestowing of rights and dignities on the millions who had for centuries been denied the merest of acknowledgements, their existence as autonomous human beings. It is fair to say, however, that at the outbreak of hostilities, the status of the enslaved, the poor, and the otherwise disenfranchised was of little concern to either.

The code of honor, as Robert E. Lee understood it, forced his hand in 1861. He said as much to Confederate Vice President Alexander Stephens shortly after he cast his lot with Virginia. Neither the protection of the institution of slavery nor the possibility that the South could achieve political independence was crucial in his decision-making process. Ulysses S. Grant believed that he was duty bound to participate in the northern effort to preserve the Union. Like Lee, he had sworn an oath of allegiance to the United States and had been educated at West Point to serve his nation; unlike Lee, no obligation to a particular state or region affected Grant's decision.[7]

This code of honor, this allegiance to duty, had a darker side that would affect how the war would be fought. Neither general had many qualms about slaughtering thousands of the enemy whose interpretation of duty was different from his own, and each was willing to sacrifice thousands in his own ranks to do so. Grant was determined to move forward no matter what the cost. After Appomattox, Lee worried about "the men who were lost after I knew it was too late." But he kept his troops in the field even though his army's defeat was inevitable. It would have been a disgrace to surrender, except as the Confederacy's dying gasp.[8]

The remainder of this chapter will set the stage for and recount the moments of decision for both Lee and Grant in the spring of 1861. Neither man could have anticipated the monumental stage unto which he would be placed, nor foreseen his particular role in the impending national tragedy.

fig. 28.
Robert E. Lee to Edward Childe, *Letter*, January 9, 1857, Stratford Hall Plantation

* * * * * * * * * *

In the 1850s, when the dilemma of slavery in America was turning into a sectionalist crisis, Robert E. Lee became concerned. He was quick to recognize that secession by the southern states would necessarily terminate his thirty-year career in the U.S. Army because he would never participate in an invasion. At the same time, disunion would destroy a nation that so many of his illustrious forebears, including his father and his wife's step-great-grandfather, had worked so hard to establish.

The political problems caused by slavery had been simmering for much of Lee's young life. The Missouri Compromise of 1820, which allowed slavery to exist in Missouri but barred it in the unorganized territory to the north and west, had postponed the dilemma for most of his professional career, including the years when he was stationed in St. Louis. But the Kansas-Nebraska Act of 1854, which overturned the status quo by returning the decision about slavery to the settlers of those territories, had worsened the situation. It led to violence that inspired the term "bleeding Kansas" and it raised the issue of the right of a state to secede, a subject that would be widely debated in the 1850s.

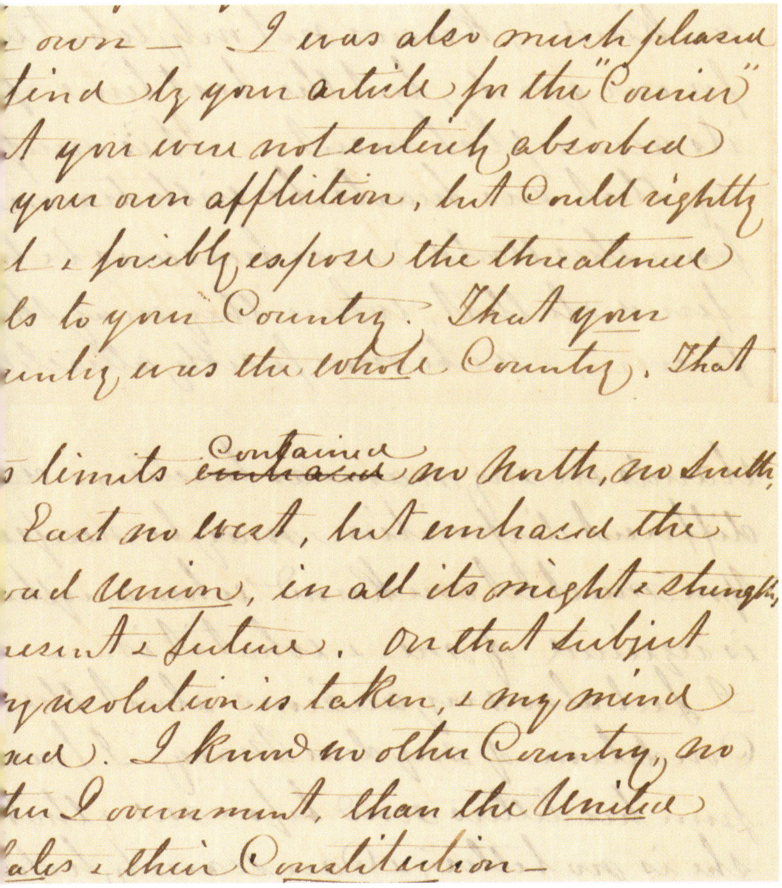
own — "I was also much pleased
find by your article for the "Courier"
t you were not entirely absorbed
your own affliction, but could rightly
& forcibly expose the threatened
ls to your Country. That your
untry, was the whole Country. That
s limits ~~embraced~~ contained no North, no South,
East no West, but embraced the
ud Union, in all its might & strength,
esent & future. On that subject
y resolution is taken, & my mind
ed. I know no other Country, no
her Government, than the United
ates & their Constitution—

One important Unionist voice was that of Lee's brother-in-law Edward Childe, a writer and political observer who had been resident in Paris with Lee's sister Mildred for more than a decade. In 1857, Childe wrote an opinion that was published in the Boston *Courier*. He argued that his country was "the *whole* Country." Lee, every bit as fervently a Unionist, sent to Childe a heartfelt letter of congratulation and endorsement (fig. 28), confirming that he too had taken a stand on the issue. At this early date, Lee unequivocally stated his position:

> I was ... much pleased to find by your article for the [Boston] "Courier" that you ... rightly feel & forcibly expose the threatened evils to your Country. That your Country was the whole Country. That its limits contained no North, no South, no East no West ... in all its might & strength, present & future. On that subject my resolution is taken, & my mind is fixed. I know no other Country, no other Government, than the United States & their Constitution.

Lee's anxiety about secession mounted in the fall of 1860 when presidential campaigning by "Black Republicans" caused some southerners to renew the threat. As in 1857, Lee was stationed with the army in faraway Texas, where he could follow events only through newspaper accounts. He reasoned that if Democrat Stephen Douglas would only withdraw and lend his support to John C. Breckinridge, Abraham Lincoln might be defeated. But, already a realist on this subject, Lee wrote to a colleague, "Politicians I fear are too selfish to become martyrs." Lincoln was elected by carrying every northern state. Four days later the South Carolina legislature called for a convention to consider withdrawal from the Union.[9]

On November 24, Lee told his son Custis that the southern states are "in a convulsion." He expressed despair that there was nothing he could do to save the Union. "I could easily lay down my life for its safety," he stated, but "that would bring but little good." A week later, on December 3, in a letter to his second son, Rooney, Lee made a statement about honor that in the coming weeks he would repeat to nearly every close acquaintance: "As an American citizen, I prize the Union very highly & know of no personal sacrifice that I would not make to preserve it, save that of honour." It is clear from his consistently pro-Unionist statements that Lee was not simply turning a pretty phrase. He was quickly becoming trapped by circumstances, and he recognized what could potentially become a personal dilemma.[10]

Lee added to Rooney, "I must trust in the wisdom & patriotism of the Nation to maintain it." He would search for that wisdom in the annual address to be delivered to Congress the next day by the president, James Buchanan. Weeks later, when the text reached him by newspaper, Lee found two arguments that he would adopt and repeat again and again. One was the idea that secession is nothing but "revolution." The other was that the sword is not the means by which to hold a nation together.[11]

When South Carolinians elected a convention made up of delegates who were ardent secessionists, Lee was distraught. Making reference to the intrusion of abolitionists into Kansas, he wrote to his oldest son that he "resent[ed]" the denial by northerners "of the equal rights of our citizens to the common [western] territory." But he was every bit as unhappy with the southern extremists who sought to break apart the Union, as well as with those who would rescind the cessation of the business of slavery:

> I am not pleased with the course of the "Cotton States," as they term themselves. In addition to their selfish, dictatorial bearing, the threats they throw out against the "Border States" as they call them, if they will not join them, argue little for the benefit or the peace of Va. should she determine to coalesce with them .... While I wish to do what is right, I am unwilling to do what is wrong, either at the bidding of the South or the North. One of their plans seems to be the renewal of the slave trade. That I am opposed to on every ground ....[12]

A week later, South Carolina seceded (fig. 28). The anger of the Lee family over this event, which more than anything else set the course for war, was expressed by Mary Custis Lee in a letter to a friend. She asked Eliza Mackay Stiles, "What is the use of a government combined such as ours, if any one part has the right ... of withdrawing? ... [This] Revolution [brought about by South Carolina warrants the] reprobation of the World." In two letters to her daughter Mildred, she expressed both the family's concern and its hope:

> With a sad heavy heart my dear child I write for the prospects before us are sad indeed & as I think both parties are in the wrong in this fratricidal war there is nothing comforting even in the hope that God may prosper the right, for I see no right in the matter. We can only pray that in his Mercy he will spare us.
>
> I pray that the Almighty may listen to the prayers of the faithful in the land & direct their counsels for good—& that the designs of ambitious & selfish politicians who would dismember our glorious Country may be frustrated—especially that our own state may act right & obtain the merit promised in the Bible to the peacemakers.

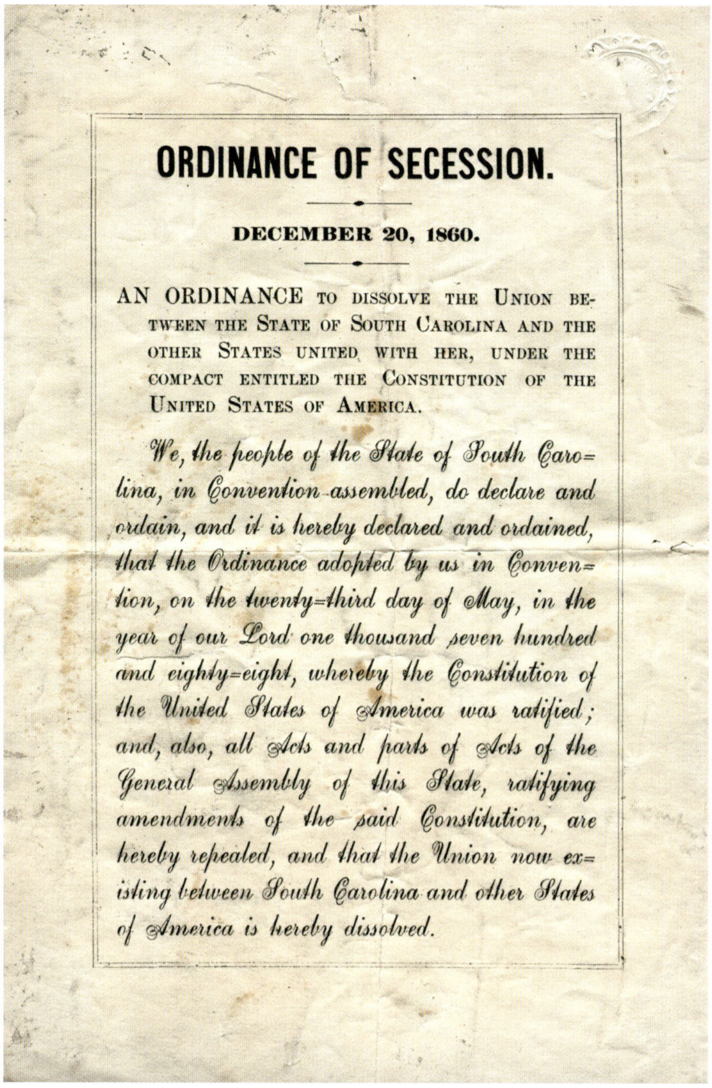
ORDINANCE OF SECESSION.

DECEMBER 20, 1860.

AN ORDINANCE TO DISSOLVE THE UNION BETWEEN THE STATE OF SOUTH CAROLINA AND THE OTHER STATES UNITED WITH HER, UNDER THE COMPACT ENTITLED THE CONSTITUTION OF THE UNITED STATES OF AMERICA.

We, the people of the State of South Carolina, in Convention assembled, do declare and ordain, and it is hereby declared and ordained, that the Ordinance adopted by us in Convention, on the twenty-third day of May, in the year of our Lord one thousand seven hundred and eighty-eight, whereby the Constitution of the United States of America was ratified; and, also, all Acts and parts of Acts of the General Assembly of this State, ratifying amendments of the said Constitution, are hereby repealed, and that the Union now existing between South Carolina and other States of America is hereby dissolved.

fig. 29.
Ordinance of Sucession, December 20, 1860, broadside, Virginia Historical Society

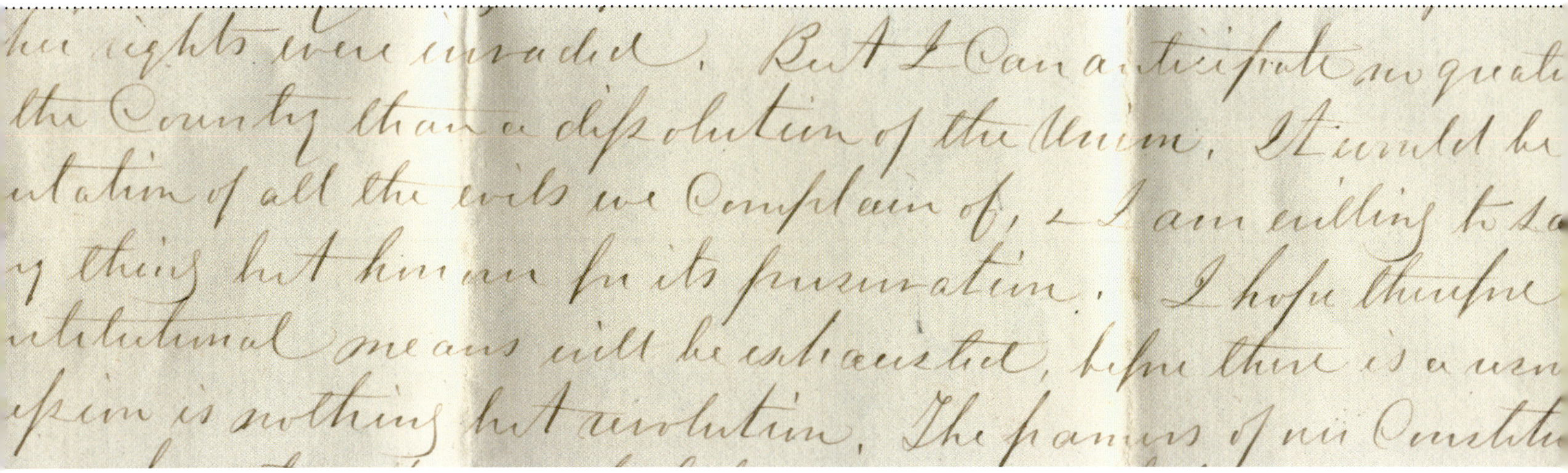

fig. 30.
Robert E. Lee, Fort Mason, San Antonio, Texas, to Rooney Lee, *Letter*, January 29, 1861, Virginia Historical Society

Mary Custis Lee's hope that Virginia would prove to be the bulwark against total war was not unrealistic. Many in the Commonwealth were against the war, and there was a real hope that should Virginia stay with the Union, a war on a grand scale might be avoided.[13]

The action by the South Carolinians, however, compelled Lee to anticipate what would be Virginia's move, and, in turn, his own should Virginia secede. It was one matter to resign rather than to fight his countrymen of the South. It was a different matter to defend one's native state against the Union army. Lee's stance was predictable. Honor would compel him to resign from the army of the United States, and it would also force him to serve in Virginia's military should his native state secede and face invasion. Lee wrote to young Annette Carter, a cousin, that he would do the first, and then wait to see if he would have to do the second: "If the Union is dissolved, I shall return to Virginia & share the fortune of my people."[14]

On January 9, Mississippi seceded, followed by Florida the next day, Alabama the next, and Georgia on the eighteenth. In the wake of those events, Lee wrote a series of thoughtful letters to the members of his immediate family that summarize his thoughts about both secession and about the duties that had been prompted by the crisis. One of the earliest letters was to Markie Williams, his young cousin and confidante, with whom he had shared his heart for decades. Lee told her that he was frustrated by the "folly, selfishness and short sightedness" of his countrymen, who would do the unthinkable: "destroy a government inaugurated by the blood and wisdom of our patriot fathers." Ever the fatalist, and conscious of the difficult moral dilemmas that had been handed down to his generation, Lee anticipated "a fiery ordeal" which the nation would "have to pass through for its sins." He also stated the arguments about honor and loyalty to Virginia that are now familiar:

> … there is no sacrifice I am not ready to make for the preservation of the union save that of honour. If a disruption takes place, I shall go back in sorrow to my people and share the misery of my native state, and save in her defence there will be one soldier less in the world than now …. I see no cause of disunion, strife and civil war and pray it may be averted.[15]

On the next day, Lee wrote a letter to his wife, the great-granddaughter of Martha Washington, in which he elaborated on the theme of the endangered legacy of the patriot fathers. Mary Custis Lee had recently sent her husband a new biography of George Washington by Edward Everett, which he said that he had read and enjoyed:

> How [Washington's] spirit would be grieved could he see the wreck of his mighty labours. I will not, however, permit myself to believe till all ground of hope is gone that the work of his noble deeds will be destroyed, & that his precious advice & virtuous example will So Soon be forgotten by his countrymen. As far as I can judge from the papers we are between a State of anarchy & Civil war. May God avert from us both …. I must try and be patient and await the end, for I Can do nothing to hasten or retard it.[16]

A week later, Lee explained his position to his son Rooney (fig. 30). By this time, he had refined his thinking to the extent that there were five points that he cared to make. The first was that no greater calamity could befall the country than dissolution. The second was that he would sacrifice everything but honor for its preservation.

The third and fourth were President Buchanan's arguments that secession is nothing but revolution, and a union should not be maintained by violence. The final point involved Lee's perceived duty to Virginia. Only in its defense would he draw his sword.[17]

The January letters are long and thoughtful; the one to Rooney mentions the christening of Lee's grandson and namesake, the health of his daughter-in-law, and the estate of his father-in-law, before he addresses the secessionist crisis:

> I can anticipate no greater calamity for the country than a dissolution of the Union. It would be an accumulation of all the evils we complain of, & I am willing to sacrifice every thing but honour for its preservation. I hope therefore that all Constitutional means will be exhausted, before there is a resort to force. Secession is nothing but revolution. The framers of our Constitution never exhausted so much labour, wisdom & forbearance in its formation & surrounded it with so many guards & securities, if it was intended to be broken by every member of the confederacy at will. It was intended for perpetual union, so expressed in the preamble, & for the establishment of a government, not a compact, which can only be dissolved by revolution or the consent of all the people in convention assembled. It is idle to talk of secession. Anarchy would have been established & not a government, by Washington, Hamilton, Jefferson, Madison & the other patriots of the Revolution. In 1808 when the New England States resisted Mr Jefferson's Embargo law & the Hartford Convention assembled secession was termed treason by Virga statesmen. What can it be now? Still a union that can only be maintained by swords & bayonets, & in which strife & civil war are to take the place of brotherly love & kindness, has no charm for me. If the Union is dissolved & the government disrupted, I shall return to my native State & share the miseries of my people & save in her defense will draw my sword on none.[18]

Also on January 29, Lee wrote to his daughter Agnes that it was difficult for him to follow the fast-moving tide of events, being so "far removed" and dependent on the New Orleans newspapers. Louisiana had seceded on January 26, and a Texas convention to consider the issue was in session; that state would secede on February 1. Lee was able to piece together enough information to confirm that the Union was fast coming apart. He could only hope that the state of Virginia would not drag him deeper into the morass that was forming. He explained his anxiety to Agnes:

> The proceedings of the Southern States in Sequestering the public property within their reach, or as it is pompously termed Capturing the U.S. Forts, Arsenals, etc. etc. wherever there is no body to defend them, I fear will not calm the angry feelings existing in the country, & except in Self defence I think unnecessary. I therefore Conclude that those States on no Condition will adhere to the Union. That their Course is taken & that they are determined to separate from the present Government …. I am particularly anxious that Virginia should keep right, & as she was chiefly instrumental in the formation & inauguration of the Constitution, so I would wish that she might be able to maintain it and to save the union.[19]

Again, his hope was that Virginia would somehow avoid being complicitous in the destruction of the Union that so many great Virginians had worked so hard to create.

Lee further told his daughter, "If the bond of the Union can only be maintained by the Sword & bayonet, instead of brotherly love & friendship, … its existence will lose all interest with me." On the next day, Lee advised Custis that on account of the secession of the Deep South states, the country "may have been plunged into civil war." As would be his course for the next four years, he turned to faith to sustain him: "May God rescue us from the folly of our own acts, save us from selfishness and teach us to love our neighbors as ourselves."[20]

The next month brought hope, concern, and eventually uncertainty for Lee. The news of four developments, all tied to February 4, eventually reached his outpost. First, a peace conference organized by the state of Virginia had opened in Washington; nothing came of it. On the same day, voters in Virginia had elected a convention made up of a two-thirds majority of delegates opposed to secession. Also on February 4, representatives of six of the seven seceded states (all but Texas) gathered in Montgomery, Alabama, to form a southern republic. This was a month before Lincoln arrived at the White House. In less than a week they had drafted a constitution, elected a provisional president and vice president, declared themselves a congress, and established the Confederate States of America. The fourth matter was announced in a letter dated February 4. It relieved Lee of duty in Texas and ordered him to report to Winfield Scott, the general-in-chief of the army in Washington, who was Lee's former commander during the Mexican War and ever since then the younger officer's mentor. Lee no doubt deduced that the cause of this unexpected change of assignment was related to the secession crisis. He hurried back, arriving at Arlington on March 1, a month earlier than his orders required.

As he anticipated his meeting with Scott, Lee considered his position. He had traveled first from Fort Mason to San Antonio, speaking to at least four fellow officers about secession and his role should Virginia decide to participate. Their accounts are consistent. To each he said that his first duty was to his family and his home state. Lee told R. W. Johnson, "it may be necessary for me to carry a musket in defense of my native state, Virginia, in which case I shall not prove recreant to my duty." He said to Captain George B. Cosby "that he had ever been taught that his first allegiance was due his mother State; [and] that … under no circumstance could he ever bare his sword against Virginia's sons." In San Antonio, he told Charles Anderson, "If Virginia stands by the old Union, so will I. But if she secedes … I will still follow my native State with my sword, and if need be with my life." And he told R. M. Potter, "When I get to Virginia I think the world will have one soldier less. I shall resign and go to planting corn." Despite the rhetoric that has been offered over the years about Lee's difficulty in making a decision in mid-April as he sat at Arlington House, there is no doubt that before he left the soil of Texas his mind was fully made up. Lee's loyalty to Virginia would take precedence over that to the federal government.[21]

Winfield Scott was a fellow Virginian who shared with Lee an abhorrence of disunion. For the prior six months he had been doing what he could to ward off civil conflict. Three months earlier Scott had published an article on the subject, *Views Suggested by the Imminent Danger, Oct. 29, 1860, of a Disruption of the Union by the Secession of One or More of the Southern States*. He advocated reinforcement of the forts and armories of the South to prevent their seizure by extremists, but he reversed that strategy following the secession of South Carolina. Scott then proposed the withdrawal of the Union force in Charleston, which was stationed at Fort Sumter, as the best means to avoid a potentially explosive situation. Ever looking to minimize the loss of life, Scott in the spring of 1861 was devising a scheme (later dubbed the "Anaconda Plan") to quell the secessionists by blockading the southern coast and controlling the Mississippi River. In this way, he would demoralize the South and deprive it of supplies. Scott is said to have reasoned that if he could muster a large enough army, with Robert E. Lee at its head, he would have found another way to intimidate the "fire-eaters" of the Deep South and thereby cause them to back away from the path toward permanent separation. Four years earlier, the general had ranked Lee as "the very best soldier that I ever saw in the field." The worst-case scenario for Scott was that so gifted a tactician would end up fighting on the opposing side.[22]

On March 2, both houses of Congress approved an amendment that guaranteed the preservation of slavery in the existing slave states. On March 4, Lincoln was inaugurated. The new president announced that he would continue to tax the South and, contrary to Scott's advice, he would not relinquish government property there. Sometime during early March, Lee and Scott held the first of their two long meetings. They talked for three hours but no record was kept of what they said. Lee must have been told of his upcoming promotion from brevet colonel to colonel (which would be signed by Abraham Lincoln on March 28) and of his assignment to command the First Cavalry regiment. Lee would fill the position held by General E. V. Sumner, who had been promoted to replace General David Twiggs. Twiggs had been removed for surrendering Texas to the secessionists.

While still in Texas, Lee had agreed with George Cosby that his meeting with Scott would no doubt have something to do with the planning of a course of military action against the seceded states. From years of duty in the Deep South, Lee knew its geography and people well. He told Cosby that if asked to confer on such a plan, he would resign. Presumably Scott and Lee conversed at length about the blockading of the South. Scott's military secretary, Colonel Erasmus Keyes, noted only that afterward the general was "painfully silent." In a letter dated March 15, Confederate Secretary of War L. P. Walker offered to Lee the highest commission then existent in the southern army, that of brigadier general. No response was made to the offer. Meanwhile, Scott and the new president communicated daily; Lee's status, no doubt, was often on the agenda.[23]

On March 23, Jeb Stuart, who was stationed with the Union army in Kansas, wrote to a friend about how he was "quietly awaiting Va's action" regarding secession, and that "Lincoln is only waiting for our [Virginia state] convention to adjoin without action decided, before he begins coercion …. Lincoln is only waiting to get firmly seated on his throne." He added that word had reached him that Scott had ordered the "distinguished" Colonel Lee to report in person. Stuart, who had been with Lee a year-and-a-half earlier at Harpers Ferry, would have known why.[24]

The first week of April brought hope to Lee that his native state would not secede. A test vote taken at the Virginia convention on April 4 measured the delegates as still opposed to secession by a two-to-one majority. Lincoln had been conferring since February with several of the Virginia delegates who were staunch unionists. In an effort to avoid a crisis at Fort Sumter, Secretary of State William H. Seward kept those talks going. On April 4, the president met with John B. Baldwin. Another of the Virginia pro-Unionists, John Minor Botts, later said that Lincoln repeated to Baldwin an offer that he had joked about before his inauguration. He would swap a fort for a state; he would remove troops from Fort Sumter if Virginia would remain in the Union. Baldwin denied that any such offer was made to him. Communication suddenly broke down, probably because Lincoln, who did not want to be the last president of the United States, had already dispatched supply ships to Fort Sumter. Even before taking office Lincoln seems to have made several momentous decisions. One was that he would not allow the expansion of slavery into any of the new territories. Another was that he would not allow the Union to be split apart.[25]

In mid-April events unfolded rapidly. In a period of one week, Lee's worst fears about disunion were realized and he had sworn allegiance to a new nation. The Confederate commander in Charleston, P. G. T. Beauregard, Lee's comrade during the Mexican War, cut off food to Fort Sumter. When Lincoln sent supplies, Confederate President Jefferson Davis ordered Beauregard to bombard the fort, thereby starting a spiral from which there would be no escape. On April 12, Americans read in broadsides that the war had commenced (fig. 31). Two days later, Fort Sumter surrendered without any loss of life. On April 15, Lincoln issued a call for 75,000 volunteers "to cause the laws to be duly executed." Virginia was expected to provide its share of those troops.[26]

In response to Lincoln's call to arms, Jefferson Davis asked for 100,000 southern volunteers to defend against invasion. The Vir-

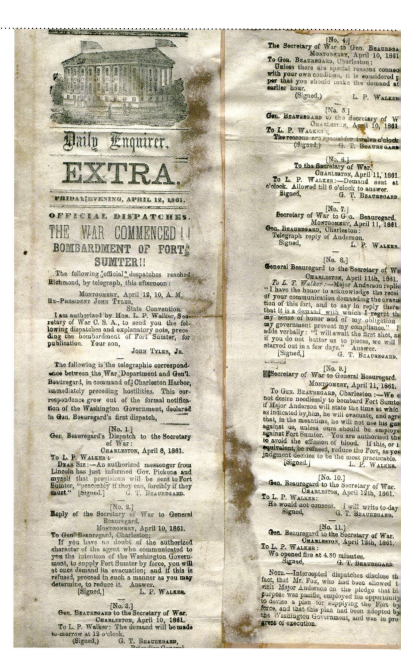

fig. 31.
Bombardment of Fort Sumter!!, April 12, 1861, broadside, Virginia Historical Society

ginia convention moved quickly into secret session. Lee was no doubt aware of this development by April 17. It was therefore no surprise that he received two letters inviting him to meetings on the very next day. The first was at the home of Francis P. Blair, Sr., who served as a spokesman for the president. The second was with Winfield Scott. The federal government clearly wanted to enlist Colonel Lee's services before the Confederacy did.

Blair, the former editor of *The Congressional Globe*, was selected by the Lincoln administration to negotiate with Lee in part because they knew one another. Decades earlier, in the late 1830s, his son, Montgomery Blair of Missouri, had befriended the young engineer when Lee served in St. Louis. The elder Blair had been conferring with Lincoln, Secretary of War Simon Cameron, and General Winfield Scott, who knew and appreciated Lee's military skills. On April 18, Blair told Lee that a large army would soon be put into the field to quell secession, and that he had been authorized by the president to offer him its command. This was Lincoln's proposed army of 75,000 volunteers. Command carried the rank of major general. The career advancement that Lee had pursued for three long decades could in an instant be fulfilled, on a grander scale than the colonel could ever have imagined. Lee in effect would succeed the aging Winfield Scott. The president had asked Blair to "ascertain Lee's intentions and feelings" on this matter.[27]

Lee's conversation with Blair was not recorded, but it was later recalled by both parties, as well as by Blair's son. Lee's account, written in 1868, is brief. It is contained in the first part of a letter that he wrote to Senator Reverdy Johnson of Maryland wherein he recounts step-by-step the process by which he left the Union army and joined the Confederate forces:

> I never intimated to any one that I desired the command of the United States Army; nor did I ever have a conversation but with one gentleman, Mr. Francis Preston Blair, on the subject, which was at his invitation, and, as I understood, at the instance of President Lincoln.
>
> After listening to his remarks, I declined the offer he made me, to take command of the army that was to be brought into the field; stating, as candidly and as courteously as I could, that, though opposed to secession, and deprecating war, I could take no part in invasion of the Southern states.[28]

The senior Blair, remembering the meeting a decade after the fact, gave more detail. Many of Lee's reported comments are not surprising.

> I told him what President Lincoln wanted him to do. He wanted him to take command of the army. Lee said he was devoted to the Union. He said, among other things, that he would do everything in his power to save it, and that if he owned all the negroes in the South, he would be willing to give them up and make the sacrifice of the value of every one of them to save the Union. We talked for several hours on the political question in that vein …. He said he could not decide without seeing his friend, General Scott. He said he could not, under any circumstances, consent to supersede his old commander. He asked me if I supposed the President would consider that proper. I said yes. Then we had a long conversation on that subject …. The matter was talked over by President Lincoln and myself for some hours on two or three different occasions. The President and Secretary Cameron expressed themselves as anxious to give the command of our army to Robert E. Lee. I considered myself as authorized to inform Lee of that fact.[29]

Lee left Blair with the impression that he would give more thought to the offer of the Union command. But his letter to Senator Johnson makes clear that the colonel's mind never wavered regarding the invasion of the southern states: "I went directly from the interview with Mr. Blair to the office of General Scott; told him the proposition that had been made to me, and my decision." Lee's mind was made up before he sat down with the general.

As with the Blair interview, no record was kept of Lee's April 18 conversation with Scott. However, a few details are known, and others can be deduced. Lee reported to the general what the president's spokesman had said. He must have admitted that the offer to command the new army was an enormous temptation. According to a conversation that Lee had in 1868 with William Allan, a professor at Washington College and former Confederate officer, Scott told Lee that he didn't think there would be a war. He showed the colonel "a mass of correspondence between himself and Lincoln and others" that was "very pacific in tone." Lee, however, would not change his stance. Scott reportedly said, "Lee, you have made the greatest mistake of your life; but I feared it would be so."[30]

Lee actually faced two crucial career decisions that April. One involved the offer of command of the Union army, which he refused. The second had to do with his commission. If Virginia did not withdraw from the Union, the colonel wanted to believe that he could perhaps continue in uniform, serving in some capacity other than with the invading force. Lee and Scott apparently discussed the situation should Virginia secede, and Lee explained that he felt strongly obligated to his family and state. According to E. D. Townsend, an aide to the general who was present during this

fig. 32.
An Ordinance to Repeal the Ratification of the Constitution of the United States of America, by the State of Virginia ..., after April 17, 1861, broadside, Virginia Historical Society

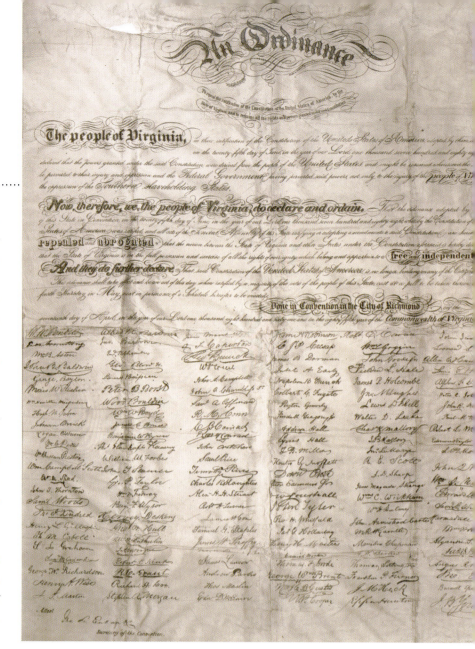

interview, the colonel stated: "The property belonging to my children, all they possess, lies in Virginia. They will be ruined, if they do not go with their State. I cannot raise my hand against my children." Scott answered that, in fact, Lee had no options. He must either resign his commission or keep it and accept whatever duty he was assigned.[31]

Scott concluded the meeting on the eighteenth with the advice that if Lee intended to resign his commission, he best do so quickly, while he could still exit with honor. Otherwise, Lee might suddenly be called to duty and have to resign under orders, which would bring disgrace. Lee had wanted to put off the decision until the Virginia convention ruled on secession. On the way home, he visited his brother Smith Lee, who was in Washington on active duty with the navy and faced the same choices himself. They discussed their respective predicaments. That night at Arlington, Lee wrestled with his decision to resign from the career that he had spent his adult life building. In her reminiscences of 1866, Mary Custis Lee wrote that this was a struggle so intense that she would "not attempt to describe it."[32]

While Lee considered what to do that evening, he did not know that the Virginia convention had already made his decision for him. When Lincoln called for 75,000 troops from all of the states, including Virginia and the non-seceding states of the South, Governor John Letcher, who had been staunchly pro-Union before April 15, was infuriated. He responded to the president, "Your object is to subjugate the Southern States …. You have chosen to inaugurate civil war, and having done so, we will meet it in a spirit as determined as the Administration has exhibited toward the South." The majority of the Virginia delegates agreed with the governor. They abruptly shifted their stance; a vote on April 17 was 88 to 55 for secession (fig. 32). On May 23 there would be a statewide referendum, but the issue was in fact settled. Lee learned of this vote in Alexandria on the nineteenth, the day following his meetings with Blair and Scott. To Lee's thinking, however, the decision was now out of his hands.[33]

A month earlier, just to be sure that Lee knew where his allegiance should lie, a group of secession-minded legislators in Richmond had concocted a strategy that would seal his fate. In mid-March, on the floor of the general assembly, they praised the valor of "Light-Horse Harry" Lee; on the twenty-eighth of that month they arranged the appropriation of funding to remove his remains from Cumberland Island in Georgia, where he had died, and return them to his native state, to be re-interred on the grounds of the Virginia Military Institute. How could Robert E. Lee possibly turn away from so high an honor awarded to his father? The disgrace associated with his father's bankruptcy and other failings would be erased. Lee might also have felt that this connection between Virginia and one of her great heroes of the Revolution would have stirred the type of Unionist sympathies that he was hoping would continue to dominate the political discussion in his home state.[34]

The type of frustration that Lee felt, entrapped as he was by circumstances beyond his control, was given vivid expression by his oldest son. On the same day that the father visited Winfield Scott, so did William Woods Averell. Averell would eventually be pro-

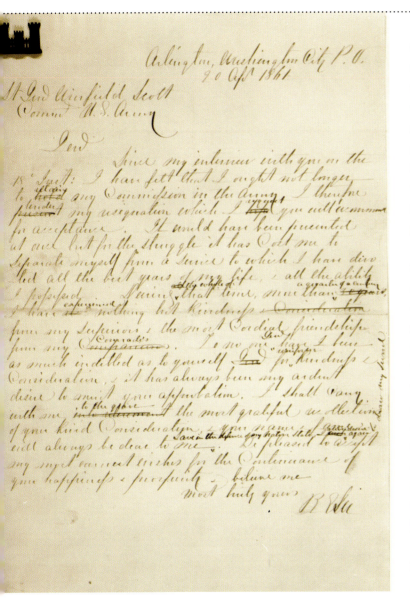

fig. 33.
Robert E. Lee to Winfield Scott, *Draft of a Letter*, April 20, 1861, Museum of the Confederacy

moted to the rank of general in the Union cavalry. He had been a cadet at West Point when Lee was superintendent there, and he knew Custis Lee. During the week of April 18, at Fort Adams just outside of Washington, Averell talked with the younger Lee and later recalled what Custis said to him:

> "Averell, that Arlington estate over the river is mine. I would give it in a moment and all I have on earth if the Union could be preserved in peace, but I must go with my State," and I left him leaning his elbows on the mantelpiece with his face buried in his hands, agitated with profound grief.[35]

Lee was angered by the failure of leadership in both the North and the South that was allowing a national tragedy to unfold. He knew that the blame lay with the politicians. During the war he would write in his journal, "Politicians are more or less so warped by party feeling, by selfishness, or prejudices, that their minds are not altogether balanced. They are the most difficult to cure of all insane people, politics having so much excitement in them." Virginia's politicians would have to shoulder their part of the blame. At the least, he may have thought, Virginia's leaders could have passed a resolution of neutrality as Kentucky did. Perhaps then, if honor permitted, he could have escaped the war.[36]

Lee recounted to Senator Johnson what happened next: "Upon reflection after returning to my home [following the Blair and Scott interviews], I concluded that I ought no longer to retain the commission I held in the United States Army; and on the second morning thereafter I forwarded my resignation to General Scott." Once he knew that Virginia had seceded, his decision was inevitable. During the following week Alexander Stephens of Georgia, the vice president of the Confederacy, asked Lee if his choice to side with the secessionists had been difficult. The general responded, "I don't believe that I had any control over it. When the time came, I could not have done otherwise." In 1866, Lee told a Congressional Joint Committee on Reconstruction, "my view [was] that the act of Virginia in withdrawing herself from the United States carried me along as a citizen of Virginia, and that her laws and her acts were binding on me."[37]

Lee penned his resignation letter on April 20, carefully choosing his words (figs. 33, 34). "I have felt that I ought no longer to retain my commission in the Army." He praised Scott and his other colleagues of "more than a quarter of a century" for their kindness and friendship. Then he stated defiantly the principle upon which he and Scott differed: "Save in defence of my native State, I never desire again to draw my sword." He almost forgot to include that sentence, which he inserted toward the end of the first draft, because he was so concerned that he adequately express the love he felt for his friend and mentor. This was an important theme of the final version:

> Since my interview with you on the 18th inst. I have felt that I ought no longer to retain my commission in the Army. I therefore tender my resignation, which I request you will recommend for acceptance. It would have been presented at once, but for the struggle it has cost me to separate myself

LEE AND GRANT

fig. 34.
Chair, which Lee used when he wrote his letters of resignation, National Park Service, Arlington House

from a service to which I have devoted all the best years of my life and all the ability I possessed.

During the whole of that time—more than a quarter of a century—I have experienced nothing but kindness from my superiors & a most cordial friendship from my comrades. To no one, General, have I been as much indebted as to yourself for uniform kindness and consideration, and it has always been my ardent desire to meet your approbation. I shall carry to the grave the most grateful recollections of your kind consideration, and your name and fame will always be dear to me.

Save in defence of my native State, I never desire again to draw my sword.

Be pleased to accept my most earnest wishes for the continuance of your happiness and prosperity, & believe me, most truly yours, R. E. Lee.

Lee next drafted a one-sentence resignation to Secretary of War Cameron: "I have the honour to tender the resignation of my Commission as Colonel of the 1st Regt. Of Cavalry." Lee added to Senator Johnson, in terms reminiscent of Washington's wish that he be allowed to return home and tend his soil, that even as he resigned his commission he remained optimistic that war might still be averted: "At the time, I hoped that peace would have been preserved; that some way would have been found to save the country from the calamities of war; and I then had no other intention than to pass the remainder of my life as a private citizen."[38]

Also on April 20, Lee wrote letters to his brother Smith Lee and to his sister Ann Marshall in Baltimore. Two days earlier he had told his brother that he was undecided. An explanation was now due. Lee's reasoning in the letter to his brother was entirely logical. He closed with what had become for him almost an oath.

The question which was the subject of my earnest consultation with you on the 18th inst., has in my own mind been decided. After the most anxious inquiry as to the correct course for me to pursue, I concluded to resign, and sent in my resignation this morning. I wished to wait until the Ordinance of Secession should be acted on by the people of Virginia; but war seems to have commenced [with the seizure of the Gosport naval yard and the arsenal at Harpers Ferry], and I am liable at any time to be ordered on duty, which I could not conscientiously perform. To save me from such a position and to prevent the necessity of resigning under orders, I had to act at once, and before I could see you again on the subject, as I had wished. I am now a private citizen, and have no other ambition than to remain at home. Save in defence of my native state, I have no desire ever again to draw my sword. I send you my warmest love.[39]

Smith Lee understood his brother's thinking. He later gave the diarist Mary Chestnut the same explanation as to his own decision: "I

62 I. THE DECISIONS OF 1861

could take no part in an invasion of the Southern States. Virginia comes first with us all, you know, so here I am."[40]

Lee told his Unionist sister in Maryland that he was "grieved" at not having been able to see her recently, and that "Now we are in a state of war that will yield to nothing." He recounted to Ann how the world they knew was unraveling, that he could never take part in an invasion of Virginia, and that he had special reason to hope that he would not have to defend the state because to do so would put him at odds with family and friends in Maryland. Lee tempered his announcement to his sister as best he could:

> The whole south is in a state of revolution, into which Virginia, after a long struggle, has been drawn; and, though I recognize no necessity for this state of things, and would have forborne and pleaded to the end for a redress of grievances, real or supposed, yet in my own person I had to meet the question whether I should take part against my native state.
>
> With all my devotion to the Union and the feeling of loyalty and duty of an American citizen, I have not been able to make up my mind to raise my hand against my relatives, my children, my home. I have therefore resigned my commission in the Army, and save in defence of my native state, with the sincere hope that my poor services may never be needed, I hope I may never be called on to draw my sword. I know you will blame me; but you must think as kindly of me as you can, and believe that I have endeavored to do what I thought right.
>
> To show you the feeling and struggle it has cost me, I send you a copy of my letter of resignation. I have no time for more. May God guard and protect you and yours and shower upon you everlasting blessings, is the prayer of your devoted brother.[41]

The move to influence Lee toward service with the armed forces of Virginia had started a month earlier when the legislature recognized his father. It accelerated dramatically following the decision to secede. On the day that Lee drafted his letters of resignation from the United States Army, an editorial in the *Alexandria Gazette* politely endorsed the idea. "We do not know, and have no right to speak for or anticipate the course of Colonel Robert E. Lee," the paper stated, but the message was clear that Virginia needed his service:

It is probable that the secession of Virginia will cause an immediate resignation of many officers of the Army and Navy from this State …. We call the immediate attention of our State to [Colonel Robert E. Lee] … [There is] no man more worthy to head our forces and lead our army … His reputation, his acknowledged ability, his chivalric character, his probity, honor, and—may we add, to his eternal praise—his Christian life and conduct—make his very name a "tower of strength." It is a name surrounded by revolutionary and patriotic associations and reminiscences.[42]

Lee's account to Senator Johnson of the momentous week of decisions that April ended with a statement concerning how he decided to pledge his allegiance to the military of Virginia. He wrote simply, "Two days after [I resigned my commission], upon the invitation of the Governor of Virginia, I repaired to Richmond; … and accepted the commission of commander of its forces, which was tendered me." Emory Thomas has pointed out that had Lee remained idle while others fought and died, he would have elected dishonor and even infamy. He would have had to spend the rest of his life explaining his inaction to deaf ears, and therefore could never have lived happily in postwar Virginia.[43]

Lee's civilian career lasted two days. On April 20, he received a message from a Richmond judge, John Robertson, who had been sent as a courier to offer Lee command of the Virginia military. Robertson was empowered by the governor, John Letcher, who was acting on behalf of the state convention. The delegates had authorized the appointment of a "commander of the military and naval forces of Virginia." On April 22, Lee boarded a train heading south. He would never set foot in Arlington again. A fellow traveler that day, T. S. Garnett, recognized an attribute of Lee that was missing from the list in the *Alexandria Gazette*. He recorded that Lee was "the noblest-looking man I had ever gazed upon … handsome beyond all men I had ever seen."[44]

Late on the twenty-second, Lee met with Governor Letcher and accepted the command. It was formally awarded on April 23 in a ceremony at the Richmond Capitol. The president of the convention, John Janney, presented a lengthy oration that was scripted to appeal to Lee's honor and sense of duty to family and state. The reference to "Light-Horse Harry" Lee's famous "first in war" eulogy to George Washington, and the suggestion that the son was the successor to the "Father of His Country," is evidence of the high

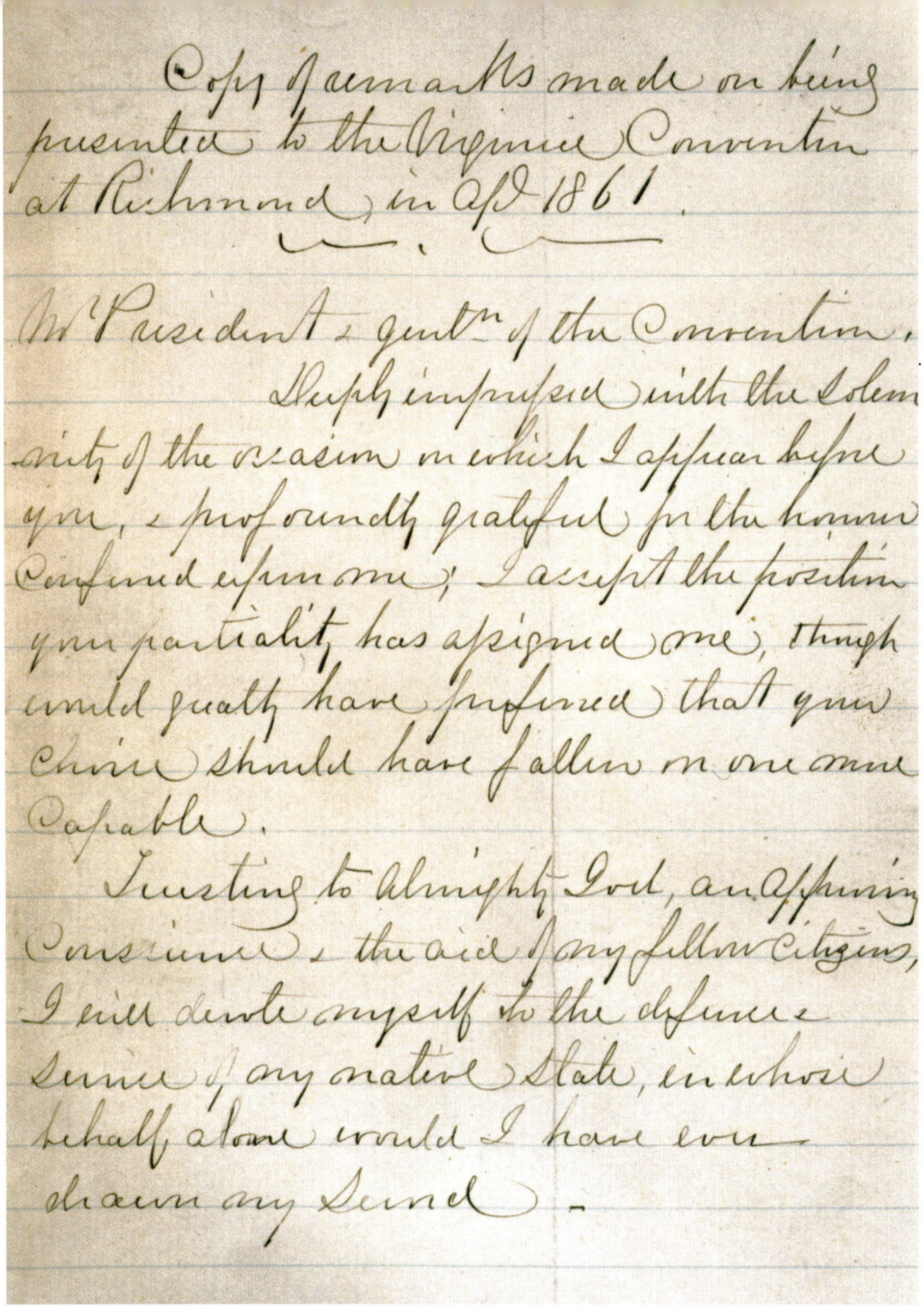

fig. 35.
Robert E. Lee, *Speech Delivered before the Virginia Convention of 1861*, April 23, 1861, Virginia Historical Society

regard held for the colonel by his peers in the gentry, who exerted the social force that obligated Lee to resign from the United States Army and cast his lot with Virginia. Janney's closing statement, parts of which we will include at length below, in essence charged Lee to fight to the death in defense of his homeland. It must have been remembered by the general in the last months of 1864 at Petersburg when he knew that the war was lost and that there was no logical reason to keep resisting:

> Major General Lee, in the name of the people of your native state, here represented, I bid you a cordial and heartfelt welcome to this Hall, in which we may almost yet hear the echo of the voices of the statesmen, the soldiers and sages of by-gone days, who have borne your name, and whose blood now flows in your veins …. We stand animated by one impulse, governed by one desire and one determination, and that is that [this commonwealth] *shall be defended*; and that no spot of her soil shall be polluted by the foot of an invader.
>
> When the necessity became apparent of having a leader for our forces, all hearts and all eyes, by the impulse of an instinct which is a surer guide than reason itself, turned to the old county of Westmoreland. We knew how prolific she had been in other days of heroes and statesmen. We know she had given birth to the Father of his Country; to Richard Henry Lee, to Monroe, and last, though not least, to your own gallant father, and knew well, by your own deeds, that her productive power was not yet exhausted.
>
> Sir, we watched with the most profound and intense interest the triumphal march of the army led by General Scott, to which you were attached, from Vera Cruz to the capital of Mexico; … and we know … that no small share of the glory of those achievements was due to your valor and your military genius ….
>
> Sir, we have, by unanimous vote, expressed our conviction that you are at this day, among the living citizens of Virginia, "first in war." We pray God most fervently that you may so conduct the operations committed to your charge, that it will soon be said of you, that you are "first in peace," and when that time comes you will have earned the still prouder distinction of being "first in the hearts of your countrymen."
>
> I will close with one more remark.
>
> When the Father of this Country made his last will and testament, he gave his swords to his nephews with an injunction that they should never be drawn from their scabbards, except in self-defense, or in defense of the rights and liberties of their country, and that, if drawn for the latter purpose, they should fall with them in their hands, rather than relinquish them.
>
> Yesterday, your mother, Virginia, placed her sword in your hand upon the implied condition that we know you will keep to the letter and in spirit, that you will draw it only in

her defense, and that you will fall with it in your hand rather than that the object of which it was placed there shall fail.

Lee could hardly have anticipated such a welcome. It demanded a response. The colonel had never before made so important a public speech. Lee's remarks were as brief as they could be. He accepted the position, demeaned his own abilities in Washingtonesque manner, and offered the sentiment about sword and state that he had repeated so many times before (fig. 35):[45]

> Mr. President & Gentlemen of the Convention,
>
> Deeply impressed with the solemnity of the occasion on which I appear before you, & profoundly gratified for the honor conferred upon me, I accept the position your partiality has assigned me, though would greatly have preferred that your choice should have fallen on one more capable.
>
> Trusting in Almighty God, an approving conscience, & the aid of my fellow citizens, I will devote myself to the defence & service of my native State, in whose behalf alone would I have ever drawn my Sword.

Alexander Stephens, the vice president of the Confederacy, was in attendance. He was impressed by what he saw:

> All the force which personal appearance could add to the power and impressiveness of words ... was imparted by his manly form and the great dignity as well as grace in his every action and movement. All these, combined, sent home to the breast of every one the conviction that he was thoroughly impressed himself with the full consciousness of the immense responsibility he had assumed.[46]

The newspapers in Richmond and Lynchburg responded with enthusiasm to Lee's appointment. Lee's character was already well known. Ironically, James G. Blaine of Maine, a veteran of Congress, looked back on Lee's assumption of the Virginia command as having been critical in determining the state's May 23 vote on the secession referendum. It "was a powerful incentive with many to vote against the Union," he later wrote. Lee's calls for troops in early May did even more to encourage a vote toward the secession that Lee had always felt would be a catastrophic mistake.[47]

Stephens visited Lee on the evening that the command was awarded. The Confederacy hoped to establish an alliance with Virginia before the May 23 referendum on secession, after which, presumably, the state would join its southern neighbors. But Lee, a Virginia major general, could then have found himself subordinate to a Confederate brigadier general. In this scenario, the Virginia convention could have refused the proposed alliance. Stephens was relieved to find that the general "did not wish anything connected with himself individually, or his official rank or *personal* position, to interfere in the slightest degree with the immediate consummation of that measure which he regarded as one of the utmost importance ...." As before when he considered Scott's offer of command, Lee was now less concerned about advancement than about honor and the fate of his native state. He knew that Virginia by itself could not halt Lincoln's army. He would fail unless Virginia allied itself militarily with the South. Two days later, on April 25, the Virginia convention approved the temporary union with the Confederacy. Lee wrote to his cousin Cassius Lee, "I fear it is now out of the power of man [to restore peace to the country]." He told his wife that war was "inevitable" and gave her instructions about her immediate course of action.

> I am very anxious about you—you have to move—& make arrangements to go to some point of safety which you must select. The Mt Vernon plate & pictures ought to be secured. Keep quiet while you remain & in your preparations. War is inevitable & there is no telling when it will burst around you— Virginia yesterday I understand joined the Confederate States .... May God keep & preserve you & have mercy on all our people is the constant prayer of your affectionate husband.[48]

Lee had vehemently opposed secession not only because it would disassemble the Union and end his career. He knew the carnage of battle and he realized that a civil war in America would not end quickly. "War is a terrible alternative and should be the very, very last resort," he stated. He warned members of the secession convention "that they were just on the threshold of a long and bloody war, and ... that he knew the Northern people well, and knew that they would never yield in that contest except at the conclusion of a long and desperate struggle." He told his wife on April 30 that this war "may last ten years."[49]

Lee's most poignant expression about the tragedy of a civil war, and about his decision-making process in 1861, is a letter that he wrote to a child in the North who had asked Lee for his photograph. The general's response was published in *The New York Times* (fig. 36). Like many Americans at this time, Lee was ready to

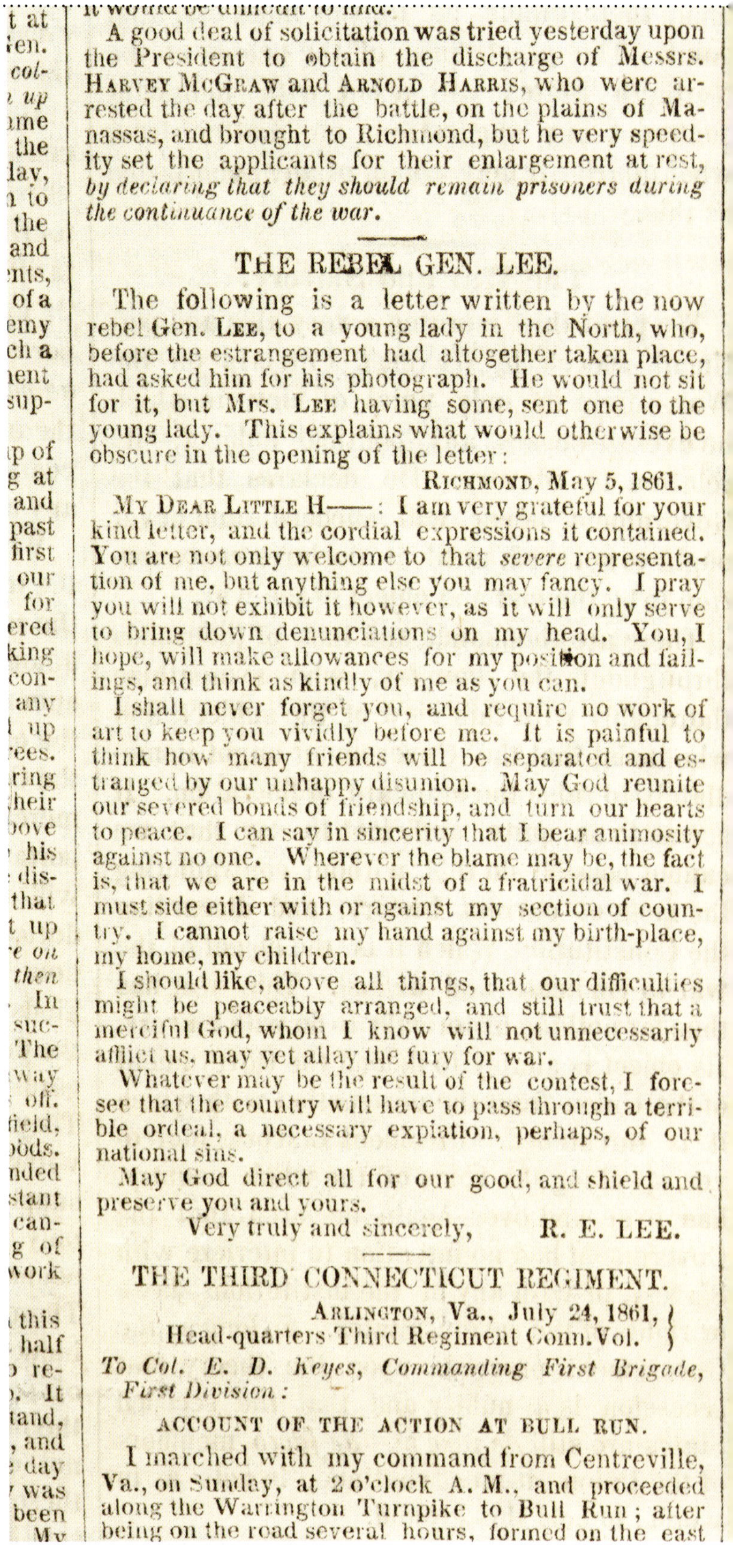

fig. 36.
Robert E. Lee, *Letter*, dated May 5, 1861, in *The New York Times*, August 6, 1861

interpret the coming death and destruction as God's punishment to Americans for their sins.

> It is painful to think how many friends will be separated and estranged by our unhappy disunion. May God reunite our severed bonds of friendship and turn our hearts to peace. I can say in sincerity that I bear animosity against no one. Wherever the blame may be, the fact is, that we are in the midst of a fratricidal war. I must side either with or against my section of the country. I cannot raise my hand against my birthplace, my home, my children.
>
> I should like, above all things, that our difficulties might be peaceably arranged, and still trust that a merciful God, who I know will not unnecessarily afflict us, may yet allay the fury for war.
>
> Whatever may be the result of the contest, I foresee that the country will have to pass through a terrible ordeal, a necessary expiation, perhaps, of our national sins.
>
> May God direct all for our good, and shield and preserve you and yours.

The decision-making process of a second Virginian, George H. Thomas (fig. 37), offers a useful comparison to Lee's story. The future generals had much in common—they had actually shared a tent while both were serving in the army in Texas—but in 1861 they reached entirely opposite conclusions as to where their allegiance should lie. Like Lee, Thomas was descended from a family rooted in Virginia since the colonial era, he was a graduate of West Point, and he served with valor in the Mexican War, after which he remained a career officer. Thomas, however, decided to retain his commission following the secession of Virginia. He ultimately became one of the most accomplished Union generals of the Civil War, serving in the western theater and earning acclaim in Tennessee as the "Rock of Chickamauga."

Some southerners believed that Thomas's decision that April was based on his interest in advancement. In March 1861, however, Governor John Letcher had offered Thomas the position of chief of ordinance for the state. He declined, stating his sense of the obligations of honor:

> I have the honor to state, after expressing my most sincere thanks to you for your very kind offer, that it is not my wish to leave the service of the United States so long as it is

fig. 37.
George N. Barnard, *General George H. Thomas*, c. 1860s (photograph courtesy of New-York Historical Society Library, gift of Charles Scribner's Sons, 1959)

fig. 38.
Sword, Awarded to George H. Thomas for Distinguished Service in the Mexican War, c. 1848–50, Virginia Historical Society, gift of the sisters of George Thomas in 1900

honorable for me to remain in it, and therefore as long as my native State Va remains in the Union it is my purpose to remain in the Army, unless required to perform duties alike repulsive to honor and humanity.

But when Virginia left the Union, Thomas stayed put.[50]

Many in Virginia judged the victories of George Thomas over Confederate armies as actions that were "repulsive to honor." In June 1861, when Jeb Stuart encountered the general in the field, he felt contempt for his former comrade. He wrote to his wife, "Old Geo H. Thomas is in command of the cavalry of the enemy. I would like to hang him as a traitor to his native state." When Thomas later asked his sisters in southside Virginia to forward to him the presentation sword (fig. 38) that he had been awarded for valor in Mexico, they refused. They had disowned him. Thomas's sisters announced to the world that they had no brother. They later gave the sword (40 years later, see caption) to the Virginia Historical Society.[51]

* * * * * * * * * *

Initially, Ulysses Grant reacted to the events of late 1860 and early 1861 much the same as did Robert E. Lee. He was appalled at the prospect of disunion, which he believed would be disastrous for the nation, and he was angered by the idea of secession, which he disdained as nothing short of revolution. But Grant's sense of duty obligated him to the nation, not to a state, and he was untroubled by the concept of a union maintained by the sword. More important to him was the nation's survival.

Grant rarely mentioned the term "honor." Instead, he often spoke of "claims" to his allegiance. In April 1861 he stated that "superior claims" by his nation should override any "motives of self-interest." He had been out of the army for seven years. Unlike Lee, he was not in a position to choose which commission he would accept. Maintaining a sense of personal dignity throughout what must have been a very painful process, Grant maneuvered through the long series of actions that would lead to his regaining a U.S. Army commission with a characteristic resolve and a firm belief that he was the type of man who could make a difference.

Grant was quite shrewd in some of his observations. He reasoned correctly that if he waited long enough, a colonelcy would come to him. He figured that the fury for war in 1861 was as strong in the South as it was in the North, but he knew that the South had fewer resources, a fact that would be its undoing. However, Grant grossly misjudged both the duration of the war—he thought it would be "short"—and the reaction, or lack thereof, of much the

LEE AND GRANT

slave population, whom Grant anticipated would "revolt" in "ninety days" if encouraged by the prospect of freedom.[52]

In the fall of 1860, Grant found himself resident in a state that had produced two of the candidates for election to the presidency. He had not lived in Illinois long enough to qualify to vote, however. Had he been, he said he would have supported the Democrat Stephen Douglas, who actually had little chance of winning. Grant recognized as had Lee that the election would be won by either the other Democrat, John C. Breckenridge, a southerner, or the sole Republican candidate, Abraham Lincoln. Also like Lee, Grant was disturbed that the Democratic Party had split into regional factions that would in all probability negate one another's votes and give the election to the Republican, which neither of the future generals wanted to happen. In 1860, Grant supported neither Abraham Lincoln nor the movement to halt the expansion of slavery. When he heard debates about whether some of the states might secede if Lincoln was elected, Grant read southern sentiment correctly. "The South will fight," he predicted.[53]

Abraham Lincoln's campaign included the pledge that he would honor the institution of slavery where it existed and he would enforce the fugitive slave law. Nonetheless, in December 1860, South Carolina seceded. Grant deplored this action, but he would later excuse the South Carolinians for this error and instead throw all the blame on Virginia. In a letter of April 29, 1861, to his sister Mary, Grant argued that his hatred for Virginia was in fact "universal" in the North. Such thinking suggests that many northerners saw the action of South Carolina as essentially inconsequential; at the least, it was not enough by itself to start a full-scale civil war. The states of the Deep South had neither the manpower nor the resources to wage either a lengthy or a formidable offensive. Grant argued:

> Great allowance should be made for South Carolinians, for the last generation have been educated, from their infancy, to look upon their Government as oppressive and tyrannical and only to be endured till such time as they might have sufficient strength to strike it down. Virginia, and other border states, have no such excuse and are therefore traitors at heart as well as in act.

Julia Grant, the daughter of a pro-southern Missouri planter and slaveholder, expressed the opinion of her father that a state had the right to withdraw from the Union. But she went along with her husband on the idea that the federal government should use force to keep that from happening.[54]

In a letter written at about the time that South Carolina cast its lot, Grant made a series of observations. He blamed the South Carolina decision on a small number of extremists. Grant thought that Jefferson Davis and his colleagues warranted the hangman's noose, and he criticized President James Buchanan for not forcefully maintaining the Union. Grant had a remarkable ability to anticipate developments by considering every contingency. In December 1860 he was able to foresee that the deployment of some "foolish policy" would rally the Border States to support the Deep South. Lincoln, not Buchanan, would be the president who did so, at Fort Sumter:

> It is hard to realize that a State or States could commit so suicidal an act as to secede from the Union, though from all the reports, I have no doubt but that at least five of them will do it. And then, with the present granny of an executive [President Buchanan], some foolish policy will doubtless be pursued which will give the seceding States the support and sympathy of the Southern States that don't go out …. It does seem as if just a few men have produced all the present difficulty. I don't see why by the same rule a few hundred men could not carry Missouri out of the Union.[55]

In his *Memoirs*, Grant further elaborated on the moment of secession. He argued that perhaps the original thirteen states had the authority to secede, but the right "certainly ceased on the formation of new States." "Florida [and] the States west of the Mississippi … were purchased by the treasury of the entire nation [and] Texas … [was] purchased with both blood and treasure." Remembering his experiences in the Mexican War, Grant added that, "It would have been ingratitude and injustice of the most flagrant sort" for Texas to withdraw. Grant reasoned that the framers "never dreamed of such a contingency" as what unfolded in 1861. Echoing the sentiments of Robert E. Lee, he argued that a "war between brothers" could have been avoided had there been rational discussion: "There is little doubt in my mind now that the prevailing sentiment of the South would have been opposed to secession in 1860 and 1861, if there had been a fair and calm expression of opinion."[56]

Grant later described the winter of 1860–61 as "one of great excitement." After South Carolina seceded, other southern states proposed to follow. But in some of those states, Grant reminded his readers, "the Union sentiment was so strong that it had to be suppressed by force." He pointed out that Maryland, Delaware, Kentucky, and Missouri, all slave states, failed to pass ordinances of secession. In 1885, Grant was able to point the blame at the hypocritical slaveholders:

> The South claimed the sovereignty of States, but claimed the right to coerce into their confederation such States as they wanted, that is, all the States where slavery existed. They did not seem to think this course inconsistent. The fact is, the Southern slaveowners believed that, in some way, the ownership of slaves conferred a sort of patent of nobility—a right to govern independent of the interest or wishes of those who did not hold such property. They convinced themselves, first, of the divine origin of the institution and, next, that that particular institution was not safe in the hands of any body of legislators but themselves.

All the while, Grant concluded, President James Buchanan "looked helplessly on and proclaimed that the general government had no power to interfere; that the Nation had no power to save its own life."[57]

In April, as other states of the Deep South were joining South Carolina in withdrawing from the Union, an apathy seemed to be taking hold in much of the nation. It was at least in part to rekindle fading northern patriotism that Abraham Lincoln allowed the situation at Fort Sumter to escalate into conflict. Grant was correct that a "foolish policy" would lure the Border States into sympathetic unity with the secessionists. But the fall of Fort Sumter also unified northern sentiment. The effect on Grant was dramatic. He knew that the moment was looming when his skills and training would be needed.

Fort Sumter was bombarded on April 12 and the garrison there surrendered on the fourteenth. On April 16, the day following Lincoln's call for 75,000 troops, events in Illinois developed rapidly. In Galena, where Grant was resident, a meeting was convened at the courthouse. In attendance were Democrats and Republicans alike, including the town's leading lawyer, John Rawlins, of the former party, and Elihu Washburne, the area's congressman and a supporter of Lincoln. Rawlins would become one of Grant's closest associates, serving on his staff throughout the Civil War and in his cabinet during his first term as president. Washburne would support Grant's career advancement on the political front, and like Rawlins would win his trust and friendship for life. On the sixteenth, Rawlins gave a rousing, patriotic speech. He declared the end of the time for compromise, and he challenged his townsmen to stand as either patriots or traitors. The country, he said, was poised to survive or collapse. Grant was moved. He told his brother Orvil, "I think I ought to go into the service." Rawlins recorded that a change came over Grant: "I saw new energies in [him] …. He dropped a stoop shouldered way of walking, and set his hat forward on his forehead in a careless fashion." Following the meeting, Grant quit for good his job at his father's leather goods store.[58]

On April 18, the day that Robert E. Lee met with Francis Blair and Winfield Scott and was offered command of Lincoln's army of 75,000, Grant's years of military service earned him a lesser reward. He was invited to preside at a second meeting at the Galena courthouse, this one to raise volunteers. Like Lee at the Richmond Capitol when he was awarded command of the Virginia military, the former captain was uncomfortable in such a setting. Few of the military figures of this era had any experience in public speaking. "With much embarrassment and some prompting, I made out to announce the object of the meeting," he later wrote. Galena was expected to field a company; in the end there would be more than a dozen regiments from Illinois. Given their prominence at the meeting, it might seem strange that neither Rawlins nor Grant volunteered, but Rawlins's wife was then dying from consumption, and Grant wanted a colonel's commission and command of a regiment. Washburne, who looked to enhance his own status through the success of anyone he endorsed, offered to help Grant to gain such a commission from the Republican governor of the state, Richard Yates.[59]

The news of Virginia's secession reached Grant on the same day that it did Lee, April 19. Both were angered by this development, but Lee was characteristically self-controlled. He told a druggist in Alexandria that he was one of the few (in the South) who "cannot see the good of secession." Grant could be more openly vehement. Like Lee he recognized the magnitude of the event, and he was shrewd enough to foresee the ripple effect of Virginia's decision. Grant immediately wrote to his pro-southern father-in-law, "Colonel" Frederick Dent, in Missouri, a border state that it was thought might follow Virginia's lead. The South is at fault, Grant said, and Virginia is the most to blame:

> No impartial man can conceal from himself the fact that in all these troubles the South have been the aggressors…. The news to-day is that Virginia has gone out of the Union. But for the influence she will have on the other border slave states this is not much to be regretted. Her position, or rather that of Eastern Virginia, has been more reprehensible from the beginning than that of South Carolina. She shoul[d] be made to bear a heavy portion of the burthen of the War for her guilt.

"Now is the time," Grant continued, "particular[ly] in the border Slave states, for men to prove their love of country." To Colonel Dent, with whom he shared a distrust of Lincoln, Grant added, "I know it is hard for men to apparently work with the Republican party but now all party distinctions should be lost sight of and evry true patriot [should] be for maintaining the integrity of the glorious old *Stars & Stripes*, the Constitution and the Union."

To Colonel Dent, who owned eighteen slaves, Grant closed with an observation about the institution that proved to be squarely on the mark:

> In all this I can but see the doom of Slavery. The North do not want, nor will they want, to interfere with the institution. But they will refuse for all time to give it protection unless the South shall return soon to their allegiance.

Like Lincoln, Grant never imagined in 1861 that an institution that had endured in America since long before the nation's birth could come so quickly to an end. Instead, he guessed wrongly that if the South did not reverse itself, the price of cotton would crash and with it the value of slaves. "Negroes will never be worth fighting over again," he said. What also becomes clear in this letter is his strong sense that Virginia has the greatest culpability for the impending conflict. For much of the second half of the war, he would make sure that Virginia suffered for her intransigence.[60]

Grant was optimistic about prospects in the North. He told Colonel Dent, "there is no mistaking the feelings of the people. The Government can call into the field not only 75000 troops but ten or twenty times 75000 if it should be necessary and find the means of maintaining them too." The son-in-law soon began to contribute to the new war effort by assisting in the mustering of the recruits in Galena who had responded to Lincoln's call.

On April 21, the day after Lee resigned his commission and lectured his brother and sister about the duties attached to honor, Grant wrote his most patriotic letter (fig. 39). It was addressed to his father. Jesse Grant was the man who had sent him to West Point. He asked for his father's advice and addressed the subject of claims to his allegiance. Grant felt sure that the right course was that he should serve his country.

> We are now in the midst of trying times when evry one must be for or against his country, and show his colors by his every act. Having been educated for such an emergency, at the expense of the Government, I feel that it has upon me superior claims, such claims as no ordinary motives of self-interest can surmount. I do not wish to act hastily or inadvisably in the matter, and as there are more than enough to respond to the first call of the President, I have not yet offered myself. I have promised and am giving all the assistance I can in organizing the Company whose services have been accepted from this place. I have promised further to go with them to the state Capital [Springfield] and if I can be of service to the Governor in organizing his state troops to do so. What I ask now is your approval of the course I am taking, or advice in the matter ….
>
> Whatever may have been my political opinions before I have but one sentiment now that is we have a Government, and laws and a flag and they must all be sustained. There are but two parties now, Traitors & Patriots and I want hereafter to be ranked with the latter, and I trust, the stronger party ….[61]

In response, Jesse Grant wrote a letter to Lincoln's attorney general, Edward Bates, in an effort to help his son win a desirable commission. He told Bates that he had written Winfield Scott to the same end "8 or 10 days ago," which would have placed that letter in the hands of the general-in-chief at about the time that Scott failed to convince Lee to remain with him. To Bates, Jesse Grant used what was clearly a very popular expression about drawing one's sword in defense of one's country:

> Yesterday I recd a letter from [the captain], he said as the Government had educated him for the military servis, & it now needed his services, he had again drawn his sword in its defence, & while his services were needed they were at the disposal of his country.

> Galena, April 21st 1861
>
> Dear Father;
>
> We are now in the midst of trying times, when every one must be for or against his country, and show his colors too, by his every act. Having been educated for such an emergency at the expense of the Government, I feel that it has upon me superior claims, such claims as no ordinary motives of self-interest can surmount. I do not wish to act hostily or unadvisedly in the matter, and as there are more than enough to respond to the first call of the President, I have not yet offered myself. I have promised and am giving all the assistance I can in organ—

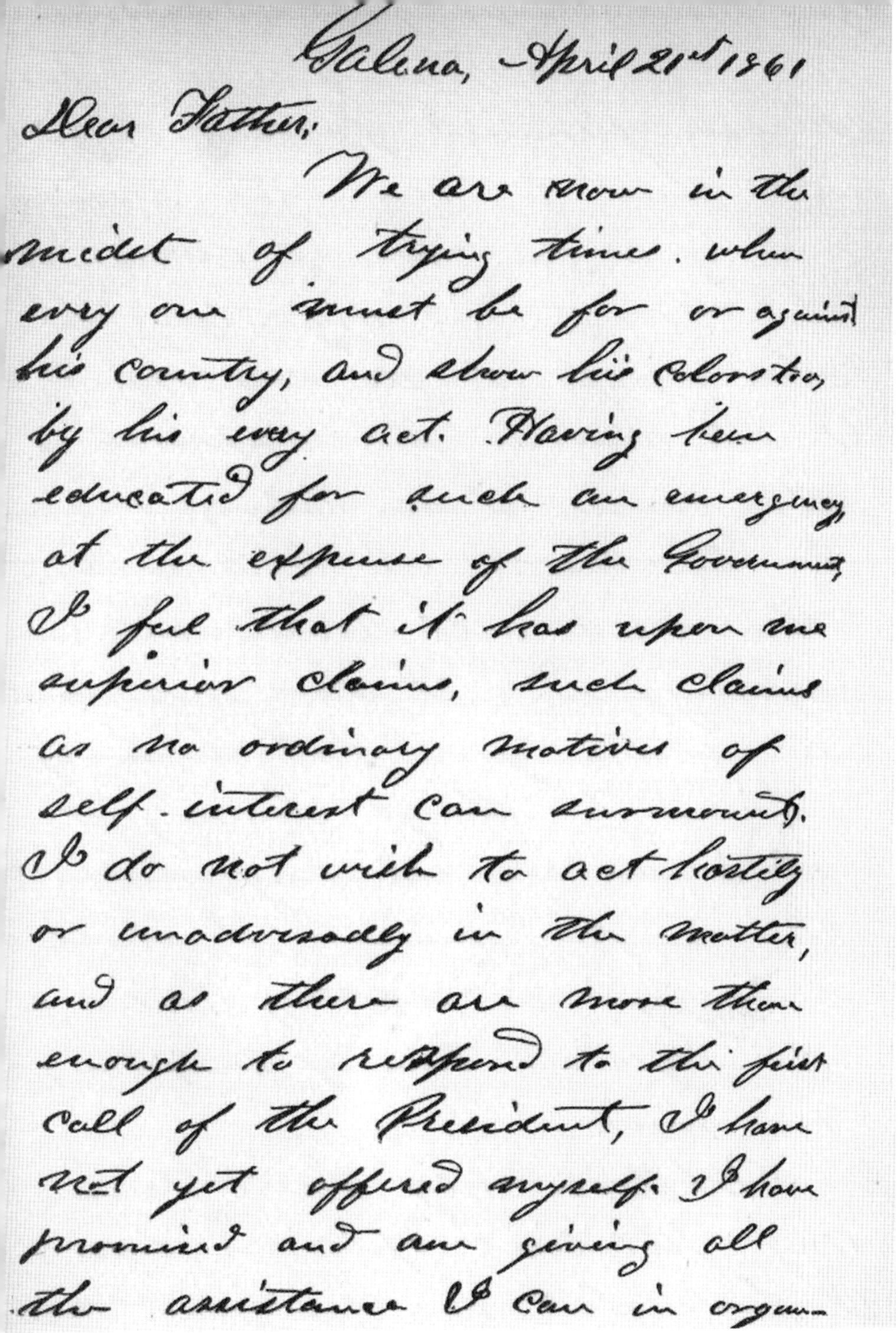

fig. 39.
Ulysses S. Grant, Galena, Illinois, to his father Jesse Root Grant, Covington, Kentucky, *Letter*, April 21, 1861, now lost, from M. J. Cramer, *Ulysses S. Grant* (1897), 25–27

Jesse Grant's letters went unanswered.[62]

Winfield Scott preferred to keep veteran officers attached to regular army units. Grant fell between the cracks of such a plan. He was no longer in the army. Beyond that, the high command did not even seem to be aware of Grant's existence, or at least of his ability. His best opportunity for a colonelcy lay with the volunteers. The Illinois governor was awarding commissions to those who would lead the new units, just as Governor Letcher was doing in Virginia. At the time when Lee was settling into his new career as a Confederate general and the commander of Virginia's military, Grant traveled to Springfield in the hope of receiving an appropriate assignment.

On the way, Grant was inspired by the patriotic response to Lincoln's call. He reported his feelings to his wife on April 27 and to his sister Mary on the twenty-ninth. "At evry station the whole population seemed to be out to greet the troops," he told Julia. "There is such a feeling aroused through the country now as has not been known since the Revolution. Evry company called for in the Presidents proclimation [sic] has been organized, and filled to near double the amount that can be received." Many southerners, of course, saw themselves as involved in a second, rightful Revolution against an oppressive federal government, but Grant saw such rebels as nothing more than traitors. He told Mary he was convinced that "if the South knew the entire unanimity of the North for the Union and maintenance of Law, and how freely men and money are offered to the cause, they would lay down their arms at once in humble submission." Grant concluded that the North no longer had any "disposition to compromise."[63]

In an April 27 letter to Julia, Grant was optimistic about his prospects in the state capital. "Mr. Washburn[e] … prevailed upon me to remain over," he reported. "The Governor told Mr Washburn[e] last night that should the legislature ask the provision for them, he wanted me to take the command and drill them until they are organized into Companies and placed in Regiments." In the meantime, Governor Yates put Grant to work in the adjutant general's office. Grant inspected weapons in the state armory, but did little more. On May 1, he complained to Julia about the inactivity: "At present I am on duty with the Governer, at his request, occupation principally smoking and occasionally giving advice as to how an order should be communicated &c."[64]

Grant also told Julia what he had read in the St. Louis papers about potential violence there between secessionists and Unionists, and about how merchants and businessmen were leaving some of the towns in northern Missouri and slaveholders were moving into the South. He still predicted that the state would become free, which must have been unsettling to Julia, who inevitably worried about her father and the slaves he owned.

In early May, newly formed Illinois regiments began to report to Springfield. Grant mustered them in at Camp Yates, which had been named for the governor. Seeing the regiments gave Grant second thoughts as to whether he should have pushed more vigorously for a command. On May 2, he wrote to his father, "I should have offered myself for the Colonelcy of one of the Regiments, but I find all those places are wanted by politicians who are up to log-rolling, and I do not care to be under such persons." He remarked again about the spirit of patriotism in the air, adding astutely, "I presume the feeling is just as strong on the other side, but they are infinitely in the minority in resources."[65]

In all the "buzz and excitement, as well as confusion" that engulfed Springfield in April and May, Grant was troubled that his approach to advancement was too passive and would founder. On May 3, he wrote to Julia,

> I don't see really that I am doing any good. But when I speak of going it is objected to by not only Governer Yates, but others.— I imagine it will do me no harm the time I spend here, for it has enabled me to become acquainted with the principle men in the state.

Grant anticipated being sent to other Illinois towns to muster in regiments from different districts, but he worried that his duties would end when the mustering was over. He wrote to his father on May 6 that he "might have got the Colonelcy," but, repeating a familiar theme, he "was perfectly sickened at the political wire pulling for all these commissions and would not engage in it." Besides, as he reasoned correctly, "I have done more now than I could do serving as a Capt. under a green Colonel, and if this thing continues they will want more men at a later day."[66]

Grant proved to be wrong on two points in this letter (fig. 40). He misjudged how long the war would last and how the slaves would react:

> My own opinion is that this War will be but of short duration ... a few decisive victories in some of the southern ports will send the secession army howling and the leaders in the rebellion will flee the country. All the states will then be loyal for a generation to come, Negroes will depreciate so rapidly in value that no body will want to own them and their masters will be the loudest in their declamations against the institution in a political and economic view. The nigger will never disturb this country again. The worst that is to be apprehended from him is now; he may revolt and cause more destruction than any Northern man, except it be the ultra abolitionist, wants to see. A Northern army may be required in the next ninety days to go south to suppress a Negro insurrection. As much as the South have vilified the North they would go on such a mission and with the purest motives.[67]

The molding of new recruits into regiments carried Grant far beyond Springfield. By May 10 he had traveled close enough to the Missouri border to cross the river into St. Louis and visit the nearby plantation of his wife's family. From there, he wrote to Julia of how he was exasperated by the pro-southern sympathies of her father and brother. He quipped that the slaves remaining at the White Haven farms might rise up. Apparently Grant was not really concerned that they would, despite his predictions of uprisings further south.

> Soon your father & Lewis Sheets will be left to themselves at the mercy of Mary and the rest of the darkeys ... I believe [John Dent] thinks of a colonelcy in the secession army. Your father says he is for the Union but is opposed to having army to sustain it. He would have a secession force march where they please uninterrupted and is really what I would call a secessionest. Aunt Fanny is strong for the Union and is distressed that your father is not so also.

On returning to Illinois, Grant set to work mustering at Mattoon. He was well enough appreciated by the new troops that they named their outpost Camp Grant. Their drillmaster, however, had not moved a single step further towards acquiring a colonelcy; the commissions continued to be awarded to others.[68]

Grant was able to provide advice of every sort, even to the design of uniforms and flags. He was one of few men in the state who knew the answers to both mundane and complex military questions. Why then was he unable to gain a colonelcy, a rank that he was more than qualified to assume? It is perhaps easier for us today to recognize the obstacles that stood in his path than it was for Grant himself to see them.

One problem was that this former farmer and leather-store clerk did not look or act the part of a high-ranking officer, which was almost mandatory in the nineteenth century. Unlike Lee, his appearance did not attract attention of the right sort. An aide to the governor complained that Grant's "features did not indicate any

fig. 40.
Ulysses S. Grant, near Springfield, Missouri, to his father Jesse Root Grant, Covington, Kentucky, *Letter*, May 6, 1861, Rosenbach Museum & Library, Philadelphia

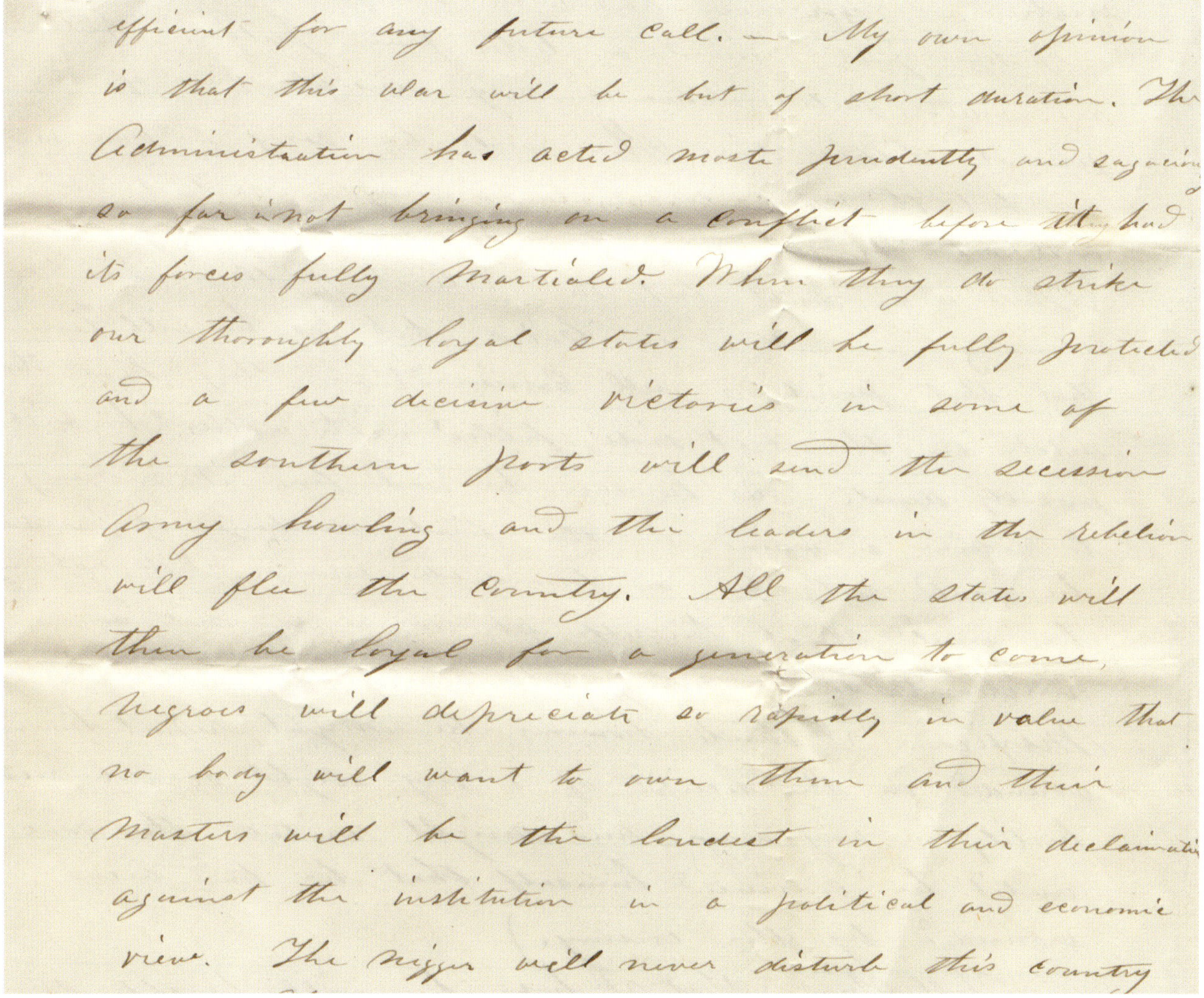

high grade of intellectuality" and that he was so "indifferently dressed" that he "did not at all look like a military man." His sad attire consisted of a worn suit and slouch hat. He smoked a short pipe behind a grizzled beard. To a colleague in the adjutant general's office, Grant appeared to be nothing but "a dead-beat military man—a discharged officer of the regular army." A second problem that thwarted Grant's advancement was the fact that by 1861 most high-ranking officials in the military had forgotten his abilities. After four years of residency at West Point and eleven years of service in the 4th Infantry Regiment, Grant had quit the army, ironically, on the same day his promotion to captain arrived. He was off the radar screen of those who would make the decisions. A final matter was the perception held by some people that Grant was a drunkard. Future general George B. McClellan had encountered Grant on the west coast and on at least one occasion was disgusted to find him drinking. Years later, Augustus Louis Chetlain, who was in competition at Springfield for a colonelcy, told Hamlin Garland, an early biographer of his colleague, that even Grant worried at this juncture that he might turn to drink in frustration. "This is the key to Grant's drinking habits," Chetlain maintained, "Whenever he was idle and depressed this appetite came upon him."[69]

In late May, Grant made renewed efforts to win a commission. On the twenty-fourth, the day after Virginia voters overwhelmingly endorsed secession in a statewide referendum, he wrote to the adjutant general in Washington, Lorenzo Thomas. If his father had no success with the army's commanding general, perhaps Grant could sway its chief administrator. With typical under-

LEE AND GRANT

statement, he pleaded for the rank that would give him command of a thousand men:

> Having served for fifteen years in the regular army, including four years at West Point, and feeling it the duty of evry one who has been educated at the Government expense to offer their services for the support of that Government, I have the honor, very respectfully, to tender my services, until the close of the War, in such capacity as may be offered. I would say that in view of my present age, and length of service, I feel myself competent to command a Regiment ….
>
> Since the first call of the President I have been serving on the Staff of the Governer of this state rendering such aid as I could in the organization of our state Militia ….

The letter to Thomas went unanswered. Grant then turned to Nathaniel Lyon, the federal commander at St. Louis, but Lyon showed no interest. Also in St. Louis was Francis P. Blair, Jr., a politician active in recruiting troops in Missouri for the Union cause. Blair was one of the sons of the man who a month earlier had offered to Robert E. Lee supreme field command of the federal forces. The younger Francis failed to see in Grant what the elder saw in Lee. Francis Blair, Jr. never did recognize Grant's talents; seven years later, in 1868, he campaigned for vice president on the Democratic ticket that opposed the general's bid for the presidency. In Covington, Kentucky, Grant tracked down William Whistler of his old regiment, the Fourth Infantry, but the colonel, at age eighty, was either too infirm or too removed from service, or both, to be of help.[70]

By the end of May, Grant was growing despondent. He had returned to Galena for a break from mustering, and for a week he sat idle. On May 30, he described to his father his agonizing sense of unfulfillment: "I have felt all the time as if a duty was being neglected that was paramount to any other duty I ever owed." He tried to rationalize that "I have evry reason to be well satisfied with myself for the services already rendered," but in truth Grant was horribly frustrated. He knew that he was capable of assuming a responsible command, and he was beginning to worry that the wave of initial flurry had left him far behind.[71]

On June 10 in Cincinnati, Grant tried to approach McClellan, by then a bright star on the rise in the army. Grant and McClellan had known each other at West Point as first-classman and plebe. Their paths had crossed again during the Mexican War, and most recently they had seen one another on the Pacific coast. McClellan remembered Grant's drinking, as well as the fact that he had quit the army. The meeting in Cincinnati, perhaps not surprisingly, never took place. McClellan later claimed that he was out of town on the two days that Grant called, but at the time the caller was told otherwise.[72]

In the end, as was almost always true with Grant, his persistence paid off. In Mattoon, the ragged group that he had mustered a month earlier wanted him back. The officers of the Seventh Congressional District Regiment had elected as their colonel Simon S. Goode, a city clerk of Decatur with no military experience. An eccentric man who carried three revolvers and a bowie knife, Goode drilled his men excessively, and even told them that he never slept. Nonetheless, a number of them routinely managed to escape at night, disturbing the townspeople and neighboring farmers with their drunken revelry. Because Goode was unable to maintain any significant discipline, and because the new recruits were unlikely to enlist for three years when so demoralized, he had to be replaced. According to an account provided by one of the commissioned officers of the regiment, they conferred with the governor and elected Grant to replace Goode. On June 17, Grant could write proudly to Julia, "I have been appointed to a Colonelcy."[73]

Grant's command of the once unruly Seventh District Regiment was effective and gave an indication of the leadership skills that he would exhibit throughout the Civil War. The colonel was low-key but firm, serious, and governed by good common sense. Rather than try to imprison the men in camp, he granted them reasonable leaves. Rather than subject them to excessive training, he required the men's timely attendance at set drill periods. For those slow to respond to his rules, the discipline was swift and sure. To Grant's thinking, he could bring an unmanageable soldier to allegiance just as in his youth he had tamed unbroken horses. The first order that he issued exhibited a characteristic mix of realistic expectation, sincerity, and resolve. He "hope[d] to receive" the "hearty support" of the civilians who had become enlisted men and he "required" the "co-operation" of his officers. Soon the regiment proudly called Grant "the quiet man." Enlistments were renewed. One of the soldiers later wrote, "We knew we had the best commander and the best regiment in the State."[74]

J. F. C. Fuller recounts the story, probably apocryphal, of a tombstone in Kentucky that marked the graves of two brothers, one who had served as a Federal and the other as a Confederate. Their father chose the epitaph, "God knows which was right." In 1861 Lee and Grant each did what he thought was right, or, at the least, what he thought was expected of him. Both would have agreed that politicians had brought the country to the brink of war, both were grieved by the state of affairs, and both saw that only armed combat would decide the issue of secession. Lee predicted a long war, Grant a short one, but both knew that Americans would have to kill Americans before it was over. It would be less than a year before Grant would be in command of the Union forces at Shiloh, to that date the bloodiest battle ever to take place on American soil.[75]

Grant opened the preface to his *Memoirs* with a profound statement: "'Man proposes and God disposes.' There are but few important events in the affairs of men brought about by their own choice." Looking back, as he fought a disease that he knew would kill him, it was important for Grant to believe that a higher power had been in control of the major events of his life, a power that he then hoped would allow him the time to complete his last great work. Lee had argued in 1861 that he had no choice but to defend Virginia: there was "no other course without dishonor" and he was "quite contented that his [God's] designs be accomplished and not mine." In the twenty-first century it is easy to dismiss such comments as rationalizations, perhaps even attempts to retreat from personal responsibility, but when each general expressed these ideas he was being candid. When they carefully weighed the pros and cons in 1861, their final decisions were seemingly no decisions at all. Each had a duty to perform, each accepted it with resignation, and then each turned his remarkable energies toward the task that lay before him. Duty and honor demanded no less.[76]

Robert E. Lee invoked George Washington when he surmised the chagrin of the "Father of His Country" at the thought of the nation's disintegration. Washington would have chosen to preserve the Union above all other considerations, and to that end would almost certainly have fought for the North had he been put in Lee's position. Because Lee felt duty bound to take the side of those who had severed the nation, he had gone against the ideals of the man upon whom he had modeled his life, in part to try to restore the reputation of his actual father and formerly aristocratic family. Ulysses S. Grant saw in his own father a tough man who demanded hard work and dedication from himself and from those around him. While he would free himself from Jesse's influence, he had learned lessons in his youth that would serve him throughout the war. In the following chapter we will examine the young life of each future general, with an eye toward better understanding the men who would answer the call to duty in 1861.[77]

II.
Youth and Early Military Careers

fig. 41.
Charles Willson Peale, *"Light-Horse Harry" Lee (1756–1818)*, 1782, oil on canvas, 22½ × 18¾ in. (57.1 × 47.6 cm.), Independence National Historical Park Collection (National Park Service), Philadelphia

fig. 42.
Hattie Mann Marshall, *Lee Family of Virginia and Maryland*, 1886, lithograph, 33 × 26 in. (83.8 × 66.0 cm.), Virginia Historical Society

The recollection of their great actions kindled a generous flame in their breasts, not to be quelled till they also by virtue had acquired equal fame and glory.

"Light-Horse Harry" Lee on the ancient Romans[1]

I never met a man with so much simplicity, shyness, and decision .... [Grant] is a soldier to the core, a genuine commoner, commander of a democratic army from a democratic people.

British journalist, March 1864[2]

The Heritage of the Lee Family

For his entire life, Robert E. Lee struggled to accept his father's uncertain legacy. He could never lay the subject to rest. "Light-Horse Harry" Lee (fig. 41) had left his children an extraordinary record of accomplishment and failure. Harry's career was too resplendent with "great actions" for the achievements not to inspire a quest for "equal fame and glory," but his life was too much a matter of public record for the errors to be forgotten. Harry Lee had been a hero of the Revolution, a dashing young soldier who was a lieutenant and friend of George Washington. He then became governor of Virginia and a congressman who exchanged correspondence with the principal political figures of the new nation. But Harry ultimately lost his fortune, his home, and even his family to bankruptcy caused by irresponsible land speculation. He was eventually attacked and mutilated by a mob. By the end of his career, many wondered if Harry Lee warranted their admiration or, in larger measure, their scorn. In the society of Old Virginia, which was governed by a rigid code of personal honor, that question gravely troubled his children. When Harry's oldest son, Henry Lee IV, created yet another scandal, a third brother, Charles Carter Lee, lamented, "I have never felt so sensibly the utter demolition of the fortune of the race of Lees."[3]

Initially, Robert E. Lee did not know a great deal about "the race of Lees" (fig. 42) who preceded his father and grandfather. As a young man he had practically no information about the family's roots in England, but he began to explore this subject in 1838. When the first project for which he served as chief engineer was beginning to yield remarkable success and bring him acclaim, the thirty-one-year-old Lee wrote from St. Louis to his cousin Cassius, "I begin in my old age to feel a little curiosity relative to my forefathers." This interest remained with him throughout his life. In his final year, Robert republished his father's massive history, *Memoirs of the War in the Southern Department of the United States*. This undertaking involved considerable research and fact gathering. Lee's preface, which is mostly a biography of his father, runs sixty-eight pages. Although the general had more to say about the Vir-

fig. 43.
Charles Willson Peale, *Richard Henry Lee* (1733–1794), 1784, oil on canvas, 30 × 25 in. (76.2 × 63.5 cm.), National Portrait Gallery, Smithsonian Institution, gift of Duncan Lee and his son, Gavin Dunbar Lee

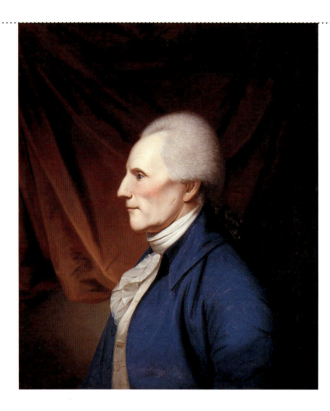

ginia Lees than the Lees of England, the opening sentence is a revealing statement of family pride.

"The Lee family in Virginia," he boasted, is "the younger branch of one of the oldest families in England. Launcelot Lee, the founder, was originally from Loudon, in France, and went to England with William the Conqueror …. Lionel Lee, the first Earl of Litchfield, raised a company of gentleman cavaliers, at the head of which he accompanied Richard Coeur de Lion in the third Crusade, in 1192." The invocation of William the Conqueror and Richard the Lionheart makes clear both the age and nobility of the family, and how its men have long made their reputations in martial pursuits.[4]

The accomplishments of the Lee family in colonial Virginia had been extraordinary. Richard Lee, the founder of the dynasty, arrived in Jamestown in 1639 or 1640. He held a series of high offices, including attorney general, burgess, member of the governor's Council, and secretary of state. Robert E. Lee was proud that during the reign of Oliver Cromwell, it was Richard who "went over from Virginia [to Breda in the Netherlands] to ascertain if [the exiled Charles II] would protect the colony." As secretary, it fell to Richard Lee to request that the king renew the appointment of the governor, William Berkeley. Richard married well, to Anne Constable, whose family enjoyed links to the crown, and he amassed considerable holdings in land, including an estate east of London at Stratford Langthorne.[5]

The next Lee, Richard II, was known as "the scholar" because of his extensive library that included fifty-seven theological texts. He was educated at Oxford University and like his father maintained close ties to the crown. In 1676, the revolutionary Nathaniel Bacon singled him out as one of the "wicked and pernicious" partners of Governor William Berkeley, whom he said had usurped the rights of the people. Lee was ultimately placed in chains for two months. A hundred years later, in the next revolution against the crown, a number of the descendants of Richard Lee II would play prominent roles.[6]

Two of his sons, Thomas and Henry, established lines at Stratford and Leesylvania. Thomas Lee was positioned by his father in such lucrative posts as collector of shipping duties on the Potomac and collection agent for the Fairfax family, the English owners of Virginia's Northern Neck Proprietary, an immense tract of land. The naval position was eventually passed along to Henry. The two worked together to acquire properties, wealth, and prominence. Thomas rose to become a burgess, a member of the governor's Council, and was acting-governor at his death.

In 1771, George Washington wrote, "I know of no country that can produce a family all distinguished as clever men, as our Lees." Four of Thomas Lee's sons at Stratford—Richard Henry, Francis Lightfoot, William, and Arthur—played prominent roles as patriots during the Revolutionary era in Williamsburg, Philadelphia, and at the courts of Europe. Later, none other than John Adams remembered "that band of brothers, intrepid and unchangeable, who, like the Greeks at Thermopylae, stood in the gap, in the defense of their country, from the first glimmering of the Revolution in the horizon, through all its rising light, to its perfect day." In the end, however, the Stratford Lees would offend many of their fellow patriots, as would "Light-Horse Harry" Lee, the most famous of the Leesylvania branch.[7]

Richard Henry Lee (fig. 43) led a family clan in the Virginia House of Burgesses that during the revolutionary period numbered seven. A fierce competitor, he often alienated his fellow legislators, at times by reversing his position on crucial matters. In 1759, he delivered one of the strongest antislavery statements of the era—he contended that blacks are "equally entitled to liberty and freedom by the great law of nature." Fifteen years later and in need of money, he took up slave trading himself. He had been a leader in the House in opposition to England's repressive policies toward her colonies, only to seek in 1764 the position of collector of the taxes that had been generated by the new Stamp Act. One of Richard Henry Lee's signature characteristics was that he enjoyed championing the opposition. He was good enough in that role to both annoy many of his colleagues and to be assured of a seat in the Continental Congress.[8]

Assisting Richard Henry Lee in Philadelphia was his brother Francis Lightfoot Lee, who was of a different temperament. Francis was rational and discreet; he served as a stabilizing force for his brother. The Lee burgesses in Williamsburg were also active. Their timing concerning Virginia's act authorizing separation enabled Richard Henry Lee to issue the momentous call for American independence. Despite that moment in the spotlight, he was subsequently denied a position on the committee that developed his motion into a declaration. The nod was given instead to Thomas Jefferson. The future president would become the nemesis of both "Light-Horse Harry" Lee and his oldest son, Henry Lee IV.[9]

Arthur and William Lee carried the family name abroad, bringing both fame and discredit to the dynasty. Arthur was the most controversial of all the Lees. He was a hostile and indiscreet man, who, like Richard Henry Lee, would take the opposite side of an issue just for the sake of battling a foe. John Adams complained of the "unhappy disposition" of this eccentric bachelor. His poor judgment "of men and things," said Adams, caused Arthur to go through life "quarreling with one person or another." Benjamin Franklin told Arthur that he had a "sick mind, which is forever tormenting itself with its jealousies, suspicions, that others mean you ill, wrong you, or fail in respect for you." Thomas Jefferson and James Madison would add their own complaints to the list.[10]

Resident in London and able to predict the policy of the Crown, Arthur and William Lee initially inspired their compatriots back home, in part by issuing pamphlets about British oppression of the colonies. Appointed, respectively, a commissioner to the French government and a commercial agent of Congress in Nantes, they soon quarreled with other American agents abroad, particularly Benjamin Franklin and Silas Deane, and just as quickly annoyed the French. Failure followed them on additional assignments to Austria, Prussia, and Spain. In the end, the international problems that Arthur and William left in their wake would actually undermine their brothers' effectiveness in Philadelphia.[11]

Following their early florescence, the four brothers from Stratford quickly left the stage. Arthur and William were summarily removed from their diplomatic assignments, while Richard Henry and Francis Lightfoot beat a retreat from Philadelphia to Virginia. All four had become too prominent, too powerful, and too arrogant. To some, it seemed that they had tried to take over the Revolution. Robert Treat Paine of Massachusetts complained:

> Gracious Heavens! Is it possible that in the infancy of our rising Republic, two brothers of one family should represent ... these United States at four of the principal Courts of Europe; and that two others of the same family should exercise the greatest acts of sovereignty in our great Council.[12]

While the Stratford Lees had attracted more than their share of the political spotlight, one member of the Spotsylvania Lees won public attention in a different arena. Henry Lee III (see fig. 41 above), the father of Robert E. Lee, became renowned for his gallantry on the field of battle. As a cavalry leader during the Revolutionary War, he conceived bold plans and executed them with such quickness that more often than not he was successful.

The life of Henry Lee is a story of achievement and failure in the extreme. He was a genuine combat hero, whose exploits earned him the epithet "Light-Horse Harry." After the war, however, as he searched to find a place for himself in a new nation that seemed to offer unlimited opportunities, Harry found that his penchant for risk taking failed him miserably in the wild business schemes that attracted his attention. On the political front, victory was again followed by defeat. His career as governor and congressman led to a dead end when his enemies were elected to power. Harry Lee would spend the last decades of his life disgruntled.[13]

Part of the legacy of "Light-Horse Harry" Lee is spelled out in the opening pages of his *Memoirs of the War in the Southern Department of the United States* (1812). Harry argued that the "honorable exertions" of the war "should be faithfully transmitted to posterity" because those "sentiments lead to the cultivation of virtue." He then included an ancient Latin passage that explains how the Romans encouraged virtue and achievement by remembering the exploits of previous generations:

> Often have I heard, that Quintus Maximus, Publius Scipio,

and other renowned men of our commonwealth, used to say, that whenever they beheld the images of their ancestors, they felt their minds vehemently excited to virtue. It could not be the wax or the marble that possessed this power; but the recollection of their great actions kindled a generous flame in their breasts, not to be quelled till they also by virtue had acquired equal fame and glory.

Robert E. Lee admired the images of Harry Lee and George Washington and often recollected "their great actions." They had left a challenge to acquire "equal fame and glory" that fueled an ambition that already was inherent in Harry's youngest son.[14]

The Revolution that provided Harry Lee with a path to "great actions" had interrupted his schooling. He was at the College of New Jersey at Princeton; on his graduation his father intended to send him to London to study law. Instead, although he was only nineteen years old in 1776, he was made a cavalry captain in a unit commanded by his cousin Theodorick Bland. Lee soon attracted the attention of the family's friend, George Washington, and he quickly became a favorite of the general, who invited him to serve as an aide. Lee preferred independence of command, however, and the opportunity he thought it would offer for fame. At the suggestion of Washington, who argued that "Lee's genius particularly adapts him to a command of this nature," and followed by the urging in Congress of cousins Richard Henry and Francis Lightfoot Lee, Harry was awarded an independent corps (fig. 44). The unit was made up of about 300 men, half cavalry and half infantry. It earned the name "Lee's Legion" and its commander soon became famous as "Light-Horse Harry."[15]

Lee proved to be a strong leader, able to instill in his troops both the pride and strict discipline that was sadly absent in many American units. Consequently, many of his soldiers volunteered for the duration of the war, which also was contrary to the norm. They were well clothed and well fed, partly because Harry contributed some of his own money to provide for them. Even their horses, which tended to be among the best mounts serving either side, were given good care. The men took pride in the reputation of their unit; there were few deserters, particularly after a grisly incident of reprisal. Lee ordered the decapitation of the body of a deserter whom he had executed. Even Washington, who was known to be unwilling to tolerate cowardice, was appalled, but Lee kept his command.[16]

"Light-Horse Harry" Lee specialized in the surprise raid. His seemingly daring maneuvers, which were actually carefully planned, brought fame to both Lee and the Legion. Robert wrote that his father's "success in impeding [British] communications, cutting off their light parties, and intercepting their supplies, drew on him the particular attention of the enemy." He added that Harry "was always

fig. 44.
Commission appointing Henry Lee ["Light-Horse Harry" Lee] a Major of a corps of partizan light dragoons ["Lee's Legion"] in the U.S. Continental Army, January 10, 1779, manuscript, 7¼ × 12 in. (18.4 × 30.5 cm.), signed by John Jay and P[eter] Scull, Virginia Historical Society

placed near the enemy," providing a service that required "coolness, address, and enterprise." Washington came to rely on Lee for intelligence as to the location, size, and movement of the enemy.[17]

Robert E. Lee took pride in publishing in the new edition of the *Memoirs of the War* a series of letters that celebrate his father's stature. He cited three from Lafayette and noted the famous comment of General Charles Lee (born an Englishman and no relation) that the major "seems to have come out of his mother's womb a soldier." Charles Lee thought that Harry should be made a lieutenant colonel and given command of the whole American cavalry. George Mason wanted his own son to serve "under the direction of a gentleman who has rendered such important services to our country, and in whose friendship I could so thoroughly confide."[18]

Historians today find the military career of "Light-Horse Harry" Lee difficult to assess. None deny that it was filled with adventure and that he demonstrated remarkable courage. Harry achieved fame early in the war for his daring attack on the enemy at Paulus Hook, a garrison that guarded the harbor of New York City, but his account was quickly challenged by subordinates who were every bit as ambitious as he was. Several even charged him with errors of command at Paulus Hook, although the charges were ultimately dismissed.[19]

Robert praised his father for his capture of enemy forts in the South, recounting how in 1781 he seized five British posts from the Santee to Augusta and took 1,100 prisoners. American victories in the Carolinas, Harry wrote, "would … demonstrate, even to a British cabinet, the folly of persevering in the hopeless, destructive conflict." Washington was joined in his admiration of Lee by the commanding general in the Southern Department, Nathaniel Greene. In short, his contributions throughout the war were significant. Why, then, did Harry Lee become so unhappy that he soon retired to private life in Virginia? Part of the reason was fatigue, both physical and emotional, the result of nearly seven years of combat. Also, following the victory at Yorktown, the war entered a phase of relative inactivity that was less glamorous to Lee. And finally, there was the issue of Harry's arrogance.[20]

"Light-Horse Harry" Lee's vanity inevitably hindered his interpersonal relationships in a burgeoning democratic society. The problem worsened when fellow officers perceived that Lee was favored by both Washington and Greene. Charitably, Greene placed the blame more on the family than on the man: "if your reputation has felt any violence, it has been owing to your being a Lee," he wrote. Greene concluded, "The people of Virginia are very jealous of your merit and growing consequence …. Your family and name must be very obnoxious that the people should refuse you the glory due to your merit and exertions." Harry Lee was too young and inexperienced to respond appropriately to this pressure. In 1782, at age twenty-six, he resigned his commission.[21]

Greene continued to cover for Lee. He wrote to the president of Congress, "I am more indebted to this officer than any other for the advantages gained over the enemy in the operations of the last campaign." He told Lee, "few officers, either in America or Europe, are held in so high a point of estimation as you are …. Everybody knows I have the highest opinion of you as an officer, and you know I love you as a friend …." Robert E. Lee printed both letters. He acknowledged that his father's behavior had become a bit irrational, but he would attribute Harry's resignation to a physical decline: "The broken health produced by his long and arduous services depressed his spirits, and caused the melancholy so apparent in his farewell letter."[22]

Lee returned to Virginia to marry a second cousin, Matilda Lee. Her uncle Richard Henry Lee escorted her down the aisle. At nineteen, she had inherited Stratford Hall. Through this marriage Harry became master of the greatest of the Lee plantations. Almost immediately, he charged into the business of land speculation. In his own words, he "calculated greatly on the advancing prosperity of the country." He imagined rapid continental expansion, internal improvements, and the growth of new cities, and he invested his wife's money accordingly. So great were his expectations that James Madison concluded rightly, "the fervor with which he pursues his objects sometimes affects the estimate he forms of them." Within two years, Lee was financially distressed. By 1789, the 6,595-acre Stratford estate that Matilda had inherited in 1775 had been reduced to 4,000 acres. In little more than two decades Henry was bankrupt.[23]

Lee had expected the national government to create a climate that would allow his investment schemes to flourish. In the 1780s he bought land not only in Virginia, but also in neighboring states and even in the faraway Mississippi country. He acquired five hundred acres at the Great Falls of the Potomac, where he envisioned a new city, not surprisingly named Matildaville. Like George Washington, Lee hoped that commerce from the Mississippi region would be funneled along the Potomac River. Allegiance of the westerners would be assured, and towns like Matildaville would flourish. Matilda, however, soon lost confidence in her husband's business schemes and changed her will to exclude him from the ownership of Stratford. His father did the same; he appointed a second son to be executor of his estate.[24]

In 1785 Lee was elected to the Virginia House of Delegates and was promptly named to the Continental Congress. In 1788 he was a delegate to the Virginia convention that debated ratification of the federal Constitution. Philosophically, Lee was at this point a nationalist. But by 1789 Harry had begun to blame the federal government for not providing what he considered the proper climate for American prosperity. The states, he said, were being suffocated by the policies of George Washington, and largely to blame was Alexander Hamilton, secretary of the treasury. "Light-Horse Harry" opposed Hamilton's plan for the federal government to fund the national debt. Ironically, Harry Lee's anti-Federalism would win him the governorship of Virginia in 1791. He served three terms of one year each. Because he worked to protect the state's frontier from Indian incursions, the westernmost county of Virginia was named Lee County.[25]

Matilda Lee had died in 1790. That loss, Harry said, "removed me from the happy enjoyment of life." He wrote to George Washington that the army would provide "scenes more congenial to my genius & to my habits." He hoped that the president would award him command of the new United States Army, which was to be deployed in the Northwest. When passed over for that job, Harry even considered a position with the army of Revolutionary France, a move Washington cautioned him against. In 1793, Harry announced to Alexander Hamilton, "I mean now to become a farmer & get a wife as soon as possible." A month later he married Ann Hill Carter of Shirley. That plantation was one of the wealthiest in the state.[26]

Ann was one of twenty children; she was twenty years old at her marriage. Ann enjoyed music and the outdoors, and she also proved to be a woman of remarkable character. Harry was thirty-seven in 1793, a war hero, the governor, and, by many accounts, irresistible. George Washington sent his blessing: "As we are told that you have exchanged the rugged and dangerous field of Mars for the soft and pleasurable bed of Venus, I do in this … wish you all imaginable success and happiness." Despite the hopes of the president, the happiness lasted for only a fortnight, at least according to a cousin of the bride. However, despite the poverty to which her husband would reduce her, Ann Lee would repeatedly deny that she was unhappy in her marriage.[27]

A year after the wedding, Harry Lee found a military command that earned him the rank of general. As governor of Virginia and titular head of the state's militia, he led that force into Pennsylvania to quiet a group of disgruntled farmers who had refused to pay their taxes on the whiskey that they sold. The "Whiskey Rebellion" was less an actual danger to the peace of the nation than a threat to the concept of federal authority. George Washington was grateful to Lee for his support in the crisis. Republicans in the Virginia legislature, however, accused Lee of abandoning his office and they replaced him with one of their own.[28]

In 1794, some Virginians had thought that Lee might succeed Washington as the state's leader. When that role was taken by Thomas Jefferson, the fortunes of "Light-Horse Harry" Lee began to decline on all fronts. His status as merely a guest and farmer on property held in trust for his son sparked old feelings of unrest. His compulsion for speculation returned; the right investment might carry him beyond the captivity at Stratford that his first wife's restrictive will had imposed on him. Unfortunately, the late 1790s was a bleak period for land dealings in the new nation. At this point Lee risked the comfort of his wife and children and his own reputation in a desperate effort to rebuild his fortune. He routinely thought he was in striking distance of financial success, investing in everything from coal mines and canals to ore fields and swamplands. Three ventures stand out as particularly significant: (1) Ever optimistic about the future importance of trade on the Potomac River, Lee participated in the purchase of some 200,000 acres of the vast Fairfax estates in the Northern Neck of Virginia; (2) he loaned the former superintendent of finance, Robert Morris, $40,000 to purchase "cheap back lands"; (3) he purchased George Washington's interest in the Dismal Swamp Company for $20,000.

The Potomac River never became the water channel for commerce that many in Virginia had hoped. Robert Morris wrote to Lee in 1801 that he was insolvent, unable to repay his debts. And although a canal was built through it, the lands of the Dismal Swamp were never reclaimed as Washington once envisioned that they would be. On at least one occasion, Lee sent Washington a bad check. The president wrote back that financial irresponsibility "is a mode of dealing to which I am not accustomed." Lee confessed, "No event of my life has given me more anguish."²⁹

In some of the land schemes the parcels had been inadequately surveyed or the same acreage was sold to more than one buyer. Harry's eldest son, Henry Lee IV, who defended his father's career with a passion, finally ran out of excuses for this lack of prudence and restraint. He acknowledged the folly of pursuing "bargains which could hardly benefit one party without injury to the other, and which were often mutually detrimental." In 1798, Harry Lee stated, "I have no money." He soon found himself in an "unprepared condition" to meet his creditors. He was forced to dispose of "a great deal of property" at half its value. The sale reduced the Westmoreland County taxable land that he controlled from 2,049 to 236 acres. He dragged his brother, Richard Bland Lee, into the financial abyss; it cost the brother his plantation. Richard's wife wrote in understatement that Harry "has produced to us anxiety and unhappiness." Charles Carter, the father of Ann Carter Lee, revised his will to protect her relatively small inheritance. This would prove to be her principal means of raising Robert E. Lee and his siblings.³⁰

Fighter that he was, "Light-Horse Harry" Lee denied defeat. In 1799 he made a brief political comeback, winning election to Congress because he was endorsed by George Washington. Harry had returned to the Federalist philosophy that he had embraced during the Revolution, and once again championed a strong central government as the means to preserve a fragile union and allow the pursuit of wealth and happiness. American prosperity "can only grow out of national identity," he wrote in 1799. Following the tumult of the French Revolution, Harry additionally valued the federal government as the preserver of internal peace. In a pamphlet entitled *Plain Truth: Addressed to the People of Virginia*, Lee wrote, "People … must determine to establish a permanent capable government or submit to the horrors of anarchy and licentiousness." He even argued for the permanence of the Union, suggesting that "no state can withdraw itself from the union. In point of policy, no state ought to be permitted to do so. The safety of those which remain would be endangered by the measure, and consequently their whole force would be exerted for its prevention." At this stage of his life he would have denied state sovereignty and the right of secession, two factors that would figure greatly in Robert E. Lee's future.³¹

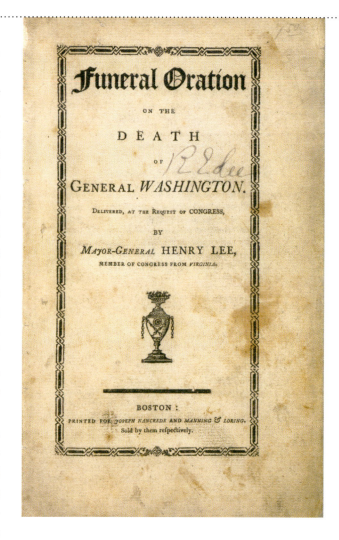

fig. 45.
Henry Lee ("Light-Horse Harry" Lee), *Funeral Oration on the Death of General Washington* (Boston, 1800), Virginia Historical Society.

At George Washington's death in 1799, the general's disciple from Virginia was chosen to present a eulogy on behalf of Congress. Harry exceeded all expectations by delivering the most stirring and best remembered of the many hundreds of addresses made nationwide. There is simplicity and truth in his evaluation of the general and president as "first in war, first in peace, and first in the hearts of his countrymen." Lee added sentiments about virtue as it was understood in Old Virginia: Washington "was second to none in the humble and endearing scenes of private life," and "the purity of his private character gave effulgence to his public virtues." Character was at the heart of the greatness of George Washington. The dignity of the inner man was what made the outer man a paragon. The eulogy was rushed into press in several cities. An edition published in Boston (fig. 45) was owned by his son, who proudly wrote "R E Lee" across the cover.³²

fig. 46.
Stratford Hall, Westmoreland County, Virginia, begun c. 1738 (photograph courtesy of Stratford Hall Plantation)

"Light-Horse Harry" Lee and Thomas Jefferson disliked one another almost from the start. During the Revolution, when Jefferson as governor fled from the advancing British, Lee was the upstart officer who spoke his mind and fought bravely against the enemy. By the turn of the century, each thought the other was a danger to the nation. Jefferson's election to the presidency in 1800 brought political ruin to Lee, at a time when he already was financially broken and on the verge of bankruptcy.[33]

The Boyhood of Robert E. Lee

Robert Edward Lee was born on January 19, 1807, one of the five children of "Light-Horse Harry" and Ann Carter Lee (fig. 47). He was named for his mother's two favorite brothers. Charles Carter, the oldest child, had been born in 1798. Sidney Smith followed in 1802. There were two sisters, Anne Kinloch and Mildred, born respectively in 1800 and in 1811. The first four children spent at least part of their childhood at Stratford Hall (fig. 46). In her will, Matilda Lee left the house and the thousands of acres of the estate to their son Henry Lee IV. Her financially inept husband was allowed occupancy until Henry reached maturity, which would be almost a decade into the nineteenth century.[34]

Charles Carter Lee was named for his mother's father. He was remembered for his wit and good humor. He studied at Harvard and practiced law in New York City before retiring to a farm west of Richmond in Powhatan County. Smith Lee, as he was known to all, was less outgoing than his older brother. He went to sea at age fifteen and in 1853 would travel with Matthew Perry to Japan. As a young man, he was strikingly handsome (fig. 48). Although few men compared favorably to Robert in terms of appearance, the diarist Mary Chestnut later wrote famously, "I like Smith Lee better, and I like his looks, too. I know Smith Lee well. Can anybody say they know his brother? I doubt it. He looks so cold and quiet and grand." During the Civil War, Smith served in the Confederate Navy. His career has an interesting parallel to that of Robert that suggests the high expectations for success that were instilled in both boys. Robert became the superintendent at West Point; Smith became the superintendent at the Naval Academy in Annapolis. The oldest sister, Anne Kinloch, lost an arm to amputation. She was married late—at age twenty-eight—to the minister William Marshall of Baltimore. He later became a lawyer and jurist. She died in

fig. 47.
Unknown artist, *Anne Hill Carter Lee*, c. 1795, oil on canvas, 28½ × 23½ in. (72.4 × 59.7 cm.), Washington and Lee University

fig. 48.
Attributed to William Edward West, *Sidney Smith Lee* (1802–1869), c. 1838?, oil on canvas, 30 × 25 in. (76.2 × 63.5 cm.), Stratford Hall Plantation

1864. Mildred Lee, the youngest child, married a wealthy Boston attorney, Edward Childe, and they lived part of their married life in Paris. She died prematurely, at age forty-five, in 1856.[35]

"Light-Horse Harry" Lee understood the two crucial factors that would shape the character of his youngest son. One was Robert's God-given instinct to behave. The other was the influence of Robert's mother. In 1817, from the West Indies, Harry wrote to his wife, "Robert is as good as ever I trust; it is his nature…." He told his son Carter, "Robert was always good, and will be confirmed in his happy turn of mind by his ever watchful and affectionate mother." Robert's "nature" would evolve into a dedication to genteel and virtuous behavior, traits for which he was known throughout his life.[36]

Douglas Southall Freeman begins his account of the general's life with a dramatic story of the family's departure from Stratford Hall in 1810. "Light-Horse Harry" Lee was heavily in debt; creditors sent by the sheriff were often at the door, which had been chained shut to keep them out. The house was nearly empty because its furniture had been impounded. The inheritance of his wife, Ann Carter Lee, was out of his reach. Henry Lee IV had come into possession of Stratford Hall in 1808. Therefore, "the only thing to do was to leave and go to Alexandria, where they could live in a simple home and send Charles Carter to the free school and find a doctor for the baby [Mildred] that was to come in February." Robert, who was three at the time, wrote at the end of his life that his father removed his family to Alexandria for the purpose of educating his children.[37]

With civil judgments ever mounting, "Light-Horse Harry" sought shelter where creditors could not reach him. He requested a government appointment to Brazil or to the West Indies, but none was to be had. In 1809, Harry was arrested for a debt of fifty-four dollars and jailed at the county seat of Westmoreland where he had once served as a justice and where George Washington had come to cast his vote in support of Harry's candidacy for Congress. Later in 1809, Lee was moved to the jail in Spotsylvania County to serve time for debts owed there. He could have taken an oath of insolvency to avoid jail, but in doing so he would have lost control of what assets remained. Such a loss would also have undermined the social standing of the family, which Lee saw as one of the few worthwhile effects left to him.

Instead, in order to obtain his release from jail, Harry Lee sold land to pay the most pressing of his debts, scheduled a plan of payments due to other creditors, and, to free his eldest son from his entanglements, surrendered his life interest in Stratford. He was set free in the spring of 1810. There was good reason for the family to relocate at this time. During her husband's absence, Ann Carter Lee had been forced to assume the management of many of the family's affairs. It was she, no doubt, with or without Harry's consultation, who made the decision to move to Alexandria. There she would find support from Lee family relatives. Robert E. Lee would later resent the loss of Stratford. During the Civil War he reminisced, "it has always been a great desire of my life to be able to purchase it."[38]

Harry Lee had made good use of his time in jail. After having solicited documents and accounts from veterans, many of whom addressed long letters to him, he wrote his 600-page account of the Revolutionary War. Harry hoped that the book would sell well enough to return him to solvency, but *Memoirs of the War in the Southern Department of the United States* was not a success, even though it was the best history of the Revolution in the South that had been written to that date.[39]

"Light-Horse Harry" Lee suffered humiliations, but through his monetary disasters he managed to preserve the social standing of his family. In 1812, however, Harry Lee endured a physical beating that was every bit as humiliating as his financial upheaval. The general was mutilated and almost murdered by a mob in Baltimore. He was stabbed in the face, nearly blinded, and his nose was practically cut off. Historian Bertram Wyatt-Brown writes that in this era, the disfigurement of a man's nose was the height of disgrace, a sort of figurative castration. From this point on Harry had to endure persistent pain. He lost clear vision and his face was scarred to the point where he often wore white bandages that actually called additional attention to his plight.

This appalling incident stemmed from Harry's bitter feud with Thomas Jefferson and the Republican party, which controlled the government after 1800. Jefferson's imposition of economic sanctions against Britain in the form of an embargo inspired Lee to publish in 1808 a thirty-eight-page attack pamphlet, *A Cursory Sketch of the Motives and Proceedings of the Party Which Sways the Affairs of the Union*. Four years later, Harry blamed the War of 1812 not on the need to protect rights or commerce or on the interest of an agricultural nation to expand territorially, but on the Republican administration of James Madison. Those sentiments were shared by Alexander Hanson, the editor of a pro-British newspaper in Baltimore. With the impetuosity that he had displayed during the Revolution, Lee linked up with a group of Maryland Federalists. This assemblage was ultimately besieged in Hanson's newspaper building. This time Lee was the one under attack.[40]

The incident in Baltimore brought an end to Lee's stature as an American patriot. Gone were the opportunities for a return to either the military or politics. Had that encounter not occurred, an officer with the experience of "Light-Horse Harry" Lee would probably have been awarded a command during the second war with Britain. Instead, in 1813, to elude his persistent creditors and despite the objections of his family, Harry Lee exiled himself to the West Indies. Robert E. Lee was six years old. Harry would spend the remaining five years of his life wandering from island to island. To his wife and son Carter he wrote twelve letters that survive. These give evidence of the remarkable intellect that had composed the hundreds of pages of *Memoirs of the War*. Harry's sons might have modeled their lives on his counsel had he mailed the letters in a timely manner. However, perhaps typically, they were kept in a trunk and only delivered to Carter in 1831.

Harry Lee's advice was derived in part from his lifelong reading. Included were ideas from great authors of the near and distant past, such as Locke, Bacon, Swift, Hume, Pope, Virgil, Homer, Lucretius, and the second-century Roman emperor Marcus Aurelius, whose *Meditations* would prove to be a favorite guide for Robert E. Lee. Harry cited passages from the *Meditations* about self-control that he perhaps should have followed: "Ease fancy; curb impulse; quench desire; let sovereign reason have the mastery." Throughout his life Robert tried to deny that his father was himself unable to "curb impulse." In 1870, Mary Custis Lee wrote to her brother-in-law Carter that Robert was "much concerned" that a new biography of Harry accused him of "want of self control & great instability of character." This, she said, was "not all consistent" with what her husband thought about his father.[41]

In the letters to Carter, Harry proposed several bits of wisdom. One can only wonder if he was trying to save his son from some of his own mistakes.

> Love virtue and abhor lying and deception.
>
> Fame in arms or art, however conspicuous, is naught, unless bottomed on virtue.
>
> Dwell on the virtues and labors of the world's great men which history presents to view. Admire and imitate them.

fig. 49.
Lee House, Alexandria (607 Oronoco Street) (photograph courtesy of Virginia Historical Society)

> Avoid debt, the sink of mental power and the subversion of independence, which draws into debasement even virtue. A man ought not only to be virtuous in reality, but he must also always appear so, said George Washington.
>
> Self command … is the pivot upon which the character, fame and independence of us mortals hang.
>
> The rank of men … stands thus: heroes, legislators, orators, and poets. The most useful and … the most honorable is the legislator …. Generally mankind admire most the hero, the most useless, except when the safety of nation demands his saving arm ….[42]

After the Civil War, Robert E. Lee entered in a journal some of his own philosophical thoughts. These reveal a sound appreciation of honor and an understanding not just of the definition of a gentleman, but also of what it meant to be a gentleman:

> The manner in which an individual enjoys certain advantages over others is a test of a true gentleman …. A true man of honor feels humbled himself when he cannot help humbling others …. He can not only forgive, he can forget.

Robert also understood a basic concept of Christianity: "The great duty of life [is] the promotion of the happiness & welfare of our fellow men." He learned these ideas early in life from his mother.[43]

Long before the trunk containing Harry Lee's letters was shipped, Robert E. Lee had received thorough instruction about virtue and honor from Ann Carter Lee, a devoutly religious woman. She was determined that the sins of the father would not be continued by the sons. Although it was the disgrace caused by Harry's misfortunes that probably did more to shape Robert's character than did any other cause, Ann's beliefs also made a powerful impression on her children. In 1816, she wrote to Carter at Harvard, "Oh! pray fervently for faith in Jesus Christ. He is the only rock of your salvation, and the only security for your resurrection from the grave!" Harry Lee wrote to Carter, "Your dearest mother is singularly pious from love to Almighty God and love of virtue, which are synonymous; not from fear of hell—a base, low influence."[44]

Ann Carter Lee readily accepted what she perceived to be God's will. Emory Thomas has posited that she probably responded to the call of the Second Great Awakening, which stirred so many in the new nation. In a society in which a woman had little if any influence over the affairs of her husband, there was no point in her worrying excessively over the problems caused by Harry Lee's reckless and irresponsible actions. She could only groom their children to become what he was not. Emily V. Mason, a close friend of Ann Carter Lee, later wrote that self-denial, self-control, and the strictest economy in all financial matters were part of the code that she taught them from infancy. Robert would confirm that statement when he said that he "owed everything" to his mother. Before he learned to read, Robert E. Lee had recited his catechism.[45]

George Washington, a miniature of whom hangs around the neck of Ann Carter Lee in her portrait (fig. 47), had wished her "success and happiness" on the occasion of her wedding. She would find neither, but she did persevere. The move to Alexandria, first to a small house on Cameron Street and then to Oronoco Street (fig. 49), more at the center of town, brought Ann close to Lee relatives who offered her sanctuary. The Oronoco address was the townhouse of William Henry Fitzhugh, a distant relative of both Ann Carter and Harry, through both the Carter and Lee families. He took an interest in his destitute "cousins" from Stratford; Robert would later honor Fitzhugh by naming his second son for him.

LEE AND GRANT

The mother and her five children had little money on which to live, only the small trust fund that Ann's father had left for her in anticipation of Harry's continued destitution. Extended visits to family helped her pocketbook as well as her spirit. Ann Carter Lee took refuge with her brothers and sisters at Shirley, with young Henry Lee at Stratford, and nearer to Alexandria, with William Henry Fitzhugh at Ravensworth, and with Fitzhugh's sister Mary Custis at Arlington. It was at Arlington that Robert discovered Mary Anna Randolph Custis, the distant cousin whom he would marry.[46]

The Carter family maintained a school for boys in the Piedmont at Eastern View, the plantation in Fauquier County of Ann's sister Elizabeth Carter Randolph. It was there that Ann first sent her sons. Next they enrolled at Alexandria Academy. Although all three showed promise, only two of the boys continued. Smith was less of a student; he remained at home until he received a midshipman's commission in the Navy. Robert demonstrated particular ability in mathematics, and he did well enough in his study of Greek and Latin literature to move easily into college. He fondly remembered William B. Leary, one of his early teachers. Lee wrote to him in 1866, "I beg to express the gratitude I have felt all my life for the affectionate fidelity which characterized your teaching and conduct toward me."[47]

By 1820, when Carter Lee was at school in Boston and Smith Lee was at sea, Robert, at age thirteen, had become the man of the house. He carried the keys, and with them the responsibilities of caring for the needs of the household. Emory Thomas believes that Ann Carter Lee, whose health had begun to fail even before Robert's birth, suffered from tuberculosis. As his mother progressed into chronic invalidism, the same plight that would await his wife years later, Robert's duties grew. His mother is reported to have said, "How can I live without Robert?"[48]

With virtually no inheritance to anticipate in either lands or funds, however, Lee soon faced a decision about his professional career. The options in the 1820s in America were limited to little beyond teaching, law, medicine, the church, and the military. The choice was apparently easy for Robert. Like his father, he may simply "have come out of his mother's womb a soldier." Also, the military probably appealed to him from the time he was old enough to understand the stories he was told of "Light-Horse Harry's" exploits. In 1857, when he considered retirement from the army, Lee cited "[military] preferences which have clung to me from boyhood."[49]

Robert's inclination was no doubt reinforced by the persistent presence in the 1820s of "Light-Horse Harry" Lee in American memory. In 1824, the year that Robert sought an appointment to West Point, Lafayette toured the country and paid a visit to Harry's widow. The town of Alexandria hosted a parade in the Frenchman's honor and Harry's youngest son participated in it. Also in 1824, Robert's half-brother Henry defended the career of their father in a bitter tome of five hundred pages, written in response to an attack upon Harry's *Memoirs of the War in the Southern Department*. William Johnson, a Supreme Court justice, had published in 1822 *Sketches of the Life and Correspondence of Nathanael Greene*, wherein he challenged Harry's assertions as "romances of his historical novel." In *The Campaign of 1781 in the Carolinas; with Remarks Historical and Critical on Johnson's Life of Greene*, Henry Lee IV fired back. Robert must have read this new book with much interest; the family's reputation was at stake. Little was left of the honor of the Leesylvania branch beyond the good war record of "Light-Horse Harry."[50]

One reason that Henry Lee IV labored so hard to produce such a massive book was that three years earlier, in 1821, he too had shamed the family with his own moral misconduct, which included the fathering of an ill-fated illegitimate child, which earned him the epithet "Black-Horse Harry" Lee. Publishing about his father seemed to him an act of atonement. At only fourteen years of age, Robert was confronted with another burden of family disgrace that he would have to bear the rest of his life. Faraway West Point was a sanctuary to which he might escape, at least temporarily. It was also a place from where he could build a career that might restore the family's good name. He would never forget the shame brought about by his father and half-brother, however; he would name none of his three sons Henry.[51]

Cousins at Arlington House

If Robert E. Lee had any second thoughts about pursuing a military career, they were no doubt set aside during his visits to Arlington House (fig. 50). The seat of his mother's distant cousins Washington (fig. 51) and Molly Custis, this plantation was maintained as almost a shrine to the memory of George Washington. So many of Washington's possessions were inherited by Custis that Arlington more resembled a museum than a residence. Little won-

fig. 50.
George Hadfield, architect, *Arlington House*, 1803–18, center interior completed in the 1850s (photograph courtesy of the National Park Service)

fig.51.
Mathew Brady, *George Washington Parke Custis*, c. 1844–49 (photograph courtesy of Library of Congress)

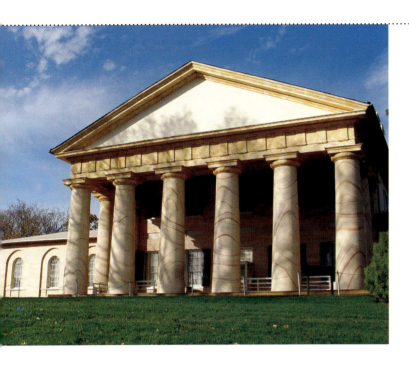

Robert E. Lee wrote in 1854 that at Arlington his "affection & attachments are more strongly placed than at any other place in the World." Part of the affection was directed to the owners, Washington and Molly Custis. During his boyhood Lee got to know them well, and he appreciated the interest they took in the plight of his mother. Molly Custis no doubt paid special attention to the widow to whom her brother William Henry Fitzhugh had given the use of his house in Alexandria. Over the years, Lee would grow particularly close to his mother-in-law because her selfless disposition matched that of his own mother and exemplified the values of duty and self-sacrifice to which he aspired; he would come to call her "Mother." Robert seems to have had mixed emotions for his father-in-law, as did many of Washy's contemporaries.

der that the daughter at Arlington would marry a military man. Ironically, his dedication to the army would ultimately cause Lee to resist taking up permanent residence there. When Mary Custis Lee inherited the plantation decades later, Robert felt for a time obliged to continue his army career far removed from Virginia.

George Washington had bequeathed to "Washy" Custis, his adopted grandson, a prime tract of riverfront land "in the vicinity of Alexandria." From its steep hills, the property offered some of the best views of the new federal city then under construction on the opposite bank. Although Custis lacked sufficient cash to complete the construction of a mansion house in a timely manner, he had the good sense to engage the most competent of architects to design one for him. This was the Englishman George Hadfield, then serving as architect of the U.S. Capitol. Hadfield brought to the highlands above the Potomac River the new Greek Revival style. He told Custis that Arlington House was modeled on the Temple of Theseus at Athens. The giant Doric portico stretches sixty feet, the width of an entire Georgian mansion of Virginia's colonial era. Behind it on the ground floor are ceilings eighteen-feet tall. Arlington was a bold design, one of the best of its style in America. Robert E. Lee appreciated it as "a House that any one might see with half an eye." Custis considered calling his plantation Mount Washington, but in the end he settled on the name of the ancestral Custis family estate on Virginia's Eastern Shore.[52]

As a child, Washington Custis was an agreeable grandson, who from his infancy won George Washington's affection. However, his resistance to education proved exasperating for his guardian. Finding the right school for him proved almost impossible; motivating the student was even more difficult. By the fall of 1796 Custis was enrolled at the College of New Jersey at Princeton, where

George Washington showered him with letters full of fatherly advice. The admonitions went unheeded; Custis did not return to school the following year. The president wrote in explanation, "From his infancy, I have discovered an almost unconquerable disposition to indolence in every thing that did not tend to his amusement." Washington next enrolled his ward at St. John's College in Annapolis. The results were the same.[53]

Several months after Washy's withdrawal from school, the president obtained for him a commission in the military. It was thought that he would serve in the threatened war with France, but he would soon resign. In 1804, Custis married Mary Lee Fitzhugh and took up farming at Arlington. He never was very good at it. At least for a while, he did try the latest scientific techniques as his guardian had done at Mount Vernon. He even inaugurated at Arlington an annual agricultural fair, mainly to show off the sheep that he bred. But he ultimately turned over the farming operation to overseers, and, unlike George Washington at Mount Vernon, paid little attention to it. The indolence that George Washington had spotted years earlier showed itself in his aversion to the hard work required of a planter.[54]

Washington Custis was eccentric. He dressed sloppily. He had a lazy but friendly manner. He turned the grounds surrounding Arlington into a park. At a spring beside the river, he built a group of picnic buildings to which he invited the public to come via steamer. The historian and writer Benson Lossing, who visited Arlington in 1853, said that "parties of from fifty to two hundred are seen there" almost every day. Oddly, almost as if to disprove his failures as a student, Custis became an effective public speaker, especially on occasions commemorating George Washington. Although he did not like to read books, he liked to write them. He wrote history, drama, and poetry. His *Recollections and Private Memoirs of Washington* (published posthumously) was well received, and his plays *The Indian Prophecy* (1827) and *Pocahontas* (1830) were good enough to be performed in Philadelphia. Custis played the violin, and he painted five panoramic canvases that celebrate General Washington's victories at Monmouth, Trenton, Princeton, Germantown, and Yorktown. The paintings are crudely rendered—as an adult Robert E. Lee would be critical of his father-in-law's dabbling—but they offer proof of both Washy's willingness to try his hand at whatever seemed amusing at the moment, and of his dedication to the memory of Washington.[55]

Benson Lossing, as did most visitors, went to Arlington to venerate George Washington. Custis had taken it upon himself to be both the keeper of Washington relics and a spokesman for his step-grandfather. "While there is much to admire in the external beauties of Arlington," Lossing wrote, "the chief attractions are the pictures within, and the precious relics of the great Patriot which are preserved there." Custis called them "Washington treasures." They were many in number, and included the early Charles Willson Peale portrait of George Washington as a colonel of the Virginia militia that was painted in 1772 (fig. 52), as well as a Peale portrait of Lafayette. The new battle scenes that Custis added to the group served as visual aids when he recounted for his guests the general's campaigns during the Revolutionary War. The decorative objects included a silver coffee pot (c. 1783), a Worcester vase (1768–70), a Chinese porcelain punch bowl with Washington's monogram (c. 1795), porcelain in the Society of the Cincinnati pattern (c. 1785), and furniture, including the bed in which Washington died. Other objects were a camp chest, Martha Washington's iron treasure chest, swords, clothing, war tents, a set of Washington's pistols, and a number of regimental flags surrendered at Yorktown. Innumerable books and papers from Mount Vernon had also been moved to Arlington. There were even a number of the Mount Vernon slaves there. Guests at Arlington were inevitably overwhelmed with thoughts of the "Father of His Country" and were challenged to live up to the legacy of achievement left by the general. Lossing praised Custis as "a living link between the patriots of the old war and the present custodians of the prize which they won." "His mind," Lossing wrote, "is thoroughly stored with a minute knowledge of the important events of the struggle." Even in his seventies, his memory remained "ever faithful."[56]

Of course, Robert E. Lee knew all about George Washington long before he ever visited Arlington. His father had been Washington's lieutenant, and his mother wore a miniature of Washington around her neck. As a child on trips to Shirley plantation with his mother, Robert saw the full-length portrait of General Washington by Charles Willson Peale that hung there. Reminders of Washington were everywhere in Alexandria. George Washington was a part of his life from its earliest moments, as he was for most boys in nineteenth-century America, who were told to emulate the character and achievements of the "Father of His

fig. 52.
Charles Willson Peale, *Washington as Colonel of the Virginia Regiment*, 1772, oil on canvas, 50½ × 41½ in. (128.3 × 105.4 cm.), Washington and Lee University

fig. 53.
Mary Anna Randolph Custis, "Enslaved Girl," 1830, watercolor on paper, 5¾ × 4 in. (14.6 × 10.2 cm.), signed "M A R Custis 1830" (lower left), inscribed "Topsy" (on the white smock), Alexander Gallery

Country." Harry Lee had called for the erection of a mausoleum that would be not only a final resting place but also a monument to Washington to help teach "our children's children that the truest way to gain honor amidst a free people is to be useful, to be virtuous." If we "imitate his virtues and his great example," we create "an opportunity of rearing some future WASHINGTON." Little could he have known how well the lessons about honor and virtue would be taken to heart by his youngest son.

The painted and sculpted depictions of George Washington and the written tributes to him were inevitably absorbed by the young Robert E. Lee. It was no surprise that he approached the great-granddaughter of Martha Washington. Lee viewed lineage as important; when he married Mary Custis, Lee became a part of the Washington family. As he matured, Lee would grow more and more into the image of Washington. The "Father of His Country" was described by his early biographers as a model of stoic virtue, whose self-discipline triumphed over a passionate nature. Lee spoke of Washington's "unfailing wisdom & spotless integrity," and the general's "wisdom & rectitude." He cultivated a reserved, aloof demeanor that some contemporaries said was modeled on that of the general. He named a horse for one owned by Washington and he often carried one of the general's swords. When he served as superintendent at West Point in the early 1850s, Lee hung a copy by Ernest Fischer of the Arlington portrait of Washington by Charles Willson Peale, and he filled his dining room with Washington relics.[57]

There was a second component of life at Arlington that would greatly influence Robert E. Lee. The plantation was a site for some of the worst abuses of the slave system. Illegitimate children were fathered there by whites. Families were separated. People were sold. Molly Custis and her daughter made earnest efforts to improve the plight of the slaves. A watercolor by Mary rendered in 1830 of an "Enslaved Girl" suggests her sensitivity and sympathy to their plight (fig. 53). Lee, however, would be exposed to all of the cruelties and privations of a working plantation. As to supervision of the field hands, Custis was lax, almost to the point of ignoring them, and so Arlington as a farm was unproductive. Decades later, when Lee became executor of his father-in-law's estate, he inherited the problems of an abused and unproductive slave force. Lee would find no solutions; he would actually be pleased to quit the plantation and return to active army duty in faraway Texas.[58]

Ann Carter Lee owned some three dozen slaves who followed her to Alexandria. Late in his boyhood, when Lee assumed command of the household operation on Oronoco Street, he supervised those people. Most Virginians during the antebellum era owned no slaves; of those who did the vast majority owned less than twenty. The Lee family was exceptional. Yet Ann Carter Lee's slave force was only half of the sixty at Arlington. In addition, Custis owned twice that number at the two plantations he inherited from his father, the White House and Romancoke, both in the Virginia Tidewater. The total number of Custis slaves at his death was 196. Because he owned more slaves than he needed, Washington Custis could be an opponent of both the international slave trade and the local auctioning of slaves. But he was a hypocrite. While he referred to "the Vulture of slavery" and said that as the "foot of the Proprietor is the best manure for the soil, so is the sweat of a *Freeman's* brow," in fact Custis sold some slaves and gave away others, but he freed few of them during his lifetime. His wife no doubt persuaded him to make this a provision in his will, which must have appealed to Custis because George Washington had done the same.[59]

Molly Fitzhugh Custis was a quiet, virtuous woman. She differed from her husband in many ways, but none more so than with respect to human bondage. Before she married, Molly alerted Washington Custis to her feelings on the subject. Her heart was "capable of sympathizing in the woes of my fellow creatures." Slavery was an affront to her religious convictions. Her cousin Bishop William Meade, with whom she was active in efforts by the American Colonization Society to return slaves to freedom in Africa, defined the evil: "[it] grows with our growth & strengthens with our strength, and will soon outgrow us & beat us to the ground." For the half-century that Molly Custis was mistress at Arlington, this opponent of the institution did what she could to better the conditions there. She taught some of the slaves to read and write so as to prepare them for an independent life, and she held religious services to ready the Arlington slaves for their eternal reward. To sanctify the family unit, she arranged wedding ceremonies at the slave quarters. Washington Custis, who was quite possibly the father of some of the mulatto children at Arlington, tolerated her efforts on behalf of the slaves but said he would not have been inclined to initiate them himself.[60]

How much Robert E. Lee knew about Washington Custis's sexual transgressions with slaves is not known. After he married into the family, he quite possibly figured it out. During Lee's boyhood visits to Arlington, however, there would have been an attempt to shelter him and his peers from the more reprehensible aspects of slavery. Back home in Alexandria, where a thriving slave trading operation was centered close to Oronoco Street, the young Lee saw other manifestations of the evils of the institution. When he left Virginia for the United States Military Academy, the most promising of the sons of Ann Carter Lee wanted to put the life of a planter behind him.

Lee at West Point

Robert E. Lee's application in 1824 to enroll at West Point was supported by William Henry Fitzhugh, the loyal cousin and protector of Ann Carter Lee and her children. "Uncle Fitzhugh" had come to know Robert well during the past decade and a half. He recognized exceptional character and ability in the seventeen-year-old; Robert already was a gentleman. He wrote an earnest letter to the secretary of war, closing with the assurance that Lee was a good candidate for the military because he was predisposed for such a career:

> He is the son of Genl. Henry Lee, with whose history, you are, of course, acquainted; and who (whatever may have been the misfortune of his latter years) had certainly established, by his revolutionary services, a strong claim to the gratitude of his country. He is the son also of one of the finest women, the State of Virginia has ever produced. Possessed, in a very eminent degree, of all those qualities, which peculiarly belong to the female character of the South, she is rendered doubly interesting by her meritorious & successful exertions to support, in comfort, a large family, and to give to all her children excellent educations.
>
> The young gentleman, whom I have now the pleasure of introducing to you, as a candidate for West-point, is her youngest son. An intimate acquaintance, & a constant intercourse with him, almost from his infancy, authorize me to speak in the most unqualified terms of his amiable disposition, & his correct and gentlemanly habits. He is disposed to devote himself to the profession of arms.

fig. 54.
George Catlin, *View of West Point (Cadets Drilling on the Plain)*, 1827, oil on canvas, 15 × 25 in. (38.1 × 63.5 cm.), West Point Museum Art Collection, United States Military Academy, West Point, New York

Years later, Robert E. Lee would name his second son William Henry Fitzhugh Lee. Often he would think fondly of his "good old Uncle Fitzhugh, whose kindness to me & all of us I shall never forget."[61]

The secretary of war in 1824 was John C. Calhoun. The fact that "Light-Horse Harry" Lee had fought with distinction in Calhoun's native South Carolina was well known to all. Calhoun received additional endorsements from five senators and three representatives, as well as from Robert's older brothers Carter and Henry. He was moved to admit the candidate, even though the allotment of cadets from Virginia was already full. Consequently, Robert would have to delay his entry to West Point until 1825.[62]

The United States Military Academy had been founded in 1802 to train the officers of the small national army that the founders had envisioned as adequate for peacetime. During war, the ranks would be supplemented by militia units from the states. This scheme would be kept in place throughout the first half of the nineteenth century, even as the nation expanded and its population grew. A tract of land at West Point, on the banks of the Hudson River north of New York City, was chosen for the school. George Washington's army had maneuvered nearby during the Revolution, and so sites like Fort Putnam would remind the cadets of an ideal to which they were to aspire. Close to the time that Lee was a student at West Point, George Catlin recorded the appearance of the still young academy (fig.54).

Engineering was a principal field of instruction at West Point. A Corps of Engineers had been established within the army because defensive fortifications, which might have thwarted the British invasion in 1812, had been absent. There were still vulnerable positions along the East Coast, and so a crucial job of the engineers was to build forts to guard the coastline. As the nation expanded, so did the duties of the engineers. They would be needed to survey territories, at times to police them, and to assist with any number of internal improvements, such as the building and maintenance of roads and canals. These assignments would also help to justify the existence of a permanent army.

Robert E. Lee was a resounding success as a cadet at West Point. His accomplishments have become legendary. No matter what effort was required of a cadet, he was up to the task. Fitzhugh Lee, the son of brother Smith Lee, in writing a biography of his uncle remembered him as "a model cadet" who "never 'ran the sentinel post,' did not go off the limits to the 'Benny Havens' of his day, or put 'dummies' in his bed to deceive the officer in charge as he made his inspection after taps." It is well known that Lee received no demerits during his four years of study and training. He was also well liked within the corps. His close friend there Joseph Johnston, another Virginian who would serve as a Confederate commander, later remembered their college years together:

> We had the same intimate associates who thought as I did, that no other youth or man so united the qualities that win warm friendship and command high respect, for he was full of sympathy and kindness, genial and fond of gay conversation, and even of fun, while his correctness of demeanor and attention to all duties, personal and official, and a dignity as much a part of himself as the elegance of his person, gave him a superiority that every one acknowledged in his heart. He was the only one of all the men I have known that could laugh at the faults and follies of his friends in such a manner as to make them ashamed without touching their affection for him, and to confirm their respect and sense of his superiority.[63]

Part of Lee's success was that he looked like an officer. Cadet Lee was called the "Marble Model." There is an old account written near the end of his life that is said to be a reminiscence of one of his classmates. If it adds some nostalgia to the facts, the point is still valid:

> His personal appearance surpassed in manly beauty that of any cadet in the corps. Though firm in his position and perfectly erect, he had none of the stiffness so often assumed by men who affect to be very strict in their ideas of what is military. His limbs, beautiful and symmetrical, looked as though they had come from the turning lathe, his step was elastic as if he spurned the ground upon which he trod.

Lee was five feet eleven inches, which was tall for his day, well proportioned, and, by all accounts, exceptionally handsome.[64]

Cadets in Lee's era at the academy were given only a rudimentary military education. They were taught more about engineering, mathematics, and science. They learned French in order to read military texts from the Napoleonic era. In his first year at West Point, Lee earned recognition for accomplishments in mathematics and in French. For his proficiency in drill he was appointed staff sergeant. With the latter award, the highest possible for a plebe, he was listed a "distinguished cadet," one of five in each class whose names were recorded in the army register. Lee finished the year third in his class.

His ability in mathematics earned Lee an assistant professorship in the subject for the next three years. Thus, for the remainder of his tenure at West Point, Lee carried academic as well as military responsibilities. He pushed his standing in his class to second during years two, three, and four. (Charles Mason, who soon after graduation would quit the army for private business in Iowa, finished first every year.) Lee's independent reading during his second year included a new edition of *Memoirs of the War in the Southern Department* and *The Federalist*.[65]

Halfway through his undergraduate career, Lee was allowed leave to visit his mother, whose health had been deteriorating. There had also been some changes in situation among his siblings. His sister Ann had married William Marshall, and his brother Charles was practicing law in New York City. When the family traveled to nearby Fauquier County to visit at Kinloch, the home of Ann Lee's cousin Edward Carter Turner, Mary Custis of Arlington happened to be there. Robert and Mary renewed their acquaintanceship. She was an attractive young lady, with no shortage of suitors. Charles, for one, had noticed her, as had others closer to her own age.[66]

Lee's continued good standing during his third year at West Point earned him the highest rank of leadership among the cadets, corps adjutant. The recipients of that designation and those just below it—quartermaster, captain, and lieutenant—were selected "for their military bearing and qualifications," according to Ulysses S. Grant, writing in his *Memoirs* about his own West Point experience. Although Lee was second in his class at graduation, he scored first in artillery and tactics, earning a maximum score in those subjects. He was exceptional even in the sketching of landscape and topography, ranking fourth in drawing. On a personal

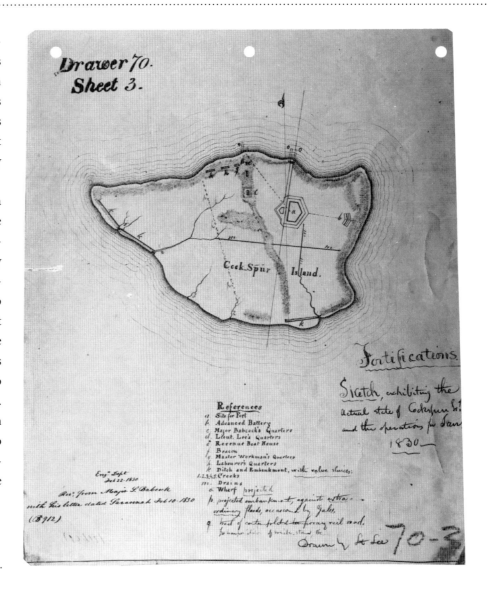

fig. 55.
Robert E. Lee, *Cockspur Island and Fort Pulaski*, 1830, sketch, National Archives and Records Administration

level, Lee excelled in frugality. He was determined not to burden his mother with expenses or set a pattern of financial irresponsibility which in any way resembled that demonstrated by his father. In part because he earned some money as a math tutor, Lee had $103 left in his account at graduation at a time when most cadets routinely overspent what they had.[67]

In the summer of 1829, Lee was awarded a brevet (temporary) second lieutenancy in the elite corps of engineers as a reward for his outstanding performance. His mother died that July at Ravensworth, the plantation of "Uncle Fitzhugh." She left some money, plus a few slaves to her children, and also a little land in southwest Virginia to her sons. Most of the slaves were probably sold along with the land; some slaves may have been hired out. Robert was twenty-two years old, without parents or a home of his own. However, he soon visited Arlington and won permission to write and court Mary Custis. To his chagrin, his first posting would put some distance between himself and the woman whom he hoped would become his wife.[68]

Engineering in the South, St. Louis, and Brooklyn

Fort Pulaski, Georgia—1829–31

Robert E. Lee began his career in the corps of engineers at a relatively opportune time. Congress had recently appropriated funding for the construction of coastal defenses. There was ample work for the army's engineers to perform. The young officers would learn to become proficient not only in engineering, but also in finance, in procurement, in handling labor, and in negotiating with the hierarchies of both the army and the local civilian communities.

Lee's first tour of duty was in Georgia at Cockspur Island in the Savannah River (fig. 55). A substantial fort was to be built on that site to defend the port of Savannah, located twelve miles upstream. The task was difficult, however, because the island in its natural state was barely habitable. It was marshland that flooded with the tides. In the heat of summer, conditions there were not tolerable. Lee assisted a major, Samuel Babcock, who delegated most of the hard physical labor to his subordinate and made decisions that even the new lieutenant could see would fail. When a gale proved that Babcock had sited the fort on the wrong part of the island, he was replaced by a pair of soldiers, Joseph Mansfield and Richard Delafield. A third engineer was not needed, so Lee was happily reassigned to Fort Monroe in Virginia.[69]

Lee's two years at Cockspur Island were occasionally relieved by the companionship of the Mackay family in nearby Savannah, to where the young lieutenant could at times escape. Jack Mackay had been one of Lee's best friends at West Point, and he remained a fre-

fig. 56.
Robert E. Lee, Cockspur Island, to Mary Randolph Custis (later Mary Randolph Custis Lee), *Letter*, November 11, 1830, private collection

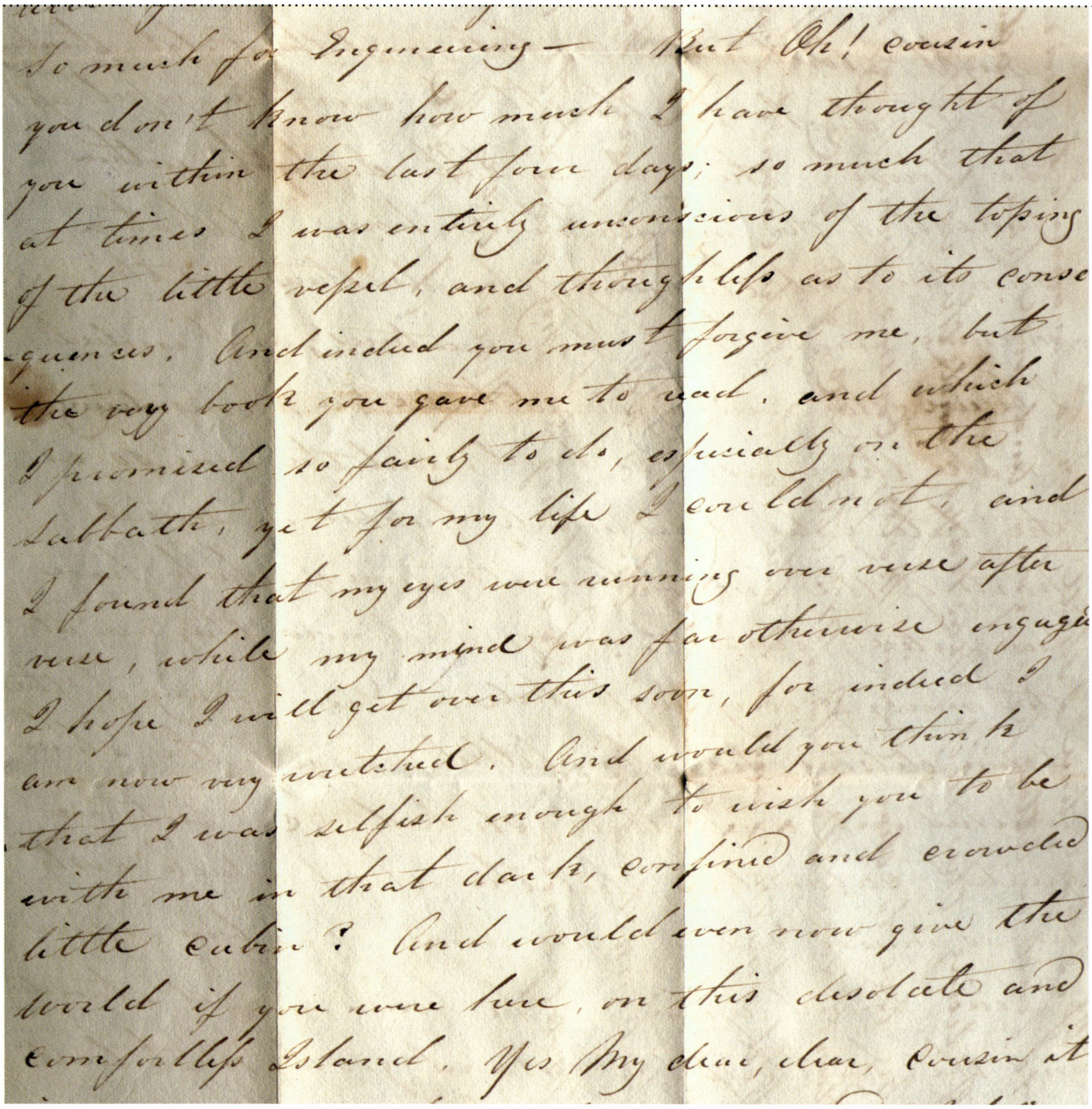

quent correspondent for several decades. Lee was accompanied to Georgia by Nat, his mother's aged coachman, a slave who had been bequeathed to Mildred. He was old and infirm, and all believed that a warm climate would help his health. However, he soon died in Georgia.

Lee lived on a boat at Cockspur Island. With plenty of time on his hands at the close of the day, he engaged in regular correspondence with Mary Custis. Several of the letters (fig. 56) have recently come to light, long hidden away in a family trunk. They are affectionate letters, proof that Robert did not propose to Mary because she would inherit wealth or because her husband would be forever linked with the illustrious family of George Washington. He married her because they had fallen in love:

> But Oh! Cousin you don't know how much I have thought of you within the last four days; so much that at times I was entirely unconscious of the tossing of the little vessel, and

fig. 57.
William Edward West, *Mary Randolph Custis Lee*, 1838, oil on canvas, 30 × 25 in. (76.2 × 63.5 cm.), Washington and Lee University

thoughtless as to its consequences …. And would you think that I was selfish enough to wish you to be with me in that dark, confined and crowded little cabin? And would even now give the world if you were here, on this desolate and comfortless Island.[70]

Fort Monroe, Virginia—1831–34

Old Point Comfort guards the entrance to both the James River and the port of Norfolk. When Lee arrived there, Fort Monroe had for the most part already been built and a garrison occupied it. He was assigned to support Captain Andrew Talcott of Connecticut in completing work there and in building a second, companion fort in the middle of the wide body of water called Hampton Roads. Hostile ships would no longer be able to pass without being in range of one of the forts. Talcott was ten years Lee's senior, and like him a graduate of West Point who had finished second in his class. The two became friends. Talcott, however, was absent on other assignments for much of the three years that Lee was there, and so many of the opportunities and frustrations of this challenging project fell to the young lieutenant.

The second outpost, to be named Fort Calhoun after the same secretary of war who had admitted Lee to West Point, was to be located a mile offshore. Decades later, when the secessionist Calhoun was out of favor, it would be renamed Fort Wool, after John Wool (with whom Lee had served in Mexico and who became a Union general of the Civil War). The site of the fort—a man-made island of fifteen acres—was under construction when Lee arrived. The island was often referred to simply as "Rip Raps" because of the stones dumped from barges on to a sand bar to create it. The foundations for the fort soon began to sink at a yearly rate of three inches. All Lee could do was to continue to bolster the foundations with additional rocks. In the process, he learned more about management than engineering. There were wharves and buildings to design and construct on the mainland, financial accounts to manage, expenses to estimate, laborers to contract with, feed, and house, superiors to report to, and even sanitation needs to resolve.[71]

Among Lee's many frustrations at Old Point Comfort were the sinking foundations for Fort Calhoun, the needless internal bickering of the administrators, and the immoral conduct of some of the workers. The officers stationed at the garrison and the engineers brought in for construction often quarreled over turf and privileges. With little to do, some of the soldiers drank and gambled. The idealistic Lee wrote Jack Mackay that when he saw "minds formed for use and ornament, degenerate into sluggishness and inactivity, requiring the stimulus of brandy or cards to rouse them to action," he was ready to "modestly retire."[72]

The return to Virginia enabled Lee to resume his courtship of Mary Custis in earnest (fig. 57). He had won her affection, but the approval of her father, who knew the scandals and financial setbacks of the Lee family, apparently took more time. Biographers of Lee have long told the story of a visit to Arlington when the young lieutenant, beneath the C. W. Peale portrait of the young Colonel Washington of the Virginia militia, read to Mary from a novel by Sir Walter Scott. Mrs. Custis sent the pair to another room for fruitcake. There the proposal was made and accepted; G. W. P. Custis was finally convinced. The couple was married at Arlington in the summer of 1831. Lee joked to Andrew Talcott that the parson dwelt on the words of the service "as if he had been reading my death warrant" and that "there was a tremulousness in the hand I held." With humor that was characteristically risqué, he added that the newlyweds' time had been passing "very rapidly"; in fact

fig. 58.
Dancing Slippers, owned by Robert E. Lee, Washington and Lee University

he was slow to write because he could not find time "for anything but _____" [the word was deleted by Lee]. His life would never be the same. Over the next fourteen years Mary would bear him seven children who became the focus of his attention and devotion. Her evangelical zeal and that of Molly Custis would reinforce the instruction in Christianity that Robert had received from his mother, such that religion would play an increasingly significant role in his life. He would also begin to see himself as a representative of the family of George Washington.[73]

Mary Lee joined Robert at Fort Monroe in married quarters, a two-room suite. She reported to her mother that he was "tender and affectionate," and that "he spends his evenings at home instead of frequenting the card parties which attract so many." Mary, however, stayed at the fort for only five months. Pregnancy was her excuse for lingering at Arlington after Christmas of 1831. A son, George Washington Parke Custis Lee, was born in 1832. Lee wrote to Talcott, "Master Custis is the most darling boy in the world." During the first eighteen months of her marriage, Mary was apart from her husband a third of the time, a pattern that would continue for the three decades of Robert's army career. The sole surviving child of overly attentive parents, she was somewhat spoiled and self-centered. "The only objection I have to this place [Fort Monroe][is that] it is so public," she wrote. "What would I give for one stroll on the hills at Arlington." She was at times careless about her appearance and that of her quarters, much like her father and the exact opposite of her meticulous husband. He wrote Talcott, "Mrs. L. is somewhat addicted to laziness & forgetfulness in her housekeeping. But … she does her best. Or in her mother's words, 'The spirit is willing but the flesh is weak.'"[74]

Lee wrote to Jack Mackay that he "would not be unmarried for all you could offer me." Marriage, however, in no way stopped him from both looking and occasionally flirting. He added to Mackay, "As for the Daughters of Eve in this country, they are formed in the very poetry of nature, and would make your lips water and fingers tingle." Marriage may even have encouraged Lee's boldness because it cut short the option to move beyond banter. He could converse and dance with other women with no fear of his intentions being misinterpreted (fig. 58). By all indications, Lee was absolutely faithful to his wife and she never doubted his fidelity. The legacy of "Black-Horse Harry" Lee was perhaps good for something. After Mackay's sister Eliza was married, Lee dared to tease her about the honeymoon: "And how did you disport yourself My child? Did you go off well, like a torpedo cracker on Christmas morning." He also wrote to Mary of his gallivanting:

> Let me tell you Mrs. Lee, no later than today, did I escort Miss G to see Miss Kate! Think of that Mrs. Lee! And hasten down, if you do not want to see me turned out a Beaux again. How I did strut along with one hand on my whiskers & the other clenching my coat tail! And my whole face thrown into the biggest grin I could muster.[75]

At Arlington, Washington and Molly Custis disapproved of the separation of the family, particularly after the birth of a child. They wanted Lee to quit the army. Mrs. Custis even suggested that he might manage the plantation, which already was in dire need of a strong hand to make it productive. She wrote to her daughter that a friend (identified only as David) "thinks as your father is so literary a character that he would find it greatly to his advantage to withdraw Robert from his present profession and yield to him the management of affairs [of Arlington]. I told him that would please me very well …." Nothing, however, came of the idea. Robert's career seemed to be on course, and he enjoyed the life of an officer.[76]

A month after Lee was married, in August 1831, the rebellion led by the slave Nat Turner unfolded in Southampton County, only forty miles southwest of Hampton Roads. Nearly sixty whites were

fig. 59.
Copied by William George Williams, *Madonna and Child*, 1830, oil on canvas, 69 × 47¾ in. (175.3 × 121.3 cm.), National Park Service, Arlington House

killed. Five companies were quickly dispatched to Fort Monroe, but the slave revolt ended as quickly as it had begun. Lee was concerned that "much mischief" might have resulted. He complained to his wife that the slaves involved "had used their religious assemblies, which ought to have been devoted to better purposes, for forming and maturing their plans."[77]

In 1834, differences between the regular military and the engineers at Fort Monroe forced the major general of the army, Alexander Macomb, and the acting secretary of war, John Forsyth, to inspect the operation. They concluded that what work remained at the fort could be completed without the engineers, who should be reduced to one officer who would reside at Rip Raps. Talcott requested and received a transfer to another post. Lee complained that he could not feed and house laborers on an empty island. After two months, he was relieved to get a new assignment in Washington. Fort Calhoun was eventually completed by others.[78]

Washington, DC—1834–37

Lee spent the middle years of the 1830s assigned to the War Department. He found a room in a boardinghouse in the city to avoid a daily commute across the Potomac River to Arlington, but he was free to be with his family as much as he wanted. He would also have the opportunity to test the purported values of plantation life while enjoying the social opportunities offered by the city. He wrote to Andrew Talcott about the young women whom he encountered at his brother Smith's wedding party: "Sweet, innocent things, they concluded I was single, & I have not had such soft looks & tender pressures of the hand for many years." But his family aroused Lee's greatest passions, particularly when a second child, Mary, was born in 1835. Lee wrote again to Talcott,

> The country looks very sweet now, and the hill at A[rlington] covered with verdure, and perfumed by the blossoms of the trees, the flowers of the garden, honeysuckles, yellow jasmine etc. is more to my taste than at any other season of the year. But the brightest flower there blooming is my *daughter*. Oh, she is a rare one, and if only sweet sixteen, I would wish myself a *cannibal*, that I might eat her up. As it is, I have given all the young ladies a holyday and hurry home to her every day.

While life at Arlington was in many ways unstructured, Molly Custis introduced some regularity there by conducting daily religious services. These were held in the parlor. Later, probably around 1838, Lee acquired for that room a nearly life-size image of the *Madonna and Child* (fig. 2.18) that still hangs there today. This remarkably ambitious canvas was painted in Italy in 1830 by Captain William George Williams, the father of Lee's cousin Markie Williams.[79]

Lee derived great joy from his two children, and while he developed an affection for the Custises, they were his ever-present in-laws and the house belonged to them. Lee's greatest concern, however, was the welfare of his wife. Mary Custis Lee suffered ill health following the birth of her daughter. She was bedridden for months. A cousin said of Lee, "I never saw a man so changed and saddened." A

fig. 60.
William Edward West, *Robert E. Lee in the Dress Uniform of a Lieutenant of Engineers*, 1838, oil on canvas, 30 × 25 in. (72.6 × 63.5 cm.), Washington and Lee University

year later, Robert wrote, "Her nervous system is much shattered. She has almost a horror of crowded places, an indisposition to make the least effort, and yet a restless anxiety which renders her unhappy and dissatisfied." Mary Custis Lee would recover sufficiently to give birth to five additional children over the next decade, but her health had begun a permanent downward spiral.[80]

At the War Department, Lee was actually less happy than he was at his previous assignments. More than anything else, it was his professional frustration that spoiled these years at Arlington. He developed considerable affection for his commanding officer, Charles Gratiot, the army's chief engineer, but Lee found that his assignments did not suit his temperament, that he needed a better salary to live the way he wished, and that he was too ambitious to be content in Washington where there was little opportunity for advancement. Congress was again debating the funding of proposed internal improvements that would expand the duties of the corps of engineers, such as the dredging of harbors and rivers and the building of forts and roads. Gratiot needed a lobbyist to argue the case for increased appropriations. The handsome son of a war hero whose name was still recognizable in Washington fit the bill. For his efforts, Lee was promoted to first lieutenant. As early as four months into his Washington tenure, however, Lee wanted out. In 1835, Gratiot placed him with Andrew Talcott on an assignment to survey the boundary line between Ohio and Michigan. This was a useful interlude, but nothing more. Two years later, Lee wrote to Talcott, "I must get away from here …. I am waiting, looking and hoping for some good opportunity to bid an affectionate farewell to my dear Uncle Sam." He admitted his own error for thinking "that said opportunity is to drop in my lap like a ripe pear," when in fact the private "companies for internal improvements" were all passing him by. Soon, however, a promising assignment within the army appeared. Town leaders in St. Louis had been pleading with Gratiot, a Missourian by birth, to save their harbor from silting. Lee wrote, "I volunteered my services … to get rid of the office in W[ashington] and the Genl. at least agreed to my going."[81]

St. Louis, Missouri—1837–40

[Lee] had none of that … petty … planning and scheming which men of little minds … use to take care of their fame. [He worked] most indefatigably, in that quiet, unobtrusive manner and with the modesty characteristic of the man.

John Fletcher Darby, former mayor of St. Louis, 1880[82]

Robert E. Lee distinguished himself by accomplishing one of the major engineering feats of the era. He was able to divert the Mississippi River from its meandering path away from St. Louis back to where it had once flowed. The harbor (fig. 61) consequently remained deep, and the boom town created by steamboat commerce resumed its development into the gateway to the West. Lee also managed to blast a channel for river traffic on a stretch of the Mississippi two hundred miles upstream. In the process of improving both the harbor and the river, Lee earned the respect of the local inhabitants, a promotion to the rank of captain, and a reputation in the army as one of its rising stars (fig. 60).

100   II. YOUTH AND EARLY MILITARY CAREERS

fig. 61.
George Catlin, *Saint Louis*, 1832, oil on canvas, 20½ × 33½ in. (52.1 × 85.1 cm.), Missouri Historical Society

Lee's task as defined by Congress when it appropriated the funding was "to build a pier to give direction to the current of the river near St. Louis" and to channel a shipping route through the rapids of the Mississippi River farther to the north. There were actually two sets of rapids above the mouth of the Ohio River that obstructed an otherwise clear path of navigation for 1,200 miles. One set was the Des Moines Rapids, an eleven-mile stretch near the town of Keokuk, Iowa, about 200 miles to the north. The other set, with the ominous name of the Rock River Rapids, was a fifteen-mile section near the later cities of Moline and Rock Island, Illinois, and Davenport, Iowa, some 350 miles upstream. While Lee's funds would be depleted before he could work much at the upper rapids, the importance of these projects to navigation on the Mississippi and to the development of the American West was obvious even to the usually tight-fisted Congress.[83]

The Mississippi assignment was the first where Lee was awarded sole command. His principal assistant for the first season would be a recent West Point graduate, Montgomery Meigs. Meigs would serve with distinction as chief engineer of the U.S. Capitol Building in the 1850s and as quartermaster-general of the Union army during the Civil War. He grew to detest the Confederacy; after the death of his son, it was Meigs who would turn the grounds around Arlington House into a cemetery. In 1837, however, the pair worked together in harmony. After Lee's death, Meigs had the highest praise for his former commander:

> [Lee was then] in the vigor of youthful strength, with a noble and commanding presence, and an admirable, graceful and athletic figure. He was one with whom nobody

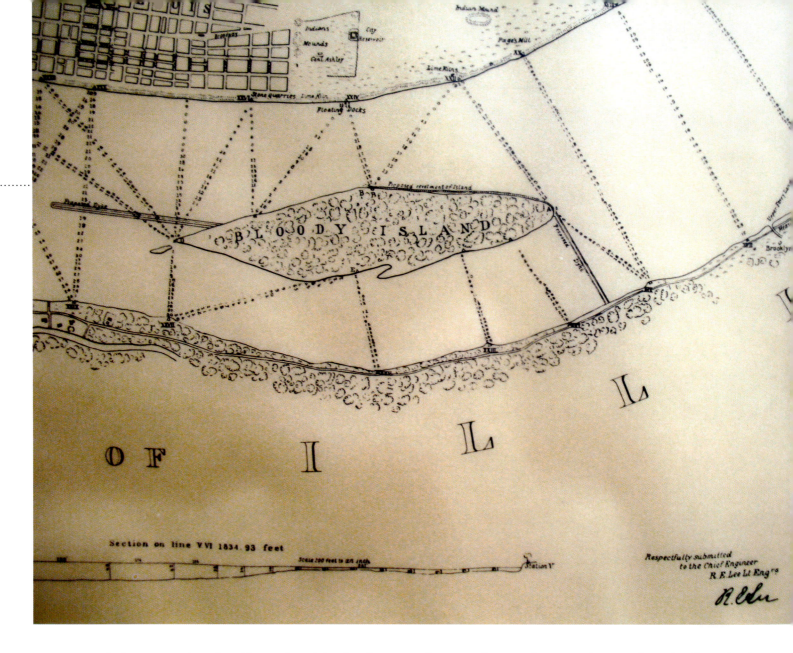

ever wished or ventured to take a liberty, though kind and generous to all his subordinates, admired by all women, and respected by all men. He was the model of a soldier and the beau ideal of a Christian man.

In August 1837, Lee explored the rapids. The water was too low so late in the season to accomplish much more than mapping and planning. He was able to see, however, "what a beautiful country it is" and to assess the importance of his assignment and the expectations that accompanied it. He wrote, "The formation of a good channel through these rapids will be of immense advantage to the country, and great anxiety seems to be felt on the subject."[84]

Lee's most important task was at St. Louis. In 1831, the city had been named a port of entry for the United States. Congress from that point forward took an interest in its development. Directly above the city, a sizable island, about a mile long and 500 yards wide, had been thrown up in the middle of the Mississippi River because of the tendency of the current to run to both banks. It was named Bloody Island because of the duels that were fought there.

By about 1818, because the current began to favor the Illinois bank, a second deposit had built up near the southern tip of St. Louis. Named Duncan's Island, this landmass was a mile long and 800 yards wide when Lee arrived. The channel between the two islands was getting increasingly shallow, threatening to create a sand bar that would cut off St. Louis from deep-water shipping (fig. 62).

The plan that Lee executed was the one devised by Charles Gratiot, who had inspected the terrain firsthand, and Captain Henry Shreve, who had worked the site before 1837. Lee made some adjustments and he implemented the scheme as well as the allocated funding and time would allow. The idea was to build: (1) a dam from the top of Bloody Island to the Illinois shore to stop the current from its path there and force it instead to the St. Louis side of the island; (2) a dike at the foot of Bloody Island to point the current directly towards Duncan's Island and thereby push it downstream; and (3) a revetment along Bloody Island, which would be vulnerable to erosion from the full force of current along its side. The task was difficult, but successful dams had recently

fig. 62.
Robert E. Lee, *Map of the Harbor of St. Louis* (detail), 1837, Stratford Hall

been constructed on the Hudson River, where a channel had been dug by a corps under Andrew Talcott after he left Fort Monroe. Both the dam and the dike would be built with piles driven into the riverbed. These were familiar to engineers as the underwater foundations for forts. Here the piles would remain above water and be linked with woven brush. Stones would then be dumped into the mix. The river would deposit brush against the dam. It was to be nearly 600 yards long, the dike 1,000 yards, and the reveted bank another 900 yards.

Lee worked from dawn to dusk in the field and long into the evenings as he developed a system of administration for so large an undertaking. His labor force numbered as many as eighty men. He was able to work well with the local population, and he pulled off the operation with seemingly little effort. It was not until the 1838 season, however, that Lee could see that his plans for St. Louis harbour would work. Once the dike at the base of Bloody Island was in place, it soon enough removed 700 feet of Duncan's Island and deepened the channel at St. Louis harbor to seven feet. The merchants of the city were elated. The building boom in the city was renewed. Local funding was collected to enable Lee to continue the project awhile longer by building the dam at the top of Bloody Island. Construction was started, but cold weather stopped the work.

The mayor of St. Louis later remembered Lee fondly. Others before Lee had tried to move the river and had failed. Sufficient progress was visible at St. Louis by the summer of 1838 for Lee to be promoted to captain of engineers. Peacetime promotions were rare because they depended largely upon vacancies; someone of higher rank had either to retire or die. Lee would not receive his next full promotion for another eighteen years, despite his continued good performance. For the time being, he stopped thinking that he would eventually have to quit the military: "I suppose the more comfortably I am fixed in the Army, the less likely I shall be to leave it."[85]

During the summer of 1839, Lee continued construction of the dam from Bloody Island to the Illinois shore. Residents on that side of the river, however, started to view the activity warily. An Illinois court order soon brought a final halt to construction. But the dike and dam already in place were yielding dramatic results. A new channel, 1,000 feet wide, was soon cut, providing steamboats with a straight path down the river. That fall Lee returned to the Des Moines Rapids. For both sets of upstream rapids, his plan was to blast along the natural channel of the river in order to expand it. At Des Moines he removed 2,000 tons of stone to open a channel four miles long. Even Lee, ever critical of himself, judged that "a tolerable season's work." His regret was the lack of time and funds to do the same at the Rock River Rapids. Lee, characteristically, was embarrassed to leave a project incomplete, but others saw the magnitude of his accomplishment. The dike and the dam at St. Louis continued to work so well that the largest of the Mississippi steamboats were soon navigating to the wharves of that city. The harbor would need additional work in the 1840s and 1850s, but, literally and figuratively, the tide had been turned.[86]

Lee had set out for the West following the birth of his third child, William Henry Fitzhugh Lee, in 1837. In 1838 he was joined in St. Louis by his wife and their two sons, who remained through the winter. In the spring of 1839, Mary and the children returned to Arlington, where she gave birth to a fourth child, Annie, in June. Lee was alone for the remainder of 1839, and again in 1840 when he returned to St. Louis to sell equipment. Though he enjoyed a great deal of satisfaction from the successful execution of his duties, his happiness was directly related to the presence of his family. When they were absent, Lee was miserable.[87]

Letters from St. Louis repeat a familiar refrain. In Washington, Lee was unhappy because his ambition had been stifled; in St. Louis, he was unhappy without his family: "I am very anxious my dear Mary to get back to see you all and learn of your proceedings, as there alone I can expect pleasure or happiness. I dream of you and the dear little children nearly every night …." (September 10, 1837). "Oh, what pleasure I lose in being separated from my children. Nothing can compensate me for that; still I must remain here, ready to perform what little service I can, and hope for the best" (October 16, 1837). "Life is too short for them and their mother to be in one place, and I in another" (October 22, 1837). "You do not know how much I have missed you and the children, my dear Mary. To be alone in a crowd is very solitary" (June 5, 1839).[88]

When the family was with Lee, the in-laws were displeased by their absence from Arlington. Lee had to defend his action: "I think it is my duty to make a sacrifice … to try and advance myself in my profession, and be thereby enabled to give our dear children such an education and standing in life as we could wish," he wrote to Molly Custis on March 24, 1838. Like her parents, Mary Custis

Lee was also uncomfortable when the family was away from Arlington, which she still considered her home. Even had her health been good, life on the frontier, without the support system of the plantation and with small children to care for, held no appeal. "Rich as [the land] is I would rather a thousand times live in Old Virginia or somewhere near it." At age thirty-one she complained to Harriet Talcott, "I am getting too old to form new friends and would rather be among those I know and love."[89]

Away from his children, Lee began to worry about the responsibilities of parenting. His worst fear was that his offspring would be raised with a lack of self-discipline. Lee began a series of long letters about parental guidance that would continue for two decades, until the seven children were grown:

> Our dear little boy [Rooney] seems to have among his friends the reputation of being hard to manage—a distinction not at all desirable, as it indicates self-will and obstinacy …. It is our duty, if possible, to counteract them and assist him to bring them under his control …. This is a subject on which I think much …. Oh, what pleasure I lose in being separated from my children. [90]

All the while, Lee kept an eye open for pretty young women. "Tell Mrs. T[alcott] there are some very pretty girls here so I will say nothing further against the country." As he put it to Jack Mackay, "[I am] in favor of the pretty girls if there are any here, and know there are, for I have met them in no place, in no garb, in no situation that I did not feel my heart open to them, like the flower to the sun." On seeing twenty-four young girls at a party, Lee wrote, "It was the prettiest sight I have seen in the West, and perhaps in my life." Lee also found a special quality in the women of the West that was more than skin deep: they had character, and so reminded him of his mother. They "subject themselves to every privation and drudgery; and … toil patiently and constantly. They are always ready to offer kindness and relief, are frugal and attentive while their rough consorts are careless unthrifty speculating lazing [sic] or worse."[91]

Lee was happy to return to Virginia in 1840. Although he had met with professional success in the West, he told his cousin Hill Carter that he headed back with joy: "I nodded to all the old trees as I passed …. and in the fulness of my heart—don't tell Cousin Mary—wanted to kiss all the pretty girls I met." He could take some satisfaction in the fact that he had established a high standing in the army. That reputation would present opportunities in Mexico that Lee would aggressively pursue during the coming war. More immediately, the success at St. Louis earned for Lee a new assignment, closer to home in a setting that his family might be able to enjoy.[92]

Fort Hamilton, New York—1841–46

Everyone says it is healthy. I am told … that the Sea breezes are very cool and refreshing … the scene is very animating & interesting. Vessels of all kinds are constantly passing, & the view is extensive …. The country in the neighborhood is fertile & well cultivated & there are quantities of handsome Country Seats in all directions.

Robert E. Lee to Mary Custis Lee, April 18, 1841[93]

Before he reported to duty at his new assignment outside New York City (fig. 63), Robert E. Lee made inquiries about the site. He reported to his wife, who had been less than content when on the frontier in St. Louis, that Fort Hamilton had much to offer with respect to its location. Its proximity to one of the largest cities in the nation, and, more importantly, the fact that his family could more easily join him there, made this posting seem ideal. As happened in Washington, however, the domestic bliss that Lee envisioned in New York would never come to pass, nor would there be the professional accomplishment that he was always seeking. Mary became pregnant three times within the six-year period of her husband's tour of duty in Brooklyn. Agnes, Robert, Jr., and Mildred were born in 1841, 1843, and 1846. Mary Custis Lee required that her pregnancies and long periods of recuperation be spent only at Arlington, where physical and emotional support was in abundance, and so Robert was not able to see his family as much as he had hoped.

As to professional fulfillment, Lee had been rewarded for his St. Louis accomplishments with an easy assignment that unfortunately provided little challenge. Fort Hamilton was important because it defended New York, a major city, one that had been a focus of British strategy during the Revolutionary War. But Lee's duties in Brooklyn provided no further opportunities for advancement.

Lee supervised not one but actually four forts that commanded "the Narrows," the stretch of water between the upper and lower bays adjacent to New York City. (Today the area is spanned by the Verrazano Narrows Bridge.) As at Old Point Comfort in Virginia, where Fort Monroe by itself could not adequately defend the wa-

fig. 63.
Jacques & Brother, New York, *Fort Hamilton Polka Redowa*, 1852, lithograph, 8 × 12¼ in. (20.3 × 31.1 cm.), New-York Historical Society Library, gift of Daniel Parish, Jr., 1900

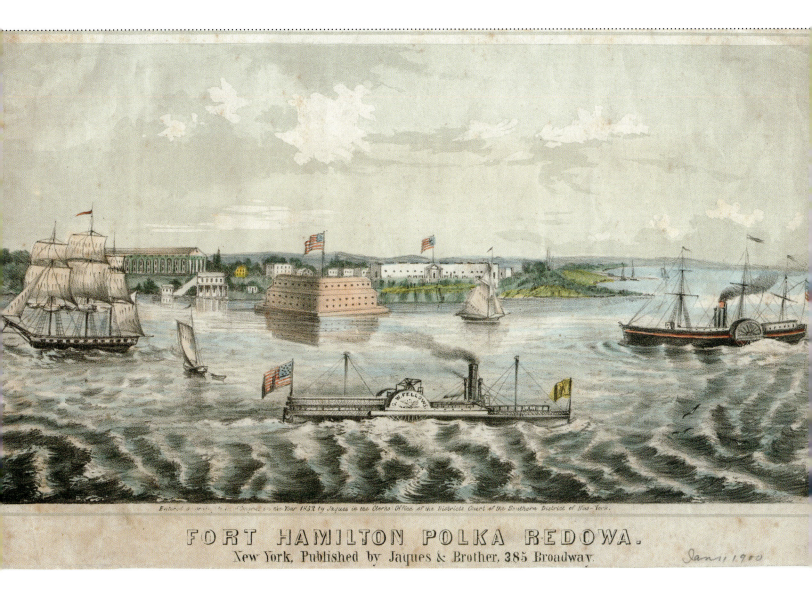

terway, "the Narrows" warranted the positioning of multiple guns. These, however, were already in place in 1841, at Battery Hudson and Battery Morton on the Staten Island side, and Forts Lafayette and Hamilton on the Brooklyn side. Lee would make his residence at Fort Hamilton and travel to the other sites by boat. Unlike his previous field assignments, where the engineering was difficult and the labor was hard, here he had only to make repairs and renovations.[94]

Henry J. Hunt, a second lieutenant of artillery stationed at Fort Hamilton while Lee was there, was impressed by the captain. He later recollected, "[Lee was] as fine-looking a man as one would wish to see, of perfect figure and strikingly handsome. Quiet and dignified in manner, of cheerful disposition, always pleasant and considerate, he seemed to me the perfect type of a gentleman."

While at Fort Hamilton, Lee was twice sent to West Point, in 1843 and again in 1844, to help in the decision concerning where to locate new barracks and to witness final examinations. There he met Winfield Scott of Virginia, the general-in-chief of the army. Scott had received his commission from President Thomas Jefferson and was a hero of the War of 1812. At six feet five inches and 230 pounds, he was an impressive figure. Cadet Ulysses S. Grant thought him in these years "the finest specimen of manhood my eyes had ever beheld." This was the first occasion when Lee would work with Scott, the man who would make good use of the captain's skills during the Mexican War and would influence him more than any other soldier. In 1845, Lee was appointed to the board of engineers for the defense of the Atlantic coastline. He had

fig. 64.
Unknown photographer (in New York City) copied by Michael Miley, *Robert E. Lee and Rooney Lee (1837–1891)*, c. 1870, from a lost photograph of c. 1845–46, Virginia Historical Society

fig. 65.
Unknown photographer copied by Michael Miley, *Agnes Lee (?) (1841–1873)*, c. 1870, from a lost photograph of c. 1845–46, Virginia Historical Society

participated in the building and maintenance of forts at critical sites. Now that expertise would be put to use in deciding where the next fortifications should be located.[95]

At Fort Hamilton, as always, Lee's children dominated his thoughts. His family had almost doubled in size. In 1846 Custis was fourteen, Mary was eleven, Rooney (fig. 64) was nine, Annie was seven, Agnes (fig. 65) was five, and Robert, Jr. (figs. 66 and 67) was three; Mary Custis Lee would give birth to Mildred that year. When the children were at Arlington, Lee would long for them and worry about their development. Following the birth of Robert, Jr., he wrote to Mary,

> It is strange how my heart yearned towards him as soon as I heard of his existence …. I am glad to hear of the well doing of those dear children. Nobody can know how I want to see them …. Tell those little daughters to get their sweet mouths ready for I shall kiss them off when I get there.

While the older children were with their father in New York, both Rooney and Annie injured themselves. Playing with straw cutters, Rooney lost the tips of two fingers. In a separate incident, Annie cut her eye. Lee blamed himself whenever the children were hurt, and he took it upon himself to nurse them back to health. He sat with Rooney through the night while the boy slept to be sure that the hand would heal without further injury. But in life's more tedious moments he longed for the type of social interaction that he had enjoyed in Virginia, and he hoped that at some point in his military career he would be able to show that he had skills beyond the assembling of bricks and mortar.[96]

Lee had kept up with the political situation in Texas, and he saw that a war on that frontier was becoming more and more likely. He soon would leave the safety of Brooklyn for the wilds of Mexico, where he would witness battle for the first time. As he approached his fortieth birthday, he thought himself as ready for the challenge.

fig. 65.
Unknown photographer copied by Michael Miley, *Agnes Lee (?) (1841–1873)*, c. 1870, from a lost photograph of c. 1845–46, Virginia Historical Society

fig. 66.
Unknown photographer (in New York City), *Mrs. Robert E. Lee and Robert E. Lee, Jr. (1843–1914)*, c. 1845–46, daguerreotype, Virginia Historical Society

The Grants of New England and Ohio

My family is American, and has been for generations, in all its branches, direct and collateral.

Ulysses S. Grant, 1885[97]

No man since Washington has better illustrated the genius of American institutions or the temper of Americans as a people.

Montgomery [Alabama] Advertizer, July 25, 1885

"I am of the eighth generation from Mathew Grant," explained Ulysses in his *Memoirs*. The first Grants in America, Mathew and his wife Priscilla, had arrived from Dorchester, England, in 1630, with a group of Puritans who named their settlement after their place of origin. (Dorchester is now a part of Boston.) Five years later Mathew and Priscilla moved to the Connecticut River to help found another town, Windsor. There Mathew served as "surveyor for [the Connecticut] colony for more than forty years" and was also town clerk. Both positions held significant responsibilities in the infant colony. After Mathew's first wife died, he married "the widow Rockwell," who had been a fellow passenger on the ship *Mary and John* that had carried them to America. Like Richard Lee I, the progenitor of the Virginia Lees, Mathew Grant enjoyed a position of prominence in his community.[98]

While Robert E. Lee proudly claimed that his family in Virginia was an offshoot of one of the oldest in England, Ulysses S. Grant began his memoirs with an equally bold assertion. The Grant family was American in all its branches; it had been American for two-and-a-half centuries and he was proud of that fact. The first Grants in America had in fact come from England, but no mention is made of English roots. Grant was a man of the present. He explains clearly that he is writing a book because he was forced to do so. He needed the money. "The rascality of a business partner" had

LEE AND GRANT

forced him into bankruptcy. There is no self-pity, no apologies. This is Grant, clear, direct, and forthright. He is going to tell his story the way that he remembered it to the best of his ability.

Mathew Grant's will tells us that he had significant land holdings, and his diary reveals that he was a man of strong religious faith and intellectual curiosity. He recorded his thoughtful considerations of the theology in Puritan sermons and included selections of poetry as well. Grant was clearly proud that his ancestor was a man of conscience who had made a place for himself in the world.[99]

Mathew's son and grandson, both named Samuel, remained in the Windsor vicinity. His great-grandson, the first Noah Grant, moved into the hills of Connecticut to a new town called Tolland. There the second and third Noah Grants were born. Captain Noah Grant (II), the great-grandfather of Ulysses, was a legitimate war hero. Noah and his younger brother Solomon fought in the French and Indian War. They "held commissions in the English army," Ulysses wrote. In 1756, the legislature awarded to Noah thirty Spanish dollars for "Ranging and Scouting the winter past; for annoyance of the Enemy near Crown Point & Discovering their motives." Later in the year, both Noah and Solomon were killed in service.[100]

The descendants of the second Noah Grant could take pride in his legacy. The story of his son is a different matter. Ulysses was proud of the third Noah as well, although his story has in recent years been questioned:

> My grandfather, also named Noah … after the battles of Concord and Lexington, he went with a Connecticut company to join the Continental army, and was present at the battle of Bunker Hill. He served until the fall of Yorktown, or through the entire Revolutionary War. He must, however, have been on furlough part of the time—as I believe most of the soldiers of that period were—for he married in Connecticut during the war, had two children, and was a widower at the close.

Grant was probably told such family lore by his father Jesse, who the son said "took a great interest in the subject [of genealogy]." When Ulysses was ten or eleven years old, Jesse Grant even traveled all the way from Ohio to Windsor, Connecticut, in a fruitless search for an entailed estate that he thought belonged to the family.[101]

In searching the records of the Connecticut State Library and the National Archives, William McFeely found no documentation whatsoever of Noah Grant's service during the Revolution. It is doubtful that Ulysses S. Grant ever questioned the story. Nor did he know of a humiliating episode in his grandfather's biography.[102]

Noah Grant's name appears in the town records of Coventry, Connecticut, for the same disgrace that befell many Americans in the new republic, including the father of Robert E. Lee. He had imagined that independence would somehow initiate a wave of settlement that would bring prosperity to those who anticipated the westward movement correctly. He speculated on land purchases, albeit on a lesser scale than did "Light-Horse Harry" Lee, but just as foolishly. Noah Grant lost so much money in the process that in 1788 he was thrown into debtors' prison ("commit[ed] unto the keeper of the gaol" of Coventry) until he paid a debt of 53 pounds. Later in the same year, he sold his farm for 400 pounds. By 1790, Noah had sold ten additional tracts of land for 900 pounds. He soon moved west, first to Pennsylvania and then to Ohio.[103]

There is no indication that Ulysses S. Grant knew of Noah's bankruptcy. If he did, the Connecticut scandal apparently never troubled him, as Robert E. Lee was tormented by the disgrace of "Light-Horse Harry's" imprisonment as a debtor. Noah Grant deftly picked up the pieces and started over in the West. (This course apparently never occurred to so established a scion of Old Virginia as Harry Lee. Admittedly, a million Virginians emigrated in the antebellum era, largely for economic reasons, but the direct descendants of the oldest families did their best to stay within the social safety of hallowed ground.)

Noah Grant began a new life in Pennsylvania. In 1792 he married Rachel Kelly, with whom he had seven children; in 1799 they moved to Ohio. The oldest of these children was Jesse Root Grant (fig. 68), Ulysses's father. Of Noah's children from his first marriage, the oldest son, Solomon, emigrated to the West Indies; the younger son accompanied Noah on the move west. Peter Grant eventually settled in Maysville, Kentucky, and became the father of nine children. Ulysses noted that he "was very prosperous" and died "one of the wealthy men of the West." In fact, Peter's wealth would soon rescue several of his half-brothers and sisters, and even his father, from poverty.[104]

In Ohio, Noah Grant settled first in East Liverpool. In 1804 he moved the family to Deerfield. The next year Rachel Grant died, leaving too many children for their father to raise on his own. Noah retreated with two of the children to the refuge offered by Peter Grant. Ulysses was charitable in his explanation: "Captain

fig. 68.
James W. Watts, after Landy, *Jesse and Hannah Grant*, c. 1850, engraving, 11 × 8½ in. (27.9 × 21.6 cm.), New-York Historical Society Library

Noah Grant was not thrifty in the way of 'laying up stores on earth,' and, after the death of his second wife, he went, with the two youngest children, to live with his son Peter" in Kentucky. More potentially distresssing was the dispersal of Rachel's other five children to "homes in the neighborhood." Jesse, at age eleven, was fortunate to be placed with a distinguished family, that of Judge George Tod, a member of the Ohio Supreme Court. The Tods lived in Youngstown.

Always the typical Yankee, Jesse Grant made the best of his situation. His foster home was apparently a good one. Ulysses said that Jesse spoke with "reverance" about Judge Tod, and his lifelong love of politics was no doubt born at the Tods. After "only a few years," however, when he was "old enough to learn a trade," Jesse left Youngstown to join the core of his family in Kentucky. Peter Grant owned a tannery. From this half-brother, Jesse Grant learned both the trade of tanning leather and how to administer a leather-goods business.[105]

"In a few [more] years," Ulysses recounts, Jesse returned to Deerfield to work and live with a local tanner, Owen Brown. This was the father of John Brown, the future abolitionist, who would later be taken into custody by Robert E. Lee at Harpers Ferry. Jesse's opposition to slavery was inevitably shaped during his tenure with the Brown family. Also, Jesse, not unlike John Brown, would become a parent inclined to impose his opinions on his children. Of John Brown Ulysses wrote:

> Brown was a boy when they lived in the same house, but [my father] knew him afterwards, and regarded him as a man of great purity of character, of high moral and physical courage, but a fanatic and extremist in whatever he advocated. It was certainly the act of an insane man to attempt the invasion of the South, and the overthrow of slavery, with less than twenty men.

While Jesse Grant mastered the trade of tanning, he also learned, largely on his own, how to read and write. He had been afforded little opportunity in his youth for formal education. Ulysses applauded his father's accomplishment of self-education:

> During the minority of my father, the West afforded but poor facilities for the most opulent of the youth to acquire an education, and the majority were dependent almost exclusively upon their own exertions for whatever learning they obtained …. But his thirst for education was intense.

> He learned rapidly, and was a constant reader up to the day of his death—in his eightieth year. Books were scarce in the Western Reserve during his youth, but he read every book he could borrow in the neighborhood where he lived. This scarcity gave him the early habit of studying everything he read, so that when he got through with a book, he knew everything in it. The habit continued through life. Even after reading the daily papers—which he never neglected—he could give all the important information they contained.

Ulysses would follow his father's example. In Ohio and later in the West Point library he studied books just as voraciously, turning to subjects beyond—often instead of—what he was assigned in class, and remembering much of what he read.[106]

Politics proved to be the outlet for Jesse Grant's intellectual energies:

> Before [my father] was twenty years of age [he] was a constant contributor to Western newspapers …. He always took an active part in politics, but was never a candidate for office, except, I believe, that he was the first Mayor of Georgetown. He supported Jackson for the Presidency; but he was

fig. 69.
Grant's Birthplace, Point Pleasant, Ohio,
lithograph, Library of Congress

a Whig, a great admirer of Henry Clay, and never voted for any other democrat for high office after Jackson.

While Ulysses S. Grant did not seek political office after the Civil War, his father's love of politics may have made his eventual decision to run less difficult.[107]

After he learned all that he could about the leather-goods business from Owen Brown, Jesse Grant set up his own tannery in nearby Ravenna. Before long he tried again, farther down the Ohio River at Point Pleasant. In the first twenty-seven years of his life, Jesse Grant had relocated six times. In 1821 he married Hannah Simpson and built the simple house at Point Pleasant that would become famous as the birthplace of Ulysses S. Grant. In a celebratory print (fig. 69), giant trees surround the idyllic homestead, and a view of the Ohio River makes the scene picturesque. A small, simple house is a castle for its industrious inhabitant. The current occupant of the Grant property (the Grants lived there for only two years) is shown to be an industrious, capable farmer. This lithograph, like those of Lincoln's birthplace, sent the clear message that in the American democracy anyone, even a president, can rise from the humblest origins.[108]

Little is known about Hannah Simpson Grant. No stories about her are offered in the *Memoirs*, nor is any mention made of either Hannah's mother or her stepmother Sarah, whom Ulysses was said to have admired. He tried to mask the omissions by providing a bit of genealogy. But this had to be brief because his mother's "family took no interest" in the subject. Hannah's father, John Simpson, who died when Ulysses was sixteen, "knew only back to his grandfather." We learn only that the family had lived in the eastern part of Pennsylvania, in Montgomery, "for several generations."[109]

In 1819, John Simpson had moved his wife and children to Clermont County in the Ohio Valley, presumably to acquire tracts of land that he and his son could profitably farm. They accumulated six hundred acres. John maintained contact with his kin in Pennsylvania and tried to duplicate the style of life that he had known there in Berks County. He and his wife were pious and lettered. It would be John Simpson's second wife, Sarah, however, who suggested the name Ulysses after reading about the ancient character in a translation (presumably) of Fénelon's *Télémaque*. It proved to be an appropriate name for a man who would take great joy in travel throughout his life.[110]

Hannah Simpson was the third of John's four children; she was more than twenty years of age when the family relocated. Her older sister and older brother both outlived Ulysses S. Grant, who took great interest in his *Memoirs* in recounting how the children of his aunt and uncle, who all remained in Clermont County, would be divided on the secession issue. Half of Grant's cousins "thought the country ruined beyond recovery when the Democratic party lost control in 1860." The rest of the cousins supported the government and believed "that national success by the Democratic party means irretrievable ruin."[111]

Perhaps the strangest fact about Hannah Simpson Grant is that she never visited her famous son at the White House during the eight years when he was president. It was not because she did not travel; she made a long journey to New York City during the same years. A reporter from Cincinnati once visited her home seeking an interview with the mother of the president. He received no response to his questions: "Not by a word or an expression … did she show that she even heard me." Ulysses S. Grant did take his children to visit "Grandma," which suggests that he held no ill feelings toward his mother. She was an exceptionally pious Methodist, and the tenets of her faith may explain her stoic nature. Jesse Grant tried to defend her abnormally quiet behavior, which complemented his talkative nature, by stating that she is "a plain, unpretending country girl." Ulysses would say nothing on the subject, although he did once tell a friend that he never saw his mother cry. One observer said that Hannah "thought nothing you could do would entitle you to praise." Whether Hannah Grant's deeply laconic nature hid a serious problem that troubled her son remains a mystery.[112]

A year after Hannah Simpson was married, Hiram Ulysses Grant was born. (His name would be changed to Ulysses Simpson Grant when he was enrolled at West Point.) The next year, 1823, when their child was only eighteen months old, Jesse Grant moved the family again, this time to Georgetown, Ohio, the county seat of Brown County. The change may have been to bring the business closer to supplies of tanning bark that were needed for the process of curing leather, or simply to allow another new start. Georgetown would remain Ulysses's home until he left to attend West Point at age seventeen.

Across the street from his new business, Jesse Grant built a small brick house that was a kitchen with a bedroom above. Five years later, when Ulysses was six, the business was sufficiently successful for his father to expand the house by adding a wing that was larger than the core. The wing contained a parlor and passage, with two rooms above. The residence had been made respectable; Ulysses later wrote that from his earliest recollections his father was "in comfortable circumstances." The extra space was needed: a brother, Samuel Simpson (known as Simpson), was born in 1825, followed by sisters Clara Rachel and Virginia Paine (called Jennie) in 1828 and 1832. A second brother, Orvil Lynch, was born in 1835, followed by sister Mary Frances in 1839. The brothers would in time assist their father in running the tanning business. Simpson would die of consumption during the Civil War, as would Clara Rachel. Jennie would become highly eligible when her oldest brother became famous. Shortly after Grant's first presidential inaugural, she married Abel Rathbone Corbin, who was seemingly a good catch, but who was soon implicated in a scheme to corner the gold market by means of insider information. In 1857, Orvil married a local woman, Mary Medary. He remained in the leather and saddlery business, moving to Chicago and then East Orange, New Jersey. Mary Frances married Michael John Cramer, who became a Methodist pastor in Cincinnati and after the war served in the diplomatic corps in Germany, Denmark, and Switzerland, where he had been born. Later in his life he taught theology at several colleges.[113]

Unlike his younger brothers, Ulysses could not tolerate the sights, sounds, and odors of the slaughtered animals whose hides were cured in lye and tannic acid. He wrote, "I detested the trade, preferring almost any other labor; but I was fond of agriculture, and of all employment in which horses were used." Ulysses was often excused from duty at the tannery because he could work effectively in the fields. His father owned, "among other lands, fifty acres of forest within a mile of the village." Each fall, woodcutters were employed to fell sufficient timber to last a year. When Grant was "seven or eight years of age" he "began hauling all the wood used in the house and shops." He was too small to load the wood on the wagons, "but I could drive, and the choppers would load, and some one at the house unload." By the time he was eleven, Ulysses was able to hold a plow. He recalled, "From that age until seventeen I did all the work done with horses, such as breaking up the land, furrowing, ploughing corn and potatoes, bringing in the crops when harvested, hauling all the wood, besides tending two or three horses, a cow or two, and sawing wood for stoves, etc …." With that experience, it is little wonder that in 1854 Grant would feel confident to quit a stalled army career to take up farming, and that as president, he dreamed of retiring to a farm.[114]

Although he worked many hours per day on the farm, Ulysses was "still attending school." Jesse Grant made certain that his boys were given a formal education. Ulysses wrote proudly in his *Memoirs*,

> Mindful of his own lack of facilities for acquiring an education, his greatest desire in maturer years was for the education of his children. Consequently … I never missed a quarter from school from the time I was old enough to attend till the time of leaving home.

Grant first attended "the subscription schools" of Georgetown. Those were practically at his doorstep in the village. In 1836–37, when he was fourteen, he returned to Maysville, Kentucky, to attend a better school, the Richeon and Rand Academy. He boarded there with the Peter Grant family. In 1838–39, Jesse tried a different school for his son, this one in Ripley, Ohio. Ulysses reflected that he "was not studious in habit, and probably did not make progress enough to compensate for the outlay for board and tuition." Among the problems were the teachers, the lack of structure, and the weakness of the curriculum. The Maysville and Ripley schools were both inadequate; Grant called them "very indifferent." They taught "the same old arithmetic which I knew every word of before," and that "a noun is the name of a thing." ("I had also heard my Georgetown teachers repeat [that statement] until I had come to believe it.") In the schools he attended, the teacher was "often a man or woman incapable of teaching much even if they imparted all they knew." A single teacher "would have thirty or forty scholars, male and female, from the infant learning the A B C's up to the young lady of eighteen and the boy of twenty, studying the highest branches taught—the three R's, 'Reading, 'Riting, 'Rithmetic." Ulysses complained that he never saw any mathematics higher than arithmetic until he was at West Point. He had bought a book on algebra in Cincinnati but could make no sense of it without a teacher ("it was Greek to me").[115]

Primarily for his diligence as both a worker and a student, Ulysses was rewarded by his father with respect and with as much freedom of movement as his spare time would allow.

> I was compensated by the fact that there was never any scolding or punishing by my parents; no objection to rational enjoyments, such as fishing, going to the creek a mile away to swim in summer, taking a horse and visiting my [Simpson] grandparents in the adjoining county, fifteen miles off, skating on the ice in winter, or taking a horse and sleigh when there was snow on the ground.

Grant made good use of these years to develop both his intellect and his agricultural skills. And even as a child, he loved to travel. While "still quite young" he visited Cincinnati, forty-five miles away, "several times, alone." He went to Maysville, Kentucky, "often," and once to Louisville (what he called "a big [journey] for a boy of that day"). He also went once to Chilicothe, about seventy miles distant. His love for horses and his remarkable competence with them made such long trips relatively easy for him.[116]

Grant proudly tells a story in the *Memoirs* about one of those trips, to Flat Rock, Kentucky, which was also seventy miles away. He traded a family horse ("I was allowed to do as I pleased with horses") for "a very fine saddle horse, which I rather coveted." He had to put the saddle horse under harness because he had traveled in a wagon. When the horse became frightened, Ulysses blindfolded him with his bandanna. Only a child and far from home, he had used his knowledge and his practical skill to solve the problem on his own.[117]

Unlike his father who killed horses for their hides, Ulysses S. Grant came to appreciate them as individuals with different personalities. If he could understand them, he could generally persuade them to work with him in harmony as he performed his chores. He also enjoyed their companionship, although this is not to suggest that Grant did not readily make friends. On the contrary, he recounts in his *Memoirs* how when he was released on furlough from West Point, he eagerly returned to Ohio to renew contact with his childhood classmates. He simply had a knack with horses, and his good horsemanship facilitated his travel to those reunions. It would also provide one of only a few opportunities for cadet Grant to excel at West Point.[118]

The Reluctant Cadet

Ulysses S. Grant did not want to attend West Point (fig. 70). The thought of doing so had apparently never crossed his mind. The military held no interest for him. He went so far as to oppose the idea of the academy when his father told him that it had been arranged. Jesse Grant had recognized that unlike his brothers, Ulysses was not disposed to work in the tannery. Another career would have to be chosen. As with Robert E. Lee fifteen years earlier, the choices were few. West Point was free, and it guaranteed for its graduates a secure career.

In 1839, Jesse Grant contacted his congressman, Thomas L. Hamer of Ohio, requesting a military appointment for his son. "Ulysses, I believe you are going to receive the appointment," his father told him. "What appointment?" Ulysses inquired, adding, "I won't go." "He said he thought I would, *and I thought so too, if he did*." Congressman Hamer did not remember the boy's first name, only the family name of Ulysses's mother, Simpson. Thus when Hiram Ulysses Grant arrived at West Point, he found that the congressman had renamed him, forever, Ulysses S. Grant.[119]

fig. 70.
George Catlin, *View of West Point (Looking South Across the Plain)*, 1827, oil on canvas, 15 × 25 in. (38.1 × 63.5 cm.), West Point Museum Art Collection, United States Military Academy, West Point, New York

Ulysses explained later in his *Memoirs* that he "really had no objection to going to West Point"; he was only afraid that he might not meet the requirements there for graduation. Whatever they were, "I did not believe I possessed them, and could not bear the idea of failing." The appointment that he received had become available because Bartlett Bailey, who had lived in the house next door in Georgetown, had flunked out. Following the initial shock, admittance to West Point appealed to Ulysses for the opportunities it offered for travel. He could see "the two great cities of the continent," Philadelphia and New York. "This was enough." The trip to the East proved to be an adventure. Grant rode on the first railroad train he had ever seen. He stopped five days in Philadelphia, "saw about every street in the city," attended the theater, and marveled at the grandest example of Greek Revival architecture then under construction in the nation, Girard College. He saw New York City "very well too." Grant arrived at West Point in 1839, at age seventeen but looking even younger. He weighed only 117 pounds and stood but five feet one inch tall. James Longstreet, a friend and later a Confederate general, described his classmate as "delicate" and thus unable to excel at any sport except riding. He did not look the part of the ideal soldier. Nor did he try to act it.[120]

Ulysses S. Grant passed the entrance exam "without difficulty," as he put it, "very much to my surprise." He wrote famously in the *Memoirs* of his disinterest in the military from the day he arrived at the academy: "A military life had no charms for me, and I had not the faintest idea of staying in the army even if I should be graduated, which I did not expect." Grant found the experience of a summer orientation encampment "very wearisome and uninteresting." It made him feel as if he had been at West Point "always," and that if he stayed to graduation, he "would have to remain always." His comments suggest a mind that was capable of deep interest in a subject, but that found many pursuits that did not

LEE AND GRANT

grab his immediate attention to be boring. As would become clear later, when Grant chose to focus on a matter at hand, he had no trouble maintaining his interest or his intellectual energy.[121]

The start of classes at West Point brought little change in his attitude. Grant wrote: "I did not take hold of my studies with avidity, in fact I rarely ever read over a lesson the second time during my entire cadetship," so bored was he with the curriculum. But he tried to make the most of the situation, and he put forward a positive public face. This ability would later inspire his colleagues to say that Grant could remain unruffled in any situation. In a letter that fall to a cousin, McKinstry Griffith, Ulysses first honed in on the importance of the site chosen for West Point. He then joked about his appearance as a cadet and worried about a demerit system that might undermine any chance he had for a very successful tenure at the academy:

Dear Coz.

So far as it regards natural attractions [West Point] is decidedly the most beautiful place that I have ever seen; here are hills and dales, rocks and river; all pleasant to look upon …. I can see Fort Putnan frowning far above; a stern monument of a sterner age which seems placed there on purpose to tell us of the glorious deeds of our fathers and to bid us remember their sufferings—to follow their examples. In short this is the best of all places—the *place* of all *places* for an institution like this. I have not told you *half* its attractions. here is the house Washington used to live in—there Kosisuseko [Thadeusz Kosciuszko] used to walk and think of *his* country and of *ours*. Over the river we are shown the dueling house of [Benedict] Arnold, that *base* and *heartless* traiter *to* his country and his God. I do love the *place* …. I study hard and hope to get along so as to pass the examination in January. this examination is a hard one they say, but I am not frightened yet …. On the whole I like the place very much, so much that I would not go away on any account. The fact is if a man graduates here he safe fer life …. I wish some of the pretty girles of Bethel were here just so I might look at them. but fudge! Confound the girles. I have seen great men plenty of them. Let us see. Gen Scott. M. Van Buren. Sec. of War and Navy. Washington Irving and lots of other big bugs …. My pants sit as tight to my skin as the bark to a tree …. my coat must always be buttoned up tight to the chin. it is made of sheeps grey cloth all covered with big round buttens. it makes me look very singulir. If you were to see me at a distance, the first question you would ask would be, "is that a Fish or an animal"?

I came near forgetting to tell you about our demerit or "black marks." They give a man one of these "black marks"

for almost nothing and if he gets 200 a year they dismiss him. The demerit system was a distraction, at least to Grant's thinking, and he simply would not take it very seriously. This letter also points out Grant's sense of the United States as "our" country, his opinion of traitors, and notes that he had seen Gen. Winfield Scott, whom he ranks first among the "big bugs."[122]

To satisfy his intellectual curiosity, Grant turned to the West Point library, reading contemporary novels, "but not those of a trashy sort." Among those he perused were "all of Bulwer's then published, Cooper's, Maryat's, Scott's, Washington Irving's works, Lever's." He often gave more time to the novels than to his textbooks, and so West Point failed to kindle the military acumen that Grant possessed. What little instruction was given in the theory of war did not interest him. When he wrote his *Memoirs*, he joked about the mismatch: "I never succeeded in getting squarely at either end of my class, in any one study, during the four years."[123]

Despite a lack of enthusiasm for life at West Point, Grant placed a respectable tenth in a class of fifty-three at the end of his second year. Twenty-four cadets had already dropped out. In math— "mathematics was very easy to me"— Grant did well, but he did poorly in French. By his own admission, he also came closer to the bottom than to the top in conduct, compiling a number of demerits (fig. 71), nor did he excel at artillery, infantry, or cavalry tactics. He did do well in art (figs. 72 and 73) and, not surprisingly, in horsemanship. Cadets were instructed in drawing by an accomplished painter, Robert W. Weir (see fig. 101 below), who in 1837 had won a commission to paint one of the large murals in the U.S. Capitol. The purpose of art instruction was to enable the future officers to record a landscape or sketch a proposed fort, dam, or foundation. Nine cadet paintings by Grant survive.[124]

At the end of two years, cadets were awarded a summer furlough, which Grant spent largely on horseback as he rode to visit former schoolmates in Ohio. He traveled back and forth from his

fig. 71.
Record of Demerits, West Point, 1843,
West Point Library, United States Military
Academy, West Point, New York

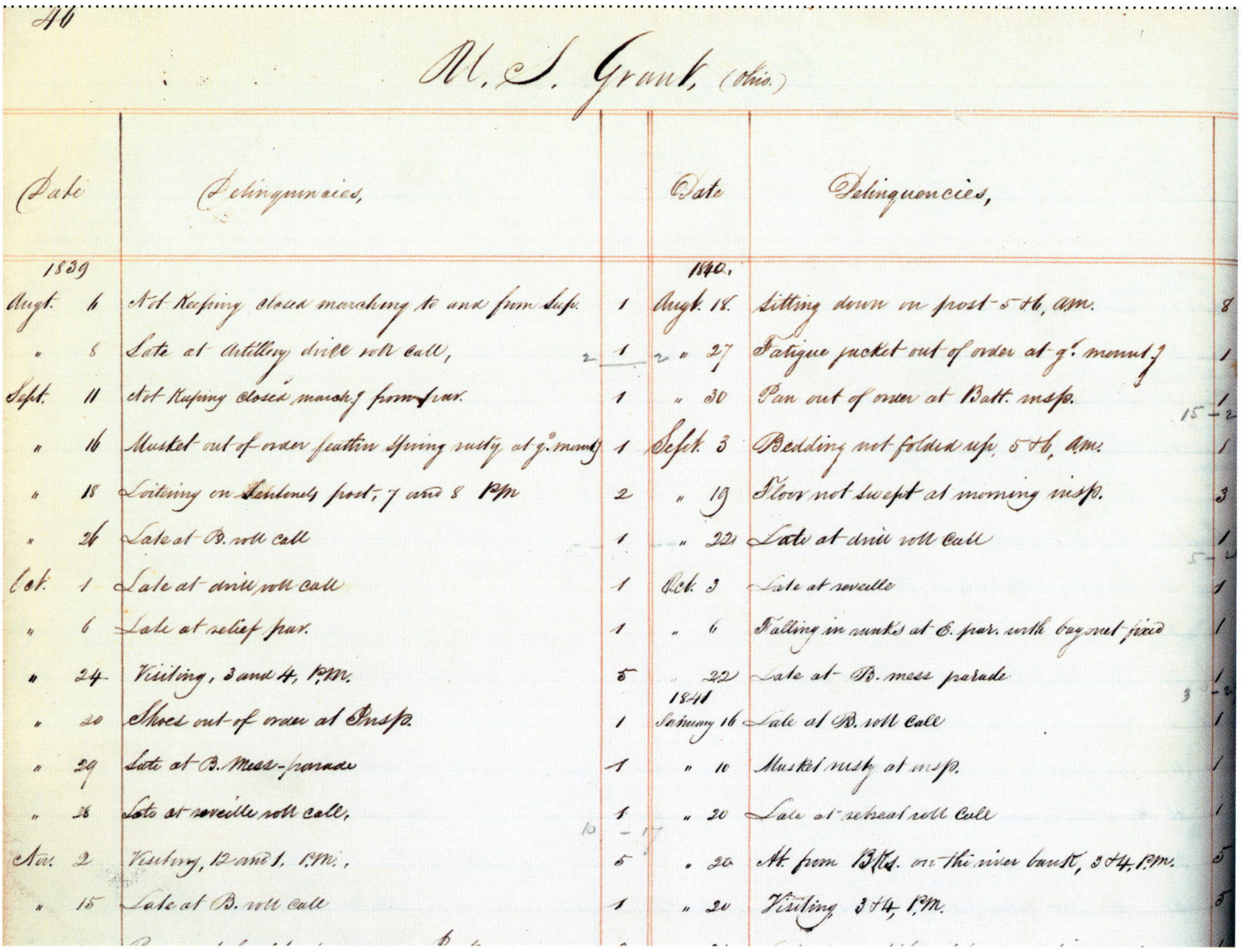
46

U. S. Grant, (Ohio.)

Date		Delinquencies		Date		Delinquencies	
1839				1840.			
Augt.	6	Not keeping closed marching to and from sup.	1	Augt.	18	Sitting down on post 5+6, a.m.	8
"	8	Late at Artillery drill roll call,	1	"	27	Fatigue jacket out of order at g. mount	1
Sept.	11	Not keeping closed march from par.	1	"	30	Pan out of order at Batt. insp.	1
"	16	Musket out of order feather spring rusty at g. mount	1	Sept.	3	Bedding not folded up, 5+6, a.m.	1
"	18	Loitering on Sentinels post, 7 and 8 P.M.	2	"	19	Floor not swept at morning insp.	3
"	26	Late at B. roll call	1	"	22	Late at drill roll call	1
Oct.	1	Late at drill roll call	1	Oct.	3	Late at reveille	1
"	6	Late at relief par.	1	"	6	Falling in ranks at G. par. with bayonet fixed	1
"	24	Visiting, 3 and 4, P.M.	5	"	22	Late at B. mess parade	1
"	20	Shoes out of order at Insp.	1	1841 January	16	Late at B. roll call	1
"	29	Late at B. Mess-parade	1	"	10	Musket rusty at insp.	1
"	28	Late at reveille roll call,	1	"	20	Late at retreat roll call	1
Nov.	2	Visiting, 12 and 1, P.M.	5	"	20	Ab. from B'ks. on the river bank, 3+4, P.M.	5
"	15	Late at B. roll call	1	"	20	Visiting 3+4, P.M.	5

father's new home in Bethel, which was twelve miles from Georgetown. "This I enjoyed beyond any other period of my life," he later recalled. Jesse Grant "had bought a young horse that had never been in harness, for my special use."[125]

On his return to West Point, Ulysses was appointed one of eighteen sergeants of the cadet corps. However, "the promotion was too much for me," Grant wrote. Demerits accumulated; these were a component of a cadet's grade. His standing in his class dropped, and in turn he was reduced in rank. He served his last year at the academy as a private. Grant's final class standing was twenty-first out of thirty-nine cadets. His senior year roommate, Frederick Tracy Dent, finished thirty-third. Four years earlier, seventy-seven cadets had enrolled. Grant had survived where a number of other young men had failed.[126]

Perhaps because he worried so little about military exercises and martial discipline, the last two years at West Point were happier for Grant than were the first two. He set the academy standard for the high-jump on horseback, a record that would last for twenty-five years. At commencement he was able to display his skill. In ceremonies in the academy riding hall, his instructor raised the bar above his head and announced, "Cadet Grant!"—"Man and beast." They cleared the height as if "welded together" noted one observer. It is understandable that so remarkable a horseman might expect that his skills would gain him entrance into the cavalry, his first choice of assignment. But only one regiment of cavalry existed in the U.S. Army in 1843, it had a full complement of officers. Grant's standing in his class was low. He was placed instead in the infantry.[127]

Grant made a few lasting friendships at West Point. Two of the best, ironically, were with future Confederate generals, James Longstreet and Simon Bolivar Buckner. Some of the more famous figures whose careers overlapped his at the academy, William Tecumseh Sherman, George H. Thomas, George B. McClellan, and Thomas J.

fig. 72.
Ulysses S. Grant, *Indians Bartering*, c. 1843–44, watercolor on paper, 10½ × 14½ in. (26.7 × 36.8 cm.), West Point Museum Art Collection, United States Military Academy, West Point, New York

fig. 73.
Ulysses S. Grant, *Landscape*, c. 1843–44, watercolor on paper, 10⅝ × 17⅜ in. (26.9 × 43.4 cm.), Gilder Lehrman Collection, Gilder Lehrman Institute of American History

"Stonewall" Jackson, barely knew him. Grant, however, had a remarkable memory, and so it is not surprising that he recalled them better than they remembered so unpretentious and diminutive a cadet.[128]

On his return to Ohio after graduation, Ulysses S. Grant was proud of his accomplishment (fig. 74). "I was impatient to get on my uniform and see how it looked, and probably wanted my old school-mates, particularly the girls, to see me in it." Two incidents, however, soon gave him "a distaste for military uniform that I never recovered from." A barefooted urchin in Cincinnati jeered at the young lieutenant, while a stableman in Bethel mimicked his dress. At the end of his life, Grant could laugh about these incidents; however, from that moment on and throughout his career, including during the famous surrender ceremony at Appomattox where much was made later about his simple and soiled attire, Grant often dressed modestly, paying little attention to the finery available to someone of his rank.[129]

Grant thought that he would stay in the army for only the four years of duty to which he was committed. He had persevered at West Point with the dream that he might teach mathematics at the academy as an assistant professor and afterwards obtain a similar, "permanent" teaching position "in some respectable college." But, he added, "circumstances always did shape my course different from my plans." A war and a wife would soon intervene.[130]

Infantry Service in Missouri, Louisiana, and Texas

Lieutenant Ulysses S. Grant was assigned to the Fourth Infantry Regiment, which was stationed outside of St. Louis at Jefferson Barracks. It was the largest military post in the nation at the time, home to sixteen companies of infantry. In command was Col. Stephen Kearney, who soon won Grant's respect. "Discipline was kept at a high standard, but without vexatious rules or regulations," Grant wrote. He would remember Kearney's approach in later years. Assignment to Jefferson Barracks especially appealed to Grant because the family of Fred Dent lived only five miles away. Fred was stationed elsewhere, but his four brothers, three sisters, and parents were there to welcome Ulysses. Just as Robert E. Lee had been able to retreat from his first assignment at Cockspur Island to the family of classmate Jack Mackay in Savannah, so Grant "soon found [his] way out to White Haven, the name of the Dent estate" (fig. 75). He thought the family "congenial" and

fig. 74.
A. H. Ritchie, *Lieutenant Grant, Age 21* [1843], 1885, engraving based on a daguerreotype and published in Grant's *Memoirs*

his visits "became frequent." When the older daughter returned home from boarding school, the visits became even more pleasant. "We would often take walks, or go on horseback to visit the neighbors, until I became quite well acquainted in that vicinity," Ulysses wrote. He and Julia Dent (fig. 76) fell in love and would marry four years later. Julia's mother apparently saw something in the young lieutenant that most did not. She approved of the pairing because she approved of the suitor: "That young man will be heard from some day." She added, "He has a good deal in him. He'll make his mark."[131]

Early in his life, Julia's father Frederick Dent (fig. 77) had worked as a merchant in Pittsburgh. There he had married Ellen Bray Wrenshall, whose father was also a merchant. In 1816, Frederick and Ellen moved to St. Louis, where he continued in business for another ten years until his profits allowed him to purchase both the thousand-acre farm that he named White Haven and enough slaves to work it. Ensconced on his plantation, Frederick Dent became "Colonel Dent" and, according to his daughter, then "passed the time … sitting in an easy chair reading an interesting book."[132]

Frederick Dent had been enterprising; he was an admirable product of the new American democracy. To Julia Dent's thinking, however, a merchant was not an aristocrat. In her memoirs, she twisted the truth, saying that her family had emigrated to Missouri from Cumberland, Maryland. She implied that her father alone had made the long trip, bringing slaves with him to transplant a southern plantation into the West.[133] Julia said that her parents loved the "repose of a country life." She remembered her childhood at White Haven as taking place at the Edenic plantation of proslavery apologists. According to her account, "Most of our colored people were from Virginia and Maryland," and they were "very happy." The war changed that: "the young ones became somewhat demoralized about the beginning of the Rebellion, when all the comforts of slavery passed away forever." Julia later looked back to a world made up largely of her own fantasies:

> … my time and sister Nellie's was passed mostly out-of-doors. I had my nurse, dear old black Kitty, and Nell had Rose, a pretty mulatto. Besides, we always had a dusky train of from eight to ten little colored girls of all hues, and these little colored girls were allowed to accompany us if they were very near.[134]

Eighteen slaves made up the work force at White Haven. "Colonel" Dent has been well described by one Grant biographer as a splendidly lazy old codger. There is no evidence that Ellen Dent, the matriarch of the family, was bothered by the holding of slaves. Julia liked to believe that her father "was the kindest of masters to his slaves, who all adored him." Her greatest concern in recounting her youth was that the readers of her memoirs be convinced of her family's wealth and social status.[135]

Julia also pointed to family pedigree. In recounting her genealogy, she sounds more like Robert E. Lee than her own unpretentious husband:

> My parents were both of English descent. My father's people came to this country in 1643, three brothers settling in Maryland …. My grandfather, George Dent … was

LEE AND GRANT 117

fig. 75.
White Haven, near St. Louis (photograph courtesy of National Park Service, White Haven)

a resident of Bladensburg. After his marriage with Susanna Marbury, he lived in Cumberland, Maryland. Miss Marbury was also of English descent. Papa always said she was a great beauty, and, by the way, I have a very pretty sketch of Marbury Hall, Cheshire, England, the homestead of the ancestors of grandmamma ….

My mother, Ellen Bray Wrenshall, was English-born and came to America when she was quite a little girl. Grandpa Wrenshall came to this country as a merchant and belonged to the firm of Wrenshall, Peacock, and Pilton. Mamma told me that they had their own ships and exported to China ….

As the first daughter behind four older brothers, Julia Dent was the delight of her father. "I was necessarily something of a pet," she confessed. She enjoyed a childhood of freedom to do whatever she pleased. The one requirement was that she attend school, where she rejected mathematics, the subject that was her future husband's joy. Free of that burden, she could honestly claim that "[her] school days [were] only pleasant memories." Like Ulysses, Julia developed a love of outdoor activities. She too was petite in appearance yet remarkably athletic. She admired and consequently pursued her brothers' sporting interests, including fishing, hunting, and horseback riding. Biographers have judged that Julia Dent was not beautiful. She was only five feet tall, and she suffered from strabismus which made her right eye look upward involuntarily. This accounts for the many photographs of her that are taken from the side. All seem to agree, however, that in general she was a good human being, that she was full of spirit, and that she became the most devoted of wives.[136]

In May 1844, Grant's regiment was transferred to Louisiana. Grant was on leave at the time, visiting family in Ohio. On his return to St. Louis, he reported to Lt. Richard Ewell, then in command at Jefferson Barracks, who gave Grant a few more days to settle his affairs. "This was the same Ewell who acquired considerable reputation as a Confederate general during the rebellion," Grant later wrote in his *Memoirs*. "He was a man much esteemed, and deservedly so."[137]

The crisis that sent U.S. Army troops to the South was the potential annexation of Texas, at this time a "subject of violent discussion in Congress, in the press, and by individuals," Grant recounted. "The administration of President [John] Tyler, then in

118   II. YOUTH AND EARLY MILITARY CAREERS

fig. 76.
Henry Bryan Hall, *Julia Dent Grant*, 1860s, engraving, 7 × 6 in. (17.8 × 15.2 cm.), New-York Historical Society Library

fig. 77.
Pach Brothers, *Colonel Frederick Dent*, detail from *General Grant and Friends*, 1872 (photograph courtesy of New-York Historical Society Library)

power, was making the most strenuous efforts to affect the annexation." A rifle regiment was already stationed at Fort Jessup, Louisiana, twenty-five miles east of the Texas border, "to observe the frontier." Grant's regiment plus another were sent to the vicinity "to await further orders" (fig. 78).[138]

The instability in Texas and the ensuing war with Mexico separated Ulysses and Julia and postponed their marriage for four long years. They would see each other only once during this interval, when Grant took a leave of absence to obtain parental consent for the wedding. Except for his tour of duty on the Pacific coast in the 1850s, Ulysses and Julia would not allow themselves to be separated again for any lengthy period, even during the years of the Civil War.[139]

Many of Grant's letters to Julia Dent from Louisiana, Texas, and Mexico, survive. Ulysses agonized during these years of separation. He looked for Julia's letters daily and thought often about her, even as he carried out his duties. In her absence he was influenced by what she might think. Some of these letters resemble those written by Lee at Cockspur Island to Mary Custis:

It has been but few days since I wrote to you but I must write again. Be as punctual in writing to me Julia and then I will be compensated in a slight degree, —nothing could fully compensate—for your absence ….

P.S. I have carefully preserved the lock of hair you gave me. Recollect when you write to seal with the ring I used to wear …. (July 28, 1844)

I am very far from having forgotten our promise to think of each other at sun setting—At that time I am most always on parade and no doubt I sometimes appear very absent minded. (August 31, 1844)

… I feel as if I [have] some one els than myself to live and strive to do well for. You can have but little idea of the influence you have over me Julia, even while so far away. If I feel tempted to do any thing that I think is not right I am shure to think, "Well now if Julia saw me would I do so" and thus it is absent or present I am more or less governed by what I think is your will. (July 11, 1845)[140]

LEE AND GRANT 119

fig. 78.
Lieutenants Ulysses S. Grant and Alexander Hays at Camp Salubrity, Louisiana, 1845 (photograph courtesy of Library of Congress)

Grant considered quitting the army as the best means to end the separation. But Julia, if we can believe her memoirs, had always longed to marry a soldier. She discouraged his resignation, perhaps because her intended had taken a genuine liking to the idea of a career in the army.

> I have always expressed myself willing you know my Dear Julia to resign my appointment in the army for the sake of overcomeing the objections of your parents, and I would still do so; at the same time I think they mistake an army life very much. No set of ladies that I ever saw are better contented or more unwilling to change their condition than those of the Army ….
>
> Your Pa asks what I could do out of the Army? I can tell you: I have at this time the offer of a professorship of mathematics in a tolerably well endowed College in Hillsboro, Ohio …. (October 1845)
>
> The Army seems to be the only objection [by your father to our getting married] and really I think there can be no happier place to live. As I told you in my last letter I am at this time thinking strongly of resigning but I do not think I will ever [be] half so well contented out of the Army as in it …. I will continue to think that when my Regiment is permanent at some post where the officers have their families that you will consent to go there too (November–December 1845).
>
> You beg of me not to resign: it shall be as you say Julia for to confess the truth it was on your account that I thought of doing so, although all the letters I get from my father are filled with persuasion for me to resign. For my own part I am contented with an army life …. (January 12, 1846)[141]

When U.S. troops moved into Texas, Grant found that he actually liked the region. He appreciated the landscape and liked the climate so much that he even talked of settling there:

> … I don't know but it would be desirable to remain in Texas. It is just the kind of country Julia that we have often spoken of in our most romantic conversations. It is the place where we could gallop over the prairies and start up Deer and prairie birds and occationally see droves of wild horses or an Indian wigwam. The climate is delightful and healthy and the soil fertile ….

That said, Grant was frustrated. Halfway through this enforced separation, he wrote, "Here it is now 1846 Julia, nearly two years since we were first engaged and still a time when or about when our marriage is to be consummated has never been talked of. Don't you think it is now time we should press your father further for his concent?" Other matters, however, would press Lieutenant Grant. He would soon be in Mexico, doing whatever was asked of him and storing images of warfare in his mind that would emerge during his bloody first engagements of 1862.[142]

When the Lee family was broken apart by the bankruptcy, desertion, and death of "Light-Horse Harry" Lee, Ann Carter Lee had kept her five children together. As they were supported by their Lee and Carter relatives, the young Robert E. Lee saw that family was the most important social bond in Virginia. In 1861, Lee would base his decision about secession on the obligation that he felt to his family first, and then to his region. By contrast, Jesse Grant had moved a number of times during his life, and he had been sent to live with nonfamily members during a time of particular trouble.

Through the stories of his father, Ulysses S. Grant came to believe that while family was important, one's relations could not always be counted on for security. Thus in 1861, Ulysses was little troubled by the divided opinions of family members on the issue of secession. He had relatives in many states, North and South, a circumstance that encouraged his view that the Civil War was a national crisis, not a split between two independent nations.

When Grant sat down to write his *Memoirs*, the last important document that he would complete in his lifetime, neither England nor Ohio were mentioned at the opening. Instead, it was important for him to stress that "My family is American, and has been for generations, in all its branches, direct and collateral." Lee, when writing the preface to his father's *Memoirs* in the year before his death, began by mentioning his family's roots in England and his sense of himself as a Virginian. From their boyhoods, through their triumphs and tragedies, to their old age, these opposing viewpoints would continue to manifest themselves. As they looked back to the crucial decisions of their lives, it would have been clear to both Lee and Grant that the choices they had made were correct and in keeping with the legacies that had been passed down to them.[143]

III.

It is true we bullied her [Mexico]. Of that I am ashamed, as she was the weaker party.

Robert E. Lee to Mary Custis Lee, February 13, 1848

I was bitterly opposed to the measure, and to this day regard the war, which resulted, as one of the most unjust ever waged by a stronger against a weaker nation.

Ulysses S. Grant, *Memoirs*, 1885

Ulysses S. Grant saw the Mexican War as an important episode both in his own life and in the history of the nation. He devoted 140 pages and ten chapters of his *Memoirs* to a discussion of the conflict that would prove to be a training ground for a remarkable number of Civil War commanders. In this account Grant emerges as more than a soldier; there is also something of the political scientist in his comments. He shows an understanding of how governments prosecute foreign affairs, as well as a conscience that suggests how such matters might be ethically conducted. This, of course, is Grant writing after he had served two terms as president. He had seen what can happen when questionable ethics are employed for personal gain.

At the time, Texans saw their revolution as parallel to the American struggle for independence in 1776. Grant, however, perceived the political underpinnings of a conflict that would add a substantial amount of territory to the United States. Texas was initially a state belonging to the republic of Mexico. Although an empire in size, it had only a sparse population until it was settled by Americans who had received permission from the Mexican government to colonize the region. The new settlers soon outnumbered the Mexicans four to one. They planted cotton and introduced slavery almost from the start, paying no attention to a Mexican law that did not sanction the institution. Soon the Texans set up their own independent government. Their claim of independence instigated a conflict between themselves and Mexico. In the most famous engagement of this campaign, Davy Crockett, Jim Bowie, William Travis, and their companions were killed by forces led by General Antonio López de Santa Anna at the Alamo in March 1836. Six weeks later, the Texans led by Sam Houston defeated the Mexican army at the battle of San Jacinto. The Republic of Texas was recognized by the United States in 1837. The Texans soon offered their country to the United States. President John Tyler (1841–45) initiated the annexation process as he left office; it would not be completed until after the inauguration of President Polk (1845–49), and after the Mexican War.[1]

Stationed with American troops near the Texas border in Louisiana "as a menace to Mexico in case she appeared to contemplate war," Grant had plenty of time to think about the developing crisis. The young lieutenant would later comment on the un-neighborly action that his country was taking in 1845:

> For myself, I was bitterly opposed to the measure, and to this day regard the war, which resulted, as one of the most unjust ever waged by a stronger against a weaker nation. It was an instance of a republic following the bad example of European monarchies, in not considering justice in their desire to acquire additional territory ….
>
> Even if the annexation itself could be justified, the manner in which the subsequent war was forced upon Mexico cannot ….

Grant interestingly allows for the possibility of American expansion. He simply disliked the methods used to force the issue.[2]

The term "Manifest Destiny" had been coined in 1845. It suggested to many expansionists that it was inevitable that the United States would continue to grow and would ultimately engulf the entire continent. The Mexican War was a crucial early test of this idea. There was resistance to the war by those who feared that it was simply an exercise meant to extend the bounds of slavery to the West. James Russell Lowell expressed his opposition in the first of *The Biglow Papers*. At the opening of "Resistance to Civil Government," Henry David Thoreau objected to a government that could be manipulated by a few individuals so as to cause the nation to become involved in a war. He was famously jailed for refusing to pay his poll tax. Congressman Abraham Lincoln challenged President Polk to justify the conflict, to identify the spot where American blood had been shed on American soil.

Robert E. Lee, by contrast, was annoyed that some questioned the right that America had to invade its southern neighbor. While he too confessed that he was "ashamed" that the United States had "bullied … [a] weaker party," Lee was among those who viewed the war as an opportunity. He also saw combat as a chance to achieve the promotion in rank that he perpetually pursued. In

fig. 79.
Edward Anthony after Mathew Brady, *Zachary Taylor*, 1849 (photograph courtesy of New-York Historical Society Library)

fig. 80.
Fanny & Seymour Palmer, *Battle of Palo Alto [1846]*, 1848, lithograph, 12¾ × 17½ in. (32.4 × 44.4 cm.), New-York Historical Society Library, gift of Charlotte Havemeyer

June 1845, he anticipated the conflict and wrote to the army's chief of the engineers, Col. Joseph G. Totten, that he was ready and willing to go to Mexico:

> In the event of war with any foreign government I should desire to be brought into active service in the field with as high a rank in the regular army as I could obtain. If that could not be accomplished without leaving the Corps of Engineers, I should then desire a transfer ....[3]

The Mexican War can actually be said to have started as early as September 1845, when Grant's Fourth Infantry Regiment was ordered by President Polk to advance from Louisiana to Corpus Christi on the Texas coast, although this was still within the region that the Mexican government had allowed Americans to colonize. Zachary Taylor (fig. 79) had been put in command of the three thousand men there. What had been an army of observation suddenly became a potential army of occupation. "We were sent to provoke a fight," Grant wrote bluntly, "but it was essential that Mexico should commence it." Once that happened, he shrewdly added, in a comment that has resonance even to this day, there would be no turning back:

> Once initiated there were but few public men who would have the courage to oppose it. Experience proves that the man who obstructs a war in which his nation is engaged, no matter whether right or wrong, occupies no enviable place in life or history. Better for him, individually, to advocate "war, pestilence, and famine," than to act as obstructionist to a war already begun.

Corpus Christi, however, was too far removed from the Mexican heartland to arouse a response. "It became necessary for the 'invaders' to approach to within a convenient distance to be struck." The army was then moved to the Rio Grande, where the bait would be taken.[4]

On May 3, 1846, after Taylor had left the encampment for the coast, General Mariano Arista attacked one of the American outposts. "The war had begun," Grant stated. Writing with typical candor, he confessed that the sound of artillery brought him considerable unease: "What General Taylor's feelings were during this suspense I do not know; but for myself, a young second-lieutenant who had never heard a hostile gun before, I felt sorry that I had enlisted." He would be even more uncomfortable five days later when Taylor's army approached Palo Alto, eight miles north of the Rio Grande (fig. 80). "An army, certainly outnumbering our little force,

fig. 81.
Ulysses S. Grant, Head Quarters Mexican Army, to Julia Dent, *Letter*, May 11, 1846, Library of Congress

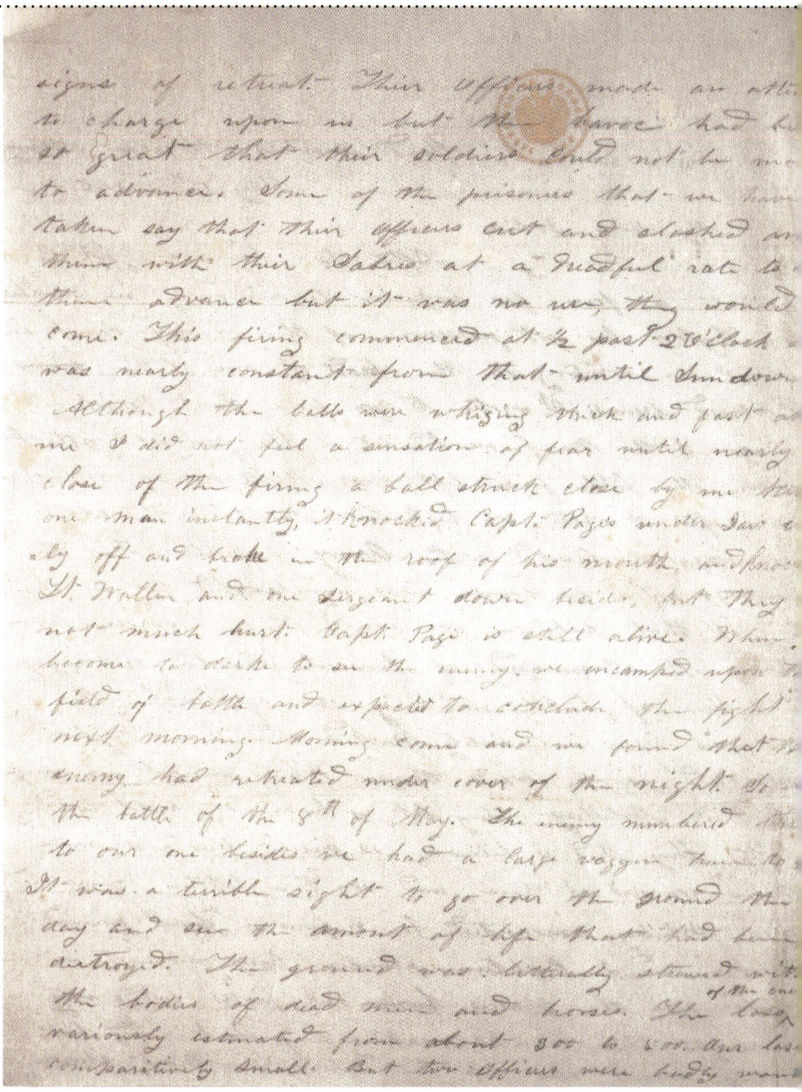
signs of retreat. Their officers made an atte
to charge upon us but the havoc had b
so great that their soldiers could not be m
to advance. Some of the prisoners that we have
taken say that their officers cut and slashed
them with their Sabres at a dreadful rate to
them advance but it was no way they would
come. This firing commenced at ½ past 2 O'clock
was nearly constant from that until Sundown
Although the balls were whizzing thick and fast a
me I did not feel a sensation of fear until nearly
close of the firing a ball struck close by me k
one man instantly, it knocked Capt. Pages under Jaw e
ly off and broke in the roof of his mouth, and knoc
Lt. Wallen and one Sergeant down besides, but they
not much hurt. Capt. Page is still alive. When
become to dark to see the enemy we encamped upon t
field of battle and expected to conclude the fight
next morning. Morning come and we found that th
enemy had retreated under cover of the night. So
the battle of the 8th of May. The enemy numbered
to our one besides we had a large waggon train to
It was a terrible sight to go over the ground the
day and see the amount of life that had been
destroyed. The ground was litterally strewed with
the bodies of dead men and horses. The loss of the ene
variously estimated from about 300 to 500. Our los
comparatively small. But two officers were badly woun

was seen …. Their bayonets and spearheads glistened in the sunlight." The Americans, however, had horse-drawn artillery, the first ever used in North America. Their twelve-pound and eighteen-pound howitzers "made a powerful armament," Grant noted. Those guns decimated the enemy before the Mexican cannons could be brought fully into range. Some cannon balls only rolled toward the American troops. Few hit their intended targets.[5]

On the following day the battle continued at Resaca de la Palma, which was closer to the Rio Grande. Though a quartermaster, Grant took the initiative to lead a charge. He characteristically downplayed the incident in his *Memoirs*:

> The ground had been charged over before. My exploit was equal to that of the soldier who boasted that he had cut off the leg of one of the enemy. When asked why he did not cut off his head, he replied: "Someone had done that before." … The battle … would have been won … if I had not been there.[6]

The fighting in Mexico would produce the highest mortality rate yet known to the American military. Of the 78,718 soldiers and sailors who served, 13,283 were killed. Grant vividly described his combat experiences. He recounted the splattering of brains and bones when a comrade was hit by cannonball, even mentioning some of the gore to Julia (fig. 81):

> After two hard fought battles against a force far superior to our own in numbers, Gen. Taylor has got possession of the Enemy's camp and now I am writing on the head of one of the captured drums ….
>
> Although the balls were whizzing thick and fast about me I did not feel a sensation of fear until nearly the close of the firing a ball struck close by me killing one man instantly, it nocked Capt. Page's under Jaw entirely off …. It was a terrible sight to go over the ground the next day and see the amount of life that had been destroyed. The ground was literally strewed with the bodies of dead men and horses ….
>
> There is no great sport in having bullets flying about one in evry direction but I find they have less horror when among them than when in anticipation.

The fact that at this stage the young lieutenant would see the anticipation of a battle as more horrible than the actual battle itself suggests that Grant had the ability to detach himself while his focus was in the moment. It would always be after the battle, once the objective was accomplished as at Shiloh, that Grant would allow himself to think about the bloodshed.[7]

Grant wrote to Julia two weeks later confident that the war would end quickly: "I think too after so sound a thrashing as our small force gave their large one, we will be able … to bring Mexico to speedy terms." Nearly five months would pass, however, before Taylor could provoke another major encounter.[8]

In August, Taylor marched his army to Monterey, the principal city in northern Mexico (fig. 82). Travel was difficult in the heat of the summer; the march took place mostly at night. "We have indeed suffered greatly but success seems now certain," Grant wrote to Julia on September 23. He added that the siege of Monterey had begun. It would ultimately fail, causing Taylor to order a series

fig. 82.
Nathaniel Currier, *Major Genl. Z. Taylor Before Monterey, Sept. 20th 1846*, 1848, lithograph, 10 × 14½ in. (25.4 × 36.8 cm.), New-York Historical Society Library, gift of Charlotte Havemeyer

of attacks that were poorly conceived. Grant suddenly found himself in the thick of the action:

> My curiosity got the better of my judgment, and I mounted a horse and rode to the front to see what was going on. I had been there but a short time when an order to charge was given, and lacking the moral courage to return to camp—where I had been ordered to stay—I charged with the regiment.

Taylor had ordered an assault on the Black Fort, which guarded the city, and in a matter of minutes one-third of his troops involved were killed or wounded. The Americans were outnumbered, about 10,000 to 6,000. "The charge was ill-conceived," Grant later concluded. The first gate could have been bypassed.

Street fighting in Monterey continued, block by block, toward the main plaza. American troops were under fire from rooftops, and in returning fire they ran low on ammunition. Grant volunteered to ride through the streets to the American line to request the needed men and supplies. Thus began a famed horseback ride under fire for which he became well known:

> My ride back was an exposed one. Before starting I adjusted myself on the side of my horse furthest from the enemy, and with only one foot holding to the cantle of the saddle, and an arm over the neck of the horse exposed, I started at full run. It was only at street crossings that my horse was under fire, but these I crossed at such a flying rate that generally I was past and under cover of the next block of houses before the enemy fired. I got out safely without a scratch.

Taylor ultimately chose not to continue his futile attack. He negotiated a settlement with his opponent, Pedro de Ampudia. The Mexican general and his men were allowed to leave Monterey with weapons and the promise of an eight-week truce.[9]

After six months, Zachary Taylor's campaign had failed to coerce Mexico to surrender the Republic of Texas. But he had done well enough for newspapers in the East to suggest that he should be the Whig candidate to lead the nation in 1848. President Polk, a Democrat, had reason to worry; he had given command to Taylor in order to keep it away from another Whig, Winfield Scott (fig. 83), who seemed to have even greater political aspirations. In May, Scott's plans for a Mexican campaign had not been approved by the administration and he had been left at home. After what was seen as a victory at Monterey, however, as Grant put it, "Something had to be done to neutralize [Taylor's] growing popularity." He could not be removed from the field when all of his engagements had been victories. "It was finally decided," Grant wrote, "to send General Scott to Mexico in chief command, and to authorize him to carry out his own original plan: that is, capture Vera Cruz and march upon the capital of the country." It was hoped by the Democrats in Washington that Scott would steal the spotlight from Taylor.[10]

Although Robert E. Lee's request in June 1845 for service in Mexico had been accepted, a year would pass before he received his orders. When they came in August 1846, this husband and father quickly made out his will (fig. 84). It would remain unchanged until his death in 1870. The will left everything to his wife and children.

Lee was concerned about how he would respond during the coming conflict, which he saw as an opportunity to match the

fig. 83.
George C. Rockwood, *Winfield Scott*, c. 1863–75 (photograph courtesy of New-York Historical Society Library)

fig. 84.
Robert E. Lee, *Last Will and Testament*, 1846, Washington and Lee University

fig. 85.
George Washington's *Mess Chest*, National Museum of American History

"fame and glory" achieved by his father. His fixation on the legacy of the American Revolution is suggested by the inclusion within his personal gear of a very special artifact. During the Mexican War, Lee had with him the mess chest that George Washington had used during the war for independence (fig. 85). It had been inherited by G. W. P. Custis and preserved at Arlington as one of the "Washington treasures." Lee would be inspired on a daily basis by the sight of Washington's knives and forks, and he was by no means modest in displaying such dazzling evidence of the extraordinary legacy that was his. More importantly, in this way Lee continuously challenged himself: "Revolutionary knives & forks were passed around the table with much veneration & excited universal attention," Lee wrote to Mary from San Antonio on Christmas Day in 1846. His pride in them was matched only by his concern about whether he would prove himself worthy of his connection to items of this significance.[11]

Captain Lee was first ordered to San Antonio to join the staff of Brigadier General John E. Wool, who served in Taylor's command. Wool would have preferred to join Taylor in confronting the principal Mexican army under General Santa Anna, but he was ordered out of the mainstream, to Chihuahua, to await further instructions. Lee was also anxious to be where the action was.

The corps of engineers had not been created for wartime service, but its officers would contribute greatly to the successful campaigns of the Mexican War. In a foreign land where maps were few, there was a genuine need for engineers who could provide geographical and topographical information about unknown territories, perform reconnaissance, evaluate enemy positions, recommend routes to be taken, and even, if necessary, lead soldiers into battle. Scouting duties would occupy much of Lee's time in northern Mexico; he would sometimes cover fifty to sixty miles a day. He traveled some 700 miles in this first campaign without ever encountering an opponent.[12]

Winfield Scott was sent to Mexico to mount a determined offensive. He was given command of some troops that had been under Taylor. Both Captain Lee and Lieutenant Grant were among them. Lee may have been recommended to Scott by Totten, who as the head of the Engineer Corps had been selected as chief engineer for the expedition. In January 1847, Lee was ordered to join Scott, who was still in the north of Mexico preparing his campaign.

Grant took full advantage of his unique opportunity to study both Taylor and Scott. He noted their styles of command and strengths as tacticians. Grant would take a particular liking to Taylor, while Lee would idolize Scott. Grant and Taylor shared the same low-key temperament, and each had spent most of his life in the West—Taylor was born in Virginia but his family emigrated to the wilds of Kentucky in the late eighteenth century when Zachary was still an infant. Lee's admiration for Scott became mutual. They were both Virginians who were proud of that heritage.

The account of Zachary Taylor in Grant's *Memoirs* is remarkable in that it could be used to describe its author. Quiet attention to the task at hand, a willingness to work under existing circumstances, calm in the face of danger, and a disdain of military ostentation, including the fineries of dress, were attitudes that would be famously adopted by Grant during the Civil War.

> General Taylor was not an officer to trouble the administration much with his demands, but was inclined to do the best he could with the means given him …. No soldier could face either danger or responsibility more calmly than he. These are qualities more rarely found than genius or physical courage.
>
> General Taylor never made any great show or parade, either of uniform or retinue. In dress he was possibly too plain, rarely wearing anything in the field to indicate his rank, or even that he was an officer; but he was known to every soldier in his army, and was respected by all.[13]

When he was transferred to Scott's campaign, Grant watched the army's general-in-chief attentively. The quick and masterful victories at Vera Cruz and Cerro Gordo were proof enough for Grant of Scott's skills. In a long career that stretched back to the War of 1812, the general had seen virtually everything that could happen in battle, and he had literally written the book on tactics. Scott's understanding of how to maneuver an army particularly impressed Grant. He pointed out that Scott's critics would be forever silenced by the general's successes: "he won every battle, he captured the capital, and conquered the government."[14]

His head-to-head comparison of the two commanders is also revealing:

> I now had been in battle with the two leading commanders conducting armies in a foreign land. The contrast between the two was very marked. General Taylor never wore a uniform, but dressed himself entirely for comfort. He moved about the field in which he was operating to see through his own eyes the situation. Often he would be without staff officers …. General Scott was the reverse in all these particulars. He always wore all the uniform prescribed or allowed by law when he inspected his lines …. His staff proper … followed, also in uniform and in prescribed order. Orders were prepared with great care and evidently with the view that they should be a history of what followed ….
>
> Taylor was not a conversationalist, but on paper he could put his meaning so plainly that there could be no mistaking it …. Taylor … gave orders to meet the emergency without reference to how they would read in history.[15]

Grant in many ways would come to resemble Taylor. Should we look to find Lee in the shadow of Scott, however, we would be disappointed. Lee was unlike either general. He had modeled himself instead on leaders from the past, his father and especially George Washington. Lee had the aloofness, gentlemanly manner, quiet intensity, and sternness of Washington. Like Taylor, he preferred to scout the terrain with his own eyes, but at the same time he learned many tactical lessons from Scott, including his manner of conducting a battle by bringing generals to the desired time and place,

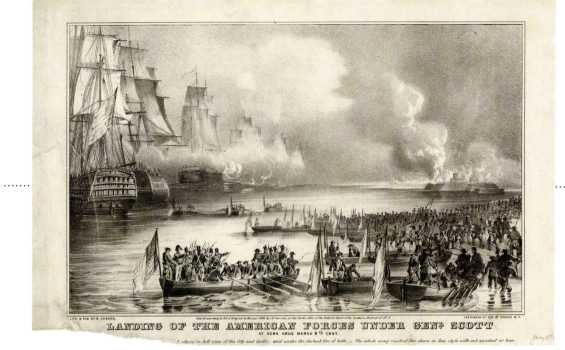

fig. 86.
Nathaniel Currier, *Landing of the American Forces under Gen. Scott at Vera Cruz, March 9th, 1847*, 1847, lithograph, 10½ × 15¾ in. (26.7 × 40.0 cm.), New-York Historical Society Library

at which point he would often leave them free to command at their own discretion. Lee also maintained a personal distance from those around him, which, while it had more to do with personality than rank, was also reminiscent of the Washington.

In February 1847, Winfield Scott sailed down the coast of Mexico to rendezvous with his invasion force and begin his campaign toward Mexico City. Lee was with him, sharing a stateroom on the ship with Joseph Johnston, the future Confederate general and his friend from Virginia and West Point. Along with Colonel Totten, the chief engineer, Lee had been selected to join Scott's "little cabinet," his inner circle of advisers. As Freeman put it, Lee stepped overnight into the planning of great enterprises. He had moved up the ladder. Other engineers in this campaign included George B. McClellan, P. G. T. Beauregard, and George Gordon Meade, all of whom would become generals and serve during the Civil War.[16]

"As soon as Gen. Scott took command everything was changed and now here we are prepairing ... to make a decent upon the City of Vera Cruze," Grant wrote to Julia Dent. The army's destination was the principal Gulf port of Mexico. For months an American fleet had been blockading the harbor. Grant showed the confidence of a twenty-five-year-old: "The general opinion now is that we will have a fight when we attempt to disembark and a big one at Vera Cruz. It is to be hoped that it will be the last!" The landing (fig. 86), actually two miles from the city, went unopposed. Grant added to Julia that word of a battle at Buena Vista had reached Scott's army: "There is a report here that Gen Taylor has had a fight with Santa Anna some place beyond Monterey and repulsed him but it is not generally believed." That battle in fact had much to do with Scott's success, because Santa Anna had diverted manpower to Buena Vista. He had hoped to raise morale by decimating a vulnerable Taylor, but his defeat instead demoralized his army.[17]

Vera Cruz was a walled city. Scott and his "little cabinet" elected to put it under siege rather than storm it. One reason was that he could readily shell it with the heavy guns of the American fleet. Lee, who to this point fretted about his not having had the opportunity to shine, and who had written to his mother-in-law that "I have done no good. I hope I have escaped any great crime," was suddenly among the engineers who would decide how to transport and where to position those guns. One of the navy's gun crews was headed by his brother, Sidney Smith Lee. The large guns were effective; after several days of bombardment and 2,500 shells, the city surrendered.[18]

Grant saw little action at Vera Cruz. "I am doing the duties of Commissary and Quarter Master so that during the siege I had but little to do except to see to having the Pork and Beans rolled about." With time on his hands, he longed all the more for Julia: "I begin to believe like some author has said,—that there are just two places in this world—One is where a person's intended is, and the other is where she is not." But, as always, Grant was looking and learning. The skills that he acquired in Mexico as a quartermaster would set him apart from most Civil War commanders. And at Vera Cruz, he studied the siege, a tactic he would use successfully at Vicksburg.[19]

Scott was determined to engage the principal Mexican army. By marching to Mexico City, he would force Santa Anna to a showdown. He had, however, a severe disadvantage in numbers. Scott had only between 11,000 and 14,000 soldiers, while Santa Anna led a massive army of some 30,000–35,000 men. Scott had to rely on his ability to maneuver an army, and he would utilize every trick he knew so as to seize the initiative and maintain the element of surprise. Grant recognized the problem that Scott faced. He wrote later in his *Memoirs*, "Twelve thousand was a very small army with which to penetrate two hundred and sixty miles into an enemy's country, and to besiege the capital; a city ... of over one hundred thousand inhabitants. Then, too, any line of march that could be selected led through mountain passes easily defended." The engineers would be called on to lead the army through those passes.[20]

Seated in Scott's "little cabinet," Lee was acutely aware of the challenge. Also, after the fall of Vera Cruz, Totten, at age fifty-nine, had retired from the field, leaving Lee virtually in charge of the en-

LEE AND GRANT   129

fig. 87.
Robert E. Lee, Vera Cruz, to Mary Custis Lee, *Letter*, April 12, 1847, Virginia Historical Society

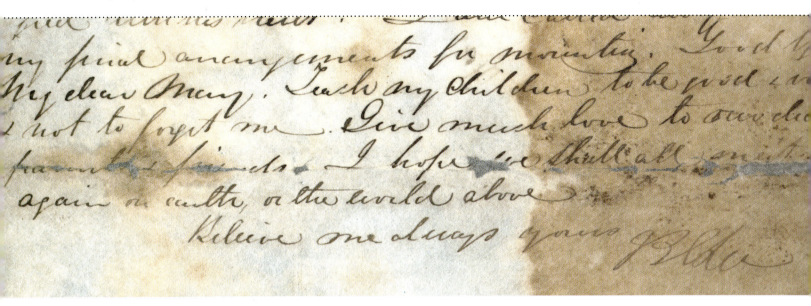

gineer corps. (Lee ranked behind Major John L. Smith, but Smith was too much in ill-health to contribute.) He had much more reason to worry about survival than did Grant the quartermaster. Less than a week before Scott engaged the enemy at Cerro Gordo, Lee wrote his wife a letter that is filled with gloom and fear (fig. 87):

> Santa Anna's force is variously estimated & varies from 2000 to 10,000. Probably the mean is near the truth …. No one at their comfortable homes can realize the exertions, pains & hardships of an Army in the field, under a scorching sun & in an enervating atmosphere. Still we must press on …. [I]f my life & strength are spared, I must see this contest to an end & endeavor to perform what little service I can to my country …. Goodbye my dear Mary. Teach my children to be good & virtuous & not to forget me. Give much love to our dear family & friends. I hope we shall all meet again on earth, or the world above.[21]

Santa Anna decided to wait for Scott at one of the highest spurs of a mountain range some fifty miles west of Vera Cruz (fig. 88). It was a formidable position from which to defend against an invading army. Scott's engineers, however, led by Lee, managed to reverse what seemed like an inevitable defeat for the Americans. Grant was impressed by what the engineers accomplished, and he left a lucid account of the battle of Cerro Gordo in his *Memoirs* and in letters home:

> The road, said to have been built by Cortez, zigzags around the mountain-side and was defended at every turn by artillery. On either side were deep chasms or mountain walls. A direct attack along the road was an impossibility. A flank movement seemed equally impossible ….[22]

> [Cerro Gordo is] a mountain pass which to look at one would suppose impregnable …. Behind this was a peak of the mountains much higher than all the others and commanded them so that the Enemy calculated that even if the Americans should succeed in taking all the other hights, from this one they could fire upon us and be out of reach themselves.[23]

Grant put the feat of the engineers into the most favorable historical context imaginable: "The difficulties to surmount made the undertaking almost equal to Bonapartes Crossing the Alps …. [I]t would have been impossible for any force in the world to have advanced."

General Scott had ordered a full reconnaissance (fig. 89). Among those assisting Lee were Lieutenants McClellan and Beauregard. Lee's assignment was to find a way to outflank the enemy. This would have to be somewhere on the Mexican left flank. Roads would have to be built to reach so high and impassable a point. Lee would then lead a division commanded by General David Twiggs to the point of attack. In the map that is fig. 89, the Mexican camp is depicted at the far left, commanding the pass to the right of it. Lee moved farther to the right, around rather than through the pass, surprising the enemy positions from the area that is at the top of the map.[24]

Grant continued his account: "Under the supervision of the en-

130 III. THE MEXICAN WAR

fig. 88.
Carl Nebel, *Battle of Cerro Gordo*, 1847, lithograph, 16⅞ × 22⅝ in. (42.9 × 57.5 cm.), published in George Wilkins Kendall and Carl Nebel, *The War between the United States and Mexico Illustrated* (New York and Philadelphia, 1851), Virginia Historical Society, Paul Mellon Collection

fig. 89.
Sketch of the Battle Ground at Cerro Gordo, 1847, pen and ink on paper, 14 × 19½ in. (35.6 × 49.5 cm.), Robert E. Lee collection, Virginia Military Institute

gineers, roadways had been opened over chasms to the right where the walls were so steep that the men could barely climb them …. The engineers, who had directed the opening, led the way and the troops followed." "With a great deal of labor," he told Julia, Twiggs's division worked its way into place. In a letter to a colleague, Grant wrote that "as soon as the Mexicans saw this hight taken they knew the day was up with them." He concluded in the *Memoirs*, "The surprise of the enemy was complete, the victory overwhelming." Lee wrote home, "All their cannon, arms, ammunition, and most of their men fell into our hands." Some $30,000 in gold also was captured, along with Santa Anna's carriage and his cork leg. Lee and Beauregard found Santa Anna's hacienda, as well as his maps and letters. The same Mexican army that had been defeated by Zachary Taylor at Buena Vista, and had then rushed a thousand miles

fig. 90.
Robert E. Lee, *Mexican Soldiers Foraging*, 1847, pencil on paper, c. 10 × 14 in. (c. 25.4 × 35.6 cm.), private collection

to Cerro Gordo, had been beaten again, this time with even more catastrophic results.[25]

The first major combat that Lee experienced had a profound emotional effect. The sight of young men dead on the battlefield made him think about his eldest son, and he realized that perhaps he was already grooming Custis to follow in his own and his father's footsteps: "I thought of you, my dear Custis … when the musket balls and grape were whistling over my head in a perfect shower, where I could put you, if with me, to be safe …. You have no idea what a horrible sight a battlefield is." Lee's accomplishment at Cerro Gordo inspired adulation worthy of his renowned father. A grateful David Twiggs praised the captain for "the invaluable services which he rendered me." He added, "I consulted him with confidence, and adopted his suggestions with entire assurance. His gallantry and good conduct on both days deserve the highest praise." Winfield Scott mentioned Lee twice in his report of the battle, singling him out for his highest praise:

> I am impelled to make special mention of the services of Captain R. E. Lee, engineers. This officer, greatly distinguished at the siege of Vera Cruz, was again indefatigable, during these operations, in reconnaissance as daring as laborious, and of the utmost value. Nor was less conspicuous in planting batteries, and in conducting columns to their stations under the heavy fire of the enemy.

"For gallant and meritorious conduct in the battle of Cerro Gordo," Lee was brevetted major.[26]

As Santa Anna retreated, Scott wanted to follow, but the move to Mexico City would be delayed for three months as Scott awaited reinforcements. His army, which had barely totaled 12,000 men at its peak size, was small for a mission that would stretch across half a nation. It would be further diminished when the terms of enlistment of several thousand volunteers soon expired. As the American army waited, the "little cabinet" held discussions for hours around the dinner table. Lee was soon better able to understand the military philosophy of his commander. Without notifying Scott, the State Department had sent Nicholas Trist to negotiate a peace, an effort that failed. During this interval, Lee also put to use the drawing skills he had learned at West Point for the amusement of his family back home (fig 90).

Soon the new major was being sent on reconnaissance missions to map the various approach routes to the capital. Once again, he was assigned a preparatory role that was critical to the success of the mission. Finally, on August 7, 1847, Franklin Pierce, the future president, arrived with 2,500 reinforcements. The army was boosted to nearly 11,000 men. On the next day, Scott sent them on the road to Mexico City.[27]

Unable to defend his line of communication to the sea, Scott decided to abandon it; he and his army would live off the land. Ulysses S. Grant would lead Scott's supply train and search for food, learning lessons that he would use sixteen years later at Vicksburg. Lee would head the team that determined how the American forces would maneuver, gaining experience that would enable his Confederate army so often to win the tactical advantage over the numerically superior Union forces.[28]

Scott chose the southern road to Mexico City. All of his advisers agreed to avoid the approach from the east because it ran on a causeway through marshes and between lakes, and was easily defended from fortified heights. But the southern route had its problems as well, ones that would take a bloody toll. Grant actually believed that Scott made a costly mistake in choosing the southern route. He expressed his concern a month later:

> From my map and all the information I acquired while the army was halted at Puebla, I was then, and am now more than ever, convinced that the army could have approached the city [Mexico City] by passing around north of it, and reached the northwest side, and avoided all the fortified po-

132   III. THE MEXICAN WAR

fig. 91.
Carl Nebel, *Battle at Churusbusco*, lithograph, 16⅞ × 22⅝ in. (42.9 × 57.5 cm.), published in George Wilkins Kendall and Carl Nebel, *The War between the United States and Mexico Illustrated* (New York and Philadelphia, 1851), Virginia Historical Society, Paul Mellon Collection.

sitions, until we reached the gates of the city at their weakest and most indefensible, as well as most approachable points.

Santa Anna had fortified the southern route to the capital. Heavy artillery at the San Antonio hacienda blocked the most direct path to Churubusco, a town that was itself heavily defended. The only other route available, the San Angel road, was farther west, beyond an immense field of hardened and seemingly impenetrable lava. Five miles wide and three miles long, this natural impediment was called the pedregal. Lee's assignment was to find out if an army could use this second route to Churubusco. When he noticed Mexican stragglers escaping into the pedregal, he decided to scout the terrain himself. He found a path across the lava, but beyond he found the enemy entrenched on a second road, near the village of Padierna. (Lee thought it was the village of Contreras, and so it was misnamed forever in the American accounts.) With the continued assistance of McClellan and Beauregard, as well as of others destined for Civil War fame, including Joseph Hooker and Thomas Jackson, Lee saw to it that the route through the pedregal was made accessible to troops and artillery. Some 3,300 soldiers soon traversed it and were poised to surprise the enemy force at Padierna.[29]

The Mexicans anticipated an attack from their south; the Americans would approach from the north. However, the commander of these troops, Persifor Smith, had Lee request from Scott a diversionary assault on the Mexican front. In total darkness, Lee had to

fig. 92.
Carl Nebel, *Storming of Chapultepec—Pillow's Attack*, lithograph, 16⅞ × 22⅝ in. (42.9 × 57.5 cm.), published in George Wilkins Kendall and Carl Nebel, *The War between the United States and Mexico Illustrated* (New York and Philadelphia, 1851), Virginia Historical Society, Paul Mellon Collection

recross the lava field. He did so successfully, and Scott responded with the requested countermove. The enemy was surprised, confused, and quickly routed. The "battle of Contreras" was another impressive American victory.

What is remarkable about Lee's journeys across the pedregal is that seven officers had previously been sent by Scott to carry messages to Smith. All had lost their way, as had two generals, David Twiggs and Gideon Pillow. Also, Lee had been in the field at that point nearly twenty-four hours. Scott described Lee's trips as "the greatest feat of physical and moral courage performed by any individual, in my knowledge, pending the campaign." In his *Memoirs* Grant did not single out Lee for credit, but he had high praise for the maneuver that Lee had orchestrated:

> This affair, like that of Cerro Gordo, was an engagement in which the officers of the engineer corps won special distinction …. The very strength of each of these positions was, by the skill of the engineers, converted into a defence for the assaulting parties while securing their positions for final attack.

However, Lieutenant Raphael Semmes of the navy wrote:

> The services of captain Lee were invaluable to his chief. Endowed with a mind which has no superior in his corps, and possessing great energy of character, he examined, coun-

selled, and advised with a judgment, tact, and discretion worthy of all praise. His talent for topography was peculiar, and he seemed to receive impressions intuitively, which it cost other men much labor to acquire.[30]

Without any opportunity to rest, Lee immediately followed Scott's next command that he scout the road to Churubusco. There the convent of San Mateo (which the Americans misnamed San Pablo) had been heavily fortified. Lee's assignment was to assess the terrain and then lead the troops across the Churubusco River and position them to the greatest effect. A frontal attack was made on the convent, and a victory was won (fig. 91). The Mexican troops fled the scene; Santa Anna lost one-third of his army. American losses, however, were heavy as well.[31]

Grant observed the action and, perhaps surprisingly, later offered a criticism of the American advance force. He wrote that Scott had "expected ... that these troops would move north sufficiently to flank the enemy out of his position at Churubusco, ... but they did not succeed in this, and Churubusco proved to be about the severest battle fought in the valley of Mexico." Grant, however, ultimately praised the engineers and the commanding general:

> Both the strategy and tactics displayed by General Scott in these various engagements of the 20th of August, 1847, were faultless as I look upon them now, ... As before stated, the work of the engineer officers who made the reconnoissances and led the different commands to their destinations, was so perfect that the chief was able to give his orders to his various subordinates with all the precision he could use on an ordinary march.[32]

For his key contributions at the pedregal, Padierna, and Churubusco, Lee earned lavish praise from every general under whom he served. Scott described him as "the gallant, indefatigable Captain Lee" and stated that he was "distinguished for felicitous execution as for science and daring." David Twiggs expressed "thanks [to Lee] for the exceedingly valuable services." Persifor Smith wrote, "I wish to record particularly my admiration of the conduct of Captain Lee of the engineers. His reconnaissances, though pushed far beyond the bounds of prudence, were conducted with so much skill, that their fruits were of the utmost value—the soundness of his judgment and personal daring being equally conspicuous." Gideon Pillow stated that Lee's "distinguished merit and gallantry deserves the highest praise." James Shields expressed "great obligations" to Lee, "in whose skill and judgment I had the utmost confidence." Franklin Pierce credited Lee with "distinguished services on both days." For his successes Lee earned the brevet of lieutenant colonel.[33]

The army could now move either to the south or the west gate of Mexico City, on one of two causeways through standing water. Lee was ordered to direct a reconnaissance. Along with all of the engineers, with the exception of Beauregard, he urged an attack on the southern gate. Scott, however, favored a move from the west. That gate was well defended by the fortress of Chapultepec, a massive stone building that sat on a ridge 190 feet high and some six hundred yards in length (fig. 92). Grant put the total height of ridge and fortress at 300 feet. It was a significant obstacle, one that the engineers rightly feared. The structure had been begun as a palace, but it was completed as a military college.[34]

To make matters worse, just in front of Chapultepec and blocking it on the same approach lay Molino del Rey (the king's mill), a grain repository. Grant described the structure as "flat roofed, and a line of sand-bags over the outer walls rendered the top quite a formidable defence for infantry." Scott's guess that the mill was lightly defended was wrong. A bloodbath ensued. Both Grant and Lee were in the thick of the action at Chapultepec. Grant "was with the earliest of the troops to enter the Mills." Careful not to exaggerate his role, he recounted how he "climbed to the roof of the building, followed by a few men," only to find that a lowly private had preceded him and single-handedly taken prisoners. The ever-observant Grant learned at this engagement that retreating forces should always be pursued:

> Worth's troops entered the Mills by every door, and the enemy beat a hasty retreat back to Chapultepec. Had this victory been followed up promptly, no doubt Americans and Mexicans would have gone over the defences of Chapultepec so near together that the place would have fallen into our hands without further loss .... I do not criticize .... The loss on our side at Molino del Rey was severe for the numbers engaged. It was especially so among commissioned officers.[35]

Lee's assignment at Chapultepec was to place four gun batteries that would shell the fortress prior to and in support of an infantry attack. McClellan assisted him; they worked through the night of September 11. The next day, Scott ordered Lee to report the effect

fig. 93.
Crucifix, early 19th century, Virginia Historical Society

of the bombardment. He then disclosed the plan of battle. Gideon Pillow's division would storm the fortress from the west, while John Quitman's troops attacked from the south. Five hundred additional soldiers would carry scaling ladders. Lee was to guide Pillow's division. Repeatedly checking on the batteries, Lee stayed up through the night a second time. He had been forty-eight hours without sleep when the battle began. Franklin Pierce commanded a brigade within Pillow's division. Joseph Johnston, James Longstreet, George Pickett, and Thomas Jackson were also engaged in what was savage combat. A Roman Catholic priest who had been mortally wounded handed Pickett a crucifix that day that he would wear for the rest of his life (fig. 93). The American troops broke through first on the west, then in the south.[36]

As with the attack on the convent at Churubusco, in retrospect the storming of the king's mill and the military college might best have been sidestepped. Grant would ultimately think so: "In later years, if not at the time, the battles of Molino del Rey and Chapultepec have seemed to me to have been wholly unnecessary …. the road running east … could have been reached easily, without an engagement." However, he also came to understand that commanders can only get the best possible information and then go with the strategy that they believe will work.[37]

On Scott's orders, Lee hastened towards the San Cosme gate to make a reconnaissance of that approach. Not having slept for fifty-six hours, he passed out from his exertions: "I could no longer keep my saddle," he wrote. Grant, however, would soon become involved in heroics that earned him his only mention in the battle reports sent back to Washington. In his *Memoirs*, Grant recounted the incident:

> I found a church off to the south of the road, which looked to me as if the belfry would command the ground back of the garita San Cosme. I got an officer of the voltigeurs, with a mountain howitzer and men to work it, to go with me …. The gun was carried to the belfry and put together. We were not more than two or three hundred yards from San Cosme. The shots from our little gun dropped in upon the enemy and created great confusion. Why they did not send out a small party and capture us, I do not know ….
>
> The effect of this gun upon the troops about the gate of the city was so marked that General Worth saw it from his position. He was so pleased that he sent a staff officer, Lieutenant Pemberton—later Lieutenant-General commanding the defences of Vicksburg—to bring me to him. He expressed his gratification at the services the howitzer in the church steeple was doing ….[38]

Lee quickly recovered. He was among the first Americans in the grand plaza of Mexico City when the U.S. flag was raised over the imperial palace. Scott and his staff arrived soon after, in full dress uniforms, providing artists with a dramatic moment to depict (fig. 94). Grant, however, described a scene that was more eerie than what the artists imagined: "The streets were deserted, and the place presented the appearance of a 'city of the dead,' except for this firing by unseen persons from house-tops, windows, and around corners."[39]

Scott had lost a huge portion of his army. Many died, often more from disease than from combat, many more were wounded, and large numbers had deserted. Less than 6,000 men remained under his command. Grant shared with Julia some thoughts about the losses:

> Since my last letter four of the hardest fougt battles that the

fig. 94.
Carl Nebel, *General Scott's Entrance into Mexico [City]*, lithograph, 16⅞ × 22⅝ in. (42.9 × 57.5 cm.), published in George Wilkins Kendall and Carl Nebel, *The War between the United States and Mexico Illustrated* (New York and Philadelphia, 1851), Virginia Historical Society, Paul Mellon Collection

world ever witnessed have taken place, and the most astonishing victories have crowned the American arms. But dearly have they paid for it! The loss of officers and men killed and wounded is frightful …. The whole Mexican army is destroyed or disbursed …. Out of all the officers that left Jefferson Barracks with the 4th Infantry [there had been twenty-one officers], only three besides myself now remain with us.

The Mexican army had been decimated by Scott's onslaught. The soldiers, followed by many members of the government, quickly dispersed. No one remained in the city to sign a peace settlement.[40]

The exultation of victory was soon diluted by dissent both at home and among the troops. Some Americans denounced "Mr. Polk's War" as a slaveholders' plot to expand the institution into the Southwest. They wanted Scott's army to withdraw and relinquish all occupied territory. Many Americans demanded the territory in dispute, while others coveted even more land. Lee bristled at the criticism of a war that had been so hard fought. He was particularly annoyed at the call for withdrawal. "We have fought well & fought fairly," he wrote to Mary Custis Lee. "We hold & can continue [to] hold their country, & have a right to enact compensation for the expenses of a war continued if not provoked by … Mexico." Lee even suggested that if the enemy rejected the peace treaty that

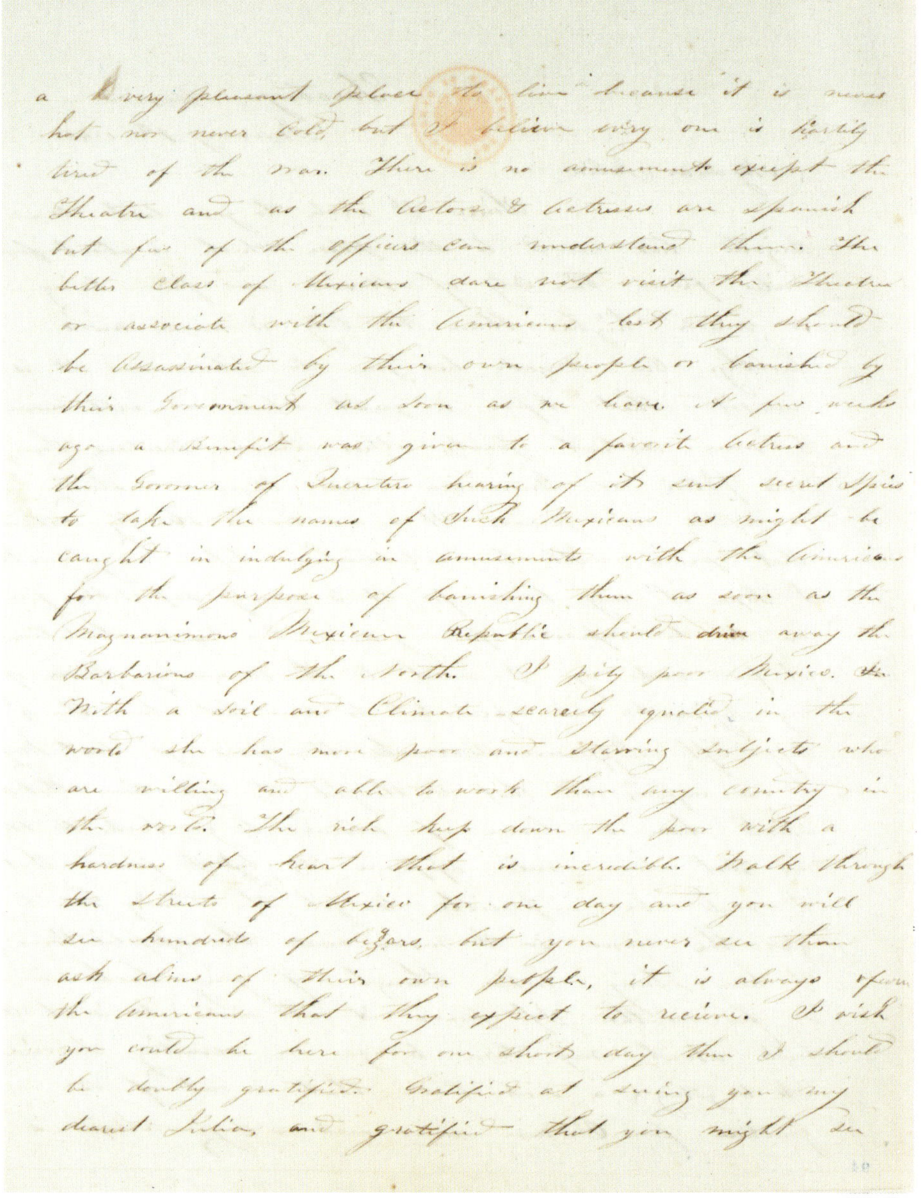

a very pleasant place the line because it is never
hot nor never cold, but I believe every one is heartily
tired of the war. There is no amusement except the
Theatre and as the actors & actresses are spanish
but few of the officers can understand them. The
better class of Mexicans dare not visit the Theatre
or associate with the Americans lest they should
be assassinated by their own people or banished by
their Government as soon as we leave. A few weeks
ago a Benefit was given to a favorite actress and
the Governor of Queretaro hearing of it sent secret spies
to take the names of such Mexicans as might be
caught in indulging in amusements with the Americans
for the purpose of banishing them as soon as the
Magnanimous Mexican Republic should drive away the
Barbarians of the North. I pity poor Mexico. she
With a soil and Climate scarcely equaled in the
world she has more poor and starving subjects who
are willing and able to work than any country in
the world. The rich keep down the poor with a
hardness of heart that is incredible. Walk through
the streets of Mexico for one day and you will
see hundreds of beggars, but you never see them
ask alms of their own people, it is always of
the Americans that they expect to receive. I wish
you could be here for one short day then I should
be doubly gratified. Gratified at seeing you my
dearest Julia, and gratified that you might see

fig. 95.
Ulysses S. Grant, Tacabaya, Mexico, to Julia Dent, *Letter*, January 9, 1848, Library of Congress

was submitted to them, the Americans should "tear up the paper" and "take the country."[41]

Both Lee and Grant shared a concern for the victims of what they considered to be American aggression, but the two officers had very different viewpoints on what should happen next. Though "ashamed" that "we bullied" Mexico, Lee suggested that the country be put "in the hands of proper people," by which he meant the hands of European immigrants instead of the resident population:

> Without a government, without an army, without money & without a revenue, these people are unable to prosecute war & have not power to make peace. They will oblige us in spite of ourselves to overrun the country & drive them into the sea. I believe it would be our best plan to commence at once. Open the ports of European immigration. Introduce free opinions of government & religion. Break down the power & iniquity of the church. It is a beautiful country & in the hands of proper people would be a magnificent one. Rich, fertile, temperate, & healthy after leaving the coast. Set our politicians to work.

Grant was better able to view the Mexican people with sympathy. He was appalled that one class ruled over another; the plight of the lowest classes immediately called to his mind that of the American slave. The Mexicans, he concluded, are "a very different race of people from ours." Yet as he waited ten months for peace to take hold, Grant developed strong feelings for these people and their land (fig. 95).

> I pity poor Mexico. With a soil and climate scarsely equaled in the world she has more poor and starving subjects who are willing and able to work than any country in the world. The rich keep down the poor with a hardness of heart that is incredible

If Texas had beckoned to Grant, it is little wonder that the "soil and climate" of Mexico did so as well. He asked Julia if she would come to Mexico if the army stayed there indefinitely. She answered that she would.[42]

Scott's increased trust in Lee had been rewarded on the long march to Mexico City. In the end, he would praise Lee more than any other officer in his battle reports, using such terms as "constantly distinguished," "conspicuous," and "daring." At a banquet following the surrender of the capital city, he would toast "the health of Captain Robert E. Lee, without whose aid we should not now be here." If he had come to Mexico to make a name for himself, Lee had certainly succeeded.[43]

The dissent within the American army following the fall of the Mexican regime could perhaps have been expected. Many of the generals had political aspirations, and they grabbed greedily for the laurels of victory. Zachary Taylor, Winfield Scott, Gideon Pillow, and William Worth all wanted a share of the credit. Amidst the quarreling that broke out, Worth brought charges against Scott, who promptly put him under arrest. Scott then brought charges against Pillow. This bickering played to attentive audiences in Washington, where the Democratic administration delighted in the opportunity to discredit Scott by dismissing him from command. In January 1848, a court of inquiry cleared Scott of plotting to accept a bribe as part of the peace settlement, but the accusation was enough to cause a political decline. It would be Taylor who would rise to the surface, and who ultimately would be elected president in 1848.[44]

Lee had testified on behalf of General Scott at the court inquiry. Convinced that President Polk was determined to reward Scott's faithful service to the nation by discrediting him, Lee despaired over the failures of the American political process. He questioned his commitment to a military career, writing to his brother Carter that he would "make a strong effort" to leave the army. He had done virtually all that was humanly possible to earn advancement in rank. He received three brevets: major for his heroics at Cerro Gordo, lieutenant colonel following Padierna (Contreras) and Churubusco, and colonel for his accomplishments at Chapultepec. But the brevets would not necessarily be converted into permanent promotions. Lee told his father-in-law that he was tired and so disgusted with the military and political hierarchies that he wanted to have little else to do with them:

> My dear father,
>
> I am much obliged to you for your kind note & for [brother-in-law William] Marshall's interest with the President in my behalf. I hope my friends will give themselves no annoyance on my account or any concern about the distribution of favours. I know how those things are awarded at Washington & how the President will be besieged by clamorous claimants. I do not wish to be numbered among them. Such as he can conscientiously bestow I shall gratefully receive, & have no doubt that those will exceed my deserts. I cannot consider myself very highly complimented by the brevet of 2 grades …. Genl Twiggs in an official letter to Genl Scott, which has fallen under my eye, & endorsed by Genl S, recommended me for two brevets for the battles of Cerro Gordo, 17 & 18 of April. So that if I performed any services at Vera Cruz, or at the battles around this capital, they will go for nought …. I wish I was out of the Army.

Four years later, another reward for his valor in the Mexican campaign would arrive. However, this would be a prize that the active Lee did not want, but was hardly in a position to turn down: the superintendency at West Point. He was assigned to this duty in 1852. His job would be to train future officers how to lead—a talent that was innate for Lee—and to teach them, if necessary, how to fight.[45]

Grant was also frustrated by his failure to win promotion. He had been brevetted first lieutenant for valor at Molino del Rey and Chapultepec, but he did not receive a permanent upgrade until one of his colleagues, Lieutenant Sidney Smith (no relation to Sidney Smith Lee), was killed in Mexico City. Like Robert E. Lee, Grant lamented the predicament of the career soldier:

> I had gone into the battle of Palo Alto in May, 1846, a second lieutenant, and I entered the city of Mexico sixteen months later with the same rank, after having been in all the engagements possible for any one man and in a regiment that lost more officers during the war than it ever had present at any one engagement.

His discouragement would increase over the next few years, when far-ranging assignments would keep Grant from his family.[46]

One day in Mexico City, as the months of American occupation slowly passed, R. E. Lee and U. S. Grant met one another. The short, young lieutenant of course remembered the moment; he wrote in his *Memoirs* that he recalled Lee "perfectly." The captain was a ranking officer, a member of Scott's "little cabinet," and one of the most acclaimed heroes of the war. His daring exploits were known to Grant, who perhaps felt a bit jealous that the Virginian, who was fifteen years his senior, had been put in positions in which he could prove himself. Grant would remind Lee of this meeting years later at Appomattox. To his surprise, his antagonist remembered him "very well" from their time together "in the old army."[47]

Both men learned a great deal during the Mexican War. Indeed, it was the only time that either of them absorbed anything of practical value about warfare. Against Santa Anna's poorly fed, ill-equipped, and often unpaid troops, the United States Army won victories by attacking. When Lee and Grant faced each other years later, armies had grown to monstrous size, with tens of thousands of men on each side in the field simultaneously, carrying rifles that had three to five times the range of muskets. No commander could view an entire battlefield, he could not be aware of every troop movement, nor would his orders always be followed with alacrity. Both Lee and Grant would adopt Scott's philosophy of command: be audacious, seize the initiative and keep it, enjoy the element of surprise when you can get it, and, when possible, decide when and where to fight. Both learned the importance of the flank movement, so that for weeks in 1864 neither could outmaneuver the other. Also, they both learned that with sound leadership a small army can beat a large one. That knowledge would keep Lee optimistic even to the end of the Civil War, and would so worry Grant that he decided he had to obliterate Lee's army and thereby give him no choice but to surrender.

The terms of the Treaty of Guadalupe-Hidalgo, which on February 2, 1848, brought a close to the Mexican War, forced the defeated nation to cede 40 percent of its territory to the United States. In return, Mexico was paid $15 million. The land acquired by power and payment included much of what is now Arizona, California, Nevada, New Mexico, Utah, and parts of Colorado and Texas. Career officers Robert E. Lee and Ulysses S. Grant would eventually receive assignments in two of those distant territories, Texas and California. Their absences from home would put a strain on their families, to the point where Grant would decide that he had lived without Julia and the children for too long. For most of the 1850s, Ulysses S. Grant's military career was a thing of the past.

The Mexican War also proved to others, but most importantly to themselves, that each man was a fighter. Lee was more than an engineer; when faced with the enemy, he knew how to respond. Grant was annoyed by some of his quartermaster duties, but when the bullets were flying around him, he was fearless and resolute. The idea to seize the belfry at San Cosme was brilliant, but as important was that Grant acted with initiative and diligence. At a crucial moment, he had gotten the job done. There would be other such moments, there would be times when his staff officers suggested disengagement or even retreat, but Grant learned in Mexico that he had it within him to stand up to discouragement, to go forward, and to succeed.

Grant added that the war taught him "many practical lessons." It "brought nearly all the officers of the regular army together so as to make them personally acquainted."

> I had been at West Point at about the right time to meet most of the graduates who were of a suitable age at the breaking out of the rebellion to be trusted with large commands …. These classes embraced more than fifty officers who afterwards became generals on one side or the other in the rebellion, many of them holding high commands. All the older officers, who became conspicuous in the rebellion, I had also served with and known in Mexico: Lee, J. E. Johnston, A. S. Johnston, Holmes, Hebert, and a number of others on the Confederate side; McCall, Mansfield, Phil. Kearney and others on the National side. The acquaintance thus formed was of immense service to me in the war of the rebellion—I mean what I learned of the characters of those to whom I was afterwards opposed. I do not pretend to say that all movements, or even many of them, were made with special reference to the characteristics of the commander against whom they were directed. But my appreciation of my enemies was certainly affected by this knowledge. The natural disposition of most people is to clothe a commander of a large army whom they do not know, with almost superhuman abilities. A large part of the National army, for instance, and most of the press of the country, clothed General Lee with just such qualities, but I had known him personally, and knew that he was mortal; and it was just as well that I felt this.[48]

As he looked back on his experiences in the Southwest, Grant saw the importance of the land acquisition to the United States, but he also foresaw that a high price would be paid:

> To us it was an empire and of incalculable value; but it might have been obtained by other means. The Southern rebellion was largely the outgrowth of the Mexican war. Nations, like individuals, are punished for their transgressions. We got our punishment in the most sanguinary and expensive war of modern times.

Lee would ultimately share Grant's view that the Civil War was inflicted on Americans by a wrathful God for their "national sins," although he did not mention the Mexican War by name. He also saw that even the ill-trained Mexican troops would fight desperately when their homeland was invaded. In the early part of the Civil War, when the defeat of what was perceived by southerners to be Lincoln's army of occupation would become a rallying cry in the Confederacy, Lee would have a confidence built on his experience in Mexico.

IV.
Crises of the 1850s

What am I to do—I fear Mary will never be well enough to accompany me in my wandering life, & it seems to be cruel to leave her.
Robert E. Lee to Anna Maria Fitzhugh, November 22, 1857

We will be much more comfortably fixed than we have ever been before and it usually happens in such cases with the Army that they are moved as soon as they are comfortable.
Ulysses S. Grant to Julia Grant, August 3, 1851

The peacetime years between the wars would bring little peace to either Lee or Grant. Both would be plagued by bouts of loneliness, self-doubt, and failure, interspersed with periods of familial bliss. Each would also come to think that the military might not be his final career. Lee pursued the elusive goal of military promotion, first while serving in Baltimore, then as superintendent at West Point, and finally with the new U.S. Cavalry in the Comanche territory of Texas. In 1857 he would take a leave from the army to attempt to manage the estate of his father-in-law, which included tending to the farming operation at Arlington, the once beautiful plantation that overlooked the nation's capital, where the potential pleasures were far outweighed by his having to deal on a daily basis with its restive slaves. Grant, after assignments in the East at Detroit and then Sackets Harbor, awoke one day in the remote Pacific Northwest having never laid eyes on his second son, "little Uly." He had bouts of boredom, and, according to some reports, would on occasion drink excessively. Grant would resign from the military in 1854 and move back home to Missouri to try his hand at farming. After five profitless years and his own interactions with slave laborers, he gave up, tried to make a living as a real estate agent, dabbled unsuccessfully in politics, and eventually settled into a career as a clerk in the family leather-goods business in Galena, Illinois. His joy at being with Julia and his children seemed to preclude a return to the wandering life of a soldier.[1]

Ambivalence Towards the Military

Lee's Pursuit of Promotion: Baltimore, West Point, and Texas

To get home from Mexico, brevet Colonel Lee took the steamship *Portland* from Vera Cruz in June 1848. From New Orleans he worked his way up the Mississippi River, then turned northeast, taking the Ohio River as far as Wheeling, in what is now West Virginia. From there he took a train, and, after missing his carriage connection, got the use of a horse to get to Arlington. His initial reward for his recent gallantry was another posting at the War Office in Washington, D. C., under now Brigadier General Joseph Totten, which allowed him to live at home in what had become a very crowded Arlington House. Lee was able to enjoy several months in Virginia prior to his deployment in mid-September to a difficult engineering task in Baltimore harbor. That summer proved to be a special time for the family, a rare interval when all seven children and their grandparents were present with Robert and Mary. The oldest child, Custis, was nearly sixteen; the youngest, Mildred, was two. Also in the house was cousin Markie Williams, then a teenager and companion of the Lee's older daughters. Robert was a loving parent, playing with and generally enjoying the company of his children. In his *Recollections* of his father that he wrote some seventy years later, Rob, the youngest son, recalled with great affection his memories of that summer:

> He was always bright and gay with us little folk, romping, playing, and joking with us. With the older children, he was just as companionable, and I have seen him join my elder brothers and their friends when they would try their powers at a high jump in our yard. The two younger children he petted a good deal, and our greatest treat was to get in his bed in the morning and lie close to him, listening while he talked to us in his bright, entertaining way. This custom we kept until I was ten years old and over. Although he was so joyous and familiar with us, he was very firm on all proper occasions, never indulged us in anything that was not good for us, and exacted the most implicit obedience. I always knew that it was impossible to disobey my father …. He was very fond of having his hands tickled, and, what was still more curious, it pleased and delighted him to take off his slippers and place his feet in our laps in order to have them tickled.

In showing the tender side of the general, Robert, Jr. helped to convert a new generation of readers to the Lee cult.[2]

Fort Carroll, Maryland: 1848–52

Assigned to engineer the underwater foundations of a new fort in the Baltimore harbor, Lee found that the drudgery and isolation of the task made for "a lonesome time." Fort McHenry, which had become famous when its defense during the War of 1812 inspired

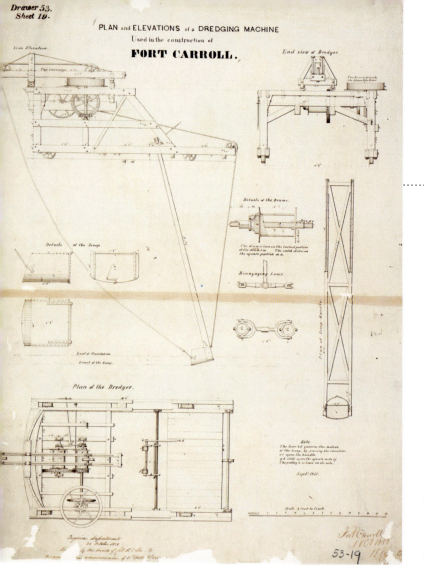

fig. 96.
Robert E. Lee, *Section of a Dredging Machine*, 1848, drawing, from the Fort Carroll collection, National Archives and Records Administration

"The Star-Spangled Banner," was located too close to the expanding city; Francis Scott Key's lyrics demonstrate Baltimore's vulnerability to naval attack. A newer structure was to be built farther downstream and named for the patriot Charles Carroll of Carrolltown, Maryland, who had lived through two wars with Britain and had earned the distinction of being the last surviving signer of the Declaration of Independence. The site, Sollers' Point Flats, had been selected, and preliminary work had begun prior to Lee's arrival in November 1848 to initiate the more difficult phases of construction. Winter weather took Lee to other assignments, including south to survey the Atlantic coast defenses with the Board of Engineers, a prestigious responsibility for the colonel. By the following spring he was back in Baltimore ready to work. For three long seasons, from 1849 to 1851, Lee devoted himself to one of the most demanding engineering tasks taken on by the army during this era.[3]

As with his assignment in Virginia at Fort Calhoun, Lee was again literally working in midstream. However, lessons had been learned at Fort Calhoun, which in 1848 was still sinking. The dumping of stone into the depths of a channel just did not work. For Fort Carroll, Lee had to develop a more scientific approach to the building of foundations. The site was on a shoal. Solid ground was some forty-five feet beneath the low-water level. The foundations would have to reach to that depth, beneath a layer of mud. Lee devised all sorts of machines for the task, including one for dredging (fig. 96), a diving bell, and a pile driver, all of which he drew and then contracted for their construction. Lee built wharves from which his men could operate as they drove the 822 piles that would be necessary. Over the piles they laid the granite footings for the fort, slowly building the five sides of the structure up to water level. By 1851 they had completed courses of masonry that were 10 feet wide, 250 feet long, and 6 feet above the foundations. That would be as far as Lee could carry the project before he was reassigned in 1852. He could not have anticipated that this would be his last engineering assignment.[4]

Working in the heat of Baltimore harbor was unpleasant. Lee wrote to his wife in June of his first year there, "It has been excessively hot [100 degrees] for the last three days, & the early part of the night has been almost as bad as the day." He added, "I have a lonesome time during 12 hours of the 24." The absence of his wife and children was difficult. Mary Custis Lee had decided to remain at Arlington in part because her mother and her mother's slaves would help with the care of her battalion of children. About the time Robert left for Maryland, she wrote to a friend, "You know what a monotonous life I lead, & how very stupid the fitting up of 7 children with winter clothes must make one." Three months later she complained to the same correspondent that the children's "little feet" were "as noisy as usual."[5]

Lee took a room in the city "hardly big enough to swing a cat in," contracted malaria, and was rejected by his wife when he requested that she join him at a Board of Engineers meeting in Newport, Rhode Island. Finally, in late 1849, his family arrived and he began to enjoy the social life of the city. His sister Ann Marshall was there, with her husband William, who had left the pulpit to practice law. Robert Lee, Jr. remembered occasions when his parents went out to entertainments:

> My father … always in full uniform, always ready and waiting for my mother, who was generally late. He would chide her gently, in a playful way and with a bright smile. He would then bid us good-bye, and I would go to sleep with this beautiful picture in my mind, the golden epaulets and all—chiefly the epaulets.

fig. 97.
George Washington Custis Lee, Jeb Stuart, and Stephen Dill Lee, 1854–55 (photograph courtesy of Virginia Historical Society)

"He was a great favourite in Baltimore, as he was everywhere," the son remembered, "especially with ladies and little children."[6]

All seven of the children at one point or another lived with their father in Baltimore. In 1850, Custis was shipped off to West Point, with reluctance matching that of Ulysses S. Grant a decade earlier. Two years later, daughters Annie and Agnes, to the delight of their maternal grandparents, were sent to Arlington to be tutored. The absence of the three children brought anxiety to their father. He did his best to parent from afar.

Having pushed himself as a cadet, but having graduated second in his class, Lee became almost obsessed with urging his oldest son to finish at the top of the class of 1854. Custis (fig. 97) responded, but was so miserable in the process that the end may not have justified the strain to both father and son. Robert wrote Custis a series of letters that are a peculiar mix of tension and concern. After a shaky start during the first ten months in school, which inspired a visit from the colonel, Custis revived his enthusiasm for his studies and for the military regimen. Lee wrote in ecstatic support in May 1851:

> Your letter … has given me more pleasure than any that I now recollect having ever received ….
>
> So long as I meet with such return from my children, and see them strive to respond to my wishes, and exertions, for their good and happiness, I can meet with calmness and unconcern all else the world may have in store for me. I cannot express my pleasure at hearing you declare your determination to shake off the listless fit that has seized you, and arouse all your faculties into activity and exertion.

Custis finished his first year at West Point second in his class. A year later, in February 1852, Lee urged his son further:

> You must press forward in your studies. You must "crowd that boy Howard." You must be No. 1. It is a fine number. Easily found and remembered. Simple and unique. Jump to it fellow.

(O. O. Howard would become a Union major general whom Lee would meet in battle.) The father, seemingly, had pushed too hard. A month later, Lee would have to attempt to rally his son from a deep depression. His advice reveals much about his own mindset:

> Why Mr. Boo, is that you that talk of being melancholy & low spirited? … Why man, when I am troubled, harassed or vexed, I think of you to cheer & support me. I feel as if I had some body to fall back upon. To stand by me. To take care of my wife & children when I am gone, when I can do no more for them. I think of you as labouring hard for your own advancement & improvement, the credit of your family, & the happiness of us all. It does not make me sad but cheerful. Shake off those gloomy feelings. Drive them away. Fix your mind & pleasure upon what is before you. Steadily, hopefully and trustfully. All is bright if you will think it so. All is happy if you will make it so.

Lee's letters to his son are remarkably similar to those written by President Washington to George Washington Parke Custis when Washy was away at college. One important difference, however, was that Custis Lee had in him the ability to succeed as a student; another was that by the fall of 1852 Lee would be at West Point as superintendent, able by his presence to stoke the fire under his son.[7]

By that spring Lee was also worrying about the education of his daughters, who were at Arlington with their grandparents. He had specific ideas at to what they should learn and how much effort they should make. Typically, he expected his children to exhibit the same perseverance that he himself had demonstrated.

> I was glad to hear that our dear little daughters [Agnes and Annie] are so diligent in their studies. I hope they will make every exertion to learn all Miss Poor can teach them.

LEE AND GRANT

fig. 93.
Martha Custis ("Markie") Williams (1827–1899) (photograph courtesy of Tudor Place Historic House and Garden, Washington, D. C.)

fig. 94.
Robert E. Lee to Markie Williams, *Letter*, May 10, 1851, Huntington Library

> I particularly desire that she will teach them to write a good hand, & to be regular, orderly, & energetic in the performance of all their duties. I also wish her to teach them to sing. I cannot admit their assertion that "they can't." They can if they try, & I say in addition they must.

He told his mother-in-law, "God punishes us for our sins here as well as hereafter. He is now punishing me for mine through my children. It is there I am most vulnerable, most sensitive." Lee often carried his parental responsibilities to an extreme, perhaps in response to his own father's shortcomings.[8]

In 1845, Lee had written to Henry Kayser, a friend from the Midwest who remembered his flirtatious streak, "You are right in my interest in the pretty women, & it is strange I do not lose it with age. But I perceive no diminution." Almost a decade later, when he was in his mid-forties, Lee remained exceptionally attractive to women. An army colleague, Lieutenant Cadmus Wilcox, called him in these years "the handsomest man in the army." Flirtation was an easy sport for him. When Markie Williams (fig. 98) grew to maturity, Lee directed much attention toward her. As Ann Hill Carter had been swept away by the handsome war hero "Light-Horse Harry," a man nearly twice her age, so Markie was overwhelmed by the interest expressed by her older cousin. The relationship was complex and remained so for many years. After Markie's father was killed in Mexico at Monterey, Lee had tracked down and sent to the daughter her father's sword belt. She had become an orphan and he became her protector, but Markie also provided an emotional outlet for Lee. When he was despondent from the monotony and strain of laying masonry at Sollers' Point Flats, it was Markie whom he told that he felt as lifeless as the stone that he worked. He expressed his admiration for her in terms that seem meant to arouse a response (fig. 99):

> You have not written to me for nearly three months. And I believe it is equally as long since I have written to you. On paper Markie, I mean, on paper. But oh, what lengthy epistles have I indited to you in my mind! Had I any means to send them, you would see how constantly I think of you. I have followed you in your pleasures, & your duties, in the house & in the streets, & accompanied you in your walks to Arlington, & in your search after flowers. Did you feel your cheeks pale when I was so near you? You may feel pale Markie, You may look pale; You may even talk pale; But I am happy to say you never write as if you were pale; & to my mind you always appear bright & rosy.

Others of Lee's letters to Markie and to Tasy Beaumont, both of an age with his eldest children, are simply risqué. Tasy was the daughter of Dr. William Beaumont, with whom the Lees had shared a house in St. Louis. In one letter, he teased her about her friends "Miss Louise" and "Alex K": "I should hate her sweet face to be hid by such hairs [Alex's whiskers] unless they were … mine," and he offered to her provocative lines of poetry about Cupid: "Although short be his arrow, slender his bow: The King Apollo's never wrought such woe." Markie, a great-great-granddaughter of Martha Washington, carried on an intimate correspondence with Lee that would last the twenty-six years until his death. He wrote to Markie in 1845, "Your good long letter … gave me infinite pleasure. I have thought upon it, slept upon it, dwelt upon it (pretty long you will say) & have not done with it yet." A year earlier, he had written her, "Oh Markie, Markie, When will you ripen." Even a much older woman who was savvy to the frivolities and subtleties of Victorian epistolary interplay might not have known how to in-

terpret such letters. Although there was never a hint of any untoward contact, Markie Williams would not marry until after Robert E. Lee died.[9]

West Point, New York: Fall 1852–55
Both to reward him further for his exceptionally valiant service during the Mexican War and to provide the cadets at the academy with an appropriate role model, Robert E. Lee was appointed superintendent of West Point in 1852. This command proved to be stressful for Lee. It was a duty that he complained about more often than he ever did about combat. A man who found the raising of his own children to be a task laden with anxiety had been assigned the duty of developing the potential of an entire corps made up of the sons of other parents. Lee took the job seriously. Jefferson Davis, the secretary of war during these years, observed his determination. Years later, Davis wrote,

[I] was surprised to see so many gray hairs on his head, he confessed that the cadets did exceedingly worry him, and then it was perceptible that his sympathy with young people was rather an impediment than a qualification for the superintendency.[10]

This post was considered both an honor and a plum, one of few available to a career officer of Lee's era. The community at the post was one of the most attractive that the army had to offer. But Lee had no wish to be an educator, and the position offered no opportunity for career advancement. The awkwardness of commanding a son whom he was prodding toward excellence may have been a further deterrent to Lee's interest in the position. He even attempted to decline the assignment. In May 1852, Lee wrote to Chief Engineer Joseph Totten that the job requires "more skill & more experience than I command." He added, getting to the point of the letter, "I would respectfully ask that some other successor than myself be

fig. 100.
Unknown artist, *View of West Point*, c. 1850, oil on canvas, 31⅛ × 41¾ in. (80 × 106.1 cm.), Boscobel Restoration, Inc

fig. 101.
Robert Walter Weir, *Robert E. Lee*, c. 1852–55, oil on canvas, 30⅛ × 25¼ in. (76.5 × 64.1 cm.), private collection

appointed to the present able Superintendent." However, even Totten could not help him. On September 1, 1852, Lee took office as the ninth superintendent of the academy. Two years later he was still complaining. He wrote to cousin Anna Fitzhugh, "The climate is as harsh to me as my duties & neither brings any pleasure."[11]

The West Point campus of 1852 was different from the one that Lee knew as a cadet a quarter-century earlier (fig. 100). A new barracks with 172 rooms had been completed only a year earlier, and a new mess hall was under construction. An observatory had been built in 1841, an academic building in 1838, and a chapel in 1836. There was not a great deal for the new superintendent to do in terms of improving the physical structure of the academy. Lee did request and receive congressional funding to build officers' quarters and stables and to enlarge the post hospital. He also set up a portrait gallery where cadets might be inspired in the way that he had been in his youth by looking at images of George Washington and other luminaries of early American history.[12]

Of the faculty in place at West Point when Lee arrived, two stand out for their later roles as Union commanders. George H. Thomas of Virginia was the instructor in artillery and cavalry, and Fitz John Porter was adjutant. Thomas would fight with great success in the West, far from his Virginia home, while Porter would face Lee in Virginia at Mechanicsville and Gaines's Mill. Robert W. Weir, who taught cadets to draw, painted Lee's portrait when he was superintendent (fig. 101). It is the second and final painted portrait from life for which Lee sat.[13]

Lee tightened both the curriculum and the discipline at West Point. All students in the graduating class would be required to pass engineering. Students with 100 demerits in a six-month period were dismissed. (Previously a cadet could accumulate up to 200 demerits in one year. Lee had none in four years.) The superintendent expected cadets to excel at both academic and military education. Many did not. Lee's standards were simply too high. Few cadets could live up to his ideal, and those who tried were often frustrated.

A fifth year of instruction, although not Lee's proposal, was tried for several years under his superintendency before it was finally abandoned. Perhaps Lee's greatest accomplishment as an administrator was to free the institution from political interference in its operation. The new president, Franklin Pierce, had been Lee's comrade in arms during the Mexican War, and the incoming secretary of war was Jefferson Davis, a West Point graduate and also a Mexican War veteran. Both were inclined to support Lee's initiatives.[14]

One of Lee's most admirable traits as an administrator was his apparent interest in every student, even though such attention was often unappreciated. If a cadet performed well within the academic and military regimen, the superintendent would offer praise but would feel less obliged to follow his progress. If a cadet's grades began to slip, however, or if he was ill, or even if he simply failed to write home, Lee would intervene. He encouraged such students to work harder and encouraged the parents to provide support. When a cadet flunked out, Lee showed great concern. The Old Virginia code of gentlemanly behavior required a display of deference to the feelings of others. Students, and especially their parents, warranted respect, particularly at the difficult time of dismissal. Lee's letters were remarkably tactful; he was often able to find something positive to say even in the worst of circumstances. If these duties gave

Lee gray hairs, he must have gained a measure of satisfaction from them as well. He would be ready to take on many of the same tasks when he assumed the presidency of Washington College in 1865. When we compare the Weir portrait to the photographs of Lee taken toward the end of the Civil War, we see the startling effect the intervening decade had on his appearance.[15]

Two episodes at West Point caused particular concern. The most trying disciplinary problem of Lee's tenure involved his nephew Fitzhugh Lee, the son of Smith Lee. Guilty of absences from the barracks and other such misdemeanors, Fitz accumulated nearly enough demerits to be expelled. He eventually graduated, forty-fifth in a class of forty-nine, and went on to become a general in the Confederate army during the Civil War. Lee's most celebrated dismissal set one of America's greatest painters on his true career path. The son of West Point graduate and engineer George Washington Whistler, cadet James Abbott McNeill Whistler was as poor a student as he was a horseman. He did not take to the military and delighted in his refusal to dine with people who discussed battles over food. Lee wrote to Totten, "I can only regret that one so capable of doing well should so have neglected himself, and must now suffer the penalty." Whistler, who enjoyed making shocking remarks, later spoke admiringly of his former superintendent, perhaps because by joining the Confederacy Lee had set a new standard for rebelling against authority.[16]

The family moved with Lee from Baltimore to the academy. Furniture was shipped from Arlington, along with paintings and decorative objects, and even the family horses. Everything was done to create the illusion of home. Agnes and Annie delayed the move for a season, and Mary and Rooney were away at school for discreet periods, but Rob and Mildred were at West Point throughout. Lee worried particularly about Agnes because of her earlier eye injury: "At dawn when I rise, & all day, my thoughts revert to you," he wrote her. The superintendent found time to take Rob on outdoor adventures, including riding, swimming, and skating. He saw Custis when he opened his quarters to cadets. Agnes wrote in her journal: "We also arrange for cadet suppers every Sat. evening, they to be sure need not be very exquisite but must be just right for Papa's scrutinizing eye." She enjoyed an environment with so many young men, as did her oldest sister. Mary caught the attention of cadet Jeb Stuart (see fig. 97), who later wrote a "Poem to Mary Lee" about "the gay old days—the West Point days."[17]

In the spring of 1853, Lee's mother-in-law died. Forever, it seemed, Mary Custis (fig. 102) had both counseled him and helped to raise the Lee children. He remembered the "tender love" that he had "felt & rejoiced in … from boyhood." The affection had been returned by Lee, who always called Mary "Mother." "As a son I have always loved her," he told his wife. "She was to me all that a mother could be, and I yield to none in admiration for her character, love for her virtues, and veneration for her memory." What most appealed to Lee about Mary Custis was her selflessness, which was a Christian virtue that his own mother had possessed. Lee described "the utter absence of every feeling of selfishness so conspicuous in her whole life." G. W. P. Custis grieved deeply over the death of his wife. Five months later Lee was able to take him to Niagara Falls for a diversion.[18]

The death of Mary Custis Lee stirred a revival of religious feeling in the family. Mary Lee wrote in her diary, "That blessed Saviour has been most faithful & now in this heavy bereavement does He draw me nearer to Himself …. May she not have died in vain for those for whom she long prayed & toiled." As a child, Robert had been drilled in religious values and beliefs by the future bishop of Virginia, William Meade, and as an adult he had attended church services with some regularity. He had even served for a time on the vestry of St. John's Church in Brooklyn. But Robert had not been confirmed. In July 1853, however, on a summer leave at Arlington, he presented himself at Christ Church, Alexandria, along with daughters Mary and Annie, who also had been moved by the recent death. From this point forward, religion became increasingly important to Lee. He read his Bible and prayer book daily. Freeman concluded that Lee believed in a God who sent both blessings and hardships, for reasons that man could not understand. That was similar to the fatalist stance that George Washington often took. Emory Thomas has concluded that Lee's response to God was based on selflessness, self-control, and service to others.[19]

In the spring of 1854, Custis Lee graduated first in his class. That rank entitled him to assignment in the prestigious Engineer Corps; his first duty would be on the coast of Florida. Robert E. Lee would leave the academy a year later. Toward the end of his tenure, the Board of Visitors of the academy was still talking about "the eminent qualifications of the superintendent for the honorable and distinguished

fig. 102.
Mrs. George Washington Parke Custis (Mary Lee Fitzhugh), c. 1850 (photograph courtesy of Virginia Historical Society)

post assigned him by the government." His "Services conspicuous in the field, and when our country was engaged in a war with a foreign nation" were not forgotten. These had "lost none of their luster in the exalted position he so worthily fills." Lee had maintained his friendship with General Winfield Scott, who visited the academy, and he had been in contact with Dennis Hart Mahan, one of three members of the academic board and a military theorist who preached the importance of trenches to modern warfare. That lesson would not be lost on Lee. The superintendent also learned a great deal about the supervision of young men, an experience that would help him both as a commander and during his later years at Washington College.[20]

Texas: 1856–57

His next assignment would take him even further from his engineering background. In 1855 Lee was placed with the Second U.S. Cavalry. He welcomed "the change from my present confined & sedentary life, to one more free & active." In Texas, however, where his unit was deployed, he would soon enough complain to Edward Lee Childe, the son of his sister Mildred, that "the separation from my dear wife & children is very grievous to me, & I do not know how long I can stand it. I fear it will eventually drive me from the service." Two cavalry units had been created by act of Congress in 1855 because a year earlier a force of Plains Indians had massacred a detachment of thirty soldiers from Fort Laramie in Wyoming. Secretary of War Davis had previously requested an expansion of the standing army, stating that the 14,000 soldiers then in uniform were inadequate to protect 800 miles of frontier from 40,000 hostile Native Americans. Davis appointed Albert Sidney Johnston to serve as colonel of the new Second Regiment. He was four years older than Lee and was a veteran not only of Mexico but also of the Black Hawk War. Lee was commissioned lieutenant colonel and placed second in command.[21]

Lee tried to explain to Markie Williams why he accepted a posting that would take him so far away. It was certainly not for "personal consideration or convenience." He claimed that if his presence was important to the family "or necessary to my children," the thought of leaving would be "bitter in the extreme." Not surprisingly, he added, "You know Markie how painful it will be to part from you." This was, however, the rare chance for career advancement. Lee probably would never have been promoted much further in the engineer corps because nine other officers outranked him. From "a military point of view," as he put it to Markie, there was "no other course." When the time comes to "act differently" and put family first, he said, "it will be time for me to quit the service."[22]

Separation from family is difficult for any career officer. "I unfortunately belong to a profession that debars all hope of domestic enjoyment," Lee wrote to Mary, "the duties of which cannot be performed without a sacrifice of personal & private relations." Robert had not been away from his family for many long stretches other than the two years in Mexico since 1840. Now he was leaving for frontier duty, which must have seemed like he was going to the end of the earth, without a Scott or a Taylor in command. Lee was now the man to whom others would turn in moments of need. He was stationed first at Fort Mason, one hundred miles beyond San Antonio. Among those deployed with him was George Thomas, with whom he would share a tent when traveling long distances on

fig. 103.
George Catlin, *Comanche Warriors, with White Flag, Receiving the Dragoons at Their Village*, 1834–35, oil on canvas, 24⅛ × 29⅛ in. (61.3 × 74.0 cm.), Smithsonian American Art Museum, gift of Mrs. Joseph Harrison, Jr.

court-martial duty. Johnston then moved Lee to the command of two squadrons of the regiment that were stationed 170 miles north of Fort Mason, at Camp Cooper, within the Comanche reserve. "We are far beyond civilization," he wrote to Agnes.[23]

Lee had little respect for the Comanches (fig. 103): "Their paint & ornaments make them more hideous than nature made them & the whole tribe is extremely uninteresting," he wrote to his wife. The chief, Catumseh, told Lee that he had six wives and would respect the colonel more if he had six as well. Lee was disgusted. "I see more of them than I desire," he commented to his old friend Eliza Stiles. Five weeks of his duty in Texas would be spent searching, unsuccessfully, for Senaco, the leader of a group of renegades. He summed up his thoughts to Mary Custis Lee, concluding that the Comanches did not warrant either his interest or his concern for their well-being: "These people give a world of trouble to man and horse, and, poor creatures, they are not worth it."[24]

The most poignant experiences for Lee in Texas involved the deaths of two children from families of soldiers under his command. He recorded one of the incidents:

> His father came to me, the tears flowing down his cheeks, and asked me to read the funeral service over his body, which I did at the grave for the second time in my life. I hope I shall not be called on again, for, though I believe that it is far better for the child to be called by its heavenly Creator into his presence in its purity and innocence, unpolluted by sin, and uncontaminated by the vices of the world, still it wrings a parents' heart with anguish that is painful to see.

Lee was further saddened to learn of the death in 1856 of his younger sister Mildred in Paris. He had much time to think while in Texas. Amidst such personal turmoil, he managed to write in his diary during these years a key tenet of his philosophy about life: "Dissimilar as are characters, intellects, and situations, the great duty of life is the same, the promotion of the happiness and welfare of our fellow men."[25]

Lee's own children suffered during his absence. Agnes wrote in her journal, "He is now in Texas O so far away he seems. I love him so much." Her father tried to convert her to his own brand of fatalism: "You must expect discomforts and annoyances all through life. No place or position is secure from them, and you must make up your mind to meet with them and bear them." Lee was particularly concerned about his absence during the upbringing of Mildred and Rob, his youngest children. He wrote a series of charming letters to the ten-year old Mildred, telling her stories about his pets, including a rattlesnake, assuring her that he missed her, and encouraging her to write back. Even these humorous letters, however, had within them lessons for his daughter to consider.

> I want to see you so much. Cannot you ... pack [yourself] up in a carpetbag & come up to the Comanche country? ... Did I tell you Jim Nooks, Mrs. Waits cat, was dead? Died of apoplexy. I foretold his end. Coffee & cream for breakfast. Pound cake for lunch. Turtles & oysters for dinner. Buttered toast for tea, & Mexican rats, taken raw, for supper! Cat nature could not stand so much luxury. He grew enormously, & ended in a spasm. His beauty could not save him.

He was also concerned that his youngest son receive the best education. Rob should "learn perfectly latin, French & arithmetic," and develop good handwriting. Robert told his wife to "let him never touch a novel":

> They paint beauty more charming than nature, & describe happiness that never exists. They will teach him to sigh after that which has no reality, & to despise the little good that is granted us in this world & to expect more than is ever given. Instill in him industry & frugality ....[26]

Mary's painful arthritis increasingly became a concern for her husband. Robert praised her for enduring her deteriorating illness with so positive an attitude: "I was much pleased & comforted to find in all your letters, that your good sense & pure piety enabled you to bear with patience & resignation this painful affliction." He charged their daughters to care for her. Lee wrote to Mildred, "Now that she is in pain & trouble, it is more than ever your duty to assist & serve her, & on no account to add to her distress." It was, for them, a test: "Perhaps God has thus afflicted her to try her children & give them an opportunity of showing their appreciation of all she has done for them." Mary Custis Lee had become nearly an invalid; she was confined to her bedroom and barely able to move. She wrote to a friend, "I almost dread [Robert] seeing me in this crippled state."[27]

Annie and Agnes were becoming more devout Christians. Lee wrote happily to their mother, "If they can lead the life of pure & earnest Christians, serving their God in spirit & in truth & doing to their neighbour all the good in their power, as if to themselves, they

fig. 104.
William Henry Fitzhugh Lee in the uniform of the U.S. Army, c. 1857 (photograph courtesy of Virginia Historical Society)

fig. 1105.
Grant as a First Lieutenant in the Fourth Infantry at Sackets Harbor, 1849, photograph from the collection of Keya Morgan, New York City

will realize the only true happiness in this world." He turned his anxiety instead to their son Rooney: "He gives me many anxious days & sleepless nights & adds more than years to the grey hairs on my head." Rooney was affectionate but thoughtless and impulsive, and he is "guided more by his feelings than his reason." Lee added, "Until I see that he has regained proper self control, & is guided by principles of duty, rather than the notions of others & feelings of pleasure, I can never feel assured of his conduct." That was vintage Lee.[28]

Unable to win an appointment to West Point, Rooney had enrolled instead at Harvard. He showed an ability to lead, but not the intellect to succeed. Henry Adams wrote famously about his classmate, describing Rooney as having "the Virginia habit of command," but being "simple beyond analysis." Mary wrote in desperation to old friend Winfield Scott, who awarded Rooney a commission as a second lieutenant in the infantry (fig. 104). Lee sent a letter of thanks to his former commander: "as you (used to) say, 'boys are only fit to be shot' & he seems to have had from infancy an ardent desire for this high privilege."[29]

Grant's Deployment in the North and Northwest

As he awaited the ratification of a peace treaty, Grant took in some of the sights of Mexico, including an expedition to Popocatapetl, which he describes as the highest volcano in America, and a visit to a bullfight. Grant was not impressed by the latter. He states, quite apologetically:

> Every Sunday there was a bull fight for the amusement of those who would pay their fifty cents. I attended one of them—just one—not wishing to leave the country without having witnessed the national sport. The sight to me was sickening. I could not see how human beings could enjoy the sufferings of beasts, and often of men, as they seemed to do on those occasions.

Grant came away feeling "sorry to see the cruelty to the bull and the horse." His regiment was eventually sent to Pascagoula, Mississippi, where he obtained leave. First Lieutenant Grant (fig. 105) married Julia Dent in St. Louis in August 1848. The couple then visited his parents and relations in Ohio, where the groom introduced his new bride. Because of his generally positive experience in Mexico, Grant had decided to remain in the army. The couple then proceeded to his next place of deployment. His regiment, the Fourth Infantry, had been reassigned to the edge of Canada, another frontier that bordered a foreign nation. Regimental head-

fig. 106.
Anthony Fleetwood after Caleb Davis, *View of the City of Detroit*, 1834, lithograph, 17 × 21½ in. (43.2 × 54.6 cm.), New-York Historical Society Library

fig. 107.
T. Birch after William Strickland, *South East View of Sackett's Harbour*, 1815, engraving, 5½ × 9 in. (14.0 × 22.9 cm.), New-York Historical Society Library

quarters were established at Detroit. Companies were stationed at outposts from Detroit to New York State. For a good part of the next four years, the Grants would be blissfully together in the North as he pursued his career.[30]

Detroit
Grant was regimental quartermaster; his duties compelled him to operate out of regimental headquarters. By mistake, however, he was initially ordered to one of the outposts, Sackets Harbor, New York. The Grants were ordered to travel there for the winter of 1848 before the error by Colonel William Whistler was corrected. By April 1849, they were in Detroit (fig. 106). Julia, who was pregnant with their first child, Frederick Dent Grant, would soon travel again. On the advice of the post surgeon, she was sent to her parents' home in St. Louis to give birth there.[31]

The two years in Detroit were spent "with but few important incidents," Grant later wrote. Best when he was active and challenged, he found life there "very dull." He told Julia that he had "nothing atal to do," and he went fishing just to pass the time. But, he confessed, her absence due to the pregnancy was the real problem: "Dearest without you no place, or home, can be very pleasant to me." At one point Grant even had a soldier fix up the garden to put it "in the nicest order" for her return.[32]

Sackets Harbor
When the Fourth Infantry garrison was transferred in the spring of 1851 to Sackets Harbor (fig. 107), Grant went with it. A month later he was brevetted captain. On the way he stopped at West Point: "I should really like very much to be stationed here," he wrote to Julia, expressing exactly the opposite sentiment found in Lee's request a year later that he not be made superintendent at the academy. Grant set up quarters at Sackets Harbor that would be comfortable for Julia and the baby, and then set about trying to coax her away from her parents. "I am highly delighted with Sacket's Harbor," he told her, mentioning the fishing, sailing, and picnicking enjoyed by the "very pleasant families in the garrison." It was only a few days' travel to Niagara Falls, New York City, Montreal, and Boston. Little Fred would be able to play on the parade ground. Grant promised to get him a dog and a wagon. At the same time, Ulysses did not shy away from the heart of the issue: your

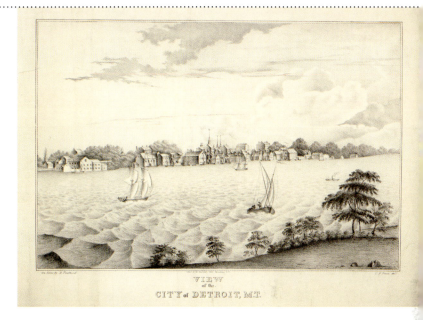

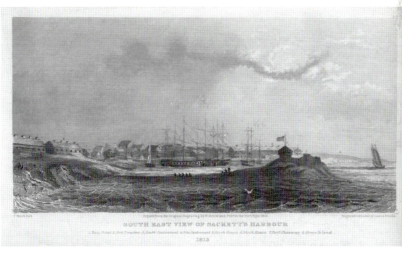

parents "know that you must come after a while and you might just as well leave soon as late." He instructed Julia to "tell Fred. to be a good boy and not annoy his grandpa & ma," and he asked, perhaps remembering his own childhood, "Is he getting big enough to whip when he is a bad boy?"[33]

In 1852, however, just when it seemed that they would "be much more comfortably fixed than we have ever been before," Grant was transferred to the Pacific Northwest. Settlement there had been spurred by the California gold rush of 1849. Troops were needed to keep order. In May 1852, the Fourth Infantry received its orders. In July, the troops set sail for Panama. Julia was pregnant with their second son, to be named for his father. Due to the difficulty of

LEE AND GRANT

fig. 108.
Thomas Sinclair, *San Francisco*, 1852,
lithograph, 7⅝ × 15½ in. (19.4 × 39.4 cm.),
New-York Historical Society Library

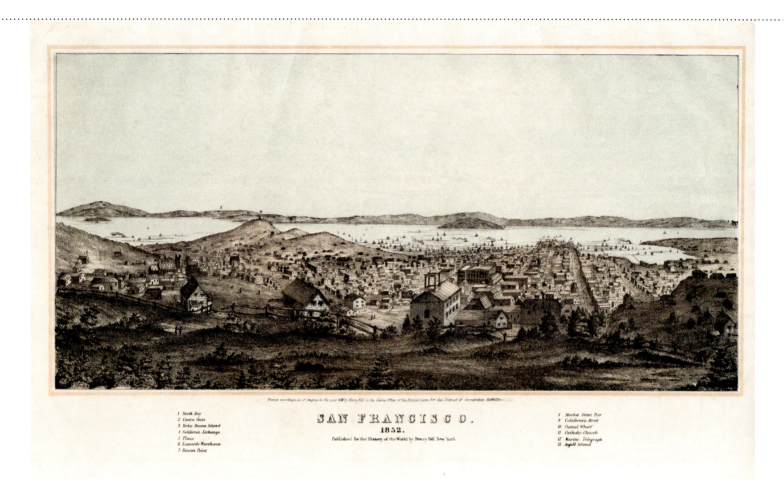

the trip, Ulysses wisely forbade her to join the other wives traveling with the group.[34]

The Northwest
During the arduous journey across the Isthmus of Panama, Grant demonstrated remarkable leadership in the midst of delays and a deadly cholera epidemic. As quartermaster he did much to bring the survivors to San Francisco. He reported to Julia the "terrible sickness among the troops" and the deaths of "one hundred persons, counting men, women & children." Those hundred made up a third of the group traveling with him. He assured her that she "never could have crossed the Isthmus at this season" and that "the horrors of the road, in the rainy season, are beyond description."[35]

After his arrival in California, Grant entered into the first of a series of business embarrassments that would undermine his expectations and preclude any possible happiness during his two-year tenure in the Northwest. He formed a partnership with a merchant he had known in Sackets Harbor, Elijah Camp. The idea was to create some sort of store or social club that would succeed in San Francisco, a city still booming from the discovery of gold four years earlier (fig. 108). In the end, Camp took Grant's money, which was all of his recent salary, and was gone. Julia reproached her husband: "Compared to you, the Vicar of Wakefield's Moses was a financier." Her reference was to Oliver Goldsmith's novel, in which Moses Primrose, the second son of the Vicar of Wakefield, was "designed for business" but was easily swindled. As biographer William McFeely has written, throughout his life there would always be an Elijah Camp in Ulysses S. Grant's business deals.[36]

Grant was soon ordered to Fort Vancouver on the Columbia River, a region that the next year would be designated "Washington Territory." "There is not a more delightful place in the whole country," he reported to Julia. He liked the climate and the scenery, and his health improved: "I have grown out of my clothes entirely." He also took a liking to the Native Americans of the Pacific

fig. 109.
Ulysses S. Grant, Columbia Barracks [Fort Vancouver], Oregon Territory, to Julia Grant, *Letter*, March 19, 1853, Library of Congress

Northwest, most of whom were friendly to Euro-Americans. He thought that if not mistreated, these "harmless and peaceable people" pose no threat at all to settlers (fig. 109). That Grant's attitude toward Indian people was entirely different from Lee's is not simply because the tribes of the Northwest seemed less militant than the peoples of the Southwest. He felt a genuine sympathy for most Native Americans. That instinct, coupled with the firsthand knowledge that he gained in the 1850s, would inspire his attempts to design more enlightened policies when he became president.[37]

Despite the initial mishap in San Francisco, Grant still looked to earn sufficient income during his free time to bring his wife and now two children west to join him. "Living is expensive but money can be made," he told Julia from Fort Vancouver, sounding like a forty-niner: "I … could enjoy myself here as well as any place that I have ever been stationed at if only you were here. " If he could "get together a few thousand dollars," he could even "go home."[38]

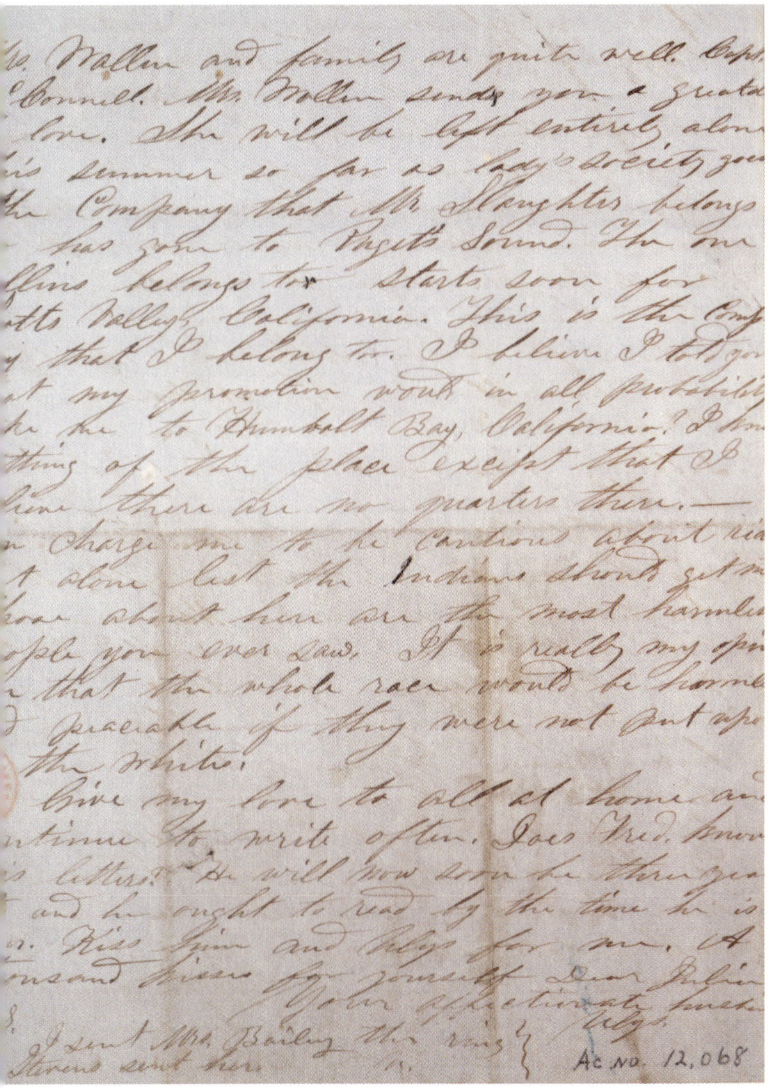

In his *Memoirs*, Grant recounted his next plan to strike it rich: "I with three other officers concluded that we would raise a crop for ourselves, and by selling the surplus realize something handsome." He would put to use the agricultural skills he had learned as a youth. Grant and his colleagues leased a farm of "about a hundred acres." They planted a field of barley and twenty acres of potatoes, as well as onions and other vegetables. They planned as well to buy, haul, and sell steamboat wood for a profit, and to buy and sell pigs, hogs, and chickens. In effect, they were speculating in agricultural commodities without any business experience. One of the officers, Captain Henry Wallen, later confessed that "neither Grant nor myself had the slightest suggestion of business talent. He was the perfect soul of honor and truth, and believed everyone as artless as himself." In this case, nature also was against them. The river flooded, destroying their crops and washing away the timber. Many of the animals died. It was a disaster; no money would be earned from this venture.[39]

In the meantime, after a death in the Adjutant General's department in July 1853, Grant was promoted to the captaincy of a company stationed at Humboldt Bay, California. The promotion was well received—there were only fifty captains on active duty then—but the change of location was not. Grant arrived in January 1854: "I cannot say much in favor of the place," he wrote Julia. "Imagine a place closed in by the sea having thrown up two tongues of land, closed in a bay that can be entered only with certain winds." He was also distracted: "The place is good enough but I have [business] interests at others [closer to Fort Vancouver] which I cannot help thinking about day and night." Little wonder that he felt "forsaken." "I do nothing but sit in my room and read and occasionally take a short ride."[40]

As a line captain, Grant's duties actually diminished in number. He had little work, which for him was a misfortune. And discipline, which he never much cared for, was more rigorous at Fort Humboldt. He began to miss his family more and more. In 1852 Grant had complained, "I am almost crazy sometimes to see [our son] Fred. I cannot be separated from him and his Ma for a long

fig. 110.
Julia Grant with Sons Buck and Fred, c. 1854, photograph from the collection of Keya Morgan, New York City

fig. 111.
Benson J. Lossing, "Arlington House, The Seat of G. W. P. Custis Esq.," *Harper's New Monthly Magazine* 7 (1853), Virginia Historical Society

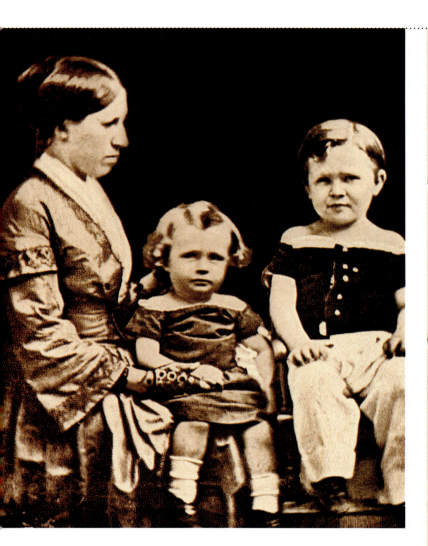

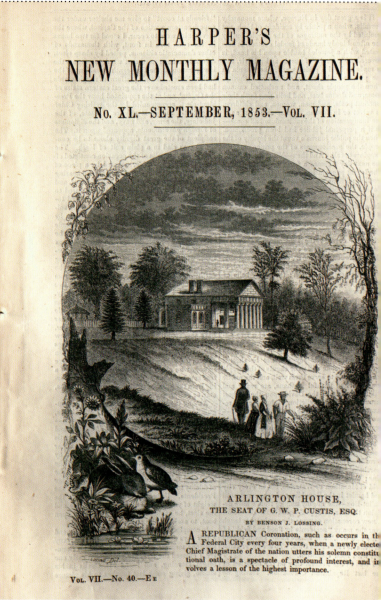

time." Now he wrote, "I feel again as if I had been separated from you and Fred long enough and as to Ulys. I have never seen him." He asked Julia to send him a photograph (fig. 110).[41]

At this low point in his life, Grant seems to have taken to serious drinking. According to Lieutenant Henry Hodges, a close friend who had served with him at Fort Vancouver, Grant had earlier recognized that he had a drinking problem and he usually abstained: "He would perhaps go on two or three sprees a year, but was always open to reason, and when spoken to on the subject would own up and promise to stop drinking, which he did." Hodges said that Grant actually quit the army because one day he appeared for duty at the pay table intoxicated. A second account, penned by another friend, Rufus Ingalls, did not specify the duty. The commanding officer, Lieutenant Colonel Robert Christie Buchanan, apparently demanded that Grant either stand trial or leave the army.[42]

If the drinking incidents are true, they point to one underlying cause behind Grant's decision to resign. In March 1854, a month before he quit the army, he wrote to Julia, "I sometimes get so anxious to see you, and our little boys, that I am almost tempted to resign." Julia, reversing her sentiments from before they were married, now apparently encouraged the move. She later wrote, "to my great delight [Captain Grant] resigned his commission … and returned to me, his loving little wife." He received his actual commission as captain on April 11, 1854, the same day on which he resigned, to take effect of July 31. He explained in his *Memoirs*:

My family, all this while, was at the East. It consisted now of a wife and two children. I saw no chance of supporting them on the Pacific coast out of my pay as an army officer. I concluded, therefore, to resign …. I left the Pacific coast very much attached to it, and with the full expectation of making it my future home.

Grant's father objected to the finality of the decision; a leave of absence should have been requested. Writing to the secretary of war, Jesse tried to undo the mistake: "I will remark that he has not seen his family for over two years, & has a son nearly two years old he has never seen. I suppose in his great anxiety to see his family he has been induced to quit the servis." Jefferson Davis did not reply. The decision had been made. Grant's army career was over.[43]

Return to Civilian Life

The Lees of Arlington

In October 1857, G. W. P. Custis died at Arlington of pneumonia. Custis Lee was on duty in San Francisco. Rooney Lee was on his way to duty in Texas. Washy's daughter Mary Lee was crippled. And so Robert E. Lee was forced to apply for a leave of absence from the army in order to return to Virginia to settle his father-in-law's estate. Once at Arlington, Lee decided to take up farming in earnest. In this effort he would have to confront the immorality, inefficiency, and injustice of slavery.

Only four years earlier, a *Harper's* article about Arlington had pictured it as Edenic (fig. 111). Over the years Lee's mother-in-law and his wife had made efforts to provide some degree of justice to the Arlington slaves, a few of whom had been freed to relocate to Africa. However, some of the slaves had showed signs of unrest and revolt even before Custis's death. His will promised bequests to his grandchildren with money that would have to be raised by the labor of his slaves. As executor, Lee would feel obliged to put the slaves to that task, with far from satisfactory results.

Lee had spent several months at Arlington in 1855. He was able then to accomplish some improvements to the house, the condition of which had deteriorated over the years. He finished the main parlor (fig. 112), had all the lower rooms painted, and installed a furnace. Despite the room's prominence and size, the parlor had been used by the Custises for half a century only for storage; it remained a wasted space. With Lee's engineering experience, the task

fig. 112.
White Parlor at Arlington (photograph courtesy of National Park Service, Arlington House)

of restoration was easy. The fact that he took it on is evidence that he considered that he might one day live full-time at Arlington. Lee filled the parlor with furniture, art, and the other accoutrements of middle-class life that he had acquired in Baltimore and West Point. A landscape painting of the Hudson River that was purchased in the North (fig. 113) is evidence that the Lees looked back upon his tenure at the academy with more pride than his letters suggest.[44]

On that earlier visit Lee had helped his father-in-law to sort out some of the business affairs at the two other Custis plantations. These too had fallen into disarray. Francis Nelson, the manager at the White House and Romancoke, had presented his employer with a bill for ten years' service without adequate records to account for

fig. 113.
Unknown artist, *Hudson River Landscape*, c. 1850, oil on canvas, 30⅝ × 44¼ in. (77.8 × 112.4 cm.), National Park Service, Arlington House

the sum requested, $6,078.95. Custis was at a loss as to what to do. Lee not only journeyed to the two plantations, but also to Richmond and Baltimore in search of records. He spent the whole month of December 1855 trying to straighten out the Arlington books, and he engaged an agent, William Overton Winston, to unravel the disorder at the two distant plantations. Winston had little success.[45]

In the end, Lee would have to devote some of his personal funds to meet the Custis debts. His dismally low army salary allowed little financial freedom, but he had been investing what he did receive in a conscious effort not to duplicate his father's bankruptcy. He bought state, city, canal, and railroad bonds. By 1846, when he set off for Mexico, he had built up a portfolio worth $38,750 that yielded some $2,000 a year, which was more than his salary from the army. Much of the portfolio would vanish during the Civil War.[46]

Lee's two-year management of the slave force at Arlington was a disastrous clash of opposing wills. The slaves thought that Custis had granted them their freedom. Lee felt compelled as the executor of the estate to follow the directives of his father-in-law's will by working the slaves until they earned the funds to pay the Custis bequests. Many of the slaves were discontented, and Lee became frustrated. He demanded of them, as he demanded of the soldiers under his command, the members of his family, and as he demanded of himself, that they work hard. Custis had apparently never asked for hard work. Lee hired out many of the able-bodied slaves as the best means to earn the always needed cash. Others ran away. He tracked them down as best he could, returned them, and asked them to perform what he thought was their duty. The worst offenders were punished, in at least one case brutally.

Lee had already spent a half-century in a slave society. He was no newcomer to a plantation. He had never worried as much about the institution as some Virginians in part because there was nothing he personally could do to alter the situation. Like his father, who dismissed slavery as a "dreadful evil which the cruel policy of preceding times had introduced," Lee had generally tried to distance himself from it. Like many of his contemporaries, he believed in a hierarchy based on race, a sort of pyramid that put the white gentry at the top, lower-class Euro-Americans in the middle, and African Americans and Native Americans at the bottom. After he had inherited several of his mother's thirty-five slaves, he wrote in 1831 to his new wife, "I do not know what to do with [them]." But, adding a comment similar to the one he would later make about the Comanches, he told Mary, "do not trouble yourself about them, as they are not worth it." Lee hired out Nancy Ruffin to his father-in-law to work at the White House, and as late as 1852 he was still hiring out another slave, Philip Meriday, in Washington. He kept personal body servants until the end of 1862, when his freeing of the Custis slaves obliged him to pay a modest wage for such help.[47]

Over the years prior to 1857, Lee's contacts with slaves other than members of the domestic staff were infrequent. A few remarks, however, reveal his views about the institution. In 1841, when Mary Custis Lee wanted to buy the freedom of a slave who had been mistreated at the plantation of her aunt Nelly Custis, Lee worried about the impact such an action would have on the other slaves, but he gave his permission: "If you determine to apply your money in this way I am ready to pay it." He was happy to liberate an occasional slave, in part because to do so was within his reach, and because the loss would not affect him. He supported his wife's efforts with the American Colonization Society, which had been established in 1816 for the purpose of returning slaves to Africa, calling the organization a "noble & Christian enterprise." In 1853, in closing a routine letter to his daughter Annie, Lee suggests a closeness to the domestic staff at Arlington: "Give much love to your dear Grdmother, Grdfather, Agnes, Miss Sue, Lucretia & all friends, including the Servants." Yet in this same decade Lee was indignant when abolitionists dared to stir up the slave population and thereby "excite some apprehensions for the peace & prosperity of the country."

fig. 114.
Robert E. Lee to Mary Custis Lee, *Letter*, December 27, 1856, Virginia Historical Society

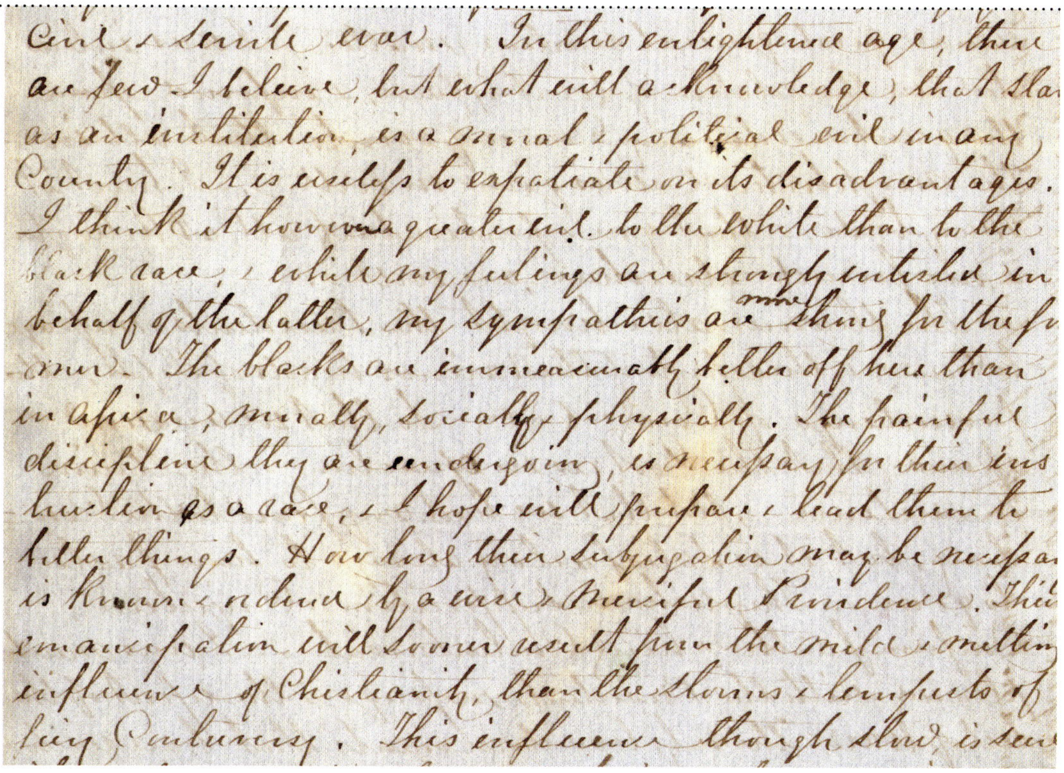

Slavery cannot be overturned, he reasoned, so why bring about discord? On learning of a cholera outbreak in 1849 among the slaves at Shirley plantation, the birthplace of his mother, Lee made a peculiar, somewhat ambiguous statement: "The poor blacks have a multitude of miseries. I hope death that must come sooner or later will end them all." If in the short term he was talking about the cholera victims, it is not a stretch to think that he might have had in mind as well the second possible meaning—that death would be better to them than life in servitude.[48]

Mary Custis Lee had been schooled by her mother to apply Christian values toward the victims of the slave system. Following the Civil War she would become bitter about the rights awarded to the freedpeople, but before that time she struggled to do what she thought was just. In 1846 she wrote to a relative who had inherited slaves, "Let no motive of worldly interest induce you to act an unkind or ungenerous part towards them." But she added, tellingly, "I well know what a trial they are, but think we are little disposed to make allowances for their peculiar ignorance and debased condition." She could never imagine that a black person could be her equal. She wrote in her diary at her mother's death of how Mary Custis had so much wanted "all the slaves [to be] enabled to emigrate to Africa," and how she had made some progress with this "sacred duty." She wanted "William & his family," "Eleanor & her family," and "Eliza" to emigrate soon, adding, "What is life worth unless you can accomplish in it something for the benefit of others, especially of those so entirely dependent upon our will & pleasure."[49]

The Lee girls had been brought up to care about the welfare of the slaves, and to help with the reading lessons and religious services. These interactions led to warm feelings. When one of the last three Mount Vernon slaves who had been owned by George and Martha Washington, "dear old Mammy," died in 1856, Agnes Lee mourned in her journal: "She was as faithful as could be. How I [miss] her …. O those nice talks! We won't have any more." Two years later, in the midst of the discontent following her father's announcement to the slaves that they were not free but must continue to labor, she added, "I am no longer the free thoughtless child at sixteen…. I am but truly commencing the … battle of life."[50]

Lee's most famous statement about slavery—that it is "a moral & political evil in any Country"—was made in a letter to his wife of December 27, 1856 (fig. 114). He wrote in sympathetic response to anti-abolitionist comments made by the outgoing president, Franklin Pierce, who was Lee's colleague during the Mexican War. Such beliefs were not new for the colonel nor were they unique. He maintained that slavery was an evil that man cannot solve. God alone will end the institution when He chooses to do so. Emancipation can only be gradual, he argued, and so he took only the smallest of steps in that direction. Lee was concerned about the welfare of blacks, but he was always more interested in the progress of whites. Abolitionists, to Lee, were simply troublemakers.

> I think it however a greater evil to the white than to the black race, & while my feelings are strongly enlisted in behalf of

fig. 115.
Robert K. Sneden, *"The Contraband Camp" below Arlington House, Va.*, November 1862, watercolor on paper, 5⅜ × 6½ in. (13.7 × 16.5 cm.), Virginia Historical Society

the latter, my sympathies are more strong for the former. The blacks are immeasurably better off here than in Africa, morally, socially & physically. The painful discipline they are undergoing, is necessary for their instruction as a race, & I hope will prepare & lead them to better things. How long their subjugation may be necessary is known & ordered by a wise Merciful Providence. Their emancipation will sooner result from the mild & melting influence of Christianity, than the storms & tempests of fiery Controversy. This influence though slow is sure …. I fear [the abolitionist] will persevere in his evil Course. Is it not strange that the descendants of those pilgrim fathers who crossed the Atlantic to preserve their own freedom of opinion, have always proved themselves intolerant of the Spiritual liberty of others?

In his way, Lee was more enlightened than many white southerners of the antebellum era. However, he did nothing to change matters, choosing instead to wait until God took a direct interest.[51]

G. W. P. Custis had mused to Markie Williams that the Arlington slaves lived better than did the lower classes in England because they had their own homes, their families were with them, they were provided with food and clothing, and, at least from his perspective, they were free to do what they pleased. The injustice portrayed in *Uncle Tom's Cabin* was, according to Custis, entirely absent from Arlington. He was being less than truthful.[52]

Owning slaves was complicated. In 1862, Robert E. Lee, Jr. wrote his sister Mildred about the slaves at the White House, the plantation he inherited from his grandfather Custis, telling her that the "most delightful thing about the place is the set of negroes. They are the real old Virginny kind, as polite as possible, devoted to their master & mistress, who are devoted to them & who do everything for them." Several years earlier, however, his mother had to write to Robert, Sr. to come home because this same son, though only a teenager, was starting to "linger near the quarters." She was worried that he might begin to do what her own father had apparently done—father illegitimate children with the slaves. There were nineteen free mulattos listed in the census records of 1850 as living on the Arlington grounds.[53]

When G. W. P. Custis died in October 1857, Lee was faced with a career decision. His wife had been awarded life occupancy at Arlington. He could live there with her and his children and lead the life of a planter, or he could return to his post. He wrote to his commanding officer in Texas, Albert Sidney Johnston, "I can see that I have at last to decide the question, which I have staved off for 20 years. Whether I am to continue in the Army all my life, or to leave it …. My preferences which have clung to me from boyhood impell me to adopt the former course, but yet I feel that a man's family has its claims too."

When he arrived at Arlington, Lee found the place in shambles. He wrote to Anna Maria Fitzhugh, "Dear Cousin Anna what am I to do? Custis I fear could not support his Gr[and]fathers name & place as he desired. Everything is in ruins & will have to be rebuilt. I feel more familiar with the military operations of a campaign than the details of a farm." Freeman describes the period of 1858–59 as one of the darkest of Lee's life. He would be troubled by both the stern measures that he adopted toward the slaves and by his failure to succeed in the role of executor of the Custis estate. When the Union soldier and artist Robert Sneden visited the plantation during the Civil War, he sketched some of the slaves, their number by then enlarged from its original ninety by the addition of runaways from other plantations (fig. 115).[54]

The Custis will, which was apparently written without the aid of a lawyer, put a heavy burden on Robert E. Lee. At the death of Mary Custis Lee, Arlington and its contents would pass to Custis Lee. White House plantation was left to Rooney, and Romancoke to Rob. Robert E. Lee was left a lot in the city of Washington. Each of the granddaughters was to receive $10,000, which was to come from the operation of the farms. When those legacies were paid, the slaves were to be emancipated, all within a period "not exceeding five years." G. W. P. Custis, however, had left $10,000 of debt, the farms were producing little income, and the will failed to provide financial support for any freed slaves. (Virginia law required freed slaves to leave the state if they were healthy, and that support be provided for those who were underage, old, or infirm.) Mary Custis Lee summed up the dilemma: "My dear father in his usual entire ignorance of the state of his affairs has left provision in his will which it will be almost impossible to fulfill even in double 5 years."[55]

All three of the Custis plantations would have to be made more productive. Colonel Lee extended his leave of absence to December 1858 and became a farmer. Custis offered him his inheritance—he even drew up a deed in February 1858 and mailed it to his father—but Robert refused it. Lee already had doubts. He wrote to a friend, Edward Turner, "I am no farmer myself & do not expect to be always here." He then, not surprisingly, gave the job his best effort. He rebuilt decaying farm buildings. Like George Washington at Mount Vernon some seventy years earlier, he instituted a scientific approach to farming, using fertilizers and deep plowing in an effort to rejuvenate tired soil. He told Rooney, however, "I succeed badly." His wife complained that he was "so harassed with the cares and troubles" of settling her father's estate that she did "not have the comfort that his presence might otherwise have afforded me." Many of the "troubles" came from the discontented slave force.[56]

Almost immediately, Lee hired out a dozen of the Arlington slaves, men and women, for the coming year. January was the traditional month to start a year's contract. His decision was quickly challenged. Lee wrote to his son Custis on January 17, 1858, that three of the men had balked at their assignment. They "returned the first on account of the work being too hard. Among them is Reuben, a great rogue & rascal whom I must get rid of some way." After three decades of service in the army, Lee was not about to put up with a refusal of orders. He soon sent three male slaves under guard to Richmond and directed his agent there, William O. Winston, to hire them out somewhere, either in the city or the country, or put them to work at the White House. (These may not have been the same three slaves—Reuben and his cohorts—because Reuben was back at Arlington by the late spring.) The next month, February 1858, Lee visited the White House and Romancoke and was discouraged to find both "dilapidated" with "nothing looking well." He told Rooney not to worry about the White House once the Custis slaves were freed because his son's future in-laws, the Wickhams, had promised to "supply you with hands." A month later he advised Rooney to be compassionate to the slaves: "attend to them & give them every aid & comfort in your power & they will be the happier."[57]

Also in February 1858, two abolitionists appeared on the Arlington property, adding fuel to a fire that was already burning. There was a near uprising, as Mary Custis Lee recounted to an acquaintance, W. G. Webster: "Scarcely had my father been laid in his tomb when two men were constantly lurking about here tampering with the servants & telling them they had a right to their freedom immediately & that if they would unite & demand it they would obtain it." Mary explained that the Custis slaves "have been so long accustomed to do little or nothing that they cannot be convinced of the necessity now of exerting themselves to accomplish the conditions of the will which the sooner they do the sooner they will be entitled to their freedom." She said that "an outbreak" was prevented only by the hand of God or "their own ineptness."[58]

Although the slaves did not revolt that spring, they did start to run away with some frequency. Seven escaped in April 1858 alone. Three were arrested and shipped to Richmond. Lee offered $10 re-

fig. 116.
Robert E. Lee, Arlington, to Rooney Lee, *Letter*, May 30, 1858, Virginia Historical Society

wards for runaways in Georgetown. In May, Reuben led another rebellion. Lee informed Rooney as part of the education of his son about the realities of slave management (fig. 116):

> I have had some trouble with some of the people. Reuben, Parks & Edward, in the beginning of the previous week, rebelled against my authority—refused to obey my orders, & said they were as free as I was, etc., etc.—I succeeded in capturing them & lodged them in jail. They resisted till overpowered & called upon the other people to rescue them.

The three were kept in jail for two months and then hired out. They probably made up part of the group of Arlington slaves who were in jail in Richmond in July 1858. "Dispose of them to the end of the year to the best advantage," Lee wrote to Winston. That summer Mary Custis Lee recorded in her diary that the slaves were causing "constant trouble in our domestic affairs." She made similar entries through the remainder of the year.[59]

Because he was making so little progress toward settling the Custis estate, Lee requested that his leave of absence from the army be extended beyond December 1858. It was a bleak winter at Arlington for the Lee family. Robert ultimately petitioned the Circuit Court to interpret the Custis will and thereby verify or negate the course he was pursuing. The court gave no answer.[60]

The troubles at Arlington peaked during the spring and summer of 1859. A rare positive moment was Rooney's wedding in March to Charlotte Wickham. But the discontent of the slave force persisted, and Mary Custis Lee's arthritis was worsening. In May, Lee wrote despondently to Custis, "I have no enjoyment in life now but what I derive from my children." Sometime in the spring, not long after Rooney's wedding, three slaves, Wesley Norris, his sister Mary, and his cousin George Parks, ran away from Arlington. Their destination was Pennsylvania. They traveled as far as Westminster, Maryland, before they were captured and imprisoned in mid-June. The trio was brought back to Arlington and whipped, then hired out to lower Virginia. The incident immediately attracted national attention. On June 21 and June 24 (fig. 117), the *New York Daily Tribune* published two critical letters that it received from anonymous contributors who claimed to be close neighbors of the Lees. The story was also carried in *The New York Times* and the *Boston Traveller*. It appeared again in 1866 in the *National Anti-Slavery Standard* under the title of "Robert E. Lee: His Brutality to His Slaves." This account was reputed to have been written by one of the victims, Wesley Norris.[61]

The first and shorter of the two letters published in New York states that the Arlington slaves were freed at the death of G. W. P. Custis but "are now held in bondage by Lee" and that he whipped Mary Norris himself. The family was no doubt also embarrassed by the accusation that "[G. W. P.] Custis had fifteen children by his slave women. I see his grandchildren every day; they are of a dark yellow." The second, longer letter suggests a reason that northern readers might accept for the flight of the three slaves. Custis, the letter stated, had told his servants on his deathbed that they would be free. After his passing they were informed by Lee that they would have to work an additional five years. Also, "they have been deprived of all means of making a little now and then for themselves, as they were allowed to do during Mr. Custis's life, have been kept harder at work than ever, and part of the time have been cut down to half a peck of unsifted meal a week for each person." Old women and old men, it was reported, were put back into the labor force. For those reasons, among others, six slaves had run away the previous year, and three had more recently set out for the

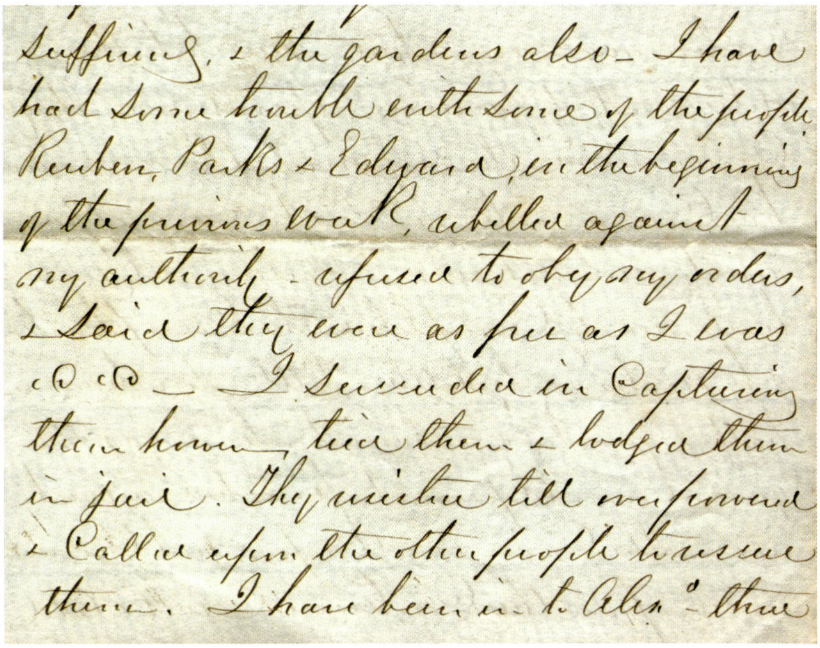

164 IV. CRISES OF THE 1850S

North. The latter were "intercepted by some brute in human form" and transported back to Arlington. Lee had them "taken into a barn, stripped, and the men received thirty and nine lashes each." Lee "himself administered the thirty and nine lashes" to the woman. The three slaves were then sent to a Richmond jail, where they are now lodged. Arlington, the writer states, is associated with the "Father of this free country." Should "never a voice [be] raised for such utter helplessness?" he concluded.

According to Wesley Norris's account of the incident, he had put up with Lee's interpretation of the will and his supervision of the Arlington slaves for seventeen months before he decided to flee. Upon his capture in Maryland and return to Virginia, Lee "demanded the reason why we ran away." The overseer at Arlington, Mr. Gwin, was ordered by Lee to give the men fifty lashes each and the woman twenty. He refused. Dick Williams, a county constable, was called in and he gave the lashes. Wesley Norris and George Parks were sent to Hanover Courthouse jail, then to Nelson County; Mary Norris was sent to Richmond. All were hired out.[62]

Some details of the various accounts are no doubt distortions of the truth, but the articles are often consistent. It would have been highly unlikely and totally out of character for Lee to have "stripped [Mary Norris] and whipped her himself," as the first letter claims, but Virginia law stipulated that it was the duty of a master to subject a runaway to a whipping, and Lee was not one to shirk his duty. Also, there is evidence to support the claims that the Norrises and George Parks were whipped. Newspaper accounts from Westminster, Maryland, in June 1859 document the imprisonment of the three Arlington slaves there. Lee's account book for the same month lists payments to Richard Williams, the "Dick Williams" mentioned in Wesley Norris's account. The question is why Williams was paid a very large sum, $321.14. The answer may lie in Lee's phrasing of the entry, "arrest, &c. of fugitive slaves." The tracking may have been extremely time-consuming, and whipping was a costly expense because few would perform such a savage task.[63]

In reporting the Norris and Parks incident to his son Custis in July 1859, Lee mentioned that other slaves had recently preceded them to "lower Virginia": "I had to send down before them, Obediah, Edward, Henry, and Austin Bingham." He added that he had to hire workers for the fields at Arlington at a "very small" price because here "we have nothing but the old men and boys."

fig. 117.
New York Daily Tribune, June 24, 1859

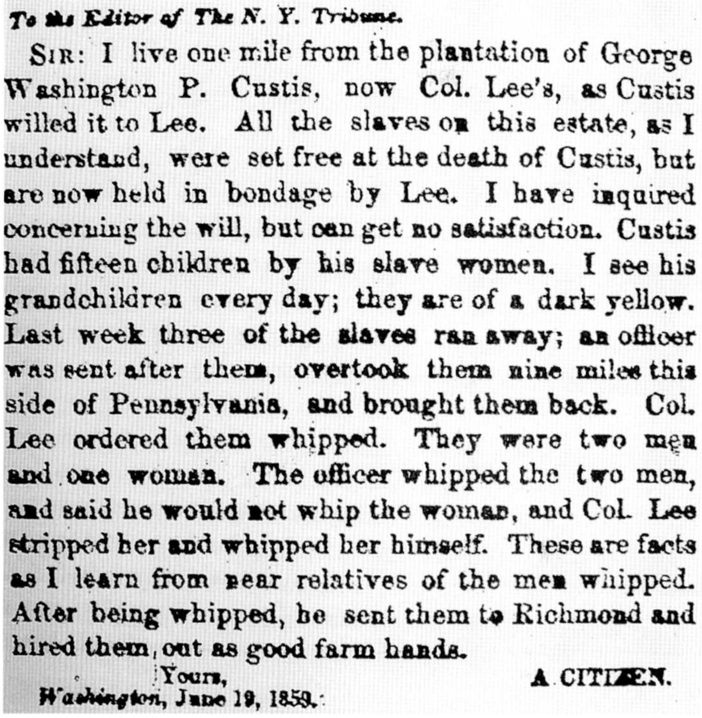

> To the Editor of The N. Y. Tribune.
>
> SIR: I live one mile from the plantation of George Washington P. Custis, now Col. Lee's, as Custis willed it to Lee. All the slaves on this estate, as I understand, were set free at the death of Custis, but are now held in bondage by Lee. I have inquired concerning the will, but can get no satisfaction. Custis had fifteen children by his slave women. I see his grandchildren every day; they are of a dark yellow. Last week three of the slaves ran away; an officer was sent after them, overtook them nine miles this side of Pennsylvania, and brought them back. Col. Lee ordered them whipped. They were two men and one woman. The officer whipped the two men, and said he would not whip the woman, and Col. Lee stripped her and whipped her himself. These are facts as I learn from near relatives of the men whipped. After being whipped, he sent them to Richmond and hired them out as good farm hands.
>
> Yours, A. CITIZEN.
> Washington, June 19, 1859.

The troublemakers, as Lee identified them, had been weeded out, and other capable workers had been hired out as simply the most efficient way to bring in money. "The *N.Y. Tribune* has attacked me for my treatment of your grandfather's slaves," Lee told his son, "but I shall not reply. He has left me an unpleasant legacy."[64]

Lee did answer the accusations after the war in a letter to an old acquaintance from St. Louis, E. S. Quirk, who had relocated to San Francisco and had defended Lee in the New York papers when the incident of the slave whippings appeared in print in 1866 (fig. 118). Lee wrote, "There is not a word of truth in it …. No servant, soldier, or citizen that was ever employed by me can with truth charge me with bad treatment." To Lee's thinking, the runaways had failed to do their duty, they had broken a law, their distant flight had cost the estate a considerable amount of money, the law stipulated their punishment, and thus he had treated them fairly, just as he would handle a soldier and as he would himself expect to be treated. He would not have defined his actions as constituting "bad treatment."

Lee's leave extended through the summer of 1859. In the July 1859 letter to Custis, he wondered if he was making the right choice to stay at Arlington: "God knows whether I have done right, or whether my stay will be an advantage. I am very doubtful on the subject and feel that I ought to be with my regiment, and this

fig. 118.
Robert E. Lee to E. S. Quirk, *Letter*, March 1, 1866, Virginia Historical Society

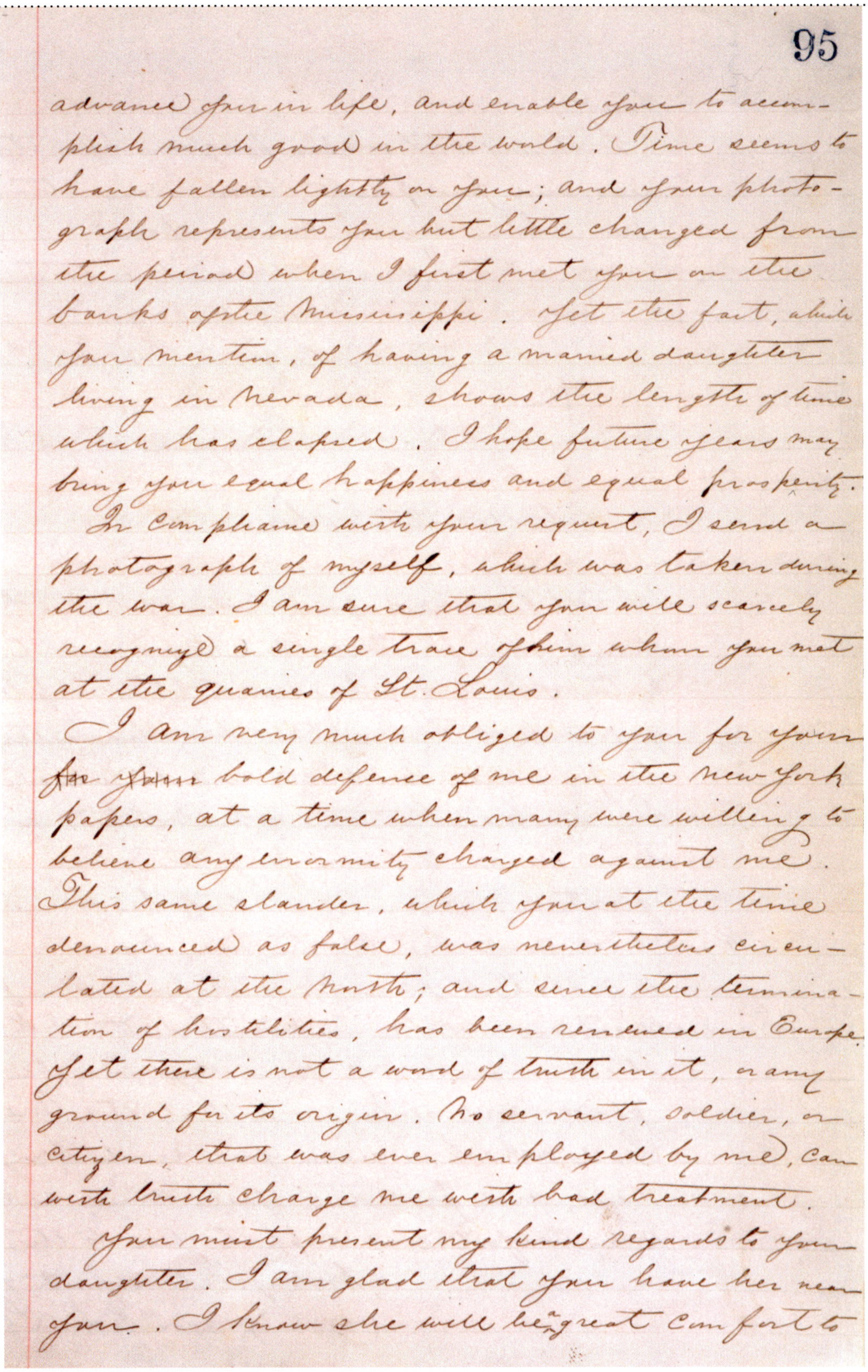

advance you in life, and enable you to accomplish much good in the world. Time seems to have fallen lightly on you; and your photograph represents you but little changed from the period when I first met you on the banks of the Mississippi. Yet the fact, which you mention, of having a married daughter living in Nevada, shows the length of time which has elapsed. I hope future years may bring you equal happiness and equal prosperity.

In compliance with your request, I send a photograph of myself, which was taken during the war. I am sure that you will scarcely recognize a single trace of him whom you met at the quaries of St. Louis.

I am very much obliged to you for your for your bold defence of me in the New York papers, at a time when many were willing to believe any enormity charged against me. This same slander, which you at the time denounced as false, was nevertheless circulated at the North; and since the termination of hostilities, has been renewed in Europe. Yet there is not a word of truth in it, or any ground for its origin. No servant, soldier, or citizen, that was ever employed by me, can with truth charge me with bad treatment.

You must present my kind regards to your daughter. I am glad that you have her near you. I know she will be a great comfort to

fig. 119.
Hardscrabble, 1854–56 (photograph courtesy of National Park Service, White Haven)

feeling deprives me of half the pleasure I should derive from being here under other circumstances." Lee spent large sums that year for the clothing, food, and medical care for the slaves. He set them to work repairing their houses, explaining to Custis, "I wish to make them as comfortable as I can." It was the whipping, however, for which he would be better remembered.[65]

The Grants of Hardscrabble

In the late summer of 1854 I rejoined my family, to find in it a son whom I had never seen…. I was now to commence … a new struggle for our support.

Ulysses S. Grant, Memoirs

Grant was no more successful at farming than was Lee. After returning from the Northwest in 1854, he had rejoined his wife and sons, settling on Dent family land near St. Louis. He took to the fields and before long set about building a modest home that he called Hardscrabble (fig. 119). For five years Grant tried to make a go of farming, but he felt that he lacked the upfront money needed to stock his farm adequately. The weather was often as uncooperative as were the market conditions. Grant had slaves to help him: he owned one slave, William Jones, and he hired others. Julia owned four slaves, Eliza, Julia, John, and Dan, who were given to her by her father and who helped with house duties.[66]

Grant's account in the *Memoirs* of his farming in Missouri is remarkably brief given the effort that he put into the venture, the length of the attempt, and the agricultural experience that he brought with him. He had little to say primarily because he failed. His father had refused repeated requests for the loan of money to give him a firm foundation. In the end he had to retreat to the security of employment in Jesse Grant's leather business. The son was embarrassed by the entire episode, taking pride only in the strong work ethic that he had demonstrated:

> In the late summer of 1854 I rejoined my family, to find in it a son whom I had never seen, born when I was on the Isthmus of Panama. I was now to commence, at the age of thirty-two, a new struggle for our support. My wife had a farm near St. Louis, to which we went, but I had no means to stock it. A home had to be built also. I worked very hard, never losing a day because of bad weather, and accomplished the object in a moderate way. If nothing else could be done I would load a cord of wood on a wagon and take it to the city for sale. I managed to keep along very well until 1858, when I was attacked by fever and ague…. It lasted now over a year, and, while it did not keep me in the house, it did interfere greatly with the amount of work I was able to perform. In the fall of 1858 I sold out my stock, crops and farming utensils at auction, and gave up farming.

Ulysses attributed his failure at agriculture in part to the illness that he suffered in 1858. But another factor was the panic of 1857, which raised the bar of difficulty for farmers large and small. The lesson about the potentially catastrophic effect of market conditions on the average citizen would be well remembered by President Grant at the time of the Panic of 1873.[67]

Biographers describe the seven-year interval from 1854 to the start of the Civil War as a low period in Grant's life, an odyssey during which he searched for work that would support his family. Yet to call these years bleak is to forget the domestic happiness that Grant enjoyed. Julia Grant made herself quite clear on this matter: "Those days were not dark but bright and charming, as it was always sunshine when he was near." A third child, Nellie, named for one of Julia's sisters, soon joined the growing family. Grant took great delight in the company of his wife and children. He played with his sons as if he was again a boy, and he lovingly admired his new daughter.[68]

Shortly after Ulysses returned to Missouri, Jesse Grant offered him a job in a store that he had established in Galena, Illinois. There was one condition: Julia and the children would have to reside with Jesse in Covington, Kentucky, ostensibly for the purpose of reducing expenses in Galena. In fact, the father and father-in-law were competing for their company. "Captain Grant positively and indignantly refused his father's offer," Julia proudly wrote. Perhaps because of that rebuff, Jesse Grant would be reluctant to hear his son's pleas for help with farming costs.[69]

The property that Grant worked initially was not the sixty-acre tract that Colonel Frederick Grant had awarded his daughter as a wedding gift. Rather, it was Wish-ton-Wish, the nearby farm of his brother-in-law Lewis Dent. The wedding-gift tract first had to be cleared of its timber. Grant had some success with his crops at Wish-ton-Wish in 1855, and the next year he worked on preparing Julia's tract and on building Hardscrabble. He apparently enjoyed his new role, pretending that he was a yeoman farmer alone on the frontier. Julia, however hated the step down; she called Hardscrabble a "cabin." Its rough-hewn timbers were "crude and homely," she recalled. "I did not like it at all, but I did not say so." She was sorry to have left Wish-ton-Wish, and would be happy when she could leave Hardscrabble.[70]

In contrast to Julia, Ulysses was upbeat at the close of 1856. He hoped to expand his farming operation, and he asked his father for financial support:

> Evry day I like farming better and I do not doubt but that money is to be made at it. So far I have been laboring under great disadvantages [building Hardscrabble] but now that I am on my place, and shall not have to build next summer I think I shall be able to do much better. This year if I could have bought seed I should have made out still better than I did. I wanted to plant sixty or seventy bushels of potatoes, but I had not the money to buy them …. I have in some twenty five acres of wheat …. My intention is to raise about twenty acres of Irish potatoes, on new ground, five acres of sweet potatoes, about the same of early corn, five or six acres cabbage, beets, cucumber pickles & melons and keep a wagon going to market evry day …. This year I presume I shall be compelled to neglect my farm some to make a living in the mean time, but by next year I hope to be independent.

Grant was speaking to deaf ears. Jesse Grant had offered his son steady employment, and these pipe dreams sounded all too familiar, reminiscent of Grant's agricultural ventures on the Pacific coast that were spectacular failures. Jesse was too experienced a Yankee businessman to be fooled into speculation on an endeavor that was subject to fluctuations in the weather and the market. Ulysses had chosen to take up residence next to White Haven; let Colonel Dent lend him the money.[71]

Grant had, in fact, shifted his political stance closer to that of his father-in-law, a change that must have annoyed Jesse. Later a staunch Republican, Ulysses went on at some length in his *Memoirs* to justify his vote in the 1856 presidential election for the Democratic candidate, James Buchanan. A remarkably savvy observer, Grant felt that the election of an antislavery Republican candidate at that date would have meant the immediate secession of the slave states, which of course is what did happen four years later. He wanted at least to postpone that showdown in the hope that "the passions of the people would subside in that time, and the catastrophe be averted altogether."[72]

Six weeks after his first request to his father, Grant tried again. He had been selling wood as fast as he could cut it but had little success at building up a financial reserve. Ulysses almost pleaded for assistance, threatening at this time to quit farming:

> Spring is now approaching when farmers require not only to till the soil, but to have the wherewith to till it, and to seed it …. To this end I am going to make the last appeal to you …. Five hundred dollars …. The fact is, without means, it is useless for me to go on farming, and I will have to do what Mr. Dent has given me permission to do; sell the farm and invest elsewhere.

He added in this letter that Mrs. Dent, his mother-in-law, had just died. Nothing would move Jesse, however. He would wait his son out.[73]

By the summer of 1857, although Ulysses had struggled, he had crops that for the most part looked promising. He wrote to his sister Mary, then age eighteen, "My hard work is now over for the season with a fair prospect of being remunerated in everything but the wheat." The "fair prospect," however, would be thwarted by the Panic of 1857, which brought a collapse of commodity prices and made his crops largely unmarketable. Grant had to pawn his gold watch for Christmas money. In St. Louis at that time, Ulysses met another West Point graduate who was in a similar financial plight. William Tecumseh Sherman had quit the army a year earlier than Grant to try a career as a banker. Sherman had lost everything in the financial panic and was trying to find some way to survive. I was "a dead cock in the Pit," he later remembered.[74]

In the following spring of 1858, more than just the weather renewed Grant's optimism. The family had expanded yet again, with the addition of a third son, named for Ulysses's father. Now a widower, Colonel Dent had decided to leave White Haven and move into St. Louis. Ulysses and Julia would take over the family home, although Dent, who was as tight-fisted as Jesse Grant, would extract rent from the couple. Grant now hoped for better luck. He leased Hardscrabble, and depended on the assistance of slave laborers at White Haven. He wrote with enthusiasm to his sister Mary:

> Little Ellen [b. 1855] is growing very fast and talks now quite plainly. Jesse R. [b. 1858] is growing very rapidly .... This Spring has opened finely for farming and I hope to do well but I shall wait until the crops are gathered before I make any predictions. I have now three Negro men, two hired by the year and one of Mr. Dents, which, with my own help, I think, will enable me to do my farming pretty well, with assistance in the harvest. I have however a large farm .... You are aware, I believe, that I have rented out my place [Hardscrabble] and have taken Mr. Dents [White Haven]. There is about 200 acres of ploughed land on it.[75]

Just when Grant's farming prospects were brightest, the weather again failed to cooperate. A record freeze on June 5, 1858, killed what crops had survived an already cold spring. In the fall, the chills and fevers that had plagued Grant as a child returned. He worried that he might have inherited a fatal ailment like the consumption that a few years later would kill both his oldest brother and his oldest sister. During the harvest season, not only was Ulysses unable to work with vigor, but sickness devastated his work force as well. He wrote to his sister on September 7, "Some seven of the negroes have been sick." The writing was on the wall: there seemed no choice but to give up farming. In conjunction with Colonel Dent, he would sell just about everything at auction, from stock and crops to farming utensils and even part of the land. He recounted the decision to his father, and asked about the employment that Jesse had offered him four years earlier:

> Mr. Dent and myself will make a sale this fall and get clear of all the stock on the place, and then rent out the cleared land and sell about four hundred acres .... I shall plan to go to Covington towards Spring, and would prefer your offer to any one of mere salary that could be offered. I do not want any place for permanent stipulated pay, but want the prospect of one day doing business for myself. There is a pleasure in knowing that one's income depends somewhat upon his own exertions and business capacity .... Mr. Dent thinks I have better take the boy he has given Julia along with me, and let him learn the farrier's business. He is a very smart, active boy, capable of making anything; but this matter I will leave entirely to you. I can leave him here and get about three dollars per month for him now, and more as he gets older.

Grant probably intended to negotiate with his father about where his wife and children would reside. However, he never made the proposed spring trip to Covington. The slavery issue may have been a factor in the decision. Jesse was staunchly antislavery, but Julia was dependent on the assistance of a slave. As Ulysses tried to explain to Jesse in a later letter, "with four children she could not go without a servant and she was afraid that landing so often as she would have to do in free states she might have some trouble."[76]

Grant looked for employment in St. Louis. He was there frequently in the fall of 1858, and during the following winter was selling firewood. James Longstreet, the future Confederate general, later told a story about meeting Grant in the city. Destitute as he was, Ulysses pressed a five-dollar gold piece into the hand of his longtime friend, a debt from fifteen years earlier, saying, "I cannot live with anything in my possession which is not mine." Grant, however, was no more successful in St. Louis than he had been at farming. He recounted one episode in his *Memoirs*:

> In the winter I established a partnership with Harry Boggs, a cousin of Mrs. Grant, in the real estate agency business .... Our business might have become prosperous if I had been able to wait for it to grow. As it was, there was no more than one person could attend to, and not enough to support two families .... I [also] was a candidate for the office of county engineer, an office of respectability and emolument which would have been very acceptable to me at that time.[77]

Thanks in part to Robert E. Lee's successes two decades earlier in St. Louis harbor, property values in the city were still soaring in 1858. Real estate must have seemed a good career to pursue. Grant tried it, but was too decent to be an effective rent collector and too honest to be a good salesman. A lawyer who worked with him at the time remembered both traits with exasperation and esteem: "He just doesn't seem to be calculated for business, but a more honest, more generous man never lived. I don't believe that he knows what dishonesty is." Grant lost a possible appointment as county engineer to politics. He was tabbed a Democrat like his in-laws; the five-man county council that made the appointment held three Free-Soilers who voted against him. He ultimately did find employment for a brief period as a clerk in the St. Louis Customs House.[78]

Ever optimistic, the Grants made the most of what amounted to two years in St. Louis. They lived frugally but comfortably. Ulysses reported to his father that he expected to do more than just make ends meet:

> I can hardly tell how the new business I am engaged in is going to sucseed but I believe it will be something more than a support …. We are now living in the lower part of the city …. The house is a comfortable little one just suited to my means. We have one spare room and also a spare bed in the childrens room so that we can accommodate any of our friends that are likely to come to see us …. Julia and the children are well.[79]

Though living close to poverty, in March 1859 Grant decided to free the slave whom he had purchased to help farm the fields at White Haven. He could easily have hired out William Jones to earn much-needed income. Instead, just as he had repaid James Longstreet a five-dollar debt because it was the right thing to do, Grant gave the man his freedom:

> Know all persons by these presents, that I Ulysses S Grant of the City & County of St Louis in the State of Missouri, for divers good and valuable considerations me hereunto moving, do hereby emancipate and set free from Slavery my Negro man William, sometimes called William Jones (Jones) of Mullato complexion, aged about thirty-five years, and about five feet seven inches in height and being the same slave purchased by me of Frederick Dent—And I do hereby manumit, emancipate & set free said William from slavery forever.

Grant had acquired Jones in 1858 from Colonel Dent. The equalizing experience of toiling in the fields side-by-side with his slaves offered Grant the opportunity to develop personal relationships with them. Jones was about the same age as Grant and not too much larger in physical size. He must have been a dependable worker. Ulysses apparently developed a rapport with him that was based on friendship and on Jones's willingness to work hard, something Grant respected.[80]

As the months went by in 1859, and despite his resilient optimism, Grant came to the realization that he was unable to provide adequately for his large family. He looked again at his father's leather-goods store in Galena, Illinois, where his brothers were already at work. This time, a job with no conditions was offered and accepted. The Grant family arrived at Galena in the summer of 1860. It seemed then that Ulysses S. Grant might spend the remainder of his life as a shopkeeper.

Prelude to War: Lee at Harpers Ferry

By the fall of 1859, Lee was ready to return to Texas. He had made progress in paying the debts of the estate and in restoring the three farms. Rooney was resident at the White House and could also manage nearby Romancoke, while Custis was able to take up residence at Arlington. All the pieces were in place. When Winfield Scott offered Lee the opportunity to remain in the area as his military secretary with the same rank of lieutenant colonel, Lee declined. His plans to leave were delayed only by a fanatical abolitionist whom some would call a martyr and others a madman.[81]

Colonel Robert E. Lee, whom fate would have it was still at Arlington, was sent in the fall of 1859 by President James Buchanan to Harpers Ferry to quell an attempt to incite a slave uprising there by John Brown and his followers. Even a minor disturbance at this nineteenth-century center of rail and water transportation (fig. 120) would have troubled many in antebellum Virginia. The town was the site of one of two federal arsenals in the country. (The other was at Springfield, Massachusetts.) The guns stored there could easily fall into the wrong hands. When John Brown (fig. 121), who was already renowned for his cold-blooded massacre of pro-slavery advocates in "Bleeding Kansas," led a band of insurgents to Harpers Ferry on a raid to free and arm slaves, rumors began to fly. Five of Brown's twenty-one men were black, but one white com-

fig. 120.
Harpers Ferry, c. 1861–65 (photograph courtesy of United States Army Military History Institute)

fig. 121.
John Brown, 1850s (photograph courtesy of Virginia Historical Society)

mentator described a mob made up partly of blacks that contained at least 500 people and perhaps as many as 3,000. A. M. Barbour, the superintendent of the arsenal, alarmed the War Department by declaring "a perfect panic here" and demanding reinforcements. Troops from Fort Monroe and the Washington Navy Yard, as well as the Maryland militia, were dispatched. Lee was ordered to command the entire relief force.[82]

Before Lee arrived, the angry townspeople had already fought a pitched battle with the insurgents, reducing their number to only eighteen. Brown and the other survivors of his group took refuge in a fire-engine house within the arsenal complex. Citizens fired sporadically into both the building and the bodies lying outside it. Some two thousand spectators, most of the population of the town plus many from nearby settlements, looked on. No doubt it was a peculiar scene that awaited Lee, but he must have been relieved that the situation was not worse.[83]

The insurgents held a number of the townspeople as hostages. For their safety, Colonel Lee delayed action until the light of day. He plotted an assault at dawn, preceded by an opportunity for "peaceable surrender." Toward that end, he drafted a note to John Brown (fig. 122):

> Colonel Lee, U.S.A. Commd the troops sent by the President of the U. S. to suppress the insurrection at this place demands the surrender of the persons in the Armory buildings.
>
> If they will peaceably surrender themselves & restore the pillaged property, they shall be kept in safety to await the orders of the President.
>
> Col Lee represents to them in all frankness that it is impossible for them to escape, that the Armory is surrounded on all sides by troops, & that if he is Compelled to take them by force he cannot assure their safety.
>
> R. E. Lee, Col. Commd U.S. Troops

Lieutenant Jeb Stuart, who had carried the original message to Lee from the War Department, then delivered Lee's note under a white flag. One of the hostages, Lewis W. Washington, a grandnephew of the president, is said to have cried out, "Never mind us,

LEE AND GRANT

fig. 122.
Robert E. Lee to the Harpers Ferry Insurgents, *Note*, October 18, 1859, National Archives and Records Administration

fig. 123.
Bowie Knife, taken from John Brown by Jeb Stuart at Harpers Ferry in 1859, Virginia Historical Society

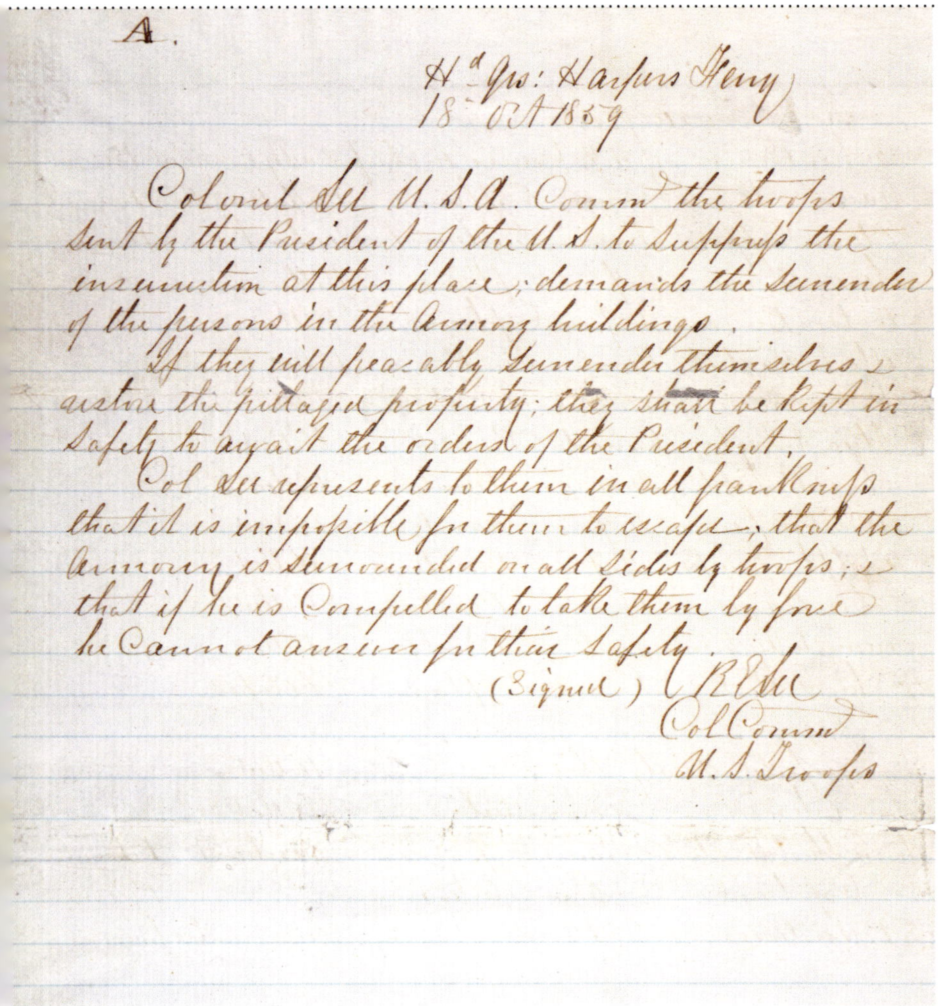

fire!" The negotiation was brief and fruitless. Stuart waved his hat to signal Lee, who ordered twelve of the marines from the Washington navy yard to rush the engine house with bayonets. Their leader, Israel Green, who had volunteered for the job, beat Brown into unconsciousness, while his men killed two insurgents and captured two others. Thanks to Lee's decisive leadership, none of the thirteen hostages was injured. Stuart took as a trophy John Brown's bowie knife (fig. 123). Lewis Washington, a proper Virginia gentleman, refused to emerge from the engine house until gloves were brought to hide his soiled hands.[84]

Lee called John Brown's raid "the attempt of a fanatic or madman." He thought it would do nothing to end slavery. But Brown understood that his mission was in part to force Americans to confront the moral issues at the root of slavery. The idea of waiting for God to end the institution was suddenly no longer acceptable. To drive home the point, Brown said, "Let them hang me …. I am worth inconceivably more to hang than for any other purpose." Visual artists and some of the nation's leading writers responded to Brown's execution. Thomas Satterwhite Noble was one of a number of painters who after the war remembered

172   IV. CRISES OF THE 1850S

fig. 124.
Thomas Satterwhite Noble, *John Brown's Blessing*, 1867, oil on canvas, 89 × 65 in. (226.1 × 165.1 cm.), New-York Historical Society Museum, gift of the children of Thomas S. Noble and Mary C. Noble

the last moments of a man they perceived to be a modern saint (fig. 124). William Cullen Bryant ranked Brown as one of the "martyrs and heroes" of our country. He was "an angel of light," said Henry David Thoreau. "Brown would make the gallows as glorious as the cross," wrote Ralph Waldo Emerson. Herman Melville called Brown the "meteor of war." Henry Wadsworth Longfellow made what proved to be a remarkably accurate prediction. He saw Brown's death as the start of "a new Revolution—quite as much needed as the old one." And even though Brown had been captured and executed, his raid made many southerners fear that all who opposed slavery would ultimately resort to bloodshed.[85]

Rejection of the Planter Lifestyle

By early 1860 Lee was in Texas; that May, Grant was in Illinois. Each was far removed from his recent troubles. Grant was still happily united with his family, and was for the moment relieved of financial worries. Galena is located in northwestern Illinois, a short distance up the Galena River from the Mississippi. A deep channel in the river allowed the town's port to compete successfully with its rival Chicago until the railroad passed the town by. In 1860, however, Galena (fig. 125) was a center of commerce. Settlers heading westward filled its 200-room hotel and more than fifty saloons. It had been a boom town since at least the 1840s, when Jesse Grant established a leather-goods store on Main Street. Ulysses and Julia Grant settled happily into a sturdy brick house nearby with the thought of staying there a long time (fig. 126). The house was not as elegant a residence as White Haven, but was a considerable improvement over Hardscrabble. Grant's only complaint would be that in his new job he had no reason to own a horse. He soon made friends, a number of whom would follow Ulysses into the Union army and even to the White House.[86]

Grant was upbeat about his prospects at the family store. After a few months he wrote to a friend in St. Louis, "I have become pretty well inniciated into the Leather business and like it well. Our business here is prosperous and I have evry reason to hope, in a few years, to be entirely above the frowns of the world, pecuniarily." He had "hope to be a partner soon." Grant later explained his optimism:

> While living in Galena I was nominally only a clerk supporting myself and family on a stipulated salary. In reality my position was different. My father had never lived in Galena himself, but had established my two brothers there, the one next younger than myself [Simpson] in charge of the business, assisted by the youngest [Orvil]. When I went there it was my father's intention to give up all connection with the business himself, and to establish his three sons in it: but the brother who had really built up the business was sinking with consumption.

Simpson Grant died a year later. Of course, by September 1861 Ulysses was pursuing a different career.[87]

John Brown was hanged on December 2, 1859. On January 10, 1860, Robert E. Lee testified before a congressional committee that was investigating the raid. By early February he was in San Antonio, in temporary command of the Department of Texas. Lee was thankful that his son Custis had returned to Arlington "to oversee the operations at the farms" and thereby remove the worries of plantation

fig. 125.
Galena, Illinois, after 1860 (photograph courtesy of Galena-Jo Daviess County Historical Society & Museum)

fig. 126.
Grant House, Galena, after 1860 (photograph courtesy of Galena-Jo Daviess County Historical Society & Museum)

fig. 127.
Robert E. Lee, San Antonio, Texas, to Annie Lee, *Letter*, 27 August 1860, Virginia Historical Society

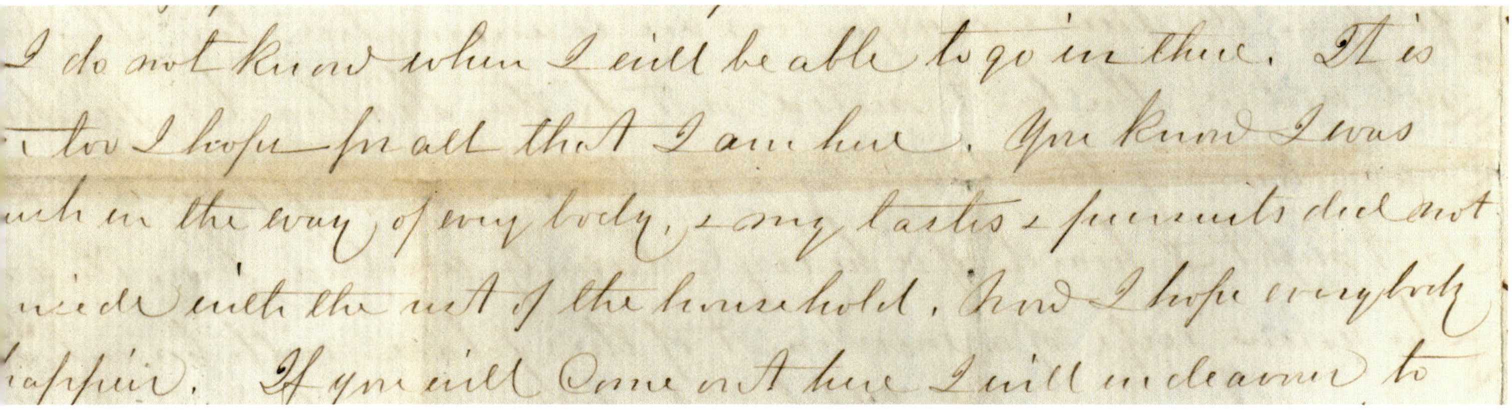
I do not know when I will be able to go in there. It is
too I hope for all that I am here. You know I was
...ch in the way of every body, & my tastes & pursuits did not
...cide with the rest of the household. And I hope every body
happier. If you will come out here I will endeavour to

management from Mary. He wrote to his wife in April that he felt better physically. He had gotten over a cold, "though I still feel its rheumatic effects, & that in my right arm seems stationary." He could not have recognized the early symptoms of a heart condition that would trouble him during the Civil War and eventually kill him.[88]

Alone on the frontier, Lee had time to contemplate what had happened at Arlington during the past two-and-a-half years. He came close to admitting defeat in his battle with the Arlington slaves. He wrote to Mary from San Antonio in March 1860 that it is "almost useless to attempt improvement [in their work ethic], or to resist the current that has been so long setting against industry & advancement." That summer he admitted to his daughter Annie that no one had liked the way he was handling the role of executor: "It is better too I hope for all that I am here. You know I was very much in the way of every body, & my tastes & pursuits did not coincide with the rest of the household" (fig. 127). He still endorsed a two-pronged approach to the treatment of slaves. "While being fair & just you must not neglect your interests," he told Custis. As to the overseer then needed at Arlington, he should be an "energetic honest farmer, who while he will be considerate & kind to the Negroes, will be firm & make them do their duty." Lee continued to try to distance himself from slavery. When he needed a body-servant that July, he told Rooney, "I would rather hire a *white* man than purchase [a black slave] if I Could."[89]

After only a few months in Texas, Lee was again frustrated with his career. He confided to his cousin Anna Fitzhugh that he was tired of failing in both his public and his private life:

> At this distance from those you love and care for, with the knowledge of the vicissitudes and necessities of life, one is rent by a thousand anxieties, and the mind as well as body is worn and racked to pieces .... A divided heart I have too long had, and a divided life too long led. That may be one cause of the small progress I have made on either hand, my professional and civil career. Success ... rarely follows a halting vacillating course. My military duties require me here, whereas my affections and urgent domestic claims call me away. And thus I live and am unable to advance either.

However, as he put it, he "must toil and trust." And as always, he would continue to do his duty, which at that moment meant that he was occupied with keeping track of the Comanches, the Kiowas, and the various Mexican bandits who threatened the order that he was entrusted to keep. Lee was far from the momentous political events that were shaking the nation but he tried his best to follow the news, even when it arrived days after the fact. He wondered often about what the politicians were doing to the country that he loved and served.[90]

Soon it would be time for both Lee and Grant to make life-altering decisions. Neither wanted the nation to divide, and neither wanted a war because each knew how horrific combat could be. But if war was inevitable, one thing was certain. The fighting men would have to be led by experienced officers. Perhaps good leaders would lessen the duration of the war and ultimately save lives.

Perhaps not.

V.
The Civil War

fig. 128.
Julian Vannerson, *Robert E. Lee*, 1864 (photograph courtesy of Virginia Historical Society)

fig. 129.
Uniform of Robert E. Lee, Sword, Scabbard, and accouterments of the general, before 1864, Museum of the Confederacy

After four years of arduous service, marked by unsurpassed courage and fortitude, the Army of Northern Virginia has been compelled to yield to overwhelming numbers and resources.

Robert E. Lee, *General Orders No. 9*, April 9, 1865

The illusion that nothing but heavy odds beat [Lee] will not stand the ultimate light of history. I know it is not true.

Ulysses S. Grant, *Interview*, Hamburg, July 6, 1878

Lee in the East; Grant in the West

Lee's First Campaign

On May 2, 1861, after the Virginia convention had voted for secession and war was all but inevitable, Robert E. Lee (fig. 128) wrote to a clergyman, Reverend Cornelius Walker, about the nation's need for God's help during the coming conflict: "If we are not worthy that it should pass from us, may he in his great mercy Shield us from its dire effects & Save us from the Calamity our Sins have produced." It is fair to say that Lee thought slavery to be among the most heinous of such transgressions, but the defense of his family and region had to come first.

While Lee would eventually prove to be the general who most perfectly matched the demands of the Confederate population for gallant military leadership, early in the war, perhaps to avoid the "dire effects" of escalation, Lee would look to achieve victory more by maneuvering troops than by engaging in desperate combat, to the point where he would be criticized for a reluctance to shed blood.[1]

Before Lee would be awarded his first field command, however, he spent the opening months of the war raising troops in Virginia. He was then assigned to Richmond to help develop and implement strategy. Lee immediately saw the need to position forces at Manassas Junction, a confluence of railroads and roads that led to Harpers Ferry and Winchester. As a result, on July 12, 1861, Confederate troops under Joseph Johnston and P. G. T. Beauregard were poised to win an important victory at the Battle of First Manassas, the field on which General Thomas Jackson earned the epithet "Stonewall" for his bravery under fire. Lee was pleased at the success but annoyed that he did not play an active part. He wrote to his wife, "I wished to partake … & am mortified at my absence but the President [Davis] thought it more important I should be here …. I could have helped … in the struggle for my home & neighborhood." The ease of the Confederate victory made some southerners overconfident and gave a false impression of the weakness of the northern forces. First Manassas, or "Bull Run," also terrified Lincoln and his government. For the remainder of the war he would encourage strategies that were overtly defensive of the city of Washington.[2]

LEE AND GRANT

fig. 130.
J. Nep Roesler, *Thunder-Storm (Big Sewell Mountain)*, 1862, lithograph, 12¾ × 16½ in. (32.4 × 41.9 cm.), published in *Album of the Campaign of 1861 in Western Virginia* (Ehrgott, Forbriger & Company, printer), Virginia Historical Society

Virginia was particularly vulnerable to a Union advance in its northwestern counties because the bulk of the Confederate troops there were under the command of amateurs. That region, what is now West Virginia, was strategically crucial because its roads connected to important centers and junctions in the East; the mountain passes were of particular significance. Union generals George B. McClellan and William S. Rosecrans had some success early in the war at Rich Mountain utilizing the flanking strategy that Lee and McClellan had learned in Mexico at Cerro Gordo. Lee was sent to the region on July 28 to coordinate the efforts of several Confederate armies.[3]

One of the passes most easily fortified because of its height was at Cheat Mountain. When Lee arrived it was already occupied by Federal forces. Lee had placed General W. W. Loring in temporary command but was unable to prompt him to action. Even when a civilian engineer found a way to attack the summit, the plan was never enacted because of the timidity of a colonel, Albert Rust, who held back his troops at the last moment. Lee wrote to his wife, "I can not tell you my regret and mortification at the untoward events that caused the failure of the plan." It seemed to some southerners, however, that it was Lee who had eschewed engaging the enemy at the crucial moment. Nor could he attempt a second maneuver; Rosecrans, advancing up the Kanawha Valley, was threatening generals Henry A. Wise and John B. Floyd, who desperately needed the help of a professional officer.[4]

Wise and Floyd were both former governors of Virginia. Although during the Buchanan administration Floyd had served as secretary of war, neither was fit to command an army. Furthermore, each wanted his own separate command and the two quarreled. Lee's inclination to avoid personal confrontations with fellow officers made him ill-equipped to resolve this problem. He wanted the two forces brought together as one army that would be less vulnerable to attack, but he failed to force the issue. In the meantime, Rosecrans attacked Floyd, who retreated, first to Big Sewell Mountain (fig. 130). Wise joined him there and remained when Floyd retreated a second time, twelve miles farther to the vicinity of Meadow Bluff. The enemy soon appeared at Big Sewell Mountain with a force twice that of Wise's 2,200 men. Lee came to examine the situation and found that Wise's position was better than Floyd's, but his troops were ill prepared for an enemy flanking attack. Lee was then left alone when Wise was recalled to Richmond by Secretary of War Judah P. Benjamin, to whom Floyd had complained. Lee fortified his position and Rosecrans quietly retreated, unwilling to assault Lee's formidable artillery. Rosecrans's "escape" was judged a second failure by Lee to take decisive action against the enemy. He did attempt to pursue an alternative offensive, but sickness, cold weather, low rations, and bad roads halted Lee, as did the remarkable printing of his plans in southern newspapers.[5]

Many of these same newspapers unmercifully attacked "Granny Lee" for his failure to grab the offensive aggressively. He was criticized for "excess of caution" by the *Richmond Examiner*. In his book *The First Year of the War* (1862), Edward Pollard castigated the general who he claimed "had never fought a battle." Lee's "extreme tenderness of blood induced him to depend exclusively upon the resources of strategy to essay the achievement of victory without the cost of life." The complaints were in part justified because, although Lee did prevent the Federals from reaching the railroad, he left western Virginia in Union hands. On October 24, representatives there voted to establish a new and separate state, West Virginia.[6]

In 1861 the southern coastline from South Carolina to Florida was badly in need of defenses. Lee's experience as an engineer who had built shoreline fortifications made him superbly qualified to remedy the situation. His reputation, however, was so bad that before Jefferson Davis could send him there in November he had to write letters of recommendation to the governors of South Carolina and Georgia. Francis W. Pickens answered from Columbia that the general was "quiet and retiring" and that "His reserve is construed disadvantageously." Lee's decision to abandon the coast as indefensible and defend farther up the rivers would in turn bring the wrath of the low country planters. From Savannah, Lee wrote to his wife the following February that the people there and throughout the South needed to arouse themselves "from ease & comfort to labour & self denial." He warned what he had said from the start: "the contest must be long & Severe & the whole Country has to go through much Suffering." While in Georgia, Lee took the opportunity to visit the grave of his father on Cumberland Island.[7]

Although many of them had served in the Mexican War, at this point Lee seemed to be one of the few officers in the Confederate chain of command who had a realistic sense of the horrors and hardships of battle. Proud of the virtues associated with their code of honor, the Confederates have been described as a restive people who wanted their military leaders to match their temperament: generals should always assume the initiative and fight with aggressiveness. In a letter of March 1862, Lee described this attitude to his brother Carter as "the feverish & excited expectation of our good people." Historian Gary Gallagher has uncovered statements by Confederates that are shocking revelations of how impassioned the people had become. A number of the officers in Lee's army were extremists in their indignation over what they saw as northern aggression. Alexander Swift "Sandie" Pendleton said after the too easy surrender of Fort Donelson, which fell to Grant in 1862, "What difference does a few hours more or less here of life make in comparison with the future destiny of the people?" Porter Alexander wrote, "[I]t is my greatest comfort to know that I have killed some of them [Yankees] with my own hands." Lee was seen by many as an anathema; he was the great hero of the Mexican War who no longer seemed to want to fight.[8]

On March 3, 1862, Lee was summoned in haste to Richmond to assist President Davis by taking over the "conduct of military operations." What that meant was never clear, and Lee did not care for the assignment, partly because it was a desk job. He wrote to his wife, "I do not see either advantage or pleasure in my duties. But I will not complain, but do the best I can." She, however, did object in a letter to a friend: "Now they have got into trouble, they send for him to help them out, and yet he never gets any credit for what he has done …. He never complains or seems to desire anything more than to perform his duty, but I may be excused for wishing him to reap the reward for his labors." The city was then threatened by a large Union army advancing from the east with little opposition under the command of George McClellan. The collapse of the Confederacy before the end of the summer was a distinct possibility. Four months earlier Lincoln had promoted Lee's Mexican War subordinate to general-in-chief, replacing the aged Winfield Scott. If Lee could not quickly muster a stout defense, the war would be over; if fighting was what the southern public wanted, Lee was about to give it to them.[9]

Grant's First Campaign

Grant is the greatest soldier of our time if not all time. He fixes in his mind what is the true objective and abandons all minor ones.

General William Tecumseh Sherman

[Grant] eclipsed us all.

General James Longstreet

Ulysses S. Grant (fig. 131) was ready from the start to do whatever was required to win. He was as appalled as anyone by the horrors of battle, but he was also a realist. Unlike Lee, who would allow a year to elapse before he accepted the fact that carnage on a grand scale was inevitable, Grant recognized that heavy bloodshed was the means not only to immediate success, but also to a quicker cessation of the overall conflict. He reasoned that the total number of lives lost would be fewer if the war ended sooner.

Grant's remarkable achievements as a commander were in no way happenstance, nor were they simply the result of his willingness to sacrifice troops. Instead, his successes during the Civil War, which eventually became regular and almost predictable, were the products of intelligence, diligence, and determination. Several factors were always at work. First, Grant set clear goals upon which he became fixated, never allowing himself to be diverted from the most important objective. Second, his time as a quartermaster made him well versed in how to attain supplies and get them to an army on the move. Third, he anticipated nearly every contingency and spent countless hours orchestrating the movements of his forces. In straightforward written directives, Grant managed his lieutenants and instructed them on how to react to unforeseen developments. Finally, he recognized that a battle is always in flux and that a commander must be ever ready to make adjustments on the fly. Grant was exceptionally good at responding coolly and quickly, and he was sufficiently confident in his abilities to be unperturbed by pressure.[10]

Grant's rise to national prominence took time; he had far to go. During the summer of 1861, the troops of the 21st Illinois regiment came to know and respect their colonel. His laid-back style of lead-

fig. 131.
Ulysses Simpson Grant, 1863
(photograph courtesy of Virginia Historical Society)

ership appealed to volunteers, who soon discerned that he was also a highly competent military leader. To some, he seemed "the best commander" in the state. Grant bragged to his father that he had worked his regiment "up to a reputation equal to the best." Those positioned above the colonel were slowly starting to notice him. His previous army experience as quartermaster, during and after the Mexican War, coupled with his inherent talent at managing detail, enabled Grant to efficiently requisition materials for his regiment. Colonel John Williams, the Illinois commissary general, told Governor Richard Yates that Grant was the only regimental commander who knew what he needed. When Elihu Washburne, Grant's supporter and congressman, pushed for his promotion to brigadier general, the request was heard—this before Grant had experienced actual combat. The new general was pleased when most of his officers requested to be attached to his command.[11]

The 21st Illinois was assigned to duty in northern Missouri as part of a Union effort to counter the activities of secessionists in a state that could potentially have been brought into the Confederacy. In early August, from Mexico, Missouri, Grant reported to his father that most of the people in that part of the state felt that they had nothing left "but to choose between two evils." He said that they were mostly secessionists who had only one idea concerning why the war was being fought: "You can't convince them but what the ultimate object is to extinguish, by force, slavery." He told his sister Mary that he no longer would try to predict the duration of the war: "I have changed my mind so much that I don't know what to think. That the Rebels will be so badly whipped by April next that they cannot make a stand anywhere I don't doubt. But they are so dogged that there is no telling when they may be subdued." He added that he "should like to be sent to Western Virginia," where he would have confronted Lee at this early stage, but he would soon be called to action much farther west.[12]

The key to victory in the West was the Mississippi River, the region's major artery of transportation and communication. Control of the river was contested from the start. Neither side, however, knew the actual strength of the other, and both were determined to pressure the enemy to stretch out his lines. Neither side could therefore build up an attack force. The state of Kentucky, having proclaimed neutrality, was vulnerable to occupation by either side. The Unionists thought that Tennessee might quickly fall if Kentucky were taken by the North. By the end of the summer, John C. Frémont, in command of the Union's military operations in the West, was ready to assume the initiative. The offensive would have to be coordinated by a capable officer who would be given control of the Federal forces in southeastern Missouri and southern Illinois. He should move into Kentucky ("occupy Columbus in Kentucky as soon as possible"), and then proceed against Memphis and Nashville. Frémont selected Grant for the position, skipping over other officers, including John Pope, who were senior:

> I believed him to be a man of great activity and promptness in obeying orders without question or hesitation …. I did not consider him then a great general, for the qualities that led him to success had not had the opportunity for their development. I selected him for qualities I could not then find combined in any other officer, for General Grant was a man of unassuming character, not given to self-elation, of dogged persistence, and of iron will.

fig. 132.
Sack Coat of Ulysses S. Grant, and accouterments of the general, 1863, Donald R. Tharpe Collection, photograph by Marc Kagan (courtesy of *North South Trader's Civil War* magazine)

fig. 133.
Presentation Sword Awarded to Ulysses S. Grant by citizens of Kentucky, 1864, Donald R. Tharpe Collection.

Grant immediately recognized the magnitude of the appointment. He wrote to his wife on August 29 in terms that made clear his own sense of personal and familial honor: "I have a task before me of no trifling moment and want all the encouragement possible. Remember that … my reputation and that of our children greatly depends upon my acts."[13]

Columbus, Kentucky, was taken by the Confederates before Grant could act, but in invading a neutral state the enemy had lost the propaganda battle. The southerners could be portrayed as the aggressors. Grant quickly responded by moving into Paducah, Kentucky, a strategically important city at the mouth of the Tennessee River. The speed of this action was typical for Grant, as was the political thought that went into the statement that he issued to the citizens of the town. Entirely on his own, Grant justified the Union presence to the Kentucky legislature. He eased the concerns of the people by assuring them "of our peaceful intentions" and of the protection of their rights. The Kentucky government, he later wrote, was rebel in sentiment but wanted to preserve an armed neutrality.

Grant issued a "Proclamation, to the Citizens of Paducah!":

> An enemy, in rebellion against our common Government, has taken possession of, and planted its guns upon the soil of Kentucky and fired upon our flag. Hickman and Columbus are in his hands. He is moving upon your city. I am here to defend you against this enemy ….

He pledged "to defend and enforce the rights of all loyal citizens." Grant wrote later in his *Memoirs* that the standard he set for the protection of private property "was evidently a relief to them."[14]

Headquartered at Cairo, Illinois, Grant looked for an opportunity to move against the Confederate positions on the Mississippi River. He had written his wife at the end of September, "I would like to have the honor of commanding the Army that makes the advance down the river," adding that "unless I am able to do it soon I cannot expect it." Frémont had ordered "demonstrations" of force and activity on the Mississippi, so as to freeze the Confederates from taking their own action, but nothing more. This was because Frémont himself intended to attack Lexington. Frémont, however, was at that moment replaced by Henry W. Halleck. Grant decided to freely interpret his orders to demonstrate at Columbus as an opportunity for him to attack Belmont, the town opposite it, on the Missouri side of the river. Only at the end of his life, in his *Memoirs*, did Grant explain why he did it.

> I had no orders which contemplated an attack by the National troops, nor did I intend anything of the kind when I started out from Cairo; but after we started I saw that the officers and men were elated at the prospect of at last having the opportunity of doing what they had volunteered to do—fight the enemies of their country. I did not see how I could maintain discipline, or retain the confidence of my command, if we should return to Cairo without an effort to

do something. Columbus, besides being strongly fortified, contained a garrison much more numerous than the force I had with me. It would not do, therefore, to attack that point.

He added that there was "a small camp of Confederates at Belmont." When Grant boldly attacked, on November 7, he was initially successful because the enemy expected to be tested instead at Columbus. His inexperienced troops, however, soon broke ranks and five Confederate regiments eventually crossed the river. This surprised Grant, and his army barely escaped. Through it all the general remained calm. He was the last man to return to the boats, using his horse-riding skills once again with dramatic effect: "There was no path down the bank …. My horse … without hesitation or urging, and with his hind feet well under him, slid down the bank and trotted aboard the boat, twelve or fifteen feet away, over a single gang plank."[15]

Casualties at Belmont were heavy for both sides. Much of the nation's press called the battle a Union victory, but in his *Memoirs* Grant remembered the negative accounts: "Belmont was severely criticized in the North as a wholly unnecessary battle, barren of results, or the possibility of them." Grant had in fact stolen the offensive from the Confederates and instilled confidence in his troops, the core of the future Army of the Tennessee, who considered the battle "a great victory" and hereafter saw themselves as "Grant's men." He wrote proudly in his *Memoirs* that those two objectives were why the battle was fought.[16]

Grant's Ascent in the West: Fort Henry, Fort Donelson, and Shiloh

The Confederate line in the West stretched for more than 500 miles. General Albert Sidney Johnston was given an army of 75,000 soldiers to defend it. The center in Kentucky was pierced by two great rivers that flow into the South, the Tennessee and the Cumberland. "The true line of operations for us was up the Tennessee and Cumberland rivers," Grant later wrote. "With us there, the enemy would be compelled to fall back on the east and west entirely out of the State of Kentucky." Tennessee would then be vulnerable. Spanning the rivers were railroads that were vital carriers of Confederate supplies, but the railroad bridges could be destroyed by Union gunboats. To halt such a "line of operation," Forts Henry and Donelson had been constructed and strongly fortified. They were sited in Tennessee close to the Kentucky border where the rivers are but eleven miles apart and troops could easily be shifted from one fort to the other. Grant quickly recognized their strategic significance. He wrote in his *Memoirs*,

> These positions were of immense importance …. With Fort Henry in our hands we had a navigable stream open to us up to Muscle Shoals, in Alabama …. Fort Donelson was the gate to Nashville—a place of great military and political importance—and to a rich country extending far east in Kentucky.

When he learned that Fort Henry was vulnerable to attack, Grant was anxious to take action. He wrote his sister Mary, "I do hope it will be my good fortune to retain so important a command for at least one battle."[17]

Henry Halleck, the new Union commander in the West, was by instinct timid in ordering offensive action. Also, his authority extended east only to the Cumberland River, where Don Carlos Buell commanded the Army of the Ohio. Therein was Johnston's advantage; he would be able to maneuver between the two Union generals. To further confuse Halleck, Johnston overstated the size of his force by two and even three times. Buell's lieutenant, the Virginian George Thomas, was making sufficient progress on Johnston's right flank to worry Halleck that perhaps he too had better take action or else be replaced. Abraham Lincoln forced the matter when he issued his General War Order No. 1 on January 27, 1862, which required "a general movement of the Land and Naval forces of the United States against the insurgent forces." This compelled Halleck to approve Grant's request to move against Fort Henry. Grant wrote to Julia on February 4 that he had "a confidant feeling of success." The fort in fact fell easily to Union gunboats under Commodore Andrew Foote, whom Grant had enlisted as a willing ally. "In little over one hour all the batteries were silenced," Grant reported. As it turned out, the fort had been flooded by the Tennessee River and was no longer defensible.[18]

Typically, Grant turned immediately to the next task at hand. Halleck said nothing so Grant went forward. The care with which he planned the assault on Fort Donelson is evident in a message that he sent to his sister a few days later: "You have no conception of the amount of labor I have to perform. An army of men all helpless looking to the commanding officer for every supply." As usual he was optimistic, writing to his wife, "We have a large force to contend

fig. 134.
Paul Philippoteaux, *General Grant at Fort Donelson*, 1863 or later, oil on canvas, 18 × 25 in. (45.7 × 63.5 cm.), Chicago Historical Society

against but I expect to accomplish their subjugation." It may be a "long job," he added: "The rebels are strongly fortified and are in very heavy force."

In the end, Grant was fortunate; Albert Sidney Johnston made a number of critical errors. Initially, Johnston had left only a small force at Fort Donelson, which he was willing to sacrifice in order to take on Grant in southern Tennessee. That strategy was sound, because a decisive Confederate defeat there might have ended the war. But Johnston reversed himself, fortified Donelson, and placed the troops under the command of two incompetent generals, John B. Floyd, the former secretary of war who had failed Lee in western Virginia and was "no soldier" according to Grant, and Gideon Pillow, who "was conceited, and prided himself much on his services in the Mexican War."[19]

Grant besieged the fort. His men endured severe weather: "The greatest suffering was from want of shelter. It was midwinter and during the siege we had rain and snow, thawing and freezing alternately." The artist Paul Philippoteaux recreated those conditions on canvas (fig. 134). Pillow led a Confederate force out of the fort to attack its besiegers, but drew back when he mistakenly thought that the battle was over. Another opponent might have retreated, but Grant counterattacked, with a bayonet charge led by Charles Ferguson Smith, who had been his commandant at West Point. Smith was proud of his former pupil and as determined as Grant. Admitting defeat, Floyd and Pillow fled on the eve of the fort's surrender. Confederate command was then assumed by Grant's friend and former classmate at West Point, Simon Bolivar Buckner. Grant showed him no favoritism, however, announcing terms of "unconditional surrender" that became part of American lore (fig. 135):

> Sir: Yours of this date proposing Armistice and appointment of Commissioners to settle terms of Capitulation is just received. No terms except an unconditional and immediate surrender can be accepted. I propose to move immediately upon your works.[20]

Fort Donelson was the first major Union victory of the Civil War. An entire Confederate army of 12,000–15,000 soldiers was taken. Grant thought this "the largest capture I believe ever made on the continent." The Confederate line in the West was broken. Half of Tennessee fell into Union hands. Grant later recalled how the "news of the fall of Fort Donelson was correspondingly depressing" to southerners. In practical terms, this meant that thousands of potential recruits in Tennessee never enlisted in the Confederate ranks. The victor became famous overnight as "U.nconditional S.urrender" Grant.[21]

fig. 135.
Ulysses S. Grant to Simon Bolivar Buckner, Fort Donelson, *Letter*, February 16, 1862, National Museum of American History

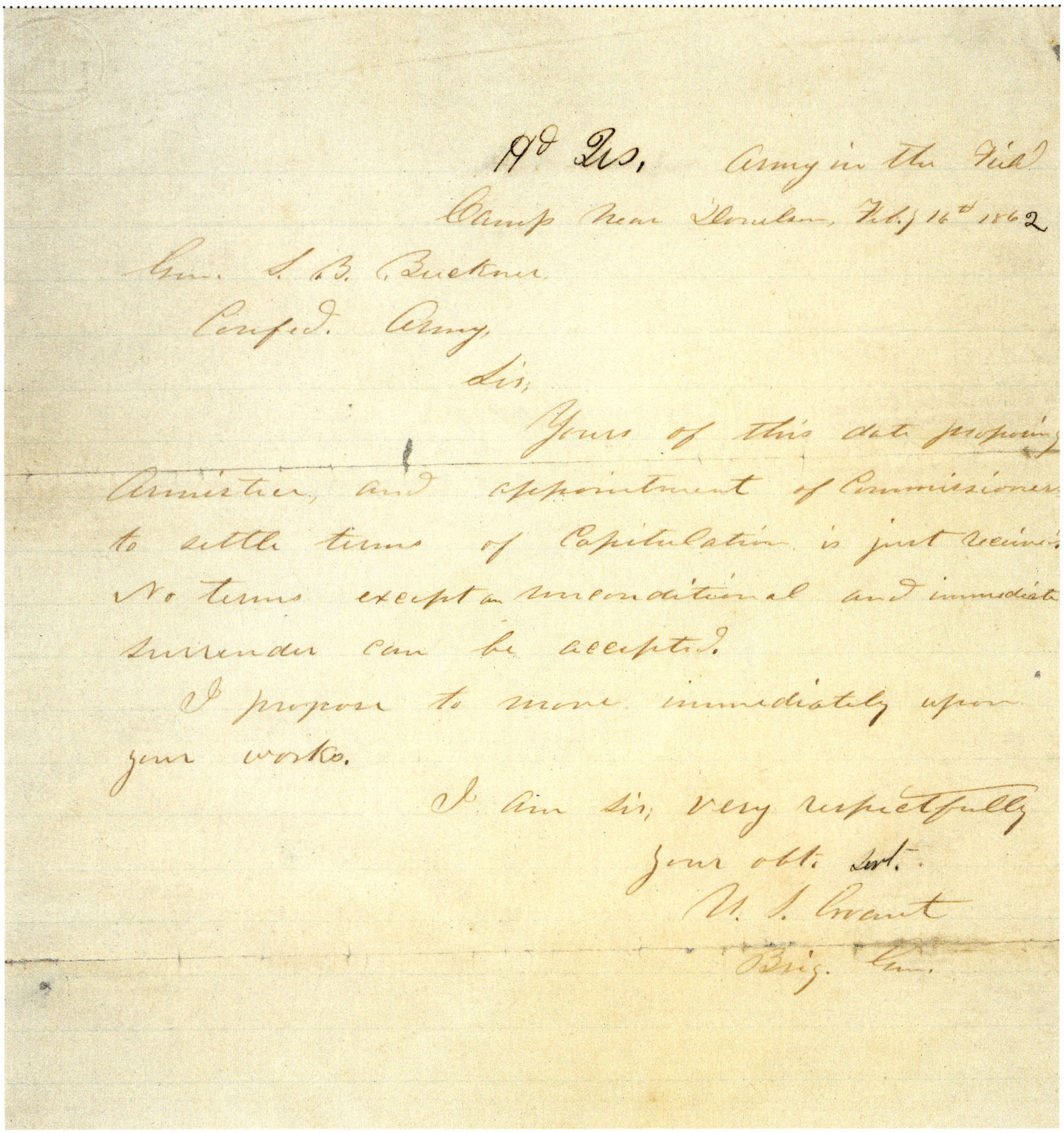

Despite his remarkable success, two matters troubled Grant. His father had doubted him on too many occasions. On receiving word of his promotion, Grant wrote to his wife with uncharacteristic sarcasm, "Is father afraid yet that I will not be able to sustain myself?" Two days later, Grant brought up to Julia his concern over the loss of so many lives: "These terrible battles are very good things to read about for persons who loose no friends …. The way to avoid it is to push forward as vigorously as possible." To attack, he thought, might bring a quicker end to the war, but he would not be allowed to do so.[22]

Halleck, seconded by General-in-Chief George McClellan, who had disliked Grant since their days on the Pacific coast, would not trust Grant to carry the war forward in the West. Grant wanted to move immediately, while the Confederate armies were in disarray. He believed that he could have ended the war by the close of the year:

> My opinion was and still is that immediately after the fall of Fort Donelson the way was opened to the National forces all over the South-west without much resistance. If one general who would have taken the responsibility had been

fig. 136.

More Glorious News. A Great Battle Fought at Pittsburgh Landing, Tenn., Victory of the Union Forces, April 9, 1862, The New York Times

in command of all the troops west of the Alleghanies, he could have marched to Chattanooga, Corinth, Memphis and Vicksburg with the troops we had then …. Rapid movements and the acquisition of rebellious territory would have promoted volunteering …. On the other hand there were tens of thousands of strong able-bodied young men still at their homes in the south-western States, who had not gone into the Confederate army in February, 1862, and who had no particular desire to go …. Providence ruled differently. Time was given the enemy to collect armies ….[23]

Grant was denied the opportunity to move on to Nashville, a huge supply center that had been evacuated. Instead, Halleck suggested to the administration in Washington that his general was guilty of misconduct. Accusations of drunkenness were raised by other enemies. Charles Ferguson Smith was instead given command of the Union forces. They would advance slowly, while Grant was ordered to remain at Fort Henry. A month would pass before Halleck set aside the problems he imagined and Grant was allowed to resume his campaign.[24]

By the middle of March 1862, Grant was again in control, and with troops "constantly arriving" his army was built to 44,000 men. Both Grant and his antagonist, Albert Sidney Johnston, anticipated what the former predicted would be "the greatest battle fought of the War." He told Julia that he thought it would be "the last in the West" and that he did not feel "the slightest doubt" that he would win. That confidence would actually prove to be the deciding factor, as it had been at Fort Donelson. Johnston had fewer troops than the combined Union forces, but, as Grant was quick to point out, "this was compensated for by the advantage of being sole commander of all the Confederate forces at the West." Johnston decided to abandon Nashville and Chattanooga, and as Grant later recounted, he "fell back into northern Mississippi, where, six weeks later, he was destined to end his career."[25]

Johnston's Confederate army was in force in Corinth, in northern Mississippi, at the junction of the two most important railroads in the Mississippi Valley. One connected Memphis and the Mississippi River with the East, while the other led south to the cotton states. Corinth, Grant wrote, was "the great strategic position at the West between the Tennessee and the Mississippi rivers and between Nashville and Vicksburg." He added, "The enemy was

MORE GLORIOUS NEWS.

A Great Battle Fought at Pittsburgh Landing, Tenn.

VICTORY OF THE UNION FORCES.

"The Hardest Battle Ever Fought on this Continent."

Beauregard and Johnston in Command of the Rebel Army.

Gen. Grant in Pursuit of the Flying Rebels.

HEAVY LOSSES ON BOTH SIDES.

CHICAGO, Tuesday, April 8.

A PRIVATE DISPATCH RECEIVED IN THIS CITY, TO-NIGHT, FROM ONE OF GENERAL GRANT'S STAFF, SAYS THAT "WE HAVE FOUGHT AND WON THE HARDEST BATTLE EVER FOUGHT ON THIS CONTINENT." THIS DISPATCH IS DATED PITTSBURGH LANDING, 6TH.

ST. LOUIS, Tuesday, April 8.

In response to a serenade to-night, Gen. HALLECK said that *Gen. Beauregard with an immense army advanced from Corinth and attacked the combined forces of Gens. Grant and Buell. The battle began at daybreak yesterday, and continued till late in the afternoon with terrible loss on both sides. We have gained a complete victory, and driven the enemy back within his fortifications.*

He also announced his departure for the field tomorrow morning.

fortifying at Corinth and collecting an army there under Johnston …. It was my expectation to march against that army." His plan was to join forces with the Army of the Ohio under Don Carlos Buell and then move against the Confederates. Johnston, however, would not oblige him by waiting.[26]

On April 5, the night before Johnston attacked, Grant wrote to Halleck, "I have scarsely the faintest idea of an attack … being made upon us." In the *Memoirs* he explained his thinking: "The fact is, I regarded the campaign we were engaged in as an offensive one and had no idea that the enemy would leave strong intrenchments to take the initiative when he knew he would be attacked where he was if he remained." Grant had established his headquarters at Pittsburg Landing, Tennessee (fig. 136). The decision by P. G. T. Beauregard, Johnston's second-in-command, to stack four corps of the assault force, rather than spread them laterally, was a mistake. The column of soldiers extended two miles. Command broke down when many of those troops, who made up most of Johnston's army, became commingled and confused. Johnston's original plan was to attack Grant's left flank, where he was weakest, and separate him from the Tennessee River. However, when reinforcements were sent in response to fierce fighting that had broken out a couple of miles from the landing at a log meeting-house called Shiloh, the Confederate forces became misdirected, moving in a northwest direction instead of northeast. That shift proved to be the second major mistake made by Grant's opponents. In the meantime, he maintained both his own composure and order within the Union ranks.[27]

The battle of Shiloh lasted two days. There was "heavy firing and generally hard fighting," Grant recounted. "It was a case of Southern dash against Northern pluck and endurance." The Union forces were pushed back the first day; a Confederate victory seemed imminent. Grant, however, saw the developments entirely differently. He wrote that he was "confident … that the next day would bring victory to our arms if we could only take the initiative." To the doubts of his officers he responded, "Retreat? No. I propose to attack at daylight and whip them." Few commanders would have made that decision, which in the end turned defeat into victory. The arrival of the first of Buell's troops in time to fight on the second day aided Grant's efforts. Of April 7 Grant wrote, "everything was favorable to the Union side …. We had now become the attacking party. The enemy was driven back all day, as we had been the day before, until finally he beat a precipitate retreat."[28]

Some 100,000 troops fought at Shiloh. Almost a quarter of them, 23,746, were killed, wounded, or captured. Grant wrote to his wife that the battle "has no equal on this continent." The heavy casualties in this one battle amounted to more than in all of America's previous wars combined. In the thick of the fighting, a bullet struck the metal scabbard of Grant's sword without wounding him. Another bullet severed an artery in the calf of Albert Sidney Johnston, causing him to bleed to death. In his *Memoirs*, Grant famously described a scene that he could never forget:

> I saw an open field in our possession on the second day, over which the Confederates had made repeated charges the day before, so covered with dead that it would have been possible to walk across the clearing, in any direction, stepping on dead bodies, without a foot touching the ground.[29]

Grant considered the Union victory at Shiloh to be "one of the most important battles in the war." Initially, he had believed that "if a decisive victory could be gained over any of the Confederate armies," the war would end "suddenly." But when the Confederates "assumed the offensive and made such a gallant effort" at Shiloh, Grant continued, "I gave up all idea of saving the Union except by complete conquest." Shiloh turned out to be significant both for the encouragement it gave to the North, and because it "broke the prestige of the Southern Confederacy so far as our Western army was concerned." As Grant stated in 1878, "From that day they never feared to fight the enemy and never went into action without feeling sure they would win." For Grant, whose own confidence never needed such reinforcement, the experience of Shiloh also brought a change of philosophy regarding the property of the rebel citizens. Henceforth, his men would "consume everything that could be used to support or supply armies." At Shiloh the Civil War was escalated to a horrifying level of bloodshed, where it would remain until the end of the conflict.[30]

The capture of Corinth had been Grant's original objective. He had wanted to seize it after the fall of Fort Donelson and Nashville, "when it could have been taken without a battle," he later wrote. "But failing then," he added, "it should have been taken, without delay, on the concentration of troops at Pittsburg landing after the battle of Shiloh." Grant, "looking for a speedy move … [that would bring]

fig. 137.
James F. Gibson, *Panorama of McClellan's Army at Camp*, 1862 (photograph courtesy of Library of Congress)

easy sailing to the close of the war," would again be denied by Halleck, a general who had never fought in a major battle or had even seen a major battlefield, and who believed in the tradition of maneuvering an army to capture geographical objectives rather than in fighting battles to destroy one's opponent. Halleck proposed to assemble an enormous army of 120,000 soldiers, under his own command, that would slowly move on Corinth. When he finally got there, with Grant unhappily second in command, they found the city abandoned. Beauregard had been allowed to escape, and the war, from Grant's perspective, had been prolonged needlessly.[31]

Once again, Grant was frustrated that the momentum he had created had not been sustained. He wrote in his *Memoirs* about what might have been achieved:

> After the capture of Corinth a movable force of 80,000 men … could have been set in motion for the accomplishment of any great campaign for the suppression of the rebellion …. [If] Buell had been sent directly to Chattanooga … he could have arrived with but little fighting, and would have saved much of the loss of life which was afterwards incurred …. [T]he battle of Chattanooga would not have been fought. The positive results might have been: a bloodless advance to Atlanta, to Vicksburg, or to any other desired point south of Corinth in the interior of Mississippi.

Grant was further displeased that some northern newspapers had attacked him both for his excessive ambition and his drinking. Lincoln dismissed the complaints: "He fights," the president stated. Lincoln cleared the way for Grant by promoting Halleck to Washington and into the position of general-in-chief, where his organizational competence could be better utilized. Grant was awarded Halleck's vast western command; he and Don Carlos Buell would report to Halleck. On the Confederate side, Jefferson Davis, who like Halleck looked to control territory rather than win victories, replaced Beauregard with a more aggressive general, Braxton Bragg. Bragg wisely chose to attack Buell rather than Grant. He retook central Tennessee and even attempted to invade Kentucky. The Union problems in Tennessee would have to await future resolution.[32]

The summer of 1862 was an anxious time for Grant. He was able, however, to enjoy the company of his wife and children. "Their visit down here in Dixie was very pleasant and they were very lothe to leave," Grant wrote to his sister Mary. The oldest son, Fred, would join his father the next spring for part of the Vicksburg campaign.[33]

Lee's Ascent in the East: The Peninsula Campaign, Second Manassas, Antietam, and Fredericksburg

By March 1862, George McClellan's colossal army of more than 100,000 men (fig. 137) had arrived at Fort Monroe aboard nearly 400 vessels. A second Federal army of close to 45,000 men commanded by Irvin McDowell was in the vicinity of Washington, but it would soon move toward Fredericksburg and threaten Richmond. Following Grant's victories at Fort Henry, Fort Donelson, and Shiloh, a fearful Confederate president Jefferson Davis had called Joseph Johnston back to the capital from Manassas. In command of close to 55,000 men who were assembled to meet the Union threats to Richmond, Johnston prepared either to take on the

invader close to the city, perhaps even from behind its heavy fortifications, or to carry the war north into Maryland. However, McClellan's "Peninsula Campaign" too closely resembled Scott's landing at Vera Cruz and move to Mexico City for Lee not to see the parallel. He urged that the Union advance be halted well before a siege could commence. Lee suggested a bold offensive thrust: send troops down the Peninsula to meet the threat there. Johnston would not agree to that plan, nor would Davis allow an offensive into Maryland.

While Johnston hesitated, McClellan advanced, landing troops at the White House and at Brandon on the James River. Mary Custis Lee had recently been in residence at the White House, the Tidewater plantation of the Custis family that was then owned by Rooney Lee. "To be enveloped in it [the landing of an army] would be extremely annoying and embarrassing," Robert calmly wrote to his wife on April 4. He advised her to leave quickly, adding with understatement, "No one can say what place will be perfectly safe or even quiet, but I think a locality within the route of an invading army will be least so."[34]

McClellan divided his army. He deployed three corps north of the Chickahominy River and two corps south of it, a dangerous arrangement were not McDowell poised to advance from Fredericksburg to join him. Lee's solution was to prevent McDowell's army from participating. Johnston would take little initiative, so Lee directed Stonewall Jackson to advance in the Shenandoah Valley. If Jackson could successfully occupy all of the Federal forces west of the Blue Ridge Mountains and thereby pose a threat to the city of Washington, then McDowell could neither be reinforced from that quarter nor move to assist McClellan. With fewer than 20,000 soldiers, Jackson engaged more than 60,000 of the enemy, winning victories at Cross Keys and Port Republic in early June 1862 and avoiding traps set by his opponents, Generals Nathaniel P. Banks and John C. Frémont. Jackson used techniques that Lee admired: rapid movement, deception, audacity, resolve, daring, and enormous risk taking, in combination with his intimate knowledge of the geography of Virginia. In mid-June, Lee moved Jackson to the outskirts of Richmond, where, surprisingly, he failed to keep up the pace. However, his achievements in the Valley contributed more than any other factor to McClellan's eventual retreat. Jackson kept McDowell from joining McClellan. Had they united, their combined force of 150,000 men would have provided a numerical superiority that may have been unbeatable.[35]

In his *First Year of the War,* Pollard laid out the fears that enveloped Richmond as McClellan's army advanced. He argued that defeat would yield "confiscation, brutality, military domination, insult, universal poverty, the beggary of millions, the triumph of the vilest individuals in these communities, the abasement of the honest and industrious, the outlawry of the slaves, the destruction of agriculture and commerce, the emigration of all thriving citizens, farewell to the hopes of future wealth, and the scorn of the world." Amidst such worry, Lee exclaimed at a cabinet meeting with Davis in May, "Richmond must not be given up; it shall not be given up!" Johnston was obliged to take the offensive. He attacked McClellan's left flank at Seven Pines (Fair Oaks) and drove it back, but in the process was severely wounded. Lee was ordered to replace him in command on June 1, 1862. He wrote with feigned modesty and actual concern to the wife of his son Rooney, "I wish that [Johnston's] mantle had fallen upon an abler man, or that I were able to drive our enemies back to their homes. I have no ambition and no desire but the attainment of this object, and therefore only wish for its accomplishment by him that can do it most speedily and thoroughly."[36]

By driving the northerners "back to their homes" Lee meant ending the war, not simply pushing an army away from the outskirts of Richmond. By doing it "speedily," he meant that the longer he delayed his offensive, the more difficulty he would have in confronting the resources of the North. Lee had deduced from his experiences during the first year of war that the Confederacy was in peril, and that southern armies had to win battles resoundingly and quickly if the new nation was to survive.

Lee had the ability and temperament to seize control of the war. A fellow officer, Joseph C. Ives, stated, "If there is one man in either army, Federal or Confederate, who is, head & shoulders, far above every other one in either army in audacity that man is Gen. Lee, and you will very soon have lived to see it. Lee is audacity personified. His name is audacity." Lee would not just attack McClellan's army; he would try to obliterate it. His goal was to win so decisive a victory or series of victories that northern sentiment would force an end to the conflict. Lee's aide Walter Taylor, however, would describe what became known as the Seven Days campaign as "a

fig. 138.
Circle of Mathew Brady, *White House, New Kent County, burned 1862*, 1864 (photograph courtesy of United States Army Military History Institute)

fig. 139.
Attributed to George Barnard and James Gibson, *Ruins of Stone Bridge, Bull Run, Va., Spring 1862* (photograph courtesy of Virginia Historical Society)

record of lost opportunities."[37]

Lee gave his command a new name, the Army of Northern Virginia, which speaks of his determination to drive the invaders from the lands that had belonged to the Lees, Custises, Fitzhughs, and Washingtons. He added troops to the army, building it to a unit of 90,000 soldiers by the end of June, only some 15,000 fewer than McClellan's force. This would be the closest to parity that Lee would ever enjoy. He left a third of his army to defend the perimeter of Richmond, while he boldly moved two-thirds of it against McClellan's right flank. There, Jackson was to link up with Lee after a march from the Valley. Jackson had been forewarned; in mid-May Lee had advised him to be prepared to support Johnston. Reconnaissance indicated that McClellan's force north of the Chickahominy was actually smaller than Lee had anticipated. He sent Jeb

Stuart's cavalry on its now-famous ride around the Union army to find out more, including the exact position of the enemy's right flank. When Jackson was late in arriving, Lee was forced to attack at Mechanicsville without his assistance, lest the Union army south of the Chickahominy seize the opportunity to dash to the capital against little resistance. Union General Fitz John Porter fell back to

Gaines's Mill. In the next day's battle, Lee was forced to send James Longstreet and A. P. Hill into action without Jackson. McClellan, who was overly cautious and fearful that Lee's army numbered twice its actual size, retreated, moving his base to the James River from White House Landing. Rooney Lee's house was burned to the ground (fig. 138). To no avail, Mary Custis Lee had posted a note on the door: "Northern soldiers who profess to reverence Washington, forebear to desecrate the home of his first married life, the property of his wife, now owned by her descendants."[38]

Lee deduced the direction of McClellan's retreat and pursued him with vigor. At Savage's Station, however, when Jackson again failed to appear, John B. Magruder was left alone and was beaten back. Jackson, Benjamin Huger, and D. H. Hill arrived too late to contribute at Frayser's Farm, a battle that ranks among the greatest of lost opportunities for the Confederacy. Lee was angry and bitterly disappointed, exclaiming "I cannot have my orders carried out!" Jackson's delay enabled McClellan to escape to Malvern Hill, one of the estates once owned by Lee's grandfather Charles Carter on the periphery of Carter's Shirley plantation. McClellan's army took a formidable position, from which A. P. Hill warned that the Union artillery could slaughter the oncoming Confederate troops. D. H. Hill described the aftermath: "It was not war …. It was murder." Although McClellan watched from a ship in panic, unable to give orders, it was Lee who blundered tactically that day and lost the most men. The campaign was "nothing but a series of blunders, one after another, and all huge," wrote Walter Taylor. The British general J. F. C. Fuller argued that the fault lay in Lee's reliance on verbal orders and his reluctance to interfere with his lieutenants once he had positioned them. McClellan retreated to the security of nearby Harrison's Landing. Two months later his army was pulled back to the north of Richmond.[39]

Lee had failed to destroy McClellan's army and bring an end to the war. He had, however, saved Richmond, and thereby saved the Confederacy from collapse. Most southerners were blind to all but the latter. The man who had been disparaged in western Virginia with various nicknames, including the "King of Spades" because of his defensive strategy, was suddenly a heroic figure to the Confederate nation, while northern papers began to wonder why he was consistently able to outthink and outfight their generals.

All the armies in Virginia, Confederate and Union, then took

time to regroup. Longstreet had proven to be dependable, while Jackson seemed not. Lee increased Longstreet's brigades from six to twenty-eight, while he reduced Jackson's from fourteen to seven. The divisions of McDowell, Banks, and Frémont were organized into a new army under John Pope, who redefined the enemy to include Confederate civilians. For that, Lee called him a "miscreant." Pope occupied Culpeper Courthouse, a railroad junction. Lee worried that McClellan's army of 90,000 might join Pope's and swell it to a force three times his own. He would again have to assume the initiative. He would fight the Yankees, under favorable conditions of his choosing, before McClellan could complete his withdrawal from the Tidewater.[40]

Lee first planned to trap Pope between the Rapidan and Rappahannock rivers. Then he devised an even more audacious plan that would move his Army of Northern Virginia even farther into the region for which it was named and which he hoped to liberate. He sent Jackson with part of Jeb Stuart's cavalry to strike at Pope's base of supplies, Manassas Junction (Bull Run), the site of the Confederate victory in 1861 (fig. 139). That move forced Pope to retreat northward. Lee daringly gave nearly half of his army to Jackson, to be positioned between Pope and the city of Washington. "Knowing the country well," as Lee recounted to William Allan after the war, he was able to bring the remainder of his army across the mountains at Thoroughfare Gap and unite with Jackson. Critics have argued that Lee should then have moved on Washington, but his goal was to defeat northern morale by winning victories and the opportunity beckoned at Manassas. Pope was thoroughly baffled as to the location of some of his own forces and most of the enemy's. Lee waited for Pope to initiate a major battle; Longstreet counseled him three times to be patient. "Lost Cause" writers set on denigrating Longstreet later critiqued his performance at Second Manassas, but in fact when the assault finally came, he responded brilliantly, mounting an effective counterattack with batteries and his entire wing. Longstreet's deployment of 30,000 men in half an hour was actually a remarkable accomplishment that was vital to the Confederate victory. The only shortcoming of Lee at Second Manassas was his failure to organize a prompt pursuit of Pope's army as it fled in retreat.[41]

Five years after the war, Lee told a cousin in Alexandria that the maneuver that followed Second Manassas was determined by his army's critical need for rations. He explained to Cassius Lee that he went into Maryland "to feed my army." Richmond would be safe from attack while his forces were so close to Washington as to pose a threat to that city; in fact, the removal of the armies to the North would allow the Confederates to strengthen the defenses around their capital. The need for rations was indeed pressing, but other factors also influenced Lee's decision. Near the top of the list was his determination to rid northern Virginia of the Union army,

fig. 140.
Alexander Gardner, *The Battle of Antietam*, September 17, 1862 (photograph courtesy of Library of Congress)

at least for a while, so that life there could return to some degree of normalcy. To move into Maryland was to take the initiative. Once in Maryland Lee could attempt to fight at the most propitious time and place. Other Confederate forces were also moving north at this time: Braxton Bragg and Edmund Kirby Smith were taking the war back into Kentucky. Lee wrote to Jefferson Davis on September 3, 1862, "The present seems to be the most propitious time since the commencement of the war for the Confederate Army to enter Maryland."[42]

Lee still sought the opportunity to win a major victory that would undermine support for the war in the North. In his determination to end the conflict, he argued on September 8 to Davis, with whom he was often at odds regarding strategy, that this was the moment for a peace initiative:

> [A peace proposal] being made when it is in our power [in Maryland] to inflict injury upon our adversary, would show conclusively to the world that our sole object is the establishment of our independence and the attainment of an honorable peace …. The proposal of peace would enable the people of the United States to determine at their coming elections whether they will support those who favor a prolongation of the war, or those who wish to bring it to a termination, which can but be productive of good to both parties without affecting the honor of either.[43]

Lee believed that when northern voters went to the polls two months later for the off-year elections they would oust the Republican majority if they were sufficiently discouraged by the course of the war. He and Davis had read enough newspapers to be aware of a strong antiwar sentiment in the North. What Lee miscalculated, however, was the extent of that movement and what it might realistically achieve. Many Democrats were unhappy with the progress of the war, but most were far from ready to agree to the disunion of their nation; only extremists would accept such a policy. More immediately, Lee also overlooked the fact that the western counties of Maryland, where he was headed, were staunchly Unionist.[44]

Lee was additionally mindful of foreign opinion. Although he routinely said that southerners could not count on foreign intervention to win their war, he was as ready to welcome it as George Washington had been during the Revolution. Military observers from England and France had joined both the Union and Confederate armies on the battlefield. Lee knew that the political leaders of those countries were keenly interested in whether or not the Confederacy was a potent enough military force to emerge into an independent nation. If it was, they wanted to be on friendly terms with a potentially important economic ally that was the leading producer of cotton in the world. Lee also knew that the South enjoyed some degree of popular support abroad. The United States Consul in Liverpool, Thomas Dudley, reported on July 19, 1862, that all of Europe was against the North and "would rejoice at our downfall."[45]

Unfortunately for Lee, his army was in many ways unready to conduct so important a campaign. Not only did his soldiers and animals enter Maryland in need of food; the men were also short of clothing and equipment. At the start they numbered only between 50,000 and 55,000, not enough to take on a much larger enemy. By the time they engaged in battle, the Army of Northern Virginia had further dwindled due to poor morale and lax discipline that allowed straggling and desertion. The army had not yet identified itself as Lee's, and they were sadly in need of self-confidence. Nonetheless, their general led them forward. To do so was his best strategic option. He told William Allan after the war that he "could do nothing more against the Yankees unless he attacked them in their fortifications around Washington, which he did not want to do, and he therefore determined to cross the river into Maryland."[46]

Once he was at Frederick, Lee issued a proclamation to the people of Maryland (fig. 141) that was similar to Grant's in Paducah, Kentucky, almost exactly a year earlier. Both generals looked beyond the battlefield into the political arena. Also as Grant had done, Lee sought to relieve public concern while at the same time win converts to his cause:

> It is right that you should know the purpose that has brought the Army under my command within the limits of your State .... [T]he people of the South have long wished to aid you in throwing off this foreign yoke, to enable you again to enjoy the inalienable rights of freemen, and restore independence and sovereignty to your State. In obedience to this wish, our army has come among you, and is prepared to assist you with the power of its arms in regaining the rights of which you have been despoiled.

The episode unfolded differently for Lee than it had for Grant. Maryland was not a neutral state that had been invaded by the enemy. Lee's excursion would rally southern morale, but it would at the same time arouse strong indignation in the North.[47]

Within a week after he issued the proclamation, Lee's military options were greatly reduced. He was forced to fight at Antietam (Sharpsburg) in part because one of his dispatches, which told of his location and intentions, had fallen into the hands of McClellan, who had uncharacteristically taken up the pursuit of the Army of Northern Virginia (fig. 140). Up until that point, Lee told Edward Clifford Gordon, his adversary was "in complete ignorance of the whereabouts and intentions of the Southern army .... Stuart with his cavalry was close up to the enemy and doing everything possible to keep him in ignorance and to deceive him by false reports, which he industriously circulated." Lee needed time to regroup after dividing his army in order to send Jackson to take Harpers Ferry, a town Longstreet said should have been bypassed. Lee believed that "if McClellan could have been kept in ignorance but two or three days longer," the Army of Northern Virginia "could have crushed" him.

At Antietam, not all of Lee's army arrived until late in the day; forces under A. P. Hill appeared only at the last moment. It was a savage battle, the bloodiest single day of the entire war, during which Lee faced frightening odds—his twenty-four brigades faced forty-four. The Army of Northern Virginia lost a third of its men. A Georgian wrote to his wife of the slaughter, "This war will have to stop before too long, as all the men will be killed off." Military historians argue that Lee showed brilliant tactical leadership on the battlefield, but that he erred badly in choosing to fight at Antietam, and that he was foolish to remain on the field a second day with his back to the Potomac River and dare a second attack from a larger army that had been reinforced during the night. Lee, however, had correctly judged McClellan's overcaution; a second attack never came. Had McClellan dared to attempt complete victory, and not let Lee "get off without being hurt" as Lincoln put it, he probably would have succeeded, Richmond would have been exposed, Confederate morale would have been destroyed, and the war might have ended.[48]

In a way the war did end at Antietam. The chance of foreign intervention on behalf of the Confederacy vanished, as most observers interpreted the Confederate withdrawal as a defeat. And with the issue of a temporary Emancipation Proclamation, the conflict was elevated to a new level of contention, from a battle simply to save the Union to an effort to determine the social and

fig. 141.
Head-quarters: Army N. Va., Near Frederick Town, 8th September, 1862. To the People of Mar[y]land, R. E. Lee, General Commanding, 1862, broadside, Virginia Historical Society

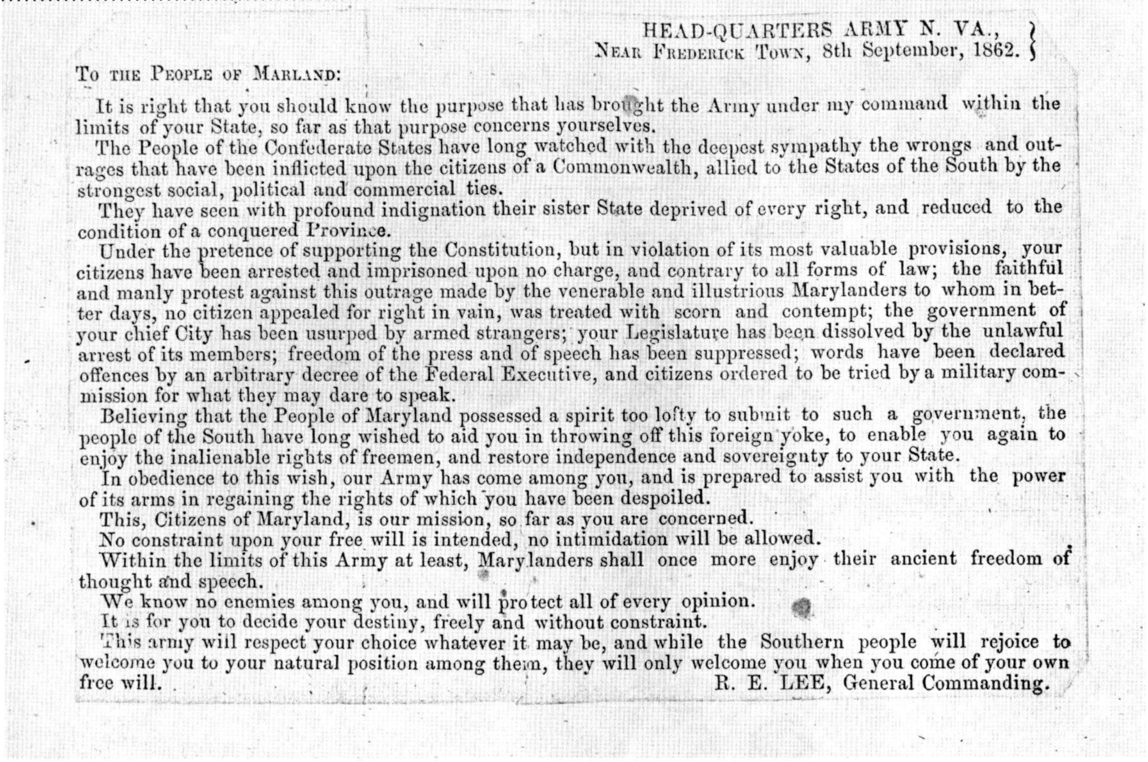

> HEAD-QUARTERS ARMY N. VA.,
> NEAR FREDERICK TOWN, 8th September, 1862.
>
> TO THE PEOPLE OF MARLAND:
>
> It is right that you should know the purpose that has brought the Army under my command within the limits of your State, so far as that purpose concerns yourselves.
>
> The People of the Confederate States have long watched with the deepest sympathy the wrongs and outrages that have been inflicted upon the citizens of a Commonwealth, allied to the States of the South by the strongest social, political and commercial ties.
>
> They have seen with profound indignation their sister State deprived of every right, and reduced to the condition of a conquered Province.
>
> Under the pretence of supporting the Constitution, but in violation of its most valuable provisions, your citizens have been arrested and imprisoned upon no charge, and contrary to all forms of law; the faithful and manly protest against this outrage made by the venerable and illustrious Marylanders to whom in better days, no citizen appealed for right in vain, was treated with scorn and contempt; the government of your chief City has been usurped by armed strangers; your Legislature has been dissolved by the unlawful arrest of its members; freedom of the press and of speech has been suppressed; words have been declared offences by an arbitrary decree of the Federal Executive, and citizens ordered to be tried by a military commission for what they may dare to speak.
>
> Believing that the People of Maryland possessed a spirit too lofty to submit to such a government, the people of the South have long wished to aid you in throwing off this foreign yoke, to enable you again to enjoy the inalienable rights of freemen, and restore independence and sovereignty to your State.
>
> In obedience to this wish, our Army has come among you, and is prepared to assist you with the power of its arms in regaining the rights of which you have been despoiled.
>
> This, Citizens of Maryland, is our mission, so far as you are concerned.
>
> No constraint upon your free will is intended, no intimidation will be allowed.
>
> Within the limits of this Army at least, Marylanders shall once more enjoy their ancient freedom of thought and speech.
>
> We know no enemies among you, and will protect all of every opinion.
>
> It is for you to decide your destiny, freely and without constraint.
>
> This army will respect your choice whatever it may be, and while the Southern people will rejoice to welcome you to your natural position among them, they will only welcome you when you come of your own free will.
>
> R. E. LEE, General Commanding.

economic structures of the slave-holding South. One thing was certain—Europeans would not join the cause to defend slavery. Only a decisive Confederate triumph on the battlefield could have perpetuated the institution of slavery, and the southern armies were simply incapable of achieving the sort of victory that would prevent an endless procession of new campaigns.

Within the South, popular opinion denied the outcome at Antietam. The battle was not a major setback but at worst a bloody stalemate. The men sacrificed in Maryland would most likely have been killed in Virginia had the Union forces not been driven away. Lee had dared to invade the North and had returned with a capable fighting force. His army was better bonded to him for the experience. Jackson had taken Harpers Ferry and 12,000 Union troops there as prisoners. Southern newspapers argued that Lincoln's emancipation policy would solidify southern opinion and eventually divide the North.[49]

Lee's sons all served in the Confederate army. By the fall of 1862, the two oldest had risen to some prominence. Custis was in Richmond on the staff of President Davis, while Rooney was promoted to brigadier general in the cavalry, with his younger brother Rob on his staff. In October, however, Lee's second daughter, Annie, died from typhoid fever at age twenty-three. Aide Walter Taylor wrote, "I was startled and shocked to see him overcome with grief, an open letter in his hand." To his wife, the general described his anguish as "agonizing in the extreme." A month later, he wrote to his daughter Mary, "In the quiet hours of the night, when there is nothing to lighten the full weight of my grief, I feel as if I should be overwhelmed."[50]

McClellan's hesitancy to pursue his enemy allowed the Army of Northern Virginia to recuperate. Lincoln then replaced McClellan with Ambrose Burnside. "We always understood each other so well," Lee remarked regarding McClellan, "I fear they may continue to make these changes till they find some one whom I don't understand." Lee anticipated that his new antagonist would move on Fredericksburg (fig. 142), which he did. Burnside delayed so long, however, that Lee had time to construct formidable fortifications that proved to be invulnerable to attack. Burnside threw repeated assaults at Lee's strong left flank. Many of Burnside's soldiers were simply annihilated. There were more than twice the number of Union than Confederate casualties. The ease of his success is said to have prompted Lee, watching from above the battlefield, to comment, "It is well that war is so terrible or we should

fig. 142.
Unidentified photographer, *Confederate Soldiers Pose at Fredericksburg*, c. 1862–63 (photograph courtesy of Virginia Historical Society)

grow too fond of it." While that remark may be apocryphal, it is certain that Lee wrote to his wife on Christmas Day of 1862, "But what a cruel thing is war. To separate & destroy families & friends …. I pray … that better thoughts will fill the hearts of our enemies & turn them to peace." The cold winter took an unexpected toll on Lee's health; by the spring he was experiencing the first signs of the heart disease that would kill him eight years later. In March he wrote to Mary, "Old age & sorrow is wearing me away, & constant anxiety & labour, day & night, leaves me but little repose." In April he told her, "I am feeble & worthless & can do but little."[51]

Grant at Vicksburg and Chattanooga

Placed in command of the Department of the Tennessee on October 25, 1862, Grant began his Vicksburg campaign a week later. As always, he would move forward quickly. His goal was ambitious: to sever the western Confederacy from the eastern states and gain control of the Mississippi River from Memphis all the way to the Gulf of Mexico. He explained in his *Memoirs*:

> New Orleans and Baton Rouge had fallen into the possession of the National forces, so that now the Confederates at the west were narrowed down for all communication with Richmond to the single line of road running east from Vicksburg. To dispossess them of this, therefore, became a matter of the first importance. The possession of the Mississippi by us from Memphis to Baton Rouge was also a most important object. It would be equal to the amputation of a limb in its weakening effects upon the enemy.[52]

Vicksburg was the key to both the geographical unity of the Confederacy and the regulation of traffic on the Mississippi River. It was both a railroad junction and the site of a seemingly impregnable river fortress that controlled the passage of shipping both north and south. Grant elaborated:

> Vicksburg was important to the enemy because it occupied the first high ground coming close to the river below Memphis. From there a railroad runs east …. A railroad also starts from the opposite side of the river, extending west …. Vicksburg was the only channel … connecting the parts of the Confederacy divided by the Mississippi. So long as it was held by the enemy, the free navigation of the river was prevented. Hence its importance.[53]

To most observers, the capture of Vicksburg seemed impossible. Situated on a high cliff above the Mississippi River on the eastern bank, the fortress was unapproachable from the west. Grant rightly called it "impregnable against any force that could be brought against its front." To the north were floodlands, "bayous filled from the river in high water." As Grant put it, "The problem was to secure a footing upon dry ground on the east side of the river from which the troops could operate against Vicksburg." After he had captured the fort and town, Grant said that from the start he knew that "Vicksburg could only be successfully turned from the South side of the City." He wrote in his *Memoirs* that during "the whole winter" of 1862–63 he contemplated "the movement by land to a point below Vicksburg from which to operate." That was more easily said than done. Grant first considered an offensive thrust directly toward the town, southward along the line of the Mississippi Railroad. Within five weeks he was halfway there, until Confederate forces under Nathan Bedford Forrest and Earl Van Dorn attacked the rear of his lines and destroyed his large supply depot at Holly Springs, Mississippi, which halted his drive. Grant then sent a large portion of his army back to Grand Junction, Tennessee, with the idea that the remainder of his army could live off the land (fig. 143). He found that the latter was easy to accomplish: "I was amazed at the quantity of supplies the country afforded."[54]

fig. 143.
Officers of the 47th Illinois at Oxford, Mississippi, December 1862 (photograph courtesy of William Whisler)

December was a low point for Grant, largely because the campaign against Vicksburg was going nowhere. It did inspire thousands of slaves to escape to freedom behind his lines, but the liberators were then confronted with the problem of what to do with those people. At the same time, merchants, many of whom were Jewish, were attempting to purchase the cotton that those slaves had been raising, with little regard for the rules that the federal government had imposed upon them. Unable to control this traffic, Grant banished the merchants: "The Jews, as a class, violating every regulation of trade established by the Treasury Department, and also [War] Department orders, are hereby expelled from the Department." Lincoln directed Halleck to command Grant to rescind his order. Remarkably honest as well as strong enough to admit a mistake, Grant soon apologized for his anti-Semitic statement.

Also at this time stories once again surfaced about his binge drinking on occasions when Julia was absent. John Rawlins, his aide from Galena, whose father was an alcoholic, looked out for Grant and defended him from such attacks. Assistant Secretary of War Charles Dana had been sent by Secretary of War Edwin Stanton to keep his eye on the general. Dana saw no alcoholic, but instead "the most modest, the most disinterested and most honest man" he ever knew. Josiah Bunting has explained the meaning of "disinterested," that "highest adjective of political praise from an earlier century":

> [Grant was] consciously devoted to Cause, not Self. He had a remarkable ability to get men to do things, the things he wanted done, as well as they possibly could, and to do so with no yelling, no threatening, no cajoling, no promises. He simply communicated a calm confidence that the mission would be done, and done successfully.[55]

The winter of 1862–63 was also a low point for many people in the North, who were disheartened by the course of a war that had extended far longer than most imagined possible. A number of anti-war Democrats had been voted into office during the midterm elections, and the longevity of the Lincoln administration was threatened. Grant came to believe that a Union victory was desperately needed. He explained in his *Memoirs* the thinking that compelled him to pursue a daring and unorthodox plan:

> At this time the North had become very much discouraged. Many strong Union men believed that the war must prove a failure. The elections of 1862 had gone against the party which was for the prosecution of the war to save the Union if it took the last man and the last dollar. Voluntary enlistments had ceased throughout the greater part of the North, and the draft had been resorted to fill up our ranks. It was my judgment at the time that to make a backward movement … would be interpreted, by many of those yet full of hope for the preservation of the Union, as a defeat, and that the draft would be resisted, desertions ensue and the power to capture and punish deserters lost. There was nothing left to be done but to go forward to a decisive victory.

He spent that winter trying to figure out how such a victory could be accomplished.

Grant had found that "marching across this country in the face of an enemy was impossible." He had allowed his engineers to try to construct canals north of Vicksburg through the delta of curving rivers. At the least, the digging kept the soldiers busy and their morale from plummeting; if the canals worked, all the better. But disease in the Mississippi lowlands was killing Union troops. Grant would have to try something extraordinary; he would maneuver deeper into enemy territory.[56]

fig. 144.
Theodore R. Davis, *The Rams "Switzerland" and "Lancaster" Running the Blockade at Vicksburg*, April 18, 1863, *Harper's Weekly*

Northern vessels had tried for some time to navigate past the Vicksburg batteries. Their success rate was not high, as illustrated in a *Harper's Weekly* account of the failure of the rams *Lancaster* and *Switzerland* to pass in late March (fig. 144): both ships were disabled; the *Lancaster* sank. Nonetheless, Grant thought the risk was worth taking. He had no authority over the navy, but as in the campaign against Forts Henry and Donelson, he soon found a sound ally. Grant would cross to the west bank above Vicksburg and then march his army south. The fleet of acting Rear Admiral David D. Porter would run the gauntlet, and then ferry Grant's army back to the east bank. Grant had high praise for Porter:

> The co-operation of the navy was absolutely essential to the success …. I had no more authority to command Porter than he had to command me. It was necessary to have part of his fleet below Vicksburg if the troops went there. Steamers to use as ferries were also essential. The navy was the only escort and protection for these steamers, all of which in getting below had to run about fourteen miles of batteries. Porter fell into the plan at once.

The admiral's fleet suffered sixty-eight hits, but only one of ten ships sank. Porter then made a second run of the batteries to bring additional transports and barges. Grant later recounted that a local black man showed the general a safe place to land on the east bank. In April, when his 33,000 men were safely across, the general "felt a degree of relief scarcely ever equaled since." The Confederate commander at Vicksburg, Lieutenant General John C. Pemberton, had no idea what his opponent was up to.[57]

Grant's enemy consisted of two armies that together outnumbered his force, one under Pemberton sent out from Vicksburg, and another under Joe Johnston, which was sent by Jefferson Davis to rescue Pemberton. But they never managed to unite, in part because Grant moved too quickly. He well understood the importance of momentum. Pemberton looked for Grant's supply line, which did not exist. (He "determined to … get between me and my base. I, however, had no base.") Neither Confederate commander imagined that Grant would attack Jackson, the capital of Mississippi, before moving on Vicksburg. In his *Memoirs*, Grant could proudly recount that in little more than two weeks, "five distinct battles … had been fought and won; the capital of the State had fallen … ; an average of about one hundred and eighty miles had been marched … ; over six thousand prisoners had been captured, and as many more of the enemy had been killed or wounded."[58]

Before laying siege to Vicksburg, Grant tried to storm the fort on May 19 and again on May 22. He made the effort, he said, out of "consideration" for his soldiers. "The troops believed they could carry the works in their front, and would not have worked so patiently in the trenches if they had not been allowed to try." He then reported to the general-in-chief that "the fall of Vicksburg … can

fig. 145.
Vicksburg. An Official Announcement to the President that Vicksburgh has Fallen, May 25, 1863, The New York Times

VICKSBURG.

An Official Announcement to the President that Vicksburgh has Fallen.

The Stars and Stripes Floating Over the Rebel Stronghold.

THE VICTORY COMPLETE.

Probable Capture of the Entire Rebel Army Under Pemberton.

Official Details of Gen. Grant's Progress After Leaving Jackson.

Two Great Battles Fought on Saturday and Sunday, 16th and 17th.

only be a question of time." The food and munitions of the Confederates "could not last always." On May 26, after newspapers had prematurely claimed victory (fig. 145), President Lincoln declared that regardless of what happened next, Grant's Vicksburg campaign "is one of the most brilliant in the world." The answer to the "question of time" proved to be six weeks. All the while, Grant was receiving reinforcements from Memphis almost daily; his force eventually reached 70,000, twice the size of his immediate enemy.[59]

With horrible conditions existing in the city, on the symbolic date of July 4 Pemberton decided to surrender rather than to suffer the humiliation of a successful assault. Grant greeted him "as an old acquaintance" because they had served together in the Mexican War. Among the terms, and so that Grant's men would be spared the "inconvenience" of transporting "over thirty thousand men ... to Cairo [Illinois]," the Confederates were paroled as prisoners of war. The officers were permitted to keep their side-arms and horses. This freed the Union army for the next important objective, the removal of Joe Johnston's army from Mississippi. Following Grant's new directive to "inflict all the punishment you can," William Tecumseh Sherman soon set about to accomplish that goal.[60]

Approximately 30,000 prisoners, 172 cannons, 60,000 muskets, and a large amount of ammunition were surrendered at Vicksburg. Grant wrote in his *Memoirs* that the campaign "gave new spirit to the loyal people of the North" and "sealed" the "fate of the Confederacy." "New hopes for the final success of the cause of the Union were inspired," he added. Although religion rarely came to the surface with Grant, he wrote at the end of his life, "It looks now as though Providence had directed the course of the [Vicksburg] campaign."[61]

Lincoln was clear in his opinion of the general: "Grant is my man, and I am his the rest of the war." Grant "doesn't worry and bother me. He isn't shrieking for reinforcements all the time. He takes what troops we can safely give him ... and does the best he can with what he has got." Grant had used virtually the same words to describe Zachary Taylor. The conqueror of Vicksburg was awarded a medal by Congress, and he was further rewarded with a promotion to major general in the regular army, the highest rank then available.[62]

Following his resounding success in Mississippi, Grant was anxious to resume the offensive and maintain momentum. However, he was again halted by Henry Halleck. In the fall of 1863, Grant was ready to take Alabama, where he would have posed a serious threat to Confederate armies and towns in Tennessee and Georgia. But,

> Halleck disapproved of my proposition to go against Mobile, so that I was obliged to settle down and see myself put again on the defensive as I had been a year before in west Tennessee. It would have been an easy thing to capture Mobile at the time I proposed to go there. Having that as a base of operations, troops could have been thrown into the interior to operate against General Bragg's army. This would necessarily have compelled Bragg to detach in order to meet this fire in his rear.

Instead, Grant spent the remainder of the summer in New Orleans as an administrator concerned with regulating trade on the

fig. 146.
Mathew Brady, *Grant and His Staff at Lookout Mountain, Tennessee*, 1863 (photograph courtesy of Library of Congress)

Mississippi River to the advantage of the Union. A serious injury to his leg that occurred when his horse fell on him added to the difficulty of Grant's next challenge.[63]

Grant recounted that he had no idea of what would be asked of him next. He soon learned of an impending disaster in Tennessee. Urged by Washington to move forward, William Rosecrans had taken Chattanooga with 60,000 troops. He then pressed on too far. At Chickamauga Creek, Georgia, Braxton Bragg's slightly larger army, reinforced by two divisions under James Longstreet, had turned the Union advance into defeat. Longstreet broke through, causing Rosecrans and most of his army to retreat to Chattanooga in panic. Heavy losses were incurred on both sides. The total of 38,000 casualties surpassed even the figure at Shiloh. Secretary of War Edwin Stanton traveled west to personally assign Grant command of a new "Military Division of the Mississippi," which was to consist of all of the territory from the Alleghenies to the Mississippi that lay north of Nathaniel Banks's command in the Southwest. Grant was allowed to replace Rosecrans with George Thomas. Thomas's Army of the Cumberland, Sherman's Army of the Tennessee, and Burnside's Army of the Ohio were all placed under his command.[64]

Grant made clear that Chattanooga must not fall. He telegraphed Thomas that he must retain the city at all hazards. "We will hold the town till we starve," Thomas responded. "A retreat at that time would have been a terrible disaster," Grant said later. "It would not only have been the loss of a most important strategic position to us, but it would have been attended with the loss of all the artillery still left with the Army of the Cumberland and the annihilation of that army itself, either by capture or demoralization." Still injured and on crutches (and "carried over places where it was not safe to cross on horseback"), Grant traveled to Chattanooga as quickly as he could. The severity of the situation concerned him. It "requires all the care and watchfulness that can be bestowed upon it," he wrote Julia. "It has all mine, and no fault shall rest upon me if we are not successful." He first opened a supply line to the city via the Chattanooga River from Bridgeport to deliver food to the besieged soldiers, noting that "It is hard for any one not an eyewitness to realize the relief this brought." He then brought in additional troops. Grant was massing his army for an attack.[65]

The spectacular high ground that surrounds Chattanooga (fig. 146) had been left to the Confederates, whose artillery commanded the approaches to the city. "The enemy, with a vastly superior force, was strongly fortified to the east, south, and west, and commanded the river below," Grant wrote. "The Army of the Cumberland was besieged." To his left they controlled Missionary Ridge, in front Lookout Mountain, and on his right Raccoon Mountain. Confederate pickets saluted Grant when he observed them; he saluted back.[66]

Grant had so dazzled the military establishment with the campaign at Vicksburg that the troops were beginning to recognize his genius. In Chattanooga, he found a group of beleaguered Union officers who were prepared to listen. Several at the time recorded their thoughts, leaving us with as good an account of the man as we will find. Horace Porter, a member of George Thomas's staff, was taken by Grant's intellect:

> So intelligent were his inquiries, and so pertinent his suggestions, that he made a profound impression upon everyone by the quickness of his perception and the knowledge which he had already acquired …. Coming to us with the laurels he had gained in Vicksburg, we naturally expected to meet a well-equipped soldier, but hardly anyone was prepared to find one who had the grasp, the promptness of decision, and the general administrative capacity which he displayed at the very start.

Porter also left a physical description of the general:

> Many of us were not a little surprised to find him a man of

slim figure, slightly stooped, five feet eight in height, weighing only 135 pounds. His eyes were dark-gray, and were the most expressive of his features. His hair and beard were of a chestnut brown color. The beard was worn full …. His voice was exceedingly musical, and one of the clearest in sound and most distinct in utterance that I have ever heard. It had a singular power of penetration, and sentences spoken by him in an ordinary tone could be heard at a distance which was surprising. His gait of walking [was] decidedly unmilitary. He never carried his body erect …. He was civil to all who came in contact with him, and never attempted to snub anyone, or treat anybody with less consideration on account of his inferiority in rank.

Another officer, Charles Francis Adams, Jr., wrote that Grant might look like a "slouchy little subaltern," but he had remarkable talents for getting work done, for managing people, and for providing leadership under stress:

> [H]e is a man of the most exquisite judgment and tact. He handles those around him so quietly and well, he so evidently has the faculty of disposing of work and managing men, he is cool and quiet, almost stolid and as if stupid, in danger, and in a crisis he is one against whom all around, whether few in numbers or a great army as here, would instinctively lean.

Major General David Hunter was impressed by Grant's work ethic, debunked the rumors about alcoholism, and pointed to Grant's ability to seize the opportunities provided by enemy mistakes:

> He is a hard worker, writes his own dispatches and orders, and does his own thinking. He is modest, quiet, never swears, and seldom drinks …. He listens quietly to the opinions of others and then judges promptly for himself, and is very prompt to avail himself in the field of all the errors of the enemy.[67]

At Chattanooga, "grave mistakes," as Grant called them, were made by the enemy. Braxton Bragg was unable to work with his lieutenants. Four corps commanders asked for his removal but instead were themselves reassigned by Jefferson Davis. The Confederate president sent James Longstreet with 20,000 of the besieging troops in pursuit of Burnside at Knoxville. There had been 70,000 Confederate soldiers looking down on Chattanooga. In an instant, their numerical superiority was removed. Grant took pleasure in pointing out Davis's poor decision: "On several occasions during the war he came to the relief of the Union army by means of his superior military genius." He also criticized Bragg for sending other troops away and for "placing so much of a force on the plain in front of his impregnable position." That was the area below Lookout Mountain, where Thomas would carry the day when Grant ordered the Union attack that freed the city.[68]

On November 21, Grant initiated what would be three days of battle. His plan was to turn one or both of Bragg's flanks and move Thomas forward at the center. (Thomas was incensed because Bragg had publicly stated, as Jeb Stuart had earlier, that the Virginian had betrayed his native state by fighting for the Union.) Grant found no success at the flanks, but Bragg's deployment of reinforcements to meet those attacks weakened the center just when Thomas moved against it with sixty regiments, some 24,000 men. Arthur MacArthur of Wisconsin, whose son Douglas MacArthur would attain much greater military fame, led the first group that reached the top of the Confederate position. Thomas's men then pushed beyond that line and routed Bragg's soldiers. Grant described their flight in his *Memoirs*:

> The retreat of the enemy along most of his line was precipitate and the panic so great that Bragg and his officers lost all control over their men. Many were captured, and thousands threw away their arms in their flight.

Grant wrote at the time, "An Army never was whipped so badly as Bragg was."[69]

As at Donelson and Shiloh, Grant had turned defeat into victory. At Chattanooga, the entire Army of the Cumberland would probably have been lost had it not been for Grant. He spelled out the broader repercussions in the *Memoirs*: "If he [Bragg] had captured Chattanooga, East Tennessee would have fallen without a struggle." Also, morale in the Confederacy was decimated. "Chattanooga, following in the same half year with Gettysburg in the East and Vicksburg in the West, there was much the same feeling in the South at this time that there had been in the North the fall and winter before." Following the victory, Grant was able to send Sherman to Burnside's relief in Knoxville. Longstreet retreated before Sherman arrived. Lincoln wrote to Grant, "I wish to tender you, and all under your command, my more than thanks, my profoundest gratitude for the skill, courage, and perseverance with which you and they, over so great difficulties, have effected that important object."[70]

Grant's remarkable success at Chattanooga inspired a public outpouring of affection. New portraits were painted and drawn of the general and new photographs were taken. (see fig. 16, above). Citizens in Galena and Jo Daviess County, Illinois, commissioned a diamond-hilted sword with a gold scabbard that was engraved with the names of battles as a gift for the general. Some members of the Democratic party asked Grant if he would allow himself to be considered a candidate for the presidency. To Lincoln's relief, Grant wrote back, "The question astonishes me …. Nothing likely to happen would pain me so much as to see my name used in connection with a political office." The president and Congress rewarded Grant by reviving for him the rank of lieutenant general, which had only been held by George Washington. On February 26, 1864, Grant replaced Henry Halleck as general-in-chief and assumed command of all of the Union armies. Halleck became his chief of staff, relieving Grant of administrative duties and enabling him to remain in the field.

Soon after Grant's seemingly instantaneous transformation from scruffy bumpkin to honored guest—after the clerk at Willard's Hotel in Washington, D.C., had read "U.S. Grant and son, Galena, Illinois" in the register book—Lincoln awarded the general his promotion at the White House. Grant replied with a fatalistic recognition of divine power that recalled the statements of the first lieutenant general: "I feel the full weight of the responsibilities now devolving on me; and I know that if they are met, it will be due to those armies, and above all, to the favor of that Providence which leads both nations and men." Grant and Lincoln later talked privately. They liked one another. Both were Midwesterners who spoke their minds clearly and directly, without pretension. A British journalist then in Washington, his name now lost, saw Grant as a symbol of the new America: "I never met a man with so much simplicity, shyness, and decision …. He is a soldier to the core, a genuine commoner, commander of a democratic army from a democratic people."[71]

Lee at Chancellorsville and Gettysburg

In early 1863, the Confederate populace began to rally behind the aggressive and capable general of the Army of Northern Virginia as their best hope for military salvation. Writing in the *Southern Literary Messenger* in January, P. W. Alexander interviewed Lee for his inquiring audience. The general talked about peace, however, not about war. He told Alexander "there was nothing he so much desired as peace and independence. All that he had and all he hoped for—all that ambition could suggest or glory give—he would freely give them all to stop the flow of blood." During the same month, Lee offered advice to his wife that is even further removed from his aggressive military instincts: "You must endeavour to enjoy the pleasure of doing good. That is all that makes life valuable."

Alexander described the general as "six feet in height, weighs about one hundred and ninety pounds; is erect, well-formed, and of imposing appearance; has clear bright, benignant black eyes, dark gray hair, and a heavy gray beard." Surprisingly, given the famed splendor of the uniform he wore at Appomattox, Lee's attire was "exceedingly plain," with little insignia and "without the usual braiding on the sleeves." "He cares but little for appearances," the writer added. "Like Washington, he is a wise man and a good man." The diarist Mary Chestnut, the wife of South Carolina congressman and presidential aide James Chestnut, never failed to notice Lee when she visited Richmond: "the man and horse and everything about him was so fine looking. Perfection—no fault to be found if you hunted for one." Although she claimed to like his brother Smith better, when Lee acknowledged her in church, "I was ashamed of being so pleased," she wrote, "I blushed like a school girl." British field marshal Garnet Wolseley, who met Lee in 1862, said, "I have met many of the great men of my time, but Lee alone impressed me with the feeling that I was in the presence of a man who was cast in a grander mould, and made of different and finer metal than all other men." In early 1863, the Confederacy longed for a hero. Lee was well suited for this role.[72]

The Confederate commander's goal was to hold off Union advances while looking for opportunities to seize the initiative and win victories that would sway public opinion in the North toward the party that favored peace. Ever optimistic, Lee wrote to his wife in April, "I do not think our enemies are so confident of success as they used to be. If we can baffle them in their various designs this year … I think our success will be certain …. If successful this year, next fall there will be a great change in pubic opinion at the North. The republicans will be destroyed." He would find an opportunity for

fig. 147.
Chancellor House, Chancellorsville, 1865 (photograph courtesy of the Massachusetts Commandery Military Order of the Loyal Legion and the United States Army Military History Institute)

success when Joseph Hooker replaced Burnside as his next antagonist and attempted too bold a campaign. Lee remembered Hooker not fondly as a colleague in Mexico who had testified in support of Gideon Pillow against Winfield Scott in the attempt to court-martial the general. Hooker's army of some 130,000 troops was twice the size of Lee's. His plan was to divide his army into wings on either side of Fredericksburg, turn Lee's flanks, get behind him, force him to retire, and then unite in pursuit. Hooker would lead the wing that attacked west of Fredericksburg at the small community of Chancellorsville, the site of an inn and little more (fig. 147).[73]

Hooker erred in thinking that Lee would not anticipate the Union offensive. His second mistake was to send his cavalry south of the enemy, thereby losing his means to determine Lee's location. The terrain at Chancellorsville is heavily wooded and appropriately named "the Wilderness"; it would also be the setting of a ferocious battle between Lee and Grant a year later. Hooker's numerical advantage was neutralized by the landscape; he would not be able to deploy all of his forces. Hooker ordered one attack, then abandoned the initiative and settled into a defensive posture. In the end, Lee did to Hooker what Hooker had tried to do to him. Lee divided his army, moved around one flank, and attacked the rear. As Lee told the story to William Allan after the war, he initially wanted simply to move directly on Hooker's right flank, but neither he nor Stonewall Jackson was able to find a place "fit to attack." Lee then decided, "we must get round on his right." Jeb Stuart found a local man within his cavalry to serve as guide. Lee held Hooker's 73,000-man front with some 14,000 men while Jackson took an army of 26,000 soldiers the ten or twelve miles around Hooker's right flank and then attacked his right rear. With the Wilderness shielding Jackson's movement of troops and no cavalry to find them, Hooker had no idea either that he missed an opportunity to destroy a divided foe or that his own army was in grave danger. While standing on the porch of the Chancellor House he was struck and dazed by a falling timber that had been hit by artillery fire. He lost the ability to command but never relinquished it. Jackson's attack on May 3 completely surprised his enemies and decimated their ranks. The battle was over quickly. Lee rode into Chancellorsville in triumph. His military secretary Charles Marshall, the grandson of John Marshall, remembered the scene: "He sat in the full realization of all that soldiers dream of—triumph; and as I looked upon him in the complete fruition of the success ... I thought that it must have been from such a scene that men in ancient days rose to the dignity of gods." However, while surveying the terrain for a possible night attack, Stonewall Jackson was mistakenly shot by one of his own sentries. Lee famously said, "He has lost his left arm; but I have lost my right arm." When Jackson died, Lee wrote to his son Custis, "It is a terrible loss. I do not know how to replace him." The Army of Northern Virginia suffered fewer casualties than did Hooker (some 13,000 to 16,000), but the loss was proportionally greater and the death of Jackson was devastating. Once again Lee was unable to pursue his beaten foe.[74]

Chancellorsville was Lee's greatest victory. It confirmed his position as the preeminent Confederate general and the only one who offered real hope for southern success. He had divided his army, attacked aggressively, and defeated a foe who had threatened Richmond with a force more than twice the size of his own. The Confederate people were uplifted both by Lee's accomplishment and by the daring that he used to carry it off. The plan and exe-

fig. 148.
Unidentified photographer, *General Rooney Lee*, c. 1862 (photograph courtesy of Virginia Historical Society)

cution of the battle have been described as more nearly flawless than any ever orchestrated by an American general. Lincoln responded, "My God! My God! What will the country say?" For an entire year Richmond would be free from a Union offensive.[75]

On June 8, Lee reviewed his cavalry, which included in its ranks his sons Rooney (fig. 148) and Rob. He wrote to his wife from Culpeper, "It was a splendid sight. The men & horses looked well. They had recuperated since last fall. Stuart was in all his glory …. Fitzhugh [Rooney] was on his black charger…. & Rob by his side." The next day at Brandy Station, in the largest cavalry battle of the war, Stuart came close to complete defeat. Rooney Lee was severely wounded. He was sent to recuperate outside of Richmond at his in-laws' plantation, Hickory Hill. From there a Union raiding party dragged him to imprisonment at Fort Monroe. Brandy Station was not to be Stuart's worst moment that summer.[76]

In 1871, the author John Esten Cooke complained that too much had already been written about the battle of Gettysburg (fig. 149): "The subject is, indeed, almost embarrassed by the amount of information collected and published; and the chief difficulty for a writer, at this late date, is to select from the mass such salient events as indicate clearly the character of the conflict." Cooke felt inundated with information, much of it conflicting. Some of the soldiers involved in what was perceived by many to be the greatest Confederate defeat had already begun to assign the blame. Longstreet, Stuart, Ewell, Hill, and Early were the suspects; southerners refused to lay any fault at the feet of their late commander. In the years since then, the literature about Gettysburg has accumulated to a size that Cooke could never have imagined. Fortunately, the publication of both Lee's own written accounts and his postwar conversations about the battle, along with some lucid modern interpretations, carry today's reader beyond the quicksand of the "Lost Cause" narratives. What emerges is that much of the responsibility must be borne by Lee. He was present during all three days of the battle, and he maintained overall control of his army's actions throughout those days, even though he did not always exercise it by following up on directives to his corps commanders. Lee's most egregious errors would occur, however, when he ordered repeated attacks against a reinforced and entrenched enemy.[77]

On the move to Pennsylvania, the Army of Northern Virginia was spirited, perhaps even overconfident, following the success at Chancellorsville. One of the general's officers, Isaac Trimble, recorded in his journal Lee's thinking in late June 1863:

> We have again out-maneuvered the enemy, who even now don't know where we are or what are our designs. Our whole army will be in Pennsylvania the day after tomorrow leaving the enemy far behind, and obliged to follow us by forced marches. I hope with these advantages to accomplish some signal result, and to end the war if Providence favours us …. I have not yet heard that the enemy have crossed the Potomac, and am waiting to hear from General Stuart …. They will come up … broken down with hunger and hard marching …. I shall throw an overwhelming force on their advance, crush it, follow up the success, drive one corps back and another, and by successive repulses and surprises before they can concentrate, create a panic and virtually destroy the army.[78]

In a long letter written to Jefferson Davis on June 10, Lee explained why he was moving north. Many of the same reasons that had carried him to Maryland a year earlier remained, including the

fig. 149.
Paul Philippoteaux, *Study for the Lee Cyclorama at Gettysburg*, c. 1884, oil on canvas, 45 × 111 in. (114.3 × 281.9 cm.), Chicago Historical Society

need for food and forage, and his determination to remove both antagonistic armies from Virginia and in the process to threaten Washington rather than defend Richmond. He still believed that only by influencing public opinion in the North by means of a decisive victory could he bring an end to the fighting. What was different, however, was that Lee no longer saw an independent Confederate nation as a realistic goal. Peace was all that was essential: "that, after all is what we are interested in bringing about." Given that Davis was adamant about winning independence—without it he would be out of a job—Lee was advancing on thin ice, close to what many would have considered dishonorable conduct. The enemy has "superiority … in numbers [and] resources," he reminded Davis, and "our resources in men are constantly diminishing …." We should not "make nice distinctions between those who declare for peace unconditionally and those who advocate it as a means of restoring the Union …. Should the belief that peace will bring back the Union become general, the war would no longer be supported …." Lee was willing to use slight of hand with the northern electorate. Let them vote for peace and stop the fighting, and then we will talk with them: "When peace is proposed to us, it will be time enough to discuss its terms." Before Lee advanced into the North, however, he had to reassign the command that Jackson had held. The solution was to divide Jackson's corps between A. P. Hill and Richard Ewell. At Gettysburg both would make decisions that would effect the outcome of that battle.[79]

Lee sent Davis a preliminary report on Gettysburg the day after the battle's end, followed by a longer account written on January 20, 1864. He reported how his two leading divisions, under the newly promoted corps commanders Hill and Ewell, unexpectedly came upon the enemy on July 1, attacked, drove the Union forces through and beyond the town, and took more than five thousand prisoners. The enemy regrouped on "a range of hills south of Gettysburg," which the Union army "immediately began to fortify" with "infantry and artillery." Being "without information" as to whether "the remainder of that army under General Meade was approaching Gettysburg" and would attack with "overwhelming numbers of fresh troops," Lee decided not to push his lieutenants. "General Ewell was therefore instructed to carry the hill occupied by the enemy if he found it practicable." Ewell declined. Lee then chose to await the arrival of Longstreet. He told Davis that he had not intended "to deliver a general battle so far from our base unless attacked, but coming unexpectedly upon the whole Federal Army, to withdraw through the mountains with our extensive trains would have been difficult and dangerous." He said he was "unable to await an attack, as the country was unfavorable for collecting supplies in the presence of the enemy." He concluded that a major battle had become "unavoidable." It began the second day.

On July 2, "we attempted to dislodge the enemy, and though we gained some ground, we were unable to get possession of his position." The reason was that "the enemy occupied a strong position, with his right upon two commanding elevations adjacent to each other" (Cemetery Hill and Cemetery Ridge) and "this ridge was difficult of ascent." Therefore Lee and his generals "determined to make the principal attack upon the enemy's left," with Longstreet in command. Ewell would move against the enemy's right flank. "About four p.m. Longstreet's batteries opened," but it was "now nearly dark" so Longstreet "determined to await the arrival of General Pickett." (In fact, several additional hours of July sunlight would have easily allowed an attack.) The generals decided that "with proper concert of action" they "should ultimately succeed" the next day.

On July 3, "a more extensive attack was made." Longstreet, reinforced by Pickett's three brigades, was ordered to attack the center of the Union line, while Ewell was "directed to assail the enemy's right at the same time." Longstreet delayed, in order "to defend his flank and rear" from a "force occupying the high rocky hills" on his extreme right. At "about 1 p.m. … a heavy cannonade was opened," but the Confederates' ammunition was nearly exhausted by the time that Pickett was ordered forward. "Owing to this fact, which was unknown to me, … the enemy was enabled to throw a strong force of infantry against our left …. A large number of brave officers and men fell." "The works on the enemy's extreme right & left were taken, but his numbers were so great and his position so commanding, that our troops were compelled to relinquish their advantage and retire." At the end of the longer report, Lee finally placed some of the blame on a subordinate: "The movements of the army preceding the battle of Gettysburg had been much embarrassed by the absence of the cavalry …. [I]t was expected that General Stuart … would soon arrive."[80]

After the war, when Confederate morale was no longer an issue, Lee spoke less guardedly about what actually happened at Gettysburg. He then put the blame for his army's defeat squarely on Jeb Stuart for failing to provide him with intelligence as to the location of the Union army, and on his corps commanders for performing poorly. On April 15, 1868, Lee told William Allan that he "could not believe" that the Federal army was upon him, "as Stuart had been specially ordered to cover his [Lee's] movement & keep him informed of the position of the enemy, & he [Stuart] had sent no word." Finding himself engaged with the entire Federal army, he felt that he "had to fight." That being determined, "victory w[oul]d have been won if he could have gotten one decided simultaneous attack on the whole line. This he tried his utmost to effect for three days, and failed." Lee was particularly displeased with Ewell for his "imperfect, halting way," and "Longstreet & Hill &c. could not be gotten to act in concert."

The subject of Gettysburg had come up with Allan because on the same day Lee was writing a response to the historian W. M. McDonald. The general told McDonald exactly what he said to Allan. The battle "was commenced in the absence of correct intelligence" and that victory "would have been gained could one determined and united blow have been delivered by our whole line." Lee added to Allan that despite the losses, he "inflicted more damage than he received, and broke up the Federal summer campaign." Going north to Pennsylvania, as he said a year earlier about Maryland, was "far better than remaining at Fredericksburg" because there he was vulnerable to yet another attack: "The position was to be easily flanked, and the plan Grant afterwards pursued might have been tried at any time." In 1870, in a later conversation, Lee told Allan that Jefferson Davis had failed him as well. Lee "had urged the Govt. before going to Penn. in 1863, to bring [P. G. T.] Beauregard to Manassas with all the troops that he could get, & threaten Washington in that quarter. Mr. Davis promised to do so, but it was never done …." Beauregard's presence close to Washington would have drained forces from Meade. Lee also told Allan that "if Jackson had been there he would have succeeded." He sincerely believed that Jackson would have taken the high ground the first day; Lee made the same statement about Jackson to his cousin Cassius.[81]

Military historians have long analyzed the three days at Gettysburg in an attempt to understand how Lee could have suffered so resounding a defeat. Criticism has been spread widely. As to day one, Stuart was absent because he needlessly circled the Union army and captured a wagon train when his job was instead to inform Lee of the enemy's movements. Stuart was at fault. But how much were Lee's other lieutenants to blame for the shortcomings of July 1? It has been argued that A. P. Hill had no authority to bring on a major battle when he followed up a chance encounter with the enemy, and that Richard Ewell refused to seize Cemetery Hill and Culp's Hill during the first day's fighting when they probably could have been taken. Lee, however, was present on day one soon after the enemy was discovered. He saw the opportunity to gain tactical advantage by seizing the high ground south of Get-

fig. 150.
Mathew Brady, *Confederate Prisoners at Gettysburg*, July 15, 1863 (photograph courtesy of Library of Congress)

tysburg. Thus Lee, not Hill, gave the order to send brigades forward and thereby bring on the battle. Lee allowed Ewell the discretion to advance alone or to not advance to the high ground. We do not know why Lee did not bring together some of Hill's troops with Ewell's and order a joint assault on the Union right flank on July 1, before that position became entrenched and reinforced overnight. Had the hills been taken on day one, the battle may have had a far different outcome.[82]

On July 2, Longstreet refused to attack the Federal left flank at dawn. Lee had ordered a coordinated assault on both flanks of Meade's army, with Ewell on Lee's left and Longstreet on the right. Hill, whose troops were tired, would only "threaten" to move against the center. Longstreet was to launch the attack, the sound of which would be Ewell's signal to begin. Time was of the essence because the enemy would reinforce and entrench, but Longstreet delayed. Finally, at 11 a.m., Lee directly ordered him to move. Five hours later, Longstreet responded. The fighting was fierce, but uncoordinated in its timing, both between Longstreet and Ewell and even within the Confederate forces fighting on each flank. The reason that Longstreet delayed was that he tried to persuade Lee to move around the Union army's far left flank and position himself between Meade and Washington. Meade later said that this was the action he most feared, because Henry Halleck had days earlier telegraphed him to "give him battle" if that happened. Lee's chief of artillery in the First Corps, Edward Porter Alexander, believed that Longstreet's delay on July 2 was the principal cause of the Confed-

erate defeat. However, Alexander further argued that Lee should have maneuvered to force Meade to attack him under more favorable conditions. He said that there was "no real difficulty" that kept Lee from abandoning the offensive on the second day. Alexander reasoned that the political climate in the North gave Lee an advantage. The governor of Pennsylvania was frantic that the Confederacy's most feared army was free in his state. "With all the prestige of victory, popular sentiment would have forced Meade to take the aggressive," Alexander wrote. He wanted Lee to retreat to South Mountain. But, as historian Gary Gallagher has argued, Lee had a predilection for aggressive action. He had momentum and morale on his side, and he wanted to fight on July 2.[83]

Lee was determined to continue the assaults by Longstreet and Ewell on July 3. He shifted Longstreet's focus from Meade's left flank to the center of the Union forces on Cemetery Ridge, where he ordered a frontal assault. By noon, however, when Longstreet had yet to stir, Ewell had already moved against Cemetery Hill and Culp's Hill on the Union right flank. Once again, the attacks were uncoordinated. Lee's style of generalship, which was often to suggest rather than to order, failed miserably at Gettysburg because his corps commanders acted with indecision. Their delays left George Pickett to charge virtually alone against impossible odds. When this last assault failed, Lee himself rode out to the beaten troops and took responsibility for the defeat. "All this has been my fault—it is I that have lost this fight, and you must help me out of it the best way you can," he said to General Cadmus M. Wilcox. The enormity of the loss shook Lee to the core. While he reported to Davis the accomplishments of the campaign—he had destroyed the plans of their adversaries, and so the Army of the Potomac would not seriously threaten Virginia again for nearly ten months—he wrote to his daughter-in-law Charlotte on July 26 that "the loss of our gallant officers and men … causes me to weep tears of blood and to wish that I never could hear the sound of a gun again." He heaped guilt on himself and his army, turning their former self-confidence into shame and even sinfulness: "Soldiers! We have sinned against Almighty God. We have forgotten His signal mercies, and have cultivated a revengeful, haughty, and boastful spirit."

Many in the South refused to view Gettysburg as a major defeat. The battle was not to be compared with Vicksburg, they said, which was admittedly a catastrophic loss. Lee had been set back in Pennsylvania but he had not been conquered. He had won a tactical victory on the first day at Gettysburg, and his men had served gallantly when they assaulted the Union positions. The artist Paul Philippoteaux later remembered that gallantry. The reality was that Lee lost approximately 28,000 men, one third of his army (fig. 150).[84]

Meade pursued Lee cautiously after Gettysburg. He followed his adversary into Virginia to the Rappahannock River where he considered taking the initiative. Lee actually hoped that he would attack, but instead Meade retired for the winter. Meanwhile, in the western theater, Ulysses S. Grant was changing the course of the war. After he took Vicksburg and entered Tennessee, Jefferson Davis wanted Lee to take command of the Confederate forces there. Longstreet ultimately went to Tennessee; Lee preferred to confront Meade in Virginia. Once Grant had defeated Braxton Bragg at Chattanooga, Lee took more notice of his future adversary. He advised Davis that a large force must be assigned to confront Grant lest he penetrate into Georgia. Joe Johnston was sent when Lee declined the assignment.

In early December 1863, Robert E. Lee was able to visit his family in Richmond. He had not seen his wife for seven months. Mary Custis Lee's health had deteriorated to the point that even with crutches she could barely move. Daughters Agnes and Mary were there, as was Custis, still on Davis's staff but anxious to gain field experience. His father refused to engage in nepotism, however, when Custis sought assignment as chief engineer with the Army of Northern Virginia. While Rooney Lee remained imprisoned (by then at Fort Lafayette, New York) his frail wife died. Mary Chestnut wrote in her diary in March 1864, "General Lee had tears in his eyes when he spoke of his daughter-in-law just dead—that lovely little Charlotte Wickham, Mrs. Rooney Lee." In December 1863 Lee could have stayed for Christmas with his family, for the first time since 1859, but he returned to the field. It was a gloomy winter. His soldiers were without adequate food and supplies. Yet they remained upbeat, out of reverence for their leader, even when Lincoln called for new Federal troops in March.

Lee positioned his army on the Rapidan River, west of the fall line, near the Wilderness. There the dense landscape might minimize his numerical weakness when the next Union campaign began at the end of the spring rains. Unlike George McClellan or Joseph Hooker, however, his new adversary would not be so easily entrapped. Ulysses S. Grant was Lee's match, and he knew how to utilize the Union advantages in men and materials.[85]

Grant versus Lee: The Wilderness to Petersburg

I never ranked Lee as high as some others of the army, that is to say, I never had as much anxiety when he was in my front as when Joe Johnston was in front.

Ulysses S. Grant, *Interview,* Hamburg, 1878

There is nothing left me but to go to see General Grant, and I would rather die a thousand deaths.

Robert E. Lee at Appomattox, 1865[86]

Ulysses S. Grant (fig. 151) and Robert E. Lee (fig. 152) were the greatest antagonists in American military history. Each was the best soldier in his army, and neither could accept defeat. Each was a brilliant, aggressive general who always looked to seize the initiative from his opponent. Each anticipated what the opponent would do by imagining how he would react in the same situation. Consequently, each commander would become enormously frustrated in May and June 1864 when they finally locked horns. Both Lee and Grant recognized that the clash between the Army of Northern Virginia and the Army of the Potomac would be a fight to the death of either the Confederacy or the old Union. In their Herculean struggle, Grant and Lee grew to both detest and respect one another. Grant particularly hated the level of acclaim that Lee was awarded and that he, the victor, was denied. Lee simply hated to lose. Each had difficulty speaking kindly of the other. Yet so much did they have in common, and so gracious was Grant at Appomattox, that for Lee the respect he came to feel for his opponent in the end outweighed the agony of his failure. Had the mythologizing of Lee diminished after the war, Grant, whose record stood for itself, might have been as gracious in remembering his greatest antagonist as he was in speaking of other former Confederate commanders. But that was not to be.

fig. 151.
Alexander Gardner, *Ulysses S. Grant*, c. 1864 (photograph courtesy of Library of Congress)

fig. 152.
Minnis and Cowell, Richmond, *Robert E. Lee*, June 1863 (photograph courtesy of Virginia Historical Society)

In his *Memoirs*, where for so many chapters Grant is refreshingly honest, modest, and self-critical, he is uncharacteristically defensive in his account of the 1864 campaign against Lee, especially from its start at the battle of the Wilderness to his bridging the James River. In fact, as he recounts the crossing he includes a paragraph about Lee that reveals his irritation at the unfair acclaim that both the press and the populace, North and South, routinely gave to Lee instead of to him. This passage also reveals his annoyance that Lee seemed to be his match on the battlefield. In the spring of 1864 Lee and Grant both seemed unbeatable. Grant would finally outmaneuver his opponent, cross the James River, and then use his advantages in numbers and materials to wear Lee into defeat. In 1885 Grant felt compelled to dress down his opponent:

> General Lee … was a very highly estimated man in the Confederate army and States, and filled also a very high place in the estimation of the people and press of the Northern States. His praise was sounded throughout the entire North after every action he was engaged in: the number of his forces was always lowered and that of the National forces exaggerated. He was a large, austere man, and I judge difficult of approach to his subordinates. To be extolled by the entire press of the South after every engagement, and by a portion of the press North with equal vehemence, was calculated to give him the entire confidence of his troops and to make him feared by his antagonists. It was not an uncommon thing for my staff-officers to hear from Eastern officers, "Well, Grant has never met Bobby Lee yet." There were good and true officers who believe now that the Army of Northern Virginia was superior to the Army of the Potomac man to man. I do not believe so.[87]

Grant's strategy for defeating the Confederacy was characteristically sound. The handling of Lee proved to be the difficult part. When Grant was made lieutenant general, he first intended to remain in the West, until he visited Washington and realized that the master plan that he had been developing for Union victory would come under too much "pressure … to pursue other [plans]" if he was so far away. Thus he would maintain his headquarters in Virginia in the field, literally beside George Meade, who, would retain command of the army that Meade knew best, while Henry

Halleck, his chief of staff, could stand in for Grant in Washington and handle the political and organizational issues.

What Grant planned was a grand coordinated spring campaign for all the Union armies. He wrote, "Before this time these various armies had acted separately and independently of each other, giving the enemy an opportunity often of depleting one command, not pressed, to reinforce another more actively engaged. I determined to stop this." Lee in Virginia and Joseph Johnston in Georgia would thereby not be able to reinforce each another. Grant would also pull together other Union troops that were being used ineffectively in order "to concentrate all the force possible against the Confederate armies in the field." He explained to the president that the soldiers holding captured territory could be better employed: "These troops could perform this service just as well by advancing as by remaining still; and by advancing they would compel the enemy to keep detachments to hold them back." Those detachments then could not threaten the principal Union commanders. Lincoln understood, "Oh, yes! I see that. As we say out West, if a man can't skin he must hold a leg while somebody else does."[88]

In a letter of April 9 to George Meade, Grant explained his master plan of "a simultaneous movement all along the line":

> So far as practicable all the Armies are to move together and towards one common center. [Nathaniel] Banks has been instructed … to move on Mobile …. Sherman will move [from Chattanooga] at the same time you do, or two or three days in advance, Jo Johnston's Army being his objective point and the heart of Georgia his ultimate aim. If successful he will secure the line from Chattanooga to Mobile, with the Aid of Banks. [Franz] Sigel … will move south [in the Valley of Virginia] …. [Benjamin] Butler will seize City Point and move against Richmond from the south side of the [James] river. His movement will be simultaneous with yours. Lee's Army will be your objective point. Wherever Lee goes there you will go also.

Johnston's army, which was defending Atlanta and the interior of Georgia, was "the first objective, and that important railroad center, Atlanta, the second." Banks was to move upon Mobile by land while the navy would close the harbor in order to "cut the Confederacy in two again, as our gaining possession of the Mississippi River had done before." But the main objective was "Lee, with the capital of the Confederacy." This was "only because the capture of Johnston and his army would not produce so immediate and decisive a result in closing the rebellion as would the possession of Richmond, Lee and his army." As Sherman put it, "He was to go for Lee and I was to go for Joe Johnston." Sherman's army of 120,000 soldiers was twice the size of Johnston's; Grant and Meade enjoyed similar odds against Lee. Banks was bogged down on the Red River in Texas, unable to move against Mobile, Sigel was defeated in the Valley, and Butler failed to attack Petersburg. However, the great armies of Grant and Sherman would be successful, and ultimately decisive.[89]

Grant's plan against Lee in Virginia was to move straight at his opponent, bring him out of his entrenchments by maneuvering towards the east, and then defeat him north of Richmond. If he was not able to do so, he would come at the Confederate capital from the south, its source of supplies. The crucial goal, however, was not to take Richmond, but to destroy Lee's army. With no army to fight him in Virginia, the war would be over. Initially, Grant "was not entirely decided" whether to "move the Army of the Potomac by the right flank of the enemy, or by his left." He later thought that if he moved to the west towards Lynchburg and avoided the Wilderness, "the war would have been over a year sooner." He "preferred" that plan, but worried that if he failed, "it would have been very serious for the country, and I did not dare the risk." He said that he hesitated because the Army of the Potomac was new to him: "[I] did not know what I could do with the generals or men," adding, "If it had been six months later … and I could have had Sherman and Sheridan to assist in the movement, I would not have hesitated for a moment." Another problem was that the land "was so exhausted of all food or forage that we would be obliged to carry everything with us." Further, by forfeiting the Tidewater rivers that his navy controlled, he would lose not only supplies but also the means to evacuate wounded soldiers, and he would sever contact with Butler's army on the James. If Grant had chosen a third alternative, to move up the rivers as McClellan had done, "Lee could have … moved on to Washington." In fact, Grant never wanted to attack Richmond because it was too heavily fortified.[90]

The key to Grant's destruction of the Army of Northern Virginia was his numerical superiority. Lee wrote to his secretary of war in August, "Without some increase of our strength, I cannot see how we are to escape the natural military consequences of the enemy's

fig. 153.
Abraham Lincoln to Ulysses S. Grant, *Letter*, April 30, 1864, Huntington Library, San Marino, California

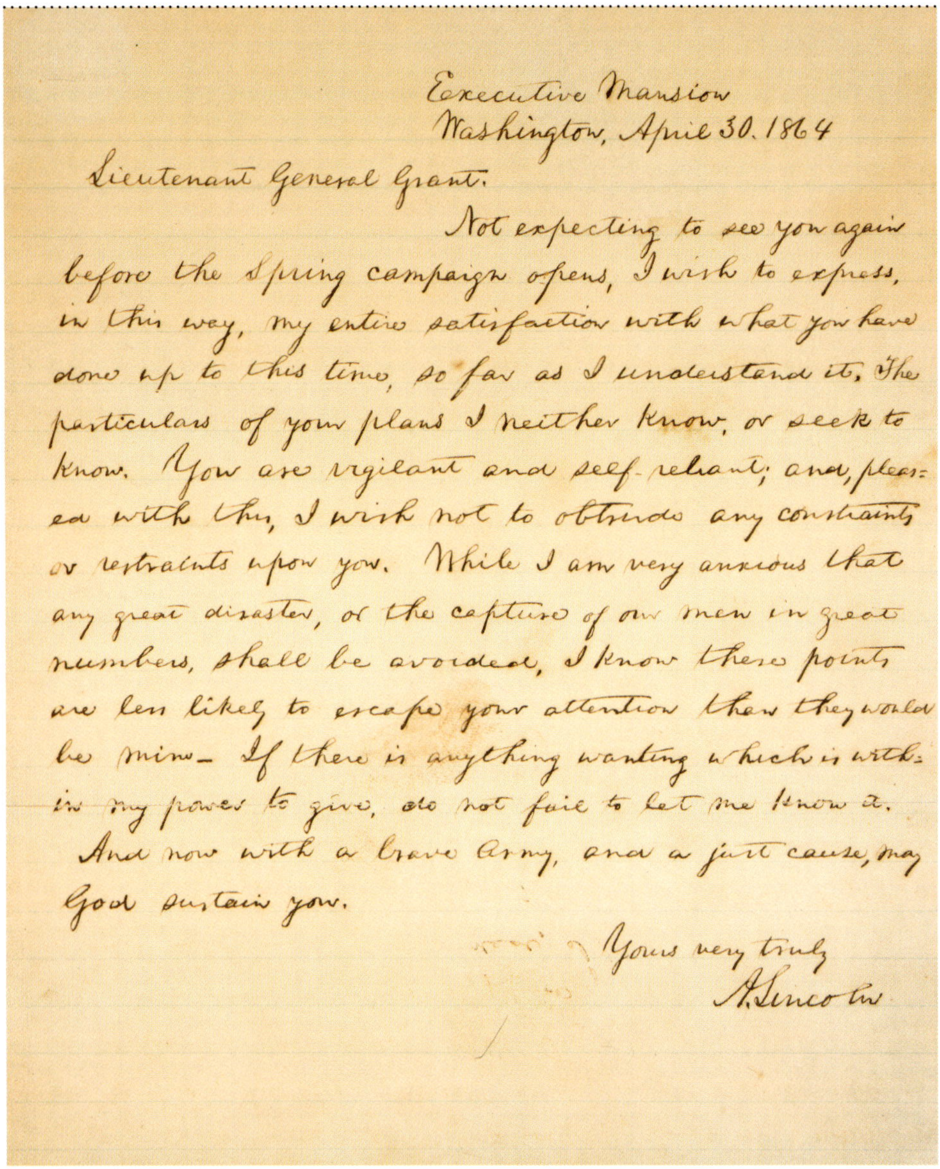

> Executive Mansion
> Washington, April 30. 1864
>
> Lieutenant General Grant.
>
> Not expecting to see you again before the Spring campaign opens, I wish to express, in this way, my entire satisfaction with what you have done up to this time, so far as I understand it. The particulars of your plans I neither know, or seek to know. You are vigilant and self-reliant; and, pleased with this, I wish not to obtrude any constraints or restraints upon you. While I am very anxious that any great disaster, or the capture of our men in great numbers, shall be avoided, I know these points are less likely to escape your attention than they would be mine— If there is anything wanting which is within my power to give, do not fail to let me know it.
>
> And now with a brave Army, and a just cause, may God sustain you.
>
> Yours very truly
> A. Lincoln

numerical superiority." Grant always denied the importance of this advantage. "The cry was in the air that the North only won by brute force; that the generalship and valor were with the South," he told the reporter John Russell Young in 1878. Many military historians today disagree with Grant's assessment: Gary Gallagher believes that considerable evidence supports the "Lost Cause" idea that superior northern numbers and resources played a fundamental role in the Confederate defeat. Grant commanded some 120,000 soldiers and Lee only 65,000 when they met on May 5, 1864. Of course, Lee had been grossly outmanned before. What was different was that Grant knew how to utilize northern resources so as to obliterate his enemy. The price would be a heavy toll in casualties on both sides, because, in Grant's words, victory "was not to be accomplished … without as desperate fighting as the world has ever witnessed." He defended the losses: they "were destined to be severe" because the armies had fought for three years and remained in "a stand-off." In his comment that there would be "heavier losses, to both armies, in a given time, than any previously suffered; but the carnage was to be limited to a single year," Grant made clear his confidence that he could bring the war to a relatively quick conclusion. "My critics say that I threw away 100,000 men in that campaign," Grant would repeatedly remind listeners, "my total losses were about thirty-nine thousand, all told … and those losses do not mean killed." (Historians today number Grant's losses at 65,000 prior to reaching Petersburg.) And "do not forget what it cost Lee," he added. "The Wilderness campaign was necessary to the destruction of the Southern Confederacy." By contrast, Lee was little blamed for his losses, partly because he was defending against an invasion. Frederick Douglass later saw the irony: "We can scarcely take up a newspaper … that is not filled with nauseating flatteries of the late Robert E. Lee …. It would seem from this, that the soldier who kills the most men in battle, even in a bad cause, is the greatest Christian, and entitled to the highest place in heaven."[91]

Before Grant moved against Lee, Abraham Lincoln sent an encouraging letter to his general (fig. 153):

> Not expecting to see you again before the Spring campaign opens, I wish to express, in this way, my entire satisfaction with what you have done up to this time, so far as I understand it. The particulars of your plans I neither know, or seek to know. You are vigilant and self-reliant; and, pleased with this, I wish not to obtrude any constraints or restraints

fig. 154.
Timothy O'Sullivan, *Troops Crossing the Rapidan River at Germanna Ford*, 1864 (photograph courtesy of Library of Congress)

upon you. While I am very anxious that any great disaster, or the capture of our men in great numbers, shall be avoided, I know these points are less likely to escape your attention than they would be mine—If there is anything wanting which is within my power to give, do not fail to let me know it. And now with a brave Army, and a just cause, may God sustain you.

Grant responded with the same sort of respect that made their working relationship effective:

Your very kind letter of yesterday is just received. The confidence you express for the future, and satisfaction with the past, in my Military administration is acknowledged with pride. It will be my earnest endeavor that you, and the country, shall not be disappointed …. I have been astonished at the readiness with which every thing asked for has been yielded without even an explanation being asked. Should my success be less than I desire, and expect, the least I can say is, the fault is not with you.

A sense of optimism pervaded the Confederate camp as well. The soldiers of the Army of Northern Virginia were as confident of victory as they had been when they moved into Pennsylvania the previous year. They trusted and revered Lee. One of the men from Georgia wrote home, "Gen Grant will go down like the rest of [the] yankey Gens, that have bin brought against this army." Many officers, however, feared Grant's numerical advantage. Captain Charles Minor Blackford of Longstreet's staff could see the inevitable: "Grant can afford to have four men killed or wounded to kill or disable one of ours. That process will destroy us at last, by using up our material." While confident of victory, Grant worried about his enemy "strongly intrenched" in a "heavily timbered" setting and perhaps grudgingly admitted that they were "commanded by the acknowledged ablest general in the Confederate army."[92]

Grant wrote, "The art of war is simple enough. Find out where your enemy is. Get at him as soon as you can. Strike him as hard as you can and as often as you can and keep moving on." Grant proceeded directly to where Lee was, the Wilderness, and set about "striking him," "hard and often," and then "moving on" to repeat the process. Of course, Lee planned the same action, and had anticipated exactly where Grant would cross the Rapidan River (fig. 154). Grant wanted to move fast through and beyond the Wilderness; Lee planned to attack him there. Lee also anticipated Grant's flanking movements that would gradually move both of them south towards Richmond. After the war, with one of the instructors at Washington College, William Preston Johnston, the son of the late Confederate commander Albert Sidney Johnston, Lee "spoke of Grant's gradual whirl and change of base from Fredericksburg to Port Royal, thence to York River and thence to James River, as a thing which, though foreseen, it was impossible to prevent."[93]

Lee had deployed Longstreet forty-two miles to the west, at Gordonsville, to protect his left flank should Grant try to turn it. Nonetheless, once the Union army moved into the Wilderness, with its cavalry off to the east in search of Stuart, Lee seized the opportunity to attack with the hope that Longstreet could return to his side in time to participate. On May 5 he sought to obliterate Grant's army and thereby to influence negatively Lincoln's bid to win a second nomination for the presidency. He had hoped to send Longstreet around the left Federal flank, much like Jackson had done a year earlier, but his general had not yet arrived. Whereas

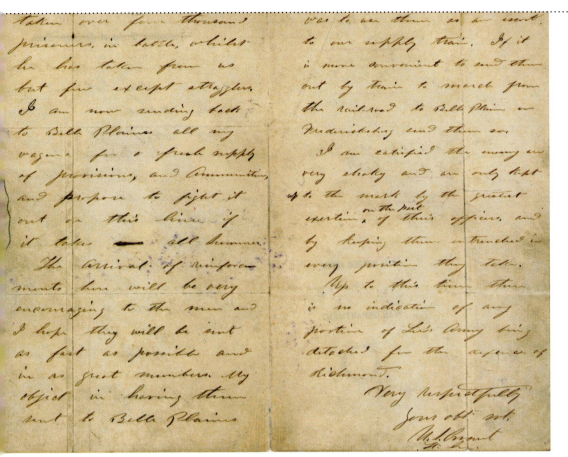

fig. 155.
Ulysses S. Grant, near Spotsylvania Court House, to Henry Halleck, *Letter*, May 11, 1864, National Archives and Records Administration

Meade might have retreated, Grant calmly took charge of his army and responded with attacks that Lee could rebuff only by a brilliant shuffling of troops. Darkness alone saved the Army of Northern Virginia from the relentless waves of attack that were without precedent in the East.[94]

On the next day Grant was determined to take the initiative: "it was my plan then, as it was on all other occasions." He ordered Winfield Scott Hancock, with "fully one-half of the Army of the Potomac," to attack at five in the morning. "We knew Longstreet with 12,000 men was on his way," Grant wrote, and he was determined to strike in advance. Lee had also planned an offensive at daybreak. In what has been called the most anxious moment of the war for the South, Hancock's massive assault overwhelmed the Confederate lines, causing many soldiers to flee "like a flock of geese" as Lee put it when he tried to rally one group. Longstreet arrived at the last possible moment with "Texas boys" at the front who would not let Lee charge with them. The famous cry of "Lee to the rear" was sounded here, and several times again at the Wilderness and at Spotsylvania. In the afternoon Longstreet tried his own assault, which was halted when he was mistakenly fired upon by his own men, just as Jackson had been shot a year earlier at almost the same spot. A bullet went entirely through his throat. At the end of the day, each commander had lost 18 percent of his army. Grant wrote that "More desperate fighting has not been witnessed on this continent than that of the 5th and 6th of May." He recorded that "The woods were set on fire by the bursting shell, and the conflagration raged. The wounded … were either suffocated or burned to death." He believed that "if the country had been such that Hancock and his command could have seen the confusion and panic in the lines of the enemy, it would have been taken advantage of so effectually that Lee would not have made another stand outside of his Richmond defences." Of course, the impenetrability of the Wilderness was the very reason that Lee chose to fight there. The battle was a draw. Had Longstreet not been wounded, Lee might have won. Grant, however, had achieved an important strategic victory; he had forced Lee to take the defensive, to use earthworks, and to look for Grant to make a mistake as his best hope. Grant sent word to Lincoln that "there will be no turning back." For the first time, a Union army was heading south after an encounter with Lee in Virginia.[95]

On May 7 Lee hoped that Grant would attack. When he did not, Lee deduced that his antagonist was retiring to Spotsylvania Court House, twelve miles to the south and directly on a line between Lee and Richmond. Walter Taylor wrote to Jeb Stuart on the same day, "the general thinks [the enemy's] intention [is] to move towards Spotsylvania Court House." Grant said that his purpose was "to get between his army and Richmond" and thereby force Lee to leave his entrenchments. He would then attack his opponent in "the open field." Grant feared that Lee might move quickly to "crush" Ben-

fig. 156.
Possibly by Andrew J. Russell, *Rebel Prisoners at Belle Plain, Spotsylvania Co.*, 1864 (photographs courtesy of Virginia Historical Society)

jamin Butler's army which had taken City Point, south of Richmond, "before I could get there." Both generals were soon heading toward Spotsylvania. Lee's troops arrived first and entrenched. Grant later wrote that Lee gained possession by accident. Lee had ordered Richard Anderson, in command of Longstreet's corps, to move to Spotsylvania the next morning, but Anderson left at night because the woods were still on fire and he had no place to bivouac. "If Lee's orders had been obeyed as given," Grant wrote, "we would have been in Spotsylvania, and between him and his capital. My belief is that there would have been a race between the two armies to see which could reach Richmond first, and the Army of the Potomac would have had the shorter line."

Anderson had shown good initiative, but his very presence in command pointed to the personnel problems that confronted Lee. These extended beyond the relatively small size of his army to his lieutenants. Not only was Longstreet now incapacitated, but Hill was ill and Ewell's poor performances at both Gettysburg and the Wilderness made Lee decide to replace him with Jubal Early. As if he did not have enough headaches, Lee was forced to adapt his style of command for the remainder of the war to fit the shortcomings of those lieutenants. The siege of Petersburg offered at least one advantage to the Confederacy: the shortage of experienced and competent generals in the Army of Northern Virginia no longer loomed as gravely important.[96]

The natural features of the terrain at Spotsylvania dictated that the Confederate entrenchments there would best take the form of an inverted U, a shape that Lee was able to put to effective use. Troops from one wing formed a reserve that could easily reinforce the other. The weakness of this breastworks was at its apex, which came to be called the "Mule Shoe"; a part of it earned an even more descriptive name, the "Bloody Angle." Grant first probed the left of Lee's lines on May 9. The next day he attacked Lee's left, and then went at that same side of the Mule Shoe. On May 11 Grant wrote to Secretary of War Edwin Stanton and to his chief of staff, "I … propose to fight it out on this line if it takes all Summer" (fig. 155). He had been sufficiently successful the day before to send Hancock's 20,000 troops against the apex of the salient on May 12. The night before that assault, Lee had made a rare mistake when he removed two dozen cannons from that section in anticipation of a Union withdrawal. Thus when Hancock launched his massive attack, the Confederate infantry lacked artillery support. Union soldiers charged over the breastworks and engaged the enemy in horrendous hand-to-hand fighting for the next eighteen hours. Caught off guard, Lee rallied reinforcements into position. He was anxious to lead charges himself until the refrain "Lee to the rear" was again heard. On one occasion John B. Gordon had to rescue him. Grant wrote, "[Lee] made the most strenuous efforts to regain the position he had lost …. Five

LEE AND GRANT

fig. 157.
Timothy O'Sullivan, *A Council of War at Massaponax Church, Virginia* (near Spotsylvania Court House), May 21, 1864 (photograph courtesy of New-York Historical Society). Grant is the standing figure at the left who leans over the shoulder of George Meade

times during the day he assaulted furiously." Reminiscent of Beauregard's bloody assault at Shiloh, Hancock's 20,000 soldiers had been launched into a space insufficient for them to maneuver—an area about the size of two football fields—some could not even lift their arms to fight. Grant then hurled another 15,000 soldiers at the Bloody Angle. The dead lay eight to ten deep in places. "All the trees between the lines were very much cut to pieces by artillery and musketry," Grant wrote. He lost 7,000 soldiers; Lee lost close to the same number, many as prisoners of war (fig. 156). Since the beginning of the campaign, Grant had sacrificed an astounding 32,000 men. Lee had lost 18,000 of his army's 60,000 soldiers. The next day, Grant wrote to his wife, "The world has never seen so bloody or so protracted a battle as the one being fought and I hope never will again. The enemy['s] … situation is desperate beyond anything heretofore known. To lose this battle they lose their cause." On the same day, Sheridan's cavalry met Stuart's six miles north of Richmond at Yellow Tavern, a battle in which Stuart was fatally wounded.[97]

Grant had initially told Meade to follow Lee wherever he goes. He had since reversed that directive to read that wherever Meade went Lee would be obligated to follow. After several days, when Lee showed no signs of moving from his entrenchments at Spotsylvania that the Union forces could not overrun, Grant decided to take action (fig. 157). He wrote, "I believed that, if one corps of the army was exposed on the road to Richmond, … Lee would endeavor to attack the exposed corps before reinforcements could come up; in which case the main army could follow Lee up and attack him before he had time to intrench." Lee did not take the bait. Instead, he again deduced where Grant was heading. The two armies drove twenty-five miles south to the North Anna River and Hanover Junction, the convergence of two rail lines important to Lee. The result of this race was vital because the river presented a formidable natural obstacle to both forces. Once again Grant met a well-entrenched Army of Northern Virginia, this time protected behind breastworks that had been constructed during the preceding winter. On May 24–26, the Army of the Potomac was dangerously vulnerable because it was separated into three components by the curves of the river. A tactical opportunity had emerged, but Lee was too ill with an intestinal malady to seize it. A year earlier he could have ordered Jackson or Longstreet into action; instead he could only mutter from his tent, "We must strike them a blow." Without aggressive leadership, nothing happened.[98]

With Lee entrenched at Hanover Junction and his own army exposed, Grant whirled again to the left, to Cold Harbor. This time he finally beat Lee to a spot, but after nearly a month of fighting his army was exhausted and therefore slow to prepare itself for yet more action. In fact, it was said that some in both armies had "gone crazy" from the extended, horrendous combat. Grant was forced to delay for a day, enabling Lee to better prepare for the anticipated attack.

Grant later wrote that Cold Harbor as a site was important to him because it controlled both the roads to his new base of supply on the York River at White House, and the roads to the James River east of Richmond. Politics, however, more than geography made

fig. 158.
Mathew Brady, *The Dead at Cold Harbor*,
April 1865 (photograph courtesy of Library
of Congress)

him fight there. As civilians in the North tired of the war, Lincoln's position became more insecure; the status of both the president and the Republican Party might ride on the success of Grant's campaign. If the general did not attack Lee, some would conclude that he was failing. Frustrated, Grant ordered a broad frontal assault at the center of Lee's seven-mile-long line, but he spread his force too wide to be effective. Many of his soldiers, aware of their impending fate, had written their names on their backs so that their corpses could be identified (fig. 158). Some 7,000 troops were slaughtered when they were exposed to relentless Confederate firepower. Grant later wrote, "I have always regretted that the last assault at Cold Harbor was ever made ... no advantage whatever was gained to compensate for the heavy loss we sustained."[99]

Grant planned to cross the James River if he was unable to have his way with Lee above it. On May 8, after the Battle of the Wilderness, he had written to Halleck, "my exact route to the James River I have not yet definitely marked out." For a month he had sparred with Lee as he worked his way toward that river, but at Cold Harbor he had sacrificed too many lives to continue the present course. With characteristic foresight, he had positioned himself so that he now could change gears. As Grant had done at Vicksburg when he crossed a great river and surprised the enemy from below, he would now maneuver across the James to Petersburg, a railroad and supply center to Richmond and a lightly defended gateway to the city. He would send Sheridan west to draw the Confederate cavalry away and thereby deprive Lee of his eyes and ears. He worked out his plans and relayed the basics to Halleck on June 5:

> My idea from the start has been to beat Lee's Army, if possible, North of Richmond, then after destroying his lines of communication North of the James river to transfer the Army to the South side and besiege Lee in Richmond, or follow him South if he should retreat. I now find after more than thirty days of trial that the enemy deems it of the first importance to run no risks with the Armies they now have. They act purely on the defensive, behind breast works …. Without a greater sacrifice of human life than I am willing to make all cannot be accomplished that I had designed outside of the City. I have therefore resolved upon the following plan …. I will move the Army to the South side of James River.

Success, he believed, "was only a question of time." Lee sensed the same. On June 4 he advised his wife to leave Richmond: "It is evident that great danger is impending over us, & therefore those not required to meet it, or who might be overwhelmed by it should it fall upon us, should get out of harm's way in time."[100]

Grant ordered all the pontoon bridging he could find to enable his engineers to build thirty miles east of Richmond the longest bridge of this type in military history. An army of 115,000 men would cross a river 700 yards wide. This was Grant's ultimate maneuver to the left, one so bold that even Lee could not counteract it. This time he would successfully outflank his opponent and begin the end of the war by threatening Richmond from the south through Petersburg. By no means was this plan easy to execute. Grant explained some of the difficulties in his *Memoirs*:

> Lee's position was now so near Richmond, and the intervening swamps of the Chickahominy so great an obstacle to the movement of troops in the face of an enemy, that I determined to make my next left flank move carry the Army of the Potomac south of the James River …. The move was a hazardous one to make …. The army had a shorter line and better roads to travel on to confront me in crossing … and … the Army of the Potomac had to be got out of a position but a few hundred yards from the enemy at the widest place.

He told his wife that this was "one of the most perilous movements ever executed by a large army." On June 14, he wrote to Halleck that all was going to plan, "Our forces will commence crossing James River to day. The Enemy show no signs of yet having brought troops to south side of Richmond. I will have Petersburg secured if possible before they get there in much force. Our movement from Cold Harbor to the James River has been made with great celerity, and so far, without loss or accident."[101]

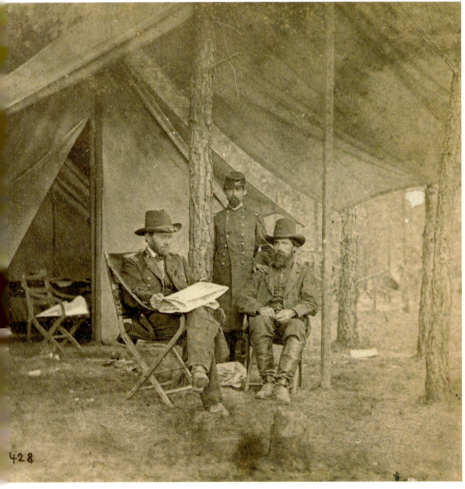

For a few days Lee did not know that on June 12 an army of 115,000 Union soldiers had abandoned its heavily entrenched front at Cold Harbor. When he discovered movement along the Chickahominy River, Lee thought that Grant would strike Richmond from there, as McClellan had tried two years earlier; he sent troops in anticipation and had them entrench. Lee had for some time suspected that the Army of the Potomac might cross the James River, and he had even written to Jefferson Davis on June 11 of that possibility. But he could not cross the James himself and leave unprotected the northern exposures of Richmond, which were under the command of his son, General Custis Lee, until he was certain that Grant had in fact crossed. Not until June 18 was Lee sure of what Grant had accomplished. Longstreet took even more time to be convinced. By then, the first attack on Petersburg, on June 15, had been made. If conducted with competence, it would have taken the city easily. Lee's biographer Freeman wrote that the success of Grant in crossing the James unhindered and the failure of Lee to reinforce Petersburg more quickly and heavily after the initial attack should be regarded as the most serious blemishes on Lee's military record, with the possible exception of

fig. 159.
Brady and Co., *Grant and His Staff at Cold Harbor*, June 11 or 12, 1864 (photograph courtesy of New-York Historical Society Library, gift of Susan E. Lyman in memory of her father Robert Hunt Lyman)

fig. 160.
Brady and Co., *Ulysses Grant, Theodore Bowers, and John Rawlins, Cold Harbor*, June 11 or 12, 1864 (photograph courtesy of New-York Historical Society Library, George T. Bagoe Collection, gift of Mrs. Elihu Spicer)

fig. 161.
David Knox, *The Mortar "Dictator" and its Gun Crew, Petersburg*, October 1864 (photograph courtesy of Virginia Historical Society)

his order for Pickett's charge at Gettysburg.[102]

When Lee realized that Grant had successfully crossed to the Southside, he knew that the Confederate cause was lost. He had stated more than once during the campaign that "We must destroy this army of Grant's before he gets to James River …. If he gets there, it will become a siege, and then it will be a mere question of time." It turned out that Petersburg became the city under siege rather than Richmond. But the end result was the same. Grant by then had destroyed so much of the Army of Northern Virginia and so many more southern soldiers had deserted that Lee's surrender was inevitable. In 1868, when Lee told Belle Stewart, a friend of his daughter Mildred, that he was sad because he was "thinking of the men who were lost after I knew it was too late," he may well have been referring to the men who died after Petersburg was put under siege. He explained somewhat cryptically to Stewart that he kept fighting then because the southern people "had to find out for themselves."[103]

General William F. Smith attacked Petersburg with 18,000 troops, but he failed to press the offensive because the city was fortified, and because Smith was apparently still stunned by the carnage at Cold Harbor. Grant wrote later, "I believed then, and still believe, that Petersburg could have been easily captured at that time. It only had about 2,500 men in the defences." Smith's failure prolonged the conflict by almost a year. By June 18, after Petersburg had been well reinforced by P. G. T. Beauregard, even Grant could not take the city; his advantages in men and material resources would not bring a quick end to the siege (fig. 161). Grant could stretch Lee's lines thin, and sporadic battles would reduce the Army of Northern Virginia's finite pool of manpower even further, but the process of forcing an evacuation of Petersburg would take ten long months. During that time, in the most celebrated of these clashes, the July 30 "Battle of the Crater," northern miners tunneled under Confederate lines to blow a gaping hole in the earth into which Union troops were launched only to be massacred. Many of the slain were United States Colored Troops. Grant described this fiasco to Henry Halleck as the "saddest affair I have ever witnessed in the war."[104]

On June 13, even before he was trapped behind the defenses of Petersburg, Lee had looked to reduce some of the Union manpower directed at him by sending troops under Jubal Early into the Valley of Virginia to threaten Washington. Initially, Early met with some success, until Grant sent Sheridan with 48,000 cavalry and infantry troops to quiet him. This region, Grant later wrote, "had been the source of a great deal of trouble to us heretofore …. I determined to put a stop to this." He directed his general not only to destroy Early's forces but also to wreak havoc on the Valley itself and thereby eradicate Lee's "storehouse." His July orders were explicit: "Eat out Virginia clean … so that crows flying over it … will have to carry their provender with them …. Do all the damage to railroads and crops you can …. Carry off stock of all descriptions, and Negroes, so as to prevent further planting. If the war is to last another year, we want the Shenandoah Valley to remain a barren waste." In the meantime, Union hopes were buoyed by Sherman's success in Georgia. As Grant put it, "the enemy [was] flanked out of one position after another." After a campaign of four months that paralleled Grant's activity in Virginia, Atlanta fell on September 2. Had not Sherman and Sheridan won their victories in Georgia and the Valley of Virginia, Abraham Lincoln might not have been re-elected in the fall of 1864. Grant believed that "these two campaigns probably had more effect in settling the election of the following November than all the speeches, all the bonfires, and all the parading with banners and bands of music in the North." Lincoln defeated George McClellan in a landslide victory. Lee despaired at the news, writing to his wife, "We must therefore make up our minds for another four years of war." Sherman's subsequent

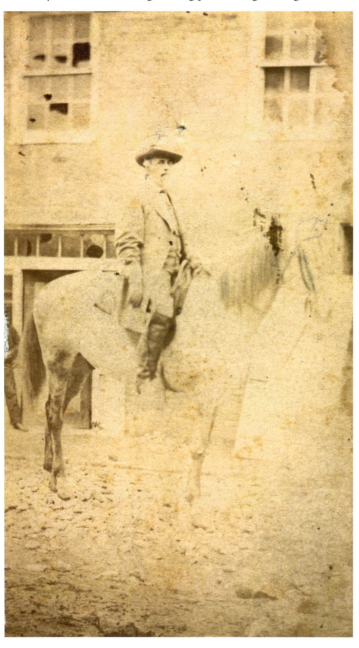

fig. 162.
Robert E. Lee on Traveller, Petersburg,
1864–65 (photograph courtesy of
Virginia Historical Society)

march to the sea, from Atlanta in October to Savannah in December, further demoralized the Confederacy.[105]

Lee persevered as best he could in Petersburg during the long months of the siege (fig. 162). The outlook was grim. In an August letter to his congressman, Elihu Washburne, Grant described the situation:

> the rebels have now in their ranks their last man. The little boys and old men are guarding prisoners, guarding railroad bridges and forming a good part of their garrisons for intrenched positions. A man lost by them cannot be replaced. They have robbed the cradle and the grave equally to get their present force. Besides what they lose in frequent skirmishes and battles they are now oozing from desertions and other causes at least one regiment per day. With this drain upon them the end is visible if we will but be true to ourselves.

Lee had lost 35,000 men since the Wilderness. Grant had lost 65,000 but was able to replenish his ranks. Lee wrote to his wife in October, "The enemy is very numerous & still increasing & is able by his superiority of numbers to move at pleasure." By late December, Grant could report to Julia, "The rebels are very despondent and say, some of them, their cause is already lost." By the start of the next year Confederate attrition reached epidemic proportions: Lee lost 8 percent of his army to desertion in January 1865 and another 8 percent in February. Grant concluded that "It was a mere question of arithmetic to calculate how long they could hold out while that rate of depletion was going on." It was this desperate need for troops that compelled Lee in January to petition state senator Andrew Hunter to endorse the enlistment of black troops by offering freedom to slaves and bounties of money and land. On January 15, the loss of the last Confederate port, Wilmington, North Carolina, stirred the Confederate Congress to remove military control from Davis and award it to Lee, who was made general-in-chief. However, rather than enlist black troops or evacuate Richmond, he did little. Lee believed that a soldier should not override the wishes of his civilian superiors. He conveyed his sense of the situation to Mary on February 21: "[The enemy is] advancing and having everything his own way. [God] does not always give the battle to the strong, I pray that we shall not be overwhelmed. I shall, however, endeavour to do my duty & fight to the last." In early March, General John B. Gordon implored Lee to beg the Confederate Congress to seek favorable peace terms while they were still in a position to negotiate. Lee traveled to Richmond but could report back only that no one in power there appreciated the situation and so it was his duty to continue to fight. On March 25 he made a desperate effort that failed to break Grant's Petersburg lines at Fort Stedman.[106]

Grant, meanwhile, was comfortably ensconced at City Point, just above Petersburg at the confluence of the James and Ap-

fig. 163.
Edward Lamson Henry, *City Point, Virginia, Headquarters of General Grant*, 1865–73, oil on canvas, 30⅛ × 60¼ in. (76.5 × 153.0 cm.), Addison Gallery of American Art, Phillips Academy, Andover, Massachusetts

fig. 164.
General Grant and the Negro Sentinel, 1888, etching, 4 × 6 in. (10.2 × 15.2 cm.), Virginia Historical Society

pomattox Rivers. There he had relocated his base of supply from the York River. The Union advantage in materiel was nowhere more visible. The artist Edward Lamson Henry painted the scene from sketches he made on the spot (fig. 163). City Point was the setting for a famed incident with one of the black soldiers who had enlisted in the Union army (fig. 164). He warned General Grant to be more careful near so many munitions: "You must throw away that cigar, sir!" As the story goes, his commander complied, happy that the soldier had performed his duty so well.[107]

Grant's wife and several of the children visited at City Point; Julia and Jesse were photographed there on an extended visit of six weeks at the end of the winter (fig. 165). Grant's correspondence with Julia during these months reveals his concern for the children's education in New Jersey and his interest in whether the family would retire after the war to a house in Philadelphia that admirers there had given him. Grant even had time to enjoy his horses (fig. 166).

On March 27, Abraham Lincoln visited, as did Sherman and Admiral David D. Porter, to discuss how to terminate the war. They met aboard the ship the *River Queen*. Lincoln and Grant each let the other lead in his arena of expertise. Sherman asked Lincoln what should be done with the enemy armies once they surrendered. In his second inaugural address, delivered earlier in the month, Lincoln had famously stated, "With malice toward none; with charity for all; with firmness in the right, as God gives us to see the right, let us strive … to bind up the nation's wounds." At City Point he said, "Let

LEE AND GRANT

fig. 165.
E. & H. T. Anthony & Co., publishers, *Lieutenant General Grant, Wife and Son, at his Headquarters, City Point, Va.*, 1864–65 (photograph courtesy of New-York Historical Society Library, George T. Bagoe Collection, gift of Mrs. Elihu Spicer)

fig. 166.
Mathew Brady, *Grant and His War-Horse "Cincinnati,"* c. 1864 (photograph courtesy of New-York Historical Society Library, gift of Susan E. Lyman in memory of her father Robert Hunt Lyman)

fig. 167.
G. P. A. Healy, *Peacemakers*, 1868, oil on canvas, 47 11/16 × 66 in. (121.1 × 167.6 cm.), The White House

them go, officers and all …. I want no one punished; treat them liberally all round. We want those people to return to their allegiance to the Union and submit to the laws." From those instructions Grant would feel justified in offering generous terms of surrender to Lee at Appomattox. The painter G. P. A. Healy later celebrated the meeting in a painting now in the collection of the White House that he titled *Peacemakers* (fig. 167). The sculptor John Rogers imagined an earlier meeting between Lincoln, Grant, and Secretary of War Edwin Stanton. He called it *The Council of War* (fig. 168). The two depictions provided viewers with a choice as to whether they would remember Lincoln as a man of peace or of war.

Grant worried during the last weeks at Petersburg that when the roads became passable in the spring Lee would escape from behind his entrenchments. Lee certainly intended to escape; he remembered that his father had written in his *Memoirs of the War in the Southern Department* that a general should never allow his army to be captured by siege, as had happened at Charleston during the American Revolution. "[Lee] had his railroad by the way of Danville south, and I was afraid that he was running off," Grant wrote in his *Memoirs*, "and that, if he got the start, he would leave me behind so that we would have the same army to fight again farther south—and the war might be prolonged another year."

On March 29 he resumed the initiative, taking personal command from Meade in order to avoid missed opportunities like that of June 15, 1864. To stretch Lee's lines even more thin at their center, he ordered Sheridan to the Confederate right to seize the road junction at Five Forks. With victory there, Grant had control of the South Side railroad. The fate of Petersburg was sealed. Lee had lost a fourth of his army at Fort Stedman and Five Forks. Thus at dawn Grant could easily storm the city, despite its fortifications that were "exceedingly strong," and so force the abandonment of both Petersburg and Richmond. On that date, April 2, he wrote to his wife (fig. 169), "this has been one of the greatest victories of the war. Greatest because it is over what the rebels have always regarded as their most invincible Army and the one used for the defince of their capitol. We may have some more hard work but I hope not." He then moved quickly to block Lee's escape: "we did not want to follow him; we wanted to get ahead of him and cut him off …. Lee ordered his troops to assemble at Amelia Court House, his object being to get away, join Johnston if possible, and to try to crush Sherman before I could get there." Grant

fig. 168.
John Rogers, *The Council of War*, 1868, plaster, 24 × 14 × 11¾ in. (61.0 × 35.6 × 29.8 cm.), New-York Historical Society Museum, gift of Mr. and Mrs. J. Edwin Huey

fig. 169.
Ulysses S. Grant [Petersburg] to Mrs. Grant, *Letter*, April 2, 1865, Library of Congress

added, "It now became a life and death struggle with Lee to get south to his provisions." On April 7, after he had beaten Lee to the route of escape, Grant wrote to his antagonist about "the hopelessness of further resistance." Lee had to agree.[108]

Appomattox

When Lee began his retreat from Petersburg, he had little more than 30,000 soldiers; Grant's army was four times larger. By the time he reached Farmville the Army of Northern Virginia was reduced to fewer than 15,000. At Appomattox there were little more than 12,000 remaining. Longstreet had agreed with Lee to hold out until all hope was gone, but other officers had suggested earlier that he negotiate a peace. As long as there remained a chance for his army to escape, however, Lee felt it was his duty to continue. It was a question of honor, the concept that had brought Lee into the war in 1861. The statement of a woman in Georgia, Sarah Hine, makes clear the feeling among many in the South: "One thing I shall glory in to the latest hour of my life," she wrote in her diary, is that "we never yielded in the struggle until were bound hand & foot & the heel of the despot was on our throats."

Lee would not sanction guerrilla warfare. Edward Porter Alexander raised the subject to his commander, who responded,

> Suppose I should take your suggestion & order the army to disperse & make their way to their homes. The men … would have to plunder & rob to procure subsistence. The country would be full of lawless bands in every part, & a state of society would ensue from which it would take the country years to recover. Then the enemy's cavalry would pursue in the hopes of catching the principal officers, & wherever they went there would be fresh rapine & destruction. And as for myself, while you young men might afford

fig. 170.
Wilmer McLean House, Appomattox Court House, c. 1865 (photograph courtesy of Virginia Historical Society)

fig. 171.
Major and Knapp, *The Room in the McLean House, at Appomattox C.H., in which Gen. Lee Surrendered to Gen. Grant*, 1867, lithograph, 19⅛ × 29 in. (48.6 × 73.7 cm.), National Portrait Gallery, Smithsonian Institution

to go to bushwhacking, the only proper & dignified course for me would be to surrender myself & take the consequences of my actions.

"I had not a single word to say in reply," Alexander wrote. "He had answered my suggestion from a plane so far above it, that I was ashamed of having made it." To Lee's credit, this decision did as much to facilitate reconciliation as did Grant's generous terms of surrender.[109]

The two antagonists met in Appomattox in the house of Wilmer McLean, who had owned a farm at Manassas but had moved away to avoid the armies (figs. 170, 171, and 172). Lee dressed in a new uniform and carried his handsomest sword. "I have probably to be General Grant's prisoner and thought I must make my best appearance," he is reported to have said, adding that he "would rather die a thousand deaths" than meet Grant to surrender. With him was his military secretary, Charles Marshall. Grant reportedly arrived "covered with mud in an old faded uniform." According to Union colonel Amos Webster, he "looked like a fly on a shoulder of beef." Many of Grant's officers came with him (fig. 173).[110]

Grant left a long and rich account of the surrender that tells a great deal about the relationship between the two generals and about the beginnings of the nation's restoration. He recalled meeting in Farmville a Dr. Smith, a Confederate officer who told him of a conversation with General Richard Ewell. This former corps commander, who knew that the cause was lost when Grant crossed the James River, held the "authorities" in Richmond responsible for the many men killed afterwards. Any further loss, Ewell believed, "would be but very little better than murder." Two days before Appomattox, Henry Wise had gone so far as to accuse Lee of murder if he persisted. Sheridan's subsequent capture of provisions desperately needed by the Army of Northern Virginia caused Grant to open correspondence with Lee on the subject of the surrender of his army.

They exchanged several letters. On April 8 Grant stated one aspect of the terms: "that the men and officers surrendered shall be disqualified for taking up arms again against the Government of the United States until properly exchanged." On April 9, Lee "request[ed] an interview." When they met at the house of McLean, Grant told a story of knowing Lee in the old army in Mexico, adding that he remembered Lee "distinctly." Grant was in "rough

garb," without a sword, because he "had not expected so soon the result that was then taking place." The Union commander wore "a soldier's blouse for a coat, with the shoulder straps of my rank to indicate to the army who I was." They shook hands and took their seats. A "good portion" of Grant's staff was present during the interview that followed. Grant wrote:

> What General Lee's feelings were I do not know. As he was a man of much dignity, with an impassible face, it was impossible to say whether he felt inwardly glad that the end had finally come, or felt sad over the result, and was too manly to show it. Whatever his feelings, they were entirely concealed from

LEE AND GRANT

fig. 172.
Table and Two Chairs from Appomattox, National Museum of American History

fig. 173.
Alexander Gardner, *Ulysses S. Grant and Staff*, 1865 (photograph courtesy of New-York Historical Society Library, gift of Harry A. Ogden)

my observation; but my own feelings, which had been quite jubilant on the receipt of his letter, were sad and depressed. I felt like anything rather than rejoicing at the downfall of a foe who had fought so long and valiantly, and had suffered so much for a cause, though that cause was, I believe, one of the worst for which a people ever fought, and one for which there was the least excuse. I do not question, however, the sincerity of the great mass of those who were opposed to us.

General Lee was dressed in a full uniform which was entirely new, and was wearing a sword of considerable value, very likely the sword which had been presented by the State of Virginia …. In my rough traveling suit, the uniform of a private with the straps of a lieutenant-general, I must have contrasted very strangely with a man so handsomely dressed, six feet high and of faultless form. But this was not a matter that I thought of until afterwards.

We soon fell into a conversation about old army times. He remarked that he remembered me very well in the old army; and I told him that as a matter of course I remembered him perfectly, but from the difference in our rank and years (there being about sixteen years' difference in our ages), I had thought it very likely that I had not attracted his attention sufficiently to be remembered by him after such a long interval. Our conversation grew so pleasant that I almost forgot the object of our meeting ….

Lee asked that the terms of surrender be written out. Grant complied (fig. 174):

> The officers to give their individual paroles not to take up arms against the Government of the United States until properly exchanged …. The arms, artillery and public property to be parked and stacked, and turned over to the officer appointed by me to receive them. This will not embrace the side-arms of the officers, nor their private horses or baggage. This done, each officer and man will be allowed to return to their homes, not to be disturbed by United States authority so long as they observe their paroles and the laws in force where they may reside.

Grant added in his *Memoirs*: "When I put my pen to the paper I did not know the first word that I should make use of in writing the terms …. As I wrote on, the thought occurred to me that the officers had their own private horses and effects, which were important to them, but of no value to us; also that it would be an unnecessary humiliation to call upon them to deliver their side arms." Lee commented that the allowance of the side arms, horses, and private property of the officers would have "a happy effect upon his army." He stated that his cavalrymen and artillerists also owned their own horses, and intimated that they would need them after the war. Grant understood that most of these men were small farmers and "that it was doubtful whether they would be able to put in a crop to carry themselves and their families through the next winter without

fig. 174.
U. S. Grant to R. E. Lee, *Terms of Surrender*,
April 9, 1865, Stratford Hall Plantation

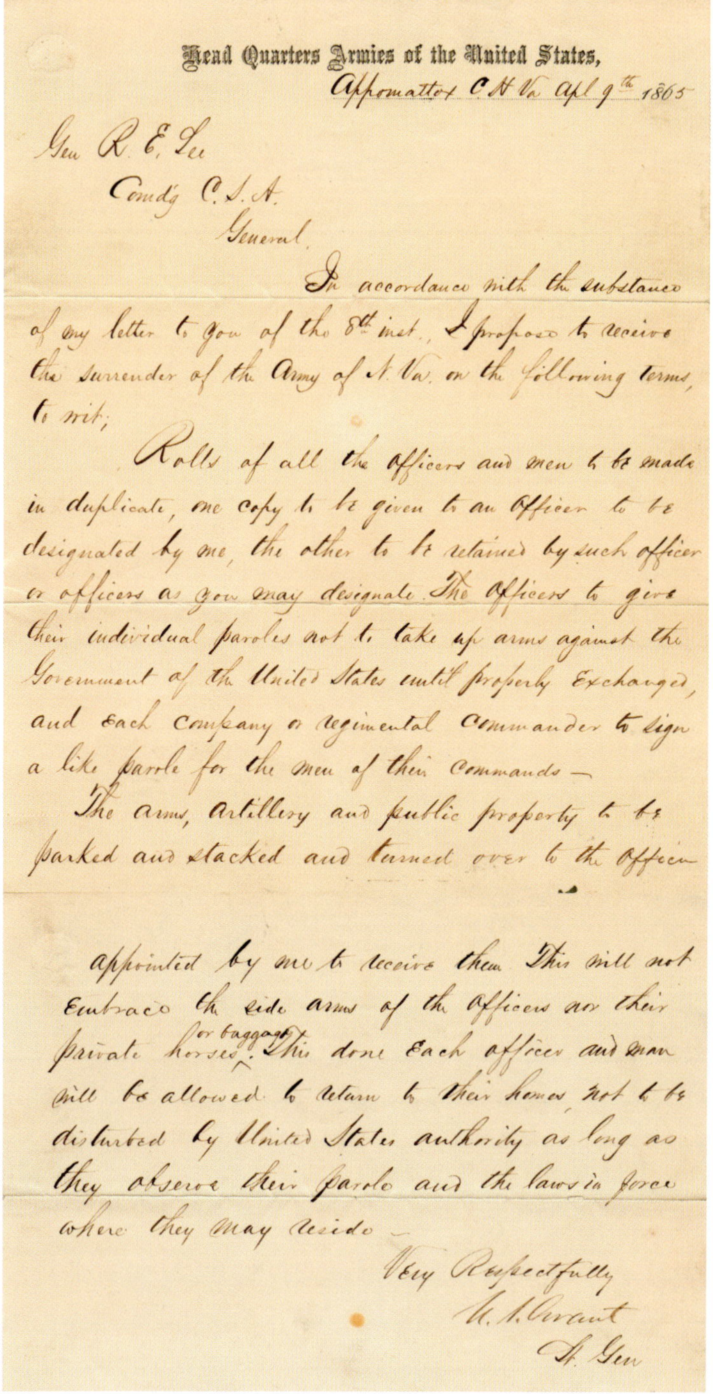

back, this and much more that has been said about it is the purest romance." The Union soldiers began firing a salute of a hundred guns in honor of the victory; Grant "at once sent word … to have it stopped." Lee departed in defeat (fig. 175).[111]

Grant wanted to talk further, so the next morning he rode to Lee's headquarters. They met on horseback and enjoyed "a very pleasant conversation of over half an hour." He recounted the discussion:

> Lee said to me that the South was a big country and that we might have to march over it three or four times before the war entirely ended, but that we would now be able to do it as they could no longer resist us. He expressed it as his earnest hope, however, that we would not be called upon to cause more loss and sacrifice of life; but he could not foretell the result. I then suggested to General Lee that there was not a man in the Confederacy whose influence with the soldiery and the whole people was as great as his, and that if he would now advise the surrender of all the armies I had no doubt his advice would be followed with alacrity. But Lee said he could not do that without consulting the President first. I knew there was no use to urge him to do anything against his ideas of what was right.[112]

Many of the soldiers in both armies could not believe that the war was over for them. New Englander Stephen Minot Weld wrote,

> To tell the truth, we none of us realize even yet that he has actually surrendered. I had a sort of impression that we should fight him all our lives. He was like a ghost to children, something that haunted us so long that we could not realize that he and his army were really out of existence to us. It will take me some months to be conscious of this fact.

Veterans of the Army of Northern Virginia felt pride even in defeat. Surgeon Lafayette Guild wrote, "To belong to General Lee's defeated Army is now the proudest boast of a Confederate soldier." Lee had Charles Marshall draft a farewell order, many copies of which were made and signed by Lee (fig. 176). The first sentence stated the southern explanation for the defeat: "After four years of arduous service, marked by unsurpassed courage and fortitude, the Army of Northern Virginia has been compelled to yield to overwhelming numbers and resources." The surrender of Lee was accepted by most Americans North and South as the surrender of the entire Confederacy. On April 26, Joseph Johnston surrendered to

the aid of the horses they were then riding." Besides, "the United States did not want them." Grant therefore volunteered to instruct his officers to let the southerners keep their horses and mules. Lee replied that this too would have "a happy effect." Grant added that "the much talked of surrendering of Lee's sword and my handing it

LEE AND GRANT

225

fig. 175.
John A. Elder, *Farewell at Appomattox*, after 1865, oil on canvas, 18 × 23½ in. (45.7 × 59.7 cm.), Washington and Lee University

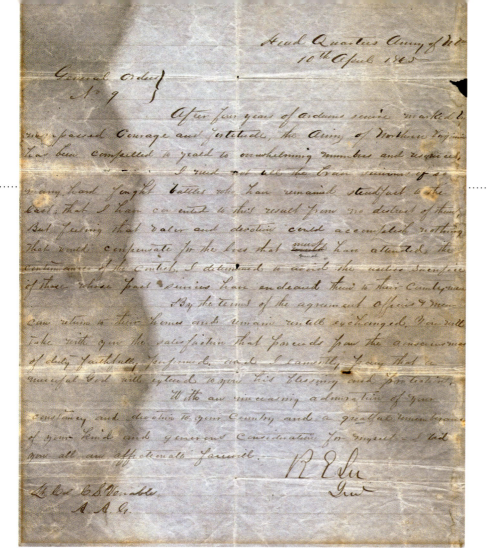

fig. 176.
Robert E. Lee, *General Orders No. 9*, April 9, 1865, Virginia Historical Society

Sherman on the same terms that Grant had given to Lee. The war was over.[113]

When on his own initiative Grant paroled the Confederate soldiers who surrendered to him, he moved the nation a giant step forward toward reconciliation. There would be no imprisonments, no trials, no witch hunts, no needless perpetuation of the bitter antagonisms that had developed during four years of horrendous warfare. Two weeks later, Grant wrote to his wife with an eye focused on the nation's future: "People who talk of further retaliation and punishment, except of political leaders, either do not conceive of the suffering endured already or they are heartless and unfeeling" (fig. 177). Grant believed that southerners had experienced more than enough agony. Others, however, did not agree. In 1867 the general was called before the Judiciary Committee of the U.S. House of Representatives as it considered the impeachment of Andrew Johnson. Grant had to defend the terms that he had awarded at Appomattox. He explained that the course he had chosen was conceived to "avoid bushwhacking & a continuation of the war." He reminded Congress that he "had a right, as Military Commander, to arrange terms of surrender, which should protect the lives of those prisoners." To squash any rebuttal, he added, "I know that Mr. Lincoln conceded it at the time."[114]

Josiah Bunting sees the actions of Lee and Grant at Appomattox as crucial to the process of bringing the nation together:

> The nature of the future of the American polity has on occasion been defined by the actions of a few citizens. In the week before the Appomattox meeting, and on the day itself, April 9, 1865, these two men, by their actions and words, largely determined the character of what would follow four years of civil war, and by their example summoned successors to heed always the counsels of their best selves. It was not only a matter of authority or stature; it was an achievement of communicated sympathy, of magnanimity and understanding on the one hand, and of transcendent courage and farsightedness on the other. Had these two men not been the makers of the surrender, had they not understood and thereafter supported the elements of that surrender, and had Ulysses Grant not served as its guarantor, the consequences for the United States would have been profoundly different.

Bunting adds that "if Grant was determined to win the war as rapidly as it could be won, he understood also that the object of the war, ultimately, was not victory but peace, and that the work of reconciliation and reconstruction must now be undertaken."[115]

The restoration of the Union would be no easy task. As the generals who were in the thick of some of the most destructive episodes of the war, and who had retained the reverence of their armies and civilian followers, Grant and Lee would be forced to remain in or near the spotlight. Ironically, the two military leaders would assume leadership roles in the political process of reunification that would consume many of the remaining years of their lives.

Lee's aggressive campaigns had been costly. In percentage of soldiers killed, to which total Lee contributed more than his share, the South suffered a staggering 37–39 percent rate. Some 258,000 died, more than one in three of 750,000–850,000 men. Northern deaths of 360,000 (17 percent), one in six of 2.2 million men, pale in a percentage comparison. However, most southerners did not complain;

fig. 177.
Ulysses S. Grant, Raleigh, to Mrs. Grant, *Letter*, April 25, 1865, Rosenbach Museum & Library, Philadelphia

fig. 178.
Timothy H. O'Sullivan, *Fugitive Slaves Crossing the Rappahannock River in Virginia*, 1862 (photograph courtesy of Library of Congress)

fig. 179.
Ulysses S. Grant, Vicksburg, to Elihu B. Washburne, *Letter*, August 30, 1863, Abraham Lincoln Presidential Library & Museum, Springfield, Illinois

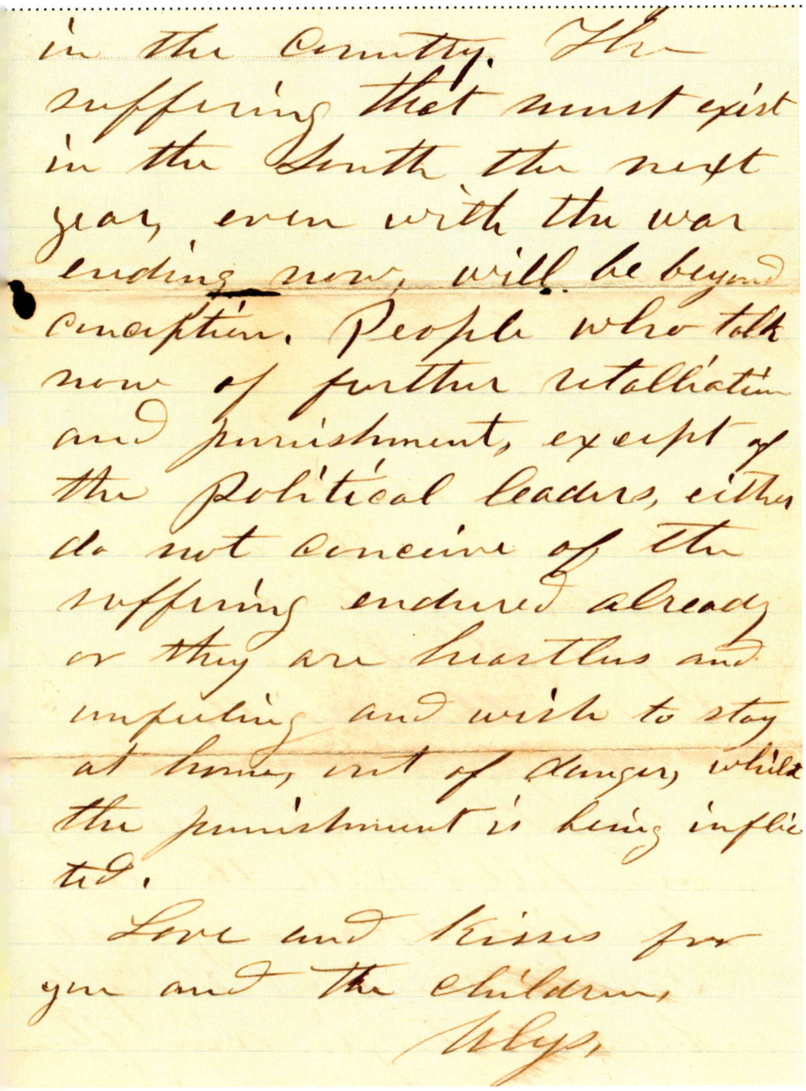

there was remarkably little criticism of the casualty rate in Lee's army, even though the South seemed to have lost a generation of young men. There was on both sides the inevitable sense that the wounds to the nation would take much time and effort to heal.[116]

There was also the need for the nation to find a way to deal with the large population of emancipated slaves. At the beginning of the war, emancipation had not been an objective. The war was being waged solely to end secession. Grant had said little about slavery before the war, but as he moved into Confederate territory and encountered thousands of black people filling his camps seeking freedom, he came to a different conclusion:

> For some years before the war began it was a trite saying among some politicians that "A state half slave and half free cannot exist." All must become slave or all free, or the state will go down. I took no part myself in any such view of the case at the time, but … I [came] to the conclusion that the saying is quite true.
>
> Slavery was an institution that required unusual guarantees for its security wherever it existed; and in a country like ours where the larger portion of it was free territory inhabited by an intelligent and well-to-do population, the people would naturally have but little sympathy with demands upon them for its protection.[117]

In November 1861, Grant wrote to his father that his "inclination was to whip the rebellion into submission, preserving all constitutional rights." Among these would be the right to own slaves. But, he added, "if it cannot be whipped in any other way than through a war against slavery, let it come to that legitimately. If it is necessary that slavery should fall that the Republic may continue its existence, let slavery go."[118]

During the months when Grant's campaign to capture Vicksburg kept him in the deep South, the general had on his own concluded that the slave system was in crisis and that its fate was sealed. During the summer of 1863, Grant explained his reasoning to Elihu Washburne (fig. 179): "it became patent to my mind early in the rebellion that the North & South could never live at peace with each other except as one nation, and that without Slavery." He added that he did not want to see a peace settlement "until this question is forever settled," explaining that "Slavery is already dead and cannot be resurrected…. Vice President Stevens [Stephens] acknowledges the corner stone of the Confederacy is already knocked out." Too many slaves had already escaped to freedom (fig. 178). "It would take a standing Army," he told the congressman, "to maintain slavery in the South if we were to make peace to-day guaranteeing to the South all their former constitutional privileges."[119]

In a conversation late in his life with the German chancellor Otto von Bismarck, Grant took the opportunity to praise two of his greatest lieutenants, but then made the perhaps surprising comment that it was actually for the good that the war lasted as least longer than the one year that some had anticipated, because if it had ended early, slavery would have been allowed to continue, only to rear its ugly head at some later date:

> A great commander like Sherman or Sheridan even then

> I never was an Abolitionist, not even what could be called anti-slavery, but I try to judge fairly & honestly and it became patent to my mind early in the rebellion that the North & South could never live at peace with each other except as one Nation, and that without Slavery. As anxious as I am to see peace reestablished I would not

might have organized an army and put down the rebellion in six months or a year, or, at the farthest, two years. But that would have saved slavery, perhaps, and slavery meant the germs of new rebellion. There had to be an end of slavery.

Although humanitarian concerns would ultimately come into his thinking, Grant's practical side had told him that slavery had to be abolished to end the possibility of another war. So he made sure that it was.[120]

Robert E. Lee had freed the 170 Custis slaves at the end of 1862 (fig. 181); the five-year deadline dictated by the will of his father-in-law had expired. This was only days before Lincoln's Emancipation Proclamation, a document that greatly angered him. Using the harshest words he ever put on paper regarding the subject of race, Lee wrote to Secretary of War James A. Seddon on January 10, 1863 asking for more troops and citing as one reason "the savage and brutal policy he [Lincoln] has proclaimed, which leaves us no alternative but success or degradation worse than death, if we would save the honor of our families from pollution, our social system from destruction." This powerful response, which Lee hoped would convince Seddon to increase the size of his army, was unusual for the general. He had expressed displeasure with slavery before 1861 and had even advocated the emancipation of all the slaves in the South to avoid war, although such comments had less to do with humanitarianism than with political and military concerns. In short, he felt that slavery was simply more trouble than it was worth. Just as the war was beginning, Lee told Bishop Joseph P. B. Wilmer, "The future is in the hands of Providence, but, if the slaves of the South were mine, I would surrender them all with out a struggle, to avert this war." He continued to advocate for emancipation. After the war he made telling statements to two veterans who were faculty members at Washington College. Lee said to William Allan that he "told Mr. Davis often and early in the war that the slaves should be emancipated, that it was the only way to remove a weakness at home and to get sympathy abroad, and to divide our enemies, but Mr. Davis would not hear of it." He stated to William Preston Johnston that "he knew the strength of the United States Government" and saw the necessity of "a proclamation of gradual emancipation and the use of the negroes as soldiers." As the war drew to a close in early 1865, Lee advised state senator Andrew Hunter that the Union army was freeing so many slaves as it advanced deep into Virginia that some action had to be taken. The enemy's "progress will thus add to his numbers, and at the same time destroy slavery in a manner most pernicious to the

fig. 180.
Johnsonville, Tennessee, Camp of Tennessee Colored Battery, 1863 or later (photograph courtesy of Library of Congress)

welfare of our people." Some 200,000 former slaves were already serving in the Union army, many as part of formidable black fighting units (fig. 180). "I think therefore, we must decide whether slavery shall be extinguished by our enemies, and the slaves used against us, or use them ourselves at the risk of the effects which may be produced upon our social institutions. My own opinion is that we should employ them without delay." Lee had favored "giving immediate freedom to all who enlist" and mentioned also bounties (money or land) to attract black men into southern service. A clerk in the Confederate War Department, J. B. Jones, wrote in his diary in January 1865, "If it really be so, and if it were generally known, that Gen. Lee is, and always has been opposed to slavery, how soon would his great popularity vanish like the mist of the morning!" Jones's statement suggests both that Lee may well have been opposed to slavery, but if he was, few southerners knew about it. By the end of the war Grant's stance on race had evolved towards that of more enlightened Americans. For Lee, it is fair to say that he would have supported emancipation to avoid the conflict. Afterward, he was ready to accept emancipation with minimal flinching and to move on to the new order.[121]

Lee had sustained the southern hope for victory well past the time when common sense and resignation should have replaced it. He and his Army of Northern Virginia took on an importance to the Confederacy that was comparable in American history only to the role that George Washington and the Continental Army served in making tangible the pursuit of American independence. And on three occasions Lee had seriously threatened to undermine northern support of the war: in the summer of 1862 when he invaded Maryland; in the spring and summer of 1863 when he repulsed northern offensives, humiliated the Army of the Potomac at Chancellorsville, and moved into Pennsylvania; and in the summer of 1864 when he stalled Grant's drive toward Richmond. Even as the end approached, Confederate faith in Lee held fast. In mid-March 1865, Thomas Conolly, a member of the British Parliament, would observe that "Genl R. E. Lee ... [is] the idol of his soldiers & the Hope of His Country .... [T]he prestige which surrounds his person & the almost fanatical belief in his judgement & capacity ... is the one idea of an entire people."

Both Lee and Grant played important roles in the evolution of the American Army. They participated in a conflict in which warfare itself changed from an attempt to secure territory to an effort to destroy both your enemy and his civilian support system. Lee inspired his men to defend their homes against the invader at all costs. At Shiloh, at the Wilderness, and on a number of other occasions, in the face of casualties that had been unthinkable in earlier wars, Grant refused to accept the apparent verdict of battle and attacked. In the first war in which reporters provided up-to-date coverage of the carnage, military deaths were reported daily, and photographers provided shocking graphic evidence of the incredible scale and brutality of the fighting, which led to questions about how much bloodshed the public could stand, Grant kept his eye on the ultimate objective. In victory Grant became the savior of the Union; in defeat Lee became the hero of the "Lost Cause." Their roles in war had been clear. It was now time for them to find ways to be of service during peacetime.[122]

fig. 181.
Robert E. Lee, *Deed of Emancipation*, December 29, 1862, Museum of the Confederacy

VI.
Restoration of the Union

fig. 182.
Mathew Brady, *Robert E. Lee*, April 1865 (photograph courtesy of Virginia Historical Society)

fig. 183.
Samuel Sartain, *Lieut. Gen. Ulysses S. Grant*, 1865, engraving, 18 × 15¾ in. (45.7 × 40.0 cm.), New-York Historical Society Library

I think it the duty of every citizen, in the present condition of the Country, to do all in his power to aid in the restoration of peace and harmony, and in no way to oppose the policy of the State or General Government directed to that object.
    Robert E. Lee to John Brockenbrough, Rector of Washington College, August 24, 1865

Let us have peace.
    Ulysses S. Grant, on accepting the Republican nomination for president, 1868

Postbellum America: Lee, Grant, and National Reconciliation

Lee and Grant (figs. 182 and 183) met face to face only once after Appomattox. This was in Washington at the White House early in Grant's first term as president. The occasion was a visit by Lee on May 1, 1869, following a trip he had made to Baltimore on behalf of the Valley Railroad Company, the only business enterprise of the postwar era to which the general offered his name and support. The company hoped to bring a railway connection to the isolated community of Lexington, Virginia. (Lee often joked that whichever wagon route you took to Lexington you wished you had taken the other.) Grant extended an invitation to his former adversary. A meeting was then arranged, at least in part because news of their continued civil conduct toward one another might help to encourage national reconciliation. Their conversation was private and went unrecorded, however, and so the newspapers gave the meeting scant coverage. The *New York Tribune* learned that the visit was a short one, perhaps fifteen minutes in duration, and was "polite and cordial" but marked by "a certain reserve." *The New York Times* reported, "They talked about the weather, about the crops in Virginia, about a railroad which General Lee is interested in, and possibly one or two other personal matters …. Not a word was said about reconstruction, and the call was entirely one of courtesy." General Adam Badeau of Grant's staff added that the president remembered jesting to Lee, "You and I, General, have had more to do with destroying railroads than building them," to which Lee refused to smile.

    Although Grant and Lee made little effort to maintain personal contact, in the wake of Appomattox they treated one another with respect. Grant may have literally saved Lee's life by personally preventing a trial for treason that could have produced a death verdict.

LEE AND GRANT

Lee always spoke respectfully of his adversary, reminding acquaintances that "General Grant has acted with magnanimity," and once rebuking a member of his faculty at Washington College with the warning, "Sir, if you ever again presume to speak disrespectfully of General Grant in my presence, either you or I will sever his connection with this university." Each man knew well that to the nation he was either the embodiment of victory or the personification of defeat. There was little Grant or Lee could do to change such perceptions. All that was possible for them was to make the best use of the present moment. History would have to take care of itself.[1]

Grant had chosen not to travel through Richmond in April 1865. He reasoned that his presence "might lead to demonstrations which would only wound the feelings of the residents, and we ought not do anything at such a time which would add to their sorrow." The contemporary historian Edward Pollard wrote that Grant "spared everything that might wound the feelings or imply the humiliation of a vanquished foe."[2]

Instead, the general traveled to Washington, where, anxious to see their children at school in New Jersey, he and Julia turned down an invitation to join the Lincolns for an evening at the theater: the play was *Our American Cousin*; the date, April 14, 1865, only five days after the surrender of Lee's army. Grant later wrote, "It was the darkest day of my life. I did not know what it meant." When he learned that Lincoln had been assassinated, the first American president to meet such a fate, he remembered that his train out of Washington had been approached by an odd stranger who could possibly have been a member of John Wilkes Booth's conspiracy. Grant would always regret his absence at Ford's Theatre that night. He imagined that he might have been able to do something to protect the life of Abraham Lincoln.[3]

Lee traveled to Richmond to rejoin his family. To add to his distress, two of his sons had been reported missing in action: General Custis Lee since the battle of Sayler's Creek and Captain Robert E. Lee, Jr. during the retreat from Petersburg. Rumors of their deaths proved to be false, but the uncertainty of both the domestic and national situations was undoubtedly stressful. A local Baptist minister, William E. Hatcher, happened to see Lee as the general rode into Richmond and he recorded the moment with the sort of emotion that would characterize many postwar accounts of the "Lost Cause": "His steed was bespattered with mud, and his head hung down as if worn by long traveling …. Even in the fleeting moment of his passing by my gate, I was awed by his incomparable dignity …. I fell into violent weeping." Lee was physically and emotionally exhausted and sufficiently depressed to spend long hours in bed or to pace the floor in the family's house on Franklin Street. Months later in Lexington he still "spoke of the Southern people, of their losses, privations, and sufferings, and also of our vain struggle." He told the mother of one of his students, "I cannot sleep, for thinking of it, and often I feel so weighted down with sorrow that I have to get up in the night and go out and walk till I thoroughly weary myself before I can sleep." His only comfort was in having fulfilled what he perceived to be his obligation. He later told former general Wade Hampton, "I did only what my duty demanded. I could have taken no other course without dishonor. And if all were to be done over again, I should act in precisely the same manner." His certainty in the correctness of his choice was undiminished.[4]

As much as Lee disliked the public spotlight, particularly in the days after the humiliation of his defeat, he agreed to sit for photographer Mathew Brady and to answer the questions of some northern newspaper reporters. Brady later wrote, "It was supposed that after his defeat it would be preposterous to ask him to sit, but I thought that to be the time for the historical picture." Lee responded, "It is utterly impossible, Mister Brady. How can I sit for a photograph with the eyes of the world upon me as they are today?" Brady then asked a prominent Richmonder, Judge Robert Ould, to speak to Mary Custis Lee, who interceded. In many of the resulting photographs (such as fig. 182), Lee "looked exceedingly robust." One northern correspondent rated him "certainly a most splendid specimen of a soldier and gentleman." Thomas M. Cook of the *New York Herald* sat down with Lee for a long interview on April 29. The general told him that Lincoln's assassination was "one of the most deplorable [events] that could have occurred. As a crime it was unexampled and beyond execration. It was a crime that no good man could approve from any conceivable motive." During this conversation Lee tried to shift the blame to the North for extending the duration of the war—the South had been "looking for some word or expression of compromise or conciliation" for the past two years. He claimed that slavery "did not lay in the way at

fig. 184.
Amnesty Oath, signed by R. E. Lee, October 2, 1865, National Archives and Records Administration

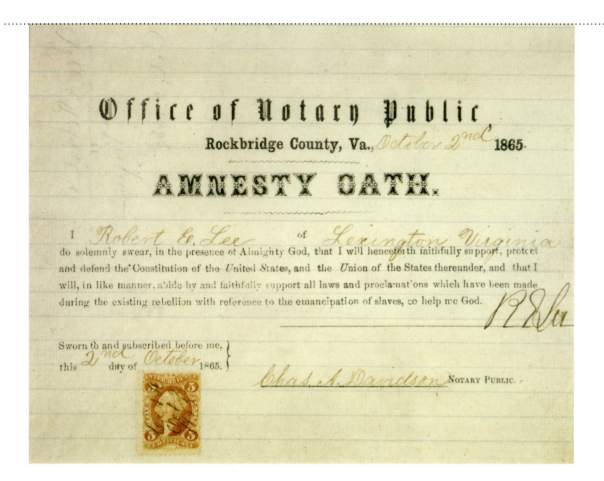

all" because the "best men of the South have long been anxious to do away with this institution." Lee had no answer to the crucial but strangely worded question, "What will you do with the freed people?," perhaps because he did not feel that he had the power to do anything with them. Cook found "most noticeable" the "strange" way that Lee "talked throughout as a citizen of the United States." He had honed in on a problem: the belief held by many southerners that they could somehow continue as U.S. citizens as if the war had never happened. This was unacceptable to many in the North. During the coming year it would incite radical elements to conceive and initiate "Reconstruction," which many southerners perceived to be a punitive policy.[5]

The citizenship issue concerned Lee as it did many other Confederate veterans. Should restoration be sought by the signing of an amnesty oath and the requesting of a pardon? Jefferson Davis swore that he would never seek a pardon; others in the South agreed with Robert Toombs of Georgia, a politician and former Confederate general, who believed that the North had started the war by invasion. He belligerently stated, "Pardon for what? I haven't pardoned youall yet." Initially Lee had no choice but to remain a paroled prisoner of war. On May 29 President Andrew Johnson offered amnesty to most southern soldiers on their taking an oath of allegiance to the Constitution. Confederate officers, political figures, and the wealthy elite (owners of $20,000 of taxable property) were allowed to apply individually. On June 13 Lee took the step that Grant had hoped he would (fig. 184). As he expressed in a May 6 letter to Henry Halleck, Grant thought that "it would have the best possible effect towards restoring good feeling and peace in the South to have him come in. All the people except a few political leaders South will accept what ever he does as right and will be guided to a great extent by his example."[6]

The idea of pardoning Robert E. Lee met with "opposition in the North." Papers there, including *The New York Times*, argued that he should be tried for treason. A federal judge in Norfolk, John C. Underwood, quickly pushed a grand jury to indict Lee and several other former Confederates. Grant immediately wrote to Secretary

fig. 185.
Ulysses S. Grant, Washington, to Robert E. Lee, *Letter*, June 20, 1865, Library of Congress

fig. 186.
E. T. Anthony & Co., *Grand Review of Returning Soldiers at Washington*, May 23–24, 1865 (photograph courtesy of New-York Historical Society Library, George T. Bagoe Collection, gift of Mrs. Elihu Spencer)

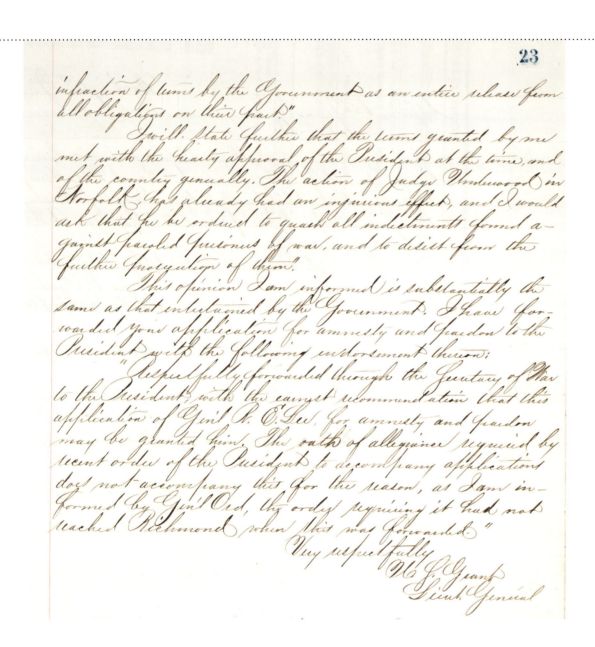

of War Stanton in protest:

> [T]he officers and men paroled at Appomattox C. H … cannot be tried for treason …. [T]he terms granted by me met with the hearty approval of the President at the time …. The action of Judge Underwood in Norfolk, has already had an injurious effect, and I would ask that he be ordered … to desist from … further prosecution.

Grant quoted his comments to Stanton in a letter to Lee (fig. 185), adding, "I have forwarded your application for amnesty and pardon to the President." On the same day, June 20, in a quarterly report to Stanton, Grant further reminded the secretary of Lee's "manly course and bearing shown in his surrender at Appomattox C.H." and of the results of that behavior: "Lee's great influence throughout the whole South caused his example to be followed, and to-day the result is that the Armies lately under his leadership are at their homes desiring peace and quiet, and their Arms are in the hands of our Ordnance officers."[7]

With Andrew Johnson, Grant later remembered, he took a strong, even defiant stand:

> Mr. Johnson had made up his mind to arrest Lee and the leading Southern officers …. I protested again and again. It would come up in the Cabinet, and the only Minister

who supported my views openly was [William] Seward. I always said that the parole of Lee protected him as long as he observed it. On one occasion Mr. Johnson spoke of Lee and wanted to know why any military commander had a right to protect an arch-traitor from the laws. I was angry at this, and I spoke earnestly and plainly to the President … a general commanding troops has certain responsibilities and duties and power, which are supreme. He must deal with the enemy in front of him so as to destroy him. He may either kill him, capture him or parole him. His engagements are sacred so far as they lead to the destruction of the foe. I made certain terms with Lee—the best and only terms. If I had told him and his army that their liberty would be invaded, that they would be open to arrest, trial and execution for treason, Lee would never have surrendered, and we should have lost many lives in destroying him. Now my terms of surrender were according to military law, to the instructions of Mr. Lincoln and Mr. Stanton, and so long as Lee was observing his parole I would never consent to his arrest. Mr. Seward nodded approval. I remember feeling very strongly on this subject. The matter was allowed to die out. I should have resigned the command of the army rather than have carried out any order directing me to arrest Lee or any of his commanders who obeyed the laws.

On this matter Grant would not back down; Johnson ultimately did. Historian Jean Edward Smith argues that if Appomattox was Grant's finest hour, his determination to protect those who surrendered there ranks a close second.[8]

Americans soon learned of the stand that Grant had taken on behalf of Lee. The *Richmond Whig* published a story, "Gen. Lee's Application for Pardon," that was reprinted in other papers, including *The New York Times*, on September 14, 1865. Grant had "responded to Gen. Lee's note promptly, and in the most complimentary and friendly terms, inclosing a letter he had addressed to the relevant officials in Washington in forwarding the petition. Grant made clear his position that under the terms of the surrender, the proceeding at Norfolk was wholly inadmissible."[9]

Grant could not be overruled on the issue of Lee's parole because of his immense popularity as the savior of the nation. After his defeat of the Confederacy, the returning hero was rewarded with parades and receptions in Washington (fig. 186), New York City, Chicago, and Galena. At West Point, the retired Winfield Scott presented Grant with a copy of his memoirs inscribed, "From the Oldest to the Greatest General." Houses were awarded to Grant by citizens' groups in Galena, Philadelphia, and Washington, and he received a check for $105,000 from supporters in New York. Unaccustomed to wealth and still scarred from his prewar financial failures, Grant told himself that he was only accepting the thanks of a grateful people; he rationalized that the largesse came with the territory. Many donors, however, saw Grant as potentially the next president and therefore worthy of cultivation.

Robert E. Lee handled such matters differently. The house built for his use at Washington College was always referred to as the President's House so that all would know that it was awarded to him for his tenure only. When he was presented with potentially lucrative positions that would only require the use of his name, such as the offer of $10,000 a year to act as the titular head of an insurance company, Lee rejected them. He would not capitalize on his celebrity. Also, his father had so soiled the family name with financial embarrassments that he was determined not to repeat such mistakes.[10]

By the end of the summer of 1865, Lee had deduced that the treason indictment against him would not be pursued; three years later, in December 1868, a general amnesty proclamation finally ended the issue. He had taken the amnesty oath on October 2, 1865, the same day he was sworn in as the head of Washington College. Lee correctly anticipated a slow response to his request. In fact, no president of the United States would consider his application for 110 years. In 1975 Gerald Ford signed an act of Congress that restored the general's citizenship. What mattered that fall, however, was that Robert E. Lee had applied for a pardon. That act turned heads everywhere in the nation. Many northerners were angered, but the well-known New York preacher and former abolitionist Henry Ward Beecher, the brother of Harriet Beecher Stowe, issued a strong statement of praise for Lee's stand. Later, the cartoonist Thomas Nast applauded as well (fig. 187). The general explained his reasoning to Captain Josiah Tatnall of Savannah, who worried that his taking the oath would endanger Jefferson Davis. Lee wrote that it is "the duty of every one to unite in the restoration of the country, and the reestablishment of peace and harmony." He added his optimistic belief that if the northern people learned why southerners seceded, they would not "consent to injustice; and it is only necessary in my opinion, that truth should be known, for the rights of every one to be secured."[11]

Having opposed secession before the war, Lee decided to work during the postwar period to restore the Union by preaching submission to authority and promoting political harmony. In a letter of August 1865, Lee made clear his philosophy of cooperation to former Virginia governor John Letcher:

> The interests of the State are therefore the same as those of the United States. Its prosperity will rise or fall with the welfare of the country. The duty of its citizens, then, appears to me too plain to admit of doubt. All should unite in honest efforts to obliterate the effects of war, and to restore the blessings of peace.

He told A. M. Keiley of Petersburg, who had proposed creating a new magazine, that such a journal should strive "to avoid controversy, to allay passion, give full scope to reason and every kindly feeling." Some of Lee's letters addressing the theme of reconciliation made their way into southern newspapers and in that way carried his message far and wide. From Vicksburg, Mississippi, former General Nathaniel H. Harris wrote (fig. 188):

> Your great and wise example of retirement and peace, obedience to government and law we are all pursuing and following …. All your old men here are peacefully at work trying to build up their shattered fortunes, and the Country, its peace and prosperity.

An editor of South Carolina's *Charleston Gazette* reported to Lee that his son was named after the general, "but it was not in the day of your glory and power he was christened—he was born and baptized six months after your dark defeat."[12]

Many Confederate leaders were emigrating to Mexico, Cuba, and Canada, and some even to such remote destinations as England, Brazil, Egypt, Romania, and Korea. Lee, by contrast, denied himself even a brief escape. He told Markie Williams, "there is much to detain me here, & at present at least it is my duty to remain …. There is nothing my dear Markie that I want, except

fig. 187.
Thomas Nast, *"With Malice towards None, with Charity to All,"* 1890, drawing, Stratford Hall

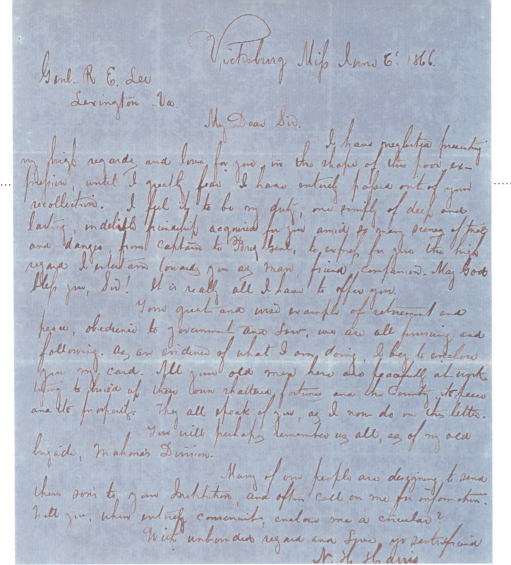

fig. 188.
Nathaniel H. Harris to Robert E. Lee, *Letter*, June 6, 1866, Washington and Lee University

to see you, & nothing that you can do for me, except to think of & love me. It would require you to become a Fairy & turn what you touched to Gold to take me to Europe." To Governor Letcher he maintained that southern citizens "should remain, if possible, in the country." They then could "qualify themselves to vote; and elect to the State and general Legislatures wise and patriotic men, who will devote their abilities to the interests of the country, and the healing of all dissensions." He wrote to Matthew Fontaine Maury in Mexico in terms reminiscent of his prewar patriotism concerning his home state:

> The thought of abandoning the country and all that must be lost in it is abhorrent to my feelings, and I prefer to struggle for its restoration and share its fate, rather than give up all as lost. I have a great admiration for Mexico … but I still look with delight upon the mountains of my native state …. [Virginia] has need for all of her sons, and can ill afford to spare you.

In a letter of October 1865 to P. G. T. Beauregard, Lee praised him for not leaving, adding, "I think the South requires the aid of her sons now more than at any period of her history. As you ask my purpose, I will state that I have not thought of abandoning her unless compelled to do so."[13]

The flight of "many thousands" of former Confederates to Mexico added to the problems that confronted the general-in-chief of the United States Army after Appomattox (fig. 189). During the Civil War, Emperor Maximilian, a puppet of Napoleon III who was supported by a French army of occupation, had provided aid to the Confederacy. Grant wanted to depose his regime and return to power the elected president, Benito Juarez. The general wrote to Secretary of War Stanton about "duty," the Monroe Doctrine, and his desire "to send an armed force to capture these [ex-Confederate] recreants who not only threaten the very existence of that Government but the future peace of our own!" Grant instead settled on a policy of massing forces on the border to pressure the government of Maximilian while providing Juarez with support in the form of munitions, some 60,000 rifles that the general had directed Sheridan to "[get] into the hands of the defenders." Grant advised Johnson, "I would openly sell, on credit, to the Government of Mexico all the arms, Munitions and clothing they want." He added, with his trademark practicality, to Sheridan, "it will be better to go to war now when but little aid given to the Mexicans will settle the question than to have in prospect a greater war, shure to come, if delayed until the Empire is established." Grant's policy was successful; by the summer of 1866 northern Mexico was in the hands of Juarez. Napoleon III withdrew the French army, and the empire of Maximilian collapsed around him. The French Impressionist painter Edouard Manet captured the execution of Maximilian (fig. 190).[14]

In the fall of 1865, Grant was optimistic that a rapid reconciliation of the North and South was possible. He toured the South "to see what changes were necessary to be made in the disposition of the Military forces of the Country … &c. and to learn as far as possible the feelings and intentions of the citizens of these states towards the General Government." Grant wrote to Julia from Richmond that "the citizens … would like to have me remain

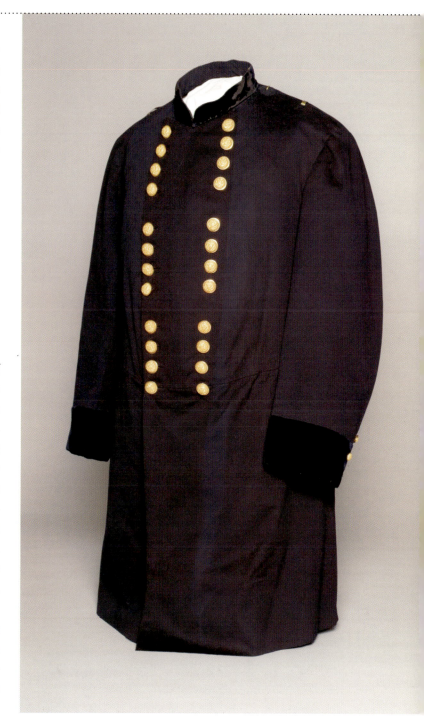

fig. 189.
Uniform of Ulysses S. Grant, post-1865, Civil War and Underground Railroad Museum of Philadelphia

over," from Raleigh that "There seems to be the best of feeling existing and nothing but the greatest desire … to secure admittence back and to please the general Government," and from Savannah that the "People all seem pleasant and at least towards me, and I thinks towards the Government, to enter faithfully upon a course to restore harmony between the sections." He reported to President Johnson:

> I am satisfied that the mass of thinking men of the South accept the present situation of affairs in good faith. The questions which have heretofore divided the sentiment of the people of the two sections, Slavery and States Rights, or the right of a State to secede from the Union, they regard as having been settled forever ….
>
> My observations lead me to the conclusion that the citizens of the Southern states are anxious to return to self government, within the Union, as soon as possible.

Grant added an ominous note to Johnson that predicted one of the problems that lay ahead: "the freedmen require for a few years not only laws to protect them, but the fostering care of those who will give them good counsel." Grant's relationship with the president had warmed; Johnson's belief that the rebel states never left the Union and thus their representatives should immediately return to their seats in Congress meshed with the general's beliefs about reconciliation. But the president, a southerner from Tennessee and a staunch racist, cared nothing for the black man and saw Reconstruction only as a means to break the slaveholding aristocracy of the Old South. A collision with a Republican Congress that was interested in the welfare of the freedman was inevitable. Grant knew which side he would take in such a confrontation.[15]

Lee was in some ways more optimistic, and more naïve, about reconciliation than was his former adversary. In looking for a quick restoration of the Union, he urged his compatriots to forgive and forget so that the pre-1861 Union might somehow be brought back. When ex-Confederates like Jubal Early expressed their bitterness, Lee urged patience: "controversy, I think, will only serve to prolong angry and bitter feelings, and postpone the period when reason and charity may resume their sway." He told Early to "Omit all epithets or remarks calculated to excite bitterness or animosity" in the North. He advised a Confederate widow, "Madam, do not train up your children in hostility to the government of the United States. Remember, we are all one country now. Dismiss from your mind all sectional feeling, and bring them up to be Americans." The first adherents to the Lee cult delighted in such lore, particularly in recounting stories about the general preaching forgiveness to clergymen. "[L]eave out all the bitter expressions against the

fig. 190.
Edouard Manet, *Execution of the Emperor Maximilian*, 1867, oil on canvas, 76 × 111 ⅘ in. (193.0 × 284.0 cm.), National Gallery, London

North and the United States government. They will do us no good," he told a minister. He reminded another that "there is a good old book which I read and you preach from, which says, 'Love your enemies.' … I have fought against the people of the North because I believed they were seeking to wrest from the South her dearest rights. But I have never cherished toward them bitter or vindictive feelings, and have never seen the day when I did not pray for them." To the historian Edward A. Pollard, author of *The Lost Cause, A New Southern History of the War of the Confederates* (1866), Lee wrote, "I have felt so little desire to recall the events of the war that I have not read a single work that has been published on the subject." To those who would memorialize a battlefield, Lee argued, "I think it wiser moreover not to keep open the sores of war, but to follow the example of those nations who endeavored to obliterate the marks of civil strife and to commit to oblivion the feelings it engendered." About his own exploits, he stated to David Macrae,

fig. 191.
Derwent, Cumberland County, post-1865 (photograph courtesy of Virginia Historical Society)

"My own life has been written, but I have not looked into it …. I do not wish to awaken memories of the past." Most Americans, however, could not forget; the late Civil War would cloud the political scene for the remaining years of his life.[16]

In the summer of 1865 Lee was in a difficult situation. The army life that he had known for almost forty years was over. He owned no home. He was not sufficiently wealthy to retire. Lee held a few bonds in the Erie Railroad that still retained their value, but what holdings he had in the Chesapeake and Ohio Canal Company would not provide an income and his Confederate and Carolina bonds were worthless. He thought first of farming: "Agriculture … seems to offer the only pursuit for obtaining a living," he told R. H. Chilton. He wrote to General A. L. Long, "I am looking for some little quiet house in the woods where I can procure shelter and my daily bread if permitted by the victor. I wish to get Mrs. Lee out of the city." An offer soon came from a wealthy widow west of Richmond, Mrs. Elizabeth Randolph Cocke, whose estate Oakland in Powhatan County contained a vacant overseer's house called Derwent (fig. 191). The Lees traveled there at the end of June. This setting allowed Lee some privacy, but its isolation and the crudeness of the accommodations discouraged his daughters. Fortunately for Mildred, then age nineteen, who wrote to a friend that her "heart & hopes [had] been withered" at Derwent, a better offer came at the end of the summer.[17]

The oldest Lee daughter, Mary, had told acquaintances that southerners were offering her father material gifts of all kinds but not a position that would allow him to work to support his family. Mary Custis Lee later referred to her husband's interest in finding "honorable support." That came, unexpectedly, from John W. Brockenbrough, the rector of Washington College in Lexington, Virginia, who offered Lee the presidency of that institution (fig. 192). He appealed to the general's sense of purpose, his virtue, and his religion. At the college Lee could "make [himself] useful to the state" and "guide [its] youth in the paths of virtue …. Knowledge & religion, not more by precept than your great example—these my dear General are objects worthy of your ambition and we desire to present you the means of their accomplishment." A note from one of Lee's former artillery generals, William Nelson Pendleton, then the rector of Grace Episcopal Church on the edge of the Washington College campus, similarly appealed to Lee's "views of duty" and recognition that "the destiny of our State & country depends so greatly upon the training of our young men." Lee had passed on offers from the University of Virginia and the University of the South, but the Lexington college was named for and associated with George Washington. Brockenbrough's offer was too good to turn down.[18]

Southerners went to the polls in the fall of 1865 and elected to the national Congress many of their prewar leaders. Four former Confederate generals and eight colonels were among those who appeared in Washington in December to take their seats. Instead, a furor erupted; their names had been omitted from the rolls, and a Joint Committee on Reconstruction was established to determine whether the rebel states were "entitled to be represented in either house of congress." Grant at that time had just completed his tour of the South that had been undertaken to "learn … the feelings and intentions" of southerners towards the federal government. The Republicans on the committee had not seen the death and suffering that the general had witnessed both during and after the war, and like many northerners they had been infuriated by the assassination of Lincoln. They were outraged to find former Confederates in their assembly when they convened, and annoyed by the policy of leniency to the South that was proposed by President Johnson, who was willing to forget the trials of the war and allow life to return as before. This would have meant putting little effort into the welfare of the freedpeople: "This country is for white men,

fig. 192.
Original Washington College Buildings, on the front campus of Washington and Lee University, photograph by Patrick Hinely

and by God, as long as I am President, it shall be governed by white men …." Congress and the president soon began to lock horns, and the inferno of Reconstruction began.[19]

The Reconstruction Committee quickly called hearings, to which Lee was summoned in February 1866 (fig. 193). Only six years earlier he had mounted the steps of the Capitol to testify regarding the John Brown insurrection. This second appearance was no doubt scheduled in part to humble the former Confederate commander, but it was also to learn the thinking of a man whose importance in the postwar nation was already apparent. Several Virginia witnesses before the committee, including Judge Underwood and the staunch Unionist John Minor Botts, had mentioned Lee in their testimony, and Colonel Orlando Brown of the Freedmen's Bureau had stated that "no man has more fully the hearts of a people than he has the hearts of Virginians." The committee had been split into four groups to investigate more fully the

different sections of the South; Virginia and the Carolinas were the purview of the subcommittee headed by senators Jacob T. Howard of Michigan and Henry T. Blow of Missouri.

Lee's testimony lasted for two hours. A few of the questions put to him were perhaps unexpected, such as those about the treatment of both northern prisoners in Confederate prisons and northern entrepreneurs in the postwar South, as well as questions about the payment of taxes with respect to both the national and Confederate debts. Lee claimed little knowledge about any of those subjects. The two senators then spent most of the time on two issues: the current sentiment in the South regarding the federal government and the attitude of the southern people toward the freedman.[20]

The senators asked about southern loyalty to the government in Washington. The general answered, "I do not know of a single person who either feels or contemplates any resistance to the government of the United States." He added that "I have heard persons … express great confidence in the wisdom of [President Johnson's] policy of restoration" as the quickest way for the government to regain the good opinion of southerners. Lee held that there was no impetus in the South to renew the war, and that, should there be a war between the United States and a foreign power, the South would not attempt to use such a conflict to again secede. On the subject of Jefferson Davis, Lee stated:

> I think it very probable that Southerners would not consider he had committed treason …. [T]hey look upon the action of the state, in withdrawing itself from the government of the United States, as carrying the individuals of the state along with it; that the state was responsible for the act, not the individual …. That was my view, that the act of Virginia in withdrawing herself from the United States carried me along as a citizen of Virginia, and that her laws and her acts were binding on me.

He concluded that politicians were largely to blame for the conflict, which "might have been avoided if forbearance and wisdom had been practiced on both sides."

Jacob Howard then pivoted to the issue of the freedpeople. Lee held that "Every one with whom I associate expresses kind feelings towards the freedmen. They wish to see them get on in the world, and particularly to take up some occupation for a living and to turn their hands to some work. I know that efforts have been made among the farmers, near where I live, to induce them to engage for the year at regular wages." In many of his statements, Lee reflected widely held opinions of the day. He felt that blacks should be educated because he had "had servants … who learned to read and write very well," but he thought that African Americans did not have a capacity equal to whites for acquiring knowledge. In his experience, black people "look more to the present time than to the future …. They are an amiable, social race. They like their ease and

fig. 193.
Alexander Gardner, *Robert E. Lee*, 1866 (photograph courtesy of Virginia Historical Society)

comfort …." On the question of voting rights, Lee thought that many southerners would object unless "these persons will vote properly and understandingly," adding that "My own opinion is that, at this time, they cannot vote intelligently, and that giving them the right of suffrage would lead to a great deal of demagogism, and lead to embarrassments in various ways. What the future may prove, how intelligent they may become, with what eyes they may look upon the interests of the state in which they may reside, I cannot say more than you can." In summation, he stated of the freedpeople that "I think it would be better for Virginia if she could get rid of them. That is no new opinion with me. I have always thought so, and have always been in favor of emancipation—gradual emancipation."[21]

The views expressed here by Lee about black people were not new; they were generally consistent with statements he had been making for years. Shortly after Appomattox, he had advised his cousin Thomas H. Carter of the Virginia Tidewater to hire white workers: "I have always observed that wherever you find the Negro, everything is going down around him, and wherever you find the white man, you see everything around him improving." Yet in that same summer of 1865, Lee knelt near a black man at St. Paul's Church in Richmond in order to mitigate a crisis that was about to unfold concerning the possibility of blacks sharing in the communion. Lee would accept the new order because he felt it was his duty, but he would keep many of his old opinions, as would many white southerners.[22]

Lee's entire Congressional testimony was published verbatim. The general had become the most visible spokesman for the South. After his visit to Washington, Lee increasingly took a stance on national issues, and his views often proved to be influential. The man who had virtually nothing to say about the constitutionality of secession in 1861 now issued opinions about the relationship of the federal government to the states, about racial issues, about his support of President Johnson, and about his optimism for the future of the South. Lee promoted reconciliation and peace. His was the voice not of a bitter and unreconstructed rebel, but of an American resident in the South who wanted the Union restored. He wrote in January 1866 to Chauncey Burr, "All that the South has ever desired was that the Union, as established by our forefathers, should be preserved, and the government as originally organised should be administered in purity and truth." To James May he argued in July 1866, "I had no other guide, nor had I any other object, than the defense of those principles of American liberty upon which the Constitutions of the several States were originally founded; and unless they are strictly observed, I fear there will be an end to Republican Government in this country." Three years later, in a letter written to his nephew Edward Lee Childe, he placed the blame for the "end to Republican Government" on the Republican Party: "It was not the form of government that was at fault, but its administration: not the constitution but the people. The former was too pure for the latter. It requires a virtuous people to support a republican government & the world has not yet reached the proper standard for morality & integrity to live under the rule of religion & reason." Lord Acton, a British historian, stated to Lee, "I deemed that you were fighting the battles of our liberty, our progress, and our civilization; and I mourn for the stake which was lost at Richmond more deeply than I rejoice over that which was saved at Waterloo." Lee responded, "If, therefore, the result of the war is to be considered as having decided that the union of the states is inviolable and perpetual under the constitution, … the existence and rights of a state by the constitution are as indestructible as the union itself." He told others that if the rights of the states, which include the liberty of the individual, were respected, then southerners would readily pledge allegiance to the Union. To George Jones he wrote in 1869, "[If the] constitution & the Union established by our forefathers [are] restored, there will be no truer supporters of that union & that constitution than the Southern people."[23]

The guarded exchanges between Lee and senators Howard and Blow regarding the policies of Andrew Johnson reflected the split that was opening between the president and the Congress. In that same month, February 1866, Congress passed a civil rights bill to protect the freedpeople from discriminatory legislation enacted by the former Confederate states; it also attempted to extend the life of the Freedmen's Bureau. Johnson vetoed both measures. The veto of the civil rights act was in turn overridden, the first override in American history for a major piece of legislation. Congress then passed the Fourteenth Amendment and extended the Freedmen's Bureau for two years. The new amendment granted citizenship to "all persons," including blacks, thereby protecting their life, liberty, and property by "due process of law" and guaranteeing "equal protection of the laws." This amendment also barred ex-Confederates from holding office. The plan being formulated by Congress was to force the former Confederate states to accept the enfranchisement of blacks as a condition of re-admission to the Union. Johnson so opposed the idea that he made it the focal point of the upcoming fall elections. Many white southerners in the cotton states reacted violently. Unrest in Alabama and Mississippi was exceeded by several days of rioting in Memphis and New Orleans. Lee blamed the problems on "the Radical party." In May he told the Marquess of Lorne, later the ninth duke of Argyll, "They are working as though they wished to keep alive by their proposals in Congress the bad blood in the South against the North." President Johnson, he thought "has been doing much to strengthen the feeling in favor of the Union among us." "If left alone," he added, "the hostility which must be felt after such a war would rapidly decrease."[24]

By the summer of 1866 matters had worsened. In July Grant issued his General Orders No. 44 to the military. Commanders in the South were directed "to arrest all persons who have been or may hereafter be charged with the commission of crimes … in cases where the civil authorities have failed, neglected, or are unable to arrest and bring such parties to trial; and to detain them in military confinement." Nast ridiculed Andrew Johnson for his poor handling of the crisis (fig. 194). Grant, now promoted to full general, another rank held only by George Washington, was obliged to tour with Johnson. He quickly lost respect for the president; in September in St. Louis, he wrote to Julia, "I never have been so tired of anything before as I have been with the political stump speeches of Mr. Johnson from Washington to this place. I look upon them as a National disgrace." He feared that "the unfortunate differences between the President and Congress" might become so violent as to spark more uprisings in the South, and he so warned his commanders to take care "that no armed headway can be made against the Union." Voters in the fall responded to Johnson's resistance to the Fourteenth Amendment by awarding the Republicans a landslide victory: 128 seats to 33 for the Democrats. Grant told a reporter for *The New York Times* that "if the Southern States had accepted the [Fourteenth] Amendment instead of rejecting it so hastily, they would have been admitted by Congress in December, but now I think they will have to take the Amendment, and manhood suffrage besides. Congress will insist on this." Grant urged the president to seek compromise and conciliation, but to no avail. Johnson's belligerent behavior and his disregard for the freedpeople, coupled with Grant's concern for his troops in the field, gradually pushed the general away.[25]

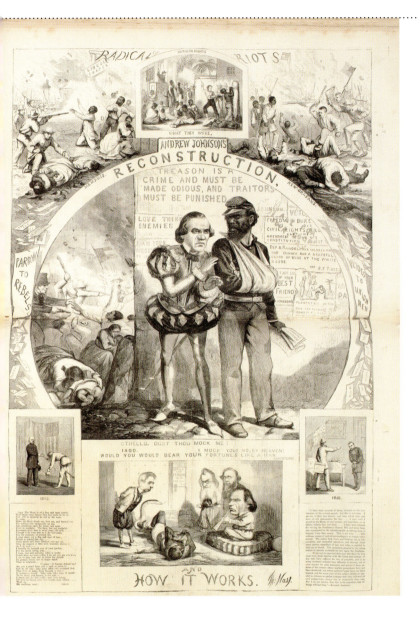

fig. 194.
Thomas Nast, *Andrew Johnson's Reconstruction and How It Works*, woodcut, *Harper's Weekly*, September 1, 1866, New-York Historical Society Library

In January 1867, the gap widened between the president and the congressional Radicals. Most southerners, including Lee, were on the side of the former; Grant was on the side of the latter. On the 7th, Congress passed a resolution that directed the House Judiciary Committee to determine if the president could be tried for "high crimes and misdemeanors," a proposal that was suspect given that Johnson's worst offense was his pursuit of a policy that was lenient towards white southerners. During the same month, Virginians rallied behind their former military leader as a candidate for governor in the hope that Johnson would be allowed by Congress to permit elections. Knowing that Lee's father had been governor of the state, Judge Robert Ould wrote to determine if the general would accept the nomination. Lee thoughtfully declined:

> I feel greatly honored at what you say is the prevailing wish of leading men in the State, that I should accept the nomination for the office of Governor of Virginia …. I candidly confess, however, that my feelings induce me to prefer private life ….
>
> I believe [my election as Governor] would be used by the dominant party to excite hostility towards the State, and to injure the people in the eyes of the country; and I therefore cannot consent to become the instrument of bringing distress upon those whose prosperity and happiness are so dear to me.

Also, the Fourteenth Amendment had banned ex-Confederates from holding public office. Lee acknowledged this in a letter two weeks later to David S. G. Cabell: "As regards my name for the next Governor, that has been finally settled by the late Bill of Congress."[26]

The Congress elected in 1866 by tradition would not have opened its session until a year later, December 1867. But its members saw themselves as on a mission to rectify the crisis of an unreconstructed South, and so they assembled on March 4, the day after the expiration of the term of the lame duck 39th Congress. Angered by the refusal of southern legislatures to ratify the Fourteenth Amendment, they passed a series of Reconstruction Acts that reduced the rebel states to little more than conquered provinces. In the eyes of the Radical Congress, the existing state governments in the South were broken beyond repair: they had brought about secession, they now were filled with ex-Confederates, and they had failed to ratify the Fourteenth Amendment. The solution was to eliminate them and start from scratch. Accordingly, each state was directed to assemble a convention that would draft a new constitution. The delegates had to be chosen by an electorate that included black voters The new constitutions had to grant black males the right to vote at a time when most northern states did not. They then had to be ratified by the voters; and the conventions had to appoint legislatures that were required to ratify the Fourteenth Amendment. On the completion of all of those requirements, each southern state could apply to rejoin the Union and enjoy representation in the national Congress.[27]

Until the new legislatures were established and functioning, the states would simply cease to be. In the words of the First Recon-

fig. 195.
Thomas Nast, *If He Is a Union Man or Freedman, Verdict, "Hang the D____ Yankee and Nigger," Harper's Weekly*, March 23, 1867

IF HE IS A UNION MAN OR A FREEDMAN.

"VERDICT", HANG THE D— YANKEE AND NIGGER."

general-in-chief for guidance, and so Grant became immersed in the process of Reconstruction. He was compelled to make difficult decisions on such civil matters as interpretations of the law, determinations of voter eligibility, and the verification of election procedures. In effect, he was given the enormous responsibility of making the policy of Radical Reconstruction work.[28]

Passage and enforcement of the Reconstruction Acts inevitably increased bitterness and racial violence in the South. By May 1867, the violence, particularly in Memphis, north Mississippi, and New Orleans, had escalated to the point that Grant felt compelled to assure Philip Sheridan that he approved of the stern actions taken by that district's commander, and by July to direct George Thomas to Memphis to "vigorously" use military force "to preserve order on election day and not to wait until people are killed and the mob beyond control before interfering." Thomas Nast ridiculed the violence and disorder (fig. 6.14). The bitter feeling in the South was recorded by Mary Lee in letters to her friend, Mrs. R. H. Chilton. In March she wrote, "The country that allows such scum [the Radicals in Congress] to rule them must be fast going to destruction and we shall care little if we are not involved in the crash."[29]

Robert E. Lee made clear his feelings about the conventions: "I think all persons entitled to vote should attend the polls & endeavour to elect the best available men to represent them in the convention, to whose decision every one should submit. The preservation of harmony & kind feelings is of the utmost importance." To General Dabney H. Maury, who was living in New Orleans, one of the hotbeds of violence, Lee stated, "The question then is shall the members of the convention be selected from the best available men in the state, or from the worst, and shall the machinery of the state government be arranged and set in motion

struction Act, "Whereas, no legal state governments exist … said rebel States shall be divided into five military districts." Virginia became Military District No. 1, under the rule of Major General John M. Schofield. The district commanders were given dictatorial powers. An additional act compelled each commander to devise and implement the means and schedules for the new constitutions to be drafted and the new legislatures to be formed. A third act empowered the commanders to remove and replace civil officials who did not comply. The commanders inevitably looked to their

fig. 196.
Robert E. Lee, Lexington, to General
Dabney H. Maury, New Orleans, *Letter*,
May 23, 1867, Virginia Historical Society

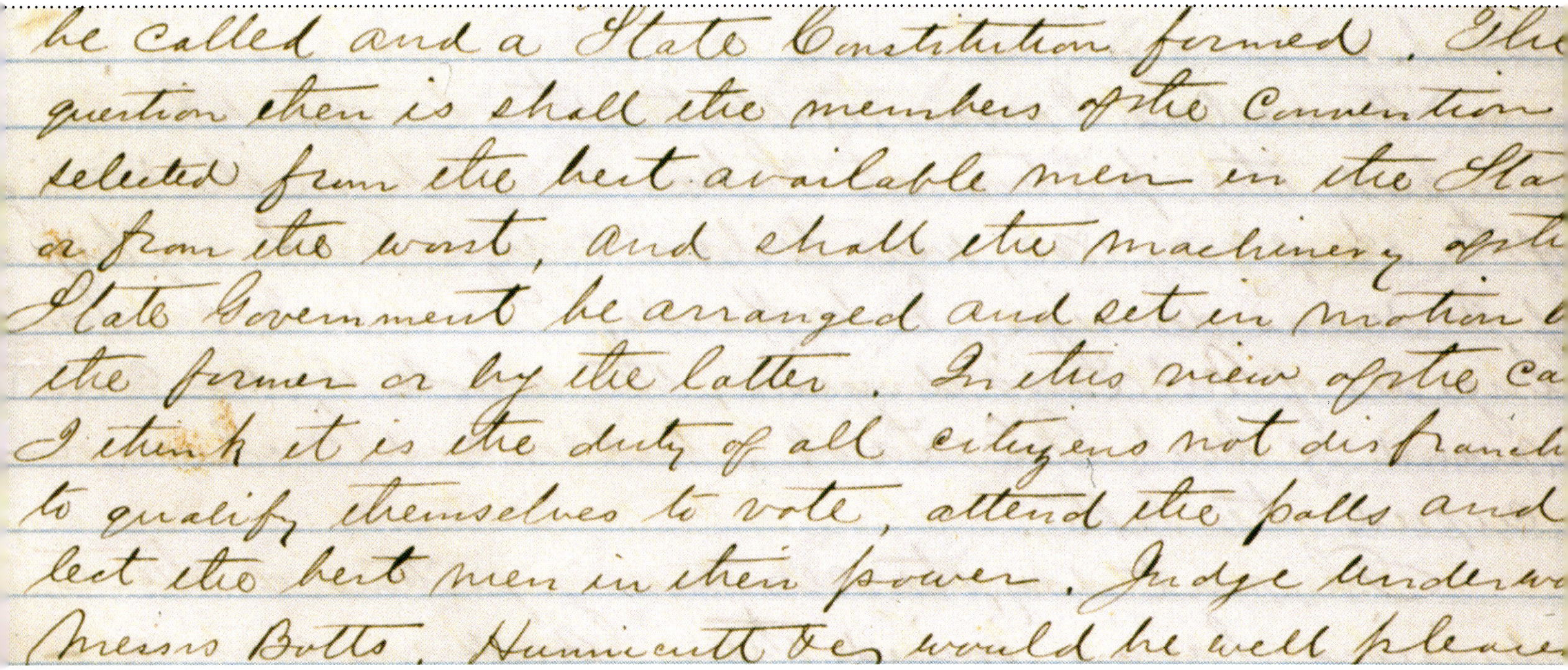

by the former or by the latter …. I think it is the duty of all citizens not disfranchised to qualify themselves to vote, attend the polls and select the best men in their power" (fig. 196). The contents of one of the spring letters appeared in both the *Richmond Dispatch* and *The New York Times* on March 23 (fig. 197) with the comment: "He thinks it is the duty of the people to *accept the situation* fully, … and that every man not actually disfranchised should not only take the necessary steps to prepare himself to vote, but to prepare his friends, *white and colored*, to vote, and to vote rightly …, and that our chief object should be to get as quickly and as quietly as possible back into the Union." The general remained optimistic; he wrote to his son Rooney in June, "Although the future is still dark, and the prospects gloomy, I am confident that, if we all unite in doing our duty, and earnestly work to extract what good we can out of the evil that now hangs over our dear land, the time is not distant when the angry cloud will be lifted from our horizon and the sun in his pristine brightness again shine forth."[30]

In his third annual message to Congress, Andrew Johnson made clear his white supremacist policy for the postwar South. In February 1868, when he tried for a second time to oust from office Edwin Stanton, the secretary of war who opposed his efforts to rescue southerners from "Negro rule," impeachment proceedings, which had been threatened a year earlier, were triggered. The House charged the president with failure to enforce the Reconstruction acts. Grant, who also opposed Johnson's policy, was pushed into the fray with Stanton. The president accused Grant of dishonesty, thereby provoking a battle that Johnson was doomed to lose. The public and press eagerly rallied behind the general, while the Radical Republicans were overjoyed to find a new champion for their cause. Grant was so disgusted with Johnson that he fired back:

> And now, Mr. President, where my honor as a soldier and integrity as a man have been so violently assailed, pardon me for saying that I can but regard this whole matter, from the beginning to the end, as an attempt to involve me in the resistance of law, for which you hesitated to assume the responsibility in orders, and thus to destroy my character before the country …. With assurances, Mr. President, that nothing less than a vindication of my personal honor and character could have induced this correspondence on my part.

The phrasing at the end is parallel to Lee's famous explanation for his becoming a Confederate, "I could have followed no other course without dishonor." In May, the impeachment of Johnson failed in the Senate by only one vote on each of three charges. In the process of battling with Johnson, Grant, the champion of both the people and the Congress, had become the obvious choice to be

fig. 197.
"General Lee—The Convention," *Richmond Dispatch*, March 23, 1867

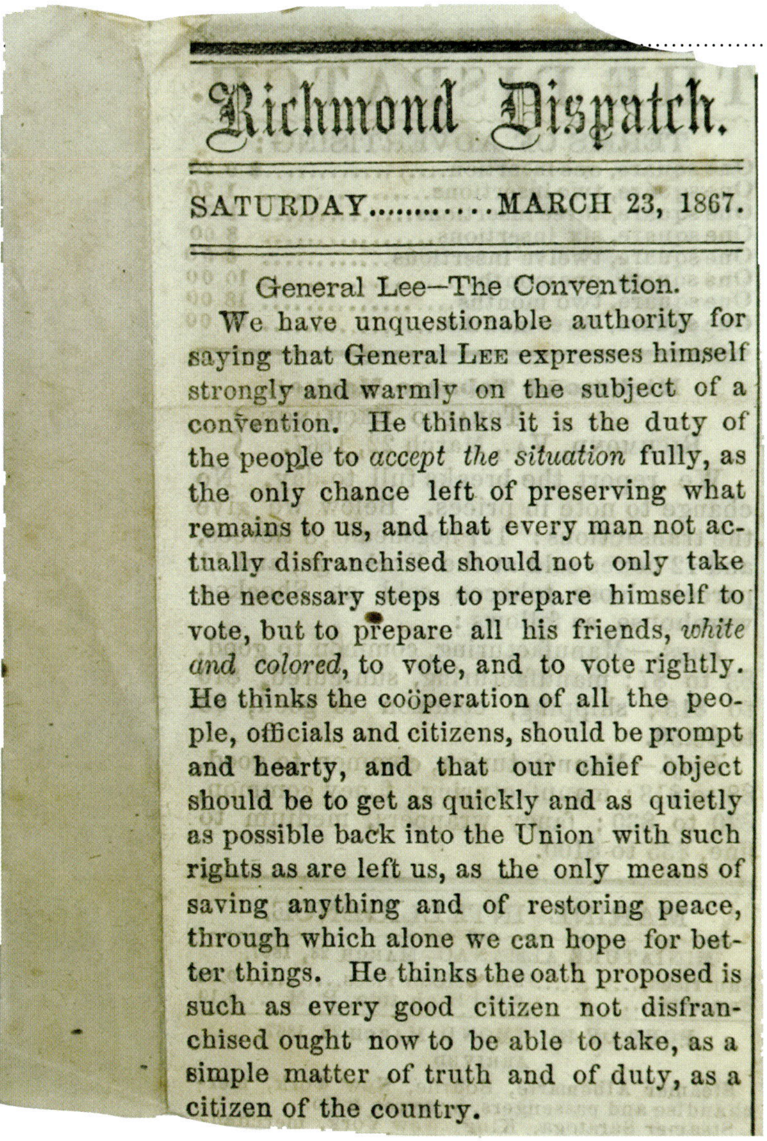

Richmond Dispatch.

SATURDAY............MARCH 23, 1867.

General Lee—The Convention.

We have unquestionable authority for saying that General LEE expresses himself strongly and warmly on the subject of a convention. He thinks it is the duty of the people to *accept the situation* fully, as the only chance left of preserving what remains to us, and that every man not actually disfranchised should not only take the necessary steps to prepare himself to vote, but to prepare all his friends, *white and colored*, to vote, and to vote rightly. He thinks the coöperation of all the people, officials and citizens, should be prompt and hearty, and that our chief object should be to get as quickly and as quietly as possible back into the Union with such rights as are left us, as the only means of saving anything and of restoring peace, through which alone we can hope for better things. He thinks the oath proposed is such as every good citizen not disfranchised ought now to be able to take, as a simple matter of truth and of duty, as a citizen of the country.

the Republican candidate in the upcoming presidential election.[31]

Lee's activities often attracted the attention of the northern press. Most had to do with his attempts to facilitate reconciliation. One story involved Erastus C. Johnston, a Union veteran whose attempts to establish a school for freedpeople in Rockbridge County was sponsored by the American Missionary Association. One day, on the North River while skating, Johnston provoked an incident with local Washington College students and other youths. Some of the students, especially the veterans, were in general prone to troublemaking, but in this instance they were outdone by Johnston, who pulled a gun on a twelve-year-old boy. Lee promptly ordered two of the students involved in the confrontation to withdraw from the college and a third left on his own. General O. B. Willcox, in command of the sub-district of Lynchburg, investigated the incident, only to report that Lee had satisfactorily resolved it. "A Resident of Lexington" wrote to *The Independent* in defense of Erastus Johnston that the professors and students of Washington College are "thoroughly rebel in sentiment," but the great majority of the published letters, which were so numerous that they prolonged the incident for two-and-a-half months, were delivered in support of both Lee and Willcox. A Captain Lacey wrote to *The New York Tribune* "to exonerate General Lee" and to praise the president of Washington College for his contribution to "the cause of education, so essential to the welfare of the south." Lacey assured his readers that Willcox "is not the man to slight his duty" and that Lexington "is as quiet as any college town in the United States."[32]

Lee must have been encouraged by the outpouring of public support for southern education that was offered at a rally in New York City in May 1868. More than thirty prominent citizens, brought together by the minister E. P. Walton, enthusiastically endorsed the fundraising efforts then being undertaken by Washington College, and they enticed some 500 people to attend a mass meeting at which letters were read and speeches delivered. The event was covered by both the *New York Tribune* and *The New York Times* (fig. 198). Governor R. E. Fenton "sympathized" with the effort of furthering education. Gerrit Smith argued that the North had been a "fellow-sinner" in the enslavement of humans— "England cursed us both with Slavery"—but all of that was finally over: "Now it only remains for us to forgive each other, to love each other, and to do all the good we can to each other. So shall we become a united people; and, profiting by our great mistakes in the past, we shall enter upon a new and happy national life." Lee's promotion of goodwill in Lexington had been noticed. Professor Roswell Dwight Hitchcock of the New York Union Theological Seminary told the audience that at Appomattox, Lee had "behaved himself as a gentleman and a Christian" and that "since the war he had acted the part of the gentleman, the patriot, and the scholar, sedulously keeping himself secluded from the public gaze …." The famed preacher Henry Ward Beecher closed the meeting with the strongest of all the endorsements. He supported Washington College because it is in Virginia and because Lee was its president. No one regretted more than he did the course that Lee had taken in 1861. With wisdom that was remarkable given the time and

fig. 198.
"Education in the South; Meeting at Cooper Institute in Behalf of Washington College, Virginia," *The New York Times*, March 3, 1868

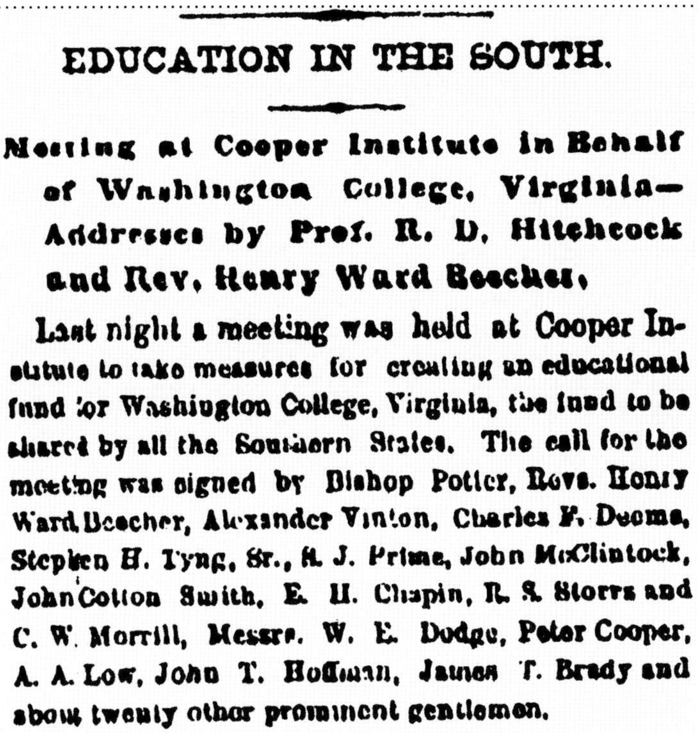

EDUCATION IN THE SOUTH.

Meeting at Cooper Institute in Behalf of Washington College, Virginia— Addresses by Prof. R. D. Hitchcock and Rev. Henry Ward Beecher.

Last night a meeting was held at Cooper Institute to take measures for creating an educational fund for Washington College, Virginia, the fund to be shared by all the Southern States. The call for the meeting was signed by Bishop Potter, Revs. Henry Ward Beecher, Alexander Vinton, Charles F. Deems, Stephen H. Tyng, Sr., R. J. Prime, John McClintock, John Cotton Smith, E. H. Chapin, R. S. Storrs and C. W. Morrill, Messrs. W. E. Dodge, Peter Cooper, A. A. Low, John T. Hoffman, James T. Brady and about twenty other prominent gentlemen.

place, Beecher said that if he had been born in Virginia and brought up amid her institutions, he might have done the same thing. Whatever his past errors, Lee had since devoted himself to the sacred cause of education, instilling patriotism and love of country in the minds and hearts of his students. Some $4,300 was raised by Walton's effort, including $1,000 from Beecher.[33]

The praise lavished on Lee by Hitchcock and Beecher provoked an angry backlash among those who sympathized with the Radicals in Washington. The *New York Independent* published an article on March 12 entitled "Education at the South" that blasted the sentiments toward reconciliation and forgiveness that had been sounded so boldly at the Cooper Institute:

> We do not think that a man who broke his solemn oath of allegiance to the United States, who imbrued his hands in the blood of tens of thousands of his country's noblest men, for the purpose of perpetuating human slavery, and who was largely responsible for the cruelties and horrors of Libby, Salisbury and Andersonville, is fitted to be a teacher of young men ….
>
> We wish to be assured, moveover, before contributing money to Gen. Lee's college, or any other similar institution at the South, that it does not tolerate the hell-born spirit of caste, by turning from its doors students of a dark complexion.

In the same paper appeared an article by the famed abolitionist William Lloyd Garrison, who wrote with bitterness:

> What of the patriotism of General Lee or Washington College? Is the vanquished leader of the rebel armies now a patriot, or disposed to teach the rebel sons of rebel parents lessons of patriotism? … Who is more dumb, or, apparently, more obdurate than himself? *He* at the head of a patriotic institution, teaching loyalty to the Constitution, and the duty of maintaining that Union which he so lately attempted to destroy![34]

The publicity given to the Cooper Institute rally and its backlash may have been what sparked Julia Anne Shearman, a northern schoolteacher who had come to Lexington in 1865 to help with the education of the freedpeople, to write in April 1868 to the *New York Independent* that she was regularly "insult[ed by] the students of Washington College," who would gawk at her as a "Yankee" and force her off the walkways "into the mud." She considered Lee to be a gentleman (this "being confirmed by his external deportment"), and so she had written to him: "I claimed the right to be treated as [a lady]," but "I received no reply." Whether or not Lee answered Miss Shearman is unknown. The claim of this one disgruntled schoolteacher, however, was insignificant in the broader picture. The peacemakers had advanced their cause. Sympathy and unity were beginning to win out over bitterness.[35]

In the summer of 1868, on the grounds that in the coming presidential election only another military figure would be able to defeat the immensely popular Grant, the *New York Herald* recommended that Lee be selected as the Democratic nominee. Lee was revered in the South and had always enjoyed support in the North. Three years earlier, in June 1865, *The New York Times* had reported that "in spite of his manifest treason, Gen. Lee has retained a strong hold upon Northern regard" and that "he had held … a sort of deified position" in the North. In 1867 in Poughkeepsie, New York, a "Lee Association" had been formed by young admirers at the Eastman Business College. Interestingly, the myth that the southern general was a better soldier than Grant was already enough in circulation by 1868 for the *Herald* to utilize it:

> But if the Democratic Committee must nominate a soldier—if it must have a name identified with the glories of

fig. 199.
Attributed to Boude and Miley, *Notables at White Sulphur Springs, West Virginia*, 1869 (photograph courtesy of Virginia Historical Society); seated, left to right, are Blacque Bey, Lee, George Peabody, W. W. Corcoran, and James Lyons. Standing, left to right, are Martin W. Gary, John B. Magruder, Robert D. Lilley, P. G. T. Beauregard, Alexander R. Lawton, Henry A. Wise, Joseph L. Brent, and James Conner

the war—we will recommend a candidate for its favors. Let it nominate General R. E. Lee. Let it boldly take over the best of all its soldier, making no palaver or apology …. He is one in whom the military genius of this nation finds its fullest development …. [T]his soldier … baffled our greater Northern armies for four years; and when opposed by Grant was only worn down by that solid strategy of stupidity that accomplishes its object by mere weight …. It is certain that with half as many men as Grant he would have beaten him from the field in Virginia, and he affords the best promise of any soldier for beating him again.[36]

Lee, of course, was not allowed by law to run for office. However, he strongly supported the Democratic Party because it was sympathetic to the efforts of white southerners to maintain the status quo. He soon found another way to attempt to contribute to the political defeat of his old adversary. Republican strategists argued that if Americans were to elect the newly chosen Democratic candidates for president and vice president, Horatio Seymour and Francis P. Blair, Jr., they would in effect undo the victory that had been won at such great sacrifice by the Union armies because the South remained uncommitted both to the Union and to the rights of the freedpeople. Those claims, it was thought, might be negated if Lee would make a statement about national unity and human justice. The Democratic strategist who conceived this scheme was the former Union general William Rosecrans, whom Grant had humiliated at Chattanooga. In August 1868, Rosecrans found Lee summering at White Sulphur Springs, now in West Virginia. (A year later Lee would be photographed there with a group of prominent northerners and southerners, fig. 199.) Feeling a duty to seize this opportunity to both further good relations with the people of the North, many of whom were themselves conflicted on racial issues, and to aid the Democratic Party, Lee accepted this challenge. He told Rosecrans to talk as well to other former Confederates who were present. Such figures as Alexander Stephens and P. G. T. Beauregard were among a group of thirty-one who convened at Lee's cottage to converse with Rosecrans and to sign a letter that had been drafted at Lee's request by Alexander H. H. Stuart, a Virginia lawyer who had been secretary of the interior under Millard Fillmore. This document expressed ideas that the general had endorsed since 1865:

> [T]he people of the South entertain no unfriendly feeling towards the government of the United States, but they complain that their rights under the constitution are withheld from them in the administration thereof. The idea that the Southern people are hostile to the negroes, and would oppress them, if it were in their power to do so, is entirely unfounded. They have grown up in our midst, and we have been accustomed from childhood to look upon them with kindness. The change in the relations of the two races has wrought no change in our feelings towards them. They still constitute an important part of our laboring population. Without their labor, the lands of the South would be comparatively unproductive ….
>
> It is true that the people of the South, in common with a large majority of the people of the North and West, are, for obvious reasons, inflexibly opposed to any system of laws that would place the political power of the country in the hands of the negro race. But this opposition springs from no feeling of enmity, but from a deep seated conviction that, at present, the negroes have neither the intelligence nor the other qualifications which are necessary to make them safe depositories of political power ….
>
> The great want of the South is peace. The people earnestly desire tranquility and a restoration of the Union. They deprecate disorder and excitement as the most serious obstacle to their prosperity. They ask a restoration of their rights under the Constitution ….

The White Sulphur Springs letter was quickly published North and South in newspapers, and enthusiastically received by millions of readers. Its call for peace actually anticipated Grant's famous proclamation. On September 7, Lee was invited by the nominating committee of the Democratic Party to speak at the Salisbury Beach Festival. The letter, Lee was told, "has been received by the people of the North as the most important document that has been put forth since the close of the Civil War." Lee declined the invitation.[37]

The White Sulphur Springs statement helped the process of reconciliation but, predictably, had no effect in turning support from Grant, who handily won the presidential election of 1868. Political prints of the period ridiculed the weakness of the Democratic candidate (fig. 200), who during the war as governor had not sufficiently suppressed the draft riots in New York City. In accepting the Republican nomination, Grant had written a one-hundred-word acceptance note that contained the most famous statement of the era, "Let us have peace." Grant told Sherman, in words reminiscent of George Washington, "I have been forced into it in spite of myself. I could not back down without, as it seems to me, leaving the contest for power for the next four years between mere trading politicians, the elevation of whom, no matter which party won, would lose to us, largely, the results of the costly war which we have gone through." A decade later, traveling in Germany, Grant repeated this sentiment: "I did not want the Presidency, and have never quite forgiven myself for resigning the command of the army to accept it; but it could not be helped." He added, "My re-election was a great gratification, because it showed me how the country felt."[38]

By the spring of 1869 a new Virginia constitution had been drafted as stipulated by the Reconstruction acts. A vote by the electorate would either approve or reject it. Universal suffrage was granted in the new document, as was an additional provision that disfranchised ex-Confederates. With language paraphrased from the Fourteenth Amendment, every man elected to office was required to take a "test-oath" whereby he would pledge that he had

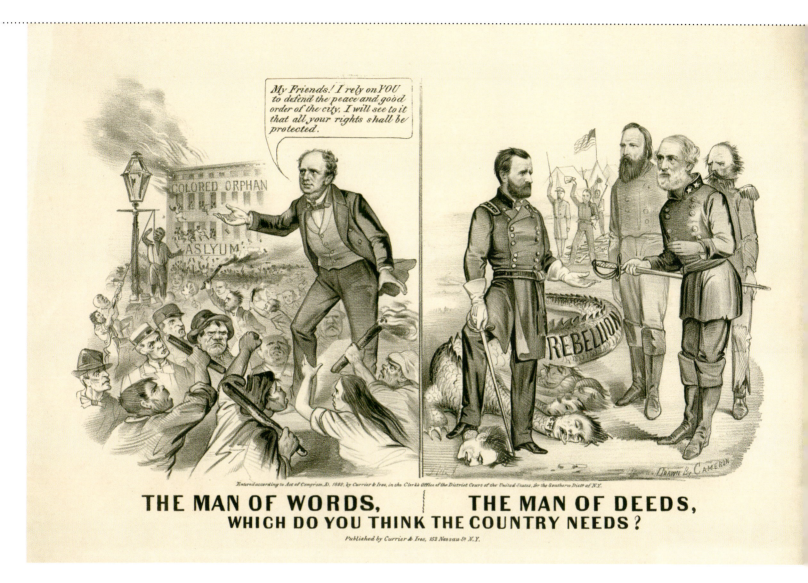

fig. 200.
James Cameron for Currier and Ives, publisher, *The Man of Words. The Man of Deeds. Which Do You Think the Country Needs?*, 1868, lithograph, New-York Historical Society Library, gift of Henry O. Havemeyer

not voluntarily aided the Confederacy. That provision jeopardized the fate of the entire document; white voters might reject it and thereby prolong military rule in Virginia. Fortunately, a compromise measure was suggested that the new president of the United States could accept: hold two separate votes, one on the constitution and one on the section that disfranchised Confederates. White voters looked to Lee: should they approve the new constitution and thereby grant the freedman the right to vote, or should they fight his enfranchisement and in the process prolong military rule in the state? The issue extended beyond Virginia. A year earlier, General John T. Morgan of Alabama had written, "Eight millions of people turn their eyes to Lexington seeking instruction and paternal advice in the severe trials they have to undergo. They read in the example of their General … the lessons of patience, moderation, fortitude, and earnest devotion to the requirements of duty, which are the only safe guides to them in their troubles." The general wrote in June 1869, "if I was entitled to vote, I should vote for the excision of the most obnoxious clauses of the proposed constitution, and for the election of the most conservative eligible candidates for Congress and the legislature …. I think all who can, should register and vote." White southerners listened. The body of the constitution was ratified, while the objectionable sections of the document were soundly defeated. On January 26, 1870, President Grant signed a bill re-admitting Virginia to the Union.[39]

fig. 201.
Frank Buchser, *Robert E. Lee*, 1869, oil on canvas, 54 × 40 in. (137.2 × 101.6 cm.), collection of the Swiss Confederation, Federal Office of Culture, Bern

Washington College

In the early fall of 1869, an accomplished Swiss artist, Frank Buchser, set out for Lexington to paint the most famous of the former Confederates. The artist had been commissioned by the Swiss government in Bern to paint portraits of the northern victors who had preserved the American Union, but Lincoln's assassination and President Grant's refusal to sit for him forced Buchser to alter his plans. His decision to paint Lee is evidence of the high international standing that the general enjoyed in the 1860s. On his way through rural Virginia, Buchser produced from life a series of images of African Americans that are remarkably sensitive depictions of a race he had come to appreciate years earlier in northern Africa. When he arrived in Lexington, if in fact he ever got there, he apparently found that Lee was as unwilling to pose for him as Grant. Buchser's portrait of Lee (fig. 201) was probably produced from photographs; the face of the sitter resembles Buchser as much as it does the general.[40]

A more accurate image of Lee was recorded in 1869 by the photographer Michael Miley, a young Confederate veteran who had settled in Lexington and developed a rapport with the general. In several of Miley's photographs, Lee shows fatigue, perhaps evidence of the heart condition that would kill him a year later (fig. 202). Miley also made duplicates of Lee photographs by others, of paintings, and even of family letters, in the event that the originals were ever destroyed. A second artist whom Lee took into his confidence and for whom the general was willing to pose was the Virginian sculptor Edward Valentine, who as a student in Germany during the war had helped raise funds to benefit disabled Confederate veterans. At Lee's death, it was Valentine who was awarded the commission to sculpt the recumbent Lee (see fig. 7). He was selected at least in part because he had visited the general in Lexington during the preceding summer and had taken studies from life.

Duty and Virtue

Washington College was in poor shape in the fall of 1865 when Lee assumed its leadership. Only four professors remained on staff, some forty students were enrolled, and the institution was nearly bankrupt. Lee's salary would be modest: $1,500 per year, plus a residence and garden, and one-fifth of the tuition of each student ($15 of $75). The position was an opportunity for the general: "I have a self-imposed task, which I must accomplish. I have led the young men of the South in battle; I have seen many of them fall under my standard. I shall devote all my life now to training young men to do their duty in life." He told his son Rooney that he "should have selected a more quiet life & a more retired abode than Lexington, & should have preferred a small farm," but Lee felt obligated to give "service to

fig. 202.
Michael Miley, *Robert E. Lee*, 1869 (photograph courtesy of Virginia Historical Society)

the country & the rising generation." He believed that "The proper education of youth [is] one of the most important objects now to be attained …." Lee wrote to John Brockenbrough about the responsibilities that all southerners faced after Appomattox:

> I think it the duty of every citizen, in the present condition of the Country, to do all in his power to aid in the restoration of peace and harmony, and in no way to oppose the policy of the State or General Government directed to that object. It is particularly incumbent on those charged with the instruction of the young to set them an example of submission to authority.

That portion of Lee's letter was released by the board of the college and was published in *The New York Times*.[41]

So much has been written about the doctrine of virtue that Lee imposed upon the students of Washington College that he may appear to modern eyes to have been little more than a relic of the prewar culture of Old Virginia. Some of his statements were written in his journal; others were passed down by apologists for the "Lost Cause". Among these were: "Obedience to lawful authority is the foundation of manly character"; "The gentleman does not needlessly or unnecessarily remind an offender of a wrong he may have committed against him. He can not only forgive, he can forget"; and "We have but one rule here, and that is that every student must be a gentleman." An honor code was developed based on Lee's personal formula: a gentleman does not lie, cheat, or steal. Custis, who taught at neighboring Virginia Military Institute and with Agnes and Mildred lived in Lexington with their parents, wrote to his brother Rob a quarter-century after the general's death, "Our father, as you well know, was simple, dignified, and kind; and was probably guilty of as few improprieties of any kind as any man living" (fig. 203).[42]

To Robert E. Lee, being a gentleman meant being a Christian. Lee's famous advice to a young mother with her baby, "Teach him he must deny himself," which repeats the words of his own mother, is close to the words of Jesus: "If any man will come after me, let him deny himself, and take up his cross daily, and follow me." To Lee, a gentleman exhibited Christian kindness, humility, and self-denial; he accepted duty (which for a student included working hard in his classes); he practiced exemplary moral and civic behavior; and he worshipped regularly and submitted to divine will. In Lexington, just as his mother-in-law had done at Arlington prior to the war, Lee held family prayers every morning before breakfast at which his Book of Common Prayer was essential (fig. 204). He attended early morning chapel services with his students and is said to have read the Bible daily. Just as Abraham Lincoln had believed that "all things most desirable for man's welfare" are found in the Bible and without it "we could not know right from wrong," so Lee said that it can satisfy "the most ardent thirst for knowledge" and for true wisdom, while teaching the only road to "salvation & eternal happiness." The general had long carried a pocket edition of the Bible and ultimately served as president of a Rockbridge County Bible society. Lee did not pretend that he was

fig. 203.
Custis Lee to Robert E. Lee, Jr., *Letter*, May 5, 1896, private collection on deposit at the Virginia Historical Society

fig. 204.
(Episcopal) Book of Common Prayer (Philadelphia, 1836), signed "R. E. Lee" on flyleaf, Virginia Historical Society

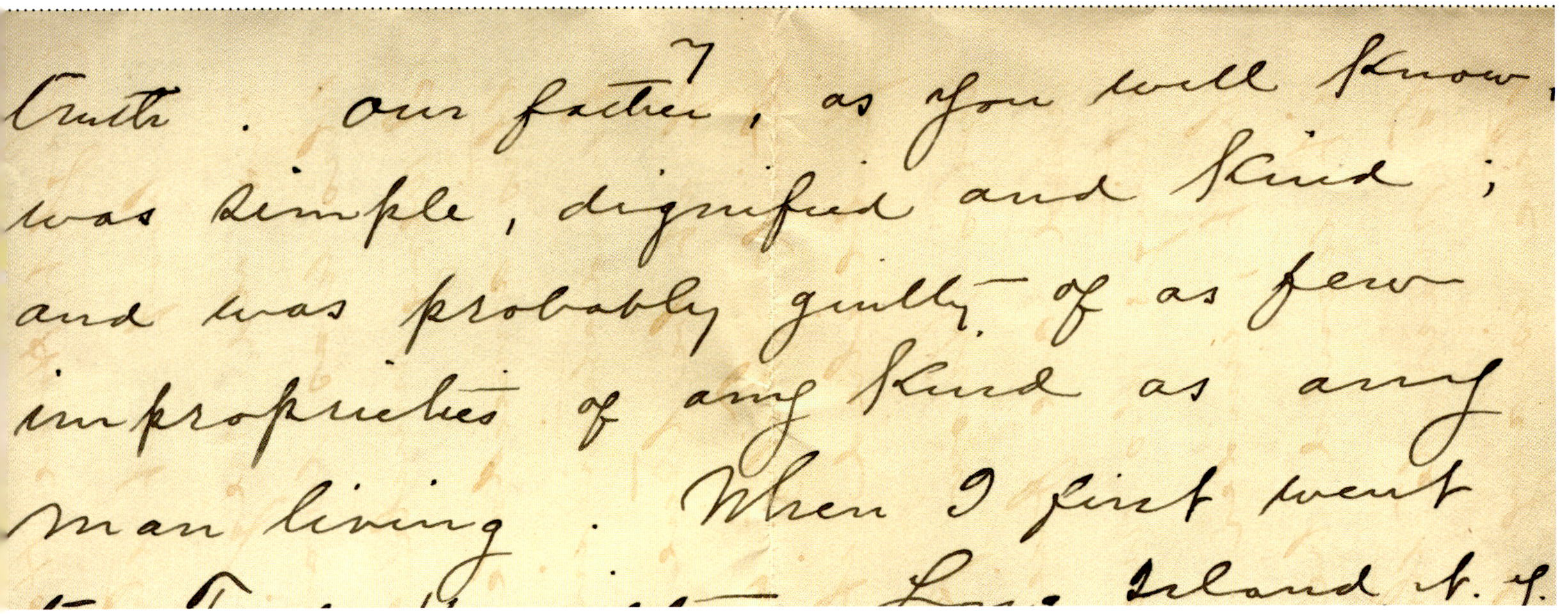

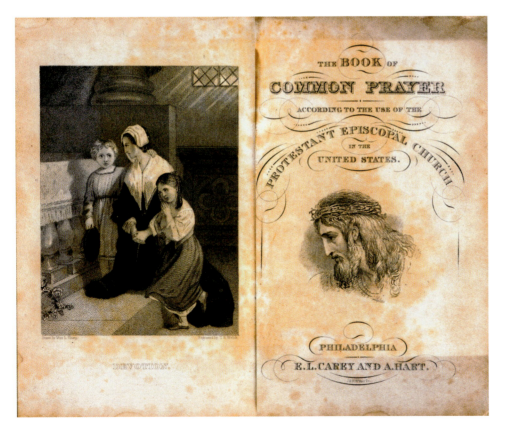

himself a model of perfection—"I find it so hard to keep one poor sinner's heart in the right way that it seems presumptuous to try to keep others"—but he felt it was his duty to help the students along the right path: "If I could only know that all the young men in the college were good Christians, I should have nothing more to desire. I dread the thought of any student going away from college without becoming a sincere Christian."[43]

Lee spoke of his "responsibility to Almighty God for these hundreds of young men." Thus, for the better practice of Christian worship and to signal the importance of religion to life at the college, he made the erection of a new chapel a priority of his presidency. It was authorized in 1866, along with a house for the president; both were dedicated in June 1868. Two engineers—the general and his son Custis—along with a second faculty member from the Virginia Military Institute (VMI), the architect Thomas Williamson, designed the structure there that today bears Lee's name (fig. 205). Its Romanesque Revival design fits well within the existing Roman Revival campus, largely due to the chapel's placement below the main run of buildings, on a site that Lee himself selected that is conspicuously opposite the center of the campus. Students were not required to attend services there because Lee hoped that his example of worship would be encour-

258 VI. RESTORATION OF THE UNION

fig. 205.
Lee Chapel, Washington College (now Washington and Lee University), photograph by Patrick Hinely

agement enough ("[let] young men ... do their duty ... voluntarily and thereby develop their characters"). His religious life extended far beyond the chapel, to include service on the vestry of neighboring Grace Episcopal Church (which would be renamed for the general after his death), and attendance in 1868 and 1869 at annual council meetings of the Protestant Episcopal Church of Virginia.[44]

Lee set high academic goals, stating his "endeavor to make [the students] see their true interest, to teach them to labor diligently for their improvement, and to prepare themselves for the great work of life." That said, one boy wrote, "he was so gentle, kind, and almost motherly, that I thought there must be some mistake about it …. It looked as if the sorrow of a whole nation had been collected in his countenance, and as if he were bearing the grief of his whole people." The general took pains to learn the names of his students so that he

LEE AND GRANT

fig. 206.
Lee's Office, Lee Chapel, Washington College (now Washington and Lee University), photograph by Patrick Hinely

could speak to them personally as their paths crossed on campus and in town. He invited students to his home for tea. When a boy performed poorly at his studies, Lee asked to see him. The president extended his courtesy to the parents as well, writing at least once a year to all and calling on those who visited Lexington. His letters that encourage self-mastery recall ones he had written to his wife thirty years earlier about their own children; other letters that address difficult situations are models of tact.[45]

Lee's daily routine at Washington College was to retire to his office (fig. 206) following chapel, and from eight in the morning until one or two in the afternoon address student issues. The general laboriously reviewed reports of each student's progress, made visits to classes, and conferred with the professors. In the afternoons he would escape the college on horseback rides, sometimes accompanied by his daughter Mildred. Correspondence consumed much of Lee's remaining time. "I have about a bushel of letters to answer," he wrote to his wife in August 1866. "I hope you do not feel obliged to reply to all these letters," his friend Margaret Preston said to him. "I certainly do," he replied. "Why should I not be willing to take the trouble to answer them? And as that is all I can give most of them, I give it ungrudgingly." It is estimated that several thousand of these responses were written, many of which remain in private collections to this day.[46]

Academic Innovation

The growth at Washington College in enrollment, size of the faculty, endowment, and number of buildings, and the expansion of the curriculum were phenomenal during Lee's presidency. The en-

fig. 207.
Lexington Gazette and Banner, December 19, 1866

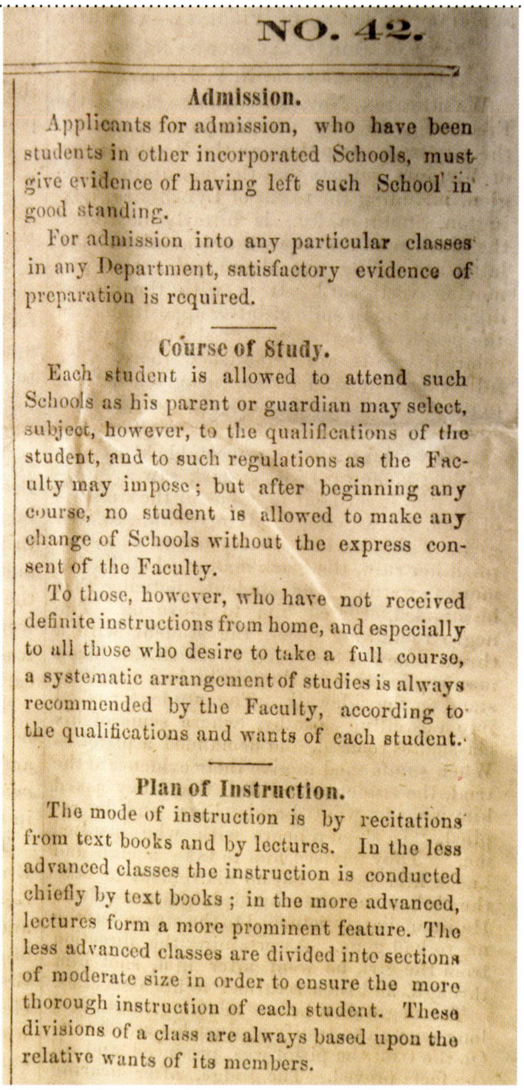

NO. 42.

Admission.

Applicants for admission, who have been students in other incorporated Schools, must give evidence of having left such School in good standing.

For admission into any particular classes in any Department, satisfactory evidence of preparation is required.

Course of Study.

Each student is allowed to attend such Schools as his parent or guardian may select, subject, however, to the qualifications of the student, and to such regulations as the Faculty may impose; but after beginning any course, no student is allowed to make any change of Schools without the express consent of the Faculty.

To those, however, who have not received definite instructions from home, and especially to all those who desire to take a full course, a systematic arrangement of studies is always recommended by the Faculty, according to the qualifications and wants of each student.

Plan of Instruction.

The mode of instruction is by recitations from text books and by lectures. In the less advanced classes the instruction is conducted chiefly by text books; in the more advanced, lectures form a more prominent feature. The less advanced classes are divided into sections of moderate size in order to ensure the more thorough instruction of each student. These divisions of a class are always based upon the relative wants of its members.

rollment of 50 students in the fall of 1865 grew to a peak of 410 in June 1868 and was noted in newspapers from Charleston to New York. The faculty grew from 4 to 22. Fundraising efforts were successful in the Virginia state legislature, in New York City, as we have seen, and with such northern philanthropists as Cyrus McCormick (born in Rockbridge County), Warren Newcomb, and George Peabody. The college was transformed from what was basically a finishing school grounded in the classics into a modern university that supplemented study in traditional subjects with new offerings in the sciences, engineering, commerce, agriculture, and the law. Lee foresaw correctly that students trained in such disciplines would be vital to the growth and economic recovery of the South.[47]

A plan to expand the curriculum of Washington College to better address the postwar needs of the South was already under consideration when Lee arrived in Lexington. Familiar with the curriculum at West Point, the general quickly endorsed the changes. Before the war the college had offered fairly traditional subject matter in six areas: political economy, philosophy, Latin, Greek, mathematics, and "natural philosophy" (chemistry and physics). The new plan was to give more emphasis to the sciences, yet at the same time to build the humanities (fig. 207). To accomplish the former, natural philosophy would be expanded into two departments, one of physics (primarily mechanical engineering, which involved the design and function of machines), and one of practical chemistry (including metallurgy and agricultural chemistry). Also, a new department of engineering (focusing on analytical mechanics, astronomy, civil engineering, and building) was to be added. New departments of modern languages (French, German, Spanish, and Italian), history, and literature would be created. These eleven departments, in which students would elect which classes to attend, essentially formed a modern university. The idea was advanced for its time when in April 1866 the trustees voted to adopt it. Insufficient funding, however, both to hire more professors and to build new classrooms, prohibited adoption of much of the new curriculum.[48]

In 1868, with Lee providing the impetus, the trustees authorized the faculty to refine plans for another extension of the scientific departments. Within a year, a report was prepared under the general's direction: "The great object of the whole plan is to provide the facilities required by the large class of our young men, who, looking to an early entrance into the practical pursuits of life, need a more direct training to this end than the usual literary courses." This time the new departments were to be agriculture (to teach the scientific management of a farm), commerce (to teach the management of commercial enterprises from banks to railroads), and applied chemistry (to teach mining and metallurgy). Lee's ideas attracted national attention. *The New York Times* reported measures "for the establishment of practical scientific departments, upon an extensive scale," and for the development and improvement of courses in civil and mining engineering. The *New York Herald* suggested that Lee's ideas about curriculum were "likely to make as great an impression upon our old fogy schools and colleges as

fig. 208.
Michael Miley, *Robert E. Lee on Traveller*, 1868 (photograph courtesy of Virginia Historical Society)

[Lee] did in military tactics upon our old fogy commanders in the palmy days of the rebellion."[49]

Historian Duncan Lyle Kinnear, writing in his *History of Virginia Polytechnic Institute*, describes a proposal in 1869 to establish an innovative agricultural school:

> One development … was a rather detailed plan proposing the establishment of a separate agricultural institute to be operated jointly by Washington College and the Virginia Military Institute. The plan called for a farm, a shop, a manual-labor feature, a complete and detailed agricultural and geological survey of the state, and a practical agricultural journal. The plan also presented ways of coordinating the work of the two colleges to prevent duplication but at the same time provide for joint faculty participation in the operation of the new institute. The proposed institute was to offer daytime instruction for youth and night classes in practical instruction to adults. In addition, all instruction was to be "open to all colors and both sexes," advanced proposals indeed, which would require nearly a century before complete achievement in Virginia.

A year earlier Lee had stated, "I am rejoiced that slavery is abolished. I believe it will be greatly for the interests of the South," adding, "I would cheerfully have lost all I have lost by the war, and have suffered all I have suffered, to have this object attained." He believed that all citizens, blacks included, must be educated so as to provide for themselves and to vote intelligently. In 1867 Lee had written to General John B. Gordon, "The thorough education of all classes of the people is the most efficacious means, in my opinion, of promoting the prosperity of the South." These statements would seem to support Kinnear's assertion that Lee endorsed the extraordinary proposal to create an integrated agricultural school. But even if he did, this is not to say that the general's views about the freedman's abilities had much changed. Lee cared about the progress of the society in which both they and he lived. His concern for the well-being of black people was part of his overall interest in the future of Virginia.[50]

The Lees in Lexington

Robert E. Lee and his wife Mary settled into their new lives in Lexington as gracefully as they could manage. The general found escape from his professional duties in his family life, in recreational horseback rides, and in attending social gatherings. Mary took joy in her children, although she worried why four remained unmarried, and she was heartened by the respect that she and her husband were awarded in Lexington. She was embittered, however, by the loss of Arlington House.

After 1865, both Mary and the general were increasingly affected by deteriorating health. "I much enjoy the charms of civil life, and find too late that I have wasted the best years of my existence," Lee wrote to Richard Ewell in 1868. He was thinking in part of how he delighted in the company of his children, particularly daughters Agnes and Mildred whom he saw daily, and sons Rooney and Rob, whose farms he visited, as well as how relieved he was to be free of his military duties. Lee also found solace in riding,

fig. 209.
Michael Miley, *Mrs. Robert E. Lee*, c. 1870 (photograph courtesy of Virginia Historical Society)

fig. 210.
Theodore R. Davis, *Soldiers' Cemetery at Arlington Heights, Virginia*, woodcut, *Harper's Weekly*, 1869.

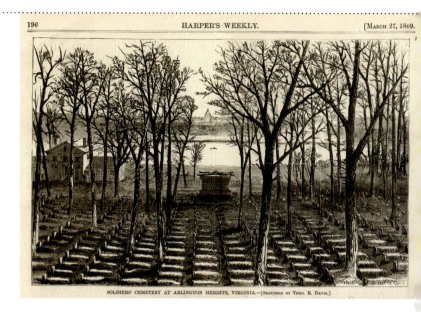

often with Mildred though sometimes alone: "my solitary evening rides … give me abundant opportunity for quiet thought." It was his idea that Michael Miley capture his love for his horse Traveller, who had carried him through the war. This proved to be the most popular photograph ever taken of the general (fig. 208).[51]

By 1865 Mary's arthritic condition had deteriorated to the point where she could no longer enjoy activities that had been important to her. She could neither ride nor garden; in fact she could barely move. Understandably she was glum (fig. 209). "It often seems to me that my affliction is peculiarly trying to one of my active temperament," she wrote to a friend. To another she said, "The greatest feat I can expect to accomplish will be to walk across my room without crutches & even that I have no hope of accomplishing." Indoors she was confined to a "rolling chair." Activities at the college and at neighboring Virginia Military Institute would have appealed, "but I am unable to mix in anything that is going on & am often very sad and lonely." The students "never seem to find time to visit me." "With the exception of my own immediate family

I am entirely cut off from all I have ever known & loved." Meanwhile, newspaper accounts of Reconstruction incited her anger and indignation. Added to that, her beloved Arlington had become the property of the United States and been converted into a soldiers' cemetery (fig. 210). "The graves of those who aided to bring all this ruin on the children and country," Mary wrote, "are even planted up to the very door [of the house] without any regard to common decency." Years later, in 1888, Mildred added, "as far as my aching eyes could see—graves—graves—graves—in memory of the men who had robbed me of my beautiful home." Mary made an effort to reclaim the Washington relics that had been left there. She wrote to President Andrew Johnson in 1868, but the story was leaked to the newspapers. Lee wrote: "I hope their [the objects'] presence at the capital will keep in the remembrance of all Americans the principles and Virtues of Washington." By the spring of 1869, Mary Custis Lee could find some enjoyment in the new "president's house" at Washington College (fig. 211), which was built with wide porches and a first-floor bedroom to accommodate her "rolling chair." Her engineer husband also equipped it with a forced-air furnace and gravity-propelled running water that was pumped to the attic.[52]

Of the Lee children, only Rooney and Robert (fig. 212) enjoyed happiness in the years after the war. Custis was plagued by health problems and emotional frustrations. None of the daughters would marry. It would appear that the general's extraordinary fame, the remarkably high standards that he set for himself and for all

fig. 211.
President's House, Washington College (now Washington and Lee University), photograph by Kevin Remington

fig. 212.
Michael Miley, *The Three Sons of Robert E. Lee*, c. 1885 (photograph courtesy of Virginia Historical Society); left to right, Rob, Custis, and Rooney Lee

chose to room with his parents, despite their concern that he have a family of his own. Apparently the general and his oldest son enjoyed a close relationship; a former student at the college remembered courtesies they exchanged: "the stately yet gracious greeting of the son and father … brought tears to my eyes." After the death of Robert E. Lee, Custis was awarded the presidency of Washington College, but this extremely shy and reticent man took more interest in the neatness of his quarters than in furthering the success of the institution or in developing personal relationships. He also suffered some from the rheumatoid arthritis that had crippled his mother. "Have all the fun you can have," he is said to have told a student at the college, "I never had any fun in my life."[53]

At the close of the war, Rooney and his younger brother Rob initially took up farming at the Tidewater plantations they inherited from their grandfather, G. W. P. Custis, but they soon were leasing their lands. Rooney's first wife, Charlotte Wickham, had died tragically in 1863 while he was a prisoner of war. His wedding to Mary Tabb Bolling in 1867 took place in Petersburg. The ceremony was an emotional episode for Robert E. Lee, who felt guilt for having to "abandon" the city in 1865. "Our son was married last night &

around him, and his extremely warm but at the same time suffocating attention to his children, was in the end more of a hindrance to them than an asset.

Custis had followed his father to Lexington to serve on the Virginia Military Institute faculty as a professor of engineering. He

fig. 213.
Michael Miley, *Mary Lee*, c. 1860s
(photograph courtesy of Virginia Historical Society)

shone in his happiness," he wrote to his incapacitated wife who remained in Lexington. He told Rooney, "when I saw the cheerfulness with which the people [of Petersburg] were working to restore their condition … a load of sorrow … was lifted from my heart." The father was pleased with Rooney's building of a new residence at the White House plantation, and with the naming of a grandson Robert E. Lee III. Rooney later moved to Ravensworth in northern Virginia and entered politics. A war hero with an engaging personality, he became an extremely popular congressman. He died prematurely, however, at age 54, in 1891. Rob lived first at Romancoke in a structure that his father described as "scarcely habitable." He courted Charlotte (Lottie) Haxall, but she died not long after their marriage. Robert, Jr. served as an executive of a Rockbridge County mining company, and in the 1890s moved to Washington. He worked in the real estate business, married a young cousin, Juliet Carter, and eventually returned to Romancoke.[54]

In 1856, when all but the youngest of the daughters was old enough to marry, Lee had written about them to his friend in Savannah, Eliza Mackay Stiles: "I know it will require a tussle for any one to get my children from me, and beyond that I do not wish to know." Margaret Preston noticed that "His tenderness to his children, especially his daughters, was mingled with a delicate courtesy which belonged to an older day than ours, a courtesy which recalls the *preux chevalier* of knightly times." He discouraged their interest in suitors: "He was apt to be critical on the subject of our young men visitors and admirers," Mildred wrote. He discouraged their travel: "I miss you very much and hope that this is the last wedding that you will attend," he wrote Agnes in 1866. He even undermined their belief that a married couple could share deep devotion; Lee wrote to Mildred in 1866, "you will never receive such a love as is felt for you by your father and mother." Mary Custis Lee, on the other hand, worried that the girls must find husbands: "I am not in the least anxious to part with them; yet think it quite time." The Lee daughters were a spirited group—"the women of the family [are] very fierce and the men very mild," Lee wrote. They took Lexington by storm, skating, sleigh riding, and boating when few ladies were so daring, and founding a Reading Club, to which male guests were invited.

Mary Lee, however, was unhappy in Lexington (fig. 213). The oldest Lee daughter wrote to a friend not long after her father's death, "I go no where, see as few people as possible, take long walks & rides in the country & teach my Sunday School." Mary, who at age five had been left behind when her parents and older brothers lived in St. Louis, now left them behind. Between 1865 and her death in 1918 she toured the world, visiting more than twenty-six countries and living abroad for most of the time. Agnes and Mildred, however, remained at home.[55]

Agnes also was unhappy with the move to the Valley. Her cousin Orton Williams, to whom she had opened her heart in the late 1850s, had been killed. She was a beautiful woman (fig. 214) with many friends in Richmond and the Tidewater. Her father had chided her in 1868, "Your uncle Smith says you girls ought to marry his sons, as you both find it so agreeable to be away from home, you could then live a true Bohemian life & have a happy time generally." Agnes died of an intestinal disorder in 1873 at age thirty-two. The loss was too much for her mother, who died a month later at age sixty-six. The deaths of both parents and Agnes left Mildred (fig. 215) in Lexington with only her brother: "Custis and I have to bear our sorrow alone … in a home once so happy, but now so desolate." She had never liked the town: "I am dreadfully lonely, know no one well," she wrote to her friend Lucy Blain in 1866; "do you know what starvation of the *heart & mind* is? I suffer & am dumb." In a second letter she added, "The number of old maids here quite appalls me. My fate was decided from the first

fig. 214.
Michael Miley, *Agnes Lee,* c. 1865–70 (photograph courtesy of Virginia Historical Society)

fig. 215.
Michael Miley, *Mildred Childe Lee,* c. 1865–70 (photograph courtesy of Virginia Historical Society)

fig. 216.
James Reid Lambdin, *Ulysses Simpson Grant,* 1868, oil on canvas, 50⅛ × 36 in. (127.3 × 91.4 cm.), New-York Historical Society Museum

President of the United States

Ulysses S. Grant (fig. 216) began his presidency immersed in the major issues of the day. He had saved the Union and had a hand in ousting a European power from Mexico. As general-in-chief of the army, Grant had determined when and where to position troops, some of whom saved the lives of freedpeople and Native Americans. He seemed to have the appropriate experience, and to be beholden to no one. Many Americans thought that the new president

moment I put my foot on shore." The little girl who had received long letters from her father when he was stationed in Texas had probably been the closest of all the children to him. "She is my light-bearer; the house is never dark if she is in it," Lee had written about Mildred. In 1879, she confided to another friend of her "need of someone to take care of me, sadly. Oh, celibacy, where are the charms!" Writing in her journal a decade later, she was still tormented by her loss and loneliness: "I have missed the tenderest, sweetest love that any daughter had from a father! … To me, he seems a Hero—& all other men small in comparison …. Most women when they lose a father replace it by husband & children. I have had nothing."[56]

would cleanse the government of its ills and inefficiencies. In the North the mood was upbeat. In a short inaugural address, Grant encouraged his constituents to anticipate a continuance of peace and the return of prosperity. He said that he would faithfully execute all duties and enforce all laws, that he would protect all citizens, including the freedpeople, that he would protect the Indians, and that he would deal fairly with foreign nations. He would pay the national debt, see that revenue due was diligently collected,

and reduce government spending. He befuddled observers with some of his cabinet selections: congressman Elihu Washburne (his longtime supporter) and merchants Alexander Stewart (who had bought Grant's Washington house at a high price and given it to Sherman) and Adolph Borie (who gave Grant a house in Philadelphia) were nominated for secretary of state, treasury, and navy respectively. Washburne and Borie quickly withdrew themselves and Stewart was ineligible to serve. That said, some of Grant's appointments were outstanding. He soon chose the talented Hamilton Fish of New York to be secretary of state, and his selection of longtime associate General Ely S. Parker, a Seneca, to be commissioner of Indian affairs was sensitive and sensible. At the same time, he made longtime friend and former Confederate general James Longstreet the surveyor of customs for the port of New Orleans, a lucrative position. The public in the North accepted all of Grant's choices because they seemed to have been made free of political influence, and also because they trusted his judgment. He then set about tackling the most pressing problems of the reconstituted nation.[57]

Human Rights

The Freedman

In his first inaugural address, Grant endorsed the right of suffrage for all citizens, black as well as white, as part of his policy to bring "the greatest good to the greatest number." The president specified the means: the ratification of an amendment that would prohibit restrictive state laws that determined voter eligibility by race. A year later, in March 1870, when the Fifteenth Amendment was passed, Grant lauded Congress with the highest praise: "A measure which makes at once Four Millions of people … voters in every part of the land, the right not to be abridged by any state, is indeed a measure of grander importance than any other one act of the kind from the foundation of our free government to the present day." This milestone was an occasion for celebration (fig. 217). The black leader Frederick Douglass praised Grant's "moral courage" in taking so bold a stand: "To Grant more than any other man the Negro owes his enfranchisement."[58]

In the short term, however, the passage of the Fifteenth Amendment actually worsened the plight of the freedpeople in the South. The Ku Klux Klan (fig. 218), among whose leaders was the former Confederate general Nathan Bedford Forrest, immediately stepped up its campaign of violence and terror throughout much of the region, particularly in the Carolinas, Louisiana, Arkansas, and the territory of New Mexico. In 1871, Attorney General Amos T. Ackerman, a Confederate veteran from Georgia who implemented Grant's programs with vigor, sent a report from South Carolina that the president forwarded to the House of Representatives. The objectives of the Klan, Ackerman concluded, are "to prevent all political action not in accord with the views of the members, to deprive colored citizens of the right to bear arms and of the right to a free ballot, to suppress schools in which colored children were taught, and to reduce the colored people to a condition closely akin to that of slavery." The use of "force and terror" would undermine Reconstruction and destroy the Republican Party in the South. Ackerman said that in some of the counties two-thirds of the white men were active members, while the other third approved or tolerated the KKK, that the "personal violence" inflicted often extended to murder, that the instances of "criminal violence" in the past year numbered in the "thousands," and that all of this had gone "unpunished." In 1870 and early 1871, Congress passed two Enforcement Acts that attempted but failed to protect the civil and political rights of the freedpeople. Grant asked for more power. He told House Speaker James G. Blaine that "there is a deplorable state of affairs existing in some portions of the South demanding the immediate attention of Congress," and he "urgently recommend[ed]" legislation to secure "life and property," assuring the representatives, "There is no other subject on which I would recommend legislation during the current session." The Ku Klux Klan Act passed on April 20, 1871; it allowed the president to use the army to enforce the law, to suspend the writ of *habeas corpus*, and to prosecute criminal violence in federal courts. Grant issued a series of proclamations to the citizens of South Carolina. He ordered troops there and he secured 3,000 indictments within the year, thereby dramatically reducing the violence.[59]

Racial troubles in the South extended through the president's first term in office. The election of 1872 was a referendum on Reconstruction as implemented by Grant. He had little interest in a second term, but he also felt a duty "to save all that has been gained by so much sacrifice of blood and treasure … [and this] could only be done through the triumph of the republican party." Grant told a

fig. 217.
Thomas Kelly, *The Fifteenth Amendment*, 1870, lithograph, New-York Historical Society Library

fig. 218.
Ku Klux Klan Robe and Hood, appliqué and painted linen, Lincoln County, Tennessee, c. 1866, Chicago Historical Society

delegation of African Americans in Philadelphia, "All citizens undoubtedly in all respects should be equal." His political opponents, some of whom he had offended by ignoring them, united as "Liberal Republicans" and attracted East Coast intellectuals and Democrats. They promoted a new policy for the South. Grant called them "soreheads & thieves who have deserted the republican party." Among the renegades was their presidential candidate, *New York Tribune* publisher Horace Greeley, whom Grant described as "a genius without common sense." Another was Senator Carl Schurz of Missouri, whom Grant labeled a "disorganizer … who can render much greater service to the party he does not belong to." They called for universal amnesty, reconciliation with the southern gentleman, and the abandonment of blacks as "worthless." Grant compared them to the howling prairie wolves of Mexico that made more noise than their numbers. Thomas Nast ridiculed Greeley and Schurz, picturing their policy as a fraudulent promise of reconciliation (fig. 219). Frederick Douglass also saw through the hype: "We will not find a candidate equal to General Grant," adding that "the Republican party is the ship and all else is the sea." Grant was returned to the White House with 56 percent of the vote, the highest endorsement for an incumbent between the presidencies of Andrew Jackson and Theodore Roosevelt. In his second inaugural address (fig. 220), Grant opined that although the former slave had been made a citizen, "Yet he is not possessed of the civil rights which citizenship should carry with it. This is wrong and should be corrected." Grant said he was tired of being "the subject of abuse and slander scarcely ever equaled in political history," and he was "looking forward with the greatest anxiety to the day when I shall be released from responsibilities that at times are almost overwhelming, and from which I have scarcely had a respite since the eventful firing upon Fort Sumter."[60]

The second presidential term was troubled by ever-increasing racial violence that culminated in massacres in Louisiana, South Carolina, Arkansas, Alabama, and Mississippi. The carnage in Louisiana was seemingly continuous. The same election of 1872 that returned the president to the White House produced contested results in the governor's race there. Grant supported his party's candidate, William P. Kellogg, with troops and proclamations. The results were disastrous. Appointees by Kellogg were "displace[d] by force" in some parts of the state, most notably in Colfax, where, in Grant's words in a report to Congress, "a butchery of citizens was committed … which in blood-thirstiness and barbarity is hardly surpassed by any acts of savage warfare." The Colfax Massacre of April 13, 1873 was the bloodiest act of the Reconstruction period. More than 100 blacks were shot to death. The next year, as Grant biographer Jean

fig. 219.
Thomas Nast, *It is Only a Truce to Regain Power ("Playing Possum")*, woodcut, *Harper's Weekly*, August 24, 1872

fig. 220.
Ulysses S. Grant, *Second Inaugural Address*, March 4, 1873, Library of Congress

fig. 221.
A. Zenneck, *Murder of Louisiana*, 1873, woodcut, Library of Congress

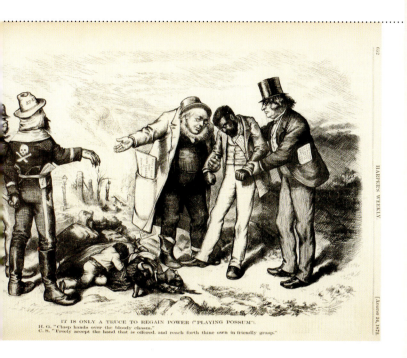

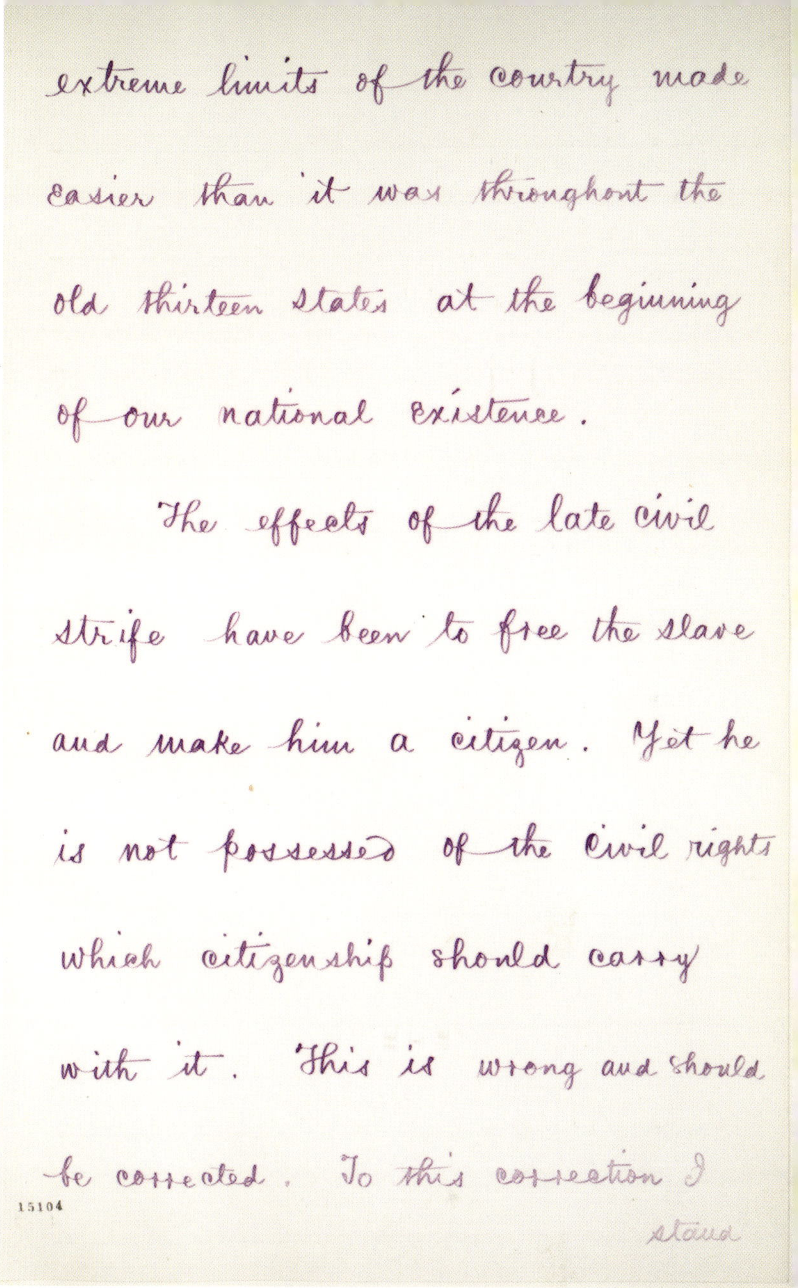

Smith writes, the situation in Louisiana went from worse to much worse. The 1874 election campaign became the most violent yet. The exasperated president sighed, "The muddle down there is almost beyond my fathoming." Some 3,400 armed White Leaguers, en route to seize the statehouse and overturn the Republican government, fought a pitched battle in the streets of New Orleans with police and black militia commanded by James Longstreet. He was wounded and eleven of his men were killed, as were twenty-one from the White League. The rebels succeeded in their coup d'état by taking the statehouse. The new governor promised peace and protection for the freedpeople if Louisiana was left alone. Grant instead issued a proclamation demanding dispersal, and he sent 5,000 troops and three gunboats to New Orleans (fig. 221). In 1875, when the White Leaguers marched again, the exasperated president called in Philip Sheridan to remedy matters as he had done in 1864 in the Valley of Virginia. "Neither Ku Klux Klan, White Leagues, nor any other associations using arms and violence to execute their unlawful purposes, can be permitted in that way to govern any part of this country," Grant told the Senate. New Orleans had experienced the iron boot of Sheridan in 1866; the revolt was quickly quashed. However, in this case hardliners in the South would be able to outlast the will of the North. In 1876 new President Rutherford B. Hayes, whose thin margin of victory could have been challenged, agreed to withdraw the army from the South, allowed the Democratic party to

extreme limits of the country made easier than it was throughout the old thirteen states at the beginning of our national existence.

The effects of the late civil strife have been to free the slave and make him a citizen. Yet he is not possessed of the civil rights which citizenship should carry with it. This is wrong and should be corrected. To this correction I stand

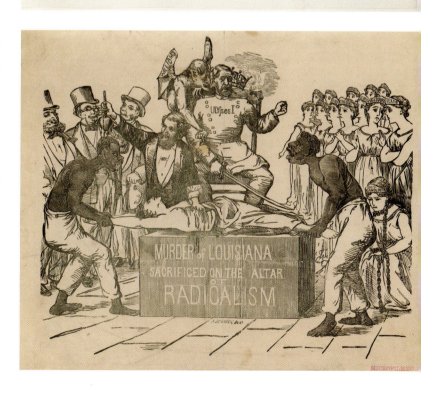

fig. 222.
Thomas Nast, *"Go On!"—U. S. Grant, The Constitution of the United States Must and Shall Be Preserved—And Protected*, woodcut, *Harper's Weekly*, September 30, 1876

fig. 223.
Ulysses S. Grant, Washington, to Governor Daniel H. Chamberlain, Columbia, South Carolina, *Letter*, July 26, 1876, South Carolina Archives & History Center

EPTEMBER 30, 1876.] HARPER'S WEEKLY. 801

"A GOVERNMENT OF THE PEOPLE, FOR THE PEOPLE, AND BY THE PEOPLE"—THAT CAN NOT PROTECT THE PEOPLE, *SHALL* PERISH FROM THE EARTH.

"There has never been a desire on the part of the North to humiliate the South. Nothing is claimed for one State that is not fully accorded to all others, unless it may be the right to kill negroes and Republicans without fear of punishment and without loss of caste or reputation. This has seemed to be a privilege claimed by a few States.... Go on—and let every Governor where the same dangers threaten the peace of his State go on—in the conscientious discharge of his duties to the humblest as well as the proudest citizen, and I will give every aid for which I can find law or constitutional power. A government that can not give protection to life, property, and all guaranteed civil rights (in this country the greatest is an untrammeled ballot) to the citizen is, in so far, a failure, and every energy of the oppressed should be exerted, always within the law and by constitutional means, to regain lost privileges and protection. Too long denial of guaranteed rights is sure to lead to revolution—bloody revolution, where suffering must fall upon the innocent as well as the guilty. Expressing the hope that the better judgment and co-operation of citizens of the State may enable you to secure a fair trial and punishment of all offenders, without distinction of race, or color, or previous condition of servitude, and without aid from the Federal Government, but with the promise of such aid on the conditions named in the foregoing, I subscribe myself, etc.,

"U. S. GRANT."

"GO ON!"—U. S. GRANT.

THE CONSTITUTION OF THE UNITED STATES MUST AND SHALL BE PRESERVED—AND PROTECTED.

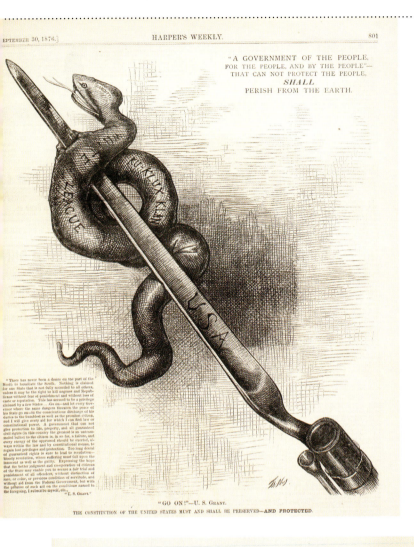

regain political control there, and abandoned the freedpeople to a life of repression.[61]

In 1874, armed, roving bands of both Republicans and Democrats in Arkansas contested the results of the recent gubernatorial race, prompting Grant to again support his party's candidate, Elisha Baxter. The president wrote to Baxter, "The United states will give all necessary protection to the legislature and prevent, as far as practicable, all violence and disturbance of the public peace." A "revolt" in Mississippi in 1875 caused Grant to complain, "The whole public are tired out with these annual, autumnal outbreaks in the South." He wrote to the governor of South Carolina, Daniel H. Chamberlain, who had complained about the murders of blacks in his state at Hamburg: "Mississippi is governed to day by officials chosen through fraud and violence, such as would scarcely be accredited to savages, much less to a civilized and christian people." He added that the seeming "right to Kill Negroes and republicans without fear of punishment, and without loss of caste or reputation" must end. He offered encouragement with a statement adopted by Nast, "Go on, and let every Governor where the same dangers threaten the peace of his State go on in the conscientious discharge of his duties to the humblest as well as the proudest citizen, and I will give every aid for which I can find law or constitutional power" (figs. 222 and 223).[62]

In 1876 both presidential candidates claimed victory. Some Democrats threatened bloodshed and possibly another rebellion if

as to my duties - Go on, and let every Governor where
the same dangers threaten the peace of his State, go on
in the conscientious performance of his duties to the
humblest as well as proudest citizen, and I will
give every aid for which I can find law, or Constitutional power.. Government that cannot give protec-

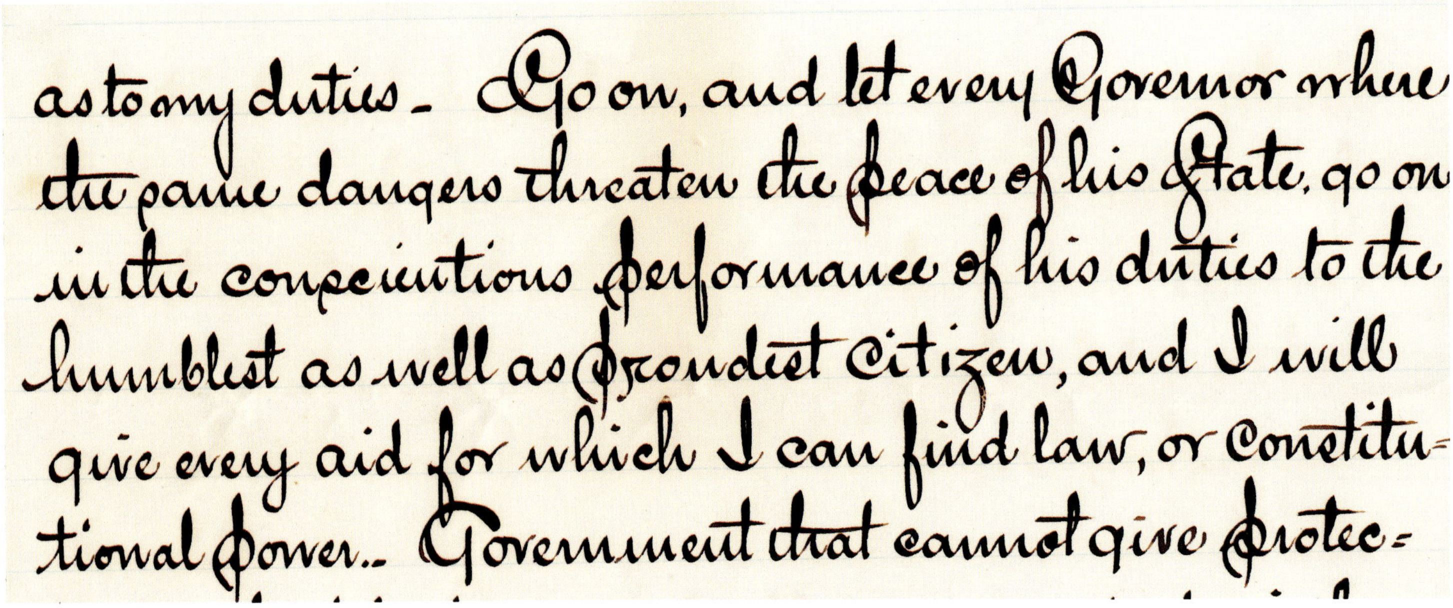

fig. 224.
Thomas Nast, *Tilden or Blood*, woodcut, *Harper's Weekly*, February 17, 1877

their candidate, Samuel J. Tilden, was not declared the winner (fig. 224). Tilden had apparently won the popular vote, but the electoral vote was undecided due to disputes in Louisiana, South Carolina, and especially Florida, where Hayes may have won but the Democratic electors had cast their votes for Tilden. Grant directed that the army in Louisiana and Florida maintain order, and he established a joint commission to decide the electoral votes of the three states. He advised General Sherman to "see that the proper & legal boards of Canvassers are unmolested in the performance of their duties," adding, "No man worthy of the office of President would be willing to hold it if 'counted in' or placed there by any fraud," and that "Either party can afford to be disappointed in the result but the Country cannot afford to have the result tainted by the suspicion of illegal or false returns." Hayes was awarded the presidency. The Democrats acquiesced in exchange for a new policy for the South. Grant had accomplished a peaceful transition of power, albeit at a high cost.[63]

There has been much debate about Grant's policies concerning the protection of African Americans. Josiah Bunting offers a useful commentary on the president's occasional distance from this controversy:

> [T]he depth of Grant's commitment to Reconstruction seemed to grow stronger as resistance to the realization of what he believed itself became more determined. The identification of the Democratic party with positions that seemed aimed on destroying the hard-won gains of black Americans seemed to the president a betrayal of all they had gained by the war and a betrayal of those who had labored to make its results permanent. Grant said, "I am a Republican because I am an American, and because I believe the

fig. 225.
Charles DeForest Fredricks, *Ely Parker*, late 1860s (photograph courtesy of New-York Historical Society Library)

first duty of an American—the paramount duty—is to save the results of the war, and save our credit."⁶⁴

While Grant may at times have been guilty of a type of conciliation, of having moments in which he seemed to step back from if not abandon his principles where the freedpeople were concerned, he stated throughout his presidency that the gains that had been made and the freedoms that had been won during the war must be retained. He dug in his heels on the issue, sanctified it as his duty, and as Frederick Douglass suggested, no other white man did so much.

The Native American

The course of Euro-American westward settlement determined the fate of many Native peoples. The Indian Removal Act of 1830 had already pushed large numbers of Native Americans west of the Mississippi River, to lands that they were told would be theirs "as long as grasses grow and water flows." In his first annual message to Congress, Grant labeled long-standing American policies against Native peoples as shameful and wasteful: "From the foundation of the Government to the present the management of the original inhabitants of this Continent, the Indian, has been one of embarrassment, and expense, and has been attended with continuous murders and wars." Lieutenant Grant had arrived in California not long after the discovery of gold had brought increased pressure on the nations there; at that time he developed an appreciation for the human rights of Indian people. During the Civil War, when he heard of the massacre of 500 Cheyenne men, women, and children at Sand Creek, Colorado, in 1864, the general labeled the act murder. To Grant, the Cheyenne War of 1868, which included George A. Custer's attack on Black Kettle's settlement on the Washita, was both ill-advised and immoral. But when Custer attacked the Indians on their reservation, Philip Sheridan commended him (figs. 226 and 227). To William T. Sherman's thinking, "The more we can kill this year, the less we will have to kill next year." Sheridan famously said in 1869, "The only good Indian is a dead Indian."⁶⁵

The new president attempted to reverse the unjust policies of the federal government. Grant's commissioner of Indian affairs was the Seneca Ely S. Parker, a lawyer and engineer, who had been his former military secretary (fig. 225). In an effort to rid the nation of corrupt Indian agents, the president accepted only Quakers and ordained ministers for such posts. To supervise the spending of federal funds allotted to the Indian, Grant established a commission made up of philanthropists and humanitarians who would purge the system of the swindling, double-dealing, and outright thievery that previously had diverted 75 percent of the money away from its intended receivers.

In messages to Congress and in private letters, Grant issued a series of emphatic statements that point to his belief that the best thing for Indian people would be assimilation: "I will favor any courses towards them which tends to their civilization, christianization and ultimate citizenship." He believed that a "system which

fig. 226.
Taylor & Huntington, publisher, *General George Custer*, 1864 (photograph courtesy of New-York Historical Society Library, George T. Bagoe Collection, gift of Mrs. Elihu Spicer)

fig. 227.
Theodore Russell Davis, *The Indian Campaign—Prisoners Captured by General Custer*, wood engraving, *Harper's Weekly*, December 26, 1868, New-York Historical Society Library, gift of Harry T. Peters

Grant's new policies were ineffective; the army still tended to do as it pleased with Indian people. His belief in the unfairness of Euro-American treatment of the Native American peoples did not wane, but in an address to Congress the president expressed what he saw as a simple fact: "No matter what ought to be the relations between such settlements and the aborigines, the fact is they do not get on together, and one or the other has to give way in the end." The soldiers who were supposed to police the frontier, perhaps

fig. 6.47

looks to the extinction of a race is too abhorant for a Nation to indulge in without entailing upon the wrath of all Christendom," adding, "I do not believe our Creator ever placed the different races on this earth with a view of having the strong exert all his energies in exterminating the weaker" (fig. 228). In terms that must have annoyed some members of the business community as well as his friends Sherman and Sheridan, the president concluded, "Wars of extermination, engaged in by people pursuing commerce and all industrial pursuits are demoralizing and wicked."[66]

feeling as though they had a soldier in the Oval Office who would side with them, were often guilty of trying to eliminate the Native peoples who were living there. Attacks on villages were common. Troopers followed the orders of Sheridan to "strike them hard" when they destroyed Heavy Runner's Piegan Blackfoot village in Montana in 1870; 158 of the 173 people murdered were women and children. The "Marias Massacre" pointed out the continuing futility of trying to manage frontier affairs from Washington.

With tensions mounting, a delegation of twenty-one Indians led

LEE AND GRANT

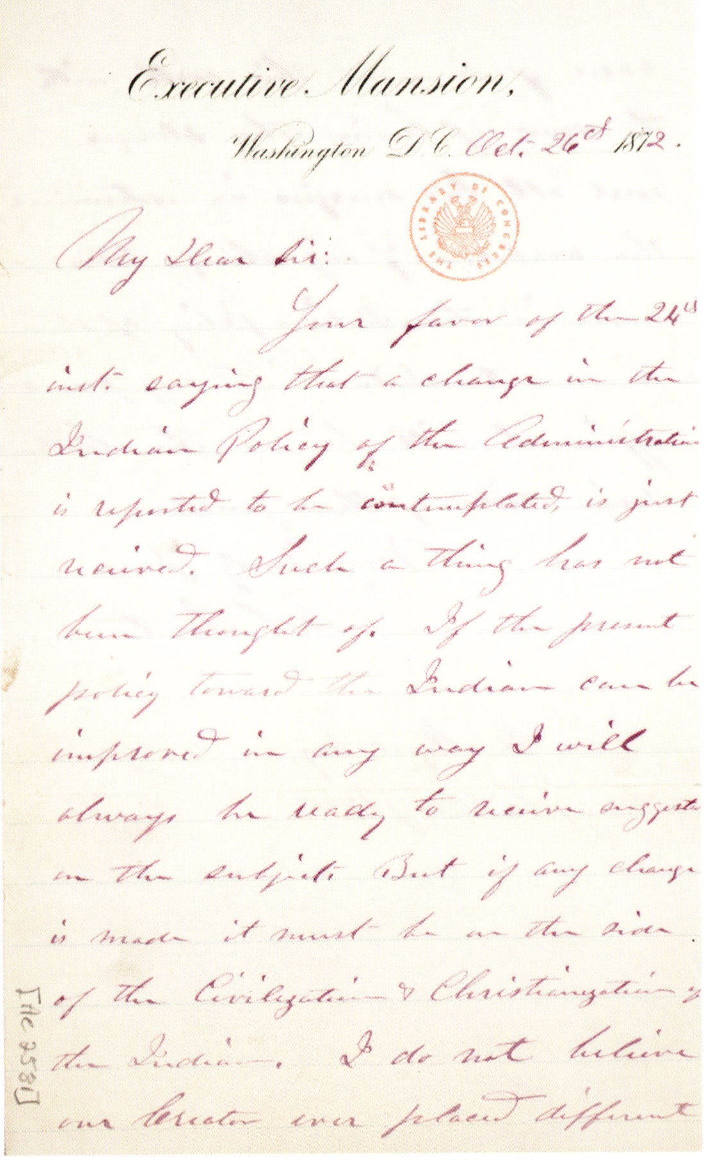

Executive Mansion,
Washington D.C. Oct. 26th 1872.

My Dear Sir:

Your favor of the 24th inst. saying that a change in the Indian Policy of the Administration is reported to be contemplated, is just received. Such a thing has not been thought of. If the present policy toward the Indian can be improved in any way I will always be ready to receive suggestions on the subject. But if any change is made it must be on the side of the Civilization & Christianization of the Indian. I do not believe our Creator ever placed different

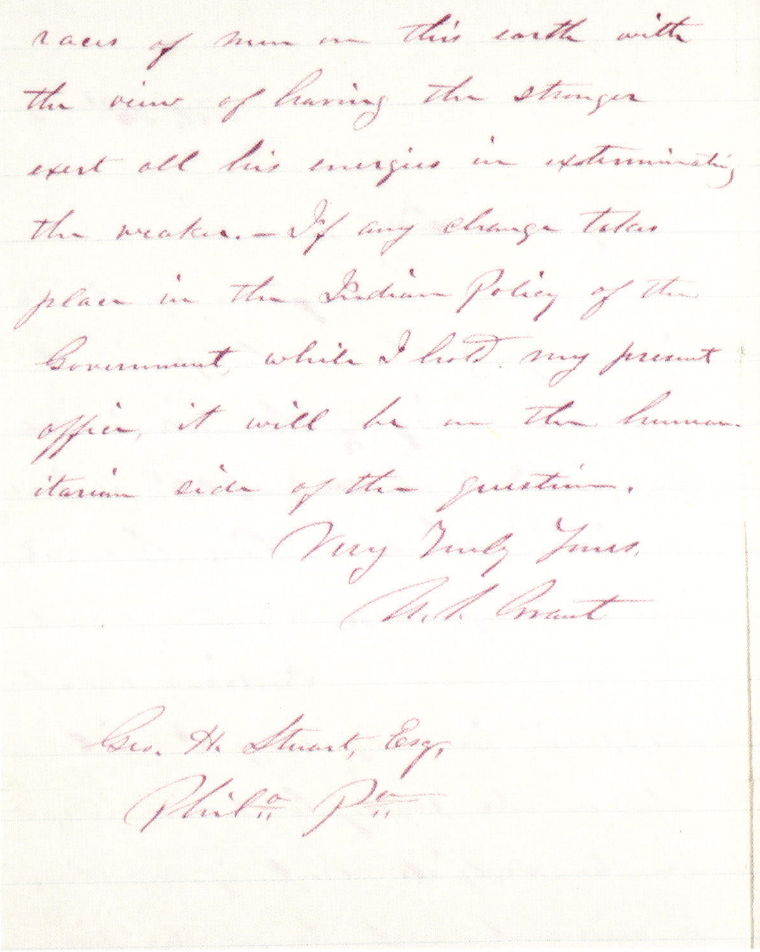

races of men on this earth with the view of having the stronger exert all his energies in exterminating the weaker.—If any change takes place in the Indian Policy of the Government while I hold my present office, it will be on the humanitarian side of the question.

Very Truly Yours,
U. S. Grant

Geo. H. Stuart, Esq.
Phila. Pa.

fig. 228.
Ulysses S. Grant, Washington, to George H. Stuart, *Letter*, October 26, 1872, Library of Congress

by the Oglala Sioux chief Red Cloud (fig. 229) traveled east to confer with Grant, a man they could respect both for his previous martial accomplishments and for his stated policies of peace toward them. Red Cloud, who in 1866–68 had led the most successful war against the United States by any Indian nation, had been promised half of South Dakota including the sacred Black Hills as part of the peace settlement. The trip became a significant public relations coup. Newspapers in the East followed Red Cloud's visit (fig. 230). "The terrible Chief of the Brule-Sioux … in company with about fifteen fierce braves and several dusky women" was taken to the Washington arsenal and navy yard. This was "to impress [him] with the powers of the 'Great Father.'" Appearing before the U.S. government's Indian Council, Red Cloud spoke "to the point" and "without ambiguity." The next day the chief visited the president in the Executive Office, "the Indians standing in a semi-circle around the room." Grant stated that "he had always and still desired to live at peace with the Indian nations." In New York City, an audience at the Cooper Institute was attracted by "curiosity … to see the most distinguished, living representatives of the race who originally possessed the American soil." The crowd gave Red Cloud "tumultuous applause." "So many liars have been sent out [west]," he told his listeners, "and I have been stuffed full with their lies." The "earnest manner" and "magnetism" of Red Cloud made "a deep impression." Many of the gifts (fig. 231) that were given to the government by Native peoples were preserved as important artifacts.

Grant, however, had little practical ability to affect matters on the ground, and little interest in preserving Indian culture. His

fig. 229.
Red Cloud, Chief of the Oglala Sioux, c. 1870 (photograph courtesy of Library of Congress)

fig. 230.
"The Indians. Red Cloud at a Council with the President," *The New York Times*, June 10, 1870

fig. 231.
Plains Indian Moccasins, c. 1870, National Museum of American History

THE INDIANS.

Red Cloud at a Council with the President—Fort Fetterman Not to be Removed.

WASHINGTON, D. C., June 9.—The Red Cloud delegation called at the Executive Mansion today, and had an interview with the President. It took place in the Executive Office, the Indians standing in a semi-circle around the room. The talk was of short duration, and was substantially a repetition of what has already been said on both sides in the conference held between the Indians and the Government officials here. RED CLOUD did not recline on the floor in this instance as he did at the council on Tuesday, but stood upright and delivered a speech to the President.

goal instead was their assimilation into the white mainstream, where he saw a better future for them.[67]

Many in the press and the public supported Grant's peace policies. At the close of 1870, the president was hopeful that a gathering of tribal leaders would succeed in establishing a self-governing Indian Territory, but Congress would not relinquish control of the lands in question. In 1872, Apaches clashed with settlers who infringed upon their lands; later that year, Commissioner Ely Parker resigned under allegations of corruption. Through such events Grant held fast to his policy of kindness and justice to the Indian and swept the vote of the plains states in the presidential election. In 1873, public furor over a Modoc uprising in California failed to shake Grant's resolve. At the close of the year, in his annual message to Congress, Grant pushed for an "Indian Territory, south of Kansas & West of Arkansas … sufficient in area and agricultural resources to support all the Indians east of the Rocky Mountains" that would have a "territorial form of government." During the next year, however, when bands of Cheyenne, Kiowa, Comanche, and Arapahoe would not be contained, the United States Army retaliated and the southern plains erupted in violence. To add to the turmoil, gold had been discovered in the Black Hills (fig. 232). In 1875, Grant offered to buy this land and to provide replacement acreage to the south. When Red Cloud returned to Washington,

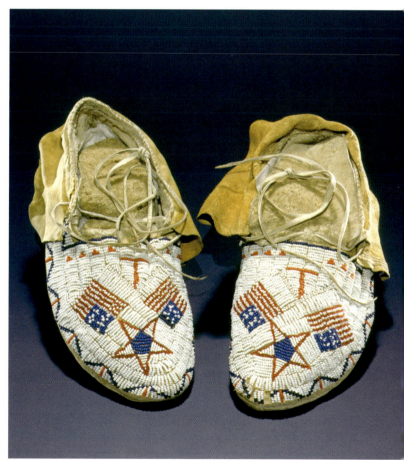

fig. 232.
Miller Studio, *Black Hills Exploration*, 1874 (photograph courtesy of New-York Historical Society Library, George T. Bagoe Collection, gift of Mrs. Elihu Spicer)

fig. 233.
Thomas Nast, *"News" in Washington*, woodcut, *Harper's Weekly*, June 19, 1875 - Penetrating Indian, "Those White Paper fellows tell Black Ink lies."
The Great Father, "Can such things be?"

Grant told him: "We have had great difficulty in keeping white people from going to the Black Hills in search of gold." Red Cloud, Spotted Tail, Little Wound, and the others in the delegation refused the offer. To further complicate the situation, a Yale paleontologist, Othniel C. Marsh, revealed widespread corruption in the procurement of supplies promised by the government to the Sioux, a matter about which Red Cloud had already intimated his concerns to Grant (fig. 233). Secretary of the Interior Columbus

Delano, who had allowed employees in his department, including his own son, to engage in land frauds, was forced to resign.[68]

Grant's policies were further jeopardized during the summer of 1876 by the battle at the Little Big Horn River in Montana, which later became known as "Custer's Last Stand." The deaths of white soldiers incited public furor when reports of a "battlefield like a slaughter pen" reached readers in the East during the Philadelphia Exposition, which had been created to celebrate the 100 anniversary of the signing of the Declaration of Independence (fig. 234). Grant had earlier directed Sheridan to force Sioux warriors back to their reservation. Sheridan seized the opportunity; he wrote to Sherman in May, "We might as well settle the Sioux matter now; it will be better for all concerned." A month later Custer, one of three commanders in a three-pronged offensive, underestimated both the size of the force he attacked and the leadership of Crazy Horse. His men were annihilated. Grant judged the massacre "a sacrifice of troops, brought on by Custer himself, that was wholly unnecessary—wholly unnecessary." This greatest victory of Indian forces over the United States military would ultimately lead to the imposition of harsher conditions on many Native peoples of the plains. By 1878 even Philip

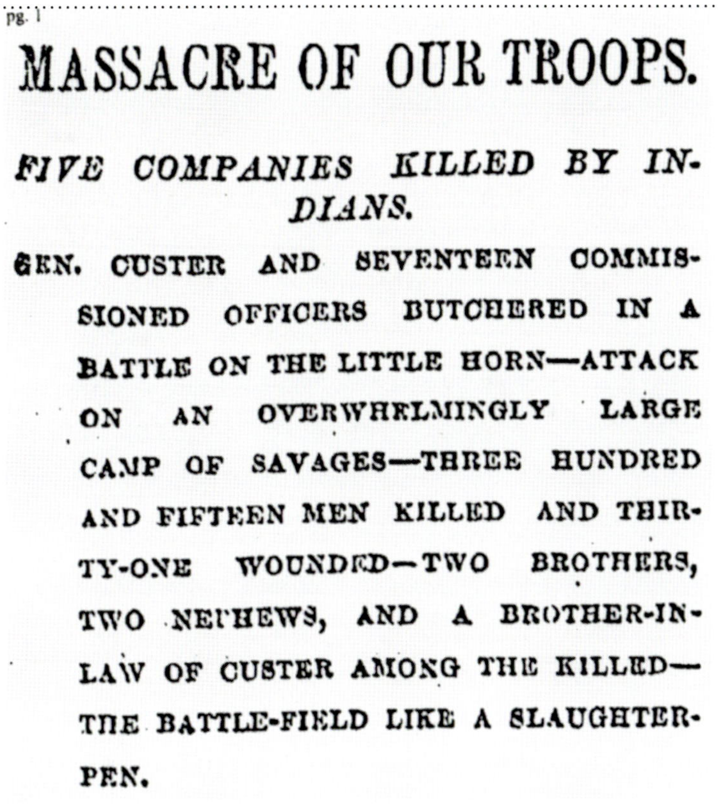

fig. 234.
"Massacre of our Troops," *The New York Times*, July 6, 1876

fig. 235.
Secretary of State Hamilton Fish, c. 1880–90 (photograph courtesy of New-York Historical Society Library)

MASSACRE OF OUR TROOPS.

FIVE COMPANIES KILLED BY INDIANS.

GEN. CUSTER AND SEVENTEEN COMMISSIONED OFFICERS BUTCHERED IN A BATTLE ON THE LITTLE HORN—ATTACK ON AN OVERWHELMINGLY LARGE CAMP OF SAVAGES—THREE HUNDRED AND FIFTEEN MEN KILLED AND THIRTY-ONE WOUNDED—TWO BROTHERS, TWO NEPHEWS, AND A BROTHER-IN-LAW OF CUSTER AMONG THE KILLED—THE BATTLE-FIELD LIKE A SLAUGHTER-PEN.

Sheridan had to admit, "We took away their country and their means of support, broke up their mode of living, their habits of life, introduced disease and decay among them, and it was for this and against this they made war. Could any one expect less?"[69]

International Affairs

Traveling in Europe after his retirement from the presidency, Grant made repeated references to his dislike for war. To Londoners he stated, "Although a soldier by education and profession, I have never felt any sort of fondness for war and I have never advocated it except as a means for peace." To the Midland International Arbitration Union in Birmingham he said much the same: "Though I followed a military life for the better part of my years, there was never a day of my life when I was not in favor of peace on any terms that were honorable." It was "my misfortune to be engaged in more battles than any other [American] general." Grant then posited a model for what would become the United Nations: "at some future day, the nations of the earth will agree upon some sort of congress, which shall take cognizance of international questions of difficulty, and whose decisions will be as binding as the decision of our Supreme Court is binding on us." In Berlin, the general told Chancellor Otto von Bismarck, "I am more of a farmer than a soldier. I take little or no interest in military affairs." When interviewed in Hamburg that same year, 1878, Grant said to a reporter, "I never liked service in the army—not as a young officer. I did not want to go to West Point. My appointment was an accident, and my father had to use his authority to make me go." One of the most successful generals of all time thought that war was useful only if it served as a stepping stone toward reconciliation. To the audience in London, Grant added, "I hope that we shall always settle our differences in all future negotiations as amicably as we did in a recent instance." He was referring to an arbitration treaty with England that averted a war and is now seen as one of the major accomplishments of his presidency.[70]

fig. 236.
Ulysses S. Grant, Kane, PA, to Hamilton Fish, *Letter,* August 14, 1869, Library of Congress

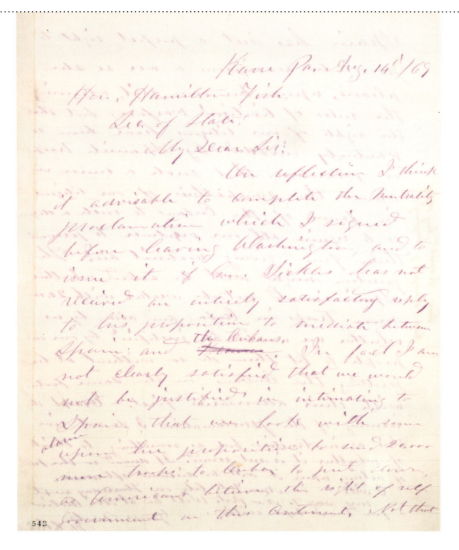

Grant stated in his first inaugural address, "In regard to foreign policy I would deal with nations as equitable law requires individuals to deal with each other." He was able to succeed in this area in large part because of the skills and integrity of his secretary of state, Hamilton Fish (fig. 235). Though very different in their backgrounds—the former governor, congressman, and senator was from a prominent New York family—the two came to admire one another greatly. After eight years of service the president wrote to Fish, "During your term of office new and complicated diplomatic questions have arisen which might readily have produced costly & bloody wars, which the country was ill prepared to meet. Through your statesmanship more than through any individual these questions have been peacibly settled." He added, "Our relations have at all times been so pleasant that I shall carry the remembrance of them through life."[71]

Cuba

A brutal rebellion against Spanish rule had broken out in Cuba, a slave state where political oppression was tolerated and many atrocities had been committed. Some Americans urged the president to intervene. They wanted as well reparations from Britain to compensate U.S. taxpayers for aid given to the Confederacy that had prolonged the Civil War, and particularly for damages to shipping that were wrought by the *Alabama* and her sister ships that had been built in British ports. As Grant pointed out to his cabinet, the two crises were related; America could hardly come to the support of rebels in Cuba and at the same time condemn Britain for having followed the same course. During his first year in office, as outlined in a letter to Fish, who was the architect of a proposal to avoid conflict (fig. 236), Grant resisted intervention, but he took two actions: he issued a neutrality proclamation and offered to mediate between the rebels and the Spanish government. As Grant convincingly explained to those in Congress who challenged him, "The insurgents hold no town or city, have no established seat of government; they have no prize courts; no organization for receiving and collecting revenues." In 1875, toward the end of his tenure in office, Grant would reiterate to Congress that in Cuba, "no … civil organization exists which may be recognized as an independent government capable of performing its international obligations and entitled to be treated as one of the powers of the earth." He added, "the conflict in Cuba, dreadful and devastating as were its incidents, did not rise to the fearful dignity of war." "[T]he good offices of the United States as a mediator," he later explained, "were tendered in good faith, without any selfish purpose, in the interest of humanity and in sincere friendship for both parties, but were at the time declined by Spain."[72]

Grant held fast to his conviction, despite his personal preference for Cuban independence. A number of Americans, including Secretary of War John Rawlins, urged or actually took part in private expeditions to Cuba to support the rebels. Rawlins had been given $28,000 in Cuban bonds by a nationalist exile group in New York

fig. 237.
Thomas Nast, *The Spanish Bull in Cuba Gone Mad. It must be stopped. If Spain can't do it, WE MUST!*, woodcut, *Harper's Weekly*, November 29, 1873

fig. 238.
Santo Domingo, 1871, from "United States—Commission of Inquiry to Santo Domingo," New-York Historical Society Library

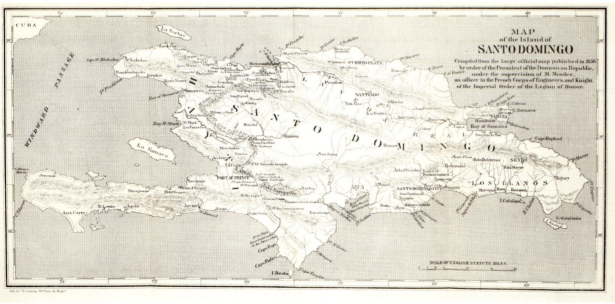

City in an attempt to purchase support. In 1873, the movement for war was particularly strong. In waters near Cuba, the Spanish not only seized the ship *Virginius*, as well as other expeditionary crafts, but also executed several dozen prisoners, some of whom claimed U.S. citizenship. Newspapers urged retribution; Civil War veterans offered their services. Grant was outraged and sent warships to Cuban waters. But rather than join the tide of the moment, as Nast had anticipated (fig. 237), Grant attempted to buy Cuba. When that failed, he and Fish skillfully maneuvered through the crisis.[73]

Santo Domingo

In 1869–70, the president directed a good deal of energy to a scheme to annex Santo Domingo (the present Dominican Republic), a country then troubled by internal dissent, poverty, and the specter of invasion from the adjoining nation of Haiti (fig. 238). To Grant's thinking, Samana Bay would provide a strategic port needed by the navy as a coaling station, and any new American states to be carved out of the island would furnish rich natural resources, as well as provide a place of refuge for freedpeople who were fed up with oppression on the mainland. Grant saw annexation as a solution to the racial hatred he had witnessed in the South. He envisioned "States … under the protection of the General Government; but the citizens would be almost wholly colored." He sent his longtime army aide Orville Babcock to gather information and to de-

LEE AND GRANT

termine if the population there really wanted annexation. He then drafted a memorandum (fig. 239) stating the benefits: "It is capable of supporting the entire colored population of the United States, should it choose to emigrate … [and] the two great necessities in every family, sugar and Coffee, would be cheapened near one half." Besides, he added, "San Domingo is weak and must go some where for protection. Is the United States willing that she should go elsewhere than to herself?"[74]

Grant neglected to present this possibility formally to the Senate, however, which particularly galled his political arch-rival, the powerful and self-righteous Charles Sumner of Massachusetts, the chairman of the Foreign Relations Committee and a man who was embittered that the president had not made him secretary of state. Sumner blocked Grant's effort. The president retaliated by appointing a special commission to explore the issue further. "I selected two men who were opposed to St. Domingo," Grant later recalled. "I also sent Frederick Douglass …. [T]hey were unanimous in favor of the annexation." He added, "It would have rendered the Cuban question more easy of solution," noting that "If two or three thousand blacks were to emigrate to St. Domingo under our Republic the Southern people would learn the crime of Ku Kluxism, because they would see how necessary the black man is to their own prosperity." This time, however, Grant's characteristic tenacity failed him. Public opinion had solidified against annexation and the idea died.[75]

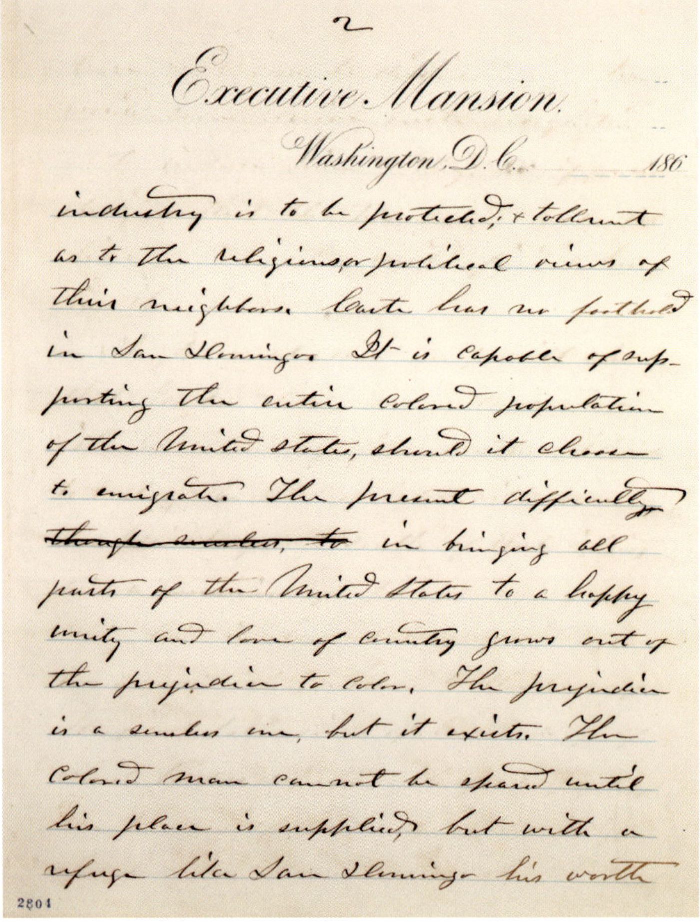
2

Executive Mansion,

Washington, D.C. 186

industry is to be protected, & tolerant as to the religious or political views of their neighbors. Caste has no foothold in San Domingo. It is capable of supporting the entire colored population of the United States, should it choose to emigrate. The present difficulty ~~though unspoken, to~~ in bringing all parts of the United States to a happy unity and love of country grows out of the prejudice to color. The prejudice is a senseless one, but it exists. The colored man cannot be spared until his place is supplied, but with a refuge like San Domingo his worth

2804

fig. 239.
Ulysses S. Grant, *Memorandum—Reasons why San Domingo should be annexed to the United States*, 1869–70, Library of Congress

Britain

Grant relied heavily on Hamilton Fish to deal with the most complex international crisis of his presidency: "I shall defer to you largely in this matter," he wrote to his secretary of state, "feeling that so much is due to you for the conception and bringing about of a settlement with the English Govt." The *Alabama* claims were at the top of the list, but the negotiators had also to settle border disagreements concerning Canada that for decades had gone unresolved. Those issues, which involved the North Atlantic fisheries, free navigation of the St. Lawrence River, damages wrought by pro-Irish raiding parties in southeastern Canada, and a determination of the northwest water boundary, would demand time and effort to sort out. Strong Anglophobic feelings stood in the way, including those of Sumner, who claimed that England's contributions to the Confederacy cost U.S. taxpayers $2 billion; he suggested that Canada be ceded to the U.S. as down payment for the debt. Grant and Fish broke with Sumner irrevocably, and ultimately managed to have him deposed from his position of power in the Senate. Fish guided Grant through the diplomatic negotiations, and Secretary of the Treasury George Boutwell helped him to appreciate how British banks could help reduce the U.S. Treasury's debt.[76]

In Britain the climate was ripe for reconciliation. William Gladstone's Liberals had deposed the Tory government of Benjamin Disraeli. Gladstone feared a renewal of fighting in the Crimea and the unforeseen consequences of the current Franco-Prussian War. He was anxious to avoid a third trouble spot, reasoning that if America was not compensated for its *Alabama* claims, it might begin to build naval cruisers for his enemies. Gladstone saw to it that a Joint High Commission was established to arbitrate the areas of contention with the United States. Grant and Queen Victoria each appointed five commissioners to meet in Washington to re-

fig. 240.
Thomas Nast, *International Law—The Better Way. "The Nations are fast becoming so Civilized as to feel that there is a Better Way to settle their difficulties than by fighting."—U. S. Grant*, woodcut, *Harper's Weekly*, 1874

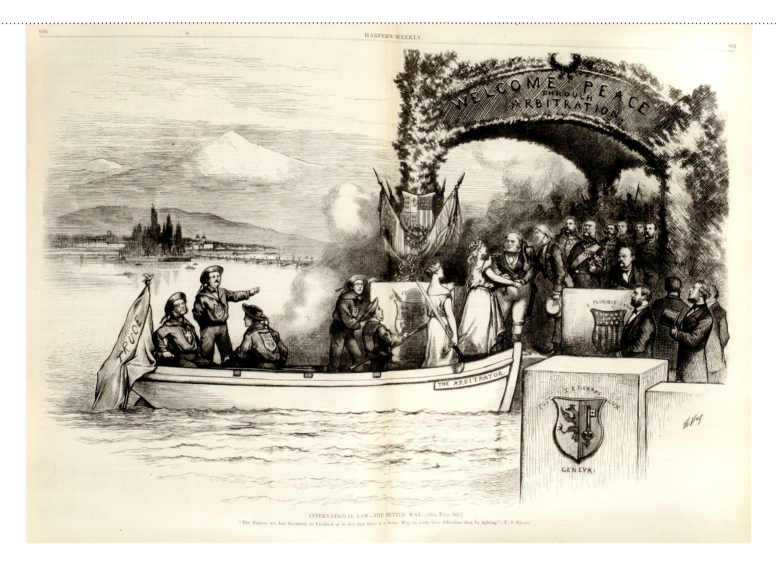

solve the differences. Fish and his counterpart, the Earl of Ripon, George Fredrick Samuel Robinson, took a liking to each other and calmly guided the project through thirty-seven half-day negotiation sessions: "This is the proudest day of my life," Ripon said at the conclusion to Fish, who felt the same gratification. The press praised the process and its results (fig. 240). *The New York Times* reported that "the 'Treaty of Washington' ought to be received with rejoicing, not only by the nations chiefly concerned, but by the whole civilized world." The two most difficult issues, the *Alabama* claims and the northwest border settlement, were sent to arbitration, the former to be addressed by a panel formed with the help of the leaders of Italy, Brazil, and Switzerland, and the latter to be decided by the emperor of Germany. In the end, the United States fared well in both decisions, winning $15.5 million for the *Alabama* claims. More importantly, a new relationship between Britain and America had been established, as was a definition of neutrality as non-involvement. Grant reported proudly to Congress, "An example has thus been set which … may be followed by other civilized nations and finally be the means of returning to productive industry millions of men now maintained to settle the disputes of nations by the bayonet and broadside." The accomplishment was unprecedented in U.S. history. In the process, Grant had ably carried the United States into the sphere of international relations.[77]

"No Bottom to Stand On": Corruption in the Grant Administration

By 1868, the federal government had grown so large in size that it was difficult to administer. What Grant said six years later regard-

fig. 241.
Thomas Nast, "This Tub Has No Bottom To Stand On," woodcut, Harper's Weekly, June 5, 1875

fig. 242.
Napoleon Sarony, *Jay Gould*, c. 1870 (photograph courtesy of New-York Historical Society Library, gift of the estate of Helen Miller Gould Shepard and Finley Johnson Shepard)

own deals, and ultimately embarrassed Grant by their indiscretions. The unfortunate consequence was that Grant's presidential terms are remembered today more for those scandals than for the valuable contributions that he made in human rights and international relations. The following incidents should be seen as exemplary of the types of management problems that Grant allowed to occur, and of some of his often-tardy attempts to correct them.[78]

ing one of the government departments could easily apply to the whole: "Its duties have been added to from time to time until they have become so onerous that without the most perfect system and order it will be impossible for any Sec. of the Int. to keep trace of all official transactions by his authority, and in his name, and for which he is held personally responsible." As is still true today, bureaucracy and perfection are terms that are rarely complementary.

Grant's inclination to reward friends and acquaintances with important political appointments and then to place what seemed like blind and irrevocable trust in their integrity at times would lead to disaster. His further inclination to accept personal gifts from the wealthy who courted him for political favors set a bad example for his appointees, some of whom shared the greed that was prevalent in the postwar era (fig. 241). A leader with impeccable integrity was needed in the White House to set a tone of high personal honor. When the highly respected Grant seemed to fail to set that standard, some in his administration felt free to make their

fig. 243.
William T. Howell, *Jim Fisk, Colonel of the 7th Regiment of the New York Militia*, 1870 (photograph courtesy of New-York Historical Society Library, gift of Edward B. Child)

fig. 244.
Currier and Ives, *The "Boy of the Period" [Jim Fisk] Stirring Up the Animals*, 1869, lithograph, 13 × 17⅛ in. (33.0 × 45.5 cm.), Library of Congress

Black Friday

In his first inaugural address Grant had stated that "The payment of this principal and interest [the national debt], as well as the return to a specie basis [gold or silver currency] … must be provided for." As one quick means to bolster the dollar, secretary Boutwell set about selling the government's growing surplus of gold for greenbacks at weekly auctions. He kept sufficient money in circulation so as not to disrupt the economy; however, he was at the same time buying back wartime bonds as well. The price of gold dropped in proportion to the amount that the government sold. Two speculators, Jay Gould and Jim Fisk (figs. 242 and 243), deduced that if they could determine beforehand the government's schedule for the sale of gold, they could make a windfall profit. Using insider information, they could buy at a low price, withhold their gold to raise its value, and then sell at an inflated price before the bubble burst. They garnered the assistance of the president's brother-in-law, Abel Rathbone Corbin. Gould also gave a $10,000 check to Daniel Butterfield, the assistant treasurer of New York, who at the close of the war had won Grant's favor when he raised $105,000 as a testimonial gift to the victorious general. Gould also tried to bribe Horace Porter, Grant's secretary, and Corbin even

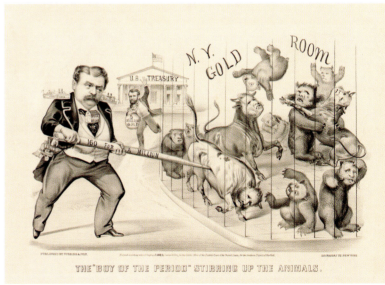

tried to give stock to Julia Grant, but both declined the offers. Gould placed gold in the bank accounts of Corbin and Butterfield, and Corbin introduced Gould and Fisk to the president, thereby creating an illusion of friendship that enhanced their effectiveness on Wall Street.[79]

Grant was oblivious to the scheme. When he figured it out, however, he acted decisively (fig. 244). He warned Boutwell in advance—"a desperate struggle is now taking place, and each party want the government to help them out. I write this letter to advise you of what I think you may expect, to put you on your guard." He

LEE AND GRANT

had Julia write to Grant's sister to "tell [your husband] to have nothing to do with Jay Gould and Jim Fisk. If he does, he will be ruined, for come what may, [the president] will do his duty to the country and the trusts in his keeping." On "Black Friday," September 24, 1869, Grant ordered Boutwell to sell gold "to save the country from a panic." *The New York Times* reported the next day, "The whole gambling fabric … fell at the single flash of the telegraph from Washington ordering an extra sale for the Treasury of only four millions [of dollars of gold]." Readers were assured that "There was not a word of truth in all that was insinuated against the high officials at Washington …. [A] gold speculation … was sure to fail." For the first time ever, the government had intervened with decisive action to control the marketplace. The economy, however, would take months to recover. On September 29, the *Times* described conditions on Wall Street as "disastrous." Brokerage firms had gone bankrupt. Farmers suffered terribly because the price of wheat dropped to nearly half of what it had been. Gould and Fisk, however, went unpunished and retained their wealth.[80]

Efforts at Civil Service Reform
To his later embarrassment, Grant too often indulged relatives and friends with political favors. His father deluged him with requests. His brother-in-law, James F. Casey, held a patronage position in Louisiana where troubles continually plagued Grant, and the placement of his brother Orvil at the Chicago Customhouse and his former staff officer George K. Leet at the New York City Customhouse caused various public relations dilemmas for the president. There were additional patronage problems in southern New York, Philadelphia, Florida, and even the Dakota Territory. While not setting a good example of incorruptibility, Grant nonetheless identified civil service reform as a priority of his presidential term. Typically realistic, he accepted political patronage as a fact of life. Rather than attempt to eradicate it, he tried instead to curb its vices.[81]

Grant was the first president to recommend a professional civil service. He advocated a merit system for federal employees, and even established a commission to develop rules and regulations to govern them. Congress, however, was unwilling to support such a policy. In 1872, Grant lectured Congress, "There is no duty which so much embarrasses the Executive and heads of departments as that of appointments, nor is there any such arduous and thankless labor imposed on Senators and representatives as that of finding places for constituents." He added, "The present system does not secure the best men, and often not even fit men, for public place." Two years later he could remind the legislators that "rules have been established to regulate the tenure of office and the mode of appointments. But without the more direct sanction of Congress these rules cannot be made entirely effective." Grant would ultimately compromise: "In lieu of competitive examinations I would rather approve of selection and then a thorough examination to test whether the person selected was fully qualified." In 1873 he complained, "there has never been any action making these rules, or any rule, binding"; in 1874, "it is impossible to carry this system to a successful issue without general approval and assistance, and positive law to support it." In the end, Grant was forced to dissolve the commission he had established and to admit a measure of defeat in his efforts to professionalize the civil service (fig. 245).[82]

The Back Pay Grab
On its final day in session in March 1873, the 42nd Congress voted to increase the salaries of its members, of the Supreme Court justices, and of the president and vice president. None of these salaries had been raised since 1852. Congress additionally awarded itself retroactively two years of salary. This so-called "Back Pay Grab" was inserted into a major appropriation bill, the one that would keep the machinery of government in motion during the coming fiscal year. Even in an age when greed was often paramount, this action crossed the line. *The New York Times* complained, "The public will not readily forget a piece of rascality so shameless, so despicable, and so conspicuous." The first order of the new Congress was to repeal the measure. It would not vote itself a raise until 1904. The *Times* did not fault Grant—"The President would be powerless to frustrate it, without blocking the wheels of the Government"—but others did blame him. Grant could have avoided a scandal by calling a special session of Congress to resolve the issue, or at the least he could have refused his own raise. Because he did neither, the "Back Pay Grab" tarnished his reputation as president.[83]

The Crédit Mobilier
Grant had no control whatsoever over the Crédit Mobilier affair, which would also be laid at his door. This scandal was named for a

fig. 245.
Thomas Nast, *No Surrender. U. S. G. "I am Determined to Enforce those Regulations,"* woodcut, *Harper's Weekly*, December 7, 1872

dummy corporation set up by the directors of the Union Pacific Railroad as a means to steal money from that company's treasury. Before Grant took office, members of Congress had been given shares of Crédit Mobilier stock to keep them quiet. When the story broke four years later, Grant typically supported his lieutenant, this time Schuyler Colfax, the vice president, who was implicated along with a dozen others: "I am as satisfied now as I have ever been, of your integrity, patriotism and freedom from the charges imputed as if I knew of my own knowledge your innocence." In the end, Colfax was not prosecuted because the incriminating evidence against him was inconclusive. For more than six months, however, newspapers followed Congress's investigation of itself. Most of the stories were critical. The appearance of Colfax before the Crédit Mobilier Committee brought some calm to the tempest, as reported in *The New York Times* in January 1873 (fig. 246): "Everybody breathes much freer since the testimony is all out …. [T]here is not an intelligent person here who believes for a moment that a particle of corruption, in motive or in action, attaches to these gentlemen." Only three members of Congress received any sort of reprimand, but the episode damaged Grant's reputation because his vice president had been involved.[84]

The Panic of 1873 and Grant's Veto of the Inflation Bill
One well-publicized episode during Grant's tenure in the White House ultimately became a political and fiscal triumph for the president. This was his handling of a crisis not of his own making, the Panic of 1873, by a bold veto of a bill that would have increased the amount of paper money in circulation. In his first Inaugural Address, Grant had given over half his speech to the financial legacy of the Civil War, the "great debt … contracted in securing to us, and our posterity, the Union." The war had been paid for with paper money, and in the process the national debt had risen from $64 million to $2.8 billion. The payment of bonds bearing 6 percent interest and the removal from circulation of $356 million in greenbacks "must be provided for," Grant told the Congress, thereby repeating the philosophy of Alexander Hamilton. "To protect the national honor every dollar of Government indebtedness should be paid in gold." The government sale of gold that had precipitated the Black Friday crisis had been implemented as one step to relieve the problem.[85]

In September 1873, however, a speculative boom caused an economic panic that shook the nation. Money became scarce, farmers lost their farms, factories and mills closed, financial institutions collapsed, and commerce inevitably shrunk. More than sixty bills were introduced in Congress to pour additional paper money into circulation. George Boutwell, who understood finance, was no

fig. 246.
"The Credit Mobilier. Testimony of Mr. Colfax Before the Investigating Committee," *The New York Times*, January 8, 1873

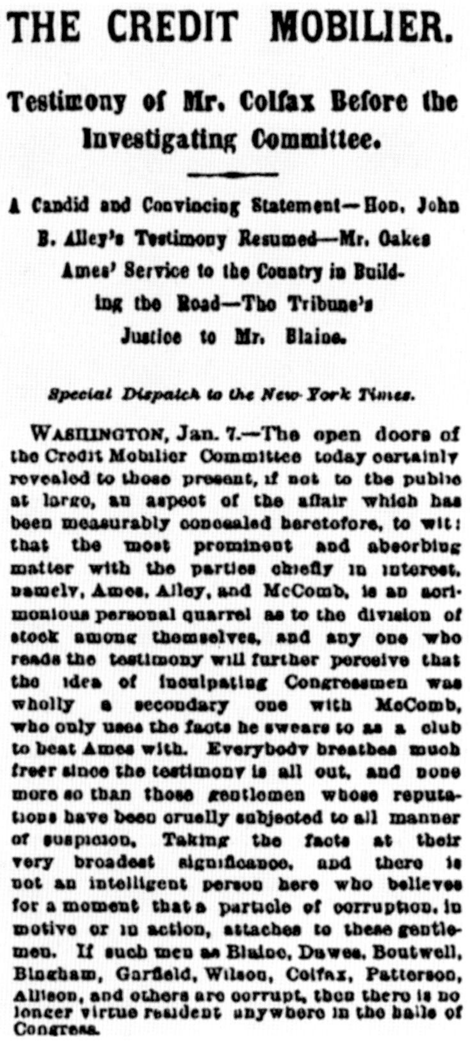

THE CREDIT MOBILIER.

Testimony of Mr. Colfax Before the Investigating Committee.

A Candid and Convincing Statement—Hon. John B. Alley's Testimony Resumed—Mr. Oakes Ames' Service to the Country in Building the Road—The Tribune's Justice to Mr. Blaine.

Special Dispatch to the New-York Times.

WASHINGTON, Jan. 7.—The open doors of the Credit Mobilier Committee today certainly revealed to those present, if not to the public at large, an aspect of the affair which has been measurably concealed heretofore, to wit: that the most prominent and absorbing matter with the parties chiefly in interest, namely, Ames, Alley, and McComb, is an acrimonious personal quarrel as to the division of stock among themselves, and any one who reads the testimony will further perceive that the idea of inculpating Congressmen was wholly a secondary one with McComb, who only uses the facts he swears to as a club to beat Ames with. Everybody breathes much freer since the testimony is all out, and none more so than those gentlemen whose reputations have been cruelly subjected to all manner of suspicion. Taking the facts at their very broadest significance, and there is not an intelligent person here who believes for a moment that a particle of corruption, in motive or in action, attaches to these gentlemen. If such men as Blaine, Dawes, Boutwell, Bingham, Garfield, Wilson, Colfax, Patterson, Allison, and others are corrupt, then there is no longer virtue resident anywhere in the halls of Congress.

longer Grant's secretary of the treasury; his successor, William Richardson, had little experience in such matters. Grant took the lead himself. He traveled to New York City to confer with financiers, to whom he then wrote letters of reassurance that were published in newspapers to help restore public confidence: "no Government efforts will avail without the active co-operation of the banks and moneyed corporations of the country …. The banks are now strong enough to adopt a liberal policy on their part, and by a generous system of discounts to sustain the business interests of the country …." He deduced that elasticity was needed in the supply of money, and so advised Congress—"[M]uch more currency, or money, is required to transact the legitimate trade of the country during the fall and winter months, when the vast crops are being removed, than during the balance of the year." The president had to decide whether or not to approve the leading bill introduced in Congress to increase the greenbacks in circulation. Businessmen and bankers were divided on the issue and gave the president mixed advice. Grant remembered his own suffering as a farmer during the Panic of 1857. He decided, however, that his duty as chief executive was to look to the long-term solution, and so he vetoed the "Inflation Bill." He told the Senate, "if in practice the measure should fail to create the abundance of circulation expected of it," its supporters would simply "clamor" for more and more paper money. Eastern financiers, who advocated the gold standard or "hard money," praised Grant's decision. Small merchants and farmers, who wanted abundant paper currency or "soft money" in circulation, were disappointed. Hamilton Fish credited Grant for his accomplishment in terms that remind us of Grant's determination as a military leader: "Never did a man more conscientiously reach his conclusions than he did in the matter of the bill …. He has a wonderful amount of good sense, and when left alone is very apt to follow it, and to 'fight it out on that line.'" Nast followed that cue, showing no mercy for the president's defeated opponents (fig. 247).[86]

Grant's decision proved to be sound. He had again acted decisively, as he had on Black Friday when he set a precedent for governmental involvement in the marketplace. In so doing he had taken what he saw as the first step toward establishing a stable currency. Congress supported him by agreeing to resume specie (coin) payment in 1879. In the last quarter of the nineteenth century the United States enjoyed unparalleled economic growth, so much so that by 1900 the American dollar had become the most stable currency in the world. Grant considered his stand on inflation to be his greatest accomplishment as president. In the process, the Republican party, its role as emancipator now behind it, had become redefined as the party of economic conservatism.[87]

The Sanborn Contracts

While Grant debated whether or not to reject the Inflation Bill of 1873, he was shaken by another scandal that touched dangerously close to the White House. It involved William Richardson and possible internal revenue fraud (fig. 249). Benjamin Butler, who had failed to win Grant's favor both during the war as a general

fig. 247.
Thomas Nast, *A General Blow Up—Dead Asses Kicking a Live Lion*, woodcut, *Harper's Weekly*, May 16, 1874

fig. 248.
Charles A. Zimmerman, *John D. Sanborn*, 1861 (photograph courtesy of New-York Historical Society Library)

what he collected he paid as bribes to public officials to keep the machinery of the fraud in motion. *The New York Times* reported that "large amounts of money, amounting to millions of dollars, due the Government" were at stake, called the Sanborn contracts "discouraging and disgusting," and concluded that the public need only decide whether the conduct of Richardson was "corrupt, or that it was inexpressibly negligent and careless" (fig. 250). Since the

and afterwards as a congressman, had inserted into an appropriations bill a measure that allowed a Massachusetts acquaintance of his, John Sanborn (fig. 248), the exceptional privilege of continuing a lucrative contract to collect back taxes from such profitable businesses as railroads, maritime shippers, and distilleries, and to keep half of the money for himself. If the actions of Butler were not criminal, those of Richardson, who had signed the contract and had directed revenue agents not to pursue delinquent accounts that Sanborn eyed, certainly were. In testimony to Congress, Sanborn exposed broader corruption when he claimed that much of

LEE AND GRANT   289

fig. 249.
Mathew Brady, *William A. Richardson*, c. 1870s (photograph courtesy of New-York Historical Society Library)

fig. 250.
"The President and the Sanborn Business," *New York Times*, May 5, 1874

THE PRESIDENT AND THE SANBORN BUSINESS.

The Committee on Ways and Means yesterday presented to the House a careful and compact report of the facts in the Sanborn business, which we publish this morning. The general conviction will be that it should make it impossible for Messrs. RICHARDSON and SAWYER to remain longer in charge of the Treasury Department. The report leaves but two judgments to be formed of the conduct of these gentlemen—that it was corrupt, or that it was inexpressibly negligent and careless. The committee say, in regard to Mr. RICHARDSON, that they find nothing to impeach the integrity of his action, and they compel us to accept the alternative conclusion. They make no distinct declaration as to Mr. SAWYER, and leave us in doubt as to whether we are to condemn him on one or the other count; but that he is to be condemned they leave no doubt at all. We shall not describe in detail the facts presented by the committee. For these we refer our readers to the report. But we call attention to a few of the most important facts, which show a condition of things in the Treasury Department that cannot be ignored with safety.

Committee on Ways and Means could "find nothing to impeach the integrity of his actions," the article continued, "they compel us to accept the alternative conclusion." Although urged by the press to demand the resignation of Richardson—"If he values the good name of his Administration … he will lose no time in exercising his power"—Grant foolishly refused to do so. However, as the scandal played out in the newspapers over a three-month period, Richardson eventually resigned on his own.[88]

The Whiskey Ring

The next scandal to rock the White House touched the president's principal secretary and aide since the Vicksburg campaign of a decade earlier, General Orville Babcock (fig. 252). The crime was yet another internal revenue fraud involving bribery and the failure to collect back taxes. It was

fig. 251.
After a photograph by Alexander Gardner, *General Benjamin H. Bristow*, 1874, wood engraving, New-York Historical Society Library

fig. 252.
After a photograph by Mathew Brady, *Orville Babcock*, c. 1875, wood engraving, New-York Historical Society Library

BRIGADIER-GENERAL O. E. BABCOCK, SHARER IN THE GENERAL ORDER SWINDLE.—FROM A PHOTOGRAPH BY BRADY.

prosecuted by the new secretary of the treasury, Benjamin H. Bristow (fig. 251), who had fought with Grant at Donelson and Shiloh. After having replaced the "negligent" Richardson, Bristow first cleaned up the Treasury Department, dismissing more than 700 employees. He then vigorously took on an issue that was related to the Sanborn contracts and was a long-standing problem for his department, the evasion of taxes due on whiskey. Precedent stretched all the way back to the time of George Washington. Bristow ordered raids on revenue offices and distilleries. Grant offered encouragement, advising, "Let no guilty man escape." He added, to his later regret, "Be specially vigilant … against all who insinuate that they have high influence to protect, or to protect them" (fig. 253).[89]

By auditing the records of distillers and shipping companies, Bristow turned up sufficient evidence to uncover "Whiskey Rings" made up of dishonest businessmen and corrupt revenue agents in Chicago, Milwaukee, Cincinnati, and St. Louis. The losses in uncollected taxes totaled millions of dollars. One of those indicted in the St. Louis district, which stretched to Texas and New Mexico and where two-thirds of the whiskey went untaxed, was former General John McDonald, a friend of Babcock. They had communicated with each other; Grant's secretary thereby appeared guilty by association. When a St. Louis prosecutor complained of "presidential interference," Grant removed him; when a friend on the grand jury gave the president privileged information, Grant rewarded the friend's son with a consulship; and when prosecutors offered immunity or leniency for testimony against Babcock, Grant directed Attorney General Edwards Pierrepont to dissuade them. When Whiskey Ring conspirators were convicted, Grant pardoned several of them. The president convinced himself that Babcock was innocent and that he, even more than his secretary, was the victim of persecution by a man (Bristow) who held presidential aspirations. Overprotective of his appointees as always, Grant gave a deposition that was read at Babcock's trial: "He had not seen or learned anything in any way connecting Gen. Babcock with the whisky rings"

LEE AND GRANT 291

fig. 253.
Ulysses S. Grant, *Endorsement*, July 29, 1875, Huntington Library

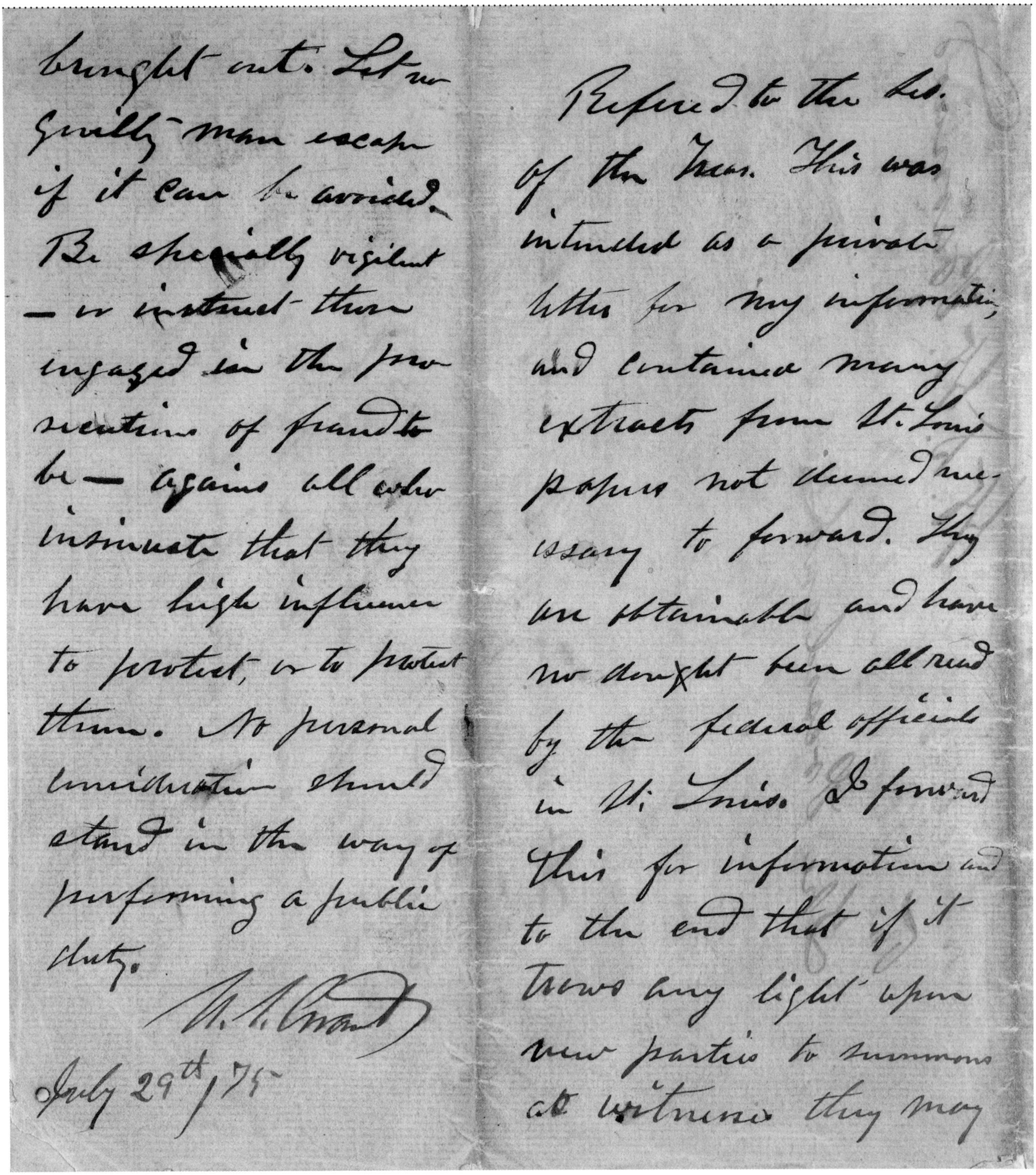

Referred to the Sec. of the Treas. This was intended as a private letter for my information, and contained many extracts from St. Louis papers not deemed necessary to forward. They are obtainable and have no doubt been all read by the federal officials in St. Louis. I forward this for information and to the end that if it throws any light upon new parties to summons as witnesses they may

brought out. Let no guilty man escape if it can be avoided. Be especially vigilant — or instruct those engaged in the prosecutions of frauds to be — against all who insinuate that they have high influence to protect, or to protect them. No personal consideration should stand in the way of performing a public duty.

U. S. Grant

July 29th /75

fig. 254.
Mathew Brady, *William W. Belknap*, c. 1865–75 (photograph courtesy of New-York Historical Society Library)

fig. 255.
"Belknap and the President," *The New York Times*, March 3, 1876.

and "he did not believe" that Babcock "had been engaged in any wrong transactions." By his testimony, the popular president silenced most of the critics and won his secretary's acquittal.[90]

The trial of Babcock excited "great popular interest" according to *The New York Times*, which put the story on the front page almost every day in February 1876. The verdict, the paper predicted, "will be received with general satisfaction throughout the country." Most Americans wanted to believe that their president and his appointees were guiltless: "it would have given a serious shock to our faith in the possibility of public virtue to find that a man occupying so honorable a position as Gen. BABCOCK should have basely betrayed the implicit trust which was reposed in him." Even though Grant had little direct involvement in the matter, such financial scandals would be remembered when the former president would later place trust in other undeserving individuals.[91]

The Indian Trading Scandal

The greed of a socially ambitious and extravagant woman, Carrie Belknap, the wife of William Belknap (fig. 254), the successor to the late John Rawlins as secretary of war, brought about her husband's downfall. The Belknaps were actually guilty of grosser abuse than Interior Secretary Columbus Delano in the handling of the government's obligations to the Native American. Military trading posts, which yielded lucrative commissions, were awarded by contract through the War Department. Carrie Belknap managed to direct the contract to trade at Fort Sill to a New York acquaintance, Caleb Marsh. The current holder of that post, John Evans, however, bribed Marsh and Mrs. Belknap to be allowed to keep his position. Marsh later testified that he paid Carrie Belknap $10,000 initially and $6,000 since. After she died months later, the payments continued to her widower. When the crime was uncovered, the secretary quickly submitted his resignation in order to avoid impeachment for accepting bribes. Grant accepted the resignation, which made it appear as

> **BELKNAP AND THE PRESIDENT.**
>
> THE EXTENT OF BELKNAP'S GUILT UNKNOWN TO THE PRESIDENT WHEN THE RESIGNATION WAS ACCEPTED—BELKNAP'S FUTURE ACTION.
>
> WASHINGTON, March 2.—The President, in conversation with friends to-night, stated emphatically that he was not aware of the enormity of the charges against Belknap at the time he tendered and the President accepted his resignation. From the hurried and incoherent manner of Belknap's communication to him, the President drew the conclusion that Mrs. Belknap, and not her husband, was the guilty party, and that the General assumed all responsibility and censure in order to shield his wife.

fig. 256.
William Cogswell, *Ulysses Simpson Grant and Family*, 1867, oil on canvas, 120 × 96 in. (305 × 244 cm.), National Museum of American History

though he was shielding his appointee. The House of Representatives presented resolutions of impeachment "for high crimes and misdemeanors in office," but the Senate acquitted Belknap.[92]

This scandal broke in March 1876, only a week after the acquittal of General Babcock. The newspapers picked it up immediately (fig. 255), reporting that the news "has already made the circuit of the world." *The Times* of London called the event "grave because it is confirmatory of the suspicion which has long prevailed among the American people," who were now speaking with "altered tones." *The New York Times* reported in Washington "a depressed and gloomy state of feeling." It labeled the scandal "a national disgrace [that] ... touches the American people without distinction of politics," and is "evidence of a debased standard of public duty." The press and the public were tired of such behavior; there had been "too many examples during the last ten years." *The New York Times* excused Grant to some extent: "the President drew the conclusion that Mrs. Belknap, and not her husband, was the guilty party, and that the General assumed all responsibility and censure in order to shield his wife," adding that "Belknap's guilt was as much of a surprise to the President as to any one else." But, the paper went on: "The country ... cannot be blind to the errors of judgment which he has at various times committed in throwing the shield of his authority over men totally undeserving of his confidence .... It is part of the duty of the President ... to tak[e] care that he surrounds himself with men by whom [the] laws are respected." By the end of Grant's second term, the press had figured out his great shortcoming as president: "Blind unquestioning confidence in one's friends may be accounted a virtue in private life, but it is nearly allied to a grievous fault in public station."[93]

The problems for the president did not end with Belknap's resignation. The interim successor in the War Department, George M. Robeson, was investigated for corruption in the Navy Department, and an examination of the trading post system turned up evidence of influence peddling by Grant's brother Orvil. The president himself, however, never broke the law. Hamilton Fish said of him, "I do not think it would have been possible for Grant to have told a lie, even if he had composed it and written it down." Attorney General Rockwood Hoar reached the same conclusion: "I would as soon think St. Paul had got some of the thirty pieces of silver [as think Grant guilty of graft]." Because of the actions of men in whom he had placed trust, however, by midway through his first term Grant was already looking forward to the day of his leaving the presidency as "the happiest of my life, except possibly the day I left West Point."[94]

The Grants in Washington

The Grant family settled comfortably into the White House. The two older sons, Fred and Ulysses, Jr. (Buck), were away at school for most of the time, but at least at the start the family could be imagined as epitomizing the American ideal of domestic bliss (fig. 256). "Our eight years in the Executive Mansion were delightful," Julia later recalled, adding with reference to the scandals, "but there were

fig. 257.
Pach Brothers, *Gen. Grant and Family at Long Branch, New Jersey*, 1870, photograph from the collection of Keya Morgan, New York City

some dark clouds in the bright sky." Nonetheless, at the end of her life she remembered the White House as seeming "as much like home to me as the old farm in Missouri, White Haven." The family's happy mood followed the example of Ulysses and Julia, whose love for each other did provide an ideal for the nation. Their children later testified that the couple never exchanged a harsh word or showed the slightest sign of hostility toward each other. In the two decades after the war they were rarely separated. In their fifties, they still held hands and insisted on being seated beside one another. Julia wrote, "[H]e was always perfection, both in manner and person, a cheerful, self-reliant, earnest gentleman. His beautiful eyes, windows of his great soul; his mouth so tender, yet so firm …. [He] was the very nicest and handsomest man I ever saw." Ulysses, who found inspiration and solace in his wife's company, felt the same utter devotion to her. They extended their kindness to their children, perhaps setting the mark so high that the younger ones would be unable to find the same fulfillment in marriage.[95]

Julia (fig. 258) complained that Andrew Johnson had left the White House in a shambles. "I found [it] in utter confusion," she wrote. "I at last had the furniture arranged in suites, so that each room would have its own set. I found it scattered widely in the upper chambers. Chairs and lounges were recovered; the hall

fig. 258.
Henry Ulke, *Julia Grant as First Lady*, c. 1869, photograph from the collection of Keya Morgan, New York City

carpets, which were much worn and so ugly I could not bear to look at them, were replaced." Following the example set decades earlier by George and Martha Washington at their residence in Philadelphia, Julia and Ulysses each received visitors at the presidential mansion once a week. "I am very fond of society and enjoyed to the fullest extent the opportunity afforded me at the White House," she remembered. Julia "felt a little shy" at her first reception, but she soon warmed to the event after inviting her husband and the wives of his appointees to join her. She described the president's levees as "brilliant," not at all what might have been expected given his relatively humble beginnings: "The senators and representatives with their families, the diplomatic corps and their families, always in full dress, officers of the army and navy in full uniform, and all of the society people of Washington in full dress, made a gay and brilliant gathering …. I have visited many courts and, I am proud to say, I saw none that excelled in brilliancy the receptions of President Grant." She wrote that she enjoyed the "excellent" state dinners, but "It is around our social private table that my memory still clings with the greatest pleasure." Julia would often place next to her at dinner parties her eighty-three-year-old father, Colonel Dent, who remained an unreconstructed southerner, "so as to engage his attention when some anecdote was being related which threw the laugh on his [Democratic] party."[96]

The two oldest of the Grant children were soon off to college, Fred to West Point and Ulysses, Jr. to Harvard. (The same schools had been chosen by the two oldest sons of Robert E. Lee.) We "saw little or nothing of [them]," Julia wrote. For the enjoyment of the younger ones, Nellie and Jess, Julia closed the back yard of the White House to the public: "the children and I had that beautiful lawn for eight years, and I assure you we enjoyed it." Ulysses "was fond of talking to them," Julia remembered, but she also commented that "The General had no idea of the government of the children. He would have allowed them to do pretty much as they pleased (hunt, swim, fish, etc.) provided it did not interfere with any duty, but his word was law always." The president set up a daily routine that resembled Robert E. Lee's postwar schedule. Breakfast was a family ritual, followed by a walk, then work at the office for five hours, which was followed by an afternoon carriage drive or stroll. Grant was still a fine horseman. He loved to drive fast trotters, and he had the opportunity in New York to take the reins behind the world champion Dexter, who was owned by his friend Robert Bonner (fig. 259). A fine carriage that the Grants used in Washington is preserved at the National Museum of American History. The family, still supported by African American servants, summered on the New Jersey coast (fig. 257):

> [A]t our cottage at Long Branch … the President enjoyed driving and gathered new strength …. Tired and weary as he was with his monotonous official duties, he hastened with delight, as soon as Congress adjourned, to its health-giving breezes and its wide and restful piazzas. What glorious drives we enjoyed on that enchanting beach! Our children were with us here too, which was a great pleasure.[97]

Frederick Grant followed in his father's footsteps to West Point and a career in the U.S. Army (fig. 260). During the Civil War, the elder Grant had on occasion taken him campaigning. At age twelve

fig. 259.
Joseph Hoover and N. Mitton, *Grant & Bonner—Dexter's Best Time 2.16¼*, 1868, lithograph, 21½ × 28 in. (54.6 × 71.1 cm.), Harness Racing Museum and Hall of Fame, Goshen, New York

he had seen the capture of Jackson, Mississippi, and the siege of Vicksburg. He received an appointment to West Point from Andrew Johnson, finishing 37th in a class of 41 and dead last in discipline. Near the end his father wrote, "I will be glad when he gets through as I know he will be. I do not want Fred to stay in the Army longer than to report for duty and serve a week or two." After graduation in 1871, Fred worked as a railroad engineer, surveying in the Rocky Mountains, until his father sent him to accompany General Sherman on a tour of Europe. Grant was pleased with his oldest son: "Fred. is a splendid fellow and I think not the least spoiled yet." In 1874 he married a Chicago socialite, Ida M. Honoré, whom Grant welcomed into the family: "Fred's wife is beautiful and is spoken of by all her acquaintances, male & female, young & old, as being quite as charming for her manners, amiability, good sense & education as she is for her beauty. Mrs. Grant and I were charmed with the young lady and her family." He added, "As my children are all leaving me it is gratifying to know that, so far, they give good promise. They are all of good habits and are very popular with their acquaintances and associates." Frederick Grant later served as minister to Austria and as New York City Commissioner of Police. During the Spanish-American War, he led troops in the Philippines. He died in 1913.[98]

fig. 260.
Pach Brothers, *Frederick Grant, Major General, U.S.A.* (photograph courtesy of New-York Historical Society Library, gift of Philip M. Plant)

fig. 261.
Ulysses S. Grant, Jr. ("Buck"), c. 1872 (photograph courtesy of Library of Congress)

Ulysses S. Grant, Jr. (fig. 261), nicknamed "Buck" after the Buckeye State of Ohio where he was born in 1852, attended the Phillips Exeter Academy, Harvard, and Columbia Law School. As a teenager in 1868, Buck saw the western plains "whilst still occupied by the Buffalo and the Indian, both rapidly disappearing now." Grant added to Julia, "Buck has enjoyed it hugely." The general appears to have provided a prudent mix of support and encouragement to Buck at Harvard: "I hope you are doing well, and, above all, are contented. I should like to hear what mark you get in your studies, and how it compares with the class generally." In 1872, Buck spent his junior year abroad in Germany, learning to speak both German and French. He then enrolled at Columbia Law School. Buck made successful investments later in the decade, some of which would help to fund his parents' post-presidency trip to Europe. He felt sufficiently confident in 1881 to start a Wall Street investment firm, in partnership with a man who seemed to be a rising star in the profession, Ferdinand Ward. The firm collapsed, however, in 1884, reducing both Buck and his parents to bankruptcy. To make a fresh start, away from the long shadow cast by his father, he moved to San Diego where he practiced law, served as an assistant U.S. district attorney, and invested in a hotel that he named after his father that still exists downtown. He married Fannie Chaffee, the daughter of a rich businessman, with whom he had five children. Four years after her death in 1909, he married America Workman Will. Buck lived to age seventy-seven.[99]

Ellen Grant was the darling of northerners during both the Civil War and the presidential terms of her famous father. A wartime print of a very young daughter and her dog with the general saw widespread circulation, as did a photograph of Nellie as the "Old Woman in the Shoe" at the Sanitary Fair of 1864 in St. Louis. There, to raise money for hospital supplies for the Union army, she helped to sell both the photograph and dolls. Nellie was sent for a short

fig. 262.
Julia Grant, Nellie Grant, Col. Frederick Dent, Jesse Grant, c. 1868 (photograph courtesy of Library of Congress, Brady-Handy Collection)

while to Miss Porter's School in Farmington, Connecticut, but for the most part was educated at home by private tutors. Just as he had sent her two older brothers to Europe, so Grant packed his daughter off at the age of seventeen: "She has been all her life so much of a companion of her mother that I feared she would want to return by the first steamer leaving Liverpool after her arrival," Grant wrote to his friend Robert Schenck, "But she writes quite the reverse of being homesick." She proved to be an excellent correspondent: "Her letters are infinitely better, as to composition and substance, than either of her older brothers can write." On the ship that carried her back home at age nineteen, Nellie became romantically attached to an Englishman, Algernon Sartoris, the son of opera singer Adelaide Kemble and a nephew of the more famous Fanny Kemble. Nellie shocked her parents by announcing her plans to marry him. The president wrote to the groom's father, "Much to my astonishment an attachment seems to have sprung up between the two young people;

fig. 263.
U.S. Institute Photography Company, *Mrs. Algernon Sartoris (Nellie Grant)*, 1886 (photograph courtesy of New-York Historical Society Library)

to my astonishment because I had only looked upon my daughter as a child." He asked about "the habits, character and prospects" of the suitor. At the White House, Nellie enjoyed a storybook wedding (fig. 263). Four children were born to the couple, who lived mostly in England and eventually divorced. Nellie and her children then lived with her widowed mother in Washington. In 1912, she married Frank Hatch Jones. She lived until 1922.[100]

Jesse Grant (fig. 262), the youngest child, was named for his paternal grandfather. He spent almost his entire youth in the glaring spotlight that shone on his father. He is pictured famously in photographs with his mother and father at City Point near the close of the Civil War (fig 165). Queen Victoria later judged him "a very illmannered young Yankee." By all accounts, Jesse was a rambunctious child by nature; he was never given the strict discipline that his personality apparently needed. When Jesse was twelve, Grant described him as "delicate" in health—"He suffers particularly from headach, and often from bleading of the nose"—but as "a very bright, as well as good, boy." At thirteen, he was sent to boarding school in Philadelphia; previously most of his education had been provided by tutors. The president wanted this son to study science at Cornell, and Jesse did well enough academically to enter the university in 1874. He was there studying engineering until 1877, when he took the opportunity to join his parents on part of their world tour. Jesse's outgoing personality was well known on the ship: "Jess has made himself a regular 'Boy-hoy' among the passengers, singing with the ladies, reading and reciting poetry to them &c." In England he continued his gregarious ways until he tired of the trip. Back home, Jesse followed his brother Buck to Columbia Law School, but stayed only a year before he pursued various business endeavors, including mining, where his father had made money as an investor. His most significant enterprise, however, was in California, where he followed Buck to manage his brother's U. S. Grant Hotel. He tried his hand at politics in 1908 without success. At age sixty-seven he wrote a memoir, *In the Days of My Father General Grant* (1925). He was twice married, to Elizabeth Chapman for thirty-four years before they divorced, and to Lillian Burns Wilkins. He outlived all of his siblings, dying in 1934.[101]

Farming had always offered Ulysses S. Grant a measure of peace and contentment going back to his days as a boy working in his father's fields. When he quit the army in 1854 and rejoined his family, he would have been perfectly content as a farmer had he been able to turn the slightest profit at Hardscrabble. Even after Grant was obliged in 1859 to give up the agricultural operation at White Haven, farming still appealed to him. Because he believed that he had to have some means by which to support himself after he retired from the government, Grant purchased acreage in the White Haven vicinity during the postwar period from his wife's family, which would become his St. Louis County farm. The president made but few of the many trips there that he had anticipated because he ultimately found Long Branch both enjoyable and convenient.

The president's personal correspondence is remarkable for the portion of it that is devoted to his farm. It reads like the papers of George Washington, who when president became in effect an absentee farmer at Mount Vernon via the mails, directing his farm managers from Philadelphia in the most minute detail about crop selection and cultivation. Grant did the same, first with an inept William Elrod, a distant relative, and ultimately with Nathaniel Carlin. A sampling of statements from Grant to his farm managers can serve here to suggest his interest and involvement during the presidential years in his St. Louis project. He began planning the farm in 1867: "I do not expect to go largely into horned stock but I do hope to raise a number of fine colts each year." He had questions for his manager in 1868: "How the crops are likely to turn out? Whether you have bought cows yet? What progress has been made on the barn, &c. do you think all the mares are in foal?" In 1869, while at Long Branch, he bought purebred cattle, and in 1870 he showed his continued interest in the livestock: "All male calves hereafter I would sell for veal and put the money, if you can spare it, into cows or young heifers." "I shall send you one of my fast mares with her youngest colt, a two year old filley and the stallion colt …. There is not one of these animals that I want ever to do a days farm, or heavy, work." "I think the place will feed 300 head of cows the horses and sheep, and pork enough for yourself and hands …. The money I now send you is the last I want to send to the farm. In fact I shall hope soon to get a dividend from it."

Despite Grant's interest and effort, the farm remained unprofitable. By 1875 he was ready to end the ordeal: "I have finally made up my mind that my farming experiment is to wind up with a great loss …. The best plan probably will be to advertise for sale." The auction, like the farm itself, failed to yield satisfactory results. Grant kept the land and leased it, with hope that a better offer to buy would come from an industrial developer. It never came. After the auction, Grant would look to investments to support himself. Although he had some successes, the collapse of Buck's business would put the family in dire financial straights. The former president would turn to his magnificent career as a general in his final effort to provide for his heirs.[102]

In the years after Appomattox, both Lee and Grant understood that their national stature carried a responsibility. Their opinions and actions could do much to restore some measure of equilibrium to the still reeling nation. If the efforts of these military men to help solve political and social problems were not always successful, there is little doubt that the history of this era would have been more tragic in their absence. Much has been made of how Robert E. Lee transformed a small, dying college into a leading force in education. Douglas Southall Freeman, however, stresses that the general's chief contribution after the war was to the cause of national reconciliation. A number of Lee's ideas for curriculum at the college were not implemented in his lifetime. Yet well past his death, Lee's stand for national unity was remembered. Thus Freeman could state that more than any other American, Lee kept the tragedy of the war from being a continuing national calamity. His only rival in this respect was Grant, who as wartime commander at Appomattox, as postwar general-in-chief, and as president tried his best to support measures that would lead to reconciliation. As illness and infirmity began to threaten the lives of each of the great commanders, both Lee and Grant would turn again to those moments in the 1860s when the survival of his nation rested in his hands. Each would also be fortunate enough to once more hear crowds cheer him and dignitaries salute him as the greatest general of his day.[103]

VII.
Remembrance

fig. 264.
Alexander Gardner, *Robert E. Lee*, 1866
(photograph courtesy of Virginia Historical Society)

Next to the deliverance of a noble people from the thralldom of a wicked foe, ... the most grateful and useful duty is to oppose your high character for truth, honor, and true Christian piety, to the thousand mendacious and hirling historians which will spring up in Yankeedom, and give to the world and posterity, a faithful history of the causes of the late terrible conflict, and the manner in which the war was conducted on either side.

Beverly Tucker to Robert E. Lee, July 11, 1865

... the most remarkable work of its kind since the Commentaries of Julius Caesar.

Samuel Clemens on Grant's *Memoirs*, 1885

Lee's Southern Tour

Robert E. Lee's health had been deteriorating since the fall of 1867 when he was jolted by what may have been a stroke. This occasioned his remark to Markie Williams, "It seems to me if all the sickness I ever had in all my life was put together, it would not equal the attack I experienced." The change in his health is visible in photographs (figs. 264 and 265). Two months after this episode Lee was thinking about death. His 1868 New Year's Day greeting to Markie was gloomy: "My interest in time & its concerns is daily fading away & I try to keep my eyes & thoughts trained on those eternal shores to which I am fast hastening." In March 1868 he wrote to the widower William Wickham, whose late wife was a cousin, "Death in its silent, sure march is fast gathering those whom I have longest loved, so that when he shall knock at my door I will more willingly follow."

The final decline in Lee's health began in October 1869 with another of his severe colds. The general confided his concern to his sons. In December he wrote to Rooney, "Traveller's trot is harder to me than it used to be and fatigues me very much." Lee's doctors diagnosed his ongoing illness as the same "inflammation of the heart-sac" that had made him bedridden in 1863. In February 1870 he wrote to his daughter Mildred, "I cannot walk much farther than to the college, though when I get on my horse, I can ride with comfort." After he had to rest on the short walk up the hill from the chapel to the president's house, he considered resignation. "My health has been so feeble this winter that I am only waiting to see the effect of the opening [of] Spring before relinquishing my present position," he wrote to M. D. Corse in March. Lee confided to several of the professors at Washington College that "he felt that he might at any moment die." The faculty suggested that he travel to the warmer climate farther south, much the same as his father had done at the end of his life. The general made it both a farewell tour and a means to reconcile himself to the prospect of death.[1]

Lee set out from Lexington accompanied by his daughter Agnes. He knew that he wanted to stop at the graves of his daughter Annie in North Carolina and his father in Georgia, and on his return trip to visit his two sons in Tidewater Virginia. Lee first went to see his

fig. 265.
D. J. Ryan, *Robert E. Lee and Joseph E. Johnston*, 1870 (photograph courtesy of Virginia Historical Society)

doctors in Richmond. John S. Mosby called on him and thought, "The General was pale and haggard, and did not look like the Apollo I had known in the army." Another caller, his former chief quartermaster Colonel J. L. Corley, would introduce needed structure to a trip that was supposed to bring relaxation but instead attracted considerable attention from both the public and the press. As the Lees traveled through North Carolina, Agnes began reporting the progress of their journey to her mother: "I wish you could travel with papa to see the affection and feeling shown toward him everywhere …. Namesakes appeared on the way, of all sizes. Old ladies stretched their heads into the windows at way stations, and then drew back and said 'He is mightily like his pictures.'" Lee asked Agnes, "Why should they want to see me?" Although he had not wished for it, he had become the premiere symbol of the Old South and the "Lost Cause." The movement to sanctify him was already out of his control.[2]

In the cemetery at Warrenton, North Carolina, the general was able to thank "the kind friends for their care of [Annie] while living and their attention to her since death." "My visit … was mournful, yet soothing to my feelings," he added in a letter to his wife. In Augusta, Georgia, a young Woodrow Wilson was in the crowd that greeted the general. There the soldiers and "the citizens generally, expressed a desire to call upon the great Captain." He rested for twelve days in Savannah where Joseph Johnston was resident. The two friends, rivals, and comrades since West Point, posed for photographs to benefit the local Ladies' Memorial Association (fig. 265). "The old soldiers have greeted me very cordially," Lee wrote to Mary, although he also noted that "I do not think traveling in this way procures me much quiet and repose." There was some improvement in his health, but the crucial problem remained: "I feel stronger than when I came. The warmer weather has also dispelled some of the rheumatic pains in my back, but I perceive no change in the stricture in my chest. If I attempt to walk beyond a very slow gait the pain is always there." The general was pleased when the Mackay family, his friends of forty years earlier, returned to Savannah. Farther south, near the Florida border, was Cumberland Island, where Lee was joined by William

fig. 266.
Abraham Bogardus, *Gen. U. S. Grant*, 1880 (photograph courtesy of New-York Historical Society Library, gift of Abraham Bogardus)

Nightingale, the grandson of General Nathaniel Greene and owner of Dungeness, the estate where "Light-Horse Harry" Lee had died. "Agnes decorated my father's grave with beautiful fresh flowers …. I presume it is the last time I shall be able to pay to it my tribute of respect." In Jacksonville, Florida, "The very silence of the multitude spoke a deeper feeling than the loudest huzzas could have expressed." By this point, however, the general was more than ready to return home.[3]

The trip back took Lee to Charleston, where a reception was held: "Old and young … were present and glad to do him honor." The Lees were next in Wilmington, then Portsmouth and Norfolk, and on up the James River. At Shirley plantation, one of the Carter cousins is said to have stated, "we had heard of God, but here was General Lee!" Mary Custis Lee, traveling with Markie Williams, joined her husband at Rooney's White House plantation. "He looks fatter," she thought, "but I do not like his complexion, and he seems still very stiff." The youngest son Rob remembered his father's stop at Romancoke: "His self-control was great and his emotions were not on the surface, but when he entered and looked around my bachelor quarters [in a former overseer's house] he appeared really much shocked." During his stay in Richmond, Lee met and sat for the sculptor Edward Valentine, who took a number of measurements. Valentine said he would come to Lexington to model the piece; Lee presciently told him to come at once. In long sittings, the general relaxed his guard with the young Virginian, telling stories that Valentine later published. The bust that he created (the basis for fig. 7) received Mary Custis Lee's approval.[4]

While the southern tour had little effect on Lee's health one way or the other, it did enhance his reputation. Many newspapers covered his progress, sometimes with appreciation and sympathy. The *New York World* wrote,

> It will be seen that the "Southern heart" is still fired by emotions that kindled the late civil strife, and it is pleasant to witness the dignified and temperate course of General Lee in the midst of these heart-felt orations. The name of Lee is identified with the most heroic deeds of the war for independence, and it is pleasant in these latter days to find it connected with words and acts of fraternal reconciliation and pacification.[5]

Although there were many in the North who had lost family members in the war and who were still bitter toward Lee, many more, it seemed, had found his efforts to bring the nation together compelling. His physical weakness was evident, but so was his dignity. He had become a larger-than-life figure. No one knew how little life he actually had left.

Grant's World Tour

In his last days in office in early 1877, Ulysses S. Grant (fig. 266) wrote to his friend Judge John Long, who was looking after his farm in St. Louis:

fig. 267.
"The Grants at Karnak, Egypt," wood engraving, *Harper's Weekly*, March 1878

I propose to remain in some place in the United States until Jesse's examination [at Cornell], in June, when he with Mrs. Grant and myself will sail for Europe. I have no plans laid either as to where we will go, or how long remain absent. We will not return however until the party becomes homesick, which may be in six months, and may not be for two years.

Money would not be a problem. Grant had made $25,000 from his investment in a silver mine in Virginia City, Nevada (the "Comstock Lode"), and Buck had made him another $60,000 on Wall Street. Grant added to Long, "I have scarcely thought of where I will make my home on my return." In May, sooner than expected, the party set sail. They did not return for two and a half years. Traveling throughout Europe, and then to northern Africa, the Middle East, the Far East, and the western United States, the Grants possibly visited more countries and peoples than anyone had before them. The general liked to wander the streets of cities, and his artistic talent made him particularly enjoy visiting art galleries and museums. For part of the trip the Grants were accompanied by a reporter for the *New York Herald*, John Russell Young, who fed to an eager audience back home a long string of stories about the adventures and triumphal receptions that the most famous soldier of his era was awarded. Grant's tour, parts of which had an ambassadorial quality, enhanced the international visibility of the emerging United States.[6]

"It has always been my desire to see all jealousy between England and the United States abated, and all sores healed up," Grant wrote soon after he was warmly received in the United Kingdom. He was justifiably proud of having settled the *Alabama* claims through arbitration, and the English people shared the warmth of that feeling. Anticipating his arrival, the London *Times* wrote, "Here he will find that his eminent services to the cause of international peace are not forgotten. He will be welcomed, not only as an illustrious soldier, but as a statesman who has always been friendly to England." The editors added, "his political errors on the other side of the Atlantic need not survive in the memories of Englishmen." Grant was awarded the key to the City of London. In one of many speeches the general gave to enthusiastic crowds, he said in Manchester, "It is scarcely possible for me to give utterance to the feelings which have been evoked by the receptions which I have had upon your soil from the moment of my arrival." The Grants were houseguests of Queen Victoria at Windsor Castle. Some moments there were awkward, both because of Jesse's behavior and because of a problem of protocol. Grant no longer held an official position; at times it was difficult to decide in what context his visit should be seen.[7]

Before returning to London and then touring Scotland, the Grants traveled to Belgium, the Rhine Valley, Switzerland, and Italy. In Rome, the general spoke with Pope Leo XIII and dined with King Umberto. Back in southern England, they visited their daughter Nellie and her English husband Algernon Sartoris. Jesse at this point returned home. Then to Paris, where Grant spent three days with Marshal Mac-Mahon, president of the Third Republic. A U.S. warship was made available to carry the general and his wife down the Italian peninsula. The Grants traveled up the Nile by boat and on donkeys (fig. 267). In Cairo, the Khedive of Egypt, Isma'il Pasha, the ruler since 1863, placed a palace at the general's disposal and provided a steamer to transport him and Julia wherever they wanted to go. In short, the Grants were honored guests no matter where they set foot.

The world tour is particularly interesting for the impressions that Grant recorded in his letters home. "All the romance given to Oriental splendor in novels and guide books is dissipated by witnessing the real thing," he wrote to Buck. "Innate ugliness, slovenlyness, filth and indolence witnessed here is only equaled, in my experience, by seeing the lowest class of Digger Indians found on the Pacific Coast." He reported to his brother-in-law Abel Corbin that "at this remote, but historically interesting quarter of the globe" he had been to the pyramids and to the Virgin's tree where she took shelter at Heliopolis. He told his son Frederick, "I have seen more in Egypt to interest me than in all my other travels," adding humorously, "your Ma balances on a donkey very well when she has an Arab on each side to hold her, and one to lead the donkey."[8]

Following visits to Jerusalem and Constantinople, and accompanied again by John Russell Young, Grant made a quick trip to Greece. His visit to the Holy Land, however, seemed to stay on his mind; he was even more disappointed with the people there than with those of Egypt. The women seemed to be treated worse than the animals that he and Julia rode. From Rome he shared his impressions with Rear Admiral Daniel Ammen, his childhood friend:

> The winter's trip has been the most pleasant of my life. It has been entirely out of the usual course of travelers abroad, and has opened a new field …. But my impression of peoples are that in the East they have a form of government and a civilization that will always repress progress and development …. The people would be industrious if they had encouragement, but they are treated as slaves, and all they produce is taken from them for the benefit of the governing classes and to maintain them in a luxurious and licentious life. Women are degraded even beneath a slave. They have no more rights than the brute. In fact, the donkey is their superior in privileges.[9]

In northern Europe, by contrast, Grant liked what he found. He wrote to Sherman, "Holland is the most interesting country—and people—that I have seen yet. The people look prosperous, free and happy, and entertain an exalted opinion of our country and countrymen." He added to Buck, "Through the Scandinavian countries,—Denmark, Norway, Sweden and Finland—my reception by the people was much like what you have seen at home soon after the war. It was by the people at every place and was most enthusiastic, with loud cheering &c." In Russia, Tsar Alexander II provided his yacht to the Grants. The general reported to Hamilton Fish, "When I called the Emperor approached me and taking me by the hand led me to a seat after which we had a talk of some twenty minutes or more." Among other matters, they mused about the future of the Plains Indians, a topic in which a number of Europeans had an interest. Grant went on to his former secretary of state, "There is no doubt but that the United States stands very high in the estimation of the Russians, from the Emperor down." In Berlin Grant met with Chancellor Otto von Bismarck. He liked Vienna: "It is one of the most beautiful cities in Europe if not the most beautiful," he told Frederick. The Grants also traveled to Spain and Portugal. "I have fallen off twenty-five pounds and feel much better for it," Grant wrote to Buck. "I can walk now like a boy—of sixty."[10]

The Grants debated whether to continue their travels to the Far East. Understandably, after a year-and-a-half away from home they longed to return, but they concluded that the opportunity to see that part of the world would never come again. They were soon pleased with their decision. Grant was enthralled by China, and once again struck up a relationship of mutual admiration with a powerful leader, in this instance the viceroy of the Middle Kingdom, Li Hung-Chang, whom the general compared to Bismarck and Disraeli. Grant was appalled by the lack of respect awarded by many western visitors to so cultured a people: "The course of the average minister, consul, and merchant in this country towards the native is much like the course of the former slave owner towards the freedman when the latter attempts to think for himself in matters of choice of candidates," he wrote to his daughter. The general foresaw a bright future for China that has only in recent years begun to come to fruition. He wrote to Adam Badeau, his former military secretary, "When it does come, China will rapidly become a powerful and rich nation. Her territory is

fig. 268.
Japanese Embroidered Picture, 1879, silk, presented to the Grants by citizens of Japan, National Museum of American History

fig. 269.
The Grant Party at the Bonanza Mines, Virginia City, Nevada, October 1879 (photograph courtesy of New-York Historical Society Library, George T. Bagoe Collection, gift of Elihu Spicer)

vast and full of resources. The population is industrious and frugal, intelligent and quick to learn. They must, however, have the protection of a better and more honest government to succeed."[11]

Japan proved to be Grant's favorite country; the couple lingered there for three months. "My visit to Japan has been the most pleasant of all my travels," he wrote to Badeau from Tokyo. "The country is beautifully cultivated, the scenery is grand, and the people, from the highest to the lowest, the most kindly and most cleanly in the world." He was taken by the progress made in recent years in the development of schools of all types, which were "as thoroughly organized" as any he had seen. Travel was as safe there "as it is in the New England States." However, even more so than in China, Grant was "struck" by the rudeness and lack of comprehension displayed by western foreigners. On the general's departure, the expressions of respect that were awarded to him were extraordinary. Emperor Meiji and his empress bid their guests a fond goodbye, which prompted Grant to reiterate the importance of Japanese independence from foreign interference. The route from Tokyo to Yokohama was lined with citizens waving American and Japanese flags like those pictured in an embroidered silk that was one of the people's gifts to the Grants (fig. 268). No better image could have been conceived to suggest the peaceful relations between the two nations that Grant's unofficial diplomacy had produced. His message of peace, delivered as it was by the man who was perceived to be the greatest warrior in the world, had inspired other, similar official affirmations and public outpourings of approval. While in the Far East, at the request of Li Hung-Chang, Grant even mediated a dispute between Japan and China over the Ryukyu Islands. When the general advised that only the western powers would benefit from a war between them, Li Hung-Chang acquiesced to the Japanese claims.[12]

The departure of the Grants from Yokohama, which included a twenty-one-gun salute from Japanese warships, was matched by the reception that awaited the couple in San Francisco. That outpouring was indicative of what the general could expect in other American towns through which he would pass as he made his way to the east coast. Young's *New York Herald* articles had captivated the American reading public, who were eager to welcome back their favorite son. The last leg of Grant's world tour allowed him a stop at the mine in Nevada that had helped fund the trip. Dressed like a miner of the Old West, Grant, pictured at the center of a souvenir photograph (fig. 269), once again suggested that he was able to adapt to any situation.

The performance of Rutherford B. Hayes as president, which had disappointed both parties, now seemed pale in comparison to Grant's tenure in office. In the meantime, the general had become a diplomat with an understanding of world affairs that few at the time could match. Grant considered running for the presidency again in 1880 if only because of the experiences he had on his trip. His friend Adam Badeau later wrote, "He had seen other countries, met the peoples and the rulers; his views were widened, and his whole character changed. In the East he had obtained knowledge of China and Japan, and conceived an Oriental policy for this country which he believed so important that a desire to achieve it was certainly one reason why he was so anxious to return to power." Julia supported his effort, but after thirty-six ballots at the Republican convention he was not offered his party's nomination.[13]

fig. 270.
Brown Brothers Studio, *Grant Residence*, New York City (photograph courtesy of New-York Historical Society Library, gift of Consolidated Edison)

fig. 271.
"Wall Street Startled," *The New York Times*, May 7, 1884

WALL STREET STARTLED

THE MARINE NATIONAL BANK CLOSES ITS DOORS.

CAUSING THE SUSPENSION OF THE FIRM OF GRANT & WARD, OF WHICH PRESIDENT FISH WAS A PARTNER.

Startling rumors swept through Wall-street at noon yesterday, and for an hour messengers from banking houses and broker's offices were kept flying hither and thither in quest of accurate information. That the Marine National Bank had closed its doors was soon ascertained. The news that followed was even more sensational. Grant & Ward, bankers and brokers, No. 2 Wall-street, announced their suspension, and ugly stories of an unaccountable deficiency of half a million dollars arose.

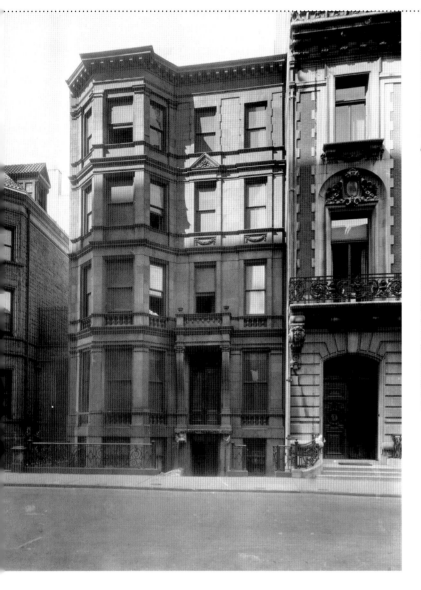

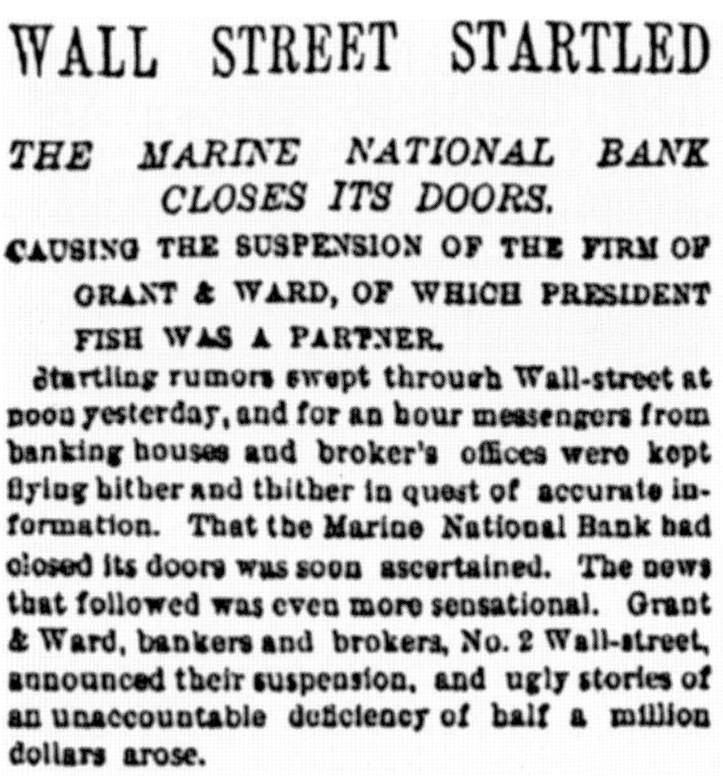

The Grants retired to Galena until admirers in New York put together yet another large trust fund, this one in the amount of $250,000, to lure the general to live in their city. The financier and steel and railroad magnate J. Pierpont Morgan gave the general an additional $100,000 to purchase the handsome brownstone at 3 East Sixty-Sixth Street that would be his residence (fig. 270). Such immense gifts stand as evidence of Grant's popularity. The house came to resemble a museum, so richly was it furnished with artifacts acquired by the general and president, and with the gifts presented to Grant on his world tour. Unfortunately, even with money and with the social life of the nation's greatest city at his doorstep, life in retirement bored a man who for the past two decades had acted on the world's stage. Grant tried suggesting policy to the new president, former general James A. Garfield, he headed a company that set out to build railroads in Mexico but actually did little, and he became a partner, in name and at the cost of $100,000, in an investment business that his son Buck co-founded. The Grant name was certain to ensure confidence and attract customers, and the firm of Grant and Ward in fact prospered from 1881 to 1884. Ferdinand Ward appeared to be a rising baron on Wall Street—he was later described as "an exceptionally shrewd man"—but his technique of using the same securities as collateral for different loans was criminal. The elder Grant thought that he was becoming a millionaire, but the firm was actually on the brink of collapse. The bubble burst when Ward could no longer make the payments due on his loans. "Startling rumors swept through Wall-street at noon yesterday," *The New York Times* reported on May 7 (fig. 271):

> Grant & Ward, bankers and brokers, No. 2 Wall-street, announced their suspension and ugly stories of an unaccountable deficiency of half a million dollars arose. The fact that ex-President Grant was interested, with his son, in the embarrassed firm became speedily known, and expressions

of sympathy were heard on every hand. Ferdinand Ward … had dragged the firm down by his extensive real estate speculations.

A week later, the paper added, "It does not appear that Gen. Grant or his sons have any part of the lost millions in their possession; on the contrary, it appears that the fortunes which they invested in the business have been lost and swallowed up." William K. Vanderbilt loaned Grant $150,000 to salvage the company, but Ward took that money and fled. Vanderbilt protected Grant's house by taking title to it. The general, however, was bankrupt, the victim of the "rascality of a business partner" as he described it. Grant would have to find a new means to earn a living. He wrote two articles for Century Magazine about the battles of Shiloh and Vicksburg that were well received, and he soon deduced that he might be able to recoup his fortune if he was willing to recount more of his wartime accomplishments.[14]

Memoirs
Few books were so greatly anticipated as Lee's history of the campaigns in Virginia. For the most part, the general held fast to his opinion that Americans should put the conflict behind them and that he should keep silent on the subject. His projected history of the war in his home state was the one exception to his self-imposed rule. In the summer of 1865, Lee received dozens of letters from southerners urging him to write his own account so that the true story would be told. Attention was given to the project by the press in both the United States and England. Publishers anticipated that a book by the premier Confederate general, who was revered in the South, respected by many in the North, and well known in England, would sell very well. When the idea was conceived during the summer after Appomattox, Lee had no career plans other than to become a farmer; he could afford to take on a demanding project. In August of that year, however, the general was unexpectedly offered the presidency of Washington College, which he perceived to be both an opportunity and an obligation.

The first known mention of the idea that the general would write a history is found in a long letter to Lee from Beverly Tucker of July 11, 1865. Tucker, a Virginian who had served as a Confederate agent, was then living in Montreal. This letter marks an early moment in the postwar battle to win the war where it would next be fought, in textbooks. It is written in the spirit of the "Lost Cause." Tucker spoke about divine purpose and duty, language that the general understood:

> God has in reserve for you a yet more noble and not less patriotic role. He has given you qualities moral and intellectual to fulfill a higher destiny. Next to the deliverance of a noble people from the thralldom of a wicked foe, … the most grateful and useful duty is to oppose your high character for truth, honor, and true Christian piety, to the thousand mendacious and hirling historians which will spring up in Yankeedom, and give to the world and posterity, a faithful history of the causes of the late terrible conflict, and the manner in which the war was conducted on either side …. [Y]our slightest utterance, would upon a statement or issue of fact, outweigh folios of yankee asseveration …. No work in the 19th century has ever had, or ever will have, such a sale. Every man, woman, & child, who can read, will deny themselves luxuries or even necessaries, if need be, to have Robert E. Lee's History of the American War.

Ironically, Tucker's sales prediction was not realized by Lee, but would be by Grant, who displayed the perseverance to complete such a book during his last days.[15]

Tucker wanted Lee to come to Canada to explore the feasibility of engaging a publisher in England. Instead, by the end of the month the general was in communication with C. B. Richardson of the University Publishing Company of New York. Lee did not feel the bitterness that enveloped Tucker; instead, if he wrote a history it would be to explain the defeat, not "to vindicate myself, or to promote my own reputation. I want that the world shall know what my poor boys, with their small numbers and scant resources, succeeded in accomplishing." That message was reassuring to former Confederates, and it would have soothed them immeasurably were they to see it in a history written by Lee. The general told Markie Williams, "My only object in writing is that truth should descend to posterity."[16]

On July 31, just before the call came from Lexington, Lee sent out a circular letter to his former officers asking for the documentary materials that he would need in order to compile his history. "I am desirous that the bravery and devotion of the army of N. Va. be correctly transmitted to posterity," he told them, adding that he had copies of his reports of the battles through the Pennsylvania campaign, but none for the last two years of the war. All had been lost or burned in the Richmond evacuation fire. "Should you have copies of the reports of the operations of your command within the period specified … send them to me." A number of Lee's lieutenants responded, but not enough documentary material was provided. Many Confederate military records had been captured at the close of the war and were being stored in Washington. The major obstacle that halted Lee's plan was the refusal of federal authorities to allow southerners to view the pertinent records.[17]

Lee's letter in effect announced his project to the world. Letters of approval and offers of assistance came to him from all parts of the country. "We have heard in Texas that you are preparing a History of the War," wrote the widow of Colonel James Reily in Houston. She added, "In common with the whole civilized world, we rejoice that there is hope of one record of that terrible conflict of the nations, which shall be characterized by the magnanimity & truth & justice that are the ruling principles of your life." Jno. R. Winston of North Carolina believed that "it will be the only true history that will be written of this painful subject." William B. Reid of Chestnut Hill, outside of Philadelphia, offered, "I implore you, not so much for our own sake, as for the sake of your Southern country, and of us in the North who felt with you and for you—not to neglect the history of the war …. [D]on't let the record fail." Lee wrote back to Reid that "All my records, reports, returns, &c, &c" are lost; "I have not even my letter or order books to which to refer."[18]

Interest in Lee's history remained high for years. A bookseller in Arkansas wrote to the general in 1866, "it is a daily thing to be asked if we have Lee's history." Letters from twenty-seven publishers seeking to sell the book remain in the Washington and Lee University archives; more would be there had not C. B. Richardson asked the general to forward offers to him in New York for refusal. When Richardson suggested that Lee write to Grant for assistance in getting the necessary records, Lee explained politely that although some of his accounts "might be found among the captured records in Washington, and Genl. Grant who possesses magnanimity as well as ability, might cause me to be furnished with copies. I have hesitated to approach him on the subject, as it is one in which he would naturally feel no interest."

Richardson then tried a new approach. He offered to publish Lee's

fig. 272.
Steamer Trunk belonging to Mary Lee, a repository for family papers, private collection

fig. 273.
Henry Lee, *Memoirs of the War in the Southern Department*, ed. Robert E. Lee (New York, 1868 ed. of 1812 original), Virginia Historical Society

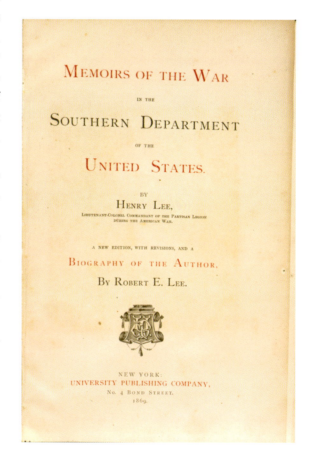

history plus a new edition of "Light-Horse Harry" Lee's *Memoirs*. The addition of a short biography of Lee's father would allow the publisher to renew the copyright to the earlier volume. The two books would be published at "the same time and in uniform style." Some of the notes that Lee prepared for the history were rediscovered in 2002, preserved in a steamer trunk (fig. 272) originally belonging to Mary Lee, the last survivor of the Lee children. At the end of her long life, she stored the papers for safe keeping in an Alexandria, Virginia, bank vault. Lee first completed the biography as an introduction to his father's *Memoirs*; this new volume appeared in 1868 (fig. 273).[19]

Charles Carter Lee advised his brother that income from his history of the war "ought to be at least $100,000." He should work quickly, however, while interest in the project was still great. A history of the Confederate campaigns was what was wanted, not their father's story: "Who cares now to dispute a big point of our revolutionary history?"

Lee was particularly anxious for data about the "effective strength at the principal battles." He asked for help from Thomas White, the former clerk in the Confederate adjutant-general's office who had prepared the field returns throughout the war, and from his former aides Charles Marshall and Walter Taylor, but their estimates did not correspond with his own memory. The project ground to a halt due to a lack of information, the drain on Lee's time caused by what had become a busy schedule at the college, and his declining health.[20]

The papers preserved in Mary Lee's trunk number about forty. On several pages are gathered statistics about troop numbers on both sides, such as:

> The aggregate amt of the Confederate Army in all Va in the Summer of 1862, was about 80,000, with which the State was reserved against 293,000, & Burnside recalled from N.C.

> McC[lellan] sets down his own loss during the M[arylan]d Campaign at about 15000, & about 13000 at Sharpsburg. But the Hospital returns of the Fed[er]al Gov[ernmen]t show an increase of 30,000 patients from his Command Consequent upon the operations of this short Campaign.

A short essay on government is roughed out. It begins,

> The fathers of the Fed[er]al Constitution intended by the Confederation of the States to provide a common agent for the equal benefit of the Confederated parties, exercising no powers except those derived from their consent, & relying upon the beneficence of its action towards them as its only guarantee. It was not supposed that the union thus formed was to be maintained by force ….

Thoughts about the meaning of the Civil War are gathered:

> The war has destroyed the bond of unity which existed in the old Confederation …. No animosity should be felt between any Section or honest man. No vain lamentations should be indulged in over the result of the war.

And nearly twenty pages recount the long retreat from Petersburg:

> It was apparent during the winter that reinforcements were continuously reaching the armies under Genl. Grant in front of Richmond, & that every preparation was being made for the early prosecution of hostilities which were suspended during intervals of inclement weather.

> Every hour would but increase the difficulty of withdrawing the army, for the superior numbers of the enemy would soon enable him to get possession of the roads to Danville & Lynchburg.

In 1868, Lee discussed with two Washington College professors the problems that hindered his progress with the history. He spoke to William Preston Johnston "of the difficulty of getting the documents to verify his statements, and his wish to be able to prove all he said," adding that it was still his "purpose to write a history of his army." With William Allan, Lee "talked of the difficulties and referred to the many errors which had become rife, and which it would be necessary for him to correct, as one of the disagreeable things that stood in his way." He specifically spoke of the mistakes in Robert Lewis Dabney's *Life and Campaigns of Lieut. Gen. Thomas J. Jackson* (New York, 1866). Perhaps for that reason, he wrote ten pages about Jackson's Valley campaign of 1862. It was a logical place to start, a chapter in the war that badly needed correct reporting, and one where the general could praise his faithful, gallant, but deceased lieutenant. This passage from Lee's account suggests the tone that the entire history might have taken:

> The bridges at White House & Columbia being burned, [Gen. John C.] Fremont & [Gen. James] Shields could not unite at New Market & it was Jackson's policy to keep them

fig. 274.
W. H. Baker, *Grant and Family at Mount MacGregor*, 1885 (photograph courtesy of New-York Historical Society Library, gift of Mrs. Lathrop C. Harper)

apart. Shields being still east of the Shenandoah, there were but two bridges by which he could join Fremont. The one at Port Republic was held by Jackson, the other at the mouth of Elk run valley, 15 miles below his directive to be burned. Before the Confederates reached the bridge, the advanced guard of Shield's army arrived, but hearing that a small body of Confederates was a few miles above, guarding their stores, they attempted their case there. The guard escaped, but the stores were captured, that when the head of his own column reached the bridge, the Confederates had arrived & the bridge was in flames. The Shenandoah still swollen was nowhere fordable, and Shields was prevented from uniting with Fremont. Jacksons object was now to seize the opportunity afforded of crushing one of his assailants while separated from the other, which no one knew better how to accomplish than he, though each was within less than a days march of his position.

Lee went on to describe in similar detail the maneuvers around

fig. 275.
John G. Gilman, *Grant on the Porch at Mount MacGregor Four Days Before His Death*, 1885 (photograph courtesy of New-York Historical Society Library)

Harrisonburg, including the death of General Turner Ashby ("he was struck in the breast by a bullet & fell dead"). At the end, he summarized the campaign, with characteristic attention to numbers of troops:

> Fifteen days previously Jackson was confronted with two armies of about 40,000 men, while his own force consisted of 15,000, & he 100 miles from his base. This battle relieved him from the presence of both & only occasioned him a loss of about 1500 men. Within 40 days he had marched 400 miles, fought four pitched battles, defeated four separate armies, in addition to several combats, captured 3500 prisoners, killed & wounded a larger number, & neutralized forces three times as numerous & detained inactive [Gen. Irvin] McDowell at Fredericksburg.

In keeping McDowell from reinforcing McClellan, who was then threatening Richmond, Jackson had achieved exactly what Lee had directed him to do. William Allan recorded that Lee told him that "he wanted to hit the Yankees in the Valley" and that "all of Jackson's

fig. 276.
Jessie Tarbox Beals, *Mark Twain* [Samuel Clemens], 1906 (photograph courtesy of New-York Historical Society Library)

movements were in accordance with letters from him (of which Dabney says nothing)." Although Jackson had on occasion failed to appear when needed, Lee was proud of what his charismatic commander had achieved in the Valley. He found that portion of the story easy and apparently invigorating to write. Lee would no doubt have further enhanced the reputations of his favorite lieutenants had he been able to execute his history in its entirety.[21]

The popularity of the two Civil War articles written by Grant for *Century Magazine*, and the ease with which the general had composed them, led the editor to propose the publication of a book. Samuel Clemens (fig. 276) intervened, convinced Grant to write his story, and offered himself as both editor and as a publisher who would award a much higher percentage of the royalties than normal to the bankrupt American hero. The Midwesterners Sam Grant and Sam Clemens became friends for the last fifteen months of the general's life. At the same moment when he was standing behind Grant, Mark Twain was introducing America to a new picture of itself in *Huckleberry Finn*. Grant would in his own way also tell a tale of a nation split over slavery.

The general knew that he was seriously ill. He put himself to the task of writing with all of the energy that he could muster. He strove for accuracy; his memory was "superb," Clemens noted, but Grant was able to check what he remembered against the official records. As summer approached and physicians advised the general to move to a cooler climate than the city, the Philadelphia banker and philanthropist Joseph Drexel of Drexel, Morgan & Co. invited the Grant family to use his country cottage at Mount MacGregor in the Adirondack Mountains (figs. 274). Photographs of the general diligently at work there on his book are poignant records of his devotion to the welfare of his wife and family (fig. 275). The two volumes were completed in 1885, only days before Grant died. Whether or not the general intended to carry his autobiography beyond 1865 is not known, but he had won the race against time by writing the portions of his life about which Americans wanted to read. The *Memoirs* were in demand in both the North and South, read by a public eager to know why the war unfolded as it did, and to learn more about the man who had defeated the Confederacy yet was magnanimous in victory. Deluxe (fig. 277) and plain editions of the *Memoirs* were published to meet the demands and income levels of different audiences, and agents were hired to hawk the book. Sales of 250,000 copies were quickly realized, enabling Clemens to present Julia, by then a widow, with the largest royalty check ever written, for $200,000.[22]

The *Memoirs* are an American literary masterpiece. Grant had somehow made a very difficult task seem simple. He had always

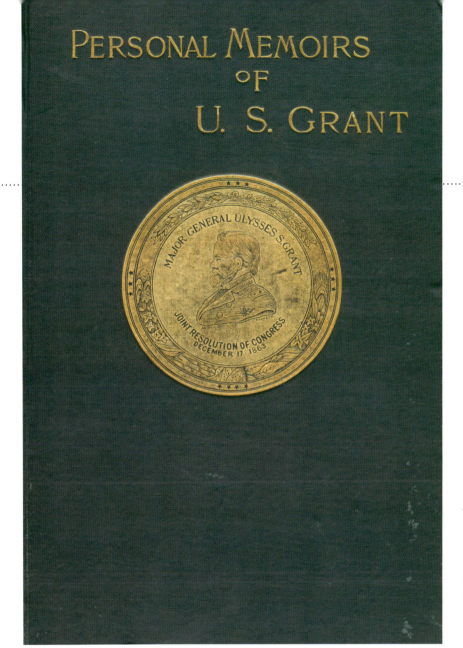

fig. 277.
Ulysses S. Grant, *Personal Memoirs of U. S. Grant,* in Two Volumes (New York, 1885), Virginia Historical Society

written with great clarity. The volumes are an impressive display of both his intellect and his humility. Even today's reader is captivated by his charm and honesty, which were well known to his family and close friends, but were less visible to the public. Compiled at the end of his life when his reputation was almost invulnerable to criticism, Grant could afford to readily admit mistakes, to be generous in his praise, and to raise himself above the pettiness of criticizing others. Samuel Clemens rated Grant's book "the most remarkable work of its kind since the *Commentaries of Julius Caesar.*" Edmund Wilson called it "a unique expression of national character," comparable to Thoreau's *Walden* and Walt Whitman's *Leaves of Grass.*[23]

The Death of Lee

Despite his early religious instruction and the combined efforts of his mother, wife, and mother-in-law, Robert E. Lee was slow to make a formal commitment to his faith. He had not sought confirmation in the Episcopal Church until 1853, when he was forty-six years old. As a young adult in the military he attended church services irregularly at best. The Civil War had changed all that. By the time the family moved to Lexington, Lee became an active participant in church activities and studied the Bible. And as we have seen, he took an active interest in the spiritual well-being of the students of Washington College.

Toward the end of September 1870, Lee (fig. 278) presided as senior warden at a vestry meeting at Grace Episcopal Church that ran late. After he had walked the short distance home, he could not speak or even cough. He apparently had suffered a stroke; pneumonia would kill him two weeks later. William Preston Johnston, Lee's chairman of history and English literature at Washington College, felt compelled to publish an account of the death that provided Victorian admirers and "Lost Cause" apologists with the sort of story that they wanted to hear: "Never was more beautifully displayed how a long and severe education of mind and character enables the soul to pass with equal step through this supreme ordeal …."

Johnston's "Death of General Lee" was published in J. William Jones's *Personal Reminiscences of General Robert E. Lee* in 1875 and then republished by later biographers. To Lee on his deathbed, Johnston attributed two "broken utterances" that became famous: "Strike the tent" and "Tell Hill he must come up!" Lee's widow wrote to a friend, "His mind wandered to those dreadful battlefields …." This was the leader who southerners wanted to imagine, the man who in his mind continued to fight the war that could not be won on the battlefield.

A moving account was written nearly two decades later by Mildred Lee, who in 1888 was still deeply affected by her father's death:

> How it rained that night & for days after … and there was darkness in our hearts! … his beautiful sad eyes always gave me a look of love & recognition, tho. his lips never uttered a sound! The silence was awful! … I remember one day as I was stroking his hand, he took mine up & kissed it …. Hour after hour Agnes & I would sit by him rubbing his dear hands in the old way he used to like, never saying a word ….

fig. 278.
Michael Miley, *Robert E. Lee*, c. 1870 (photograph courtesy of Virginia Historical Society)

fig. 279.
Michael Miley, *Funeral of Robert E. Lee*, 1870 (photograph courtesy of Virginia Historical Society)

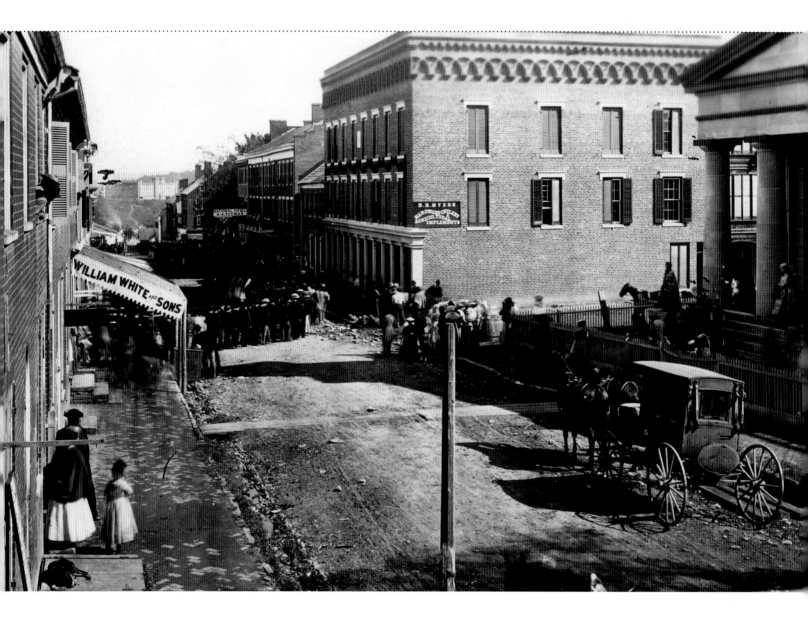

Custis came from the Institute & nursed him tenderly, being with him when we could not. My poor suffering mother would be rolled in, in her chair, to sit by his side, having the hardest part to act, that of being passive when she would have given her life to do something! … Another awful day—everyone frightened & crying—the doctors striving to give life to a dying man—consternation in all our faces. I remember nothing distinctly until that night—that last night! … Dr. Pendleton was there & read the prayer for the dead—the doctors—Mr. Harris standing—my mother, Custis, Agnes & I kneeling around his bed—he was breathing hard & painfully & seemed unconscious …. In a moment he was dead.

Then my mother gave way for the first time & in his room, putting her arms around me, said, "do be kind to me now"! Oh how my heart aches at the memory of those words & the need for them …. How quiet he lay in the darkened room—the battle of life forever over! Then he was taken away from us to the college Chapel so that all the people could see his face once more—the people he had died to save![24]

The family gathered together to support Mary Custis Lee as word spread of the general's demise (fig. 279). Three days after Lee's death, Markie Williams wrote to "My darling little Agnes" from Philadelphia, "You know how my heart is sorrowing for you all & for myself …. I think so much of you all—your dear dear mother—

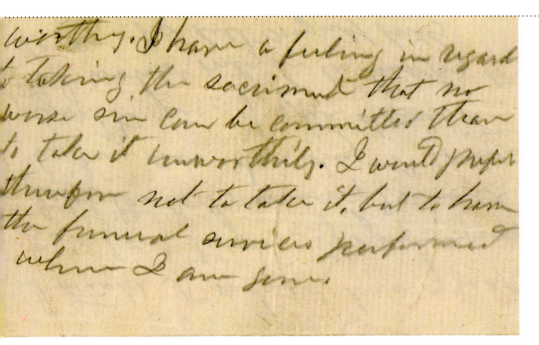

fig. 280.
Ulysses S. Grant, *Note*, 1885, United States Military Academy Library, West Point, New York

this is the overwhelming sorrow of her life, and she is so helpless. My heart bleeds for her."[25]

The Death of Grant

When Samuel Clemens first discussed with Grant the publication of the *Memoirs*, he was disturbed to see how thin and frail the general had become. It seemed that Grant's health had deteriorated rapidly, but in fact the general had postponed consulting with doctors after he realized that something serious was wrong with his throat. The pain that he had discovered while eating a peach turned out to be cancer, apparently developed from years of smoking cigars. It was a painful malady, one that would have halted most people from undertaking a monumental project. But he loved Julia dearly, and she would need financial protection. The completion of a one-thousand-page book under the duress of a time schedule set by the approach of the author's own death was a remarkable accomplishment, a testament to Grant's extraordinary courage, intellect, memory, and his characteristic focus on a singular goal and persistence to reach it.

Friends came to visit Grant that summer, including Sherman, Sheridan, and the former Confederate Simon Bolivar Buckner, whose surrender Grant had accepted at Fort Donelson. Julia remembered, "How affected they both were! As General Buckner took General Grant's hand at parting, the only words were 'Grant,' 'Buckner.'" In his last days Grant, like Lee in this respect, could not speak. But his mind remained clear and he kept writing. Notes were his only means to converse with his family. Of the scraps of paper that have been preserved, one to Julia addresses the question of last rites. It sheds light on his religious views at the end (fig. 280). Grant refused the sacrament with characteristic logic, honesty, and humility:

> "I would only be too happy to do so if I felt myself fully worthy. I have a feeling in regard to taking the sacrament that no worse sin can be committed than to take it unworthily. I would prefer therefore not to take it, but to have the funeral services performed when I am gone."

Julia bravely endured the death process. In her own memoirs she recounted the last days: "after sitting awhile with us, he would take out his little tablets and write, 'It is very pleasant to be here, but I must go to my writing or I fear my book will not be finished.' And so he wrote on and on … that he might leave a home and independence to his family." Julia wrote her own memoirs as a way to return some meaning to her life in the years following the death of her husband. The book is more than anything else a tribute to her Ulysses. She closes it with a remembrance:

> For nearly thirty-seven years, I, his wife, rested and was warmed in the sunlight of his loyal love and great fame, and now, even though his beautiful life has gone out, it is as when some far-off planet disappears from the heavens; the light of his glorious fame still reaches out to me, falls upon me, and warms me.[26]

The American public remembered Ulysses S. Grant with every honor that could be bestowed. The remarkable outpouring of appreciation expressed at his funeral in New York City (fig. 281) and the ideas about how his burial place might be made a fitting memorial have been discussed above in the Introduction. The completion of the monumental tomb (fig. 282) in 1897 was marked by a show of affection that matched the public outpouring twelve years earlier at Grant's funeral. Dignitaries and tens of thousands of Americans once again attended. The Grant that they best re-

fig. 281.
Pach Brothers, *The Catafalque, with Gen'l. Grant's Remains, Leaving City Hall, New York,* August 8, 1885 (photograph courtesy of New-York Historical Society Library)

membered was the successful general who was unconquerable in war but who championed peace (fig. 283).

The deaths of both commanders were reported in detail by the national media. Life came virtually to a halt in the former Confederacy when Lee's death was pronounced. Businesses and government offices closed throughout the region and correspondents across the South recorded that entire cities were in mourning. The greatest symbol of the "Lost Cause," and of a way of life that had been ripped from its citizens, was gone. For better or worse, an era was over.

Many in the South took the opportunity to continue the deification of Lee. The *Richmond Dispatch* ended its report with the reflection, "If the heathen could say that 'whom the gods love die young,' we may say that there is in contemplating Gen. Lee's death the sad consoling reflection that it is not now possible for him to do aught to diminish the esteem in which his name is held by mankind …. He is now safe in the pantheon of his admiring countrymen." Some papers in the North took this moment to reconsider his entire life. *The New York Times*, while making clear his great error in 1861, chose to take a broader view (fig. 284):

> Intelligence was received last evening of the death at Lexington, Va., of Gen. Robert E. Lee, the most famous of the officers whose celebrity was gained in the service of the Southern Confederacy during the late terrible rebellion.…
>
> [H]is wife declared that he "wept tears of blood over this

fig. 282.
Grant's Tomb, c. 1900 (photograph courtesy of Library of Congress)

fig. 283.
"Let Us Have Peace," poster commemorating the dedication of the Grant Memorial Tomb, April 27, 1897, New-York Historical Society Library

fig. 284.
"Gen. Robert E. Lee," *The New York Times,* October 13, 1870

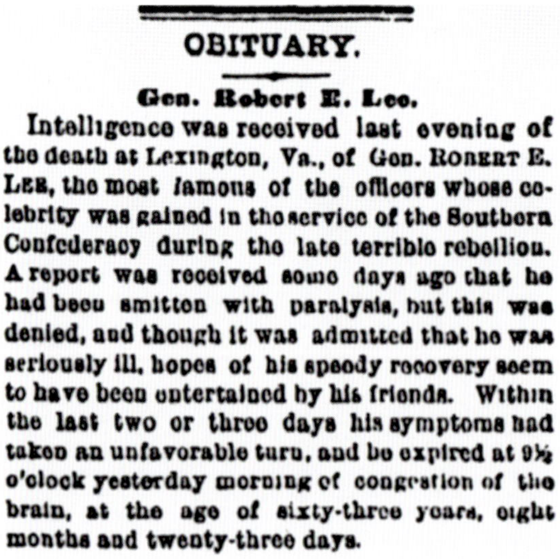

terrible war." There are probably few who doubt the sincerity of his protestation, but thousands have regretted, and his best friends will ever have to regret, the error of judgment, the false conception of the allegiance due to his Government and his country, which led one so gifted to cast his lot with traitors, and devote his splendid talents to the execution of a wicked plot to tear asunder and ruin the Republic in whose service his life had hitherto been spent ….

Not long after his surrender he was invited to become the President of Washington University, at Lexington, Va., and was installed in that position on the 2d of October, 1865. Since that time he has devoted himself to the interests of that institution, keeping so far as possible aloof from public notice, and by his unobtrusive modesty and purity of life, has won the respect even of those who most bitterly deplore and reprobate his course in the rebellion.[27]

Lee would continue to have his detractors. However, because of both his postwar efforts to bring the nation together and the elements of his character that he had maintained throughout his life, Lee was often remembered with respect.

The death of Grant set off a period of national mourning. The front-page story in the *The New York Times* included a description of his last moments, comments on how the family was bearing up, and a discussion of why New York would be the proper site for his memorial: "Here, in the Nation's real capital, which he himself had selected as his residence for his declining years, it was regarded as

322   VII. Remembrance

fitting that his tomb should be." Even in the South there were heartfelt tributes. The *Richmond Dispatch* (fig. 285) made clear that "The news of the sad event created profound sorrow throughout the country." In a section of the announcement called "Southern Opinion: How Grant's Life and Character are Viewed by ex-Confederates," A. H. H. Stuart states that upon hearing of his death, "Political and sectional differences were at once forgotten. His many generous and manly qualities were remembered, and every heart was filled with grief for his afflictions and sympathy with his family in their bereavement." Special trains left from various points in Tennessee, Alabama, and Georgia for people who wanted to attend his funeral.[28]

While the outpouring for Grant was far greater in scope than that for Lee, it was no more fervent. Each man had died in his sixty-third year having accomplished much, having survived many potentially devastating assaults on his reputation, and having had the rare honor of seeing himself elevated far above the great majority of his contemporaries. Lee, of whom much was expected, and whose Civil War heroism was enhanced by the long odds against his success, came to be seen by his adherents as representing attributes that outshone anything that could be achieved by an individual man at any particular moment in history. His character, sense of honor, and devotion to duty became the stuff of legend. Grant, of whom comparatively little was expected, had accomplished more in the martial and political worlds than had anyone before him with the possible exception of George Washington. To his contemporaries in the North, and, more grudgingly, to many in the South, he was the greatest hero of his age.

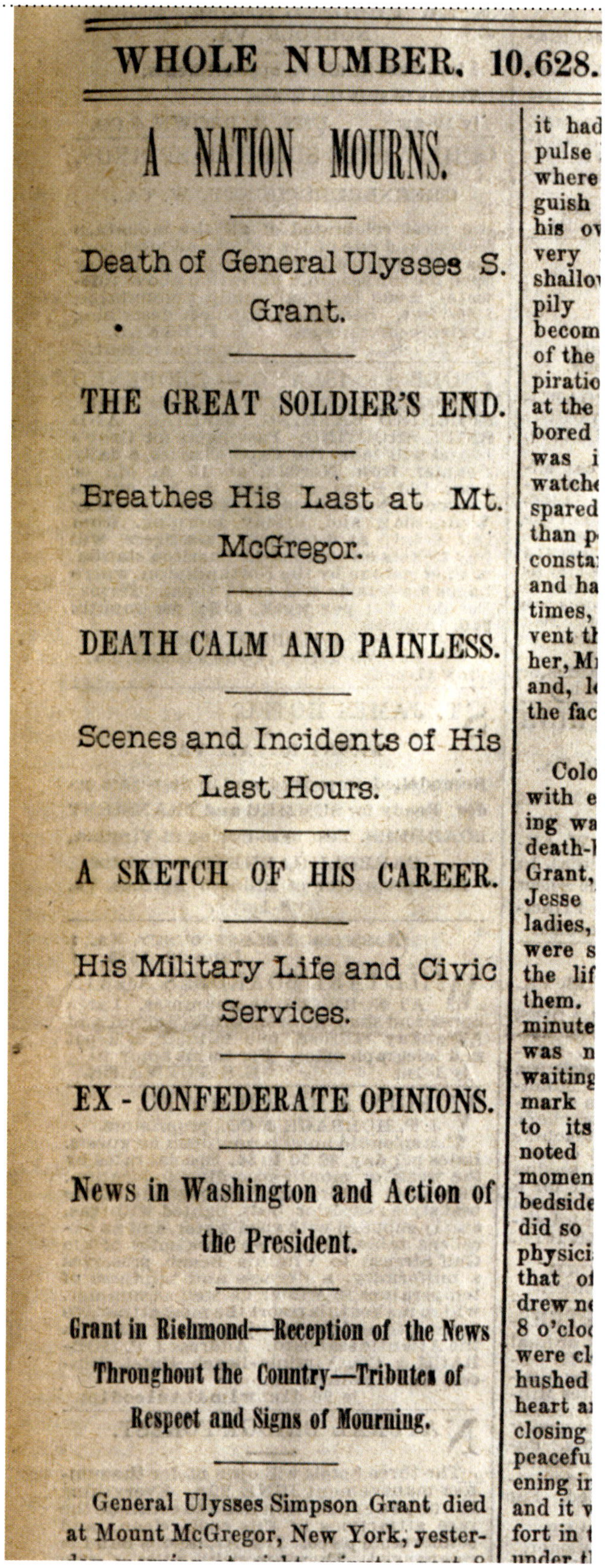

WHOLE NUMBER. 10.628.

A NATION MOURNS.

Death of General Ulysses S. Grant.

THE GREAT SOLDIER'S END.

Breathes His Last at Mt. McGregor.

DEATH CALM AND PAINLESS.

Scenes and Incidents of His Last Hours.

A SKETCH OF HIS CAREER.

His Military Life and Civic Services.

EX-CONFEDERATE OPINIONS.

News in Washington and Action of the President.

Grant in Richmond—Reception of the News Throughout the Country—Tributes of Respect and Signs of Mourning.

General Ulysses Simpson Grant died at Mount McGregor, New York, yester-

fig. 285.
"A Nation Mourns. Death of General Ulysses S. Grant. The Great Soldier's End," *Richmond Dispatch*, July 24, 1885

Conclusion

A Messenger comes from its President and from General Scott, commander-in-chief of its army, to tender him supreme command of its forces …. Since the Son of Man stood upon the Mount, and saw "all the kingdoms of the world and the glory of them" stretched before him, and turned away to the agony and bloody sweat of Gethsemane, and to the Cross of Calvary beyond, no follower of the meek and lowly Saviour can have undergone more trying ordeal, or met it with higher spirit of heroic sacrifice….

John Warwick Daniel[1]

But the history of his country will ever hold his name:
It will ever stand out bold on the pages of its fame.
Grant was a man like Moses in the Bible, for
He could not talk, but was mighty in a war.
Eloquence of speech can often charm the mind,
But all good qualities in a man we very seldom find.

Adrian Hitt[2]

Given their prominent roles in the enactment of America's greatest tragedy, it may seem odd that Lee and Grant were so quickly revered. To praise them, however, was to give importance to their respective causes, and thereby to deflect attention from the 618,000 lives that had been sacrificed and the suffering of countless thousands of others. Adulation of Lee allowed people in the South to hide from the humiliation of defeat, while giving due honor to the nation's savior reminded northerners that their cause had been just. Comparisons of Lee's 1861 decision to turn down the offer made by Winfield Scott to Christ's turning down the offer made by Satan during the Temptation as described in Matthew, or of Grant's leadership during the Civil War to that of Moses, who was called upon by God to free his entire nation from bondage, may seem like the wildest sort of hyperbole, but these passages do give modern readers a sense of the esteem in which Robert E. Lee and Ulysses S. Grant were held by many of their contemporaries.

To John W. Daniel, Scott offered Lee everything he had ever wanted. Had Lee taken command of the Union forces in the spring of 1861, the war would certainly have come to an end much more quickly. Lee would then have been the great hero of the nation, and it is probably not a stretch to imagine him following Washington, Jefferson, Madison, Monroe, W. H. Harrison, Tyler, and Taylor to become the eighth president of the United States from Virginia. This was in his grasp, but he let it go to preserve his personal honor and to defend his home and his family. Those who would argue that he chose to fight for slavery rather than against it—and that this is all one needs to know about Lee—lose sight, perhaps purposely, of the extent of the sacrifice that he made. With the chance to follow in the footsteps of his idol George Washington, and to expunge, once and for all, every stain on the Lee family honor made by actions of his father and half-brother, Lee said no. It was not about defending slavery, an institution that he had often spoken out against. Indeed, the irony is that had Lee taken Scott up on his offer, and had he quickly brought the cotton states of the Deep South to heel, there is a good chance that slavery, which Lincoln had no intention of ending in 1861, would have had a much longer history in the United States than it did.

It is sometimes difficult for twenty-first century Americans to understand that Lee's decision was based on his lifelong desire to do what he thought was right. He explained this to P. G. T. Beauregard in October 1865:

> I need not tell you that true patriotism sometimes requires of men to act exactly contrary, at one period, to that which it does at another, and the motive which impels them—the desire to do right—is precisely the same …. Washington himself is an example of this. At one time he fought against the French, under Braddock, in the service of the King of Great Britain; at another, he fought with the French at Yorktown, under the orders of the Continental Congress of America, against him. He has not been branded by the world with reproach for this, but his course has been applauded.[3]

During the war years the *Richmond Whig*, the *Southern Literary Messenger*, and the *Illustrated London News* all compared Lee to George Washington in prominent articles. In early 1865, when things were looking bleak for the Confederacy, the *Richmond Dispatch* said of Lee: "Providence raises up the man for the time, and a man for the occasion, we believe, has been raised up in Robert E. Lee, the Washington of the second American Revolution." General Henry Wise told Lee, "you certainly play the part of Washington to perfection." Historian Edward Pollard called Lee "a modern copy of Washington," and Colonel Clement A. Evans noted in his diary in 1864, "Lee is regarded by his army as nearest approaching the character of the great & good Washington than any man living." Lee took pride in this association. He had married into Washington's family and, after turning down other offers, he accepted the presidency of Washington College so that his work there would "constitute a tribute to the memory of Washington." It was Herman Melville, in his poem "Lee in the Capitol," who allowed his readers to see darker repercussions of this comparison. Writing of the moment in 1866 when Lee was compelled to testify before Congress, and when the term traitor was in the air, Melville demands that we probe more deeply into this connection:

> In his mien
> The victor and the vanquished both are seen—
> All that he is, and what he late had been.
> Awhile, with curious eyes they scan
> The Chief who led invasion's van—
> Allied by family to one,
> Founder of the Arch the Invader warred upon:
> Who looks at Lee must think of Washington;
> In pain must think, and hide the thought,
> So deep with grievous meaning it is fraught.[4]

If Lee is a traitor to his nation, what was Washington? To Melville, such dangerous thoughts have to be buried. The poem concludes with Lee asking the senators to "Avoid the tyranny you reprobate," and the narrator's affirmation that "Faith in America never dies," but in this difficult poem Melville makes clear that in questions of individual conscience versus national allegiance, there are no easy answers.

Robert E. Lee has proven to be very adaptable as a symbol. People felt that they knew him at the time of the Civil War, they knew him at the turn of the twentieth century, they knew him during the Civil Rights Movement in the 1960s, and they know him today. He seems easily graspable. Although Emory Thomas, in his essay "The Malleable Man," has shown the danger of reading Lee too simplistically, there continues to be a sense that he can be reduced to a single basic term. He fought for the South. The South had slavery. Therefore, he fought *to defend* slavery. One of the questions in mind when we began this study was whether it would be possible for Lee to be seen as the complex individual that he was, or whether such an attempt would fail to raise the boulder of contemporary public perception. Many modern Americans believe that whatever Lee's reasoning, it does not excuse the fact that had he won the war, slavery, albeit in a separate nation, would have continued.[5]

Ulysses S. Grant was not a simple man, but he was a straightforward man. If he was interested in something, he would bring marvelous talents of observation and dedication to it. If he had a job to do, he generally got it done. Grant saw to the heart of matters. He wrote with clarity and a beautiful economy of language, whether addressing his family, his officers, or his reading public. At the end of his life he saw that while he was a product of an old America, he was a symbol of the new. The Union victory had been rooted in the industrial North, but he believed that it had achieved a democracy for all of the people that would not be based on race or wealth or descent. Grant epitomized the highly capable Yankee. He was hardworking, rarely self-serving, and often humble about his accomplishments. He did not stand on pretense, and believed in moving forward toward the completion of a task in a direct and logical manner. To outsiders, like the British journalist who in 1864 saw in Grant a "genuine commoner" and "a commander of a democratic army," all of this was obvious. Grant's admirable qualities eventually became clear to Americans across the country, such as the Montgomery, Alabama, newspaper editor who at his death in 1885 identified the general's "genius" and "temper" as traits of America's national character.[6]

Grant was annoyed by the notion that the Confederacy did not lose, but simply "gave out from sheer exhaustion." Such thinking allowed southerners to maintain that their cause was just and that the fight had been worth any sacrifices that were made. Grant's hope was that "As time passes, people, even of the South, will begin to wonder how it was possible that their ancestors ever fought for or justified institutions which acknowledged the right of property in man." By the time he wrote his *Memoirs* he was tired of hearing about the "Lost Cause." If he knew that Lee and most southerners did not fight the war to preserve slavery, they did fight to justify a government that would have sought to preserve the institution indefinitely. The South, as Bruce Catton famously put it, had become enveloped in a fury in which such concepts as honor, duty, and the rights of man had become confused. To Grant, looking back twenty years later, it was simple. The Union had to be preserved. He made sure that it was. After the war laws had to be enforced. He did his best to assure that they were. He would be one of the first presi-

fig. 286.
The Meditations of Marcus Aurelius Antoninus the Roman Emperor, Concerning Himself. Treating of a Natural Man's Happiness: Wherein It Consisteth, and the Means To Attain It (Glasgow, 1749), College of William and Mary

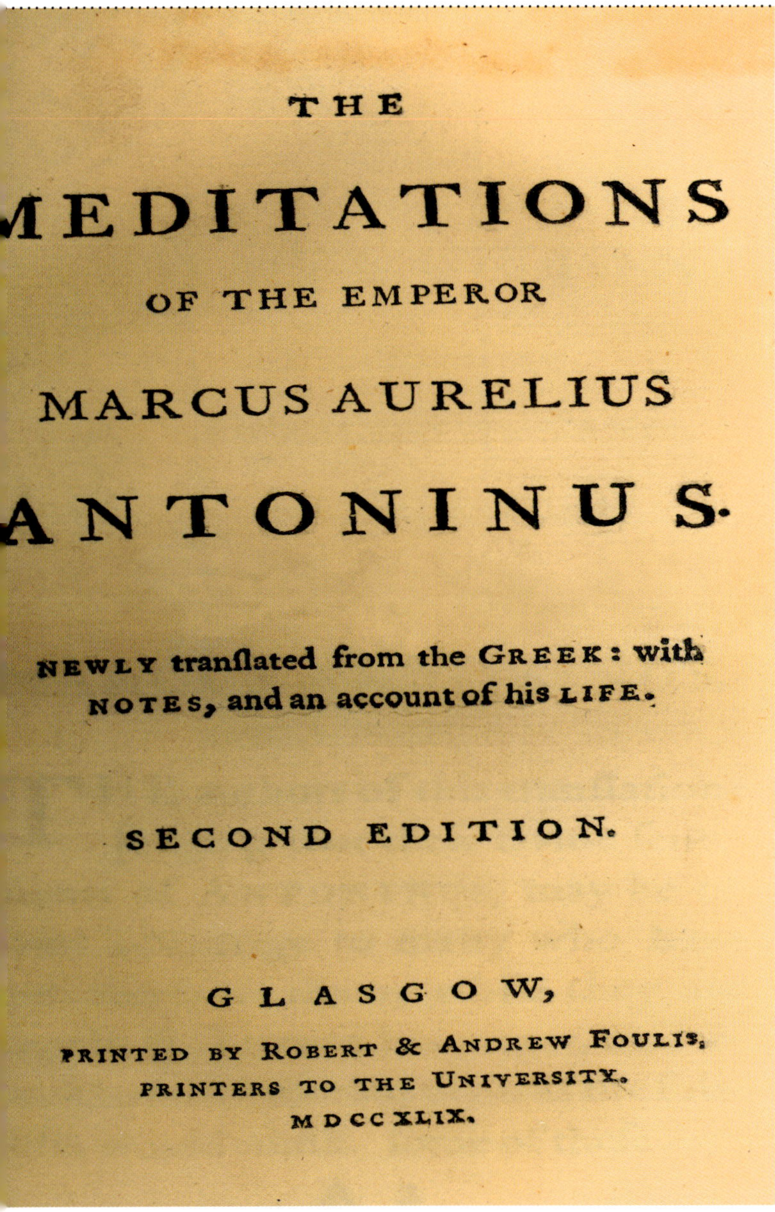

THE

MEDITATIONS

OF THE EMPEROR

MARCUS AURELIUS

ANTONINUS.

NEWLY tranflated from the GREEK: with NOTES, and an account of his LIFE.

SECOND EDITION.

GLASGOW,

PRINTED BY ROBERT & ANDREW FOULIS, PRINTERS TO THE UNIVERSITY.

MDCCXLIX.

dents to use Federal troops against terrorists; he would try to protect the rights of Native Americans; he would suppress the Ku Klux Klan and other such organizations; and he would defend the rights of the freedpeople. The Klan would not rise again for a generation, and African Americans would not again have as much freedom to vote as they had in 1876 until 1968. Few Americans today, however, remember Grant with the reverence that Frederick Douglass awarded him.[7]

Edward Valentine had been intimidated at the prospect of working with so renowned a figure, but Robert E. Lee quickly put the young sculptor at ease. A conversation about the traditional poverty of artists led Lee to begin to think philosophically about how one should deal with adversity. Valentine recounted a story of one of their portrait sessions in 1870 in which, as the general was speaking about the aftermath of the war, he stated, "misfortune nobly borne is good fortune." Only later did Valentine realize that Lee had quoted from the *Meditations* of the second-century Roman emperor and Stoic, Marcus Aurelius—"Remember too on every occasion which leads thee to vexation to apply this principle: not that this is a misfortune, but that to bear it nobly is good fortune." The *Meditations* (fig. 286) was one of several books that Lee reportedly kept on his desk for daily reference. Marcus Aurelius had written the volume as a means to develop a code of ethics, and both "Light-Horse Harry" Lee and his son used it for the same purpose. The general had found in his support of efforts toward reconciliation and in his acceptance of the presidency of Washington College ways in which his own misfortune could be made useful. If he could set an example of noble behavior in the face of adversity, his students might be able to profit by it.[8]

While it seems as though the unconscionable behavior of some of his friends, many of his enemies, and who knows how many unnamed bureaucrats would have undermined President Grant's belief in himself or his way of doing his job, he never wavered. Grant too saw himself as a model. If he worked hard, if he weeded out corruption when and where he saw it, and if he focused on doing the most good for as many people as he could, things would be all right. If he was at times overly naïve, or if he put too much trust in subordinates, the public would understand that there was never any malice in it, nor was there any overt attempt to profit from any of his political endeavors (fig. 287).

When thinking about the commonalities shared by Lee and Grant, one thinks first of their seeming reticence. Lee used his bearing, his reserve, and even his gentility to keep others at bay. Grant's quiet intensity and his rural scruffiness—the fact that he didn't look the part of the commanding general and so few Union officers knew how to approach him—allowed him to maintain his working distance. Both Lee and Grant valued home and family above all else, both listened to advice but rarely took it, both tended to give a good deal of responsibility to subordinates, both held politicians largely responsible for the onset of hostilities, and it is fair

fig. 287.
Thomas Nast, "The Hero of Our Age—Dead," woodcut, *Harper's Weekly*, August 1, 1885

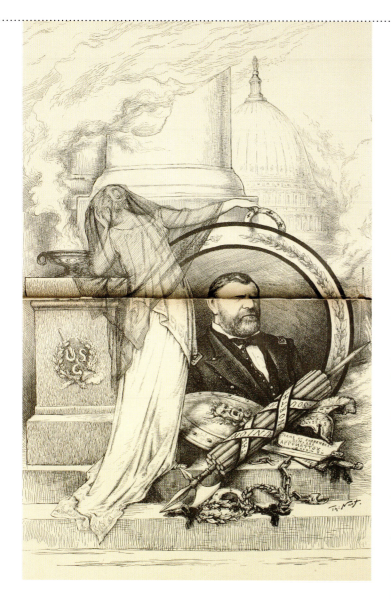

to say that both believed that once they explained their actions, people would understand what they did and why they did it. They would be surprised that we now often choose not to take them at their words. Perhaps it is easier to view the then Colonel Lee as a racist and traitor and President Grant as a patsy than to try to understand why they made the decisions they did. In so doing, however, we lose sight of another commonality. What made each of them great was an adherence to a personal code of honor. Although many of their choices seem not to have stood them in good stead in the post-Civil Rights and post-Watergate eras, for each man the crucial concern was to make decisions that would allow him to deal with his toughest critic, himself.

Our effort here, made by a Richmonder and a New Yorker, was to try to reacquaint ourselves and our readers with the actual men and the world that they shared. We have provided so many passages in their own words in part to allow them to explain themselves once again, to make their beliefs and intentions known, and to see how they judged their own successes and failures. We have tried to avoid apologizing for either Lee or Grant. Their triumphs, of which each had many, are apparent; their mistakes and misjudgments, consequential and trivial, which have been the focus of much scholarship and the bases for waves of popular opinion, have been, we hope, expressed in a manner that will allow readers to form their own opinions.

Many modern Americans detest Lee for supporting a proslavery government, and they think little one way or the other about Grant. Yet each general, in his own way, personified many admirable qualities. It is difficult to review Lee's remarkable devotion to what he perceived to be his duty, or to follow his pursuit of virtue, his "Christian values," without appreciating his dedication to what he believed were the highest of ideals. Similarly, few can read Grant's *Memoirs* without coming to like and admire the man. He is clear and honest, and so modest is his own review of his fabled military career that it is almost shocking. While both made innumerable errors in judgment—as most of us do—the achievements of Grant and Lee far outweigh their flaws. Perhaps the most important thing to remember about them is that their accomplishments and shortcomings are tied to the values of the regions that bred them during the periods in which they lived. We believe that Americans are better off setting aside the regional appreciation of one general over the other and attempting to recognize their respective vices and to appreciate their respective virtues.

Lee and Grant lived through eight decades of almost unimaginable change. During their tenure as commanders, war became as much about destroying your enemy and his civilian support systems as it was about capturing territory. By 1870, the nation was quite unlike the loose conglomeration of the antebellum years. Black people were free. The power of the central government had been confirmed and strengthened. New lands had been opened up for settlement, and a transcontinental telegraph and railroad had come into service. It was a larger, yet in some ways a smaller country, that was united in a way that it had never been before.

fig. 288.
Arlington National Cemetery (photograph courtesy of the National Park Service)

Grant is perhaps easier for twenty-first-century Americans to deal with. His vision from the start was national. In 1861 you were a patriot or a traitor. You had to choose. Lee's absolute dedication to Virginia might seem somewhat antiquated, although there are undoubtedly those who will see his not wanting to lead an army of invasion and occupation against his home state as an exemplary display of regional patriotism. What became clear to us is that as they fought against each other, each man saw himself as fighting for the identical fundamental rights and freedoms that the first generation of American revolutionaries had fought for and that the framers of the Constitution intended for Americans to have. And in the end, it should be remembered that both called for unity and reconciliation.

When next you visit Stratford Hall, or Arlington House (fig. 288), or Lee Chapel at Washington and Lee University, or White Haven plantation, or Grant's house in Galena, or his tomb in New York City, you will find preserved the memory of each man as an individual. Our attempt has been to place them in their personal and historical contexts in order to better understand not only the men who sat across the table from each other at Appomattox, but also what got them there, and what allowed them to go on to the productive lives that each led after the war. When figures of such stature are involved, the line between myth and history easily disappears. If we have been able to sketch in parts of that boundary, then our efforts will have had some measure of success.

Special Lenders to the Exhibition

Washington and Lee University in Lexington, Virginia, holds the largest collection of Lee family objects, including life portraits of Robert E. Lee, his wife, and his mother, and portraits and objects owned by George Washington that were inherited by Mary Custis Lee. All were carried to Lexington following his acceptance of the presidency of Washington College in 1865. After Lee's death, the collection was given to the university by his family, along with many of the general's papers. Lee assumed the presidency fearful that his leadership of the Confederate armies "might draw upon the College a feeling of hostility," but he added, "I think it the duty of every citizen in the present condition of the Country, to do all in his power to aid in the restoration of peace and harmony." The building now called Lee Chapel is the most visible evidence of the general's tenure at the college. It was constructed during his presidency, and he attended daily services there with the students. In 1883, a massive sculpture of the recumbent general by Edward Valentine was made the focal point of the building's interior. Below is a crypt that holds the remains of Lee and members of his immediate family. Also on the lower level are Lee's office, preserved as he left it in 1870, and a museum that honors the general's contributions to the university. Lee Chapel has become a national historical monument that is visited annually by thousands. In his five years as president of the college, Lee expanded the curriculum to include courses in business and journalism and he added a school of law. The greatest legacy that he left the college, however, was his institution of a code of honor that remains the guiding principle of life there.

The Museum of the Confederacy in Richmond, Virginia, holds one of the premier collections of artifacts, documents, and photographs related to the life and career of Robert E. Lee. The items illustrated in this catalog—including the frock coat and sword that Lee wore to his meeting with Grant at Appomattox, his April 1861 draft letter written to Winfield Scott, and the document emancipating his father-in-law's slaves—are among its highlights. Just as much of the museum's overall collection has been received as gifts from families, so most of the Lee items came directly from the general's immediate kin, notably his son George Washington Custis Lee and his nephew Fitzhugh Lee. His youngest daughter Mildred was the regent for the museum's Virginia Room from 1896 to 1905, succeeded by another daughter, Mary Lee. Many of the Lee artifacts are on permanent display in the museum's flagship installation, *The Confederate Years*. In 2000, the museum organized a major show on the life and military career of Lee with the benefit of loans from the Virginia Historical Society, Lee Chapel Museum, and the Leyburn Library of Washington and Lee University. In turn, the museum is pleased to make available a few of its most significant Lee items for the enjoyment of visitors to the traveling exhibition *Lee and Grant*.

The Civil War and Underground Railroad Museum in Philadelphia interprets the struggle for freedom, equality, and national unity in nineteenth-century America. Founded in 1888 by veteran officers of the Union Army, Navy, and Marine Corps, it is the oldest chartered Civil War institution in the United States created to preserve the history of that conflict and to promote public education through the collection, preservation, and display of artifacts, documents, and photographs. With nine galleries of displays and exhibits, the museum's holdings include more than 3,000 artifacts and 7,000 photographs, hundreds of art works, and some 400 cubic feet of archival material. Firearms, edged weapons, uniforms, paintings, photographs, and flags are among the many objects on permanent display. A library with in excess of 7,000 volumes constitutes one of the foremost collections of material related to the Civil War. In all, the museum maintains one of the largest assemblages of Civil War related material.

Arlington House, The Robert E. Lee Memorial, was the home of Lee and his family for thirty years, from the time of his marriage until 1861. During the Civil War, when combat and troop movements forced the Lee family to vacate the property, the estate was confiscated. The grounds were ultimately turned into Arlington National Cemetery. Some of the objects in the house remained there during and after the war; others that had been seized by the federal government were ultimately returned. Arlington House is uniquely associated with the Washington, Custis, and Lee families. George Washington Parke Custis built the house to be both his home and a memorial to George Washington, his step-grandfather. In 1925, Congress decreed that the house be preserved as a memorial to Lee. It became part of the National Park System.

Stratford Hall, The Birthplace of Robert E. Lee, was the home of Lee for the first four years of his life. The house was built c. 1740 by Thomas Lee, Robert's great-great-uncle. In 1929, the Robert E. Lee Memorial Foundation was established to acquire and restore the property. Today, the Robert E. Lee Association interprets the house itself and discusses life on the Stratford plantation. The dominant theme is that the ideals and leadership of generations of the Lee family helped to shape democracy in the United States. The mission of the Association is to foster preservation, research, and education.

Notes

INTRODUCTION

1. This painting has been traditionally known as *Sketch of General Lee*. Grant, who is clearly present, was not, to Eakins's mind, the crucial subject.
2. For the quote about "Bobby Lee," see Ken Burns, *The Civil War* (New York, 1996), 271. For Grant's remarks about Lee, see Ulysses S. Grant, "Interview," Hamburg, July 6, 1878, cited in John Y. Simon, ed., *The Papers of Ulysses S. Grant* (Carbondale, IL, 1967–), 28:419.
3. Theodore Roosevelt to Hilary Abner Herbert, et al., Jan. 16, 1907, cited in *The Letters of Theodore Roosevelt*, ed. Morison & Blum (Cambridge, MA, 1952), 553–55.
4. W. E. B. DuBois, "Robert E. Lee," *The Crisis*, Mar. 1928, 97.
5. The portrait of Lee by Edward Caledon Bruce was owned in 1898 in New York City by Charles Broadway Rouss.
6. A photograph of the design is now lost, but it is cited in a letter to Brooke of 1864. See Pamela H. Simpson, *American Sculptors in Lexington* (Lexington, VA, 1977), 27–29. Brooke was well known for his involvement in developing the ironclad CSS *Virginia* and for his design and production of heavy rifled guns.
7. Mary Lee to Gen. R. H. Chilton, Dec. 12, 1870, cited in Douglas Southall Freeman, *R. E. Lee* (New York, 1934), 4:528.
8. John Esten Cooke, *A Life of General Robert Edward Lee* (New York, 1871), 307, 324.
9. In several respects, Jubal Early resembled Lee. He was a West Point graduate, a veteran of the Mexican War, and an opponent of secession. But Early became embittered and defiant after Appomattox. Rejecting the restored Union, he fled to Mexico and then to Canada, while he directed other southerners to New Zealand. Early had not been incompetent as a general, but he proved to be a more effective and a much more feared writer. He even gained credibility as an historian, when he served as first president of the Southern Historical Society. For a quarter of a century, Early preached his heavily biased and regionalist doctrine, becoming arguably the most influential figure in nineteenth-century Civil War writing, North or South. Early originated the theory that a southern victory was denied because of Longstreet's tardiness in obeying Lee's command to attack the enemy on the morning of July 2 at Gettysburg. The idea to blame Longstreet would be accepted even by Lee's principal biographer, Douglas Southall Freeman. See Thomas L. Connelly, *The Marble Man: Robert E. Lee and His Image in American Society* (New York, 1977), 51, 88–89.
10. J. William Jones, *Personal Reminiscences, Anecdotes and Letters of Robert E. Lee* (New York, 1874), Preface.
11. Christopher Roland Lawton, "Myth and Monument: The Sculptural Image of Robert E. Lee and the Ideology of the Lost Cause" (master's thesis, University of Georgia, 2000), 22.
12. John Warwick Daniel, *Robert E. Lee, An Oration Pronounced at the Unveiling of the Recumbent Figure at Lexington, Virginia* (Savannah, GA, 1883), 41, 13.
13. Early, cited in Jones, *Personal Reminiscences of Lee*, 49.
14. Emory Thomas, "The Malleable Man," in Peter Wallenstein and Bertram Wyatt-Brown, eds., *Virginia's Civil War* (Charlottesville, VA, 2005), 9.
15. Lawton, "Sculptural Image of Lee," 53–70; *New York Times*, May 10, 1890, 1–2.
16. *Richmond Planet*, May 21, 1890, 1, cited in Lawton, "Sculptural Image of Lee," 147. See also Kirk Savage, *Standing Soldiers, Kneeling Slaves: Race, War and Monument in Nineteenth-Century America* (Princeton, NJ, 1997).
17. Ervin L. Jordan, *Black Confederates and Afro-Yankees in Civil War Virginia* (Charlottesville, VA, 1995), 62–63, 65, 238–39, 243, 245–46, 249–50, 261; W. E. B. Du Bois, "Robert E. Lee," *The Crisis*, Mar. 1928, 97.
18. Connelly, *Marble Man*, 65, 103–9.
19. Woodrow Wilson's commentary on Lee is cited in Connelly, *Marble Man*, 162.
20. Thomas Connelly has chronicled the mania. See *Marble Man*, 99–122.
21. Daniel to Valentine, Dec. 13, 1907, copy in curatorial files, U.S. Capitol.
22. The Vannerson photograph was one of the images taken during the war that had been sent to the young Edward Valentine in Germany. One version of the Pine portrait hangs in the Asheville-Buncombe Library in Asheville, North Carolina.
23. From the 1907 lecture by Adams in Lee Chapel, Lexington, Virginia.
24. Gamaliel Bradford, *Lee the American* (Boston, 1912), 265–66.
25. Connelly, *Marble Man*, 125–26. Less attention was devoted in the New York press to the massive granite relief of Jefferson Davis, Lee, and Stonewall Jackson that in these years was being carved on the face of Stone Mountain in Georgia. The largest ever of its type, it competed for the support of the same southern dollars. The sculpture was begun in 1916 by Gutzon Borglum and not completed until 1972. In 1922, Franklin Riley, a professor at Washington and Lee University, published *General Robert E. Lee after Appomattox*. Riley revived and expanded the defunct "Lee Memorial Volume," that had been projected in 1870. His purpose was to disseminate more information about Lee's tenure in Lexington.
26. Stephen Vincent Benét, *John Brown's Body* (New York, 1928), 230–35.
27. *New York Times*, Feb. 10, 1935.
28. Freeman, *Lee*, 4:494, 505.
29. Connelly, *Marble Man*, 145. Like Freeman's biography, Margaret Mitchell's novel *Gone with the Wind*, which won the Pulitzer Prize in 1936 and enjoyed widespread acclaim, also appealed to an audience that suffered during the Depression. For the enlistees during the summer of 1942, see July 15, 1942 radio broadcast on Richmond, Virginia radio station WRVA, Library of Virginia, # 38210.
30. Winston Churchill, *A History of the English Speaking Peoples*, vol. 4, *The Great Democracies* (London, 1958), 135.
31. Dwight D. Eisenhower to Leon W. Scott, Aug. 9, 1960, written from the White House (http://www.federalobserver.com/archive.php?aid=8455).
32. Among the many followers of Freeman was Clifford Dowdey, whose *Lee* was published in 1965. Dowdey carried the study of Lee's interaction with slaves and freedmen little further than had Freeman or any of his predecessors. He told the story from the white perspective only. Slaves are anonymous beings. Dowdey tried to give focus to the character of Lee, which had long been shown to be the persona that northerners could bear to tolerate. One critic for *The New York Times* had suggested that only "after-gleaners" could follow Freeman, and some passages from Dowdey suggest that there actually was little substantive left to say about Lee by those who would glorify him (*New York Times*, Feb. 10, 1935, cited in Connelly, *Marble Man*, 152).
33. Connelly, *Marble Man*, xiv–xv.
34. President Gerald R. Ford signed the bill restoring Robert E. Lee's citizenship on August 5, 1975, commenting then on the strength of Lee's character.
35. Craig Timberg, "Lee's Portrait Opens Wounds in Richmond," *Washington Post*, June 4, 1999, B1; Timberg, "Richmond is Seeking Civil Solution," *Washington Post*, June 17, 1999, B4.
36. *Richmond Times-Dispatch*, June 14, 1999.
37. "City Council Supports Mural of Lee on Floodwall," *Richmond Times-Dispatch*, July 27, 1999; Douglas Wilder, quoted in the *Washington Post*, June 17, 1999.
38. *Richmond Times-Dispatch*, Nov. 14, 2003.
39. Michael Fellman, *The Making of Robert E. Lee* (New York, 2000), xviii, xx, 306, 307–8.
40. Thomas, "Malleable Man," 9–18. Most recently, scholars have started to rebut the rebuttals of Freeman. In a book review that followed Alan Nolan's 1991 *Lee Considered*, Emory Thomas complained that the author "reveals a spirit mean and sad, and neither of these adjectives applies to Lee." Of *The Making of Robert E. Lee*, Thomas writes, "Fellman seems to me to be so much in thrall to—repelled by—the Lee legend, myth, hagiography, that he spends most of his energy and ink protesting what Lee was not rather than elucidating what Lee was" (Thomas, "Malleable Man," 12–13). In 2001, in the Preface to *Lee & His Army in Confederate History*, Civil War scholar Gary W. Gallagher alerts the reader to a new direction in Lee studies: "My own research over the years indicated that Freeman might have been closer to the mark than many of those who insisted Lee and his army had been overrated" (ix). Then, in a series of essays, Gallagher gives impressive evidence that suggests that Freeman's instincts were correct. What is different to a reader in the twenty-first century is that Gallagher exudes credibility, which a work published in 1934 perhaps inevitably lacks because it is more than half a century old.
41. Theodore Roosevelt, speech delivered at Galena, Illinois, Apr. 27, 1900.
42. Ernest Hemingway, *For Whom the Bell Tolls* (New York, 1940), 227.
43. Antrobus was commissioned in Chicago by a northern friend and admirer of Grant, J. Russell Jones.
44. The Antrobus painting is less successful than the similar imitation of Lee in the guise of George Washington painted by Edward Caledon Bruce of 1864 (fig. 4).
45. Balling also painted, from studies in Washington in late 1864, a portrait of Grant as he might have stood at Vicksburg. That canvas is in the National Portrait Gallery, Washington.

46. Balling must have observed the general on his mount Cincinnati, because the image is convincing. Grant was renowned for his skill as a rider.
47. One example of the new wave of prints is the etched and engraved image by John C. McRae that surrounds a portrait of Grant with scenes of his triumphs. This print is illustrated on the National Portrait Gallery website (http://npgportraits.si.edu).
48. Albert D. Richardson, *A Personal History of Ulysses S. Grant* (Reading, PA, 1868), x–xi; Henry C. Deming, *The Life of Ulysses S. Grant, General United States Army* (Hartford, CT, 1868), 527–28.
49. Simon, "Introduction," in Simon, ed., *Papers of Grant*, 1:xxxii.
50. James P. Boyd, *Military and Civil Life of Gen. Ulysses S. Grant* (Philadelphia, 1885), 3–5; Simon, "Introduction," in Simon, ed., *Papers of Grant*, 1:xxxii.
51. The map is illustrated in *The New York Times*, Aug. 5, 1885. For the low fares, see *New York Times*, Aug. 3, 1885.
52. Harold Holzer, *Prang's Civil War Pictures: The Complete Battle Chromos of Louis Prang* (New York, 2001), 37–38.
53. Walt Whitman, "The Silent General" [1879], *Specimen Days*, in *Prose Works* (Philadelphia, 1892), available at http://www.bartleby.com/229/1200.html (accessed Jan. 17, 2007).
54. Karl Gerhardt, "Grant's Memorial: What Shall It Be," *North American Review*, Sept. 1885.
55. David M. Kahn, "The Grant Monument," *Journal of the Society of Architectural Historians* 41, no. 3 (1982), 21–31. (The root of the Latin word mausoleum is taken from the name of King Mausolus because of his renowned tomb.)
56. Grant penned a letter to the governor of Rhode Island, former general Ambrose Burnside, recommending Franklin Simmons "to make some statuary for your Capital," July 24, 1866, Simon, ed., *Papers of Grant*, 16:256.
57. The first standing marble statue of Grant, larger than life-size, is now at the Portland Museum of Art. The commissioning of a sculpture of Robert E. Lee for the same Capitol building in Washington began three years later. "Lee the statesman" was preferred by his turn-of-the-century admirers to "Lee the soldier."
58. Dennis Montagna, "The Ulysses S. Grant Memorial in Washington, D.C.: A Monument for the New Century," in *Critical Issues in Public Art: Content, Context, and Controversy*, ed. Harriet Senie and Sally Webster (New York, 1992), 115–27; article posted on the Internet under its title, 2006.
59. Hamlin Garland, *Ulysses S. Grant, His Life and Character* (New York, 1898), v–vii.
60. Jean Edward Smith, *Grant* (New York, 2001), 475.
61. "[Assistant Secretary of War] Breckenridge Asks Better Defenses," *New York Times*, June 1, 1915; Allan Sinclair Will, "America Famed For War Leaders," *New York Times*, Oct. 28, 1917.
62. "Keen Debate for 13 Hours," *New York Times*, Apr. 5, 1917; "Wilson Foresees War of Grimness," *ibid.*, May 13, 1917; "Sees Enemy Plot in War Loss Scare. Casualties Exaggerated by Pro-Germans, Senator Saulsbury Says, to Deter America," *ibid.*, Oct. 22, 1917; Arthur S. Link, *American Epoch, A History of the United States since the 1890's* (New York, 1963), 1:198; Charles Willis Thompson, "Grant, The Master Strategist, A British Military Critic Rates Him the Greatest of His Age," *New York Times*, Dec. 29, 1929; for use of the term "butcher" see also Stephen Vincent Benét, *John Brown's Body* (New York, 1928), 218; J. F. C. Fuller, *Grant & Lee, A Study in Personality and Generalship* (New York: 1933), 7.
63. B. L. Duffus, "Some Political Scandals in the History of the Nation, Oil Disclosures Bring to Mind Aaron Burr's Plot, the Credit Mobilier, the Whisky Ring, and the Ballinger Case," *New York Times*, Feb. 10, 1924.
64. William E. Woodward, *Meet General Grant* (New York, 1928), 25–26, 29–30, 99.
65. Stephen Vincent Benét, *John Brown's Body* (New York, 1928), 210, 218–19, 310–12, 386–88, 437–38.
66. Charles Willis Thompson, "Grant, The Master Strategist, A British Military Critic Rates Him the Greatest of His Age," *New York Times*, Dec. 29, 1929.
67. Fuller, *Grant & Lee*, 57–58.
68. William Best Hesseltine, *Ulysses S. Grant: Politician* (New York, 1935).
69. "Roosevelt Bitter in Beginning War on the President," *New York Times*, Oct. 29, 1918; "Unconditional Surrender," *ibid.*, Oct. 31, 1918; "Says Germany Will Quit. Unconditional Surrender Within Six Months Predicted by Taft," *ibid.*, Nov. 3, 1918; "Sends Out Victory Appeal. Stone Issues Message to 'Unconditional Surrender Club,'" *ibid.*, Nov. 6, 1918; Maj. J. Stewart Richardson, "Pershing, in Spirit, Is Again Over There," *ibid.*, Aug. 13, 1944.
70. "Grant's Struggle Viewed as Lesson," *ibid.*, Apr. 29, 1940; "Aid for Britain Urged by Veterans' Groups," *ibid.*, Apr. 28, 1940.
71. Drew Middleton, "Leaders Go By Air. Aim at 'Unconditional Surrender' by Axis, President Says," *ibid.*, Jan. 27, 1943; "Pacific War Talks," *ibid.*, Aug. 11, 1944; "Enemy Gets His First Taste of 'Unconditional Surrender.' Germans in Bizerte Area Yielded to American General Who Offered No Terms," *ibid.*, May 11, 1943; Henry Stuart Clark, "Definition of Intent Needed," *ibid.*, Sept. 6, 1943; "Japan's Peril," *ibid.*, June 10, 1945.
72. Gertrude Stein, "The New Hope in Our 'Sad Young Men,'" *ibid.*, June 3, 1945.
73. Lloyd Lewis, *Captain Sam Grant* (Boston, 1950), 430.
74. Bruce Catton, *Grant Moves South* (Boston, 1960), 3.
75. Major General Ulysses S. Grant, III, *Ulysses S. Grant, Warrior and Statesman* (New York, 1969), 9–10.

I

1. Lee wrote to his son about honor on May 4, 1851 when Custis was a cadet at West Point. Bertram Wyatt-Brown, *Southern Honor: Ethics and Behavior in the Old South* (New York, 1982), 109; Wyatt-Brown, "Robert E. Lee and the Concept of Honor," in Peter Wallenstein and Bertram Wyatt-Brown, *Virginia's Civil War* (Charlottesville, VA, 2005), 34. See also Wyatt-Brown, *Yankee Saints and Southern Sinners* (Baton Rouge, LA, 1985), Wyatt-Brown, *Honor and Violence in the Old South* (New York, 1986), and Wyatt-Brown, *The Shaping of Southern Culture: Honor, Grace, and War, 1760s–1890s* (Chapel Hill, NC, 2001).
2. Wyatt-Brown, *Southern Honor*, 34–37, 45; Wyatt-Brown, "Lee and the Concept of Honor," 29, 55; Wyatt-Brown, *Yankee Saints and Southern Sinners*, 210–11.
3. Rachel Grant Tompkins, June 5, 1861, cited in M. J. Cramer, *Ulysses S. Grant: Conversations and Unpublished Letters* (New York, 1897), 27, 159–82, and in turn cited in John Y. Simon, ed., *The Papers of Ulysses S. Grant* (Carbondale, IL, 1967–), 2:15. If a relation lived outside the region, however, the code of protection did not apply. In 1862 and again in 1863, Lee's Army of Northern Virginia invaded Maryland. There his sister Ann Marshall was resident, in Baltimore. Her son was enlisted in the Union army. Lee wrote Ann Marshall in 1861 that he could not raise his hand against his relatives. A year later she must have wondered how she got left out of the equation. Not only did Ann Marshall's son fight for the Union, but so did distant cousins of Lee. Lee's decision making, obviously, was governed by more than simple duty to family. All of the Grant papers cited below are published in the volumes edited by Simon.
4. Wyatt-Brown, "Lee and the Concept of Honor," 37; Wyatt-Brown, *Southern Honor*, 110–14. The Mary Lee quote is Douglas Southall Freeman, *R. E. Lee* (New York, 1934), 1:442. The Henry Lee quote is J. F. C. Fuller, *Lee & Grant, A Study in Personality and Generalship* (New York, 1933), 98.
5. Wyatt-Brown, *Southern Honor*, 89, 107, 108; Wyatt-Brown, "Lee and the Concept of Honor," 29, 34, 39. The Richmond *Dispatch* reported in April 1861 that a "more heroic Christian, noble soldier and gentleman could not be found" (cited in Gary W. Gallagher, *Lee and His Generals in War and Memory* [Baton Rouge, LA, 1998], 6).
6. Wyatt-Brown, *Yankee Saints and Southern Sinners*, 176, 184, 5, 198, 212; Wyatt-Brown, "Lee and the Concept of Honor," 35; Wyatt-Brown, *Southern Honor*, 5.
7. Wyatt-Brown, "Lee and the Concept of Honor," 38.
8. Wyatt-Brown, "Lee and the Concept of Honor," 37, 40. The statement about men "lost after I knew it was too late" was made in 1868 outside Lexington to Lee's riding companion Belle Stewart, later Mrs. Joseph Bryan, a close friend of Lee's daughter Mildred. Belle had asked, "Why are you so sad, General Lee?" See J. Bryan, III, *The Sword Over the Mantel*, 81; cited in Nelson Peabody Rose, *Robert E. Lee of Virginia, The Anguish of Conflicting Loyalties* (Cleveland, 1985), 21.
9. Lee to Major Earl Van Dorn, July 3, 1860, Library of Congress, cited in Freeman, *Lee*, 1:413.
10. Lee to Custis Lee, Nov. 24, 1860, cited in Freeman, *Lee*, 1:414; Lee to Rooney Lee, Dec. 3, 1860, Virginia Historical Society.
11. Buchanan stated that secession is "neither more nor less than revolution." He further told Congress that the Union "can never be cemented by the blood of its citizens shed in a civil war .... Congress possesses many means of preserving it by conciliation, but the sword was not placed in their hands to preserve it by

11. force." Cited in Freeman, *Lee*, 1:416; Nelson Peabody Rose, *Robert E. Lee of Virginia: The Anguish of Conflicting Loyalties* (Cleveland, 1985), 108.
12. Lee to Custis Lee, Dec. 14, 1860, cited in Freeman, *Lee*, 1:417.
13. Mrs. Lee to Eliza Mackay Stiles, Feb. 9, 1861; Mrs. Lee to Mildred Lee, Feb. 19 and 24, 1861, Virginia Historical Society.
14. Lee to Annette Carter, Jan. 16, 1861, Washington and Lee University. Annette Carter was the daughter of Lee's first cousin Charles Henry Carter.
15. Lee to Markie Williams, Jan. 22, 1861, cited in Freeman, *Lee*, 1:421.
16. Edward Everett, *The Life of George Washington* (New York, 1860); Lee to Mrs. Lee, Jan. 23, 1861, Virginia Historical Society.
17. A similar, now lost letter that apparently was addressed to Custis Lee is printed in Freeman, *Lee*, 1:420–21.
18. Reference to "perpetual union" is not made in the U.S. Constitution but in the preamble to the Articles of Confederation.
19. Lee to Agnes Lee, Jan. 29, 1861, Virginia Historical Society.
20. Lee to Custis Lee, Jan. 30, 1861, cited in Freeman, *Lee*, 1:423.
21. Lee made a seemingly contradictory statement to R. W. Johnson, "I shall never bear arms against the Union, but it may be necessary for me to carry a musket in defense of my native state, Virginia, in which case I shall not prove recreant to my duty." What he meant was that as a unionist he would never assume the offensive and thereby undermine the nation, but as a man of honor he would defend Virginia from invasion. (Lee to R. W. Johnson, Feb. 13, 1861, cited in Freeman, *Lee*, 1:425.) Captain George B. Cosby recalled, "[Lee] said that … if [Virginia] failed [to avert civil war] and determined to secede, he would offer her his services. That he had ever been taught that his first allegiance was due his mother State; that … under no circumstance could he ever bare his sword against Virginia's sons. As he spoke his emotion brought tears to his eyes, and he turned away to avoid showing this emotion which was greater than he afterwards showed when he lost or won some great battle." (Cosby's recollections were printed in the *Confederate Veteran*; cited in Freeman, *Lee*, 1:426.) Lee told Charles Anderson of Kentucky that he disapproved of everything about secession, but his duty was to Virginia: "my loyalty to Virginia ought to take precedence over that which is due the Federal government. And I shall so report myself at Washington. If Virginia stands by the old Union, so will I. But if she secedes (though I do not believe in secession as a constitutional right, nor that there is sufficient cause for revolution), then I will still follow my native State with my sword, and if need be with my life. I know you think and feel very differently, but I can't help it. These are my principles, and I must follow them." (Cited in Freeman, *Lee*, 1:427.) As to his statement to R. M. Potter about planting corn, when he left Texas, Lee was searching desperately for an escape from the dilemma brought by the action of the Deep South. His statements to the others in Texas indicate that he did not really believe that retirement would resolve his dilemma. In fact, Lee worried that duty to Virginia would soon prevent most white men in the state from planting corn. (Cited in Freeman, *Lee*, 1:429.)
22. A popular cartoon of the time, entitled "Scott's Great Snake," depicts a giant snake enveloping the South. This was the source of the term "Anaconda Plan." The origin for the belief that Scott suspected that the threat of a powerful army under Lee's command would end the prospect of war is the general's military secretary, Colonel Erasmus Keyes (cited in Freeman, *Lee*, 1:433). Scott wrote to Secretary of War John Buchanan Floyd, May 8, 1857, "I hope beg to ask that one of the vacant 2d. Lieutenancies may be given to W. H. F. Lee, son of Brevet colonel R. E. Lee at present on duty against the Comanches. I make this application mainly on the extraordinary merits of the father—the very best soldier that I ever saw in the field" (Virginia Historical Society). Another of Scott's Mexican War lieutenants, P. G. T. Beauregard, was already in command of secessionist forces in South Carolina and Scott did not want another to join him.
23. Freeman, *Lee*, 1:432.
24. Jeb Stuart, Fort Riley, Kansas, to John Overton Steger, Mar. 23, 1861, Virginia Historical Society.
25. Daniel W. Crofts, *Reluctant Confederates: Upper South Unionists in the Secession Crisis* (Chapel Hill, NC, 1989), 301–6; Rose, *Lee*, 103–5, 46.
26. Official Records, cited in Freeman, *Lee*, 1:435; Emory Thomas, *Robert E. Lee, A Biography* (New York, 1995), 187.
27. Freeman, *Lee*, 1:434–35.
28. Robert E. Lee to Senator Reverdy Johnson, Feb. 25, 1868. The letter is lost. It is cited in J. William Jones, *Personal Reminiscences of General Robert E. Lee* (New York, 1874), 141. Lee wrote his account of the 1861 interview because his name had recently been slandered on the floor of Congress by Senator Simon Cameron, the former secretary of war. In response, Senator Johnson of Maryland had defended the honor of Lee. The general wrote Johnson a letter of thanks, assuring him of his good "conduct on the occasion referred to." What had incurred the wrath of Cameron was debate over the admission of a newly elected senator from Maryland, Philip Thomas, who was said to have sympathized with Confederates in 1861. In trying to defend Thomas, Johnson had offered Lee's actions as a comparison, only to incite from Cameron a bitter recounting of the Blair interview. A full account of this incident is in Freeman, *Lee*, 4:360–62.
29. In 1866, Montgomery Blair, the son, wrote an account of the interview that confirms the other two (Freeman, *Lee*, 1:634–35.) The comment by Lee about freeing slaves, which is mentioned by both of the Blairs, was confirmed by Bishop Joseph P. B. Wilmer of Louisiana, who spoke with Lee at the start of the war. Lee told him that "if the slaves of the South were mine, I would surrender them all without a struggle, to avert this war" (Jones, *Reminiscences*, 142).
30. "Memoranda of Conversations with General Robert E. Lee," William Allan, Apr. 15, 1868, in Gary W. Gallagher, ed., *Lee the Soldier* (Lincoln, NE, 1996), 9–10; Freeman, *Lee*, 1:437. Freeman's source for the Scott quote is the early literature on Lee. Freeman concluded that Mrs. Lee must have approved it as being accurate.
31. Lee's conversation with Scott as recorded by E. D. Townsend (published in *Anecdotes of the Civil War*, 29) is cited in Freeman, *Lee*, 1:437. Freeman "hesitated to cite Townsend as witness" because Townsend gave the wrong date for the interview (by a day) and Freeman thought that the sentence about Lee's children being ruined "does not sound like Lee." However, Freeman got the quote wrong. Lee did not say "They will be ruined, if *I* do not go with their State"; he said, "They will be ruined, if *they* do not go with their State."
32. Cited in Thomas L. Connelly, *The Marble Man: Robert E. Lee and His Image in American Society* (New York, 1977), 37.
33. Rose, *Lee*, 70; Freeman, *Lee*, 1:439. The May 23 referendum for secession passed five to one. By then, too many steps toward war had been taken, including the seizure in late April of the federal naval yard at Gosport, near Norfolk, and the federal arsenal at Harpers Ferry. A letter written on April 19 from Agnes Lee, at Arlington, to her sister Mildred Lee (Virginia Historical Society) records the family's discovery of the secession decision: "Papa, Mamma, and Mary went to Alexandria this morning. Helen & I learned out walking today. Virginia has seceded! I cannot yet realize it, it seems so dreadful. But she had to take one side or the other & truly I hope she has chosen the right one. It is a very solemn step & I fear we will have to go through a great deal of suffering …. Our poor country & our Fathers & brothers need all of our prayers."
34. For the honor to Lee's father, see *Acts of the General Assembly of Virginia*, 1861, 58, cited in Freeman, *Lee*, 1:466–67, note 15.
35. William Woods Averell, *Ten Years in the Saddle*, cited in Rose, *Lee*, 74.
36. Robert E. Lee, *Journal*, c. 1861–65, Virginia Historical Society.
37. For the Stephens quote, see Guy Emery, *Robert E. Lee*, 108, cited in Rose, *Lee*, 11; *Report of the Joint Committee on Reconstruction at the First Session Thirty-Ninth Congress* (Washington, DC, 1866), 133.
38. Lee to Johnson, cited in Jones, *Reminiscences*, 141.
39. Apr. 20, 1861, cited in Freeman, *Lee*, 1:444.
40. Charles B. Flood, *Lee: The Late Years* (Boston, 1981), 47.
41. Apr. 20, 1861, cited in Freeman, *Lee*, 1:443.
42. April 20, 1861, cited in Freeman, *Lee*, 1:444–45.
43. Lee to Johnson, cited in Jones, *Reminiscences*, 141. Lee's full statement ("I repaired to Richmond; found that the convention then in session had passed the ordinance withdrawing the State from the Union; and accepted the commission …") included an error of memory. Lee had actually learned that secession had been voted on April 19, before he left Arlington. Thomas, *Lee*, 190.
44. Freeman, *Lee*, 1:445, 462–64, 450.
45. Freeman, *Lee*, 1:466–67, 468.

46. Freeman, *Lee*, 1:468.
47. Freeman quotes long passages from the *Richmond Dispatch* ("A more heroic Christian, noble soldier and gentleman could not be found ….") (Apr. 26 and May 1, 1861), and the *Lynchburg Virginian* ("We rejoice that this distinguished officer and worthy son of Virginia has withdrawn from Lincoln's army and thrown himself upon the bosom of his native State. It was what we expected of the man.") (quoted in *Richmond Enquirer*, Apr. 25, 1861). The *Richmond Enquirer* reported Scott's disappointment (he would rather have received the resignation of every other general) (Apr. 27, 1861). See Freeman, *Lee*, 1:468–69, 493.
48. Freeman, *Lee*, 1:470, 487, 475. The letter to C. F. Lee was dated Apr. 25, 1861. Lee to Mrs. Lee, Apr. 26, 1861, Virginia Historical Society.
49. The quote about war being a terrible alternative is cited in Flood, *Lee*, 119. The letter to Mrs. Lee and the statement to members of the secession convention are in Freeman, *Lee*, 1:475. The latter is supported by the recollection of aide Walter Taylor that Lee "alone, of all those then known to me … expressed his most serious apprehensions of a prolonged and bloody war"; cited in Thomas, *Lee*, 197.
50. George Thomas to John Letcher, Mar. 12, 1861, University of Virginia.
51. Jeb Stuart to Flora Cooke Stuart, June 18, 1861, Virginia Historical Society.
52. Grant to Jesse Root Grant, and Grant to Mrs. Grant, both May 5, 1861 and both cited in more detail below.
53. Brooks D. Simpson, *Ulysses S. Grant: Triumph over Adversity, 1822–1865* (Boston, 2000), 75.
54. Grant to his sister Mary Grant, Apr. 29, 1861. He said as well to her, "The conduct of eastern Virginia has been so abominable through the whole contest that there would be a great deal of disappointment here if matters should be settled before she is thoroughly punished."
55. Simpson, *Grant*, 76; Grant, letter of Dec. 1860 to an unknown addressee. Simpson has deduced that this letter was addressed to Charles W. Ford, a friend in Missouri.
56. Ulysses S. Grant, *Personal Memoirs of U. S. Grant* (New York), 1:218–22.
57. Grant, *Memoirs*, 1:225–26.
58. Simpson, *Grant*, 77; William S. McFeely, *Grant, A Biography* (New York, 1981), 73.
59. Grant, *Memoirs*, 1:230–34; McFeely, *Grant*, 75–76.
60. Grant to father-in-law Frederick Dent, Apr. 19, 1861.
61. Grant to Jesse Root Grant, Apr. 21, 1861, lost, reproduced in Cramer, *Grant*, 25–27.
62. Jesse Root Grant to Edward Bates, Apr. 25, 1861, cited in Simon, ed., *Papers of Grant*, 2:8. In 1861, "defense" meant what it means today. Our national Department of Defense engages in offensive action as part of a defensive strategy.
63. Grant to Mrs. Grant, Apr. 27, 1861; Grant to Mary Grant, Apr. 29, 1861.
64. Grant to Mrs. Grant, May 1, 1861.
65. Grant to Jesse Root Grant, May 2, 1861.
66. Grant to Mrs. Grant, May 3, 1861; Grant to Jesse Root Grant, May 6, 1861.
67. Grant to Jesse Grant, May 6, 1861. Writing to his wife on the same day, Grant repeated his misconceptions about both the magnitude of the war ("there will be much less bloodshed than is generally anticipated") and slave uprisings ("The worst to be apprehended is from Negro revolts"). It was in this letter that Grant worried that "the secessionest contemplated making an attack upon this state but the preparations that have been made here will probably prevent it." See Grant to Mrs. Grant, May 6, 1861. To be fair to Grant, had he been given complete control of all the Union armies in 1861, his predictions might not have been so far off the mark. Even in 1864, however, it took him more than ninety days to defeat the Confederacy, and rarely did slaves break free from bondage beyond where the Union lines reached out to them.
68. Grant, Wish-ton-Wish (neighboring White Haven), Missouri, to Mrs. Grant, May 10, 1861. Grant repeated this theme in a letter to Julia of May 15: "… your father professes to be a Union man yet condemns evry measure for the preservation of the Union."
69. Simpson, *Grant*, 79, 82; McFeely, *Grant*, 74; Grant, *Memoirs*, 1:239. Grant received his commission as captain on Apr. 11, 1854 and resigned on the same day, to take effect on July 31.
70. Grant, Galena, Illinois, to Bvt. Brig. Gen. Lorenzo Thomas, Washington, DC, May 24, 1861.
71. Grant to Jesse Root Grant, May 30, 1861.
72. Simon, ed., *Papers of Grant*, 2:40–41, Grant to Mrs. Grant, 10 June 1861, and note 2; McFeely, *Grant*, 75.
73. Grant to Mrs. Grant, June 17, 1861.
74. Simpson, *Grant*, 84–85; Jean Edward Smith, *Grant* (New York, 2001), 111, 108.
75. Fuller, *Grant & Lee*, 95.
76. Lee to Bishop Joseph P. B. Wilmer of Louisiana, 1861, written at the time of the outbreak of the war; cited in Jones, *Reminiscences,* 142–43.
77. George Washington stated that if the Union split apart into North and South, "he had made up his mind to remove and be of the Northern." He made the comment to his secretary of state, Edmund Randolph; it was recorded by Thomas Jefferson. See Julian P. Boyd et al., eds., *The Papers of Thomas Jefferson*, 30 vols. (Princeton, NJ, 1950–), 28:568, "Notes of a Conversation with Edmund Randolph," dated by the editors "after 1795." Cited in Henry Wiencek, *An Imperfect God: George Washington, His Slaves, and the Creation of America* (New York, 2003), 362.

II

1. Henry Lee, *Memoirs of the [Revolutionary] War in the Southern Department of the United States*, edited by Robert E. Lee (New York, 1868), 81–82.
2. Jean Edward Smith, *Grant* (New York, 2001), 290–91. The identity of the journalist is lost.
3. Paul Nagel, *The Lees of Virginia: Seven Generations of an American Family* (New York, 1990), 202.
4. Douglas Southall Freeman, *R. E. Lee* (New York, 1934), 1:159; Richard McCaslin, *Lee in the Shadow of Washington* (Baton Rouge, LA, 2001), 37; Henry Lee, *Memoirs of the War*, 1. Having the founder be named Launcelot and the Crusader be named Lionel, both the names of famed knights, no doubt appealed to Lee. As Robert tells us, "This pedigree of the Lee Family is abridged from a narrative written by Mr. William Lee in London, September, 1771, and obtained from his daughter, Mrs. Hodgson. He was American Minister at the Hague during the Revolution."
5. Nagel, *Lees of Virginia*, 2–15; Henry Lee, *Memoirs of the War*, 11. Satisfactory biographies of the members of the Lee dynasty in Virginia have not been written, but Paul Nagel has been able to put together penetrating accounts of the principal figures.
6. Nagel, *Lees of Virginia*, 24.
7. Brian Holden Reid, *Robert E. Lee, Icon for a Nation* (London, 2005), 45; Nagel, *Lees of Virginia*, 98.
8. Richard Henry Lee was schooled in England and then enjoyed the luxury of five years of reading and contemplation in the Stratford library. Though frail from epilepsy and too much drink, he became a powerful political figure who was vicious to his many enemies. They in turn curtailed his ascent. The seven Lees serving in the House of Burgesses were Richard Henry and brothers Francis Lightfoot, Philip, and Thomas, plus Squire Richard Lee from Lee Hall and Henry Lee of Leesylvania, the father of "Light-Horse Harry" (Nagel, *Lees of Virginia*, 77–84).
9. Ibid., 99.
10. Ibid., 107–11.
11. Arthur Lee had traveled to London to study medicine, then law. William Lee had established himself there as a merchant and was elected a sheriff. See Nagel, *Lees of Virginia*, 69, 94, 99.
12. Ibid., 110–11.
13. Charles Royster, *Light-Horse Harry Lee and the Legacy of the American Revolution* (New York, 1981), 15–18.
14. Henry Lee, *Memoirs of the War*, 81–82. Oil portraits of Robert's father were probably lost to creditors following Harry's bankruptcy, so that the son would have spent most of his life looking only at engravings of the portraits.
15. Royster, *Light-Horse Harry Lee*, 16, 21.
16. Ibid.,18.
17. Ibid., 21; Henry Lee, *Memoirs of the War*, 16. For Washington's use of "Lee's Legion," see, for example, the letter from George Washington, in Germantown, Pennsylvania, to Lee, July 11, 1780, at the Virginia Historical Society. Washington directs Lee to "proceed to Monmouth and establish yourself in that vicinity," look "for a French fleet expected at the Hook, … give such assistance in this as will be necessary, … instantly impress every kind of refreshment the Country affords; cattle, vegetables &ca. for the use of our allies, … [and] advise me instantly of any thing important that happens on the Coast."
18. One letter from Lafayette congratulated Major Lee on the award of a special corps ("I have admired your enterprising spirit"). Another asked for intelligence about enemy troop movement ("to you I have recourse for obtaining that end"). A third was a request to locate boats ("if it can be done by any human being it will be executed by Major Lee"). Robert E. Lee also published a letter from George

Washington that urged the President of Congress, at the time of Harry Lee's move to duty in the South, not to remove the Legion's independence by incorporating it into a regiment: "Major Lee has rendered such distinguished services, possesses so many talents for commanding a corps of this nature, and deserves so much credit for the perfection in which he has kept his corps as well as for the handsome exploits he has performed, that it would be a loss to the service and a discouragement to merit to reduce him" (Royster, *Light-Horse Harry Lee*, 27–30).

19. Harry Lee was not only exonerated of the charge of committing errors at Paulus Hook but even awarded a medal by Congress. The most audacious of the raids that he planned, to attack St. John's Island in South Carolina, never happened: a contingent of Lee's men lost their way. His performance at the battle of Eutaw Springs has received mixed reviews. Some said he was absent at critical moments; others reported that at least at one point he carried the tide (Nagel, *Lees of Virginia*, 161; Royster, *Light-Horse Harry Lee*, 40, 43, 46; Henry Lee, *Memoirs of the War*, 247).

20. Harry Lee added in his *Memoirs of the War*, 247, 322, "Destroy the army of Greene, and the Carolinas with Georgia inevitably became members of the British Empire." Virginia, "the bulwark of the South, would be converted first into a frontier, then into the theatre of war."

21. Nagel, *Lees of Virginia*, 161; Royster, *Light-Horse Harry Lee*, 41, 42.

22. With self-pity perhaps befitting his youth, Harry Lee complained that he was unappreciated. Sounding like his Stratford cousins, he cited "the persecution of my foes." Greene had noticed the "melancholy." He could only hope that his young and impulsive friend would return to his "former good humour and cheerfulness." "Your complaints [have] originated more in the distresses of the mind than in the ruins of your constitution," he advised, "Give yourself time to cool." See Nagel, *Lees of Virginia*, 163; Royster, *Light-Horse Harry Lee*, 53, 39; Henry Lee, *Memoirs of the War*, 550, 39–41.

23. Matilda was said to have an agreeable disposition. She played the harpsichord. See Nagel, *Lees of Virginia*, 160, 164; Royster, *Light-Horse Harry Lee*, 57, 74, 76.

24. Royster, *Light-Horse Harry Lee*, 71, 75; Nagel, *Lees of Virginia*, 166, 167. Of his father's heavy financial losses, Robert E. Lee probably knew little of the details, some of which remain murky even today. For example, one of the schemes began with Lee's borrowing of $5,000 from the Spanish government that he would never repay. When a vote came in Congress on the opening of the port of New Orleans to upriver trade, which was favored by his own state (Kentucky was still a part of Virginia), Lee was inclined to capitulate to Spain and vote against the measure. Royster states that Lee did not capitulate, but followed state instructions and voted for opening the port. Nagel found evidence that Lee actually voted against the opening of New Orleans, and the Virginia assembly consequently removed him from office. Lee complained about the difficulty of "life in the precarious tenure of a democratic assembly." Then in 1786, he reversed himself on the port issue. See Royster, 75; Nagel, 167–69.

25. Nagel, *Lees of Virginia*, 169–71; Royster, *Light-Horse Harry Lee*, 105. Before Lee's anti-Federalist shift, Hamilton had rebuffed Lee when Lee asked for insider information about the sale of government securities at low prices.

26. Harry Lee told Alexander Hamilton that combat offered "the best resort to my mind in its affliction." See Royster, *Light-Horse Harry Lee*, 64–65, 125–26; Nagel, *Lees of Virginia*, 174–75; Emory Thomas, *Robert E. Lee, A Biography* (New York, 1995), 24.

27. Freeman, *Lee*, 1:22; Thomas, *Lee*, 26. Samuel Storrow, a cousin of Ann Carter Lee, wrote to his sister on Sept. 6, 1821 that in a fortnight Ann Carter Lee's "affections were trampled on by a heartless & depraved profligate." This letter is cited in Elizabeth Pryor in "Torn to Pieces," a chapter in her forthcoming biography, *Reading the Man: A Portrait of Robert E Lee Through his Portraits* (New York, 2007). In 1799, Ann Carter Lee had contended to her companion in financial destitution, the wife of her brother-in-law Richard Bland Lee, that at Stratford her life of isolation (and debt) was acceptable: "I do not find [my life] in the slightest degree tiresome: my hours pass too nimbly away. When in company, if agreeable company, I greatly enjoy it: when alone my husband and Child excepted, I am not sensible of the want of society. In them I have enough to make me cheerful and happy" (Freeman, *Lee*, 1:11, 22).

28. Nagel, *Lees of Virginia*, 176. George Washington wrote: "It gives me sincere consolation amidst the regret with which I am filled, by such lawless and outrageous conduct … that you are disposed to lend your *personal* aid to subdue this spirit, and to bring those people to a proper sense of their duty," Washington to "Light-Horse Harry" Lee, Aug. 26, 1794, Virginia Historical Society.

29. Freeman, *Lee*, 1:9; Royster, *Light-Horse Harry Lee*, 59, 6, 72, 171–73, 175–76, 178.

30. *H. Lee's Observations*, 179; cited in Freeman, *Lee*, 1:10; Royster, *Light-Horse Harry Lee*, 175; Nagel, *Lees of Virginia*, 179; Thomas, *Lee*, 30. When Mildred, one of Ann's sisters, died in 1807, she too positioned money "free from the control of [Ann's] husband General Lee."

31. Thomas, *Lee*, 26; Royster, *Light-Horse Harry Lee*, 87, 93, 99, 100, 111–12.

32. Harry Lee, *Memoirs of the War*, 51.

33. Nagel, *Lees of Virginia*, 177; Royster, *Light-Horse Harry Lee*, 138–40.

34. The first son of Harry and Ann Lee died in infancy. Charles was the second.

35. Nagel, *Lees of Virginia*, 232–34; Thomas, *Lee*, 28; Thomas, *Robert E. Lee, An Album* (New York, 2000), 61. Smith Lee's peculiar name was taken from the New Jersey family that charitably housed his mother at the time of his premature birth.

36. "Light-Horse Harry" Lee to Charles Carter Lee, Feb. 9, 1817; "Light-Horse Harry" Lee to Anne Hill Carter Lee, May 6, 1817, Virginia Historical Society.

37. Freeman, *Lee*, 1:1; Henry Lee, *Memoirs of the War*, 53.

38. Freeman, *Lee*, 1:12–13; Nagel, *Lees of Virginia*, 181, 197; Royster, *Light-Horse Harry Lee*, 181; Thomas, *Lee*, 31; McCaslin, *Lee in the Shadow of Washington*, 85.

39. Years earlier, at the death of Nathaniel Greene in 1786, Harry Lee had considered publishing a biography of the general. He had too few sources in 1809 to pursue that subject, so he wrote instead about the southern campaigns, which he knew firsthand from his own participation in many of them (Royster, *Light-Horse Harry Lee*, 190).

40. Bertram Wyatt-Brown, "Robert E. Lee and the Concept of Honor," in *Virginia's Civil War*, ed. Peter Wallenstein and Wyatt-Brown (Charlottesville, VA, 2005), 31; Royster, *Light-Horse Harry Lee*, 154–67, 204, 209; Nagel, *Lees of Virginia*, 182; Thomas, *Lee*, 30; Freeman, *Lee*, 1:16. Lee said that he had traveled to Baltimore in search of a publisher for his *Memoirs of the War*.

41. Henry Lee, *Memoirs of the War*, 61; Mary Lee to Charles Lee, August 1, 1870, cited in McCaslin, *Lee in the Shadow of Washington*, 20.

42. Henry Lee, *Memoirs of the War*, 56–73; Thomas, *Lee*, 33–36; Nagel, *Lees of Virginia*, 183. Robert E. Lee would not follow in his father's steps as a legislator, as important and "honorable" as that vocation has always been. In 1861, at least part of him must have regretted the decision, when the failure of others altered his life and that of the nation. "Light-Horse Harry" Lee died in 1818 on Cumberland Island, Georgia, at the estate of his former commander, Nathaniel Greene. He had attempted to return home to die. He suffered from some sort of disorder in his abdomen, possibly a result of the beating in Baltimore. He was sixty-two and prematurely old.

43. The statement about a true gentleman was written in a different journal, probably after the war. The entry about the great duty of life is in a diary of 1857.

44. Ann Carter Lee's statement is cited in Thomas, *Lee*, 45 (Anne Carter Lee to her son Charles Carter Lee, July 17, 1816). See also Freeman, *Lee*, 1:29.

45. Freeman, *Lee*, 1:23; Thomas, *Lee*, 38. Douglas Southall Freeman did not recognize Ann Carter Lee's faith as evangelical Christianity, probably because in his lifetime the magnitude of the evangelical movement was less understood than it is today. See Thomas, *Lee*, 45. The listener to Robert's catechism, the rector of Christ Church in Alexandria, would enjoy a career as illustrious as that of his candidate. William Meade would become the bishop who in the next decades almost single-handedly resurrected the faltering Episcopal Church in Virginia.

46. William Fitzhugh III of Chatham had sold that house and built Ravensworth so that he could live closer to his friend George Washington. His son William Henry Fitzhugh inherited Ravensworth in 1809. One result of the move was the marriage of William's daughter to G. W. P. Custis, the grandson of Martha Washington.

47. Ever since the colonial era, gentry children in Virginia were given their first education in family schools that were tied to extended family networks, like those of the Carters and Lees. The

47. Carter family maintained a school for girls at Shirley (Freeman, *Lee*, 1:30. See also Thomas, *Lee*, 38–41).
48. Thomas, *Lee*, 34–35, 37, 41, 44.
49. On learning of his father-in-law's death, which affected his decision as to whether to remain in the military or not, Lee told Albert Sidney Johnston that he preferred the military. See McCaslin, *Lee in the Shadow of Washington*, 63; Freeman, *Lee*, 1:37.
50. Freeman, *Lee*, 1:116.
51. In the War of 1812, the conflict in which his father might have participated, Henry Lee IV had served honorably, as a major. On his return, the son was reminded that the legacy of "Light-Horse Harry" included Stratford reduced to its bare bones. Little money, little acreage, and few furnishings had escaped the creditors. The slave population had dwindled to a small size. In 1817, Henry Lee IV decided to marry an heiress (and orphan) of the county, Ann McCarty. Her sister Betsy accompanied her to Stratford, as a ward of Henry. In 1818, Ann McCarty Lee gave birth to a daughter, but two years later the infant died in a fall down the front steps. The distraught mother took to morphine to mask her grief. "Black-Horse Harry" Lee then earned his epithet: he fathered an illegitimate child with his ward. At the same time he even squandered a portion of Betsy McCarty's inheritance. In 1821, the unwanted child died mysteriously. Its body was found when fourteen-year-old Robert Lee was at Stratford, visiting his half-brother.

    The second scandal at Stratford went little noticed for almost a decade. But in 1830, when "Black-Horse Harry" sought an appointment from President Andrew Jackson as consul in Algiers, the incident became public knowledge. On the floor of the United States Senate, John Tyler of Virginia, Lee's friend and college-mate, denounced the incident. Every senator present voted against the appointment. "Black-Horse Harry" had never denied his error. He admitted it in the local court, which ruled, "Henry Lee hath been guilty of a flagrant abuse of his trust in the guardianship of his ward Betsy McCarty." To restore Betsy's inheritance that he had lost, he had sold Stratford the following year, in 1822. Six years later, the same Betsy McCarty, then married to Henry Storke, purchased the plantation. For the next fifty years, she would reign as mistress of Stratford, the role that her sister had all too briefly owned. Historian Elizabeth Pryor has located a Lee family letter dated Sept. 6, 1821 that mentions the gruesome discovery of the dead child and the presence of Robert at the house. See Pryor's upcoming biography, *Reading the Man: A Portrait of Robert E. Lee through his Private Letters*. See also Thomas, *Lee*, 36–41, 59; Nagel, *Lees of Virginia*, 207.
52. In 1802, at the death of his grandmother, Martha Washington, George Washington Parke Custis tried to buy Mount Vernon, the best of the relics left by the "Father of His Country." That house was bequeathed by the president to his nephew Bushrod Washington, whose father had cared for the estate during the Revolutionary War. Bushrod, a prominent justice of the Supreme Court, chose not to sell.
53. George Washington wrote the president of St. John's College about Custis's "indolence of mind," but at the same time he praised the boy as free of "drinking and gaming" and all other vices. He credited him as "generous and regardful of truth." Soon, Custis wrote home that his "habits of indolence and inattention [were] so unconquerable, that he did not expect to derive any benefit" from further schooling. He returned to Mount Vernon in 1798 with a sense that he had failed or had at least sorely disappointed his step-grandfather. George Washington placed him with his secretary, Tobias Lear, for tutoring that would continue his education.
54. Washington Custis was made a "cornet," or standard-bearer, in a mounted troop commanded by Lawrence Lewis, the husband of his sister Nelly Custis. To Lafayette's son, George Washington wrote, "[Custis] prefer[s] a Military career to literary pursuits." He concluded that his step-grandson lacked the perseverance to excel: "I believe Washington [Custis] means well, but has not resolution to act well." For an account of George Washington's trials in raising Custis, see William Rasmussen and Robert Tilton, *George Washington, The Man Behind the Myths* (Charlottesville, VA, 1999), 250–52. A miniature painting of Custis by Robert Field, 1801 (watercolor on ivory, 2¾ × 2½ in), at the Virginia Historical Society, depicts him as a young adult serving in the military. It is inscribed on the reverse in Custis's hand, "Remember Mount Vernon." It was presented to Lafayette in 1824–25 when he visited Arlington and later requested by and returned to Custis's daughter, Mrs. Robert E. Lee.
55. Lossing, "Arlington House, The Seat of G. W. P. Custis," *Harper's New Monthly Magazine* (Sept. 1853), 437; Freeman, *Lee*, 1:129–30. Lossing recorded that "Mr. Custis was an eloquent and impressive speaker, and always entertaining his company with pleasing oratory." See also Lossing, "The Historic Buildings of America. The Arlington House," *Potter's American Monthly* 6:50 (Feb. 1876). See Robert E. Lee's letter to Charles Carter Lee: "The Major is busy farming. His corn field is not yet enclosed or ploughed but he is rushing on all he knows. [His play] 'Montgomerie' failed. The 'big Picture' has been exhibited in the Capitol, and attracted some animadversions from the Critics, which he says were levelled at his Politics!!" (May 2, 1836, University of Virginia).
56. Lossing, "Arlington House," 437, 435. George Washington had stipulated in his will that his slaves be freed at his wife's death, when he anticipated that Martha would do the same for the many slaves she owned. Clearly she did not liberate the ones who soon were living at Arlington, but instead bequeathed them to her grandson.
57. McCaslin, *Lee in the Shadow of Washington*, 30–31, 1. See Robert E. Lee's letter to Mrs. Mary Custis, Mar. 17, 1852, Virginia Historical Society.
58. The watercolor by Mary Lee descended in the collection of Jeb Stuart. It was recently found amongst Stuart's collection of West Point autographs and watercolors; it is believed to have been given to him when he was a cadet there and Mrs. Lee's husband was superintendent. This information is courtesy of Alexander Gallery, New York City.
59. Freeman, *Lee*, 1:92. We are indebted to Elizabeth Pryor for sharing information about the Arlington slaves. For Custis's statement about the "Vulture of slavery," made in a letter to T. S. Skinner, Mar. 23, 1827 (Huntington Library), and more on this subject, see Pryor's "The Family Circle," a chapter in her forthcoming biography, *Lee*.
60. For Molly Fitzhugh's letter to Custis, probably 1803 or 1804, and more on her feelings about slavery, see Elizabeth Pryor's "The Family Circle," a chapter in her forthcoming biography, *Lee*. See also William Meade to Mary Fitzhugh Custis, Apr. 9 and May 30, 1825, Virginia Historical Society.
61. Letter of W. H. Fitzhugh, Feb. 7, 1824, in Freeman, *Lee*, 1:39. The quote about "good old Uncle Fitzhugh" is repeated in Michael Fellman, *The Making of Robert E. Lee* (New York, 2000), 140.
62. Freeman, *Lee*, 1:39, 42. The scandal of "Black-Horse Harry" Lee was not publicly known at this date.
63. Fitzhugh Lee, *General Lee* (New York, 1894), 23; Freeman, *Lee*, 1:74.
64. For the term "Marble Model," see General L. L. Lomax, quoted in Walter Watson, *Notes on Southside Virginia*, 245, cited in Freeman, *Lee*, 1:68. See "An Old Dragoon [Cadet]," in the *Lexington [Virginia] Gazette*, July 24, 1867. See also Thomas, *Lee*, 54–55. Lee's feet were remarkably small for a man his size (4½ C by nineteenth-century measure).
65. Freeman, *Lee*, 1:61, 62, 64, 65, 72. Hamilton's *Federalist* was printed in the second volume of his *Works*, which Lee borrowed from the library nine times that spring.
66. Thomas, *Lee*, 51; Freeman, *Lee*, 1:93.
67. Freeman, *Lee*, 1:74, 82; Thomas, *Lee*, 52–54; Ulysses S. Grant, *Personal Memoirs of U. S. Grant* (New York, 1885), 1:40–41.
68. Thomas, *Lee*, 56.
69. Cockspur Island is named for a thorny plant. Joseph Mansfield had finished second in his class four years ahead of Lee. He would be killed in the Civil War at Antietam, fighting Lee. See Freeman, *Lee*, 1:96–100.
70. Thomas, *Lee*, 57; Lee to Mary Randolph Custis, Nov. 11, 1830.
71. Freeman, *Lee*, 1:103, 119–22; Thomas, *Lee*, 69, 74.
72. Freeman, *Lee*, 1:122; Thomas, *Lee*, 69, 74.
73. Freeman, *Lee*, 1:104; Lee to Talcott, July 13, 1831, Virginia Historical Society.
74. Thomas, *Lee*, 69; Lee to Talcott, Nov. 1, 1834; Mrs. Mary Lee to Mrs. Mary Custis, "Sunday 1831"; Lee to Talcott, Apr. 10, 1834, all Virginia Historical Society.
75. Thomas, *Lee*, 72; Freeman, *Lee*, 1:113, 117–18. Lee to Jack Mackay, June 26, 1834; Lee to Eliza Mackay Stiles, Jan. 4, 1832; Lee to Mrs. Lee, Apr. 24, 1832, Virginia Historical Society.
76. Mrs. Mary Custis to Mrs. Lee, Oct. 6, 1831, Virginia Historical Society.
77. Freeman, *Lee*, 1:111–12.
78. Thomas, *Lee*, 69–74. Fort Calhoun still stands, visible today from the southern end of the modern Hampton Roads Bridge-Tunnel. The island continues to

79. Lee to Andrew Talcott, Feb. 10, 1835, in Freeman, *Lee*, 1:133; Lee to Andrew Talcott, May 5, 1836, Virginia Historical Society. The *Madonna and Child* is inscribed on the rear: "Copied from the original picture in the Corsini Palazzo, Rome, Italy in the year 1830 by Lieut. W. G. Williams—and by him presented as a token of affectionate esteem to Col. J. L. Abernathy, Corps of the Topographical Engineers in 1838." Like Lee, William George Williams was an officer in the Engineers Corps and married to a great-granddaughter of Martha Custis Washington. Mrs. Williams was the former America Pinckney Peter of Tudor Place in Washington.
80. Thomas, *Lee*, 84.
81. Freeman, *Lee*, 1:135, 138; Thomas, *Lee*, 77, 82; Lee to Talcott, Feb. 2, 1837, Virginia Historical Society.
82. Freeman, *Lee*, 1:183.
83. *Ibid.*, 1:137; Thomas, *Lee*, 86.
84. Thomas, *Lee*, 87; Lee to Andrew Talcott, Oct. 11, 1837, Virginia Historical Society.
85. Freeman, 1:145–47; Thomas, *Lee*, 91; Lee to Mrs. H. Hackley, Aug. 7, 1838, Virginia Historical Society. For the Des Moines Rapids, Henry Shreve had proposed more work than would prove necessary, the removal of ten times the amount of rock and earth in order to create an artificial channel. At the Rock River Rapids, the natural channel takes sharp turns. Lee believed that he could blast and remove enough rock there to make the stretch navigable.
86. Lee wanted to slant the dam at the top of Bloody Island more towards the north, away from a line perpendicular to the Illinois shore, so that it would be less vulnerable to winter ice. The army's chief engineer, Joseph Totten, however, overruled him. In the spring of 1840, Lee awaited a vote by Congress on continued funding for the Mississippi River. When nothing was appropriated, he was ordered to return to St. Louis to sell equipment and close accounts. "I anticipate no pleasure on the trip," he wrote to Jack Mackay. See Thomas, *Lee*, 96–97; Freeman, *Lee*, 1:173–79. Totten had replaced Charles Gratiot, who had been dismissed because of an accounting scandal. Lee was distressed that a man he had appreciated as a substitute father had fallen from grace.
87. Two-year-old Mary Lee was left at Arlington when the rest of the family traveled to St. Louis in 1837. As if to make up for the lost trip, she traveled incessantly as an adult.
88. Lee to Mrs. Lee, Sept. 10, 1837, Virginia Historical Society; Lee to Mrs. Lee, Oct. 16, 1837, in Freeman, *Lee*, 1:141; Lee to Jack Mackay, Oct. 22, 1837, in Thomas, *Lee*, 92; Lee to Mrs. Lee, June 5, 1839, cited in Freeman, *Lee*, 1:172.
89. Lee to Molly Custis, Mar. 24, 1838, Virginia Historical Society; Mrs. Lee to Molly Custis, 1838, in Thomas, *Lee*, 94; Mrs. Lee to Harriet Talcott, Jan. 1839, in Thomas, *Lee*, 96.
90. Cited in Thomas, *Lee*, 103. Rooney was only a toddler, less than a year old.
91. Freeman, *Lee*, 1:180; Thomas, *Lee*, 89.
92. Freeman, *Lee*, 1:177, 179.
93. Lee to Mary Lee, Apr. 18, 1841, University of Virginia.
94. Freeman, *Lee*, 1:186–90; Thomas, *Lee*, 101.
95. Freeman, *Lee*, 1:191–94; Thomas, *Lee*, 110; Grant, *Memoirs*, 1:41.
96. Lee to Mrs. Mary Lee, Oct. 31, 1843, Virginia Historical Society; Freeman, *Lee*, 1:196; Thomas, *Lee*, 103–4.
97. Grant, *Memoirs*, 1:17.
98. Grant, *Memoirs*, 1:17–18. The spelling of "Mathew" is taken from Grant's *Memoirs*.
99. William S. McFeely, *Grant, A Biography* (New York, 1981), 3–4.
100. McFeely, *Grant*, 4.
101. Grant, *Memoirs*, 1:18–22; McFeely, *Grant*, 4–5.
102. *Ibid.*
103. McFeely, *Grant*, 5.
104. Grant, *Memoirs*, 1:19.
105. Grant, *Memoirs*, 1:19–20; McFeely, *Grant*, 5–6.
106. Grant, *Memoirs*, 1:20.
107. Grant, *Memoirs*, 1:21–22.
108. Grant's father, according to the *Memoirs*, actually "tilled considerable land" while he ran his tanneries.
109. Grant, *Memoirs*, 1:22–23.
110. McFeely, *Grant*, 8; Brooks D. Simpson, *Ulysses S. Grant: Triumph over Adversity, 1822-1865* (New York, 2000), 2–3.
111. Grant, *Memoirs*, 1:22–23.
112. McFeely, *Grant*, 8–9; Simpson, *Grant*, 7.
113. Grant, *Memoirs*, 1:25; McFeely, *Grant*, 7–8; *Ulysses Grant Genealogy*, Ulysses Grant Association Web page.
114. Grant, *Memoirs*, 1:26.
115. Grant, *Memoirs*, 1:24–25; McFeely, *Grant*, 10.
116. Grant, *Memoirs*, 1:26–27.
117. *Ibid.*, 1:27–29.
118. *Ibid.*, 1:27.
119. *Ibid.*, 1:32. Italics by Grant. The general later denied that the "S." stood for anything.
120. *Ibid.*, 1:32, 35, 37–38. Contrary to his remark about enjoying travel, Grant later joked that he was hoping that his steamboat would blow up on the way to West Point.
121. McFeely, *Grant*, 14; Grant, *Memoirs*, 1:38.
122. Ulysses S. Grant, West Point, to cousin McKinstry Griffith, Sept. 22, 1839, John Y. Simon, ed., *The Papers of Ulysses S. Grant* (Carbondale, IL, 1967–), 1:4–8. The emphasis is in the original letter. At the end of the year, Congress debated closing the academy, and Grant hoped that it would. Later he reversed his opinion. All of the Grant papers cited below are published in the volumes edited by Simon.
123. Grant, *Memoirs*, 1:38–39: McFeely, *Grant*, 15.
124. Grant, *Memoirs*, 1:38–39: Smith, *Grant*, 27; McFeely, *Grant*, 15, 17–18.
125. Grant, *Memoirs*, 1:40.
126. Simpson, *Grant*, 17.
127. *Ibid.*, 16–17; Grant, *Memoirs*, 1:40–42.
128. McFeely, *Grant*, 20.
129. Grant, *Memoirs*, 1:43–44.
130. *Ibid.*, 1:40.
131. *Ibid.*, 1:45, 46; Simpson, *Grant*, 20.
132. Simpson, *Grant*, 18; John Y. Simon, ed., *The Personal Memoirs of Julia Dent Grant* (Carbondale, IL, 1975), 42.
133. *Memoirs of Julia Dent Grant*, 34–36.
134. McFeely, *Grant*, 20–22; *Memoirs of Julia Dent Grant*, 34–36. Julia's analysis seems all the more absurd when it is compared with the situation at Arlington, where the slaves threatened to rebel in mass during the time when Robert E. Lee served as executor of the Custis estate. A number of them in fact ran away then.
135. Simpson, *Grant*, 19; McFeely, *Grant*, 22; *Memoirs of Julia Dent Grant*, 42.
136. *Memoirs of Julia Dent Grant*, 40, 35–36; Simpson, *Grant*, 19–20; McFeely, *Grant*, 23–24.
137. Grant, *Memoirs*, 1:49.
138. *Ibid.*, 1:47.
139. *Ibid.*, 1:51.
140. Grant, Camp Salubrity, Louisiana, to Julia Dent, July 28, 1844; Grant, Camp Necessity, Louisiana, to Julia Dent, Aug. 31, 1844; Grant, New Orleans Barracks, Louisiana, to Julia Dent, July 11, 1845.
141. *Memoirs of Julia Dent Grant*, 38–39; Grant, Corpus Christi, Texas, to Julia Dent, [not dated] Oct. 1845; Grant to Julia Dent, Nov.–Dec. 1845; Grant to Julia Dent, Jan. 12, 1846. See also Grant to Julia Dent, June 5, 1846 ("I think it probable though that I shall resign as soon as this war is over and make Galena [Illinois] my home. My father is very anxious to have me do so [and work in his new leather-goods store there].").
142. Grant to Julia Dent, Oct. 10, 1845; Grant to Julia Dent, Jan. 2, 1846. Robert E. Lee would be stationed in Texas a decade later and find little there to please him. His opinion was almost the exact opposite of the one expressed by Grant.
143. Grant, *Memoirs*, 1:17.

III

1. Ulysses S. Grant, *Personal Memoirs of U. S. Grant* (New York, 1885), 1:54–56.
2. *Ibid.*, 1:53–56.
3. Lee to Mrs. Lee, Feb. 13, 1848; Lee to Joseph Totten, June 17, 1845, both Virginia Historical Society.
4. Grant, *Memoirs*, 1:68.
5. *Ibid.*, 1:92, 94–95.
6. *Ibid.*, 1:98.
7. Jean Edward Smith, *Grant* (New York, 2001), 36.
8. Grant to Julia Dent, May 11, 1846 and May 24, 1846. These letters, and all of Grant's papers cited below, are published chronologically in John Y. Simon, ed., *The Papers of Ulysses S. Grant* (Carbondale, IL, 1967–).
9. Grant to Julia Dent, Sept. 23, 1846; Grant, *Memoirs*, 1:110–12, 115–16; William S. McFeely, *Grant, A Biography* (New York, 1981), 33; Smith, *Grant*, 57.
10. Grant, *Memoirs*, 1:119–20.
11. Richard B. McCaslin, *Lee in the Shadow of Washington* (Baton Rouge, LA, 2001), 47; Douglas Southall Freeman, *R. E. Lee* (New York, 1934), 1:213–14.
12. Emory Thomas, *Robert E. Lee, A Biography* (New York, 1995), 113–16, 111; Freeman, *Lee*, 1:217.
13. Grant, *Memoirs*, 1:99–100.
14. Two books in the Virginia Historical Society library that showcase Scott's skill in tactics are Col. Pierce Darrow, *National Militia Standard, Embracing Scott's Militia Tactics, or the Duty of Infantry, Light Infantry, and Riflemen* (Hartford, CT, 1822), and Winfield Scott, *Infantry Tactics: or, Rules for the Exercise and Manouvres of the United States' Infantry* (New York, 1840). See Grant, *Memoirs*, 1:166.
15. Grant, *Memoirs*, 1:138–39.
16. Thomas, *Lee*, 119; Freeman, *Lee*, 1:219, 226.
17. Grant to Julia Dent, Feb. 1, 1847 and Feb. 25, 1847; Smith, *Grant*, 59–60; Thomas, *Lee*, 120.
18. Freeman, *Lee*, 1:217, 223, 226, 229–34; Robert E. Lee to Mrs. Mary Custis, Feb.

19. Grant, Vera Cruz, to Julia Dent, Apr. 3, 1847; Grant, Island of Lobos, to Julia Dent, Feb. 25, 1847. See also Grant to Julia Dent, Apr. 3, 1847 ("Julia aint it a hard case that this Mexican war should keep me two long years as it has done from seeing one that I love so much").
20. Freeman, *Lee*, 1:235–37; Smith, *Grant*, 64; Grant, *Memoirs*, 1:129.
21. Lee, Vera Cruz, to Mrs. Lee, Apr. 12, 1847, Virginia Historical Society.
22. Grant, *Memoirs*, 1:131–32.
23. Grant to Julia Dent, Apr. 24, 1847.
24. Grant to John W. Lowe, May 3, 1847; Freeman, *Lee*, 1:238–42.
25. Grant, *Memoirs*, 1:131–33; Grant to Julia Dent, Apr. 24, 1847; Grant to John W. Lowe, May 3, 1847; Freeman, *Lee*, 1:245–46; Thomas, *Lee*, 127.
26. Freeman, *Lee*, 1:246–47; Lee to Custis Lee, Apr. 25, 1847.
27. Freeman, *Lee*, 1:249–52.
28. Smith, *Grant*, 64.
29. Grant to unknown addressee, Sept. 12, 1847; Freeman, *Lee*, 1:252–61.
30. Freeman, *Lee*, 1:263–66, 256, 272; Grant, *Memoirs*, 1:143.
31. Thomas, *Lee*, 132; Freeman, *Lee*, 1:267, 279: Smith, *Grant*, 65.
32. Grant, *Memoirs*, 1:145–46.
33. See Freeman, *Lee*, 1:271–72; Thomas, *Lee*, 133.
34. Freeman, *Lee*, 1:273–74, 277–79; Grant, *Memoirs*, 1:149.
35. Grant, *Memoirs*, 1:149, 152–53; Smith, *Grant*, 65.
36. Freeman, *Lee*, 1:278–83; Thomas, *Lee*, 134; Smith, *Grant*, 66.
37. Grant, *Memoirs*, 1:154–55. During the Civil War, Grant proved that he could be every bit as hardheaded as was Scott, on occasion forcing a showdown unnecessarily. His worst error of this sort was at Cold Harbor, as he himself later admitted. Lee was guilty of the same, particularly at Gettysburg. Three of the best generals in American history were at fault for allowing a focus on the greater objective of complete and final victory to blur the immediate decision-making process.
38. Freeman, *Lee*, 1:283; Grant, *Memoirs*, 1:157–59.
39. Grant, *Memoirs*, 1:162–63.
40. Freeman, *Lee*, 1:285; Grant, City of Mexico, to Julia Dent, [not dated] Sept. 1847.
41. Thomas, *Lee*, 136; Lee, City of Mexico, to Mrs. Lee, Feb. 13, 1848, Virginia Historical Society.
42. Lee to Mrs. Lee, Feb. 13, 1848, Virginia Historical Society; Lee to John Mackay, Oct. 2, 1847, Virginia Historical Society (typescript); Grant to Julia Dent, Jan. 9, 1848; Smith, *Grant*, 50–51, 70.
43. Thomas Connelly, *The Marble Man: Robert E. Lee and His Image in American Society* (New York, 1977), 193.
44. Freeman, *Lee*, 1:286–88; Thomas, *Lee*, 138.
45. Thomas, *Lee*, 139; Freeman, *Lee*, 1:285, 303; Lee, City of Mexico, to G. W. P. Custis, Apr. 8, 1848, Virginia Historical Society. Lee did not become a non-brevet lieutenant colonel until March 1855 and a full colonel until March 1861.
46. Grant, *Memoirs*, 1:162–63.
47. Ibid., 2:488–90. Grant wrote that Lee was Winfield Scott's chief of staff, which technically he was not, although he was one of the officers on whom the general most relied.
48. Ibid., 1:191–92.
49. Ibid., 1:54–56.

IV

1. Lee to Anna Maria Fitzhugh, Nov. 22, 1857; Grant to Mrs. Grant, Aug. 3, 1851.
2. Douglas Southall Freeman, *R. E. Lee* (New York, 1934), 1:301; Emory Thomas, *Robert E. Lee: A Biography* (New York, 1995), 143–45; Captain Robert E. Lee, Jr., *Recollections and Letters of General Robert E. Lee* (New York, 1924), 9–10.
3. Freeman, *Lee*, 1:303, 305, 308; Thomas, *Lee*, 146.
4. Freeman, *Lee*, 1:306–8, 314–16; Thomas, *Lee*, 147. We are indebted to Elizabeth Pryor for sharing with us her discovery in the National Archives of Lee's previously unpublished drawings of machinery for use at Fort Carroll.
5. Lee to Mrs. Lee, June 23, 1849, Virginia Historical Society (Lee found "little amusement in the ev[ening]s killing muskitoes & watching kittens playing with their tails," and he could not read because light attracted "so many insects."); Mrs. Lee to Cora Caroline Peters, Oct. 26, 1848 and Jan. 1849, Washington and Lee University.
6. Freeman, *Lee*, 1:305–6, 309; Thomas, *Lee*, 146; Captain Robert E. Lee, *Recollections*, 10–11.
7. Lee to Custis Lee, 4 May 1851, 1 Feb. 1852, and 28 Mar. 1852 (Virginia Historical Society). See Freeman, *Lee*, 1:309–10, 312; Thomas, *Lee*, 149–50.
8. Lee to Mrs. Mary Custis, Mar. 17, 1852, Virginia Historical Society.
9. Lee to Henry Kayser, June 16, 1845, in Thomas, *Lee*, 106; ibid., 145, 149; Lee to Markie Williams, May 10, 1851, cited in Avery Craven, ed., *"To Markie": The Letters of Robert E. Lee to Martha Custis Williams* (Cambridge, MA, 1933), 24–27; Lee to Tassy Beaumont, Mar. 11, 1843, in Thomas, *Lee*, 106; Lee to Markie Williams, Sept. 2, 1844 and Sept. 17, 1845, in *ibid.*, 106. Once when riding the New York City sleighs, which in winter replaced coaches, he gave his seat away rather than have "a lady in [his] lap." He told John Mackay, "I thought it would not sound well if repeated in the latitude of Washington, that I had ridden down B. D. [Broadway] with a strange woman in my lap" (Lee to John Mackay, Jan. 30, 1846, cited in Freeman, *Lee*, 1:197–98).
10. Jefferson Davis, former Secretary of War, *North American Review*, Jan. 1890, cited in Freeman, *Lee*, 1:339.
11. Lee to Joseph Totten, May 28, 1852, Virginia Historical Society; Lee to Anna Fitzhugh, Apr. 3, 1854; Freeman, *Lee*, 1:317.
12. Freeman, *Lee*, 1:319–22, 324, 347. For the portrait gallery at West Point, see "U.S. Army," a chapter in Elisabeth Brown Pryor's biography, *Reading the Man: A Portrait of Robert E. Lee Through His Private Letters* (New York, 2007). The site of West Point had been selected at least partly because of its associations with the Revolutionary War, as Ulysses Grant explained in a letter that he wrote when a cadet.
13. Freeman, *Lee*, 1:319–20.
14. Ibid., 347–48, 327; Thomas, *Lee*, 154.
15. Cadets at West Point caricatured Lee and criticized his strict regimen. A number of Lee's letters to parents could be cited for their tact. For example, "He is a youth of such fine feelings and good character that I should not like to subject him to the mortification of failure, to which he might give more value than it deserves. For I consider the character of no man affected by a want of success, provided he has made an honest effort to succeed." See Freeman, *Lee*, 1:340–44.
16. Freeman, *Lee*, 1:332, 334, 337; Thomas, *Lee*, 156. Lee's letter to Totten was dated July 8, 1854.
17. Freeman, *Lee*, 1:331, 323; Thomas, *Lee*, 157; Lee to Annie Lee, Feb. 25, 1853, Virginia Historical Society. For the poetry, see Jeb Stuart, "Poem to Mary Lee," Mar. 19, 1862, Virginia Historical Society: "It chanced to-night on outpost duty–/ I found an album with thy name in:/ So full of gems of love and beauty/ I looked it o'er till lo' there came in–/ My muse–so long forgot–neglected–/ A form I least of all expected./ In the gay old days–the West Point days,/ She led me o'er its sweet romance …."
18. Freeman, *Lee*, 1:328; Thomas, *Lee*, 159; Lee to Mrs. Lee, May 2, 1853 and Apr. 27, 1853, Virginia Historical Society.
19. Mrs. Lee, *Diary*, June 1853, Virginia Historical Society; Freeman, *Lee*, 1:330–31; Thomas, *Lee*, 160.
20. Freeman, *Lee*, 1:346–47, 351, 353, 358; Board of Visitors, West Point Military Academy, June 1854, cited in Freeman.
21. Lee to Markie Williams, Mar. 14, 1855, cited in Craven, ed.,"*To Markie*," 52–53; Lee to Edward Lee Childe, Nov. 1, 1856, Jan. 7 and 9, 1857, Stratford Hall, in Michael Fellman, *The Making of Robert E. Lee* (New York, 2000), 184; Freeman, *Lee*, 1:347–50.
22. Lee to Markie, Mar. 14, 1855, cited in Craven, ed.,"*To Markie*," 52–53; Lee to Mrs. Lee, Mar. 7, 1857, Virginia Historical Society; Freeman, *Lee*, 1;347–50. Before Texas, Lee was drawing the pay of a colonel, by brevet, so that the move to the cavalry did not better him financially.
23. Freeman, *R. E. Lee*, 1:368, 363–64; Thomas, *Lee*, 167.
24. Richard B. McCaslin, *Lee in the Shadow of Washington* (Baton Rouge, LA, 2001), 57; Lee to Mrs. Lee, Apr. 12 and Aug. 25, 1856, in Freeman, *Lee*, 1:363–68; Thomas, *Lee*, 167.
25. Freeman, *Lee*, 1:365–68, 375–76; Lee, *Diary*, 1857, Virginia Historical Society.
26. Agnes Lee, *Journal*, Mar. 16–27, 1856; Lee to Agnes Lee, Aug. 11, 1885, in Freeman, *Lee*, 1:361–62; Lee to Mildred Lee, Mar. 22, 1857, Virginia Historical Society. See also the letter of Apr. 28, 1856: "My rattlesnake, my only pet, is dead! He grew sick & would not eat his frogs, etc. & died one night," and Lee to Mrs. Lee, Aug. 18, 1856, both Virginia Historical Society.
27. Lee to Mrs. Lee, and Lee to Mildred Lee, both Jan. 9, 1857, and Mrs. Lee to Mrs. Hackley, Feb. 19, 1857, all Virginia Historical Society; Freeman, *Lee*, 1:379.
28. Lee to Mrs. Lee, May 18, 1857 and Dec. 20, 1856, both Virginia Historical Society.
29. Lee to Winfield Scott, Aug. 11, 1857, Virginia Historical Society. See Thomas, *Lee*, 164, 171.
30. Ulysses S. Grant, *Personal Memoirs of U. S. Grant* (New York, 1885), 1:175–90, 193.
31. Jean Edward Smith, *Grant* (New York, 2001), 73-75; John Y. Simon, ed., *The*

Papers of Ulysses S. Grant (Carbondale, IL, 1967–), 1:173, 175–77. All of the Grant papers cited below are published in the volumes edited by Simon.

32. Grant, *Memoirs*, 1:193; Grant to Mrs. Grant, Apr. 27, 1849.
33. Grant to Mrs. Grant, June 29 and Aug. 10, 1851.
34. Grant to Mrs. Grant, Aug. 3, 1851; Smith, *Grant*, 76.
35. Grant to Mrs. Grant, Aug. 9, 1852.
36. Smith, *Grant*, 81; William S. McFeely, *Grant, A Biography* (New York, 1981), 48.
37. Grant to Mrs. Grant, 20 Aug. 1852, 14 Sept. 1852, 4 Mar. 1853, and 19 Mar. 1853.
38. Grant to Julia Grant, 7 Oct. 1852, 20 May 1853.
39. Grant, *Memoirs*, 1:203; Smith, *Grant*, 81.
40. McFeely, *Grant*, 55; Grant, *Memoirs*, 1:206; Grant to Mrs. Grant, Jan. 18, 1854; Smith, *Grant*, 85.
41. Grant to Mrs. Grant, 2 Feb. 1854, 20 Aug. 1852; Smith, *Grant*, 85.
42. Smith, *Grant*, 87.
43. Grant to Mrs. Grant, Mar. 6, 1854; McFeely, *Grant*, 50; Grant, *Memoirs*, 1:210; Smith, *Grant*, 83; Simon, ed., *Papers of Grant*, 1:331.
44. Thomas, *Lee*, 164.
45. *Ibid.*, 164–68.
46. Thomas, *Lee*, 107–9, 159. The states in which Lee invested were Virginia, Ohio, Kentucky, and Missouri. The cities were Pittsburgh and St. Louis. The railroads were the New York & Erie and the Hudson River. Lee had accumulated a small income in the early years of his career from the sale and rental of the few slaves whom his mother bequeathed to him.
47. McCaslin, *Lee in the Shadow of Washington*, 58. In the 1831 letter to his wife, Lee referred to the slaves in question as "our Georgetonians," in reference to his mother's move late in her life to Georgetown. He owned at least four women from his mother's bequest, but he complained to his wife about the quality of their work. One of them, Nancy Ruffin, he would not take himself as a cook, and he had rented her out instead. He freed Nancy and her children in his will that he wrote when he departed for Mexico. Philip Meriday is mentioned in a contract with James Eveleth, Washington, August 1, 1852, Virginia Historical Society. See Elizabeth Pryor, "Humanity and the Law," in *Lee*; Thomas, *Lee*, 72, 107, 173; Lee to Mrs. Lee, Apr. 24, 1832, Virginia Historical Society; and Lee to Sidney Smith Lee, Mar 18, 1852, Library of Congress. The authors would like to thank Elizabeth Pryor who generously allowed us to read parts of the manuscript of her forthcoming biography. A good deal of the information concerning Robert E. Lee and slavery is given more in-depth discussion in Pryor's book.
48. Lee to Mrs. Lee, Apr. 18, 1841, University of Virginia; Lee to Annie Lee, Feb. 25, 1853, Virginia Historical Society; and Lee to Mrs. Lee, July 8, 1849, Virginia Historical Society. For the abolitionist episode, see Thomas, *Lee*, 110. Lee had sent his father-in-law a newspaper clipping about the annual meeting of the Anti-Slavery Society in New York. He criticized the "evil passions" of such men.
49. Charles Bracelen Flood, *Lee, The Last Years* (Boston, 1981), 139; Mrs. Lee, *Diary*, June 1853, Virginia Historical Society. The teaching of reading and the conducting of religious services became more difficult after 1847, when the portion of the District of Columbia that contained Arlington was ceded back to Virginia. Tight laws that prohibited such leniency had been enacted following the Nat Turner rebellion of 1831.
50. Agnes Lee, *Journal*, Mar. 23, 1856 and Jan. 3, 1858, Virginia Historical Society.
51. Freeman, *Lee*, 1:370–73; Thomas, *Lee*, 173.
52. See the diary of Markie Williams, Nov. 2, 1853, and the letter from Mrs. Lee to Robert E. Lee, Mar. 17, 1857, Library of Congress, both cited in Pryor, *Lee*.
53. Robert Lee, Jr. to Mildred Lee, Jan. 5, 1852, Library of Congress; Mrs. Lee to Robert E. Lee, Sept. 3, 185_ (possibly 1858 or 1859), Duke University; both cited in Pryor, *Lee*. See also Seventh U.S. Census (1850).
54. Lee to Albert Sidney Johnston, Oct. 25, 1857, Tulane University; Lee to Anna Maria Fitzhugh, Nov. 22, 1857; Freeman, *Lee*, 1:382; Thomas, *Lee*, 144. See also "Inventory of Personal Property at Arlington," Jan. 1, 1858, Washington and Lee University, and Seventh U.S. Census (1850).
55. Freeman, *Lee*, 1:380–84; Thomas, *Lee*, 175–77; Mrs. Lee to W. G. Webster, Feb. 17, 1858, Museum of the Confederacy.
56. The will was probated Dec. 7, 1857. Lee to Edward Turner, Feb. 13, 1858; Freeman, *Lee*, 1:380–84; Thomas, *Lee*, 274–75; McCaslin, *Lee in the Shadow of Washington*, 58; see also Pryor, *Lee*.
57. Lee to Custis Lee, Jan. 17, 1858 and Mar. 17, 1858, both Duke University and cited in Thomas, *Lee*, 177; Thomas, *Lee*, 176–78; Lee to Rooney Lee, Feb. 24, 1858 and Mar. 12, 1860.
58. Mrs. Lee to W. G. Webster, Feb. 17, 1858, Museum of the Confederacy; in Thomas, *Lee*, 177.
59. See Pryor, *Lee*. Lee wrote to Winston on July 8, 1858.
60. Freeman, *Lee*, 1:386–88.
61. Thomas, *Lee*, 179; Lee to Custis Lee, May 30, 1859, in Freeman, *Lee*, 1:388; Pryor, *Lee*; John W. Blassingame, *Slave Testimony: Two Centuries of Letters, Speeches, Interviews, and Autobiographies* (Baton Rouge, LA, 1977), 467–68. The slaves may have fled as early as March, and they were heading beyond Maryland. Lee stated in a letter of July 2 to his son Custis that they "absconded some months ago … making their way to Pennsylvania." Printed in Freeman, *Lee*, 1:392; "Robert E. Lee: His Brutality to His Slaves," *National Anti-Slavery Standard*, Apr. 14, 1866, cited in Pryor, *Lee*.
63. This information is taken from Pryor, *Lee*. For fees paid to Richard Williams, see Custis Estate, 1859, Alexandria Will Book #7, 488, 491. In 1858 Lee had paid Richard Williams only $57.25 to arrest and detain three of that season's runaways, plus $37.12 to transport them to Richmond.
64. Lee to Custis Lee, July 2, 1859; cited in J. William Jones, *Life and Letters of Robert Edward Lee* (New York, 1906), 100–102.
65. Pryor, *Lee*. In 1859 Lee spent $301.73 for medical care (Alexandria Will Book #8, Alexandria County, Virginia, 93).
66. McFeely, *Grant*, 62.
67. Ulysses S. Grant, *Memoirs*, 1:210–11.
68. Julia Grant to Hamlin Garland, Dec. 26, 1896, in Simon, ed., *Memoirs of Julia Dent Grant*, 18; McFeely, *Grant*, 63.
69. McFeely, *Grant*, 58–59.
70. *Ibid.*, 59–61.
71. Grant to Jesse Root Grant, Dec. 28, 1856.
72. Grant, *Memoirs*, 1:213–15.
73. Grant to his father Jesse Grant, Feb. 7, 1857.
74. Grant to his sister Mary Grant, Aug. 22, 1857; Smith, *Grant*, 92.
75. Grant to Mary Grant, Mar. 21, 1858.
76. Grant to Mary Grant, Sept. 7, 1858. Grant had three slaves to assist him at planting time, but for harvesting he hired additional slaves. The number is not known, but apparently it was many if seven were sick. See also Grant to his father Jessie Grant, Oct. 1, 1858, and Mar. 12, 1859.
77. Smith, *Grant*, 92–93; Grant, *Memoirs*, 1:211–12.
78. Grant, *Memoirs*, 1:211–12; Smith, *Grant*, 94.
79. Grant to his father Jessie Grant, Mar. 12, 1859.
80. Grant, "Document of Manumission," Mar. 29, 1859.
81. Thomas, *Lee*, 179; Freeman, *Lee*, 1:393.
82. Freeman, *Lee*, 1:394–95; Ervin L. Jordan, Jr., *Black Confederates and Afro-Yankees in Civil War Virginia* (Charlottesville, VA, 1995), 1–3; A. M. Barbour, Superintendent of the Arsenal at Harpers Ferry, telegram to the Secretary of War, Oct. 19, 1859, National Archives and Records Administration. With more troops dispatched than he could use, Lee quickly cancelled the order for a contingent from Fort Monroe.
83. Freeman, *Lee*, 1:394–98; Thomas, *Lee*, 179–81.
84. Freeman, *Lee*, 1:399–400; Thomas, *Lee*, 182; Lee to the Harpers Ferry Insurgents, *Note*, Oct. 18, 1859, National Archives and Records Administration. The militia of Virginia and Maryland had all declined to rush the insurgents.
85. Report of Oct. 19, 1859, cited in Freeman, *Lee*, 1:402; Thomas, *Lee*, 182; Nelson Peabody Rose, *Robert E. Lee of Virginia, The Anguish of Conflicting Loyalties* (Cleveland, 1985), 37–38. Thomas Hovenden's *The Last Moments of John Brown*, 1884, at the Metropolitan Museum, New York, is perhaps the best-known in this genre of painting.
86. Smith, *Grant*, 96; McFeely, *Grant*, 65–66.
87. Grant to Mr. Davis, Aug. 7, 1860; Grant to unknown addressee, Dec. 1860; Grant, *Memoirs*, 1:215–16.
88. Lee to Mrs. Lee, Apr. 25, 1860, Virginia Historical Society.
89. Lee to Mrs. Lee, Mar. 3, 1860, Library of Congress, and Lee to Custis Lee, Dec. 14, 1860, Duke University, both cited in Pryor, *Lee*; Lee to Annie Lee, Aug. 27, 1860, Virginia Historical Society. For the comment about a white servant, see Lee to Rooney Lee, July 9, 1860, Virginia Historical Society.
90. Lee to Mrs. Anna Fitzhugh, June 6, 1860, cited in Freeman, *Lee*, 1:410; Thomas, *Lee*, 183–85.

V

1. Lee, *General Orders* No. 9, Apr. 9, 1865, Virginia Historical Society; Grant,

1. "Interview with John Russell Young," *New York Herald*, Hamburg, July 6, 1878, in John Y. Simon, ed., *The Papers of Ulysses S. Grant* (Carbondale, IL, 1967–), 27:419–20; Lee to the Reverend Cornelius Walker, May 2, 1861, Virginia Historical Society. All of the Grant papers cited below are published in the volumes edited by Simon.
2. Lee to Mrs. Lee, July 27, 1861, Virginia Historical Society.
3. Emory Thomas, *Robert E. Lee: A Biography* (New York, 1995), 201.
4. Lee to Mrs. Lee, Sept. 1861, cited in Thomas, *Lee*, 206–7.
5. Douglas Southall Freeman, *R. E. Lee* (New York, 1934), 1:579–604.
6. Freeman, *Lee*, 1:597, 602–3; Thomas, *Lee*, 209–10; Edward Pollard, *The First Year of the War* (Richmond, VA, 1862), 168.
7. Lee to Mrs. Lee, Feb. 8, 1862, Virginia Historical Society.
8. Gary W. Gallagher, *Lee and His Generals in War and Memory* (Baton Rouge, LA, 1998), 10; Thomas, *Lee*, 216; Gallagher, *The Confederate War* (Cambridge, MA, 1997), 72, 105.
9. Thomas, *Lee*, 211 16; Lee to Mrs. Lee, Mar. 13, 1862; Mrs. Lee to Mrs. William H. Stiles, Mar. 8, 1862, Lee Papers, Colonial Dames, Georgia, cited in Thomas L. Connelly, *The Marble Man: Robert E. Lee and His Image in American Society* (New York, 1977), 36.
10. Of his preparatory work, Grant wrote to his sister Mary Grant on Sept. 11, 1861: "My duties are very laborious and have been from the start. It is a rare thing that I get to bed before two or three o'clock in the morning and am usually wakened in the morning before getting awake in a natural way."
11. Jean Edward Smith, *Grant* (New York, 2001), 111, 113; Grant to Jesse Grant, Aug. 3, 1861.
12. Grant to Jesse Grant, Aug. 3, 1861; Grant to his sister Mary Grant, Aug. 12, 1861.
13. Smith, *Grant*, 117–18; Grant to Mrs. Grant, Aug. 29, 1861.
14. Smith, *Grant*, 118–120; "Proclamation, to the Citizens of Paducah!," Sept. 6, 1861; Ulysses S. Grant, *Personal Memoirs of U. S. Grant* (New York, 1885), 1:266.
15. Grant to Mrs. Grant, Sept. 22, 1861; Grant, *Memoirs*, 1:271, 278–79.
16. "The two objects for which the battle of Belmont was fought were fully accomplished. The enemy gave up all idea of detaching troops from Columbus .... The National troops acquired a confidence in themselves at Belmont that did not desert them through the war" (Grant, *Memoirs*, 1:280–81).
17. Grant, *Memoirs*, 1:284–86; Grant to his sister Mary Grant, Jan. 23, 1862.
18. Grant to Mrs. Grant, Feb. 4, 1862; Grant to Capt. John C. Kelton, Feb. 6, 1862; Abraham Lincoln, *The Collected Works of Abraham Lincoln*, ed. Roy P. Basler (New Brunswick, NJ, 1953), 5:111; Smith, *Grant*, 134–48.
19. "General Halleck did not approve or disapprove of my going to Fort Donelson. He said nothing whatever to me on the subject" (Grant, *Memoirs*, 1:296); Grant to his sister Mary Grant, Feb. 9, 1862; Grant to Mrs. Grant, Feb. 13, 1862; Grant, *Memoirs*, 1:308–9.
20. Grant, *Memoirs*, 1:299; Smith, *Grant*, 149–66.
21. Grant to Mrs. Grant, Feb. 16, 1862; Grant, *Memoirs*, 1:316.
22. Grant to Mrs. Grant, Feb. 22 and Feb. 24, 1862. Relations with his father would remain strained. Later in the year, during the Vicksburg campaign, Grant wrote that Jesse was embarrassing him by "denouncing other General officers" ("keep quiet on this subject") and that his "condescending" talk about Julia "is not pleasing to me." See Grant to Jesse Grant, Sept. 17, 1862 and Nov. 23, 1862.
23. Grant, *Memoirs*, 1:317–18.
24. Smith, *Grant*, 167–68; Simon, ed., *Papers of Grant*, 4:112, 54, 117–18.
25. Grant to Mrs. Grant, Mar. 29, 1862, Apr. 3, 1862; Grant, *Memoirs*, 1:322, 324.
26. Grant, *Memoirs*, 1:330–31.
27. Grant to Henry Halleck, Apr. 5, 1862; Grant, *Memoirs*, 1:333, 338.
28. Grant, *Memoirs*, 1:342, 348, 350; Grant to Col. James McPherson, Apr. 6, 1862. Grant's comments about the "hard fighting" were written with specific reference to the second day of the battle but actually apply well to both days.
29. Grant to Mrs. Grant, Apr. 8, 1862; Grant, *Memoirs*, 1:355–56; Smith, *Grant*, 184–206.
30. Grant, "Interview with Young," in Simon, ed., *Papers of Grant*, 28:419–20; Grant, *Memoirs*, 1:368–69.
31. Grant, *Memoirs*, 1:374; Grant to Mrs. Grant, Apr. 15, 1862, Apr. 25, 1862; Smith, *Grant*, 206–12. Halleck even wrote a book about the cautious strategy that he endorsed, *Elements of Military Art and Science* (New York, 1846).
32. Grant, *Memoirs*, 1:383–84; Grant to Mrs. Grant, Apr. 15, 1862; Smith, *Grant*, 212–19.
33. Grant to his sister Mary Grant, 19 Aug. 1862. See also Grant to Mrs. Grant, 30 Apr. 1862, 20 and 24 May 1862, 16 June 1862, 18 Aug. 1862; Grant to Jesse Grant, 3 Aug. 1862. For Fred's visit during the Vicksburg campaign, see Grant to Mrs. Grant, 6 and 30 Mar. 1863, 3, 20, and 28 Apr. 1863, 3 May 1863, 9 June 1863 ("Fred has enjoyed his campaign very much").
34. Lee to Mrs. Lee, the White House, Apr. 4, 1862, Virginia Historical Society.
35. Gallagher, *Lee and His Generals*, 108.
36. Thomas, *Lee*, 274, 223; Lee to Charlotte Wickham Lee, June 2, 1862, cited in Freeman, *Lee*, 2:76–77.
37. Thomas, *Lee*, 226–27; Joseph Christman Ives to Edward Porter Alexander, spring 1862; cited in Alexander, *Fighting for the Confederacy* and in turn in Thomas; J. F. C. Fuller, *Grant & Lee, A Study in Personality and Generalship* (New York, 1933), 266, 128.
38. Gallagher, *Lee and His Generals*, 250; Thomas, *Lee*, 230; Freeman, *Lee*, 2:86–165.
39. Thomas, *Lee*, 241–43. Lee aide Walter Taylor tried to place the blame on the absence of good maps ("The Confederate commanders knew no more about the topography of the country than they did about Central Africa"), as if to suggest that the Union officers active on enemy soil had better. Taylor is cited in J. F. C. Fuller, *Grant & Lee*, 162.
40. Thomas, *Lee*, 247–51.
41. Thomas, *Lee*, 251–55; "Memoranda of Conversations with General Robert E. Lee," William Allan, Apr. 15, 1868 and Feb. 19, 1870, in Gary W. Gallagher, ed., *Lee the Soldier* (Lincoln, NE, 1996), 16–17, 23–24; Fuller, *Grant & Lee*, 164; Gallagher, *Lee and His Generals*, 155–57.
42. Freeman, *Lee*, 4:473; Gallagher, *Lee and His Generals*, 29.
43. Gallagher, *Lee & His Army*, 174–77; Freeman, *Lee*, 2:358; Emory Thomas, "Ambivalent Visions of Victory: Davis, Lee, and Confederate Grand Strategy," in Gabor S. Boritt, ed., *Jefferson Davis's Generals* (New York, 1999), 27–45; Steven E. Woodworth, *Davis and Lee at War* (Lawrence, KS, 1995).
44. Gallagher, *Lee and His Generals*, 27.
45. Gallagher, *Lee and His Generals*, 23–24; Ervin L. Jordon, Jr., "Queen Victoria's Refugees: Afro-Virginians and Anglo-Confederate Diplomacy," in Peter Wallenstein and Bertram Wyatt-Brown, eds., *Virginia's Civil War* (Charlottesville, VA, 2005), 152–64.
46. Gallagher, *Lee and His Generals*, 30–35; "Memoranda of Conversations with Lee," William Allan, and General Viscount Wolseley, "General Lee," 1887, both cited in Gallagher, ed., *Lee the Soldier*, 7, 105.
47. Freeman, *Lee*, 2:358.
48. "Memorandum of a Conversation with General Robert E. Lee," Edward Clifford Gordon, Feb. 15, 1868, in Gallagher, ed., *Lee the Soldier*, 8, 25–27; Gallagher, *Lee and His Generals*, 36–37, 40–43.
49. Gallagher, *Lee and His Generals*, 38; Gallagher, *Lee & His Army*, 6–8, 11, 13, 18, 32, 37, 39.
50. Lee to Mrs. Lee, Oct. 26, 1862, Virginia Historical Society; Thomas, *Lee*, 266.
51. Thomas, *Lee*, 268. The comment about war being terrible is probably the creation of the apologist authors of the Lost Cause literature (e.g., John Esten Cooke, *A Life of Gen. Robert E. Lee* [New York, 1871], 84). It is well enough accepted to be listed in *Bartlett's Quotations*. Lee to Mrs. Lee, Dec. 25, 1862, in Clifford Dowdey and Louis A. Mannarin, eds., *The Wartime Papers of R. E. Lee* (Boston, 1961), 379–80; Mar. 9, 1863 and Apr. 19, 1863, in Thomas, *Lee*, 277–78.
52. Grant, *Memoirs*, 1:383.
53. *Ibid.*, 1:422.
54. *Ibid.*, 1:435, 437, 446, 460; Grant to Col. John C. Kelton, Asst. Adj. Gen., July 6, 1863; Smith, *Grant*, 223–25.
55. General Orders No. 11, Oxford, Mississippi, Dec. 17, 1862; Smith, *Grant*, 223–25, 231–32; Josiah Bunting III, *Ulysses S. Grant* (New York, 2004), 51.
56. Grant, *Memoirs*, 1:442–43, 455; Smith, *Grant*, 228.
57. Grant, *Memoirs*, 1:461, 463, 478, 480, 492; Smith, *Grant*, 236.
58. Grant, *Memoirs*, 1:511, 532–33.
59. *Ibid.*, 1:531–32; Grant to Halleck, 24 May 1863; Grant to Jesse Grant, and Grant to Mrs. Grant, both June 15, 1863; Grant to Mrs. Grant, June 29, 1863; Smith, *Grant*, 234.
60. Grant, *Memoirs*, 1:558, 560, 561; Grant to Henry Halleck, 4 July 1864; Smith, *Grant*, 258. Grant wrote to his father, "My troops were not allowed one hours idle time after the surrender but were at once started after other game" (Grant to Jesse Grant, July 6, 1863). In contrast to Grant's understanding of his mission, Jeb Stuart at this same time lost focus of the larger picture on his way to Pennsylvania, when he allowed the capture of 100 wagons to slow his

progress to Gettysburg and thereby contribute to the Confederate defeat there.

61. Grant, *Memoirs*, 1:571–72, 568, 525.
62. Smith, *Grant*, 259.
63. Grant, *Memoirs*, 1:578–79.
64. Union Gen. George Thomas held his ground, gaining acclaim as the "Rock of Chickamauga." Grant, *Memoirs*, 2:18; Smith, *Grant*, 262–65.
65. Grant, *Memoirs*, 2:26, 24, 28, 38; Grant to Mrs. Grant, Nov. 14, 1863.
66. Grant, *Memoirs*, 2:34–35, 42.
67. Smith, *Grant*, 267, 269, 282. Decades after the war, Adams praised Robert E. Lee for entirely different virtues.
68. Grant, *Memoirs*, 2:85, 87; Smith, *Grant*, 269–71.
69. Grant, *Memoirs*, 2:81; Grant to J. Russell Jones, Dec. 5, 1863. Grant elaborated to his wife: "I went with the advance, in pursuit over twenty miles. Every mudhole for that distance showed evidence of the utter route and demoralization of the enemy. Wagons, & Caissons would be found stuck in the mud and abandoned in the haste of the enemy to get away. Small arms were found everywhere strewn. We have now forty-two pieces of Artillery taken from the enemy and over six thousand stand of small arms and no doubt many more will be found. The number of prisoners taken is about seven thousand" (Grant to Mrs. Grant, Nov. 30, 1863). See also Grant to Henry Halleck, Nov. 27, 1863; Smith, *Grant*, 273–81.]
70. Grant, *Memoirs*, 2:97, 98. Lincoln's letter to Grant was dated Dec. 8, 1863.
71. Grant to B. Burns, Dec. 17, 1863; Geoffrey C. Ward, Ric Burns, and Ken Burns, *The Civil War* (New York, 1990), 276; Grant, *Memoirs*, 2:100, 115–16; Smith, *Grant*, 290–91.
72. P. W. Alexander, *Confederate Chieftains*, in *Southern Literary Messenger*, Jan. 1863; Robert E. Lee to Mrs. Lee, Jan. 29, 1863, in Dowdey and Mannarin, eds., *Wartime Papers of Lee*, 395–96; Nelson Peabody Rose, *Robert E. Lee of Virginia: The Anguish of Conflicting Loyalties* (Cleveland, 1985), 199, 204; Field Marshal Viscount Wolseley, "General Lee," 1887, in Gallagher, *Lee the Soldier*, 95, 105, 108–9; Gary W. Gallagher, *Lee & His Army in Confederate History* (Chapel Hill, NC, 2001), 172. The laudatory descriptions of Lee are numerous. See also Dr. Samuel Merrifield Bemiss, camp near Fredericksburg, to his children: "He is a tall, robust, fine-looking man with white beard all over his face and white hair, always polite and agreeable, and thinking less of himself than he ought to, and thinking indeed of nothing, hoping and praying for nothing but the success of our cause and the return of a blessed peace. I know you would all love him if you saw him, but with a deep quiet admiration which would find expression in a desire to imitate his actions" (Apr. 10, 1863, Virginia Historical Society). Lee's hair color had gone from gray to white during the difficult winter that brought him health problems.
73. Lee to Mrs. Lee, Apr. 19, 1863; Thomas, *Lee*, 279.
74. Thomas, *Lee*, 283–87 (Hooker was "Hit by a large timber from the column" beside where he was standing); "Memoranda of Conversations with Lee," William Allan, in Gallagher, ed., *Lee the Soldier*, 9.
75. Gallagher, *Lee and His Generals*, 13; Freeman, *Lee*, 2:508–63; Thomas, *Lee*, 275–86; Gallagher, *The Confederate War*, 138.
76. Lee to Mrs. Lee, June 9, 1863, Virginia Historical Society; Thomas, *Lee*, 277.
77. Cooke, *Lee*, 298. See Gary Gallagher's recent writings that are cited in the following notes.
78. Thomas, *Lee*, 292–93; Gallagher, *Lee and His Generals*, 56, 14.
79. Gallagher, *Lee & His Army*, 101–2, 173–74: Freeman, *Lee*, 3:34–35; Thomas, *Lee*, 288.
80. Lee's two reports on Gettysburg are printed in Dowdey and Manarin, eds., *Wartime Papers of Lee*, 538–39, 574–80.
81. "Memoranda of Conversations with Lee," William Allan, in Gallagher, ed., *Lee the Soldier*, 13–15, 16–17, 23–24; Lee to W. M. McDonald, Apr. 15, 1868, in Freeman, *Lee*, 4:476; Gallagher, *Lee and His Generals*, 165. Gallagher writes that it is highly improbable that Jackson's presence at Gettysburg would have brought a result that altered appreciably the strategic balance of power (*Lee and His Generals*, 113).
82. Gallagher, *Lee and His Generals*, 158–59, 172–73, 177–81, 65, 165.
83. Gallagher, *Lee and His Generals*, 60–61, 66–68, 72–73; Gallagher, ed., *Lee the Soldier*, xxx. Alexander had full knowledge of the difficulties of maneuvering long wagon trains and thought they could be moved under the enemy's eyes.
84. Thomas, *Lee*, 293–303; Gallagher, *Lee and His Generals*, 257; Gallagher, *Lee and His Army*, xi, 88, 104–5, 179; Lee to General Cadmus M. Wilcox, July 3, 1863, in Thomas, *Lee*, 300; Lee to Charlotte Wickham Lee, July 26, 1863, in J. William Jones, *Life and Letters of Robert Edward Lee, Soldier and Man* (New York, 1906), 277–78; Lee to the Army of Northern Virginia, Aug. 1863, in Thomas, *Lee*, 308; Thomas, *Lee*, 303–4; Marc E. T. Rasmussen, "Gettysburg," unpublished research paper, 2006.
85. Thomas, *Lee*, 313–316, 319; Rose, *Lee*, 200; Gallagher, *Lee & His Army*, 135–38.
86. Grant, "Interview with Young," in Simon, ed., *Papers of Grant*, 28:415; Thomas, *Lee*, 483. Young added that the fame of Lee seems to grow every day, especially in Europe.
87. Grant, *Memoirs*, 2:291–92.
88. *Ibid.*, 2:116, 127, 129, 142–43.
89. *Ibid.*, 2:130, 119–20, 146; Grant to George G. Meade, Apr. 9, 1864; Smith, *Grant*, 296–98.
90. Grant, *Memoirs*, 2:141, 134–37; Grant, "Interview with Young," in Simon, ed., *Papers of Grant*, 28:413.
91. Robert E. Lee to Secretary of War James Seddon, Aug. 23, 1864; cited in Gallagher, *Lee & His Army*, 271, ix, 259, 276, 275; Grant, "Interview with Young," in Simon, ed., *Papers of Grant*, 28:415, 413; Grant, *Memoirs*, 2:177–78; Smith, *Grant*, 376.
92. Abraham Lincoln to Grant, Apr. 30, 1864; Grant to Abraham Lincoln, May 1, 1864; Gallagher, *Lee & His Army*, 115, 119, 122, 129, 132–33, 135–38. Regarding his soldiers' adoration of Lee, a woman in Richmond said, "It is delightful to see how they reverence him and almost as much for his goodness as for his greatness." Grant, *Memoirs*, 2:126.
93. "Memoranda of Conversations with General Robert E. Lee," William Preston Johnston, May 7, 1868, in Gallagher, ed., *Lee the Soldier*, 29. Lee anticipated that Grant would cross at either the Germanna or the Ely ford; Grant crossed at both. For the remainder of his life, Grant believed he had taken Lee by surprise. See Smith, *Grant*, 312.
94. Thomas, *Lee*, 324–26; Smith, *Grant*, 316–24.
95. Grant, *Memoirs*, 2:193, 196, 197, 201, 204; Smith, *Grant*, 327–28, 333–34, 336–38, 343; Thomas, *Lee*, 324–26. Of the 800 Texans who fought, only 250 survived. The bullet through Longstreet's throat was a serious wound, causing him to cough up blood as he breathed. Grant lost 17,666 casualties, Lee lost 11,000.
96. Walter Taylor to Jeb Stuart, 7 May 1864, cited in Fuller, *Grant & Lee*, 216; Grant, *Memoirs*, 2:208–12; Gallagher, *Lee & His Army*, 191–94, 196–98, 200–205, 211. At Spotsylvania, Ewell's unsatisfactory performance continued. His loss of composure there was a sin that Lee would not condone. He chastened him, "General Ewell, you must restrain yourself; how can you expect to control these men if you have lost control of yourself?"
97. Grant, *Memoirs*, 2:231–32; Gallagher, *Lee & His Army*, 192–93; Smith, *Grant*, 345–55; Thomas, *Lee*, 327–29; Grant to Henry Halleck, May 11, 1864; Grant to Mrs. Grant, May 13, 1864. The report of Union wagons on the move was sent to Lee by his son Rooney. The wagons were in transit only to bring back supplies.
98. Grant, *Memoirs*, 2:241–42, 244; Gallagher, *Lee & His Army*, 212; Smith, *Grant*, 358–59. Regarding the photographs of himself at Massaponax Church, Grant wrote to his wife on June 19, 1864 that he was sending "three stereoscopic views taken at Mattaponix Church, near Spotsylvania Court House. Brady is along with the Army and is taking a great many views."
99. Grant, *Memoirs*, 2:259, 264, 272, 276; Smith, *Grant*, 360–64; Thomas, *Lee*, 330.
100. Grant to Henry Halleck, June 5, 1864; Lee to Mrs. Lee, June 4, 1864, Virginia Historical Society; Smith, *Grant*, 364, 367–74.
101. Grant, *Memoirs*, 2:279–80; Grant to Mrs. Grant, June 15, 1864; Grant to Henry Halleck, June 14, 1864; Smith, *Grant*, 372.
102. Thomas, *Lee*, 336, 338; Freeman, *Lee*, 3:411–13, 438; Smith, *Grant*, 369. In a postwar conversation with William Allan, Lee complained that "he had written to L[ongstreet] several times telling him that the enemy had mostly left his front and were on the South side, but that L[ongstreet] would not be convinced, and insisted they were still before him" ("Memoranda of Conversations with Lee," William Allan, in Gallagher, ed., *Lee the Soldier*, 16).
103. Smith, *Grant*, 370; J. Bryan, III, *The Sword Over the Mantel*, 81, cited in Rose, *Lee*, 21.
104. Grant, *Memoirs*, 2:293–94; Thomas, *Lee*, 431; Smith, *Grant*, 373–74, 381; Ervin L. Jordon, Jr., *Black Confederates and Afro-Virginians in Civil War Virginia* (Charlottesville, VA, 1995), 276–78. Grant had sent orders also to Winfield Scott Hancock that failed to reach him;

105. Thomas, *Lee*, 335; Smith, *Grant*, 379–80; Grant to Henry Halleck, July 14, 1864; Grant, *Memoirs*, 2:316–17, 164, 173–74; Gallagher, *Lee and His Generals*, 258–59; Gallagher, *The Confederate War*, 9–10; Lee, Petersburg, to Mrs. Lee, Nov. 12, 1864, Virginia Historical Society.
106. Grant to Elihu B. Washburne, Aug. 16, 1864; Lee, Chaffins, to Mrs. Lee, Oct. 9, 1864, Virginia Historical Society; Grant to Mrs. Grant, Dec. 26, 1864; Smith, *Grant*, 376, 390; Grant, *Memoirs*, 2:426; Lee to Robert Hunter, Jan. 11, 1865, Museum of the Confederacy, in Thomas, *Lee*, 347; Lee to Mrs. Lee, Feb. 21, 1865, in Dowdey and Manarin, eds., *Wartime Papers of Lee*, 907; Freeman, *Lee*, 116. On Jan. 31, a group of Confederate peace commissioners had visited Grant but could accomplish nothing because they were not empowered to yield to Lincoln's demands that the Union be restored and slavery be abolished; see Grant, *Memoirs*, 2:420.
107. The etching *General Grant and the Negro Sentinel* is published in Joseph T. Wilson, *The Black Phalanx: A History of the Negro Soldiers of the United States* (Hartford, CT, 1888).
108. Grant, *Memoirs*, 2:424–25, 456–58, 467; Grant to Mrs. Grant, Apr. 2, 1865; Grant to Lee, Apr. 7, 1865.
109. Smith, *Grant*, 395–401 (Smith cites the figures of 15,000 and 12,000 soldiers); John S. Wise, *The End of an Era*, 434–35, cited in Rose, *Lee*, 25; Gallagher, *The Confederate War*, 158; Thomas, *Lee*, 362; Freeman, *Lee*, 484.
110. Freeman, *Lee*, 483; Smith, *Grant*, 404.
111. Grant, *Memoirs*, 2:477–78, 483, 486, 488–94.
112. *Ibid.*, 2:497.
113. Gallagher, ed., *Lee the Soldier*, xx.
114. Gallagher, ed, *Lee the Soldier*, xviii; "Testimony of Grant before the Judiciary Committee, U.S. House of Representatives, Washington," July 18, 1867; Grant, Raleigh, NC, to Mrs. Grant, Apr. 25, 1865; Smith, *Grant*, 405.
115. Bunting, *Grant*, 69.
116. Gallagher, *The Confederate War*, 28–29, 53. The Confederate percentage of deaths would have translated to six million American deaths in World War II.
117. Grant, *Memoirs*, 2:542.
118. Grant, Cairo, IL, to Jesse Grant, Nov. 27, 1861.
119. Grant to Elihu B. Washburne, Aug. 30, 1863. In his *Memoirs*, Grant actually states, "since the war is over, reviewing the whole question [of abolition], I have come to the conclusion that the saying is quite true." His memory failed him (a rare instance), because the letter to Washburne proves that by 1863 he had already "come to the conclusion" that slavery had to be abolished.
120. Grant, "Conversation with Otto von Bismarck," Berlin, 1877, in John Russell Young, *Around the World with General Grant: A Narrative of the Visit of General U. S. Grant, Ex-President of the United States, to Various Countries in Europe, Asia, and Africa, in 1877, 1878, 1879* (New York, 1879), 1:416–17, cited in Smith, *Grant*, 610.
121. Lee to James A. Seddon, Jan. 10, 1863, in Dowdey and Manarin, eds., *Wartime Papers of Lee*, 388–90; "Memoranda of Conversations with Lee," William Allan, "Memoranda of Conversations with Lee," William Preston Johnston, both in Gallagher, ed., *Lee the Soldier*, 12, 29–30; Lee to Hunter, Jan. 11, 1865, Museum of the Confederacy; Gallagher, *Lee & His Army*, 169–70; Howard Swiggett, ed., *A Rebel War Clerk's Diary at the Confederate States Capital by J. B. Jones* (New York, 1935), 2:398.
122. Grant, *Memoirs*, 1:191–92; Gallagher, *Lee & His Army*, 189; Gallagher, *The Confederate War*, 116; Gallagher, *Lee and His Generals*, 20; Lee to James A. Seddon, June 8, 1863, cited in Dowdey and Manarin, eds., *Wartime Papers of Lee*, 504–5; Gallagher, *Lee and His Generals*, 4–5, 18.

VI

1. "Washington: General R. E. Lee's Visit to the President—Misrepresentations of Its Character and Import," *New York Times*, May 4, 1869; Douglas Southall Freeman, *R. E. Lee* (New York, 1934), 4:395, 401, 520–21, 196; Charles Bracelen Flood, *Lee, The Last Years* (Boston, 1981), 188. The *New York Tribune*, reprinted in *The National Intelligencer*, May 4, 1869, is cited in Freeman. The epigraphs are cited below in this chapter.
2. Jean Edward Smith, *Grant* (New York, 2001), 408–10.
3. Ulysses S. Grant, *Personal Memoirs of U. S. Grant* (New York, 1885), 2:508–10.
4. Flood, *Lee*, 3, 152; Freeman, *Lee*, 4:161, 188, 367 (Lee to Wade Hampton, May 27, 1867).
5. Had elected officials in the postwar South quickly ratified the Fourteenth Amendment, which gave citizenship and protection to all, they might have been spared some of the effects of Reconstruction. Flood, *Lee*, 44, 49; Freeman, *Lee*, 4:164.
6. Nelson Peabody Rose, *Robert E. Lee of Virginia, The Anguish of Conflicting Loyalties* (Cleveland, 1985), 185–86; Emory Thomas, *Robert E. Lee, A Biography* (New York, 1995), 309, 371; Smith, *Grant*, 416–18.
7. Grant to Henry Halleck, May 6, 1865, in John Y. Simon, ed., *The Papers of Ulysses S. Grant* (Carbondale, IL, 1967–); Freeman, *Lee*, 4:201, 206; Grant to Edwin Stanton, June 16 and June 20, 1865; Grant to Lee, June 20, 1865. All of the Grant papers cited below are published in the volumes edited by Simon.
8. Grant, "Interview," Hamburg, July 6, 1878, in Simon, ed., *Papers of Grant*, 28:421; Smith, *Grant*, 418.
9. *New York Times*, Sept. 14, 1865.
10. When it was known that Grant might live in Philadelphia and commute weekly to Washington, the Union League there purchased for him a house and furnished it. A family friend from Missouri, Abel Rathbone Corbin, who had been successful in the stock market and would marry Grant's sister Jennie, bought him a house in Washington. Major General Daniel Butterfield of New York City raised the $105,000 check. See Smith, *Grant*, 419–20; Freeman, *Lee*, 4:244.
11. The peculiar timing of Lee's pardon actually mattered little because when the Fourteenth Amendment was finally approved by the voters of Virginia, Lee and others formerly in the Confederate hierarchy were barred from holding state or Federal office. When a new state constitution was adopted, Lee was allowed to vote, but he never did so. Ironically, given Grant's account of Secretary of State Seward's support of a tolerant policy for Lee, the general's actual signed oath was lost after the document reached the desk of Seward, who gave it to a friend as a souvenir (see Thomas, *Lee*, 380). Flood, *Lee*, 65, 102; "Rev. Henry Ward Beecher on Reconstruction … Kind Words for General Robert E. Lee …," *New York Times*, Oct. 23, 1865; Lee to Captain Josiah Tatnall of the Confederate navy, Sept. 7, 1865, in Freeman, *Lee*, 4:221.
12. Lee to John Letcher, Aug. 28, 1865, in Freeman, *Lee*, 4:220; Thomas, *Lee*, 381; Flood, *Lee*, 64, 101, 145; Nathaniel H. Harris to Lee, June 6, 1866.
13. Flood, *Lee*, 102; Lee to Markie Williams, May 2, 1865, in Thomas, *Lee*, 372; Freeman, *Lee*, 4:219; Lee to Matthew Fontaine Maury, Sept. 8, 1865, in J. William Jones, *Personal Reminiscences, Anecdotes and Letters of Robert E. Lee* (Richmond, VA, 1989 reprint of 1875 ed.), 206; Lee to Beauregard, Oct. 8, 1865, in Jones, *Lee*, 207. Lee said much the same to Robert W. Lewis, Jr. (Apr. 6, 1866, Virginia Historical Society): "As regards the advice you ask on the subject of emigrating to Mexico or Brazil, … I considered that the South required the presence of her sons more then than at any former part of her history, to sustain and restore her …. I have therefore invariably advised all who could remain, to adhere to their homes and friends."
14. Simon, ed., *Papers of Grant*, 15:xiii–xv, 16:xii–xv; Smith, *Grant*, 415; Grant to Edwin Stanton, June 20, 1865; Grant to Sheridan, July 25, 1865; Grant to Andrew Johnson, Sept. 8, 1865.
15. Grant, Richmond, to Mrs. Grant, Nov. 28, 1865; Grant, Raleigh, to Mrs. Grant, Nov. 29, 1865; Grant, Savannah, to Mrs. Grant, Dec. 4, 1865; Grant to Andrew Johnson, Dec. 18, 1865; Smith, *Grant*, 420–22.
16. Early had stated, "I hate a Yankee this day worse than I have ever done & my hatred is increasing every day." Jubal Early, Mexico City, to Lee, Jan. 25 1866, Washington and Lee University; Lee to Early, Mar. 15 and Oct. 4, 1866, in Flood, *Lee*, 144. See also Flood, *Lee*, 152; Freeman, *Lee*, 4:237, 206, 412; Jones, *Lee*, 195–96; Lee to Edward A. Pollard, Baltimore, Jan. 24, 1867, Virginia Historical Society; Lee to the Honorable D. McConaughy of the Gettysburg Battlefield Memorial Association, Aug. 9, 1869, Washington and Lee University.
17. Freeman, *Lee*, 4:207, 235, 209–12.
18. *Ibid.*, 4:215–19; Rector John W. Brockenbrough of Washington College to Robert E. Lee, Aug. 10, 1865, Washington and Lee University; Thomas, *Lee*, 374, 380; Flood, *Lee*, 83; Rose, *Lee*, 66.
19. Flood, *Lee*, 116; Smith, *Grant*, 421–22; 443.
20. Freeman, *Lee*, 4:249–51.
21. *Report of the Joint Committee on Reconstruction, at the First Session Thirty-Ninth Congress* (Washington, 1866), 129–36; Flood, *Lee*, 117.
22. Thomas, *Lee*, 371–72; "Negro Communed at St. Paul's Church," *Confederate Veteran* 13 (1905): 360.

For a different interpretation of the incident at the communion rail, see Nelson Lankford, *Richmond Burning: The Last Days of the Confederate Capital* (New York, 2002), 243–44. The racist aspect of Lee's testimony was mild in comparison to some of his wife's statements. See, for example, her letter to Emily Mason, May 20, 1866: "We are all here dreadfully plundered by the lazy idle Negroes who are lounging about the streets doing nothing but looking what they may plunder during the night …. When we get rid of the freedmen's Bureau & can take the law in our hands we may perhaps do better. If they would only take all their pets north it would be a happy riddance" (Museum of the Confederacy, cited in Thomas, *Lee*, 371–72). In 1866, Mary Lee wrote "My Reminiscences of the War Waged Against the South by the United States Abolitionist Faction Immediately After the Election of Lincoln" (in Connelly, *Marble Man*, 36).

23. Lee to Chauncey Burr, Jan. 5, 1866, in Freeman, *Lee*, 4:303; Lee to James May, July 9, 1866, in Jones, *Lee*, 217–18; Lee to Edward Lee Childe, Feb. 11, 1869, Stratford Hall Plantation; Lee to Lord Acton (Sir John Dalberg Acton), Dec. 15, 1866, published in Lord Acton's *Correspondence* in 1917, in Freeman, *Lee*, 4:303–4, 516–17; Lee to George Jones, Mar. 22, 1869, in J. William Jones, *Lee*, 273–74.

24. Smith, *Grant*, 422–23: Simon, ed., *Papers of Grant*, 16:xiii–xv; Freeman, *Lee*, 4:300–302; Grant to Andrew Johnson, Mar. 14, 1866.

25. Smith, *Grant*, 423–30; Simon, ed., *Papers of Grant*, 16:xiii–xv; Grant, *General Orders No. 44*, July 6, 1866; Grant, St. Louis, to Mrs. Grant, Sept. 9, 1866; Grant to Philip H. Sheridan, Oct. 12, 1866; Grant to Edwin M. Stanton, Jan. 29, 1867; Grant, "Interview," *New York Times*, Feb. 20, 1867.

26. Flood, *Lee*, 148; Freeman, *Lee*, 4:310–11, 208; Lee to Robert Ould, Virginia Senate, Richmond, Feb. 11, 1867, Virginia Historical Society; Lee to David S. G. Cabell, Feb. 25, 1867, in Freeman, *Lee*, 4:311. (A two-thirds vote of Congress, an unlikely occurrence, would have allowed a former Confederate officer to take office.)

27. Simon, ed., *Papers of Grant*, 17:xiii–xv; Smith, *Grant*, 431; Flood, *Lee*, 148–49; Freeman, *Lee*, 4:312.

28. Simon, ed., *Papers of Grant*, 17:xiii–xv; Flood, *Lee*, 148; Freeman, *Lee*, 4:312; Smith, *Grant*, 435–39.

29. Grant to Philip Sheridan, May 26, 1867; Grant to Secretary of War Edwin Stanton, July 23, 1867; Mrs. Lee to Mrs. Chilton, March 10 and May 6, 1867, in Freeman, *Lee*, 4:312. See also Mary Lee to Emily Mason, Feb. 22, 1867: "What a farce all the proceedings of the Washington Congress are. We have almost ceased to read them …. I should think soon all decent white people would be forced to retire from that city & give the place to the dominant race" (in Thomas, *Lee*, 385). In a May letter Mary added, "They still desire to grind [the South] to dust & wish to effect this purpose by working on the feelings of the low & ignorant Negroes many of whom do not even comprehend what a vote means. My indignation cannot be controlled."

30. Lee to Robert Ould, Virginia Senate, Richmond, Mar. 29, 1867, in Freeman, *Lee*, 4: 313–14; Lee to General Dabney H. Maury, New Orleans, May 23, 1867, Virginia Historical Society (see also Lee to R. I. Moses, Columbus, Georgia, Apr. 13, 1867, Virginia Historical Society); "General Lee—The Convention," *Richmond Dispatch*, Mar. 23, 1867; Lee to Rooney, June 8, 1867, in Freeman, *Lee*, 4:315.

31. Simon, ed., *Papers of Grant*, 18: xiii–xv; Smith, *Grant*, 443–58; Grant to Andrew Johnson, Feb. 3, 1868. Johnson's efforts to dismiss Stanton were in violation of the Tenure of Office Act, which Congress had passed in 1867 to block the president from removing Republican appointees. Grant temporarily assumed Stanton's position as secretary of war, to keep the post from falling into the hands of someone who would support Johnson's policy against the rights of African Americans. Johnson tried to force a new appointee, Lorenzo Thomas, into place, without conferring with Congress. A compromise was reached when John Schofield accepted the position, with Grant's approval, and stated that he would enforce Reconstruction (see Smith, *Grant*, 453–55).

32. Freeman, *Lee*, 4:343–47, 353–57; Thomas, *Lee*, 388, 393–95; *New York Tribune*, Apr. 20, 1868. Lacey's letter was printed as well in the *New York Independent*. See also John M. McClure, "The Freedmen's Bureau School in Lexington versus 'General Lee's Boys,'" in Peter Wallenstein and Bertram Wyatt-Brown, *Virginia's Civil War* (Charlottesville, VA, 2005), 189–200.

33. "Education in the South; Meeting at Cooper Institute in Behalf of Washington College, Virginia—Addresses by Prof. R. D. Hitchcock and Rev. Henry Ward Beecher," *New York Times*, Mar. 3, 1868; Freeman, *Lee*, 4: 348, 350–51, 358.

34. Freeman, *Lee*, 4:351, 354.

35. *Ibid.*, 4:354. It is possible that if he received her letter, Lee did not respond to Julia Shearman because her plight did not win his sympathy; many in the postwar South felt that the education of the freedpeople did not fall within the purview of northerners. We do know that Lee paid little attention to those African Americans in the Lexington area who were victimized by Ku Klux Klan activity. Klan violence was sadly characteristic of life throughout Virginia and the South during the Reconstruction era, and Lee would have had difficulty controlling it even had he tried. That he did not should be no surprise, because it was always Lee's choice to avoid personal confrontation and always his style to lead by example. He would avoid condemning those who joined the Klan just as during the war he had avoided embarrassing officers who were doing their best. Rather than condemn the general for not intervening with the KKK, probably the more important point to make, as historian Richard McCaslin has done, is that Lee himself refused to have anything to do with that organization, unlike so many former Confederates who did. His absence from the Lexington group was a glaringly visible example for his neighbors to follow. See Richard B. McCaslin, *Lee in the Shadow of Washington* (Baton Rouge, LA, 2001), 212. Historian Ervin Jordan has found evidence that in 1868 in Virginia the Ku Klux Klan advertised its meetings in Richmond newspapers, issued posters to intimidate black voters in Goochland County (west of Richmond), assaulted the pastor and trustees of Galilee Baptist Church in their homes in Appomattox County, opened fire on black voters in Southampton County, and issued death threats against black and white delegates to the state constitutional convention in Richmond. See *Report of the Joint Select Committee Appointed to Inquire into the Condition of Affairs in the Late Insurrectionary States* (Washington, 1872), 1:20; Stanley Fitzgerald Horn, *Invisible Empire: The Story of the Ku Klux Klan, 1866–1871* (Boston, 1939), 281–84; Richard L. Morton, ed., "Life in Virginia by a 'Yankee Teacher,' Margaret Newbold Thorpe," *Virginia Magazine of History and Biography* 64 (April 1956), 185.

In May 1868, the *Lexington News Gazette* carried a story that failed to interest editors in New York City who did not republish it. The incident was the shooting of Francis Brockenbrough, a younger son of the rector of Washington College, by a black youth, Caesar Griffin. Students quickly captured Griffin and paraded him to the courthouse with a rope around his neck. According to one witness, Lee appeared and was able to disperse the crowd and turn the accused over to authorities. Two days later, when a rumor circulated that the victim's death would be a signal for students to storm the jail, Lee acted again to restore order. Francis Brockenbrough did not die; Caesar Griffin was accordingly sentenced to only two years in prison (Freeman, *Lee*, 4:358–59; Thomas, *Lee*, 389).

36. "Excellent Examples," *New York Times*, June 17, 1865 (the paper's editors were pleased that the Confederate general had "the good sense to acknowledge his sins and ask for forgiveness" in the form of a pardon); Flood, *Lee*, 151.

37. "White Sulphur Springs, Virginia—Gen. Rosecrans and Gen. Lee," *New York Times*, Aug. 22, 1868; "Gen. Lee's Reply to Gen. Rosecrans—Meeting in Norfolk," *New York Times*, Sept. 14, 1868; Freeman, *Lee*, 4:373, 377–78, 382; Flood, *Lee*, 196; Lee, White Sulphur Springs, to William S. Rosecrans, Aug. 26, 1868, Virginia Historical Society (letterbook); Isaac Hale, Jr., to Lee, Sept. 7, 1868, Washington and Lee University. In 1868, six northern states still refused blacks the vote (see Flood, *Lee*, 197).

38. Grant to Joseph R. Hawley, May 29, 1868 (acceptance of the nomination); Grant to William T. Sherman, June 21, 1868; Grant, "Interview," Hamburg, July 6, 1878, in Simon, ed., *Papers of Grant*, 28:429.

39. Freeman, *Lee*, 4:413; John T. Morgan to Robert E. Lee, cited in Ollinger Crenshaw, *General Lee's College: The Rise and Growth of Washington and Lee University* (New York, 1969), 149; for Lee on "impartial suffrage," see "Memoranda of Conversations with General Robert E. Lee," William Preston Johnston, May 7, 1868, in Gary W. Gallagher, ed., *Lee the Soldier* (Lincoln, NE, 1996), 30; Lee to Giles Crook, June 11, 1869, Virginia Historical Society.

40. Flood, *Lee*, 217–24. Buchser wrote a

41. detailed account of lengthy sittings with Lee that probably never took place; there are no mentions of Buchser in Lee's correspondence during the several weeks when Buchser was supposedly with him. The artist's entries probably were fabricated to impress his patrons back home. Marilyn von Kuhlberg, a student of the literature on the general, has conducted an extensive survey of both Lexington newspapers and Lee family correspondence in search of any mention of Buchser; she has found no evidence that the artist even stepped off the coach in Lexington. For Buchser's images of blacks, see William M. S. Rasmussen and Robert S. Tilton, *Old Virginia: The Pursuit of a Pastoral Ideal* (Charlottesville, VA, 2003), 161.

41. Freeman, *Lee*, 4:223–24, 258, 296; Thomas, *Lee*, 375; Lee to Rooney Lee, Oct. 30, 1865, Virginia Historical Society; Lee to G. W. Leyburn, Mar. 20, 1866; Lee to John Brockenbrough, Aug. 24, 1865, Washington and Lee University; *New York Times*, Sept. 7, 1865.

42. Thomas, *Lee*, 397; Freeman, *Lee*, 4:278, 499, 503; Custis Lee to Robert E. Lee, Jr., May 5, 1896, Virginia Historical Society.

43. Freeman, *Lee*, 4:279–83, 297, 505; Jones, *Lee*, 433, 480; Rose, *Lee*, 211; Franklin L. Riley, *General Robert E. Lee after Appomattox* (New York, 1922), 25; Thomas, *Lee*, 398.

44. Freeman, *Lee*, 4:276, 278, 299, 365, 406–7; Thomas, *Lee*, 384.

45. "If he [W. E. Cater] fails now to obtain the self control & self denial which he will be called on to exercise in life, I fear it will be difficult, unless under some great necessity, for him to acquire it." "I do not think it would be to his [John Lapsley's] advantage to continue here without reaping an adequate return for the expenditure of his time and money." "He is a youth of good capacity, candor and truth. These qualities have endeared him to the members of the Faculty, and I trust his future course will reinstate him in their good opinion, and in the confidence of his comrades." Thomas, *Lee*, 377, 395; Freeman, *Lee*, 4:287, 294–96; Flood, *Lee*, 104; Lee to Mrs. F. S. Cater, Apr. 2, 1869, Virginia Historical Society; Lee to Col. J. W. Lapsley, Selma, AL, June 5, 1866, Virginia Historical Society; Lee to unidentified parents, Mar. 8, 1867, in Freeman, *Lee*, 4:290.

46. A portion of the correspondence that was immensely important had nothing to do with the college. Already we have seen letters of advice regarding political matters. Lee sent as well personal advice both to young parents who wrote to him and to their children. "It is my great desire that he should … learn obedience, perfect & cheerful obedience, to his parents, masters & spiritual teachers. This is the first step. Other virtues will follow & I hope that truthfulness, honesty, & integrity will lead the way to pure & true religion." "[L]isten to your parents; obey their precepts; and from childhood to the grave, pursue unswervingly the path of honor and of truth. Above all things, learn at once to worship your creator and to do His will, as revealed in His Holy book." Freeman, *Lee*, 4:231, 271, 274; Lee to Fanny French, Apr. 29, 1866, Lee to Robert E. Lee Mooty, La Grange, GA, May 29, 1866, both Virginia Historical Society.

47. A report in the *Charleston Mercury* was reprinted in the *New York Times* of June 7, 1868; Freeman, *Lee*, 4:233, 245, 248, 259, 266, 299, 344, 367–68, 378, 420, 438, 471; Flood, *Lee*, 175; Thomas, *Lee*, 376, 399.

48. Freeman, *Lee*, 4:231, 262–66; Thomas, *Lee*, 376, 399; Flood, *Lee*, 112.

49. Lee also introduced innovative ideas in the areas of elementary and secondary education, by serving on a committee of the Educational Society of Virginia. He wrote to one of his colleagues, Professor J. B. Minor of the University of Virginia, "In its broad & comprehensive sense, education embraces the physical, moral & intellectual instruction of a child from infancy to manhood." The general had moved into the first rank of American educators. Freeman, *Lee*, 4:420–28, 471; Flood, *Lee*, 205; Thomas, *Lee*, 399; *New York Times*, Jan. 22 and Feb. 1, 1869; *New York Herald*, 1869, in Freeman, *Lee*, 4:428; Lee to J. B. Minor, Charlottesville, Jan. 17, 1867, Virginia Historical Society.

50. Freeman, *Lee*, 4:400–1, 420, 425; Duncan Lyle Kinnear, *The First 100 Years: A History of Virginia Polytechnic Institute and State University* (Blacksburg, VA, 1972), 28. The late Duncan Kinnear does not cite his source; the authors have enlisted the assistance of special collections librarians at Washington and Lee University, Virginia Military Institute, Virginia Tech, the Virginia Historical Society, and the Library of Virginia in search of the "detailed plan," but nothing has been found. See also *The Farmer*, Feb. 1867, 59 ("That the negro ought to be educated is we think beyond dispute, that he will be taught by somebody and in some way, is, we think, equally evident; … the sooner and more earnestly we set about this work, the better for the prosperity of ourselves and our State"), and the *Lexington Gazette and Banner*, Jan. 15, 1868 ("a resolution to sell the Virginia Military Institute buildings to educate little piccaninies, was offered by a colored delegate").

51. For Lee, the "charms of civil life" included the flirtations he conducted via letters and at the springs. He sent photographs to young girls, who responded ("I will frame it with a glass over it, so that I can kiss it as often as I wish without wearing it away"). He encouraged his daughters to recruit visitors ("as to the young ladies, tell them that I want to see them very much"). He encouraged his sons to marry and he even wrote to their girl friends ("I have been looking for you and Annette all the spring …. You ought not to disappoint me, Carrie, for I cannot stand broken promises like the young men."). Christina Bond published a popular story about Lee's instructions to southern belles at White Sulphur Springs to show no resentment to northern guests ("we were on our own soil and owed a sacred duty of hospitality"). She concluded, "Apparently, he felt among the maidens a safety from intrusion which he could not have among those to whom his personality, and the great issues which he represented, were uppermost thoughts." Of course, it was more than that. As Mrs. Lee put it, "No one enjoyed the society of ladies more than himself. It seemed the greatest recreation in his toilsome life." Freeman, *Lee*, 4:320, 325, 329, 331, 345, 363, 372, 380, 410; Thomas, *Lee*, 379, 386, 391–92, 404; Flood, *Lee*, 140, 162–63, 165; "Nettie" (?) to Lee, Feb. 12, 1869, Virginia Historical Society; Lee to Agnes Lee, Mar. 28, 1868, Virginia Historical Society; Lee to Caroline (Carrie) Stuart, July 4, 1868, Washington and Lee University.

52. On his trip to Baltimore in 1869, Lee purchased a carriage for Mary. Until then, the woman who had accompanied her husband to faraway St. Louis and New York City had considerable difficulty traveling to the nearby springs; there she would endure therapeutic treatment and dine alone in her cottage while her husband socialized. Travel farther was not feasible: "I know you long sometimes for the banks of the Potomac and James," Mary wrote to Mrs. R. H. Chilton in 1867, "I confess I do. These mountains seem to shut out all I used to know and love." She added, "yet I am thankful we have found an asylum here and such kind people." Flood, *Lee*, 126; Freeman, *Lee*, 4:242, 323, 325, 382–86, 408; Thomas, *Lee*, 386, 402; Connelly, *Marble Man*, 34; Mildred Lee, "Journal," Aug. 21, 1888, Virginia Historical Society.

53. Freeman, *Lee*, 4:411; Thomas, *Lee*, 377; Mary P. Coulling, *The Lee Girls* (Winston-Salem, NC, 1987), 184, 193; Roy Blount, Jr., *Robert E. Lee* (New York, 2003), 162.

54. Thomas, *Lee*, 378, 405; Freeman, *Lee*, 4:333, 340–41, 364; Coulling, *Lee Girls*, 190–91; Lee to Mrs. Lee, Nov. 29, 1867, Lee to Rooney Lee, Nov. 29, 1867, and Lee to Charlotte Haxall, Sept. 27, 1867, all Virginia Historical Society.

55. Flood, *Lee*, 73–74, 30, 129–31; Freeman, *Lee*, 4:411.

56. Mary Custis Lee to Jo Lane Stern, May 8, 1871 or 1872, Washington and Lee University; Lee to Agnes Lee, Nov. 16, 1865 and March 26, 1868, both Virginia Historical Society; Mildred Lee to Lucy Blain, Feb. 7, 1866, Mildred Lee to Emily Hay, Jan. 6, 1879, both Washington and Lee University; Mildred Lee, *Journal*, Aug. 21, 1888, Virginia Historical Society; Freeman, *Lee*, 4:344, 372, 411; Coulling, *Lee Girls*, 179, 187–89, 193–97.

57. As an active retailer, Stewart was barred from service by a statute enacted in 1789 by Alexander Hamilton that established the treasury department and said it could not be headed by a person engaged in trade or commerce. Grant's other appointments were Jacob Cox of Ohio (Interior), John Creswell of Maryland (Postmaster General), Judge Ebenezer Rockwood Hoar and George Boutwell of Massachusetts (Attorney General and Treasury), and his aide Gen. John Rawlins (War). See Smith, *Grant*, 464–73; Simon, ed., *Papers of Grant*, 19:xi–xiv.

58. Simon, ed., *Papers of Grant*, 20: xi–xii; Grant, "Inaugural Address," Mar. 4, 1869; Grant, "Message to Congress," Mar. 30, 1870. The Fifteenth Amendment prohibited states from denying suffrage because of race but permitted the survival of such other restrictions as those based on education,

59. Simon, ed., *Papers of Grant*, 21:xi–xiii, 22:xi–xiii; Smith, *Grant*, 542–47; Grant to Rep. James G. Blaine, Mar. 9, 1871; Grant, "Presidential Message," Mar. 23, 1871; Grant, "Proclamation," Mar. 24, May 3, Oct. 12, and Oct. 17, 1871; Grant to Secretary of War William W. Belknap, May 13, 1871; Grant, "Annual Message to Congress," Dec. 4, 1871; Grant, "Message to the House of Representatives," Apr. 19, 1872. In protecting the freedpeople, Grant bypassed Secretary of War William Belknap, who had no interest in their welfare, and gave orders directly to the army.

60. Simon, ed., *Papers of Grant*, 22:xi–xiii, 23:xi–xiv, 24:xi–xiv; Smith, *Grant*, 547–51; Grant to Schuyler Colfax, Aug. 4 and Nov. 14, 1871; Grant to Henry Wilson, Nov. 18, 1871; Grant, "Second Inaugural Address," Mar. 4, 1873. Greeley died shortly after the election; Grant attended his funeral as a gesture of national reconciliation.

61. Grant, "Message to the Senate," Jan. 13, 1875; Grant to Secretary of War William W. Belknap, 15 Jan. 1871, 5 Jan. 1872, 2 Sept. 1873; Grant to Henry L. Dawes, Jan. 12, 1872; Grant, "Message to Congress," Feb. 25, 1873; Grant, "Proclamation," May 22, 1873, and Sept. 15, 1874; Simon, ed., *Papers of Grant*, 24:xi–xiv, 25:xi–xvi; Smith, *Grant*, 563–68. Seventy-two of the Colfax murderers were indicted, but only three were convicted and they in the end were turned free by a ruling of the Supreme Court. In the Zenneck cartoon, the devil who directs Grant is identified as Attorney General George H. Williams. Northern merchants are the figures at the left; South Carolina is pictured in chains at the right.

62. Grant to Elisha Baxter, May 11, 1874; Grant, "Proclamation," May 15, 1874 and Oct. 17, 1876; Grant to Attorney General Edwards Pierrepont, Sept. 13, 1875; Grant to Daniel H. Chamberlain, July 26, 1876; Simon, ed., *Papers of Grant*, 25:xi–xvi, 26:xi–xvi, 27:xi–xvii; Smith, *Grant*, 596.

63. Grant to W. T. Sherman, Nov. 10, 1876; Simon, ed., *Papers of Grant*, 28:xi–xvi; Smith, *Grant*, 598–605. The joint commission was composed of five Democrats and five Republicans from Congress, plus five Supreme Court justices, two from each party plus one independent. When the independent justice left to take a Senate seat offered to him by the Illinois legislature, only Republican justices remained on the court. One joined the commission, and Hayes was given the three states and the election.

64. Josiah Bunting III, *Ulysses S. Grant* (New York, 2004), 114.

65. Grant, "First Annual Message to Congress," Dec. 6, 1869; Smith, *Grant*, 516–20.

66. Grant, "Inaugural Address," Mar. 4, 1869; Grant, "First Annual Message to Congress," Dec. 6, 1869; Grant to George H. Stuart, Oct. 26, 1872; Grant, "Second Inaugural Address," Mar. 4, 1873; Smith, *Grant*, 521–27; Simon, ed., *Papers of Grant*, 19:xi–xiv.

67. Grant, "First Annual Message to Congress," Dec. 6, 1869; Smith, *Grant*, 527–31. The Marias Massacre is central to the denouement of James Welch's *Fools Crow*. See also "Red Cloud," June 15, 1870; "The Indians," June 5, 1870; "The Appeal of the Red Man," June 8, 1870; "The Indians," June 10, 1870; "The Story of the Indians," June 13, 1870; "The Great Chief: Red Cloud Meets His White Brethren at Cooper Institute," June 17, 1870; "The Last Appeal of Red Cloud," June 17, 1870, all *New York Times*.

68. Simon, ed., *Papers of Grant*, 21:xi–xiii, 22:xi–xiii, 24:xi–xiv, 25:xi–xvi, 26:xi–xvi; Smith, *Grant*, 534–37, 586. See also Richard H. Dillon, *Indian Wars, 1850-1890* (New York, 1984).

69. Simon, ed., *Papers of Grant*, 27:xi–xvii; Smith, *Grant*, 516–20, 538–41. See also Richard Slotkin, *The Fatal Environment: The Myth of the Frontier in the Age of Industrialization, 1800-1890* (New York, 1985).

70. Grant, "Speech," London, June 15, 1877; Grant, "Speech to the Midland International Arbitration Union," Birmingham, England, Oct. 16, 1877; Grant, "Conversation with Otto von Bismarck," Berlin, June 30, 1878.

71. Grant, "Inaugural Address," Mar. 4, 1869; Grant to Hamilton Fish, Mar. 9, 1877. See also Grant to Adolph E. Borie, Nov. 22, 1871.

72. Grant to Hamilton Fish, Aug. 14, 1869; Grant, "Memorandum," Aug. 31, 1869; Grant, "Annual Message to Congress," Dec. 7, 1875; Simon, ed., *Papers of Grant*, 19:xi–xiv, 23:xi–xiv; Smith, *Grant*, 491–92, 498.

73. Simon, ed., *Papers of Grant*, 24:xi–xiv; Smith, *Grant*, 493–98.

74. Grant, "Memorandum—Reasons Why San Domingo Should Be Annexed to the United States," 1869–70; Grant, *Memoirs*, 2:550; Simon, ed., *Papers of Grant*, 20:xi–xiii; Smith, *Grant*, 499–501.

75. Grant, "Interview," Hamburg, July 6, 1878; Smith, *Grant*, 501–6.

76. Grant to Hamilton Fish, Aug. 26, 1871; Simon, ed., *Papers of Grant*, 23:xi–xiv; Smith, *Grant*, 508.

77. *New York Times*, May 12, 1871; Grant, "Message to Congress," Dec. 4, 1871; Grant, "Proclamation," July 4, 1871; Smith, *Grant*, 509–15; Simon, ed., *Papers of Grant*, 23:xi–xiv.

78. Grant, "Draft Annual Message to Congress," Dec. 7, 1874; Simon, ed., *Papers of Grant*, 20:xi–xiii, 21:xi–xiii.

79. Grant, "Inaugural Address," 1869; Smith, *Grant*, 480–85.

80. Grant to George S. Boutwell, Sept. 12, 1869; *New York Times*, Sept. 25 and 29, 1869; Smith, *Grant*, 486–90.

81. For Grant's personal patronage dilemmas, see Simon, ed., *Papers of Grant*, 19:xi–xiv, 23:xi–xiv.

82. Grant, "Draft of Annual Message to Congress," 5 Dec. 1870, 2 Dec. 1872, 1 Dec. 1873, and 7 Dec. 1874; Grant, "Second Inaugural Address," Mar. 4, 1873; Smith, *Grant*, 587–89; Simon, ed., *Papers of Grant*, 22:xi–xiii.

83. "Helping Themselves," *New York Times*, Mar. 8, 1873; Smith, *Grant*, 552–53.

84. "The Credit Mobilier—Testimony of Mr. Colfax before the Investigating Committee," *New York Times*, Jan. 8, 1873; Smith, *Grant*, 552–53. The House censured Oakes Ames of Massachusetts and James Brooks of New York, and the Senate expelled James W. Patterson of New Hampshire.

85. Grant, "Inaugural Address," Mar. 4, 1869; Smith, *Grant*, 480.

86. Grant to Horace Claflin and Charles Anthony, Sept. 27, 1873; Grant to Nathaniel Cowdrey, President of Continental National Bank, New York City, Oct. 6, 1873; Grant, "Draft Annual Message to Congress," Dec. 1, 1873; Grant, "Veto to the Senate of the United States," Apr. 22, 1874; Grant, "Memorandum [to Senator John Sherman]," June 1, 1874; Grant, "To Congress," Feb. 3, 1877; Hamilton Fish to General L. Schuyler, Apr. 25, 1874; Simon, ed., *Papers of Grant*, 24:xi–xiv, 25:xi–xvi; Smith, *Grant*, 575–80.

87. Smith, *Grant*, 581–82

88. "Facts in the Sanborn Case," Apr. 2, 1874; "The President and the Sanborn Business," May 5, 1874; "The Sanborn Contracts," May 27, 1874, all *New York Times*; Smith, *Grant*, 577.

89. Grant, "Endorsement," July 29, 1875; Simon, ed., *Papers of Grant*, 26:xi–xvi, 27:xi–xvii; Smith, *Grant*, 582–83, 585, 590.

90. "The Trial of Gen. Babcock, The President's Deposition," Feb. 13, 1876, *New York Times*; Grant to Annie Campbell Babcock, Dec. 17, 1875; Simon, ed., *Papers of Grant*, 27:xi–xvii, 28:xi–xvi; Smith, *Grant*, 584–86, 590–93.

91. "Western Whiskey Trials," Feb. 8, 1876; "The Trial of Gen. Babcock; Opening of the Defense," Feb. 17, 1876; "Gen. Babcock's Acquittal," Feb. 25, 1876, all *New York Times*.

92. "The Secretary of War; Painfully Damaging Testimony," Mar. 2, 1876; "The Case in the House; Presentation of Resolutions of Impeachment," Mar. 3, 1876, both *New York Times*; Simon, ed., *Papers of Grant*, 26:xi–xvi, 27:xi–xvii; Smith, *Grant*, 593–95.

93. "Ex-Secretary Belknap," Mar. 3, 1876; "Belknap and the President," Mar. 3, 1876; "The Belknap Case Abroad; Opinions of the French Press—The Scandal Deplored," Mar. 4, 1876; "The Case of Gen. Belknap; Sentiment in Washington," Mar. 4, 1876; "The President's Responsibility," Mar. 4, 1876; "The Belknap Case Abroad; Opinions of the London Press," Mar. 5, all *New York Times*.

94. "Post Tradeships; The Charge against Mr. Orvil Grant denied by Traders," *New York Times*, Mar. 7, 1876; Simon, ed., *Papers of Grant*, 21:xi–xiii; Smith, *Grant*, 592.

95. John Y. Simon, ed., *The Personal Memoirs of Julia Dent Grant* (Carbondale, IL, 1975), 182, 174, 75.

96. Smith, *Grant*, 473–74; Simon, ed., *Memoirs of Julia Grant*, 174–77.

97. Simon, ed., *Memoirs of Julia Grant*, 174, 162, 177; Grant to John Rawlins, Sept. 1868 ("I am getting fat, weigh now over 160 pounds"); Grant to Sophia C. Page, Mar. 23, 1877 ("I have grown much older and some forty pounds larger [since 1865]").

98. Grant to Ulysses S. Grant, Jr. [Buck], Dec. 8, 1870; Grant to Mary Grant Cramer, Oct. 26, 1871; Grant to Abel Corbin, Sept. 13, 1872; Grant to Adam Badeau, Oct. 25, 1874; Simon, ed., *Papers of Grant*, 21:xi–xiii, 22:xi–xiii, 23:xi–xiv, 25:xi–xvi.

99. Grant to Mrs. Grant, July 17 and 21, 1868; Grant to Ulysses S. Grant, Jr., Oct. 23, 1870; Grant to his father Jesse Grant, June 2, 1872; Simon, ed., *Papers of Grant*, 21:xi–xiii, 25:xi–xvi.

100. Grant to Robert C. Schenck, May 17, 1872; Grant to Abel Corbin, Sept. 13, 1872; Grant to his father Jesse Grant, June 2, 1872; Grant to Edward J. Sartoris, July 7, 1873; Simon, ed., *Papers*

of Grant, 24:xi–xiv, 25:xi–xvi, 26:203; Smith, *Grant*, 573–75. The print of Grant and Nellie is pictured in William S. McFeely, *Grant, A Biography* (New York, 1981), 172; the photograph of the "Old Woman in the Shoe" is pictured in Simon, ed., *Memoirs of Julia Grant*, 186–87.

101. Grant to Ulysses S. Grant, Jr. , 24 Nov. 1870, 26 May 1877, 17 June 1877, and 25 Aug. 1877; Simon, ed., *Papers of Grant*, 25: xi–xvi, 26:xi–xvi, 27:xi–xvii.

102. For Grant about his farm, see for instance Grant to William Elrod, 14 Nov. 1867, 24 Aug. 1868, 23 Aug. 1869, 27 Mar. 1870, 23 Oct. 1870, 24 Nov. 1870, 28 Feb. 1871, 15 Mar. 1872; Grant to Charles W. Ford, 3 May 1871, 23 Apr. 1872, 15 June 1873; Grant to Nathaniel Carlin, 27 Oct. 1873, 7 June 1874; Grant to John Long, 9 Nov. 1874, 13 July 1875; Simon, ed., *Papers of Grant*, 19:xi–xiv, 21: xi–xiii, 26:xi–xvi, 27:xi–xvii, 28:xi–xvi.

103. Freeman, *Lee*, 4:482–84; Connelly, *Marble Man*, 30.

VII

1. Lee to Markie Williams, Oct. 4, 1867 and Jan. 1, 1868; Lee to William F. Wickham, Mar. 4, 1868; Lee to Rooney Lee, Dec. 2, 1869; Lee to Mildred Lee, Feb. 2, 1870, Virginia Historical Society; Lee to Gen. M. D. Corse, Mar. 18, 1870, Washington and Lee University; Douglas Southall Freeman, *Robert E. Lee* (New York, 1934), 4:272, 440, 442; Emory Thomas, *Robert E. Lee, A Biography* (New York, 1995), 387, 405–6. The epigraphs are cited below in this chapter.

2. Agnes Lee to Mrs. Lee, Apr. 3, 1870; Captain Robert E. Lee, *Recollections and Letters of General Robert E. Lee* (New York, 1924), 388; Charles Bracelen Flood, *Lee, The Last Years* (Boston, 1981), 235; Freeman, *Lee*, 4:444; Thomas, *Lee*, 406–7.

3. Captain Robert E. Lee, *Recollections* (New York, 1924), 390; "Gen. Lee's Reception in Augusta," *New York Times*, Apr. 4, 1870; Lee to Mrs. Lee, Apr. 2, 11, and 17, 1870; *Jacksonville Union*, Apr. 13–16, 1870; Freeman, *Lee*, 4:446–53, 465; Flood, *Lee*, 241; Thomas, *Lee*, 408. From Savannah, Lee wrote famously to his wife about Agnes, "You know she is like her papa—always wanting something," an apparently simple reference to the difficulties of leading a life of self-restraint that has been much discussed by Lee's biographers (Captain Robert E. Lee, *Recollections*, 395).

4. *Charleston Courier*, Apr. 28, 1870; Freeman, *Lee*, 453–64, 469–70; Thomas, *Lee*, 409; Flood, *Lee*, 248. In one of the stories, a sculptress, possibly Harriet Hosmer, had enclosed in a letter to Lee photographs of the scantily clothed figures she made and asked when she could come to do a bust. Lee told Valentine that "a friend suggested July or August, as the most of her works seemed to have been done in the summer time."

5. *New York World*, reprinted in *Richmond Enquirer*, May 4, 1870, in Freeman, *Lee*, 4:467.

6. Grant to Judge John F. Long, Jan. 28, 1877; John Y. Simon, ed., *The Papers of Ulysses S. Grant* (Carbondale, IL, 1967–), 28:xi–xvi; Smith, *Grant*, 606–13. All but a few of the Grant papers cited below (the ones dating to the end of his life) are published in the volumes edited by Simon.

7. Grant to George W. Childs, June 6, 1877; *Times* (London), May 23, 1877; Grant, "Speech," Manchester, May 30, 1877; Simon, ed., *Papers of Grant*, 28:208.

8. Grant to Ulysses Grant, Jr., Jan. 7, 1878; Grant to Abel Corbin, Jan. 13, 1878; Grant to Frederick Grant, Jan. 25, 1878.

9. Grant to Daniel Ammen, Mar. 25, 1878.

10. Grant to William T. Sherman, July 7, 1878; Grant to Ulysses Grant, Jr., Aug. 4, 1878; Grant to Hamilton Fish, Aug. 22, 1878; Grant to Frederick Grant, Aug. 22, 1878; Grant to Ulysses Grant, Jr., Sept. 14, 1878.

11. Grant to Nellie Sartoris, Aug. 10, 1879, Grant Papers, Carbondale, IL; Grant to Adam Badeau, July 16, 1879; both cited in Jean Edward Smith, *Grant* (New York, 2001), 612.

12. Grant to Adam Badeau, Aug. 1 and 25, 1879; both cited in Smith, *Grant*, 612–13.

13. *Ibid.*, 614.

14. "Wall Street Startled," May 7, 1884; "Ward's Transactions," May 19, 1884, both *New York Times*; Smith, *Grant*, 614–18. Mrs. Grant sold the New York brownstone in 1893 and thereafter lived in Washington; in 1926 the property was demolished and replaced by a twelve-story apartment house.

15. Allen W. Moger, "General Lee's Unwritten 'History of the Army of Northern Virginia,'" *Virginia Magazine of History and Biography* 71 (July 1963), 341–42.

16. J. William Jones, *Personal Reminiscences, Anecdotes and Letters of Robert E. Lee* (Richmond, VA, 1989 reprint of 1875 ed.), 180; Avery Craven, ed., *"To Markie": The Letters of Robert E. Lee to Martha Custis Williams* (Cambridge, MA, 1933), 66; both cited in Moger, "Lee's History," 342–43.

17. Moger, "Lee's History," 343.

18. *Ibid.*, 344–48.

19. *Ibid.*, 344–48.

20. *Ibid.*, 349, 356.

21. "Memoranda of Conversations with General Robert E. Lee," in Gary W. Gallagher, ed., *Lee the Soldier* (Lincoln, NE, and London, 1996), 30, 15–16. The material in the Lee trunk is privately owned.

22. Smith, *Grant*, 624–28. See Mark Perry, *Grant and Twain: The Story of an American Friendship* (New York, 2004).

23. Smith, *Grant*, 624–28.

24. J. William Jones, *Lee*, 446–52; Freeman, *Lee*, 4:491; Thomas, *Lee*, 411–13; Mildred Lee, "My Recollections of My Father's Death," Aug. 21, 1888, Virginia Historical Society.

25. Markie Williams to Agnes Lee, Oct. 15, 1870, Virginia Historical Society.

26. John Y. Simon, ed., *The Personal Memoirs of Julia Dent Grant* (Carbondale, IL, 1975), 329–31.

27. "Death of Robert E. Lee," *Richmond Dispatch*, Oct. 13, 1870; "Gen. Robert E. Lee," *New York Times*, Oct. 13, 1870.

28. "A Hero Finds Rest: Gen. Grant's Peaceful, Painless Death," *New York Times*, July 24, 1885; "A Nation Mourns: Death of Ulysses S. Grant," *Richmond Dispatch*, July 24, 1885.

CONCLUSION

1. John Warwick Daniel, *Robert Edward Lee, An Oration Pronounced at the Unveiling of the Recumbent Figure at Lexington, Virginia, June 28th, 1883* (Savannah, GA, 1883), 7.

2. Adrian Hitt, *The Grant Poem (*New York, 1886), 11.

3. Lee to Beauregard, Oct. 8, 1865, in J. William Jones, *Personal Reminiscences, Anecdotes and Letters of Robert E. Lee* (Richmond, VA, 1989 reprint of 1875 ed.), 207–8

4. The *Richmond Whig* made the comparison between Lee and Washington in July 1862. Peter Alexander compared Lee to Washington in the *Southern Literary Messenger*, Jan. 1863. The *Illustrated London News* made the comparison in a front-page article on June 4, 1864. The article in the *Richmond Dispatch* appeared on Feb. 7, 1865. See Richard B. McCaslin, *Lee in the Shadow of Washington* (Baton Rouge, LA, 2001), 85, 106, 162, 181, 186, 202, 210; Herman Melville, "Lee in the Capitol," 64–73, 200, 211.

5. Emory Thomas, "The Malleable Man," in Peter Wallenstein and Bertram Wyatt-Brown, eds., *Virginia's Civil War* (Charlottesville, VA, 2005), 9–18.

6. *Montgomery Advertiser* [Alabama], July 25, 1885.

7. Ulysses S. Grant, *Personal Memoirs of U. S. Grant* (New York, 1885), 1:170; Bruce Catton, *The Coming Fury* (New York, 1961), cited in Nelson Peabody Rose, *Robert E. Lee of Virginia: The Anguish of Conflicting Loyalties* (Cleveland, 1985), 72. Douglass had said that "To Grant more than any other man the Negro owes his enfranchisement," and in 1872 that "We will not find a candidate equal to General Grant" and "the Republican party is the ship and all else is the sea."

8. Douglas Southall Freeman, *Robert E. Lee* (New York, 1934), 4:412; Marcus Aurelius, *Meditations* 4.15; Elizabeth Gray Valentine, *Dawn to Twilight: The Work of Edward V. Valentine* (Richmond, VA, 1929), 108–9.

Index

Page numbers in *italics* indicate illustrations

A

Ackerman, Amos T., 268
Acton, Lord, 247
Adams, Charles Francis, Jr., 25, *25*, 200
Adams, Henry, 42, 154
Adams, John, 25, 78, 79
Adams, John Quincy, 25
African Americans, 16, 22, 29, 31, 42, 54, 70, 72, 160-7, 219, *219*, 243, 245-7, 256, 268, 270, 272, 274, 281-2, 327
Alabama, 198, 247, 270, 323
Alabama (ship), 280, 282-3, 306
Alexander, Edward Porter, 179, 206, 222-3
Alexander II, Tsar, 307
Alexander, P. W., 201
Alexandria, Virginia, 60, 69, 85-86, 87, 89, 92, 191, 313; Academy, 88; Christ Church, 150
Alexandria Gazette, 63
Allan, William, 59, 191, 193, 202, 205, 229, 313, 315
Amelia Court House, Virginia, 220
American Colonization Society, 92, 160
American Missionary Association, 251
American Revolution, 220
Ammen, Daniel, 307
Amnesty Oath, 235
Ampudia, Pedro de, 126
Anderson, Charles, 57
Anderson, Richard, 213
Andersonville Prison, Georgia, 252
Annapolis, Naval Academy, 84; St. John's College, 90
Anthony, E. T. & Co. *Grand Review of Returning Soldiers at Washington*, 236, *236*
Anthony, E. & H. T., & Co., *Lieutenant General Grant, Wife and Son, at his Headquarters, City Point, Va.*, 220
Anthony, Edward, *Zachary Taylor* (after Mathew Brady), 124
Antietam (Sharpsburg), battle of, *192*, 193, 313
Antrobus, John, *General Grant on the Battlefield*, *33*, 34
Apaches, 277
Appomattox, 13, 16, 18, 25, 34, 38, 39, 52, 116, 139, 201, 207, 220, 222-27, *222*, *223*, *226*, 233, 236, 237, 240, 246, 251, 257, 301, 311
Appomattox River, 219
Arapahoe, 277
Arista, Mariano, 124
Arkansas, 268, 270, 272
Arlington, Virginia, 143; Robert E. Lee Memorial, 26
Arlington House, Virginia (later Arlington Cemetery), 26, 57, 88-92, *88*, 95, 97, 101, 143, 145, 159-67, 170, 173, 175, 257, 262, 263, 329, *329*
Army of the Cumberland, 199, 200
Army of Northern Virginia, 190-230
Army of the Ohio, 183, 187, 199
Army of the Potomac, 206, 207, 209, 212-15, 230
Army of the Tennessee, 183, 199

Arnold, Benedict, 114
Arthur, Chester A., 36
Ashby, Turner, 315
Asheville, North Carolina, 24
Astor, Lady, 26
Atlanta, Georgia, 188, 218
Augusta, Georgia, 304
Austria, 297
Averell, William Woods, 60-61

B

Babcock, Orville, 281, 290-94, *291*
Babcock, Samuel, 95
Bacon, Nathaniel, 78
Badeau, Adam, 233, 307-9
Bailey, Bartlett, 113
Baker, Joseph Edward, *Ulysses S. Grant*, *32*, 34
Baker, W. H., *Grant and Family at Mount MacGregor*, 314
Baldwin, John B., 58
Balling, Ole Peter Hansen, *Grant and His Generals*, 34, *35*
Baltimore, Maryland, 17, 86, 143, 144-45, 150, 159, 233
Banks, Nathaniel P., 189, 191, 199, 209
Barbour, A. M., 171
Barnard, George N., *General George H. Thomas*, 67
Bates, Edward, 70
Baton Rouge, Louisiana, 195
Battery Hudson, 105
Battery Morton, 105
"Battle of the Crater", 217
Baxter, Elisha, 272
Beals, Jessie Tarbox, *Mark Twain* (Samuel Clemens), *316*
Beaumont, Tasy, 146
Beaumont, William, 146
Beauregard, P. G. T., 58, 129, 130, 131, 133, 135, 177, 187, 188, 205, 214, 217, 240, *253*, 254, 325
Beecher, Henry Ward, 238, 251-2
Belgium, 306
Belknap, Carrie, 293-94
Belknap, William W., 293, 293-94
"Belknap and the President", 293
Belmont, Kentucky, 182-83
Benét, Stephen Vincent, 26-8, 32; *John Brown's Body*, 44
Benjamin, Judah P., 178
Berkeley, William, 78
Berks County, Pennsylvania, 110
Berlin, 279, 307
Bethel, Ohio, 115, 116
Bey, Blacque, *253*
Big Sewell Mountain, Virginia, 178, *178*
Bingham, Austin, 165
Birch, T., *South East View of Sackett's Harbour* (after William Strickland), 155
Bismarck, Otto von, 228, 279, 307
Black Friday, 285-86, 287, 288
Black Hawk War, 151
Black Hills, 277-78, *278*

Black Kettle, 274
Blackford, Charles Minor, 211
Blain, Lucy, 265
Blaine, James G., 65, 268
Blair, Francis P., Jr., 74, 253
Blair, Francis P., Sr., 58-60, 69, 74
Blair, Montgomery, 59
Bland, Theodorick, 80
Bloody Angle, 213-14
Bloody Island, 102-3
Blow, Henry T., 245, 246
Blue Ridge Mountains, 189
Bogardus, Abraham, *Gen. U. S. Grant*, 305
Boggs, Harry, 169
Bolling, Mary Tabb, 264
Bombardment of Fort Sumter!!, 58
Bonner, Robert, 296, 297
Book of Common Prayer, 257, 258
Booth, John Wilkes, 234
Borie, Adolph, 268
Boston, 155
Boston Traveller, 164
Botts, John Minor, 58, 244
Boude and Miley (attrib.), *Notables at White Sulphur Springs, West Virginia*, 253, *254*
Boutwell, George, 282, 285-6, 287-8
Bowie, Jim, 123
Bowie Knife (John Brown's), 72, *172*
Boy Scouts of America, Robert E. Lee Council, 31
Boyd, James P., 36
Braddock, Edward, 325
Bradford, Gamaliel, *Lee the American*, 25
Brady, Mathew, *124*, 234; *Confederate Prisoners at Gettysburg*, 206; *The Dead at Cold Harbor*, 215; *George Washington Parke Custis*, 89; *Grant and His Staff at Lookout Mountain, Tennessee*, 199; *Grant and His War-Horse "Cincinnati"*, 220; *Orville Babcock*, 291; *Robert E. Lee*, 233; *William A. Richardson*, 290; *William W. Belknap*, 293
Brady & Co., *Grant at Headquarters, Cold Harbor, Virginia*, 13, *15*; *Grant and His Staff at Cold Harbor*, 217; *Ulysses Grant, Theodore Bowers, and John Rawlins, Cold Harbor*, 217
Bragg, Braxton, 188, 192, 198-9, 200, 207
Brandon, Virginia, 189
Brandy Station, Virginia, 203
Brazil, 283
Breckenridge, John C., 68
Breda, Netherlands, 78
Brent, Joseph L., *253*
Bridgeport, Connecticut, 199
Bristow, Benjamin H., 291
Britain, 279, 280, 282-83, 306
Brockenbrough, John W., 233, 243, 257
Brooke, John Mercer, 17
Brown, John, 109, 170-73, 244
Brown, Orlando, 244
Brown, Owen, 109, 110
Brown Brothers Studio, *Grant Residence*, 310

Brown County, Ohio, 111
Bruce, Edward Caledon, *Robert E. Lee*, 16-17, *17*
Bryant, William Cullen, 173
Buchanan, James, 54, 56, 68-69, 168, 170, 178
Buchanan, Robert Christie, 158
Buchser, Frank, *Robert E. Lee*, 256, *256*
Buckner, Simon Bolivar, 36, 115, 184, 320
Buell, Don Carlos, 183, 187, 188
Buena Vista, 129, 131
Bunker Hill, battle of, 108
Bunting, Josiah, 42, 196, 227, 273
Bunting, Josiah III, 47
Burnham, D. H., 40
Burnside, Ambrose, 194, 199, 200, 202, 313
Burr, Chauncey, 246
Butler, Benjamin, 209, 212-13, 288-89
Butterfield, Daniel, 285

C

Cabell, David S. G., 248
Cairo, Egypt, 307
Cairo, Illinois, 182, 198
Calhoun, John C., 93
California, 277
Cameron, James, *The Man of Words. The Man of Deeds*, 255
Cameron, Simon, 59, 62
Camp Cooper, Texas, 152
Camp Grant, Illinois, 72
Camp Yates, Illinois, 72
Canada, 154, 282
Carlin, Nathaniel, 301
Carroll, Charles, 144
Carrolltown, Maryland, 144
Carter, Ann Hill. *See* Lee, Ann Carter
Carter, Annette, 55
Carter, Charles, 83, 84, 190
Carter, Hill, 104
Carter, Juliet, 265
Carter, Thomas H., 246
Carter family, 305
Casey, James F., 286
Catlin, George, *Comanche Warriors, with White Flag*, 152; *Saint Louis*, 101; *View of West Point*, 93, *93*, 113
Catton, Bruce, 326; *Grant Moves South*, 46; *Grant Takes Command*, 46
Catumseh, 152
Cemetery Hill, Pennsylvania, 205, 206
Cemetery Ridge, Pennsylvania, 205, 206
Century Magazine, 311, 316
Cerro Gordo, battle of, 127, 129-32, 134, 139, 178
Chaffee, Fannie, 298
Chamberlain, Daniel H., 272, *272*
Chancellor House, Charlottesville, 202
Chancellorsville, Virginia, 17, 202, *202*, 230; Chancellor House, 202
Chapman, Elizabeth, 300
Chapultepec, battle of, 135-36, 139
Charles II, King, 78
Charleston Gazette, 238

LEE AND GRANT

Charleston, South Carolina, 57, 220, 305
Chattanooga, Tennessee, 186, 209, 254; battle of, 34, 39, 188, 199–200, 207
Chautauquan, 23
Cheat Mountain, Virginia, 178
Chesapeake and Ohio Canal County, 243
Chestnut, James, 201
Chestnut, Mary, 62, 84, 201, 207
Chetlain, Augustus Louis, 73
Cheyenne, 274, 277
Cheyenne War, 274
Chicago, 111, 173, 238, 291; Lincoln Park, 39
Chickahominy River, 189–90, 215–16
Chickamauga Creek, Georgia, 199
Childe, Edward, 53, 85
Childe, Edward Lee, 151, 247
Childe, Mildred *see* Lee, Mildred (later Childe)
Chilicothe, Ohio, 112
Chilton, Mrs R. H., 249
Chilton, R. H., 18
China, 307, 309
Churchill, Winston, 29, 45
Churubusco, battle of, 133, 135–36, 139
Cincinnati, 116, 291
Cincinnati (Grant's horse), 40, *41*, 220
City Point, Virginia, 24, 209, 213, 218–19, 300
Civil War, 140–1, 160, 177–231, 274, 280, 296, 300, 313, 326
Clay, Henry, 110
Clemens, Samuel (Mark Twain), 38, 303, 316, *316*, 317, 320; *Huckleberry Finn*, 316
Clermont County, Ohio, 110
Cleveland, Grover, 36
Cocke, Elizabeth Randolph, 243
Cockspur Island, Georgia, 95–96, 116, 119
Cogswell, William, *Ulysses Simpson Grant and Family*, 294
Cold Harbor, Virginia, 214–16
Colfax, Schuyler, 287
Colfax, Louisiana, Massacre, 270
Colorado, 140
Columbia Law School, 298, 300
Columbus, Kentucky, 180, 182–83
Comanches, 152, 175, 277
Concord, battle of, 108
Confederate Bureau of Naval Ordnance and Hydrography, 17
Confederate Congress, 218
Confederate Navy, 84
The Congressional Globe, 58
Connecticut State Library, 108
Connelly, Thomas, *The Marble Man*, 29–31
Conner, James, 253
Conolly, Thomas, 230
Conrow, Wilford S., *Ulysses S. Grant*, 44, 45
Constable, Anne, 78
Constantinople, 307
Continental Congress, 79, 82
Contreras, battle of, 133–34, 139
Cook, Thomas M., 234–35
Cooke, George S., *Jubal Anderson Early*, *19*
Cooke, John Esten, 18, 21, 23, 203
Cooper, James Fenimore, 114
Cooper Institute, 252
Corbin, Abel Rathbone, 111, 285, 307
Corcoran, W. W., 253
Corinth, Mississippi, 186, 187, 188
Corley, J. L., 304
Cornell University, 300, 306
Corpus Christi, Texas, 124
Corse, M. D., 303
Cosby, George B., 57
Courier (Boston), 53
Coventry, Connecticut, 108

Covington, Kentucky, 74, 169
Cramer, Michael John, 111
Crawford, Thomas, *George Washington*, 17–18, 21, 22
Crazy Horse, 278
Crédit Mobilier, 286–87
The Credit Mobilier. Testimony of Mr. Colfax, 288
Crimean War, 282
Crockett, Davy, 123
Cromwell, Oliver, 78
Cross Keys, Virginia, 189
Cuba, 280–81
Culpeper Courthouse, 191
Culpeper, Virginia, 203
Culp's Hill, Pennsylvania, 205, 206
Cumberland Island, Georgia, 60, 179, 304–5
Cumberland River, 183
Currier and Ives, *The "Boy of the Period" (Jim Fisk) Stirring Up the Animals*, 285
Currier, Nathaniel, *Major Genl. Z. Taylor Before Monterey*, 126
Custer, George Armstrong, 34, 274, *275*, 278
"Custer's Last Stand", 278
Custis, George Washington Parke ("Washy"), 56, 88–90, 88–92, *89*, 97, 98, 127, 139, 150, 159–60, 162, 163, 164, 229, 264; *The Indian Prophecy*, 90; *Pocahontas*, 90; *Recollections and Private Memoirs of Washington*, 90
Custis, Mary Anna (Anne) Randolph. *See* Lee, Mary Anne Randolph Custis
Custis, Mary Lee Fitzhugh (Molly), 88–9, 92, 98, 103, 129, 146, 150, *151*, 161
Custis family, 50, 52, 189, 190

D
Dabney, Robert Lewis, *Life and Campaigns of Lieut. Gen. Thomas J. Jackson*, 313, 316
Dakota Territory, 286
Dan (Grant slave), 167
Dana, Charles, 196
Daniel, John Warwick, 19, 20–21, 23–24, 325
Danville, Virginia, 220
Darby, John Fletcher, 100
Davis, Jefferson, 13, 58, 68, 147, 148, 151, 159, 177, 179, 188, 189, 192, 197, 200, 203, 204, 205, 206, 207, 216, 235, 238, 245
Davis, Theodore Russell, *The Rams "Switzerland" and "Lancaster" Running the Blockade at Vicksburg*, 197; *The Indian Campaign - Prisoners Captured by General Custer*, 275
Deane, Silas, 79
Deerfield, Ohio, 108–9
Delafield, Richard, 95
Delano, Columbus, 278, 293
Delaware, 69
Deming, Henry C., 35
Denby, Edwin, 43
Denmark, 307
Dent, Ellen (née Ellen Bray Wrenshall), 117, 118, 168
Dent, Colonel Frederick, 50, 69–70, 72, 117, *119*, 168, 169
Dent, Frederick Tracy, 115, 116–17, 299
Dent, George, 117–18
Dent, John, 72
Dent, Lewis, 168
Dent, Nellie, 117
Dent, Susanna (née Marbury), 118
Derwent, Cumberland County, 243, *243*
Des Moines Rapids, 101–3
Detroit, Michigan, 143, 155, *155*
Dexter (horse), 296
Dismal Swamp Company, 82

Disraeli, Benjamin, 282, 307
Dorchester, England, 107
Douglas, Stephen, 53, 68
Douglass, Frederick, 210, 268, 270, 274, 282, 327
Dowdey, Clifford, 47
Downing, A. J., 40
Drexel, Joseph, 316
Drexel, Morgan & Co., 316
Du Bois, W. E. B., 16, 22
Dudley, Thomas, 193
Duncan, John, *Grant's Tomb*, 38–39, *38*
Duncan's Island, 102–3
Dungeness, 305

E
Eakins, Thomas, 13; *Sketch of Lee and Grant at Appomattox*, 13, *14*
Early, Jubal Anderson, 19, *19*, 20, 21, 25, 203, 213, 217, 241
East Orange, New Jersey, 111
Education in the South, 252, *252*
Edward (Lee slave), 164, 165
Eggleston, George Cary, 23
Eisenhower, Dwight David, 29
El-Amin, Saad, 31
Elder, John A., *Farewell at Appomattox*, 226
Eleanor (Lee slave), 161
Eliza (Grant slave), 167
Eliza (Lee slave), 161
Elk Run Valley, 314
Elrod, William, 301
Emerson, Ralph Waldo, 173
Erie Railroad, 243
Evans, John, 293
Evans, Clement A., 325
Everett, Edward, 55
Ewell, Richard, 118, 203, 204–6, 213, 223, 262

F
Fairfax family, 78, 82
Fall, Albert, 43
Farmington, Connecticut, Miss Porter's School, 299
Farmville, Virginia, 222, 223
Fauquier County, Virginia, 94
The Federalist, 94
Fellman, Michael, *The Making of Robert E. Lee*, 31–32
Fénelon, François de, *Télémaque*, 110
Fenton, R. E., 251
Ferris, Jean Leon Gerome, *Let Us Have Peace*, 26, *27*
Fillmore, Millard, 254
Finland, 307
First Manassas, battle of (Bull Run), 177
Fischer, Ernest, 91
Fish, Hamilton, 268, 282, 288, 294, 307
Fisk, Jim, 285, 285–86
Fitzhugh, Anna Maria, 143, 148, 162
Fitzhugh, William Henry, 87, 88, 89, 92–93, 95
Fitzhugh family, 50, 190
Five Forks, Virginia, 220
Flat Rock, Kentucky, 112
Fleetwood, Anthony, *View of the City of Detroit* (after Caleb Davis), 155
Florida, 273, 286
Floyd, John B., 178, 184
Foote, Andrew, 183
Ford, Gerald R., 31, 238
Foreign Relations Committee, 282
Forrest, Nathan Bedford, 195, 268
Forsyth, John, 99
Fort Calhoun (later Fort Wool), Virginia, 97, 144

Fort Carroll, Maryland, 144
Fort Donelson, battle of, 34, 45, 179, 183, 184, 186, 187, 188, 200, 291, 320
Fort Hamilton, New York, 104–6, *105*
Fort Henry, Virginia, battle of, 34, 183, 186, 188, 196, 197
Fort Lafayette, New York City, 105
Fort Laramie, Wyoming, 151
Fort McHenry, Baltimore, Maryland, 143–4
Fort Mason, Texas, 57, 151
Fort Monroe, Virginia, 95–6, 97–9, 104–5, 171, 188, 203
Fort Pulaski, Georgia, 95–96
Fort Putnam, New York, 93, 114
Fort Sill, Oklahoma, 293
Fort Stedman, Virginia, 218, 220
Fort Sumter, South Carolina, 57, 58, 68–9, 270
Fort Vancouver, Washington, 156, 157, 158
Franco-Prussian War, 282
Franklin, Benjamin, 79
Frayser's Farm, 190
Fredericksburg, Virginia, 188, 202, 205, 211, 315
Fredricks, Charles DeForest, *Ely Parker*, 274
Freedmen's Bureau, 244, 247
Freeman, Douglas Southall, 301; *R. E. Lee*, 22, 25–26, 28–29, 46, 85, 129, 150, 163, 216
Frémont, John C., 180, 182, 189, 191, 313–14
French, Daniel Chester, 40
French, Daniel Chester, and Potter, Edward Clark, *General Ulysses S. Grant*, 39, *39*
Friedrich Wilhelm III, King of Prussia, 20
Fuller, John Frederick Charles, 44–45, 74–75, 190; *The Generalship of Ulysses S. Grant*, 44; *Grant & Lee, A Study in Personality and Generalship*, 44

G
Gaines's Mill, Virginia, 148, 190
Galena, Illinois, 69, 70, 143, 170, 173, 196, 201, 238, 310, 329
Galena, Illinois, 174
Galena river, 173
Gallagher, Gary, 179, 206, 210
Gardner, Alexander, *The Battle of Antietam*, 192; *General Benjamin H. Bristow*, 291; *Robert E. Lee*, 246, *303*; *Ulysses S. Grant*, 208; *Ulysses S. Grant and Staff*, 224
Garfield, James A., 310
Garland, Hamlin, 40–41, 73
Garnett, T. S., 63
Garrison, William Lloyd, 51, 252
Gary, Martin W., 253
"Gen. Lee's Application for Pardon", 237
"Gen. Robert E. Lee" (news of death), 322
General Grant and the Negro Sentinel, 219
General Lee - the Convention, 251
General Rooney Lee, 203
George Washington Custis Lee, Jeb Stuart, and Stephen Dill Lee, 145
Georgetown, Ohio, 109, 111–12, 113, 164
Georgia, 178–79, 198, 207, 208, 211, 222, 268, 303, 323
Gerhardt, Karl, "Grant's Memorial: What Shall It Be?", 38, 39
Germany, emperor of, 283
Gettysburg, battle of, 17, 18, 21, 200, 203–7, 213, 217
Gibson, James F., *Panorama of McClellan's Army at Camp*, 188
Gilman, John G., *Grant on the Porch at Mount MacGregor Four Days Before His Death*, 315
Gladstone, William, 282

348 INDEX

Going My Way, 45
Goldsmith, Oliver, *The Vicar of Wakefield*, 156
Goode, Simon S., 74
Gordon, Edward Clifford, 193
Gordon, John B., 213, 218, 262
Gordonsville, Virginia, 211
Gould, Jay, *284*, 285–6
Grand Army of the Republic (G.A.R.), 39, 40
Grand Junction, Tennessee, 195
Grant, Clara Rachel, 50, 111
Grant, Ellen (Nellie) (later Sartoris), 167, 169, 296, 298–300, *299*, 300, 306
Grant, Frederick, 46, 297, 307
Grant, Frederick Dent, 155, 157, 168, 188
Grant, Hannah Simpson, *109*, 110–11
Grant, Jesse Root, 49, 70–1, 72, 75, 108–12, *109*, 120–1, 159, 167, 168, 173, 180, 185, 286
Grant, Jesse Root, Jr., 169, 219, *220*, 296, *299*, 300, 306; *In the Days of My Father General Grant*, 300
Grant, Julia Dent, 117–20, *119*, 138, 140, 154, 155–6, *158*, 168, 173, 196, 219, *220*, 285–6, 294–6, *295*, *296*, *299*, 306, 307, 316, 320, 321; *The Personal Memoirs of Julia Dent Grant*, 47. *See also* Grant, Ulysses S., letters to Julia Dent Grant
Grant, Mary Frances, 71, 111, 168, 169, 180, 183, 188, 286
Grant, Mathew, 107–8
Grant, Mrs (earlier Rockwell), 107
Grant, Noah I, 108
Grant, Noah II, 108
Grant, Noah III, 108–9
Grant, Orvil Lynch, 69, 111, 173, 286, 294
The Grant Party at the Bonanza Mines, Virginia City, Nevada, *309*
Grant, Peter, 108–9
Grant, Priscilla, 107
Grant, Rachel (née Kelly), 108, 109
Grant, Samuel, and Samuel, Jr., 108
Grant, (Samuel) Simpson, 111, 173
Grant, Solomon (son of Noah Grant I), 108
Grant, Solomon (son of Noah Grant III), 108
Grant, Ulysses S., *14*, *15*, *27*, *32*, *33*, *35*, *37*, *39*, *40*, *41*, *43*, *44*, *49*, *180*, *208*, *214*, *220*, *233*, *295*, *297*, *305*, *314*, *315*; *Endorsement*, *292*; funeral, *36*; *Indians Bartering*, *116*; *Landscape*, *116*; memorandum on Santo Domingo, 282; *Note*, *320*; *The Papers of Ulysses S. Grant*, 42, 47; *The Personal Memoirs of U. S. Grant*, 36, 68, 75, 94, 110–39 *passim*, 157, 158, 167–9, 182, 183, 187, 188, 195–8, 200, 208, 215, 220, 224, 316–17, *317*, 320, 326, 328; Second Inaugural Address, 270, *271*; *Terms of Surrender*, 224, *225*; tomb, *38*, 320, *322*, 329
Grant, Ulysses S., letters, to Daniel Ammen, 307; to Adam Badeau, 307, 309; to Elisha Baxter, 272; to George Boutwell, 285–6; to Daniel H. Chamberlain, 272, *272*; to Frederick Dent, 69–70; to Hamilton Fish, 280, *280*, 282, 307; to Frederick Grant, 307; to Jesse Grant, 70, *71*, *73*, 225; to Julia Dent Grant, 71–2, 74, 119–20, 125, *125*, 129, 131, 136, *138*, 143, 155–8, *157*, 182, 183–4, 185, 186, 199, 214, 218, 219, 220, *221*, 227, *228*, 240–1, 247, 298; to Mary Grant, 169, 180, 188; to McKinstry Griffith, 114; to Henry Halleck, *212*, 213, 235; to Andrew Johnson, 240, 241, 250; to Robert E. Lee, 236, *236*; to Abraham Lincoln, 211; to John Long, 305–6; to George Meade, 209; to Robert Schenck, 299; to Philip H. Sheridan, 240; to William T. Sherman, 273, 307; to Edwin Stanton, 213, 240; to George H. Stuart, *276*; to Elihu B. Washburne, 228, *229*
Grant, Ulysses S. (Buck), Jr., 143, 155, 158, *158*, 294, 296, 298, 300, 301, 306, 310; letter to Simon Bolivar Buckner, *185*; *Ulysses S. Grant, Warrior and Statesman*, 46–7
Grant, Virginia Paine (Jennie), 111
Grant & Ward, 310–11
Grant family, 50–1
Grant House, Galena, *174*
Grant Monument Association, 38
Grant as a First Lieutenant in the Fourth Infantry at Sackets Harbor, *154*
"The Grants at Karnak, Egypt", *306*
Grant's Birthplace, Point Pleasant, Ohio, *110*
Gratiot, Charles, 100, 102
Greeley, Horace, 270
Green, Israel, *172*
Greene, Nathaniel, 81, 305
Griffith, McKinstry, 114
Guadalupe–Hidalgo, Treaty of, 140
Guild, Lafayette, 225
Gwin, Mr., 165

H

Hadfield, George, 89, *89*
Halikarnassos, tomb of Mausolus, 39
Hall, Henry Bryan, *Julia Dent Grant*, *119*
Halleck, Henry W., 34, 182, 183, 187, 188, 198, 201, 206, 209, 215, 217, 235
Hamburg, 279
Hamer, Thomas L., 112
Hamilton, Alexander, 82, 287
Hampton, Wade, 234
Hampton Roads, 97, 98
Hancock, Winfield Scott, 212
Hanover Courthouse, 165
Hanover Junction, Virginia, 214
Hanson, Alexander, 86
Harding, Warren, 13, 43
Hardscrabble, Missouri, 167–70, 173, 300
Harper's, 23, 159
Harpers Ferry, West Virginia, 109, 170–3, 177, 193, 194
Harper's Weekly, 197
Harris, Mr., 319
Harris, Nathaniel A., letter to Robert E. Lee, 238, *240*
Harrison, W. H., 325
Harrisonburg, Virginia, 315
Harrison's Landing, Virginia, 190
Harvard University, 154, 296, 298
Hatcher, William E., 234
Haxall, Charlotte, 265
Hayes, Rutherford B., 36, 271, 273, 309
Healy, G. P. A., *Peacemakers*, 220, *221*
Heavy Runner, 275
Hebert, Paul, 140
Hemingway, Ernest, 32; *For Whom the Bell Tolls*, 45
Henry, Edward Lamson, *City Point, Virginia, Headquarters of General Grant*, 219, *219*
Henry (Lee slave), 165
Hesseltine, William B., *Ulysses S. Grant: Politician*, 45
Hickory Hill, Virginia, 203
Hill, A. P., 190, 193, 203, 204–6, 213
Hill, D. H., 190
Hillsboro, Ohio, 120
Hine, Sarah, 222
Hitchcock, Roswell Dwight, 251–2
Hitchcock, Gilbert M., 42
Hitt, Adrian, 325
Hoar, Rockwood, 294
Hodges, Henry, 158
Holland, 307
Holly Springs, Mississippi, 195
Holmes, Theophilus H., 140
Homer, 50
Honoré, Ida M., 297
Hooker, Joseph, 133, 202, 207
Hoover, Joseph, and Mitton, N., *Grant & Bonner - Dexter's Best Time 2.16*, *297*
Houston, Sam, 123
Howard, Jacob T., 245, 246
Howard, O. O., 145
Howell, William T., Jim Fisk, *Colonel of the 7th Regiment of the New York Militia*, *285*
Hudson River, 103, 159
Hudson River Landscape, *160*
Huger, Benjamin, 190
Humboldt Bay, California, 157
Hunt, Henry J., 105
Hunter, Andrew, 218, 229
Hunter, David, 200

I

I fought for Virginia (poster), 30
Illinois, 69, 180
Illustrated London News, 325
The Independent, 251
Indian Council, 276
Indian Removal Act (1830), 274
"The Indians. Red Cloud at a Council with the President", *277*
Ingalls, Rufus, 158
Ingram, Barbara, 31
Ipsen, Ernest Ludwig, *Brevet Colonel Robert E. Lee, Superintendent USMA*, 26, *27*
Irving, Washington, 114
Isma'il Pasha, 307
Isthmus of Panama, 156, 167
Italy, 283, 306
Ives, Joseph C., 189

J

Jackson, Andrew, 270
Jackson, Thomas J. "Stonewall", 109–10, 115–16, 133, 136, 177, 189–91, 194, 202, 204, 214, 313–16
Jackson, Mississippi, 197, 297
Jacksonville, Florida, 305
Jacques & Brother, *Fort Hamilton Polka Redowa*, *105*
James River, 97, 189, 190, 209, 211, 214, 215, 216, 218–19, 223, 305
Janney, John, 63–65
Japan, 309
Japanese Embroidered Picture, *308*
Jefferson, Thomas, 79, 82, 84, 86, 105, 325
Jerusalem, 307
Jews, 196
Jo Daviess County, Illinois, 201
John (Grant slave), 167
Johnson, Andrew, 227, 235, 236–7, 241, 245, 246, 250, 263, 295, 297
Johnson, R. W., 57
Johnson, Reverdy, 59, 61, 62, 63
Johnson, William, *Sketches of the Life and Correspondence of Nathaniel Greene*, 88
Johnsonville, Tennessee, Camp of Tennessee Colored Battery, *230*
Johnston, Erastus C., 251
Johnston, Albert Sidney, 140, 151–52, 162, 183, 184, 186–87, 211
Johnston, Joseph E., 36, 94, 129, 136, 140, 177, 188–89, 197, 198, 207, 209, 220, 225–27, 304
Johnston, William Preston, 211, 229, 313, 317

Joint High Commission, 282–83
Jones, Frank Hatch, 300
Jones, George, 247
Jones, J. B., 230
Jones, J. William, *Personal Reminiscences, Anecdotes and Letters of General Robert E. Lee*, 19–20, 317
Jones, William, 167, 170
Juarez, Benito, 240
Julia (Grant slave), 167
Julia Grant, Nellie Grant, Col. Frederick Dent, Jesse Grant, *299*
Julia Grant with Sons Buck and Fred, *158*

K

Kanawha Valley, 178
Kayser, Henry, 146
Kearney, Stephen, 116, 140
Keiley, A. M., 238
Kellogg, William P., 270
Kelly, Thomas, *The Fifteenth Amendment*, *269*
Kemble, Adelaide and Fanny, 299
Kentucky, 69, 109, 180–83, 188
Keokuk, Iowa, 101
Key, Francis Scott, 144
Keyes, Erasmus, 57
Kinloch, 94
Kinnear, Duncan Lyle, *History of Virginia Polytechnic Institute*, 261
Kiowas, 175, 277
Knox, David, *The Mortar "Dictator" and its Gun Crew*, *217*
Knoxville, Tennessee, 200
Kosciuszko, Thadeusz, 114
Ku Klux Klan, 268, 282, 327
Ku Klux Klan Robe and Hood, *270*

L

Lacey, Captain, 251
Ladies' Lee Monument Association, 21
Ladies' Memorial Association, 304
Lafayette, Marquis de, 81, 88, 90
Lambdin, James Reid, *Ulysses Simpson Grant*, *267*
Lancaster (ram), 197, *197*
Lawton, Alexander R., *253*
Leary, William B., 88
Lee, Agnes, 56, 104, 106, *106*, 145, 150, 153, 160, 161, 257, 262, 263, 265, *267*, 303, 304, 305, 317, 318
Lee, Ann Carter, 82, 85–8, *85*, 92, 94, 95, 120, 146
Lee, Ann Kinloch. *See* Marshall, Ann
Lee, Annie, 103, 106, 145, 150, 153, 160, 175, 194, 303, 304
Lee, Arthur, 78, 79
Lee, Cassius, 65, 77, 191, 205
Lee, General Charles, 81
Lee, Charles Carter, 77, 84, 85, 86, 88, 93, 94, 139, 179, 313
Lee, Charlotte (née Wickham), 164, 189, 206, 207, 264
Lee, (George Washington Parke) Custis, 49, 53, 61, 98, 103, 106, 132, 143, 145, *145*, 150, 159, 163, 165, 167, 170, 173, 175, 194, 202, 216, 234, 258, 263–4, 265, 296, 319; letter to Robert E. Lee, 257, *258*
Lee, Fitzhugh, 21, 94, 150
Lee, Francis Lightfoot, 78, 79, 80
Lee, Henry ("Light-Horse Harry"), 36, 50, 60, 63, 64, 77, *77*, 78, 79–87, 90–3, 108, 120, 146, 160, 179, 248, 303, 305, 313, 327; *A Cursory Sketch of the Motives and Proceedings...*, 86; *Funeral Oration on the Death of George Washington*, 83,

83; *Memoirs of the War in the Southern Department of the United States*, 77, 79–80, 81, 86, 88, 94, 220
Lee, Henry IV ("Black-Horse Harry"), 77, 78, 83, 84, 85, 88, 98; *The Campaign of 1781 in the Carolinas*, 88
Lee, Launcelot, 78
Lee, Mary Anne Randolph Custis 18, 20, 21, 26, 50, 54, 159, 249, 60, 86, 88–89, 92, 94, 96–98, *97*, 99–100, 103–4, *107*, 143, 150, 153, 161, 163, 164, 190, 207, 234, 243, 262–3, 305, 319. *See also* Lee, Robert E., letters to Mary Custis Lee
Lee, Mary Anne Randolph Custis, *Enslaved Girl*, 91, *91*
Lee, Mary Custis, 22, 99, 103, 150, 194, 207, 243, 265, 313
Lee, Matilda, 81–82
Lee, Mildred Childe, 54, 104, 106, 143, 150, 217, 243, 257, 260, 262–3, 265, 266–7, *267*, 303, 317
Lee, Mildred (later Childe), 53, 84, 85, 96, 151, 153, 162
Lee, Richard I, 78, 107
Lee, Richard II, 78
Lee, Richard Bland, 83
Lee, Richard Henry, 64, 78–9, *78*, 80, 81
Lee, Robert E., *14*, *15*, *17*, *18*, *20*, *22*, *24*, *27*, *28*, *43*, *49*, *100*, *106*, *208*, *218*, *233*, *246*, *253*, *256*, *257*; chair, *62*; *Cockspur Island and Fort Pulaski*, *95*; dancing slippers, *98*; *Deed of Emancipation*, *231*; *General Orders No. 9*, *227*; *Last Will and Testament*, *126*, *127*; *Map of the Harbor of St. Louis*, *102*; *Mexican Soldiers Foraging*, *132*; *Section of a Dredging Machine*, *144*; *Speech Delivered before the Virginia Convention of 1861*, *64*; *To the People of Maryland* (broadside), *194*
Lee, Robert E., letters, to William Allan, 205; to Tasy Beaumont, 146; to P. G. T. Beauregard, 240, 325; to John Brockenbrough, 233, 257; to David S. G. Cabell, 248; to Annette Carter, 55; to Edward Lee Childe, 151; to M. D. Corse, 303; to G. W. P. Custis, 139; to Molly Custis, 103, 146; to Maury H. Dabney, 249–50, *250*; to Jefferson Davis, 203; to Richard Ewell, 262; to Anna Maria Fitzhugh, 143, 148, 162–3, 175; to John B. Gordon, 262; to Harpers Ferry insurgents, *172*; to Reverdy Johnson, 59, 61; to A. S. Johnston, 162; to Henry Kayser, 146; to Agnes Lee, 56, 256; to Annie Lee, 166, *175*; to Cassius Lee, 65, 77, 191, 205; to Charles Carter Lee, 179; to Charlotte Lee, 206; to Custis Lee, 132, 145, 163, 164, 165–7, 175, 202; to Mary Anne Randolph Custis Lee, 55, 96–7, *96*, 98, 103, 104, 106, 119, 123, 127, 130, *130*, 137, 144, 145–6, 150, 151, 153–4, 160, 175, 177, 179, 189, 195, 203, 217, 218, 260, 265, 304; to Mary Custis Lee (daughter), 194; to Mildred Lee, 153, 162, 303; to Rooney Lee, 55–6, *55*, 163, 164, *164*, 175, 250, 256–7, 265, 303; to John Letcher, 240; to A. L. Long, 243; to W. M. McDonald, 205; to Jack Mackay, 98; to David Macrae, 242; to Ann Marshall, 62, 63; to Matthew Fontaine Maury, 240; to E. S. Quirk, 165, *166*; to Winfield Scott, 61–2, *61*; to James A. Seddon, 229; to Belle Stewart, 217; to Eliza Mackay Stiles, 153, 265; to Andrew Talcott, 99; to Joseph Totten, 124, 147–8, 150; to Edward Turner, 163; to Cornelius Walker, 177; to William Wickham, 303; to Markie Williams, 146–7,

147, 151, 238–40, 303, 311; to Joseph P. B. Wilmer, 229; to W. O. Winston, 164; in *New York Times*, 66
Lee, Robert E., Jr. (Rob), 104, 106, *107*, 143, 144, 150, 153, 162, 163, 194, 203, 234, 257, 262, 263, 265, 305; *Recollections and Letters of General Robert E. Lee*, 24, 41
Lee, Robert E. III, 56, 265
Lee, Rooney (William Henry Fitzhugh), 49, 53–4, 55, 87, 93, 103, 104, 106, *106*, 150, 154, *154*, 159, 163, 164, 170, 175, 189, 190, 194, 203, *203*, 207, 250, 256, 262, 263, 264–5, *264*, 296, 303, 305
Lee, (Sidney) Smith, 60, 62, 70, 84, *85*, 88, 94, 99, 150, 201, 265
Lee, Stephen Dill, 145
Lee, Thomas, 78
Lee, William, 78, 79
Lee family, 190
Lee County, Virginia, 82
Lee Memorial Association, 19, 20
Lee Monument Association, 21–22
Lee Navy Volunteers, *30*, 31
Lee's Legion, 80–1, *80*
Leesylvania, 78, 88
Leet, George K., 286
Leo XIII, Pope, 306
"Let Us Have Peace" poster, *322*
"Let Us Have Peace." The Golden Anniversary, April Ninth, 1865-1915, *43*
Letcher, John, 60, 63, 66, 71, 238, 240
Lever, Charles, 114
Lewis, Lloyd, *Captain Sam Grant*, 45–46
Lexington Gazette and Banner, 261
Lexington, Virginia, 19, 21, 25, 182, 233, 251, 255, 303, 305, 317, 321; battle of, 108; Grace Episcopal Church, 19, 243, 259, 317; Virginia Military Institute, 17
Li Hung-chang, 307, 309
Lieutenants Ulysses S. Grant and Alexander Hays at Camp Salubrity, Louisiana, *120*
Lilley, Robert D., *253*
Lincoln, Abraham, 13, 19, 23, 32, 34, 36, 38, 40, 42, 51, 53, 57–60, 65, 68, 69, 70, 110, 123, 141, 177, 179, 183, 188, 198, 200, 201, 217, 219–20, 227, 229, 234, 237, 243, 256, 257; letter to Grant, 210–11, *210*
Lincoln, Mary Todd, 234
Litchfield, Lionel Lee, Earl of, 78
Little Big Horn, battle of, 34
Little Big Horn River, 278
Little Wound, 278
Logan, John A., 46
London, 279, 306
Long, A. L., 243
Long Branch, New Jersey, 296, 300–301
Longfellow, Henry Wadsworth, 173
Longstreet, James, 18, 19, 113, 115, 136, 169, 170, 179, 190, 191, 193, 199, 200, 203–6, 211–13, 214, 222, 268, 271
Lookout Mountain, Georgia, 199, *199*, 200
Loring, W. W., 178
Lorne, Marquess of, 247
Lossing, Benson J., 90; "Arlington House, The Seat of G. W. P. Custis Esq.", *158*
Louisa, Queen of Prussia, 20
Louisiana, 19, 118, 119, 123, 124, 268, 270–1, 273
Louisville, Kentucky, 112
Lowell, James Russell, *The Biglow Papers*, 123
Lynchburg, Virginia, 65, 209, 313
Lyon, Nathaniel, 74
Lyons, James, *253*
Lytton, Bulwer, 114

M
Mac-Mahon, Marshal, 307
MacArthur, Arthur, 200
MacArthur, Douglas, 200
McCall, George A., 140
McClellan, George B., 17, 34, 44, 73, 74, 115, 129, 130, 133, 135, 178, 179, 185, 188–90, 194, 207, 209, 216, 217, 313, 315
McCormick, Cyrus, 261
McDonald, John, 291
McDonald, W. M., 205
McDowell, Irvin, 188, 189, 191, 315
McFeely, William S., 47, 108, 156
Mackay, Eliza, 98
Mackay, Jack, 95–96, *97*, 98, 104, 116
Mackay family, 304
Mackenzie, Ross, 31
McKinley, William, 39
McLean, Wilmer, 223
Macomb, Alexander, 99
Macrae, David, 242
Madison, James, 79, 81, 86, 325
Magruder, John B., 190, *253*
Mahan, Dennis Hart, 151
Major and Knapp, *The Room in the McLean House, at Appomattox C. H.*, *223*
Malvern Hill, 190
Manassas Junction, Virginia, 177, 191, 205, 223
Manchester, England, 306
Manet, Edouard, *Execution of the Emperor Maximilian*, 240, 242
Mansfield, Joseph, 95, 140
Marbury Hall, Cheshire, 118
Marcus Aurelius, *Meditations*, 51, 86, 327, *327*
"Marias Massacre", 275
Marryat, Frederick, 114
Marsh, Caleb, 293
Marshall, Ann (Ann Kinloch Lee), 70, 84, 84–5, 94, 144
Marshall, Charles, 19, 202, 223, 225, 313
Marshall, Hattie Mann, *Lee Family of Virginia and Maryland*, *77*
Marshall, John, 202
Marshall, William, 84, 94, 139, 144
Martha Custis ("Markie") Williams, *146*
Maryland, 69, 171, 189, 192, 193, 194, 203, 205, 230, 313
Mason, Charles, 94
Mason, Emily V., 87
Mason, George, 81
"Massacre of our Troops", *279*
Mattoon, Illinois, 72, 74
Maury, Dabney H., 249–50, *250*
Maury, Matthew Fontaine, 240
Maximilian, Emperor, 240
May, James, 246
Maysville, Kentucky, Richeon and Rand Academy, 112
Meade, George Gordon, 129, 204, 206, 207, 208, 209, 212, 214, *214*, 220
Meade, Bishop William, 92, 150
Meadow Bluff, Virginia, 178
Mechanicsville, Virginia, 148, 190
Medary, Mary, 111
Meigs, Montgomery, 101–2
Meiji, Emperor, 309
Melville, Herman, 173; "Lee in the Capitol", 326
Memphis, Tennessee, 180, 186, 195, 198, 249
Mercié, Jean-Antonin, *Lee Monument*, 22–23, *22*
Meriday, Philip, 160
Mexican War, 105, 123–41, 147, 148, 161, 179, 180, 184, 198, 223

Mexicans, 175
Mexico, 104, 119, 120, 154, 178, 240, 270, 310; Gulf of, 195
Mexico City, 129, 132, 135, 136, 138–9, 189
Mexico, Missouri, 180
Midland International Arbitration Union, Birmingham, 279
Miley, Michael, 20; *Agnes Lee*, *266*; *Agnes Lee (?) 1841–1873* (copied), *106*; *Mary Lee*, *265*; *Mildred Childe Lee*, *266*; *Robert E. Lee*, *256*, *318*; *Robert E. Lee, Jr.* (copied), *107*; *Robert E. Lee and Rooney Lee (1837–1891)* (copied), *106*; *Robert E. Lee on Traveller*, *262*, *263*
Miller Studio, *Black Hills Exploration*, *278*
Milwaukee, 291
Minnis and Cowell, *Robert E. Lee*, *208*
Missionary Ridge, Chattanooga, Tennessee, 199
Mississippi, 186, 198, 247, 249, 270, 272
Mississippi River, 100–103, 143, 180, 183, 186, 195, 199, 209, 274
Missouri, 69, 69–70, 71, 143, 167, 180
Mobile, Alabama, 198, 209
Modoc, 277
Molino del Rey, battle of, 135, 136, 139
Monroe, James, 64, 325
Monroe Doctrine, 240
Montana, 275, 278
Monterey, Mexico, siege of, 125–26, *126*, 129, 146
Montreal, 155
More Glorious News. A Great Battle Fought at Pittsburgh Landing, Tenn. Victory of the Union Forces, *186*
Morgan, John T., 255
Morgan, J. Pierpont, 310
Morris, Robert, 82
Mosby, John S., 304
Mount MacGregor,, *314*, *315*, 316
Mount Vernon, Virginia, 90, 161, 163, 300
Mrs. George Washington Parke Custis (Mary Lee Fitzhugh), *151*
Mrs. Robert E. Lee and Robert E. Lee, Jr., *107*
Mule Shoe, 213
Muscle Shoals, Alabama, 183
Mussolini, Benito, 45

N
Nantes, 79
Napoleon III, Emperor, 240
The Narrows, 104–6
Nashville, Tennessee, 180, 183, 186, 187
Nast, Thomas, 238, 288; *Andrew Johnson's Reconstruction and How it Works*, 247, *248*; *A General Blow Up - Dead Asses Kicking a Live Lion*, *289*; "Go On! - U. S. Grant", 272, *272*; "The Hero of our Age - Dead", *328*; *If He is a Union Man or a Freedman...*, 249, *249*; *International Law - The Better Way*, *283*; *It is Only a Truce to Regain Power*, 270, *271*; "News" in Washington", *278*; *No Surrender*, *287*; *The Spanish Bull in Cuba Gone Mad*, *281*; "This Tub Has No Bottom To Stand On", *284*; *Tilden or Blood*, *273*; "With Malice towards None, with Charity to All", *239*
Nat (coachman), 96
National Anti-Slavery Standard, 164
National Archives, 108
National Museum of American History, 296
Native Americans, 152, 156–7, 160, 229–30, 267, 268, 274–9, 293, 298, 307, 327
Nebel, Carl, *Battle at Churubusco*, *133*; *Battle of Cerro Gordo*, *131*; *General Scott's*

Entrance into Mexico [City], 136, *137*; *Storming of Chapultepec - Pillow's Attack*, *134*
Nelson County, Virginia, 165
Nelson, Francis, 159–60
Nevada, 309, *309*
New Jersey, 234
New Mexico, 268, 291
New Orleans, Louisiana, 143, 195, 249, 268, 271
New York City, 18, 104, 113, 155, 238, 251, 261, 280, 288, 310, 320, *321*; Brooklyn, 106; Cooper Institute, 276; St. John's, Brooklyn, 150; Union Club, Brooklyn, 39; Verrazano Narrows Bridge, 104
New York (state), 286
New York Daily Tribune, 164, 165
New York Herald, 234, 252, 261, 306, 309
New York Independent, 252, *252*
The New York Times, 22, 27, 28, 42, 43, *43*, 65–66, 66, 164, 235, 237, 247, 250, *251*, 257, 261, 283, 286, 287, 289, 294, 310, 321, 322, 322–23
New York Tribune, 233, 251, 270
New York Union Theological Seminary, 251
New York World, 305
Newcomb, Warren, 261
Newport, Rhode Island, 144
Niagara Falls, 150, 155
Niehaus, Charles, 21–22
Nightingale, William, 304–5
Nile, river, 307
Noble, Thomas Satterwhite, *John Brown's Blessing*, 172–73, *173*
Nolan, Alan T., *Lee Considered: General Robert E. Lee and Civil War History*, 31
Norfolk, Virginia, 97, 305
Norris, Mary, 164–65
Norris, Wesley, 164–65
North Africa, 45
North American Review, 38, 39
North Anna River, 214
North Atlantic, 282
North Carolina, 245, 268, 303
North River, 251
Northern Neck Proprietary, 78
Norway, 307

O
Oakland, Powhatan County, Virginia, 243
Obadiah (Lee slave), 165
Officers of the 47th Illinois at Oxford, Mississippi, *196*
Oglala Sioux, 276
Ohio, 109, 154, 298
Ohio River, 101, 143
Old Point Comfort, Virginia, 97, 104
An Ordinance to Repeal the Ratification of the Constitution..., 60
Ordnance of Secession, 54
Original Washington College Building, *244*
O'Sullivan, Timothy H., *A Council of War at Massaponax Church*, *214*; *Fugitive Slaves Crossing the Rappahannock River in Virginia*, *229*
Ould, Robert, 234, 248
Our American Cousin (Taylor), 234

P
Pach Brothers, *The Catafalque, with Gen'l Grant's Remains, Leaving City Hall New York*, *321*; *Colonel Frederick Dent*, *119*; *Frederick Grant, Major General, U.S.A.*, *298*; *Gen. Grant and Family at Long Branch, New Jersey*, *295*

Padierna, 133, 135, 139
Paducah, Kentucky, 182, 193
Page, Thomas Nelson, 23
Paine, Robert Treat, 79
Palmer, Fanny & Seymour, *Battle of Palo Alto*, *124*
Palo Alto, battle of, 124–25, *124*, 139
Paris, 306–7
Parker, Ely S., 268, 274, *274*, 277
Parks, George, 164–65
Partridge, William Ordway, 39
Pascagoula, Mississippi, 154
Paulus Hook garrison, 81
Peabody, George, *253*, 261
Peale, Charles Willson, *"Light-Horse Harry" Lee*, *77*; *Richard Henry Lee*, *78*; *Washington as Colonel of the Virginia Regiment*, 90, 91, *91*, 97
Pemberton, John C., 136, 197, 198
Pendleton, William Nelson, 19, 243, 319
Pendleton, Alexander Swift "Sandie", 179
"Peninsula Campaign", 189
Pennsylvania, 110, 203, 206, 207, 211, 230
Pennsylvania campaign, 17, 18, 312
Perry, Matthew, 84
Pershing, John J., 45
Petersburg, Virginia, 209, 210, 213, 215–20, 222, 313
Philadelphia, 13, 39, 113, 219, 238, 268, 286, 296, 300; Fairmont Park Art Association, 39; Girard College, 113
Philadelphia Exposition, 278
Philippines, 297
Philippoteaux, Paul, *General Grant at Fort Donelson*, 184, *184*; *Study for the Lee Cyclorama at Gettysburg*, *204*, 207
Phillips Exeter Academy, 298
Pickens, Francis W., 178
Pickett, George, 18, 136, 205, 206, 217; crucifix, 136, *136*
Pierce, Franklin, 132, 136, 148, 161
Pierrepont, Edwards, 291
Piegan Blackfoot, 275
Pillow, Gideon, 134, 135, 136, 139, 184, 202
Pine, Theodore, 26; *Robert E. Lee*, 24–25, *24*, 25
Pittsburg Landing, Tennessee, *186*, 187
Plain Truth: Addressed to the People of Virginia, 83
Plains Indians, 151, 307
Plains Indians Moccasins, *277*
Point Pleasant, Ohio, 110, *110*
Polk, James A., 123, 124, 125, 137, 139
Pollard, Edward A., *The First Year of the War*, 178, 189, 234; *The Lost Cause: A New Southern History of the War of the Confederates*, 242, 325
Poor, Miss, 145–46
Pope, John, 180, 191
Popocatapetl, 154
Port Republic, 189, 313
Port Royal, South Carolina, 211
Porter, Horace, 285
Porter, David D., 197, 219
Porter, Fitz John, 148, 190
Porter, Horace, 199
Portsmouth, Virginia, 305
Portugal, 307
Potomac River, 81, 82, 89, 193, 203
Potter, R. M., 57
Poughkeepsie, New York, Eastman Business College, 252
Prang, J., & Co., 38
Presentation Sword Awarded to Ulysses S. Grant by citizens of Kentucky, *182*

"The President and the Sanborn Business", 290
Preston, Margaret, 260, 265
Princeton, College of New Jersey, 80, 89–90
Protestant Episcopal Church of Virginia, 259

Q
Quirk, E. S., 165
Quitman, John, 136

R
Raccoon Mountain, Chattanooga, 199
Raleigh, North Carolina, 241
Randolph, Elizabeth Carter, 88
Randolph, Sarah Nicolas, 22
Rapidan River, 191, 207, 211
Rappahannock River, 191, 207, *229*
Rauch, Christian Daniel, 20
Ravenna, Ohio, 110
Ravensworth, Virginia, 88, 95, 265
Rawlins, John, 69, 196, 280, 293
Rebisso, Louis, 39
Record of Demerits, West Point, 115
Red Cloud, 276–77, *277*
Red Cloud, Chief of the Oglala Sioux, *277*
Red River, 209
Reid, Brian Holden, 32
Reid, William B., 312
Reily, James, 312
Resaca de la Palma, 125
Reuben (Lee slave), 163, 164
Rhine Valley, 307
Richardson, Albert D., 34–35
Richardson, C. B., 311–13
Richardson, William, 288–91, 290
Richmond, Virginia, 17, 21, 63, 65, 163, 165, 177, 188–91, 195, 202, 204, 207, 209, 211, 214–18, 223, 230, 234, 240, 247, 304, 305, 313, 315; Capitol, 21, 63, 69; Hollywood Cemetery, 21; Libby Prison, 252; Monument Avenue, 31; St. Paul's Church, 246
Richmond Dispatch, 250, *251*, 321, 323, 325
Richmond Examiner, 178
Richmond Planet, 22
Richmond Times-Dispatch, 31
Richmond Whig, 237, 325
Ripley, Ohio, 112
Ripon, George Fredrick Samuel Robinson, Earl of, 283
Ritchie, A. H., *Lieutenant Grant, Age 21*, 116
River Queen, 219
Robert E. Lee on Traveller, Petersburg, *218*
Robertson, John, 63
Robeson, George M., 294
Rock River Rapids, 101–3
Rockbridge County, Virginia, 251, 261, 265; Bible Society, 257
Rockwood, George C., *Winfield Scott*, *127*
Rocky Mountains, 297
Roesler, J. Nep, *Thunder-Storm (Big Sewell Mountain)*, *178*
Rogers, John, *The Council of War*, 220, *221*
Roland, Charles, 32
Romancoke plantation, Virginia, 92, 159–60, 163, 170, 265, 305
Rome, 306
Roosevelt, Theodore, 16, 32, 42, 45, 270
Rosecrans, William S., 178, 199, 254
Ruffin, Nancy, 160
Russia, 307
Rust, Albert, 178
Ryan, D. J., *Robert E. Lee, and Joseph E. Johnston*, 304
Ryukyu Islands, 309

S
Sack Coat of Ulysses S. Grant, and accoutrements of the general, *181*
Sackets Harbor, New York, 143, 155–56; Elijah Camp, 156
St. Lawrence River, 282
St. Louis County, 300
St. Louis, Missouri, 59, 74, 100–104, 116, 117, 146, 155, 169, 170, 173, 247, 265, 291, 301, 305; Customs House, 170; Jefferson Barracks, 116, 118, 137; Sanitary Fair, 298
Saint-Gaudens, Augustus, 21–22
Salisbury Beach Festival, 254
Salisbury National Cemetery, North Carolina, 252
San Antonio, Texas, 57, 127, 133, 151, 173, 175
San Cosme gate, 136, 140
San Diego, California, U. S. Grant Hotel, 298, 300
San Francisco, California, 156, *156*
San Jacinto, battle of, 123
San Mateo, convent of, 135
Sanborn, John, 289
Sand Creek, Colorado, 274
Santa Anna, Antonio López de, 123, 127, 129–34, 140
Santo Domingo, *281*
Santo Domingo (later Dominican Republic), 281–82
Sarony, Napoleon, Jay Gould, 284
Sartain, Samuel, *Lieut. Gen. Ulysses S. Grant*, *233*
Sartoris, Algernon, 299–300, 306
Savage's Station, 190
Savannah, Georgia, 178, 218, 238, 265, 304
Savannah River, 95
Sayler's Creek, battle of, 234
Schenck, Robert, 299
Schofield, John M., 249
Schurz, Carl, 270
Scotland, 306
Scott, Sir Walter, 97, 114
Scott, Winfield, 57–61, *61*, 64–65, 69–71, 105, 114, 126–40, *127*, 151, 154, 170, 179, 202, 325; *Views Suggested by the Imminent Danger...*, 57
Second Manassas, 191
Secretary of State Hamilton Fish, *279*, 280
Seddon, James A., 229
Semmes, Raphael, 134
Senaco, 152
Seven Days campaign, 189
Seven Pines (Fair Oaks), 189
Seventh Congressional District Regiment, 74
Seward, William H., 58, 237
Seymour, Horatio, 253
Shearman, Julia Anne, 252
Sheets, Lewis, 72
Shenandoah Valley, 189, 217, 313
Sheridan, Philip H., 34, 36, 209, 214, 215, 217, 220, 223, 228–9, 240, 249, 271, 274, 275, 278–9, 320
Sherman, William Tecumseh, 34, 36, 41–2, 115, 169, 179, 198, 199, 200, 209, 217, 219, 220, 227, 228–9, 254, 268, 273, 274, 275, 297, 320
Shields, James, 135, 313–14
Shiloh, battle of, 34, 75, 125, 187, 188, 199, 200, 214, 230, 291, 311
Shirley plantation, Virginia, 88, 90, 161, 190, 305
Shrady, Henry Mervin, *General Ulysses S. Grant Memorial*, 40, *41*
Sigel, Franz, 209

Simmons, Franklin, *General U. S. Grant*, 39–40, *40*
Simon, John Y., 47
Simpson, Brooks D., 47
Simpson, John, 110
Simpson, Sarah, 110
Sinclair, Thomas, *San Francisco, 156*
Sioux, 278
Sketch of the Battle Ground at Cerro Gordo, 131
Smith, Charles Ferguson, 184, 186
Smith, Dr. (Confederate officer), 223
Smith, Edmund Kirby, 192
Smith, Edward C., 31
Smith, Gerrit, 251
Smith, Jean Edward, 47, 237, 270–1
Smith, John L., 130
Smith, Persifor, 133, 135
Smith, Sidney, 139
Smith, William F., 217
Sneden, Robert K., *"The Contraband Camp" below Arlington House, Va., 162,* 163
Society of the Army of the Tennessee, 40
Society of the Cincinnati, 90
Sollers' Point Flats, 144, 146
Sons of Confederate Veterans, Virginia Division, 31
South, University of, 243
South Carolina, 68, 178, 238, 245, 268, 270, 273
South Dakota, 276
South Mountain, Pennsylvania, 206
Southampton County, Virginia, 98
Southern Literary Messenger, 201, 325
Spain, 307
Spanish-American War, 297
Spotsylvania County, Virginia, 79, 85, 212; Court House, 212–14
Spotted Tail, 278
Springfield, Massachusetts, 170
Springfield, Missouri, 70, 72, 73
Stanton, Edwin, 196, 199, 213, 220, 236, 237, 240, 250
Stein, Gertrude, 45
Stephens, Alexander, 52, 61, 65, 228, 254
Stewart, Alexander, 268
Stewart, Belle, 217
Stiles, Eliza Mackay, 54, 152, 265
Stowe, Harriet Beecher, 238; *Uncle Tom's Cabin*, 162
Stratford Hall, Westmoreland County, Virginia, 26, 81, 82, 83, *84*, 85–86, 87, 329
Stratford Langthorne, 78
Stuart, Alexander H. H., 254, 323
Stuart, Jeb (James Ewell Brown), 19, 57–8, 67, 145, 150, 171, 190, 191, 200, 202, 203, 205, 212, 214
Sumner, Charles, 282
Sumner, E. V., 57
Suzuki, Kantaro, 45
Sweden, 307
Switzerland, 283, 306
Switzerland (ram), 197, *197*
Sword, Awarded to George H. Thomas…, 67

T

Table and Two Chairs from Appomattox, *224*
Tacitus, 50
Taft, William H., 45
Talcott, Andrew, 97, 98, 99, 100, 103
Talcott, Harriet, 104
Tate, Allen, 32
Tatnall, Josiah, 238
Taylor & Huntingdon, *General George Custer, 275*

Taylor, Walter, 189, 190, 194, 212, 313
Taylor, Zachary, 124–9, *124*, *126*, 131, 139, 151, 198, 325
Teapot Dome, Wyoming, 43
Tennessee, 180, 183, 188, 198, 200, 207, 323
Tennessee River, 182, 183, 187
Texas, 106, 118–19, 119, 120, 123, 126, 140, 143, 151–54, 267, 291
Thomas, Emory, 32, 87, 88, 150; "The Malleable Man", 326
Thomas, George H., 66–67, *67*, 115, 148, 151, 199, 200, 249
Thomas, Lorenzo, 73–74
Thoreau, Henry David, 173; "Resistance to Civil Government", 123; *Walden*, 317
Thoroughfare Gap, 191
Thulstrup, Thure de, *Grant from West Point to Appomattox, 37,* 38
Tidewater Plantation, Virginia, 191, 264, 303
Tiemann, H. N., & Co., *The Funeral of Ulysses Grant, 36*
Tilden, Samuel J., 273
The Times (London), 294
Tod, George, 109
Tokyo, 309
Tolland, Connecticut, 108
Tompkins, Rachel Grant, 50
Toombs, Robert, 235
Totten, Joseph G., 124, 128, 129, 143, 147–48, 150
Townsend, E. D., 59–60
Traveller (Lee's horse), *218*, 262, 263, 303
Travis, William, 123
Trenton, New Jersey, 16, 34
Trimble, Isaac, 203
Trist, Nicholas, 132
Trumbull, John, 16, 34
Tucker, Beverly, 311
Tuggle, Robert A., 31
Turner, Edward, 163
Turner, Edward Carter, 94
Turner, Nat, 98
Twain, Mark *see* Clemens, Samuel
Twiggs, David, 57, 130, 132, 134, 135, 139
Tyler, John, 118–19, 123, 325

U

Umberto, King of Italy, 306
Underwood, John C., 235–6, 244
Uniform of Robert E. Lee, Sword, Scabbard, and accouterments of the general, 177
Uniform of Ulysses S. Grant, 241
Union Pacific Railroad, 287
United Nations, 279
United States, House of Representatives, Judiciary Committee, 227; Institute Photography Company, *Mrs. Algernon Sartoris (Nellie Grant), 300;* Treasury, 282, 291; War Department, 99–100
University Publishing Company of New York, 311

V

Valentine, Edward Virginius, 256, 305, 327; *Robert E. Lee* (bronze), 23, *24*; *Robert E. Lee* (marble), 20, *20*, 21
Valley Railroad Company, 233
Valley of Virginia, 217, 313
Van Buren, Martin, 114
Van Dorn, Earl, 195
Vanderbilt, William K., 311
Vannerson, Julian, *Robert E. Lee,* 13, *15*, 24–25, 31, *177*
Vera Cruz, Mexico, 125, 127, 129, 130, 132, 139, 143, 189

Vicksburg: An Official Announcement to the President that Vicksburgh has Fallen, 198
Vicksburg, Mississippi, 238; battle of, 34, 39, 129, 132, 186, 188, 195–9, 200, 207, 215, 290, 297, 311
Victoria, Queen, 282, 300, 306
Vienna, 307
View of West Point (unknown artist), 148
Virginia, 178, 204, 207, 208, 209, 212–17, 229, 240, 245, 246, 253, 255, 256; Historical Society, 67; House of Burgesses, 78; House of Delegates, 82; Military Institute, 60; University of, 243
Virginia City, Nevada, 306, *309*
Virginia Military Institute (VMI), 258, 262, 263
Virginia Tidewater, 246
Virginius, 281
Volck, Frederick, 17; *Robert E. Lee*, 17–18, *18*

W

Walker, Rev. Cornelius, 177
Walker, L.P., 57
"Wall Street Startled", *310*
Wallen, Henry, 157
Walton, E. P., 251–52
Ward, Ferdinand, 298, 310–11
Ward, John Quincy Adams, 21
Warrenton, North Carolina, 304
Washburne, Elihu, 69, 71, 180, 218, 268
Washington, George, 16, 17–18, 22, 23, 29, 32, 34, 36, 42, 49, 55, 62, 63, 65, 75, 78, 80–3, 85, 87, 88–92, 93, 96, 98, 114, 128, 150, 161, 163, 190, 192, 199, 201, 208, 230, 247, 254, 291, 296, 300, 323, 325, 326; mess chest, 127, *127*
Washington, Lewis W., 171–72
Washington, Martha, 55, 91, 146, 161, 296
Washington family, 50, 190
Washington, D. C., 39, 99–100, 143, 177, 188, 189, 191, 234, 238, 246, 265; American University, 31; Capitol, 23, 40, 89, 114; Ford's Theatre, 234; Navy Yard, 171; White House, 189, 233, 294–96, 300; Willard's Hotel, 201
Washington College, Lexington, Virginia (later Washington and Lee University), 17, 20, 25, 59, 150, 151, 229, 238, 243, 251, 252, 256–62, 258–9, 303, 311, 312, 317, 322, 325, 329; President's House, 263, *264*
Washita River, 274
Watts, James W., *Jesse and Hannah Grant, 109*
Webster, Amos, 223
Webster, W. G., 163
Weir, Robert W., 26, 114, 148, *149*, 150; *Robert E. Lee,* 149
Weld, Stephen Minot, 225
West, William Edward, *Mary Randolph Custis Lee,* 97; *Robert E. Lee in the Dress Uniform of a Lieutenant of Engineers,* 100; (attr.) *Sidney Smith Lee,* 85
West Point, United States Military Academy, 22, 26, 38, 51, 61, 70, 74, 84, 88, 92–5, 97, 105, 109, 111, 112–16, 132, 139, 140, 143, 145, 147–51, 154, 155, 159, 169, 184, 261, 279, 294, 296, 297, 304
West Virginia, 178, 180
Westminster, Maryland, 164, 165
Westmoreland County, Virginia, 64, 83
Wheeling, West Virginia, 143
"Whiskey Rings", 291
Whistler, George Washington, 150
Whistler, James Abbott McNeill, 150
Whistler, William, 155
White Haven, Missouri, 116, 117, 168, 169,

173, 295, 300
White Haven, near St. Louis, 118, 329
White House plantation, Virginia, 92, 159–60, 162, 163, 170, 190, 214, 265, 305
White League, 271
White Parlor at Arlington, 159
White Sulphur Springs, West Virginia, 254
White, Thomas, 313
Whitman, Walt, 38; *Leaves of Grass*, 317
Wickham, William, 303
Wickham family, 163
Wilcox, Cadmus, 146, 206
Wilder, L. Douglas, 31
Wilderness, Virginia, 211, 213, 218, 230
Wilkins, Lillian Burns, 300
Will, America Workman, 298
Willcox, O. B., 251
William Henry Fitzhugh Lee, 154
William (Lee slave), 161
Williams, John, 180
Williams, Martha Custis ("Markie"), 55, 99, 146–47, *146*, 151, 162, 238, 305, 311, 319–20
Williams, Orton, 265
Williams, Richard (Dick), 165, 166
Williams, William George, *Madonna and Child* (copied), 99, *99*
Williamsburg, Virginia, 78, 79
Williamson, Thomas, 258
Wilmer, P. B., 229
Wilmer McLean House, Appomattox Court House, 223
Wilmington, North Carolina, 218, 305
Wilson, Edmund, 317
Wilson, Woodrow, 23, 42, 304
Winchester, Virginia, 177
Windsor Castle, 306
Windsor, Connecticut, 107
Winston, William Overton, 160, 163, 164
Wise, Henry A., 178, 223, *253*, 325
Wish-ton-Wish, Missouri, 168
Wolseley, Garnet, 201
Woodward, Clark, 45
Woodward, William, 43
Wool, John E., 97, 127
Worth, William, 136, 139
Wrenshall, Peacock, and Pilton, 118
Wyatt-Brown, Bertram, 49, 51, 86

Y

Yates, Richard, 69, 71, 180
Yellow Tavern, Virginia, 214
York River, 211, 214
Yorktown, battle of, 81, 325
Young, John Russell, 210, 306, 307, 309
Youngstown, Ohio, 109

Z

Zabriskie, George A., 45
Zenneck, A., *Murder of Louisiana,* 271
Zimmerman, Charles A., *John D. Sanborn,* 289